THE YANKEE PAUL
ISAAC THOMAS HECKER

ISAAC THOMAS HECKER

From the original portrait by
George P. A. Healy in Catholic
Information Center, Boston.

THE·
YANKEE PAUL

Isaac Thomas Hecker

VINCENT F. HOLDEN, C.S.P.

THE BRUCE PUBLISHING COMPANY
MILWAUKEE

IMPRIMI POTEST:

WILLIAM A. MICHELL, C.S.P.
Superior General

NIHIL OBSTAT:

JOHN A. SCHULIEN, S.T.D.
Censor librorum

IMPRIMATUR:

✠ ALBERTUS G. MEYER
Archiepiscopus Milwauchiensis

die 12ª Junii, 1958

Library of Congress Catalog Card Number: 58-12230

Foreword

THE plans of Divine Providence do not always follow the well-marked directions which lead to success in human endeavors. Again and again in the history of the Church we find patterns of tension and struggle, of mystifying departure from the norms of human prudence, which appear in retrospect to be clearly defined steps in the realization of a supernaturally conceived goal. No one who has been an instrument of God's grace in the missionary activity of the Kingdom of God on earth has been able in his own lifetime to grasp the significance of what he has accomplished. Nor have the contemporaries of the great builders for God always bestowed upon them the honor and praise which a grateful posterity recognizes to be due them for their honest and self-sacrificing labors. Those who give their lives to God receive their richest rewards in eternity rather than in time.

Isaac Thomas Hecker is without question one of the most important figures in the early growth of the Catholic Church in the United States. It has been said of him that he smuggled his way into the Church. It might be even more truthfully said that he forced his program for the conversion of non-Catholic America into the framework of Catholic action against the wishes of those who might have seemed more obviously destined for the work which he aimed to accomplish. Isaac Hecker has been compared on the one hand to Ignatius Loyola and on the other to Cardinal Newman. Like both of these champions of the faith, Hecker had an irresistible tendency to dedicate himself totally to what seemed an impossible task. Like them, he suffered keenly from the misunderstanding of those among whom he labored. Like them, he became the center of a movement which has turned the course of history. Like Ignatius, Hecker became the founder of a congregation of priests whose ministry reflects even today the spirit which he breathed into it. Like Newman, Hecker had a sense of his mission to those outside the Church and a conviction of the power of revealed truth to answer the objections of Protestantism.

This new life of Father Hecker is the fruit of long years of patient research and scientific synthesis. The author, Father Vincent Holden, unfolds in this volume the amazing career of Father Hecker up to the year 1858, when he founded the Missionary Society of St. Paul the Apostle. Almost a century has passed since Father Hecker's death, and the limitations under which previous lives of the founder of the Paulists were written have been largely removed. We may confidently expect, therefore, that Father Holden's work will come to be regarded as the definitive life of Father Hecker, and that it will take its place in the ever increasing library of American Catholic Church history as a source which future historians may consult with assurance.

I am happy for several reasons to write these few words of introduction for Father Holden's work. Father Hecker belongs to the Archdiocese of Boston in a very special way. It was to Boston that he came in the early years of his restless search for the truth which finally brought him into the Catholic Church. At the age of twenty-two he met another Bostonian by adoption, Orestes A. Brownson. It was Brownson who sent young Isaac Hecker to Brook Farm in West Roxbury. From Brook Farm he wandered to Fruitlands, another Massachusetts experiment in practical sociology. The turning point in Hecker's progress toward the Church was reached while he sojourned at Concord, in close association with Emerson, Alcott, and Thoreau. It was an interview with the third Bishop of Boston, John Bernard Fitzpatrick, that proved decisive in convincing young Hecker that he should become a Catholic. Another Bostonian, later to become His Eminence Cardinal O'Connell, spoke strongly in Father Hecker's defense at a time when so many others seemed to misunderstand his motives and to misinterpret his efforts to bring the truth of the Church's teaching into relation with American life and customs. Thus it was that when we invited the Paulists to come to Boston in 1945, the spirit of Father Hecker began to pervade an area in which the earliest origins of the Paulists can be discovered and in which the work to which they are dedicated has always found a sympathetic response.

Another reason, somewhat more personal, prompts me to welcome this new life of Father Hecker. My own labors as a priest and bishop have led me into the fields in which Father Hecker achieved his greatest success. I have always been convinced that the Church can thrive in America only to the extent that it meets the needs and hopes of the people to whom the age-old truths of the Gospel are preached. This was the fundamental principle of Father Hecker's apostolate. The character and the spirit of our people, he argued, must find themselves at home in our Church as they have in every other land; it is only thus that the Catholic religion can make progress in our country.

Hardly a century ago this tendency was condemned in many quarters. Men of Father Hecker's ideals were suspected of being American to the point of becoming non-Catholic. In this our day, however, the growth of the Church in America, contrasted with its precarious condition in other lands in which formerly it was prosperous, has proved beyond doubt that Father Hecker's policies were sound. Catholicism has flourished instead of deteriorating as Yankee priests have pleaded its cause according to methods which differed from those of the Old World.

Ut Cognoscant Te — this thought has been the inspiration of my own humble efforts to serve God and the Church. I find great consolation in reflecting that this was likewise the dominant theme of Father Hecker's ministry. That non-Catholics might know the truth about the Catholic Church — this was the burning desire that sustained his zeal, the standard by which he measured the usefulness of his efforts to save souls. As I view the American scene today, I am filled with deep admiration for Father Hecker's forward-looking understanding of the future that was in the making in his own lifetime. In the functioning of the Church in America I have never been able to find any indication of the independence which leads to schism. Among the American bishops of the present day there is an astonishing sense of loyalty to the Holy See. I doubt if anywhere in the world there can be found a body of prelates who are more completely united in their determination to think and act in accordance with the traditions of the Universal Church and in conformity with the directives of the authority of St. Peter. The principle *sentire cum Ecclesia* has penetrated every aspect of the organic vitality of the Church in America. Our seminaries are free of those doctrinal deviations which have caused so much concern elsewhere in the world. Our Catholic colleges and universities have resisted successfully the efforts of modern pagan educators to indoctrinate future leaders with the dubious principles of materialism and skepticism.

We cannot, to be sure, underestimate the dangers which threaten our spiritual integrity and we must not rest in false complacency as a proud and conceited cult of scholarship runs wild in an arbitrarily designated domain of academic freedom. I feel certain, however, that the plan of campaign which Father Hecker mapped out will continue to be successful, and that in years to come he will be vindicated in his claim that the irresistible truth of Catholicism will be accepted wherever it is vigorously and resourcefully diffused.

Two traits in Father Hecker's character impress me as fundamental to his extraordinary success: his restless dissatisfaction with any solution of life's problems that could not withstand reasonable objection, and his sympathetic patience with those who were groping for the truth in the darkness and confusion of erroneous belief.

It is said that one of young Isaac Hecker's first preoccupations upon reaching intellectual maturity was to establish with certainty the reality of his own thoughts. This had been the central problem for the German idealists whose works Hecker had read so avidly as he pushed a baker's cart for his elder brothers. Kant and Hegel failed to throw light on the mystery and Hecker became stranded for the moment in the dismal mire of skepticism. He had too much basic common sense, however, to conclude that philosophy was but a system of phenomenal relationships with no bearing at all on a real world. He was deeply religious; the antirealist tendencies of his day could not destroy his belief in the absolute reality of a personal God. His love of God impelled him to regard the speculation of philosophy as directed toward the discovery of God's purposes in creating man a little lower than the angels.

It was thus that he was drawn into the Catholic Church. He had been playfully nicknamed "Ernest the Seeker" by his companions at Brook Farm. His quest led him through much the

same experiences as those of Justin Martyr. Having passed from
one school of philosophy to another, he found satisfying answers
to philosophy's questions in a divinely revealed religion. His approach to the Catholic Church was not purely intellectual; yet
once he found the Church, the truths of faith brought deep and
lasting satisfaction to the inquiries of his troubled mind.

Hecker's sympathy with non-Catholics made it possible for
him to be successful in a work which few others could have undertaken. The Paulists were the first congregation of priests to be
founded in the United States. From the beginning their efforts
were dedicated to the conversion of non-Catholics who lived on
American soil and experienced the influence of American democratic institutions. For such a work intolerance would have been
disastrous. It has been well said that heresy is truth gone astray.
It may be said with equal significance that everyone who thinks
at all has his mind orientated toward the truth. Thinking minds
are not to be ridiculed or condemned. They must be welcomed
with an open sincerity; their non-Catholic associations must not
be erected into a barrier of enmity against the gentle persuasiveness of supernatural charity. It was because Father Hecker understood this that he succeeded where others had failed and opened
up the doors of the Church to non-Catholics who were willing
to think themselves into its fold.

When Father Hecker came back from Rome in 1858, having
been rescued from repudiation and oblivion by the penetrating
missionary vision of Pope Pius IX, he was able to transform his
personal zeal into the spirit of a congregation which would carry
his work far into the future, and bring it, over rough and disappointing roadways, to be sure, but with nonetheless certain
direction, to triumphant achievement for which he never dared to
hope. This volume gives proof of the strength of the foundations
upon which the Paulists have been able to build. Whatever judgment may be passed upon it by discerning historians, it will
make the Paulists better known and more highly respected and
admired. Their influence on the growth of the Catholic Church
in America has been far out of proportion to their numerical
strength. They have now reached the point at which their identifica-
tion with the future of American Catholicism is assured. It is
my earnest hope that this volume of the life of Father Hecker

may be well received, and that Father Holden may bring to successful completion the stirring account of a courageous pioneer whose thinking and apostolic zeal were a century in advance of the age in which he lived and worked.

Archbishop of Boston.

Preface

ONE of the most ardent apostles of the Catholic Church in the United States during the second half of the 19th century was an American convert, Isaac Thomas Hecker. After he had traveled the tortuous road from the darkness of unbelief to the light and freedom of the children of God, Father Hecker, like his illustrious patron, St. Paul, counted no cost and spared no efforts to bring the great riches of Christ to his fellow countrymen. His great and all consuming passion was his love for the Church and second to that his love for America. He firmly believed that if America knew the Church as it really was, America would become Catholic. He was on fire to tell his countrymen that the Church as they knew it was not the Church at all, but a caricature of the divine work of Christ. He wanted to cry out from the housetops that Catholicism was no enemy of freedom, but its ardent defender. It was no foe of liberty, but the parent and the friend of the liberty that we have through sonship with Christ. It did not trample on the rights of human personality but endowed them with the privileges of the children of God. All his priestly life he worked tirelessly to carry this message to his fellow citizens. As a missionary, a lecturer, a writer and editor, a trusted adviser of American bishops, clergymen, and laity, he extended the sphere of his influence to almost every corner of the United States. When he died in 1888, his hopes and ambitions were not interred with his remains, but live on in the religious community he had founded, the Paulist Fathers, the first native American community of priests formed in this country. The noted historian, Dr. Peter Guilday, called this achievement of Father Hecker: "America's first gift to the great legacy of religious orders and congregations in the Church."

When I first undertook to write the life of this American apostle, I knew instinctively that a single volume could never describe the remarkable character, the enduring achievements, and the prodigious activity of this dedicated son of the Church and devoted American patriot. As the work progressed, I realized that there was a natural division, clear cut and sharp, that produced almost two Isaac Heckers: Hecker the precursor and Hecker the apostle. In 1858 with his release from the Redemptorist Community Hecker the precursor gave way to Hecker the apostle with the beginning of the Paulist Community. The years that preceded this transition were momentous ones as he prepared for the work that almighty God had called him to do. He had come to know intimately and personally the problems and difficulties of various classes outside the Church. He had worked with the laboring man, he had mixed with members of various religious groups, he had associated with social reformers and had mingled with the intellectual leaders of his day. In short, he had become well acquainted with that phenomenon he later called "the American Mind." He knew what that mind sought and he was convinced that only in the Catholic Church could it find peace and solace.

In his struggle to reach out and bring the truth of Christ to his fellow Americans, Father Hecker had come up against a problem somewhat akin to that of St. Paul. As the great Apostle of the Gentiles went up and down the coasts of Asia Minor winning souls for Christ, he found his labors somewhat impeded by certain groups among his co-religionists who wanted to saddle Jewish customs and observances on the newly won Christians. St. Paul resisted any such attempt, declaring that no one had to accept the customs and traditions of the land in which Christ was born before they received His sacraments. Father Hecker, traveling over the widely scattered areas of the United States, sensed that some of his fellow Catholics were identifying Catholic truth with the social and political patterns of the land where Catholicism had bloomed. He strenuously maintained that Americans did not have to Europeanize before they would become Catholics. Saint Peter, the first Vicar of Christ on earth, approved St. Paul's stand and urged him to continue his mission to the pagans of the ancient world. Pius IX, the two hundred and fifty-sixth Vicar of Christ on earth, approved Father Hecker's stand and encouraged him to go forth among the pagans of his own country. For this reason I have chosen to call this volume which deals with Father Hecker's pre-Paulist days THE YANKEE PAUL. The second volume which will describe his Paulist labors is now in progress and will, I hope, appear shortly.

When I asked the Archbishop of Boston, the Most Reverend Richard J. Cushing, to write the foreword and he graciously accepted, I was delighted. A devoted friend of the Paulists, with many characteristics of mind and heart reminiscent of Father Hecker, the Archbishop was the ideal person to introduce this volume to the American public. I am deeply grateful for the honor he has conferred on me in accepting this task.

It is only a truism to say that no book such as this biography could be written without co-operation and encouragement. In my efforts I have received an abundant share of both. I owe more than I could ever dare hope to express to the Paulist Community which deserves every last bit of credit for any success that I may have achieved in the priesthood. To list all the advantages and opportunities I have received since the first day I started wearing a Paulist habit would be an almost endless litany of favors. While I pass over many of these in silence I cannot refrain from expressing others. I am deeply indebted to our Superior General, the Very Reverend William A. Michell, who not only asked me to write the Hecker biography, but who followed every step of its progress with his kindly, interested, and constant support. He did everything possible to make my labors the most pleasant of tasks. So too did my confrere of seminary days, Father John B. Sheerin, editor of the *Catholic World*. Despite his taxing journalistic duties, he found time to read every line of this volume and offered numerous and excellent suggestions and corrections that could come only from the pen of a stylist of his recognized ability. Our Paulist Novice Master, Father Frank R. McNab was not only hospitality incarnate during my stay at the novitiate where this book was written but he too read every chapter and aided me with valuable recommendations and counsels. I owe a deep debt of gratitude to other Paulists who put at my disposal their expert knowledge of languages. Father Theodore C. Petersen, a scholar of the first rank, had no diffi-

culty deciphering almost illegible scripts in German and gave
me professional translations of documents in that language, as
well as those in Dutch. Father Martin Lombardi rendered not
only the meaning but the flavor of those in Italian, and Father
John Overend assisted me with those in French, while Father
Edward Peters was always available to solve any difficulties I
encountered in German, French, or Italian manuscripts. When
puzzling questions dealing with ecclesiastical law and procedure
beset me, Father James A. McVann took pains to answer and
clarify them for me.

During the course of this work, I made many friends outside
the Paulist Community who were magnanimous in the aid they
gave me. Especially is this true of the Redemptorist Fathers. I
could never have written this account if the Very Reverend Father
William Gaudreau, the Rector Major of that Community, had
not given me free access to all Redemptorist archives. This was
the first time since Father Hecker and his confreres separated
from the Redemptorists that a Paulist had the opportunity of
seeing these all-important sources. Credit for this privilege must
be given to Father Gaudreau, the first American-born Superior
General of the Redemptorist Community. Without his co-operation,
no candid and unprejudiced account of this separation, which I
have attempted to give, could have been written. The Redemptorist
General Archivist, Father Andreas Sampers, was extremely helpful.
A man of rare intellectual attainments, he searched his archives
for every possible scrap of evidence bearing on Father Hecker's
days as a Redemptorist. While I was in Rome, Father Sampers,
with his facility in speaking five languages, accompanied me to
the various Roman depositaries while we searched for all documents bearing on the Hecker case. While he cannot in any sense
be held responsible for what I have written of Father Hecker's
days as a Redemptorist, he gave me excellent suggestions and
marvelous advice on the treatment of the material. With his ex-
quisite sense of humor, he lightened the oftentimes dreary burden,
all the more discouraging when unsuccessful, of going from one
manuscript collection to another and he thus made my five weeks'
stay in Rome a delight.

The same courtesy and kindness that I received from the
Redemptorists in Rome, I experienced at the hands of these

Fathers in other parts of Europe and in the States. Father Van Couwenberg in St. Trond where Father Hecker had made his novitiate showed me what was available there. Father Van Ouwerkerk in Wittem produced all the available records of the studentate and took care of the photostating of necessary material; the venerable historian of the Redemptorists, Father De Meulemeester, spent several hours with me in Brussels discussing various aspects of the life of Father Hecker; Father Holloway at Clapham, England, showed me the documents relative to Father Hecker's stay in England and arranged for the photostating of pertinent papers. Here in the States, the Baltimore Provincial archivist, Father Rudolph Reiss, gave me complete access to the Provincial Papers, as well as providing me with a glossy print of Father Bernard. Father Michael J. Curley, the Provincial historian, gave me interesting insights into Redemptorist history and called my attention to documents that I might have otherwise missed.

Many absorbing episodes of American Catholic history are buried away in the manuscript depositaries of Rome. Of these, none is more important than the Propaganda archives, the Congregation that for so many years had jurisdiction over the Church in America. Monsignor Giuseppe Monticone, the capable and scholarly archivist of this documentary collection, made available to me all the material dealing with Father Hecker and permitted me to have photostatic copies of letters and documents necessary for this study. Time and again, he went out of his way to lend valuable aid and suggestions. I can say the same of Father Gerard McSorley of the Irish College who gave me complete access to the Kirby papers and showed me every kindness.

My colleagues in the States working in the field of American Catholic history also offered me marvelous co-operation. Father Thomas T. McAvoy, C.S.C., archivist of the University of Notre Dame, with whom I had worked in 1938, put at my disposal the Brownson, Cincinnati, and Hartford papers in that valuable collection of Americana; Father Harry Browne of the Archdiocese of New York, and formerly archivist of the Catholic University of America, provided me with copies of Hecker material in the Hughes papers; Father Colman J. Barry, O.S.B., not only opened for my inspection the valuable treasure of the

Smith papers but gave me the hospitality of St. John's Abbey during my stay at Collegeville; Father Patrick Ahern of the Archdiocese of St. Paul extended the same privilege when I went through the Keane and Ireland collection at the archdiocesan seminary; Father Paul Love, the archivist of the Baltimore Archdiocesan archives, gave me easy access to the Kenrick, Spalding, and Bayley papers; Monsignor John L. Manning, the chancellor of the Charleston Diocese allowed me to search for Hecker material in the numerous Lynch papers housed in the chancery building.

When I wanted a photograph of Brook Farm to include in this biography, Mr. Henry Harrison, curator of the Fruitlands Museum, obtained for me a glossy print of the Josiah Wolcott painting in the possession of Mrs. Robert Blake Weston of Belmont, Massachusetts. For her permission to use a copy of this painting and his kindness in securing it, I am very grateful. Mr. Harrison also secured for me a photograph of Fruitlands. Father John de Louchry performed a similar service in securing Archbishop Connolly's photograph from an original in St. Mary's Basilica rectory, Halifax.

An important and hitherto unused source of information for data on the Hecker family was the material in the Hall of Records in New York City. Because of the specialized character of the arrangement of this material, I needed the advice of one familiar with the recording of these legal documents and called upon my companion of high school days, Mr. Robert J. McGinn. With characteristic unselfishness he gave of his time and talents in assisting me to secure these records.

When it came to the tedious and time-consuming task of proofreading and preparing the index, I was extremely fortunate to be able to call upon the capable and experienced Miss Katherine Crofton who for a number of years was editorial assistant to Father Gillis in the *Catholic World*. Graciously and willingly she took this exacting work off my hands.

Miss Katherine M. Richardson in her characteristically efficient manner typed this book in manuscript from a copy that to many others would have been illegible. I cannot refrain at this time from expressing my sincere gratitude to this extraordinarily competent assistant who for the past fifteen years has helped me generously and zealously in promoting Catholic causes and always in an unsalaried capacity. She served with me at the Paulist Information Center in New York City, was with the *Catholic World* for a time, and is currently in the archives serving as secretary and doing excellent work in cataloguing and calendaring the Hecker papers and other administrative collections.

As I write these lines, there is a lurking fear that my memory may have missed someone who has co-operated in the production of this volume. If I have overlooked anyone, I should like, in the eloquent words of Cardinal Newman which appear in the closing paragraphs of the *Apologia,* to express my appreciation of those "who have been so faithful to me; who have been so sensitive of my needs; who have been so indulgent to my failings; who have carried me through so many trials; who have grudged no sacrifice, if I asked for it; who have been so cheerful under discouragements of my causing; who have done so many good works and let me have the credit of them."

VINCENT F. HOLDEN, C.S.P.

Illustrations

Contents

THE YANKEE PAUL

ISAAC THOMAS HECKER

CHAPTER I

The Birth of a Conviction

AT THE beginning of the 19th century, America was beginning to find herself. She had weathered the difficult days of her formation and had succeeded in consolidating thirteen independent colonies into a national unit. She had formulated her Constitution, established her government, and strengthened her national defenses. She was now a new country, a new nation, vigorous, resourceful, teeming with ideas of democracy and equality. The newly elected Jefferson dramatized the pattern of the future when he rode to the inauguration astride his favorite white horse, Wildfire, and not, as Washington had done, in an imported coach emblazoned with a coat of arms and drawn by four white horses accompanied by outriders. Many an aristocratic Whig witnessing this scene tossed his head in scorn, but the disdainful tilt of a powdered wig was powerless to stop the surge of democracy and the rise of the common man. Equal opportunity for all was the Republican slogan when Jefferson took over the reins of government from John Adams.

With the development of trade and commerce, stories of the land of golden opportunity across the sea began to trickle through to the Old World. These reports were heard especially in shipping centers where seamen, sitting around in taverns, entertained their listeners with stories of a land free of kings and lords and dukes. They told of a country where the government proclaimed that all men were created equal and endowed by their Creator with inalienable rights to life, liberty, and the pursuit of happiness. America, they declared, was a land where men of ability and

1

industry, no matter what their rank or class, would find not only a challenge, but an almost certain chance of success.

Accounts of the new and fabulous land reached Rotterdam, a seaport in southwestern Netherlands, where John Hecker, a young metalworker, followed his trade. Trained by his father, he had learned quickly but before he could qualify as a *schmeidmeister* he had to make his journeymanship. Leaving his native town of Schwalbach, about seventy miles southwest of Bonn in Germany, he went first to Wetzlar, then to Niederlahnstein, and finally to Rotterdam. Here in the year 1800, he decided to try his fortune in the New World and set sail for America.[1]

During that long ocean voyage of forty-two days, while John Hecker was looking anxiously but hopefully into the future, he could reflect, perhaps with some regrets, on certain events of the past. His ancestors had not always been of the working class. There was a time when they held vast estates in Holland and bore the title Barons of the Empire. They were ranked high among the aristocracy and married into the families of the various Princes of Orange and the Dukes of Franconia, Cleves, and Egmond. But their future changed radically when one of John's forebears, Henry van Hecker cast his lot with William, Prince of Orange, in 1567. He followed him to Dillenburg in Eastern Germany and under the influence of the Prince's father and mother, both fervent Protestants, Henry and his family renounced Catholicism and became stanch Lutherans. This move caused a wide breach between them and their Catholic relatives and they were soon cut off from their inheritance in the rich Hecker-Udal estates in Holland. From plenty they were plunged into need and had to earn their living. Two hundred years later their descendants were still in Dillenburg working in various trades. They then moved to Wetzlar where they stayed but a short time until they settled in Schwalbach where John was born, November 7, 1782. Had it not been for the change of religion, he might have been raised in Holland, the revered son of a nobleman, instead of an unknown journeyman on his way to America. Religion had wrenched his family from positions of distinction and honor and cast them into insignificance and obscurity.

So far as the records show, John Hecker had no relatives or close friends in America. He came, a lone emigrant, to make his way as best he could. He was strictly on his own. Shortly after his arrival in New York, he found work at his own trade in the foundry and machine shop of James P. Allaire in Cherry Street, between Corlears Hook and Walnut Street, where in a few years he became foreman of the foundry. This shop was close to the shipyard of Charles Brown who had been engaged by Robert Fulton to construct the hull of the first successful steamboat ever to navigate the Hudson, the *Clermont*. Allaire was given the task of installing the London-made engine. Working on this project, John came into contact with one of Brown's carpenters, a young immigrant by the name of Frederick Friend. He was born in Elberfeld in Rhenish Prussia of a family that once occupied an important place among the vassal-nobles of the Tyrol. He had come to America in 1797 with his mother, father, and six sisters. They had settled down in Hester Street, between Christie and Forsyth, where his father, Engel Friend,* opened his own brass foundry. He had a successful business and his family lived in comfort.[2]

The young carpenter and the metalworker became close friends and John Hecker was a frequent visitor at the Friends' home. He met all Fred's sisters, but Susan Caroline became his favorite. She was a tall, fair-haired, rather good-looking girl, with great energy of character and a gracious disposition. Although she was fourteen years younger than John — she was born March 2, 1796 — her easy and friendly manner quickly appealed to the young immigrant. Before long the familiar pattern began to unfold: friendship, courtship, and finally marriage, which took place July 21, 1811, in the Old Dutch Church in the Swamp.[3]

After his marriage, John Hecker opened a brass foundry at 83 First Street, between First Avenue and Avenue A. He remained there about a year and then moved down to 128 Hester Street, between Forsyth and Christie Streets, next door to his father-in-law.[4] In the early 1800's, this area was one of the desirable spots of the city, since it was close to the ocean whose refreshing breezes were a blessed relief in the sultry, summer heat. Trees

---

* The German form of the name was Freund but soon after coming to America Engel Freund changed it to Friend. In Longworth's *New York Register and City Directory,* and in the *Books of Conveyances* in the Hall of Records, New York City, as well as in Engel's will, the family name is spelled Friend.

shaded the homes and shops on either side of the street and shrubbery acted as natural dividers to mark off the boundaries of the individual dwellings. It was a delightful spot for a newly married couple to make their home.

The success that John Hecker had hoped for and dreamed about as he sailed across the Atlantic was not slow in coming. He had a thriving business, a devoted wife, and a family destined to do him honor. His two sons, John and George, later organized a flour and milling business that would not only make them wealthy, but would perpetuate the Hecker name as a household word for many years to come.*

John, the oldest of the Hecker boys, was born on July 25, 1812. Aggressive, gifted with unusual business initiative, and shrewd in financial matters, he was quick to grasp an opportunity and adroit in turning it into a successful enterprise. George, born January 5, 1818, seems to have had, like his father, a great deal of original mechanical ability which he later used to great advantage in the baking business. He was a very generous and considerate person who believed in practicing charity without any fanfare. He had his mother's intense and dogged determination and whenever he gave himself to an enterprise he never relaxed until he made a success of it.

The youngest child, Isaac, born December 18, 1819, bore the closest resemblance to his mother.[5] He was a good-looking youngster with blond hair and blue eyes, a square, high forehead, an oval face with a full mouth and regular chin. Decidedly sanguine in temperament, he had a kindly and cheerful disposition, with an attractive and winning personality which quickly won him friends. A happy, courageous disposition, with unusual sincerity, a great earnestness of character and frankness of manner, this was the heritage young Isaac received from his mother.

The Hecker family was a compact unity, with George and Isaac particularly devoted to each other. From earliest years, they seemed to have the same ideals and interests. As years went on, the friendship became stronger and richer. They appeared to go

---

* There were two other children born to the Heckers. One was a boy, Henry, who died soon after his birth, August 15, 1814; the other was the only girl in the family, Elizabeth, who was born October 12, 1816. All extant accounts have little to say of the part she played in the family.

through life supporting and encouraging each other. One could turn to the other with the confident realization that he would always understand and appreciate in a way impossible to anyone else. No matter what the difficulty or problem, George would give to Isaac material or moral support, prudent advice, wholehearted and sincere co-operation. And Isaac was George's closest confidant to whom he bared his deepest thoughts, his highest hopes and ambitions.[6]

The dominant influence of the home was unquestionably that of the mother who governed the household with kindness and firmness. Hers was a discipline by affection, rather than severity, and she taught her children to respond to kindness rather than threats of punishment. Isaac once said that the severest punishment she ever inflicted on him was once or twice to tell him she was angry with him. This made him so utterly miserable that he sat down on the floor completely overcome "and so remained" until after a time she relented and restored him to her good graces.[7] Yet she did not allow her children to develop their own ideas of right living. She instilled into their minds strict rules about lying and stealing and other vices.

Although Mrs. Hecker could and did take care to condition her children against harmful moral influences, physical disorders were beyond her control. When the yellow-fever epidemic swept the city in 1822, claiming thousands of victims, she managed to keep her children safe from its ravages, but, some time after that, Isaac was stricken with confluent smallpox. The disease progressed rapidly until there was little hope that the lad could survive. His mother told him of the seriousness of his condition. With simplicity and utter confidence, the sick boy replied: "No mother, I shall not die now. God has a work for me to do in the world and I shall live to do it."[8]

At first glance, we might be tempted to dismiss these words as the delirious outpouring of a youthful mind racked with fever. But as subsequent events proved, they represented a firm conviction burned deep into the consciousness of this youngster that God had selected him for a special work. As he lay in his sickbed with his devoted mother seated beside him, neither he nor she knew, nor could surmise, what his work would be. Years would pass, years of trying and soul-searching experiences, before he would know clearly the precise nature of that special work.

He recovered from the disease but not without some permanent aftereffects. His face was pock-marked and his eyesight was impaired, the smallpox leaving him nearsighted. For some years he was able to get along without glasses, but after he passed his twentieth birthday he had to wear them; he discovered he was passing friends on the street without recognizing them.[9]

While still a youngster, one place above all others that Isaac liked to visit was his grandfather's shop next door to his home. Engel Friend was a kindly, warmhearted old gentleman, with a strong affection for his grandson. He was a clockmaker as well as a smith and he would talk to the boy by the hour as he worked over clocks. The two spoke in German, since Engel Friend, as he himself said, "never had time to learn English."[10] Isaac watched him as he put each little wheel in place and wound the spring that set them all in motion. Fascinated, the youngster asked questions and waited for explanations. After watching the old man at work for some time and having asked him a thousand questions, the young lad said he too would like to make a clock. Cheerfully, half amused, his grandfather taught him. The year before Engel Friend died on April 20, 1832, twelve-year-old Isaac could proudly boast of having made a clock. It was a good one and gave many years of service, ticking faithfully for more than forty years until it was accidentally destroyed by fire.[11]

A lively, active boy, Isaac did not spend all his time in his grandfather's shop. One of his favorite sports was climbing the trees that lined the walks. He and his young playmates took part in various games around the neighborhood. Their gathering call was a little verse that sounds tame in comparison with the raucous yells of today's youngsters!

> Boys and girls come out to play,
> The moon does shine as bright as day;
> Come with a whoop, come with a call,
> Come with a good will, or don't come at all.[12]

Their games were often interrupted by the clang of the fire engines from Engine 19. Isaac would take to his heels and follow them like a hound chasing a fox.

When he had reached the age of six required for admission to grade school, Isaac was sent in the fall of 1826 to Public School 7 in Christie Street between Pump and Hester Streets.[13] His school day began at nine and continued until five. He learned to form the letters of the alphabet first in sand. When he had mastered this, he was instructed in reading and given Murray's First Book. After acquiring a little skill in reading, he advanced to writing, first on slate, then on paper. If his later penmanship is any criterion, he was not too careful in forming his letters. He apparently learned to write rapidly and was much more concerned about getting his thoughts on paper than about producing a legible script. When he had acquired some proficiency in reading and writing, he was advanced to the study of arithmetic and first principles of English grammar.[14]

While young Hecker was learning the three fundamental R's of a basic education, the fourth R, religion, was not neglected. Although his father, nominally a Lutheran, paid little attention to religion, his mother was supremely conscious of its importance. She had been raised a Lutheran, but shortly after her marriage became a Methodist and was very fervent and devout in that faith. It was only natural that Isaac would attend her church in Forsyth Street between Walker and Hester Streets just a short distance from both his school and his home. Here he became acquainted with fundamental Methodist doctrine and with the Methodist form of worship. The clock that Isaac had made hung in this church for almost forty years until the building was torn down.[15]

Sometime after Isaac's twelfth birthday, his schooling was brought to a close. His father's business began to fail, the family's financial situation became grave, and he was called upon to lend what assistance he could. He had scarcely progressed beyond primary training when he exchanged the schoolroom for the workshop. This was by no means unique or unusual in the 1830's. The average boy of that day rarely went beyond the bare essentials of education and very few pursued any of the higher branches of learning.[16] Although young Hecker had but six years of formal education in a classroom, his departure from school was not a signal for a farewell to books and study. He was an avid reader and devoted as much time as he could spare from work to follow the thoughts and ideas of others on the printed page. He always wanted to study, which he said later on was "the secret desire of my heart."[17]

The reason for John Hecker's failure in business, which interrupted his son's education, is difficult to discover. Apparently it was not due to any business recession since he had weathered the hard times of 1819, the aftermath of the War of 1812. His brass foundry flourished and his family were in comfortable circumstances from 1814 to 1822 when they lived at 128 Hester Street. After that, as the *City Directory* shows, he moved from one location to another. Early in 1823, he moved to 63 Pump Street between Forsyth and Christie Streets, a block away from his former residence and that of his in-laws. The next year he located in 20 Eldridge Street between Pump and Walker, about five blocks from the Friend family. For the next three years, the *Directory* contains no mention of him. It seems quite likely that he lost his foundry sometime in this period. His name reappears in 1828 when he opened a shop farther uptown at 269 Broome Street between Orchard and Allen Streets. He remained here two years and then once again his name disappears from the *Directory*.

The reason for all these changes, each one taking him farther away from his wife's people, remains unknown. It is a curious fact that the only information we have about him concerns his family background and his first few years in this country.[18] Although several visitors to the Hecker home record their impressions of the family, especially the character and personality of the mother, they make no mention of the father.[19] There are numerous letters of Isaac to his immediate family, some to his relatives, quite a few to his friends, but only one to his father.[20] This is a very strong and impassioned plea begging him to overcome "the habit that has governed you for so many years past" and which has given so much "pain to those who love you as we all do." He asks him to open his mind "to Mother, to John, to George, when you do not feel strong enough to resist, and follow their advice."

Although Isaac is quite detailed in the remedy he offers his father to overcome this "wicked passion" he does not name it or indicate its nature. Whatever it may have been, there can be little doubt that it played a part in John Hecker's business failure. The burden of supporting the family fell to his sons.

D E A R   M E M B E R

We are very pleased to send you this volume as a free book dividend, to which you are entitled by reason of your completion of a four book purchase.

We believe it is a book you will enjoy reading and be proud to add to your library.

Manager

THE CATHOLIC LITERARY FOUNDATION

YANKEE PAUL

John, who was nineteen at the time, had been working for three or four years for his uncle, Christopher Schwab, the husband of Mrs. Hecker's sister Marie. Schwab had his own bakery at 108 Hester Street.[21] George, who was six years John's junior, joined his brother and the two learned the business in all its details from their uncle.

Young Isaac, just turning thirteen, found an opening in the publishing house of the *Christian Advocate and Journal and Zion's Herald* at 14 Crosby Street, just off Broadway.[22] This was a Methodist weekly issued by the Methodist Book Concern. John B. McMaster says it "had a weekly circulation of fifteen thousand copies, the largest it was claimed, then reached by any paper in the world, the *London Times* not excepted."[23] It also had a large mail subscription list and the papers had to be folded and prepared for mailing. This was light work and needed no experience, so young Hecker was given the job.

Up until this time, none of John Hecker's sons had followed in the family trade which he, his father, and his grandfather had chosen, that of a metalworker. So it fell to the lot of his last born to continue the tradition. After a year with the Methodist publication, Isaac went to work in a type foundry in Thames Street to learn the trade. But the Hecker brothers soon realized that their hope for the future lay not in bronze and metal but in bread and flour. John, who by this time was a skillful baker, had reached his majority and decided it was time to strike out on his own. He rented a place in 56 Rutgers Street, between Cherry and Monroe, and set up his own shop,[24] which required the combined efforts of all three boys. George went with him and so did Isaac, forsaking forever a career in metals. All three gave of their talents and labor to make the new enterprise a success.

In the beginning, Isaac knew little of the business, so he functioned mainly as a delivery boy. Gradually he was initiated into more and more of the intricacies of the trade. His brothers taught him how to make yeast, how to mix the ingredients, how to determine the necessary quantities, and a host of other things a successful baker needed to know. Years later he could recall this training and remarked how hard he worked preparing for holidays, especially New Year's Day: "Three weeks in advance,

we began to bake New Year's cakes — flour, water, sugar, butter
and caraway seeds. We could never make enough. How I used
to work carrying the bread around in my baker's cart. How often
I got stuck in the gutters and in the snow! Sometimes some good
soul, seeing me unable to get along, would give me a lift."[25]

Intense application and perseverance on the part of all three
brothers began to have its effect. Their business was expanding
but still there was an air of uncertainty about its future. The
Heckers were merely tenants in 56 Rutgers Street and at any
time they could be asked to vacate the premises. John decided
to take up the matter with Abraham Larue, the man from whom
he rented the property early in 1835. Larue had a twenty-one
year lease from the owner, Mary Hedges, and there were still
seventeen years to run on the lease which had begun May 1,
1831. This was the type of long-term secure rental that John
wanted. After some delay, Larue agreed to assign his lease to
Hecker at a cost of three thousand, two hundred and fifty dollars.
The papers were drawn up November 9, 1835, and the amount
"duly paid."[26] The sum of money John paid out indicates the
thriving business the Heckers had established, for even if John
did not have that much capital on hand, his assets must have been
sufficiently great to permit him to raise that amount.

In 1838 the Heckers opened a new shop at 483 Pearl Street,
sufficiently distant from their original location to cater to new
customers.[27] As the volume of business increased, they required
a larger supply of flour and in a time of crisis it was not easy to
obtain as they had learned during the 1837 panic. So in 1842 they
decided to build their own mill on the corner of Cherry and
Pike Streets which they named the Croton Flour Mill.[28] By 1843,
the Heckers had establishments in 111 Broadway, 123 Houston
Street, 483 Pearl Street, and 68 Spring Street. The three were now
in partnership, John, George, and Isaac forming the firm, Hecker
and Brothers.[29] This was the beginning of the enterprise which
later became widely known as the Hecker Flour Company.

Although Isaac worked long hours in the bakery and threw
himself wholeheartedly into the business, he never forgot the
conviction he had voiced as a youngster stricken with smallpox:
"God has a work for me to do in the world." He realized that
this call was not to bake bread for paying customers, or to make

money in the business world. Just exactly what the special work was, he did not know. All he could be sure of was the conviction. Often while lying on the shavings before the ovens in the bake-house, he would become acutely aware of it. Stirred by its reality, he would run out of the shop and wander along the wharves of the East River, speculating and asking himself: "What does God want of me? What has He sent me into the world to do?"[30] Time and again he would ask these questions, but no answer was forthcoming.

The divine call in the soul of Isaac Hecker was temporarily muted by the more immediate cry of victimized humanity. This began to sound in his ears as he noticed all about him the sufferings and injustices inflicted on the laboring man and his family. It was, in a sense, a summons to action, both economic and political. Economic, because of the miserable condition of the workingman; political, because the politician seemed to be the only person that could bring about reform.

Before young Hecker was ten years old and while he was still in school, notable changes were taking place in his native New York and in the New England States. For some years these areas had been largely shipping centers handling vast numbers of im-ports and exports. But during the Embargo and the War of 1812 they turned to manufacturing. After the Tariff of 1828, the process of conversion was in full force. They had, as James Truslow Adams notes, "swung over to the factory from the ship."[31] The factories built industry which in turn created industrialists who were reaping fortunes on the rapidly expanding American markets. This new moneyed class depended especially on the laborers who would turn out the products the public was seeking at as small a cost as possible to the owner. The workers got starvation wages while fat profits went into the till of the exploiting industrialist. The rising tide of immigrants supplied cheap labor in ever growing amounts.

Almost immediately the newcomers were absorbed into the laboring class. If they wanted to exist, they had no choice but to accept whatever occupation they could find. Manufacturer and industrialist welcomed them and put them to work manning machines, excavating ditches for gas and water mains, digging canals, or mining coal and ore. Their brawn was laying the foundation for the new material civilization of America and it was only for their brawn that they were sought. Little if any consideration was given to them as human beings. Their hours were long, their salary meager, their working conditions miserable.[32]

The rise of the modern capitalist at the expense of labor had its effect not only on the immigrant but on the native American workers as well. They were beaten down in the labor market as low as possible with the club of cheap immigrant labor. Their working hours were not noticeably shorter than those of the newly arrived foreigner, extending ordinarily ten hours and often twelve and fourteen. The salary the workers received for such arduous and extended labor was at most one dollar a day.[33]

This was the situation when young Hecker left school and began to earn his first dollar. Rubbing shoulders with the workers, he had an excellent opportunity to know and appreciate their problems. He was one of them. At the same time his innate sympathy roused him to try to improve the lot of the workers. The desire for social reform began to haunt him as the cry of oppressed humanity grew louder in his ears. He began to loathe a system whereby the rich became richer and the poor poorer. Even when the Heckers had advanced from the status of employee to that of employer, Isaac was still actuated by the same ideal — the amelioration of the economic and social conditions of the laboring class.

Essentially a person of action, he was not content to sit around and merely talk about the need for reform. He must do something about it. But what could he, a mere youth of sixteen or seventeen, hope to accomplish? Alone he would be powerless but by joining his efforts with those of others having the same goal, he might achieve some improvement.

Like so many of his own age, he turned to the one organized group which seemed capable of fighting labor's cause, a political party. He joined forces with an offshoot of the Tammany Democrats, the Loco-Focos, who were ardent defenders of the rights of labor and the immigrant. Early in 1836 they had organized and had recruited their members largely, and almost solely, from the working classes in New York City. Small grocers and shopkeepers, mechanics and laborers formed a major part of the organization. About a half-dozen physicians and a few dissatisfied officeholders completed their number.[34] Anyone could become a member of the party who accepted the Declaration of Principles which had been drawn up in February of 1836 by Moses Jacques "the Venerated Patriarchal leader of the Loco-Focos." It was a very interesting document which disclaimed any intention of instituting a new party but declared that their members were the original Democratic Party according to the mind of the "revered" Jefferson. Since the Loco-Focos were unalterably opposed to monopolies and vested rights, the Declaration maintained that the true foundation of Republican government was the "equal rights of every citizen in his rights and property, and in their management." It limited the power of legislation to the declaring and enforcing of natural rights and duties, but denied that legislators could deprive their fellow men of any of these rights. The Declaration also affirmed "unqualified and uncompromising hostility to bank notes and paper money" because gold and silver were the only safe and constitutional currency.[35]

Such a statement of principles appealed very strongly to Isaac Hecker. The excessive and arbitrary use of authority, no matter whether it came from the state or any other human power, was abhorrent to him. He preferred, as he said later on, "to suffer from the excesses of liberty rather than from the arbitrary actions of tyranny." The Declaration embodied these ideas and he willingly accepted it. With his brothers, he worked enthusiastically and unselfishly in the interests of the organization which had so many commendable principles.[36]

By the time the Heckers became actively associated with the antimonopoly faction, the party was well organized. It had its own party organ, a penny paper called the *Democrat* with Clinton Roosevelt as editor. Isaac Hecker was a faithful reader of this journal and kept a complete file of it for years after the party was only a memory. The year before his death, he quoted from the first issue to show the principles and aims which he embraced wholeheartedly.

> We are adherents of democracy. We are in favor of a government by the people. Our objects are the restoration of Equal Rights and the prostration of those aristocratical institutions existing in the state of monopolies and exclusive privileges of every kind. . . . The means we rely on to carry our principles into effect are a faithful exhibition of

them to the reason and judgment of our fellow men and warnings of the fearful and inevitable consequences of . . . monopoly legislation.[37]

All monopolies, but especially banks, this group condemned. When the Democrats instituted and championed state banks, the Loco-Focos raised their voices loudly against this form of monopoly. They had watched certain individuals secure a charter from the legislature, receive gold and silver on deposit, and then issue paper money greatly in excess of their collateral.[38] The ones who suffered most from this chicanery were the workers and their families, and through their political organization they opposed this practice and took a firm stand on the question of public finance.

The Hecker brothers joined the Loco-Focos in their fight against the misuse of paper money and the abuse of legislative power which approved and tolerated such mischief. Although John was the only one of the three old enough to vote, George and Isaac had other ways of showing their opposition. They bought a hand printing press and set it up in the garret of their home in 56 Rutgers Street. Then they took all the paper money received from their customers, smoothed the bills out, and printed on them the words: "Of all the contrivances to impoverish the laboring classes of mankind, paper money is the most effective. It fertilizes the rich man's field with the poor man's sweat." The banks soon found out what was going on and tried to have the enthusiasts punished for defacing the currency. But as George Hecker, who related the story, bantered: "We beat them. We didn't deface it; we only printed something on the back of it."[39]

In their fight against the banks and in their struggle for equal rights, the Loco-Focos were arousing considerable attention. They might have become a power in city politics if they had not made a fatal move in the fall of 1837. Shortly after President Van Buren, in opposition to national state banks, proposed the subtreasury plan with the government taking charge of its own funds instead of handing them over to others, the Loco-Focos enthusiastically endorsed his proposal. So too did the Young Men's Committee of Tammany, but their action was opposed by the Old Men's Committee, and another split in Tammany Hall was evident.[40] After the Loco-Focos had selected their slate of ten candidates for the November elections of 1837, they discussed the advisability of uniting with the Young Men's Committee for greater strength. To explore the possibilities of such a move, the Loco-Focos appointed a committee of five to confer with the Tammany group and to find out if the Tammanyite candidates would subscribe to the Loco-Foco principles. But this committee far exceeded its powers. When Tammany nominated five Loco-Focos to run on their ticket, the committee reciprocated by putting five Tammanyites on the Loco-Foco ticket. To carry through this plan, five of the Loco-Focos who were not selected by Tammany would have to resign. But no resignations were forthcoming. The little group was in a desperate plight with the elections close at hand. A resolution was finally introduced to support the joint ticket thus forcing the resignation of the five unwanted candidates. The resolution carried by a vote of 71 to 22.[41]

The minority group in this convention was furious at this betrayal and accused their former cohorts, whom they called Buffaloes, of selling out to Tammany. In indignation, they bolted the party and formed their own group which the Tammanyite Loco-Focos scornfully labeled as Rumps. The split in the Equal Rights Party in New York City was now complete with the Buffaloes in the majority. The Heckers refused to go with the Tammanyite Loco-Focos and threw in their lot with the Rumps. They attended meetings to propose their candidates and when the ticket was chosen, they worked like Trojans to put it over. Isaac and George went around the city posting handbills long after the people had retired for the night. They worked at this up until about three o'clock in the morning, but as Isaac said later: "this hour was not so inconvenient for us, for we were bakers."[42] When election day dawned they doubled their energies, working at the polling booths, especially in their own ward, the old seventh. But despite all their efforts, their candidates were defeated. Tammany, however, also lost; the Whigs won the city.

This election sounded the death knell of the purists in the Loco-Foco faction. They never again met as a corporate body, but gradually merged into the Democratic Party. It also dispelled the hopes of the youngest of the Hecker boys, even before he reached his eighteenth birthday, for any effective and lasting social reform through politics alone. He had acquired, through his activity with the party, a firsthand knowledge of the political machine and its inner workings. He saw how much reliance could be put on politicians and ward-heelers in a time of crisis. He watched them compromise the very cause they had enthusiastically embraced, just as soon as it served their purpose. As he wrote, some twenty years later: "Not much was to be hoped from political actions, as politicians were governed more by selfishness and a thirst for power than by patriotism and the desire of doing good to their fellow citizens."[43]

It is a striking coincidence that this same thought about the politicians of the time was voiced by a man whom Hecker had not yet met but who would figure largely in his life — Orestes A. Brownson. This celebrated philosopher, writing in the January, 1841, issue of his own periodical, *The Boston Quarterly Review*, observed in scathing words: "People . . . distrust the politician, because they believe him cool, calculating, crafty, selfish, cowardly, destitute of bravery and enthusiasm, as most politicians have been and are."[44] Allow them to control government as they please, he warned, and they will cater to special interests and disregard the ordinary citizen. Society must restrain and guide them. "Our chief concern is with society and our main endeavor should be to create a true public opinion and that exaltation of public sentiment which will carry society with resistless force towards the completion of its destiny. This is to be done by moral, religious, and intellectual influences."[45]

Through the pages of his *Review* and in public speaking engagements, the Boston Reformer endeavored to help in the attainment of this goal. In March of 1841, he came to New York to give a lecture on Christian democracy. In his audience were the Hecker brothers and Isaac listened to the speaker's forceful and logical presentation with rapt interest.[46] After the lecture, Hecker met Brownson and was immediately attracted to him. Little could either man imagine, as they exchanged greetings, how their lives would be drawn together. For over thirty years, the two were the closest of friends, spending countless hours together, exchanging ideas, sharing the richness of their experiences, aiding and encouraging each other in their search for the truth, and then uniting their efforts to convey to their fellow men the truth they had found.

Though sixteen years apart in age, the two men were strangely alike, and yet quite different. They were similar in background since neither had much formal education, having been forced by necessity to start work at an early age. Brownson had overcome this handicap through personal study and application to books. At the time Hecker met him, he had acquired a brilliant command of the English language and he could write with fluency, directness, and vigor. He had mastered French which he read easily and had a fair knowledge of German. He had plunged into philosophy and had become one of the foremost disciples of Cousin in America.[47] Hecker had made no further advance over the limited education he had received at P.S. No. 7. He wrote English with difficulty in a very stilted and artificial style as his first known letter reveals. He knew German but had done very little reading at this time in either language. And as to philosophy, he was, in his own words, "as yet unborn."

The one strong bond between them was their dedication to the restoration of equal rights and opportunities, and their passionate love of liberty and freedom. Each had an insatiable thirst for truth and they were ready to sacrifice personal considerations and ambitions in their quest for its fulfillment. It was this affinity of minds and ideals that drew the two reformers together. This meeting had a profound influence on the course of Hecker's life. It broadened his horizon, introduced him to new realms of thought, and turned his attention to philosophy and religion as effective agents for social reform.

CHAPTER II

The Break with the Past

WHEN Brownson came to New York in March of 1841, he was at the height of his career. He had been roundly attacked for his "Essay on the Laboring Classes" which he published in July during the heat of the 1840 presidential campaign.[1] His doctrines were regarded as obnoxious because he advocated the destruction of the ministry, Catholic and Protestant alike; the abolition of the outward visible church; the elimination of banks and great business corporations; a complete renovation of the credit system; and a total revision of property distribution. The Whigs seized upon the article as typical of Democratic sentiment and policy since it emanated from the pen of a prominent Democrat; the Democrats disowned Brownson and protested the injustice of holding them responsible for his eccentricities. When the Democrats lost the election, no small share in the defeat was attributed to Brownson. His days of public favor seemed to be at an end. But when he published a defense of the laboring class in the *Boston Quarterly Review* for October, 1840, he gained far more attention than before the attack. As he remarked in *The Convert:* "In the three years that followed, I gained more than I had lost, and I never stood higher, commanded more of public attention, or had a more promising career open before me."[2]

In 1841 Brownson was riding the crest of the wave of popular approval when he lectured in New York. On March 4th, in Clinton Hall, he spoke to a "numerous and fashionable audience" on "The Democracy of Christ" and the following night on the "Reform Spirit of Our Age."[3] Years later Hecker recalled these lectures and

18

remembered Brownson as a "handsome man, tall, stately and of grave manners. . . . As he appeared on the platform and received our greeting, he was indeed a majestic man. . . . He never used manuscript or notes; he was familiar with his topic and his thoughts flowed out spontaneously in good, pure, strong, forcible English. He could control any reasonable mind, for he was a man of great thoughts and never without some truth to impart." Young Hecker was immediately struck by the force of this extraordinary man who was six feet two inches tall, with black hair brushed straight back from his forehead and deep-set eyes of mixed gray and hazel that seemed black when he grew excited. Hecker summed up the message Brownson left with him in the words: "The life and teachings of Our Saviour Jesus Christ were brought into use and the upshot of the lecturer's thesis was that Christ was the big Democrat and the Gospel was the true Democratic platform."[4]

Hecker did not know, nor was the audience aware, that Brownson was experiencing a new realization of the need for a deeper and more vital religious creed than he possessed. He was still searching, still unsure of himself, and proceeding with caution and reserve. And well he might. From his youth, his religious views had undergone radical changes. Revolting against the doctrines of total depravity and predestination in Calvinism, he abandoned Congregationalism and Presbyterianism and took refuge in Universalism. His devastating logic soon pierced the shallowness and abstraction of that sect but left him stranded in the web of skepticism. Through a chance reading of William Ellery Channing's *Likeness to God* he regained some of his faith and became a Unitarian minister. From 1832 to 1838 he preached regularly, but, discouraged by the attitude of the Boston clergy, resigned his pulpit and devoted himself unreservedly to social reform, attempting to establish the kingdom of God on earth. But after the election of 1840 and the reception accorded his "Essay on the Laboring Classes," he was coming to the conclusion that people, as a whole, were incapable of seeking the good if left to merely human means. They needed the vitalizing force of divine help, the source which Brownson was now seeking very cautiously.[5]

Hecker had a further opportunity to know Brownson when the latter returned to New York the following July 4th to deliver an Independence Day address. In fact it was the Heckers who had arranged the engagement and secured Brownson's consent.[6] There was nothing startling or unusual about the address the Boston Reformer gave. He hammered home the theme that: "The great principle involved in the American Revolution, and the mission of this country, was the alleviation of the condition of the laborer, giving to him an equality of rank with the mercantile and feudal lords, so that man should everywhere be recognized as man." He then graphically and forcefully presented the deplorable condition of the worker and his family. This he had done many times before in his articles in the *Boston Quarterly* and *Christian Examiner*. Injecting a new note, he turned to the question of intellectual freedom exclaiming: "But what is it to me that my country is free from England, if I have the chain on my mind and the padlock on my hand? You may bind my limbs, but if you leave my mind free, I may still be a man; and though you bind my limbs with cords like the green withes with which Samson was bound, yet if a man dare to think, he will not be long a slave. . . . A power has grown out that wealth cannot command — the power of thought."[7]

Undoubtedly this was a new idea to young Hecker. Previously, he had looked solely to action as a way of helping mankind; now Brownson was directing his attention to a new world, the world of ideas. And the source for these ideas, the lecturer continued, was the literature of France and Germany. "The literature of the Old World is becoming thoroughly democratic. . . . You may turn to the most popular literature of Paris at this moment: you will find that thousands are unwilling for Americans to read it — why is this? Not because it is impure, not because it is demoralizing but because it is *democratic!*"[8]

Literature was at that time an unknown source of hope for young Hecker. Previously he had looked to the ballot, now he would turn to a book. It might be the key that would unlock the mystery of man's destiny and reveal the secret of achieving it. French, he could not read, but since he was familiar with German he turned to the authors he could find in that language. It is quite likely that he requested of Brownson some direction in the books he would select, since the lecturer spent the evening at the Hecker home. However, Hecker has not said whether or not the noted author gave him any suggestions. It is clear though that his brothers were not so much concerned with literature. They were more interested in another project. They felt that the Reform movement in New York needed the direction and inspiration Brownson would give it. He must return for further engagements, particularly a full course of four lectures. They offered to call on the president of the New York Lyceum in time for the fall series, and have Brownson put on the regular schedule. Before he left New York, Brownson agreed.[9]

The Heckers soon found that the directors of the New York Lyceum did not share their high opinion of the editor of the *Boston Quarterly*. In an interview they had with the president of the organization, they learned that Brownson's "peculiar opinions" were so unpopular "they would be an injury to the course in a pecuniary point of view." Turned down on this score, the Heckers sounded out their friends who were quite unanimous in the opinion that Brownson should come. But since no one was taking any initiative, the Heckers made the decision. On November 14, 1841, they outlined their plans in a letter to Brownson. They would get the hall, take care of all the publicity, and be responsible for the success of the course. They left the subject to him, and suggested a time after the holidays.[10]

The letter, though it was signed "Hecker and Brothers" was written by the youngest of the family speaking in his own name and that of John and George.[11] There are characteristic phrases in this letter that reveal the spirit and temperament of Isaac. He tells Brownson "whatever you make up your mind to do we are always ready to cooperate with hearty cheer." One of the outstanding traits that marked him all his life was the enthusiasm and optimism which at this early date accompanied his efforts for reform.

The last paragraph of this letter indicated that young Hecker had dipped into some of the German authors and had begun to dabble in philosophy. He sent Brownson a copy of Orville Dewey's last two sermons which he had "the pleasure of hearing prior to his departure for Europe." Then he adds "Dr. Rev. Dewey we suppose is gone to meet the german Saviour so as to preach the Gospel of design at Boston to those german Transcendental mystics. Look out now you metaphysicians get your Cognition faculty in order so as to envisage time a Priori a Posteriori by intuition subjectively in your understandings."* This paragraph must have amused Brownson who would recognize that his youthful admirer had taken his advice to turn to literature, but who very obviously had understood little of what he had read. Isaac had seized upon words, but the juxtaposition in which he placed them showed unmistakably that he had little comprehension of their meaning.

When Brownson returned to New York, he selected as his general subject "Civilization and Human Progress" which he developed in four lectures on January 17, 19, 25, and February 2, 1842. The Heckers had hired Clinton Hall and had arranged for the publicity. The New York press, especially the *Tribune,* the *Evening Post,* and the *New Era,* gave generous space to reports of these talks which were generally quite commendatory. They noticed not only that there was a good audience, but that it was "penetrating and highly gifted."[12]

Of all the ideas Brownson enunciated, the one that had the greatest fascination for Hecker was the emphasis on the need of religion and philosophy. For at this stage of his life, religion had sunk down, not out of sight, but out of practical prominence.[13] He had attended the Unitarian Church of the Messiah and listened to its enlightened and popular pastor, Orville Dewey, not because he attached any importance to religion, but "because Dewey was a smart fellow and I enjoyed listening to him."[14]

As well as paying close attention to the logical development of Brownson's thought as he spoke earnestly and at times eloquently from the platform, Hecker had the further opportunity of intimate and personal conversation with the Boston Reformer who made the Hecker household his home during his stay in New York. Isaac had many earnest discussions with him at various times during the day "often during or after breakfast, dinner, or supper."[15] They reviewed the failure of workingmen's parties to achieve effective reform because, as Brownson reasoned, man could not elevate himself by human effort alone, no matter how concentrated or widespread it might be. "No man can rise above himself or lift himself by his own waistband."[16] Human reason could aid, but as he had written in the *Boston Quarterly*

---

* In Hecker's early letters and diary, there are mistakes in grammar, spelling, and punctuation due to his incomplete education. To make his meaning clear I have corrected his spelling and punctuation but not the grammar.

for that same month of January: "We have seen enough of mere individual reason. It is impotent when it has not for its guide and support, the reason of God, speaking not only to the heart, but through revelation and the traditions of the race."[17]

This immediately brought into prominence a vast range of philosophical questions that were soon to challenge Hecker's attention. How can anyone be sure of the validity of spiritual realities? How can he be certain that the voice of God speaking to the heart is not an illusion? Where is man to obtain the help he needs to elevate himself? Some of these questions Brownson had solved for a time with the aid of the French philosophers, Benjamin and Victor Cousin, who had given him grounds for faith in the reality of the spiritual world which exists outside of and independent of the individual.

But on closer examination, and pushing his thoughts to their logical conclusion, Brownson found that Cousin led him to the despairing dilemma, subjectivism and pantheism, neither horn of which he could accept. In pantheism he could not explain the evils of human life, for the divinity could not be as imperfect as he saw it in some of its modes. Subjectivism was just as untenable for Brownson from a point of view both of common sense and his own experience.[18]

In truth, Brownson could not answer the questions he himself raised either to his own or Hecker's full and complete satisfaction. And when Hecker put to him the basic difficulty he found in this whole matter of religion: "How can I be certain of the objective reality of the operations of my soul?" Brownson could only offer the weak and unsatisfactory reply: "If you have not yet reached that period of your mental life, you will do so before many years."[19]

For a further solution of these difficulties, Hecker went deeper into German philosophy. Whether he did it at the older man's suggestion, we have no means of knowing. Hecker does tell us that he read avidly Kant, Fichte, and Hegel, and became further ensnared in subjectivism.[20] Of course he was poorly equipped to deal with the works of these authors. He was not familiar with philosophical writings; his mind was unaccustomed to mental abstractions and he failed to see the sophisms latent in the writings he was so hungrily devouring.

This was not true of Brownson who had been studying philosophy for more than ten years. His mind at thirty-eight, enriched by experience, was sharper and more subtle than that of his young friend at twenty-two, who, until the last year, had expended his mental energies almost entirely on baking and politics. It is not surprising then to learn, as Hecker remarked some years later: "It took very little to lift him out of it [subjectivism] but it took much to lift me."[21]

Brownson's path opened out before him after he had studied Leroux's philosophical treatise, *L'Humanité*. A thorough understanding of Leroux's analysis of thought convinced him of the reality of the spiritual world outside himself and the validity of his thought processes. Within three months after he stayed in Rutgers Street, Brownson really grasped the significance of Leroux's doctrine of objectivity.[22] Hecker was not quite so fortunate. Although he could not read French, he could follow Leroux's ideas through the pages of the *Boston Quarterly Review* and see its theological implications in Brownson's letter to Channing on *The Mediatorial Life of Jesus* published in June, 1842. Perhaps Hecker might have become more certain of spiritual reality much sooner than he did if certain unusual events had not occurred in his own life. They created a deeply personal problem that drew his attention away from the social question to a profound scrutiny of his own impulses and thoughts. He began a soul-searching analysis of these thoughts and impulses to determine if he should ignore or obey them. Vaguely he began to realize that the call of humanity was giving way to the call of God sounding once more in his soul.

Until the summer of 1842, Isaac Hecker's way of life paralleled that of most young men of his age. With his brothers, he took an active interest in their rapidly expanding baking business and discussed with them its future possibilities. He was sensitively aware of social injustices and saw their effect on his fellow men. To the limit of his ability, he did what he could to remedy these evils, actively associating himself with movements for social reform. In all of this, his world was bound by the material things of life as they came within the range of sense experience.

After meeting Brownson, Hecker had his first introduction to the world of ideas and the realm of abstraction. But even though he became mentally active along metaphysical lines, he was anything but an introvert. His thought was stimulated by books and lectures, conversations and discussions. His energies were directed outside of himself and to others. He was a "window mind" rather than a "mirror mind." But about June of 1842 a complete change took place.[23] The focus of his attention, interest, and concern shifted from social reform and the physical problem of the reality of the universe, to the intensely individual problem of himself and his Creator.

A new life, a new world had suddenly burst upon his consciousness. It mystified him, it distressed him. He could not understand it nor explain it to himself, much less to others. This change was not the result of logic or a critical analysis of his own thoughts and ideas. He had not proceeded methodically from one premise to another, arriving at the conclusion that there is more to life than what his senses perceived. Nor had he stopped to evaluate his religious position, to analyze his grounds for belief, or indeed to question seriously if he had any strong or vital creed. Had he gone through any such process, he would have been able to trace more or less logically, as did Brownson, the various steps that had led to the awakening of his spiritual life. He was puzzled and bewildered because his transition resulted from intuitive and mystical factors rather than rational or philosophical. It was not gradual and consecutive, but sudden and recurrent. It was not a passing fancy issuing from a vivid imagination and leaving only a momentary effect on him. It was real and genuine with lasting results that altered the entire course of his life.[24]

Though young Hecker could not understand the cause, he could recognize the effect. He had suddenly become aware, how or in what way he does not reveal, of the only True Reality, God. Aside from this, everything else was meaningless and empty for him. His whole nature was slowly being drawn to his new-found Reality, why or for what purpose he could not answer. He found his interest was not in the bake shop, not in the ordinary things of his life, but diverted to "commune with other beings" whose nature he could not define. Time that should be given to his work he was devoting to contemplation, to prayer. This frightened him, especially when he realized that he was losing interest in all he formerly found so absorbing. He became more and more aware of "an irresistible force" drawing him away from the life of those around him.

Alarmed at seeing his former interests slipping away from him, he fought against the new influence and redoubled his efforts to concentrate on the ovens before him, the bread and cake he was baking, the people coming into the shop. He tried to tell himself this inner revolution was only temporary, that it would pass and he would be his old self again. For a while he entertained doubts that this "new world" opening before him was real. It must be imaginary, a phantasy of his mind, anything but genuine. But the more he fought against it, the stronger and more imperious this influence became.[25]

All his efforts to dismiss this change, to disregard the desire for prayer and contemplation, to question the truth of what he was experiencing, were useless. It was real; he knew it. It was a life given him by God; he could not deny it. He must surrender completely to its influence or he would never be true to himself. He must submit to its purifying guidance or he would never be at peace.[26]

The whole course of his life had suddenly taken a violent and abrupt twist. Previously religion had meant no more to him than a pious sentiment or a pleasant emotion. Now it was a vital force influencing his every action and demanding almost all his time and energy. It would brook no interference nor admit any alien interest. Its demands and its requests must be satisfied before all else and at all costs. His life must be transformed.

Slowly and in great agony of mind he began to realize that he could no longer continue his work. He must give up forever any hope of a business career. With this realization new problems arose. What would he tell his brothers? How could he explain to them what had happened, so they would not be puzzled and confused, or even distrustful of him? What language could he use that would be expressive and descriptive of the new life within him? He feared they might even interpret this new development as self-induced, as something he wished and sought. He did not expect them to understand, but he fervently prayed they would not misunderstand or, worse still, misinterpret his intentions.[27]

While he was debating what course to adopt toward his family, the situation was made more complex after the summer of 1842 by a series of dreams. They were not just ordinary dreams, or reveries conceived in a shadowy subconscious state which he could quickly forget, for he protests:

> How can I doubt these things? Say what may be said, still for all, they have to me a reality, a practical good bearing on my life. They are impressive instructors, whose teachings [are] given in such a real manner that they influence me, would I or not. . . . If I should not follow them I am altogether to blame. I cannot have such advisers upon earth; none could impress me so strongly with such peculiar effect, and at the precise time most needed.[28]

One and only one of these dreams does he explain or attempt to relate in any detail. This he does in his diary, some ten months after it happened.

> I saw (I cannot say I dreamt for it was quite different from dreaming as I thought [since] I was seated on the side of my bed) a beautiful, angelic, pure being and myself standing along-side of her, feeling a most heavenly pure joy. And it was [as] if . . . our bodies were luminous and they gave forth a moonlike light which I felt sprung from the joy that we experienced. We were unclothed. pure, and unconscious of anything but pure love and joy, and I felt as if we had always lived together and that our motions, actions, feelings and thoughts came from one center. And when I looked towards her I saw no bold outline of form but an angelic something I cannot describe, but in angelic shape and image. It was this picture [which] has left such an indelible impression upon my mind; and for some time afterwards I continued to feel the same influence, and do now so that the actual around me has lost its hold on me. . . . Now this vision continually hovers over me . . . I am charmed by its influence, and I am conscious that if I should accept anything else, I should lose the life which would be the only existence wherein I could say I live.[29]

This description bears a striking resemblance to some of the supernatural visions of genuine mystics such as St. Francis of Assisi and Henry Suso and St. Teresa. It attempts to clarify by resorting to human analogy but then abstracts from it; it makes use of the prevalent mystical symbol of a luminous background; it employs the use of angelic image and asserts the absence of form and shape; it speaks of heavenly joy and love coming from one center. It particularly stresses the lasting impression for good that remains after the vision has retreated.[30] If Hecker had been reading mystical treatises, if he had been familiar with the lives of the saints in which similar events had occurred, there might be a danger that he was re-enacting in his own life what he had learned from the experience of others. But at this time, he was totally unfamiliar with mystical phenomena, he was completely ignorant of the heroic lives of men and women of extraordinary holiness. He could not be accused of reliving incidents remembered from something he had read. It was to him a vivid, realistic, and effective occurrence that drew him away more and more from the life around him.

This is the first experience that he records which gives him great joy and happiness. Previously he is concerned about the pain and difficulty of renunciation of a business career which he makes reluctantly but sincerely. After this vision he forsakes any hope of marriage, but he does it willingly and eagerly that he might retain "this vision" and its "beauty." There is no struggle because "the charm of its influence" more than counterbalances any attraction of a human being.[31]

The luminous figure did not, however, dispel the darkness before him. He could not see where the new life was leading him. It was taking him away from everything but directing him to no certain goal. Repeatedly he observes that all is dark before him. Of one thing only is he sure; he is being led by the Spirit and he must, at all costs, follow that guidance.[32] He could no longer continue living his life of the past twenty-three years. The one problem still to be solved, the one he dreaded facing, was how to tell his family.

By this time, Isaac's older brother John was fairly well established as the head of the household. He apparently made all the decisions and directed the destinies of the family. So it was natural that Isaac should acquaint him first with the new turn his life had taken. How much the young sufferer revealed of his difficulties we do not know. John was sympathetic with his younger brother and sincerely concerned about the problem. He had noticed the change in him, how he seemed to withdraw into himself and become lost in thought when he should be engrossed in business. John also had an explanation for Isaac's action, one which gave little attention to religious or supernatural reasons, but traced the whole cause to books and study which resulted in "too much exercise of mind." He strongly recommended that Isaac check that tendency and he would be all right.[33] The advice seemed simple enough but for Isaac it was impossible. "How can I keep my life from flowing on?" he asked himself.[34]

Mrs. Hecker did not entirely agree with John and saw more than a mental state. She supposed, in characteristic Methodist fashion, that the upheaval was the result of a religious awakening which "all persons must have before they are Christians in a more or less degree." She felt that her son wanted "a giving up of his whole mind to Christ" and then he would be all right.[35]

Isaac's forebodings were realized: his family could not understand. Any attempt at expressing himself made him appear singular and eccentric, since those around him were neither subject themselves to his experiences nor familiar with such inner unrest in others. Rather than distress his family with any further attempts to bare his soul, he kept all to himself. But this did not solve the problem. He became worried and upset. The tenseness of the situation brought on severe nervous depression, his appetite was affected and he soon became ill. The physician who was called advised the patient to engage in some occupation that would be a happy combination of mental and physical labor. He further told him to take a renewed interest in social life, to associate more with young people of his own age, and to plan to marry.[36]

All this well-intentioned but patently professional advice was useless because it failed to probe the heart of the matter. Part of it was repugnant to Hecker, for he was convinced he would never marry. Since the time of his vision, he had no desire for marriage. He knew the only companion he wanted was the Spirit guiding him; the only life, communion with God. But this he could not have as long as he continued as he was.

Unassisted by medical aid, unimproved by friendly advice, Isaac's condition grew worse. To encourage him, the family gave him his own way, hoping that some unforeseen circumstance would restore him. They noticed that he always felt better when he was expecting something or contemplating a journey. But when he received what he was expecting or finished whatever he undertook, he experienced severe spells of despondency. To help him as much as possible, the family took care not to cross him but gave him encouragement in his undertakings. They treated him with utmost kindness and compassion, as Isaac observed on several occasions,[37] hoping that time would solve the problem and he would then be "as he once was."[38] But despite all their willingness to help, Isaac felt that they could not give him what he needed most — compassionate understanding. Only one who could understand him could help him.

In his distress he thought of Brownson with whom he had spent many an interesting and enlightening hour the past winter. The first opportunity to see him came in December when Brownson arrived in New York to deliver three lectures. He stayed with the Heckers from December 6th to the 19th.[39] During this time Isaac could discuss his difficulties with one whom he not only admired and respected, but whose judgment he highly regarded. How much of his interior Hecker revealed to Brownson, or with what detail he explained the new life within him, or whether he told him of his dreams, we have no way of knowing. The nature of his experience was so intimate and personal, the relationship between his soul and the Spirit guiding him was so tender and delicate, it seems highly unlikely that he could, even if he would, lay it bare even to his closest friend.

Since Brownson had come to the deep realization of the need of religion in the life of all men, as well as in his own, he was sympathetic and understanding with Hecker. His spiritual sense too had deepened, but in a way quite different from that of his young friend. Brownson's religion was of the head, logical and intellectual; Hecker's was of the heart, spontaneous and mystical. Brownson's religious advance was gradual, evolving slowly from one syllogism to another; Hecker's was sudden, awakened and quickened by the ever mysterious action of God. Brownson's religion was social, looking to the interest of others; Hecker's was personal, dealing with his own soul.[40]

Hecker wanted to discuss a wide range of questions but Brownson could give so little time during this hurried lecture tour, that the older man suggested a visit to Boston. Isaac promptly accepted and planned to leave for Boston the week after Brownson had returned home, but he was temporarily delayed by illness. This time Dr. William H. Channing (whose church Hecker was attending) suggested another doctor who "pretends to have the power to discover any disease of the system or any tendency the mind may have to excessive excitement." Hecker had little faith in the "intended experiment . . . yet I feel it my duty that if there is any medicinal remedy I ought to try it, because living out a complaint, if I may say so, is not only a very slow process but at the same time wretched and rather unpleasant living."[41] Isaac held out little hope of improvement from medicine, for he knew that the cause of his illness was not physical but spiritual. He felt that the only remedy for his troubles would be a satisfactory solution to two questions: (1) How could he harmonize his present with his former life? (2) What did God want of him? In search of these answers he went to Boston.

A few days before Christmas, Isaac Hecker arrived at Brownson's home where he was greeted with cordiality and friendship.[42] The Boston Reformer was then living in Mt. Bellingham in Chelsea. He had discontinued his *Boston Quarterly Review* with the October issue of 1842, merging it with the *Democratic Review* at the suggestion of the editor, Mr. J. L. O'Sullivan. Brownson was to function as contributing editor.[43] He had also returned to the pulpit in April of 1842 and every Sunday he preached in Boston. His sermons, Hecker recalled years later, were the main feature of the service and attracted a class of men and women "who were thinkers rather than worshippers. . . . There was more original thinking in that congregation than in all the rest of Boston put together."[44]

One of the subjects that Brownson had written about in the July, 1842, number of his *Review* fascinated Hecker and he wished to discuss it further with Brownson. This was Leroux's doctrine of communion which Brownson had found invaluable in solidifying his own religious thought and removing all vestiges of subjectivism. Hecker, though convinced of the reality of his own inner feelings and the existence of a spiritual world outside of himself with which he communed, was lacking in solid rational arguments to prove their existence. The experience of his own consciousness he could not deny, but neither could he confirm it with philosophic reasoning. This Brownson gave to him, walking the streets of Boston, on the ferry as they crossed the harbor, and from the ferry wharf up the hill to Mt. Bellingham, and in his home. Back and forth the conversation went, analyzing and comparing Leroux and Constant with the more abstruse reasoning of Kant and Hegel.[45]

Finally Hecker had firm, philosophical grounds on which to base the validity of his intuitions. But he had more. Through Leroux's arguments, Brownson had shown him the need for man to commune with reality outside of himself, to come in contact with the power and strength of God. It was logical to infer from this that Hecker's recent experience was not altogether unique. It should be the lot of mankind. This was consoling news for Isaac, coming from one of the most powerful minds he had ever known and backed with the force and authority of basic logical arguments. He had found the understanding heart and the sympathetic mind.

Then he turned his thoughts to the first of the two practical questions clamoring for attention — his return home. He had come to the definite and convincing conclusion that he could never harmonize the new life he had received with the old life he had lived. They were not only mutually opposed but utterly irreconcilable. Were he to attempt it, he would be torn apart by mental anguish. He was certain of this. Now he must convince his family who still cherished the hope that his condition was only temporary. The day after Christmas he wrote a long and ardent letter to his brothers making unmistakably clear his decision and its final character. It was written firmly, but not easily. As he said "it is done in tears."[46] He writes "in a sense I have never spoken to you before," and he attempts the tortuous process of opening his "inmost life." Abruptly he comes to the crux of the situation and voices the thought uppermost in his mind: "Truly can I say a new life has opened to me and to turn back would be death. . . . My mind has lost all disposition to business. My hopes, life, existence all are in another direction." He realizes the responsibility involved in this decision and "to give up as I have to do, my highest aims and hope" is a tremendous sacrifice that will entail suffering and heartache. But he is powerless to control it. "It is not my will but my destiny." Then, lest any of them should think that the new life was unmitigated renunciation and sorrow, he speaks, but only a word, of a new found joy, "a communion" he had never known before. He looks ahead to the future with resignation: "How this will end I know not, but cannot but trust in God."[47]

Since this was the first attempt he had made to reveal to those at home what had been going on for many months, he was terribly concerned that he might be misunderstood. "When I say my mind cannot be occupied now as formerly, do not attribute this to my wishes. This is my fear, which makes me almost despair — makes me feel that I would rather die than live under such thoughts."[48]

Brownson was aware of his visitor's agony of mind and knew he was announcing his decision to his family. He could not help realizing that the intensity of Isaac's inhibited feelings would break out in his letter and cause his family great distress. So, unknown to the young man, he wrote an accompanying letter to John Hecker to cushion the shock they would all experience from this unexpected outburst.[49] It was not a long letter nor did it say too much other than to give a few hopeful words of comfort. He explained that Isaac was excited and disturbed when he wrote and that this was to some degree responsible for the vehemence of his words. But they should have no worry. He was taking a fatherly interest in Isaac and would do all he could for him.[50]

There was not much Brownson could say for he himself was somewhat puzzled by the sudden change in the young reformer whom he had met in New York. He did not disclose to the Heckers that, though he could not doubt Isaac's sincerity about the new life within him, he thought it was still too new and too fervent to permit any definite and far-reaching decision. But he also recognized without saying so to the Heckers that an immediate return home would be detrimental to Isaac's health as well as to his state of mind. As a practical expedient it would be too dangerous, so in his own mind he was weighing the advisability of a temporary sojourn at Brook Farm in West Roxbury.* There, away from the environment and associations that had led to his

---

* Brook Farm was an attempt at a co-operative society through a natural union between intellectual and physical labor. It aimed to combine the worker and the thinker in the same individual. The following chapter will discuss the project more in detail.

unrest, Brownson hoped Isaac would become more calm and settled. Then he could plan for the future.

When Isaac's letter reached Rutgers Street, it startled the family. It was so definite, so final, that they feared he was breaking away from the family. What should they do about it? What could they do? What was leading him on? These and a number of other frightening questions leaped from the pages their devoted brother had written. They were somewhat reassured after they read Brownson's letter. It gave them hope that perhaps Isaac's condition was only temporary and under Brownson's careful guidance it would shortly disappear.[51]

While Isaac was waiting for a reply to his first letter, he wrote again on December 28th, a further explanation of his mind. He was more restrained but nonetheless definite, stressing the permanent character of his change and the impossibility of any compromise.

> What is the state of my mind? This I have mostly stated in my former letter, but will add that what is there said is to me a permanent state, not a momentary excitement. You may think that in a little time this would pass away and then I would be able to resume my former life; or at least so adapt it [at] home that, although I should not precisely occupy myself as then, still it might be so arranged as to give that which I feel necessary so as to live at least somewhat contented. I am sorry to say that I can in no way conceive such an arrangement of things at home. Why? I hate to say it, yet we might as well come to an understanding between us. I have grown out of the life which can be received through the accustomed channels of the circle that has surrounded me. I am subject to thoughts and feelings which those around me had no interest in — hence they could not be expressed. This had not need be told; you must all have seen it. How can I stop my life from flowing on? You must see the case I stand in. . . . Do not think this is imagination; in this I have had too much experience. The life that was in me had no one to commune with, and I felt it was consuming me. . . . It is a life in me which requires altogether different circumstances to live it. This is no dream. If it is, then have I never had such reality. What course can I adopt to secure it? That is not perfectly clear to me as yet. When I wrote my last letter, it struck me I might secure it at Brook Farm.[52]

At this point he was interrupted by the arrival of his brother

John's answer to his earlier letter. Acting on the information Brownson had given him, he wrote carefully and did not reveal the family's alarm. Isaac read and reread it and summed up its message in one sentence: "What object have you in contemplation?" In answer, he simply stated: "None further than to live a life agreeable to the mind I have and which I feel under a necessity to do."[53] Although this sounded somewhat vague and indefinite, Isaac Hecker had grasped its practical significance and took a realistic view of the situation. He could not spend all his time in contemplation. He would need something else to engage his mind, but something that would add to, rather than detract from, the life within him. Further, he could not stay on indefinitely as a guest in the Brownson home. But where could he go? Brownson suggested Brook Farm which offered many advantages. He could have solitude when he wanted it and the opportunity to study when his mind was free. This would allow him to probe further into philosophy and dip into theology which would not divert but swell the stream of thought flooding into his mind.[54]

In his last letter home, Isaac had mentioned Brook Farm as a possible residence. The more he thought of it, the more the idea appealed to him. But before committing himself, he made up his mind to go to West Roxbury for a visit and investigate for himself. He would look it over carefully, taking a few days to get as complete a picture as he possibly could. Then, if he found it satisfactory, and his brothers acquiesced in his going, he would stay at Brook Farm until his views clarified a little more.

Brownson gave him a letter of introduction to George Ripley, the founder, and on January 4, 1843, Isaac presented it.[55] He liked the place immediately, with its pine groves, located near the winding Charles River. He was impressed with the simplicity and sincerity of the people he saw there, especially the kindly and gracious Mr. Ripley. He could study at his leisure, particularly languages which would give him the necessary background to read outstanding thinkers in their own tongue. The terms he considered quite reasonable. The rate was four dollars a week, which covered room, meals, washing, mending, and whatever kind of education he wished. When Mr. Ripley found out that he was a baker, he explained that if he cared to do the baking that would reduce his expenses.[56] Isaac was at first noncommittal on this offer. He did not want to engage himself immediately in work he found so unsatisfactory at home. But he did not rule it out entirely. As a result of his investigation, Isaac came to the conclusion that this might be just the place he needed. He liked Brook Farm and Brook Farm liked him. At the meeting of the directors held three days after Hecker arrived, his name was proposed for membership in the "family" of the Farm. The decision was favorable and the director was authorized to receive him, "on such terms as may be agreed upon."[57] All he needed now was his brothers' consent.

Isaac's letter with the mention of Brook Farm and study had by this time reached New York.* It struck no sympathetic chord in his brother John. He was already convinced that books and abstractions were the source of Isaac's trouble and he was ready to register strong disapproval. After a little reflection he decided to leave the decision to Brownson. "If you think it would do him no harm to stay at Brook Farm and study I will be satisfied and I will do for him what is necessary."[58]

When John's letter arrived in Boston, Isaac was much relieved. He felt "more settled than I have been for some time."[59] He had even come to the conclusion that he would do the baking at the Farm, though he was cautious in telling this to the family. He wrote and asked them to send him "the best of my working clothes (for I may help them in our business)."[60] He did not want them to write and ask if he could bake in West Roxbury, why not in New York. Of course, the two situations were in no sense comparable, but since his family were so anxious for his return, he had no intention of raising that question. Moreover, he was not sure that Brook Farm would be entirely suitable; he only hoped it would.

The first of the two problems he had brought to Boston was settled; he would not return home immediately. He then turned to the second: What did God want of him? All his life he had

---

* The mere mention of Brook Farm without any explanation in this letter and the absence of any questions about it in John's letter to Brownson, indicate that the family had some knowledge of the project. They may have read the account of it in the January 28, 1842, issue of the *Tribune* or in the article which Brownson wrote for the *Democratic Review,* November, 1842.

been convinced that God had a work for him to do, but until the summer of 1842, it had been quiet conviction that had caused him no worry. But after his first awareness of the Presence of God, that conviction burst into a flame that consumed not only his life, but all that touched his life. This progress of purification he attempted to chart in the first diary he kept. He confided his thoughts to loose scraps of paper on two successive days while he was still at Brownson's home. They are outpourings of mingled joy and sorrow, fervent protestations of love and sacrifice, ardent longings for light and guidance.

The first day he asks himself: "Could I but reveal myself unto myself, what shall I say? Is life dear to me? No. Are my friends dear to me? I could suffer and die if needs be for them, but yet have none of the old attachment that I had for them. I would clasp all to my heart, love all for their Humanity, but not as relations or individuals." He had passed through a period of purgation during which he was separated from everything he had always cherished, family, friends, marriage, and business prospects. He had broken all his attachments. "My love of all worldly things is gone." No longer did they interest or delight him. Now, cleansed of all affection for the things of the world, he finds "all around" him a darkness which mystifies and concerns him. And he asks the eternal why and wherefore. He begs for divine aid and prays "O Lord, open Thou my eyes to see the path Thou wouldst [have] me walk on. Thy Spirit has led me in all my present judgments but I have not looked unto Thee for light, which I hope I may have the faith to ask in the right spirit, so I can receive Thy blessing of wisdom." He closes this entry with a spirit of resignation to the divine will of God.[61]

The second day, he dwells not so much on the fact of his purification, but its results: "Things below have no hold on me further than that they led to things above." He would not take it upon himself to say that he has been "born again, but I know that I have passed from death to life. . . . I have no conception of a life insensible to that which is not above."[62]

This gradual detachment resulted in a complete conversion of his whole being. He was no longer subject to the usual temptations. Now they were of a different kind. "I am led to be untrue to my life; if I am not on my guard I become cold." What is this life? "One continuous prayer, an unceasing aspiration after the holy . . . it is only by unuttered prayer that my bosom is unburthened." He has a terrifying fear that he might do anything to diminish or disturb this life. "Oh, I hope of all [things] my *life* will be continued which I now have. . . . I would rather be taken from this stage of action than lose it."[63]

He then turns to the God of love who has drawn him to Himself and asks: "Who can fathom the blessing of God? It is infinite in its source and its kind. . . . He that is without God has nothing but that which is an injury, a curse to his soul." Then fastening his thought on the suffering of Christ, not in His passion and death, but in man's rejection of His divine help, he wrote: "He would give them life, but they would not receive. He would save them, but they rejected Him. He loved them and they despised Him. . . . His love, goodness, mercy were unbounded." Then he finishes with a prayerful plea "O Lord, may I daily come in closer and closer communion with Thy Son, Jesus Christ."[64]

If, at this crisis in his life, Isaac Hecker had been in touch with anyone familiar with the ways of the spiritual life, he would have received some helpful information on his state of soul. Ascetic theology would have told him that the very nature of God's love is purifying and ennobling. When it touches the soul in any pronounced degree, it cleanses that soul of earthly attachments and preoccupation with the things of the world. This is a preparation for the greater infusion of divine love which soon absorbs the attention and interest of the soul's energies. It can no longer be satisfied with anything created. God is the whole center and object of its attentions. The greater the infusion of divine love, the more consuming becomes its operation and the soul yearns with ever increasing desire for greater participation in the divine life.

The guidance Hecker needed, but did not receive, would have warned him that he could expect alternate periods of what he called darkness and light. These would result from the divine action of God revealing or concealing Himself and the course of this action no man can chart. It would come and go according to the design of God and His plan for the soul, and for this reason should cause no undue anxiety. The wise director would have counseled him to remove any hindrance and avoid any obstacle that might impede God's action, without trying to force or hurry the hand that is leading him.

The only one to whom Hecker could turn at this time of his life, the only one with whom he could discuss something of his interior struggle, was Orestes Brownson. Considerate, kindly, sympathetic as Brownson was to him, he could give no beneficial spiritual guidance, for he was a philosopher, not a director of souls. He did what lay within his power, which Hecker ever appreciated, and he always carried a deep and heartfelt sense of gratitude to Brownson. He felt he owed more to him than to any other man he met during these trying days.[65]

Hecker had brought to Brownson a difficulty and the philosopher found it was too much for him. Hecker realized this more than a year later when he wrote in his diary: "Brownson is a friend to me and the most critical periods of my experience have been known to him. He has advised and frequently given me his sympathy, yet he never moves my heart." Then, after speaking of Brownson's tremendous mental activity, "he thinks for a dozen men," Hecker adds this significant sentence, "It is too late for him to give his time to contemplation and interior recollection — he is a controversialist."[66] There was no place for controversy in Hecker's problem, but there was need for guidance and enlightenment. The philosopher could give neither. All he could do was to turn his head in the direction of West Roxbury and point his finger in the direction of Brook Farm. There, he hoped this bewildered young man might find the answers to the questions of his soul.

CHAPTER III

Search Among the Utopias

THE panic of 1837 had shaken the confidence of many an American in the wisdom of the businessman and the strength of the capitalistic system. The struggle for economic survival and the anguish of insecurity had awakened an interest in a new and different kind of society where love of man would replace love of mammon. As John Morley put it: "A great wave of humanity, of benevolence, of desire for improvement, — a great wave of social sentiment, in short, — poured itself among all who had the faculty of large and disinterested thinking."[1] Utopian hopes and aspirations were breaking through the social unrest and finding expression in co-operative rather than competitive living. After 1840 associations in which members lived a community life began to appear in various forms and in widely separated areas of the nation.[2]

One of the most famous was Brook Farm, the creation of the scholarly and idealistic mind of George Ripley. A graduate of the Harvard Divinity School, he had labored as a Unitarian minister for more than fourteen years to infuse the spirit of disinterested charity into the lives of his congregation. Meeting with little success, he resigned his pulpit and decided to gather together individuals with ideas similar to his own and to establish a more Christian way of life. His aim was to create "a society of liberal, intelligent and cultivated persons whose relations with each other would permit a more simple and wholesome life than can be led amidst the pressure of our competitive institutions." Knowing

40

that although man does not live by bread alone, he cannot do without food, Ripley hoped "to insure a more natural union between intellectual and manual labor than now exists; to combine the thinker and the worker, as far as possible, in the same individual."[3]

In April of 1841 with his wife and fifteen others, he began his idyllic experiment on a farm of 192 acres which he had bought in West Roxbury, nine miles west of Boston. With its sloping hills, its trees and shrubbery, its extensive untouched acres crying for cultivation, the location seemed ideal for the new community. A pleasant little brook ran through the property and very soon the old estate was called Brook Farm.[4]

The Utopia of George Ripley had been flourishing a little more than a year when Isaac Hecker boarded the coach at Scollay's Square in Boston which took him out to Brook Farm. The ride was a pleasant one through the New England countryside, during that third week of January, 1843. The picturesque white houses with green shutters soon gave way to pleasant farms surrounded by stone walls enclosing fruit and shade trees. The scenery became more beautiful the nearer he came to his destination. Soon he saw the buildings of the New Eden. Hecker remembered from his first visit, the poetic names Ripley had used when pointing them out; the Hive, the Eyrie, the Cottage, the Pilgrim House, and the Nest.[5] Except the Hive, the original farmhouse, all the others were newly built to provide for increasing membership. By the time Hecker arrived, there were ninety boarders who came from all walks of life.* George William Curtis recalled some years later: "The society of Brook Farm was composed of every kind of person. There were the ripest scholars, men and women of the most aesthetic culture and accomplishment, young farmers, seamstresses, mechanics, preachers."[6]

The roster of permanent members, those who made Brook Farm their home and their life, included such illustrious names as the Harvard scholars, George P. Bradford, Charles A. Dana, and

---

* There were two types of boarders: partial and full. The former did work around the farm and, according to the amount they did, their expenses were reduced. The latter paid the full amount and engaged in no labor. These were mainly students who provided the largest source of revenue at the Farm. Some income came from the sale of farm products.

John S. Dwight. Grouped with them were lesser lights, but nonetheless important in the success of the new movement: the head
farmer, William Allen; the guestmaster, Christopher List; the
shoemaker, Lewis Ryckman; the recreation leaders, Charles New-
comb and Amelia Russell.[7]

For the first few weeks Hecker did not take an active part
in Brook Farm life. He had come, not to make friends or engage
in social activities, but to work out a solution of his spiritual
problem. All he asked of Brook Farm was to be left alone until
he could adjust himself to his new life. The Brook Farmers, who
abhorred intruding themselves into anyone's personal affairs, respected Hecker's wishes. All treated him very kindly, but they
realized that though he was at Brook Farm, he was not of it.
Hecker was aware of this when he wrote in his diary: "Evidently
I am not one of their spirits. The tone of their speech to me is
different. 'Mr. Hecker' is pronounced in tones different from the
tone in which they address others."[8]

Within a few days after his arrival, Hecker became the community baker. Any visitor to the Hive could see in the kitchen
this thoughtful young man, six feet tall, who looked even taller
with his regulation baker's cap perched on the top of his head,
his long blond hair reaching his shoulders, his blue eyes set in
an oval, pock-marked face which Ora Gannett described as "not
handsome, but . . . earnest, high-minded and truthful."[9] His
predecessor at the ovens was not skilled and the bread had been
"very poor."[10] Isaac knew he could do much better, for as he
later told George Curtis: "I am sure of my livelihood because I
can make good bread."[11] He prepared his own baker's yeast and
turned out fifty or sixty pounds of bread a day in one batch. The
results of Isaac's work at the ovens pleased everyone, and whatever else the members thought of the newcomer — they had found
out that he was "a baker by profession and a mystic by inclination" — they agreed that he made excellent bread.[12]

One of the reasons for Hecker's choice of Brook Farm was the
opportunity he would have to study. While he was still a youngster, his mother had said to John: "Let Isaac go to college and
study." These words made no impression on John, but they went
through Isaac like "liquid fire" which never burned itself out.[13]
At home he had neither the opportunity nor the circumstances to

CROTON FLOUR MILLS

ORESTES A. BROWNSON

BROOK FARM   From original painting of Josiah Wolcott
now in the possession of Mrs. Robert Blake Weston,
Belmont, Massachusetts.

FRUITLANDS   Courtesy Mr. Henry Harrison.

feed that flame, but at Brook Farm it could burn brightly, for, there, intellectual development was considered the torch of freedom. Complete courses which prepared young men for college attracted students from such widely separated areas as Cambridge and Havana, New York and Florida. The curriculum even merited the approval of Harvard College.[14] Excellent and well-trained scholars made up the faculty. George Ripley taught philosophy and mathematics; Bradford, Literature; Dwight, assisted by his two sisters Marianne and Frances, taught Latin and music; Dana, Greek and German; Sophia Ripley, history and modern languages; Hannah Ripley, drawing; and Amelia Russell, dancing. All students did not take the full course of studies, but selected those subjects which most appealed to them.[15] Since Hecker was not preparing for college, he was one of this group. His first interest was music so he attended Dwight's singing school. Occasionally he would drop in on Mr. Ripley's philosophy classes.[16]

At first, Isaac did not feel that his mind was free enough to attempt any serious study and he was still too unsettled to commit himself to follow even one particular course for any length of time. Moreover, his inner life was demanding a large share of his attention. Conscious of an influence drawing him away from those around him, he would spend hours in his room in prayer and contemplation asking God: "Raise me up from this world, for I am becoming unsuited for it. I exist not in this life. I commune not with man. . . . It is only in Thee I find communion. O Lord, grant that this may be uninterrupted and that I may drink deeper and deeper in Thy Spirit."[17]

Anxiety about the future still filled his soul. He felt himself drawn to a life beyond this world, but still forced to live in it. At a loss to harmonize the two, he begged: "What I want is that I may live in any one direction; not that I shall see where or whence this direction will lead me, but that I may walk in the road and leave the end for the end." He felt that he was "tossed about on the sea of life without knowing which way to steer." The conviction that God had a work for him was deeper and stronger than ever and he was aware that in some mysterious way his present condition was a prelude to that future work. Ardently he longed for the moment "when the dawn of day would break upon my soul that I might see unto what I was born." Once or twice the thought crossed his mind that perhaps at Brook Farm this burst of light might pierce the darkness surrounding him but he dismissed this as wishful thinking when he realized: "Here is not my life; it is only a temporary resting place; perhaps an intermediary place suitable for my condition at present." If the spirit should drive him from West Roxbury, and he felt sure it would, where could he go? To return home "would be death." He resolved to leave the future to God. "Into Thy hands, O Lord, I commit myself, and Thou dost with me as seemeth good in Thy sight. But grant, O Lord, Thy Spirit to me, that I may be willing to do Thy will and not strive against it. Give me power that I may walk in Thy direction and teach me how to pray that I may receive Thy blessing."[18]

This act of resignation brought peace to Isaac's soul and he decided to remain at Brook Farm until spring. On January 26, 1843, he wrote to his brothers telling them of this intention and asking their consent. The tone of the letter indicated that he expected no opposition from the family and his request for a three months' subscription to the *Weekly Herald* suggested the length of his stay. His money was almost gone, so he asked from $30 to $50 from his account in the business.* John, with his insistence that study caused Isaac's trouble, must have groaned when he saw the imposing list of books that Isaac asked for: "Flugel's German Dictionary, an English Dictionary, Arndt's Geist der Zeit, Levan or Ersiegenungslehre, Goets von Berlichen-gen, Kant's Anthropologie, Davy's Algebra and Geometry, the Grammar . . . Schiller's Prosaische Schriften and Treck's Dich-tund."[19] However, since the family had agreed with Brownson to let Isaac go to Brook Farm temporarily and study, they decided to send him the books. But they were not happy about his intention to remain for three months and wondered why he did not come home. Before asking that question, George wrote a letter "full of news" in which he inquired about Isaac's health.[20] "I do not know that I can be better than I am in my physical health," he answered, adding that his mind was more settled than it had been for some time. These were the beneficial effects of his stay

---

* Since the business was a partnership, the profits were divided among the three and credited to each one separately on the books. Later on Isaac objected to this and wanted a common account.

at Brook Farm and he trusted "the future will have much more."[21]

When the Heckers received this letter, it touched off anew the delicate question of Isaac's return. He had left home in poor health and since he had recovered, they assumed that most of his difficulties had vanished. His place, then, was with his family in New York, not among strangers in West Roxbury. John wrote and told his younger brother he could no longer be reconciled to his absence, since his health was so much improved. Now that he was well, he should return. Such a prospect filled Isaac with horror and showed him how little his family understood his problem. His illness had not caused his new life, as they seemed to think, but was the result of his attempt to stifle it. His health returned only when he was able to live that life through prayer and contemplation as he was doing at Brook Farm. To deny him the privilege of communing with "the Spirit" would not only inflict on him excruciating pain, it "would be death."[22]

This tug of war between Isaac and his family was sure to continue until either he could open his soul to them or they could penetrate the meaning of his words. He realized he could find no words to express himself, and they had no background to understand what he was trying to say. But he felt that since "it is my duty towards you not to keep back my life from you," he makes the futile attempt to clarify his state of soul in a letter dated February 22nd. He sums up his life in one sentence that must have further mystified them, though undoubtedly he thought it would enlighten them: "All appears to me as a seeming to be, nothing real, nothing that touches that life in me which is seeking for which I know not." Some power is guiding him, he is certain of that; but where or why, he cannot answer. "All before me is dark, even as that which leads me now and has led me before." All he can do is submit to it, since he has not even the strength "to wish myself out of this state. I have no will to do it — not that I have or do desire it. I am in it is all I can say and in it, I am."[23]

Isaac's family never doubted for a moment that he was "in it." Their problem was how to get him out of it and they sincerely believed that their hope of success would be far greater if he were at home rather than at Brook Farm. Their first thought was to have him return not in obedience to a command, but voluntarily.

At this point, they stopped to evaluate the whole situation. Why had Isaac left? Was it solely because of a profound religious experience, or rather was it not their attitude toward that experience? With the best of intentions and the finest of motives, they had wounded his spiritual sensitivity by refusing to discuss religious questions and brusquely dismissing the thoughts he haltingly tried to express. With perhaps the least sympathy of any member of the family, John had insisted that his younger brother devote all his time to the active work of the bakery and forget his inner life. Unwittingly, they had driven him into himself and away from them. No wonder, they concluded, Isaac felt rejected by his own and in desperation turned to strangers. The family's desire for Isaac's restoration to his place at home undoubtedly caused them to paint in the most somber colors their part in his difficulty because they sincerely believed they were responsible for his leaving.[24]

To clarify the whole situation, George wrote a long letter to Isaac explaining the family attitude and assuring him that now the spirit at home was entirely different. During his absence they had taken a greater interest in religion, were reading the Oxford tracts, and John had all but made up his mind to become an Episcopalian. If he would come home, and all the family agreed he should, he would find not only sympathy but understanding.[25]

The mail had brought the olive branch from New York, but Isaac could not accept it. His family, he knew, was entirely mistaken in assuming they had treated him badly and they should not reproach themselves for what they had done. He admitted, in his reply of March 6th, that they had not understood him, but "it is useless to conjecture what might have happened if things had been different." He insisted that their attitude was not worthy of blame; they had nothing to regret. Emphatically he protests that they did not force him from the bosom of the family. A power greater than man, which neither they nor he could control, drew him:

> What then was the reason of my going, or what made me go? The reason I am not able to tell. But what I felt, I can say. There was a dark, irresistible influence which was upon me, which led me away from home. What it was I know not. What keeps me here I cannot tell. It is only when I struggle against it that a spell comes over me. If

I give up to it, nothing is the matter with me. But when I look to my past, my duty toward you all, and what this may lead me to, and I attempt to return, I get into a state which I can not speak of . . . I mean by attempt to return, to return to my old life, for so I have to call it — that is, to get clear of this influence. And yet, I have no will to will against it. Still, I do not desire it [or] its mode of living, and [I] am opposed to its tendency. What bearing this has upon the question of my coming home, you will perceive. As soon as I can come home, I will come. If I should come now, it would throw me back to the place from which I started from home. Is this fancy with me? All that I can say is, it is just as much as the last nine or ten months of my life have been fancy, which is too deep for me to control. When do I expect to return? As soon as possible. How long may that be? Perhaps this month — perhaps longer. Hence you see that under these circumstances for me to state the precise time when I will come home is doubtful. I hope you will not misunderstand what has been written. To answer your thought I have stated to you my condition, which I hope you can see, but which I do not expect you to feel, not because of want of sympathy on your part, but perhaps [because of] not having had to pass through the same life.[26]

Shortly after Isaac mailed this letter, new fears began to prey upon his tortured soul. Would his family look upon his desire to remain at Brook Farm as proof that his love for them had cooled? Would they think he preferred the company of his newly found cultured and intelligent friends to the simple and unaffected atmosphere of his home? Would they wonder if he was conscious of the worry he had brought upon them? Without waiting to find out if his fears had any foundation, Isaac sat down at his desk on the chilly afternoon of March 14th and wrote a very warm and affectionate letter to "My good relatives." No one, he told them, could ever replace them in his affections. Because they were all very dear to him, he had suffered great agony in separating from them. From the depths of his heart, he deplored the rift he had created in the harmony of the home and the sorrow he had inflicted on those he loved so much. Their unhappiness was his "greatest pain." In desperation he asked what could he do? He was torn apart by his obligation to them and his duty to God. He begged them to think seriously over this and then to give him advice and counsel.[27]

At this critical stage of his relationship with his family, Isaac began to realize that correspondence was a very poor substitute for conversation. He was sure that he could more easily clear this fog of misunderstanding in an hour's discussion than in a month of letter writing. He decided he would go home for a visit and explain everything in a full and open exchange of ideas in the presence of all the members of the family. Then, if they objected to his remaining any longer at Brook Farm, he could explain why he could not return home immediately. If they agreed to let him live in West Roxbury for a "period," he would require some time in New York to settle some of his affairs.[28] Early in the last week of March, he left Brook Farm and went directly to his home in Rutgers Street.

Unfortunately, he has left no record of that visit other than to express his gratitude to his relatives for having received him with so much kindness and for allowing him to return to Brook Farm.[29] Undoubtedly the family noticed how much Isaac had improved physically since the last time they had seen him. He was not so nervous, seemed to be more settled and more in control of himself. Brook Farm had been good for him and they agreed to let him return and study, at least through the summer. This decision lifted a great weight from Isaac's soul and he felt more at peace.

A few weeks before Isaac had made his visit to New York, he wrote his brothers that the Brook Farmers "are not acquainted with me."[30] Little did Hecker realize how well they knew and liked him. The night of his return, April 13, 1843, they met him at the door of the Hive and gave him an enthusiastic and hearty welcome. "They shook me from all sides" was the way he described it and he was at a loss to explain their kindness.[31] Hecker was not aware that his new-found companions had recognized this shy and somewhat serious youth as a searcher after truth. They called him Ernest the Seeker,* a name George Curtis had given him because of his eager inquisitiveness. But his preoccupation with his personal problems did not cloak his easy and frank manner, his friendly disposition, and his winning smile. He was liked by all and became a general favorite at the Farm.[32]

Among his close friends were George and Burrill Curtis, sons

* In 1843 William Henry Channing published in the *Dial* a story of mental unrest with the title "Ernest the Seeker." The story, Curtis thought, bore a striking resemblance to Hecker and he began to call him Ernest the Seeker.

of the wealthy president of the Bank of Commerce of New York, who had come to West Roxbury in the spring of 1842 as students. Although both boys were younger than Hecker — Burrill was twenty-one, George nineteen — they seemed older than their years.[33] A particularly strong attachment grew up between Isaac and George which lasted after Hecker had left Brook Farm. They corresponded regularly even after Isaac had gone to Europe to study for the priesthood.[34] Like Hecker, the Curtis boys were interested in social reform though not convinced that Ripley's scheme was the answer. They spent many hours discussing philosophy, music, and literature and often walked into Boston to hear Brownson preach, or to browse through Green's bookstore.

Charles Dana, the brilliant Harvard scholar who later became editor of the New York *Sun,* was also close to Hecker whom he affectionately called "Mein liebster Isaac." After Hecker had given up the bread baking at the Farm,* he accepted Dana's invitation to become his roommate and moved over from the Hive to the Cottage.[35]

The young ladies at the Farm also discovered that the young baker from New York was very interesting company. Occasionally, they would stroll through the pine groves with him, discussing Leroux's philosophy of the heart, literature, or the latest development in the co-operative movement. Swedish-born Ida Russell, whose father had been American minister to Sweden, often accompanied Hecker and, while he talked, she worked away at her embroidery, answering now and then with scattered words of interest and sympathy.[36] Their relationship was rather formal, she calling him Mr. Hecker, though after he left the Farm, she begged him when writing to her, not to begin the letter "Dear and Respected Miss Russell."[37] Much more personal was Isaac's friendship with Deborah Gannett whom Hawthorne described as "a bright, vivacious, dark-haired, rich-complexioned damsel."[38] The niece of Ezra S. Gannett, she had left the Farm before Hecker arrived but came back often to visit her friends. She caught her first glimpse of Hecker while he was working at the

* Shortly after his return from New York, Hecker relinquished his post as baker. He decided on this when he found out that it would only cost him two dollars a week more than he was paying. This amount would not require his brothers to work any harder and since his stay was only for a few months, he would devote all his time to study and reflection. Had he planned on remaining longer, he wrote in a letter to his brothers May 12, 1843, he would have continued as baker.

ovens and was immediately attracted by his earnest and "high-minded" expression.[39] She had much in common with Isaac since she too was a searcher for peace and truth. Together they discussed the trials and perplexities of life, the emptiness and dissatisfaction of their souls. After Hecker left Brook Farm they corresponded regularly on "high spiritual themes." When Hecker became a Catholic, she frequently asked him about the Church and if it satisfied him. Writing years later, she confessed his persuasiveness almost made her a Catholic.[40]

There is no doubt that Ora, as she was called at the Farm, fascinated Isaac for with great warmth he described her in his diary as "one of the loveliest, most love-natured beings that has met my heart. There is more heart in her bosom, more heaven in her eyes than I have felt or seen in any other person. She is not lovely but love itself."[41] This effusive and impassioned sentiment never blossomed into romance for, as she wrote him, "you are a brother to me."[42] Moreover, since the time of his vision of "the angelic being" Hecker had been careful to guard his heart and avoid "a person whom I felt I might or would love" and marry.[43]

Isaac came perilously close to breaking that resolution within a short time after his return to Brook Farm. A charming and very beautiful woman, Mrs. Almira Barlow, had separated from her husband after he refused to settle down in any one place. Tiring of a nomadic existence, she and her three sons came to Brook Farm and lived at the Hive, the same building in which Hecker had his room. She was very popular with the men, but not with the women who looked upon her as a flirt tugging at the heartstrings of any man who caught her fancy.[44] John S. Dwight was very much in love with her, but she held him at arm's length,[45] while she turned all her charm on the young baker, twelve years her junior.

Isaac had been warned about her and advised to keep her at a distance,[46] but Almira shortened that distance very quickly. During the last weeks before he made his visit to New York, she often went out to the kitchen to talk to him, and then took to strolling with him in the woods. He had no sooner returned to the Farm than she decided to open her heart to him. The afternoon of April 17th — he had come back on the 13th — he was sitting in his room when she stopped by to visit him. After a few words of greeting she began to blurt out her love for him. Hecker started to record the conversation in his diary but then abruptly stopped and tried to scratch out her name.[47]

The attention Mrs. Barlow was giving to Ernest the Seeker did not escape the attention of the Brook Farmers. It is an interesting fact that less than two weeks after she began her ardent pursuit of Hecker, the directors of the Farm voted to convert her quarters in the Hive to a large parlor, requiring her to move out of the Cottage.[48] But a change to another building at the Farm in no way checked the romance. She was in love with Hecker and he was fond of her. He speaks of her in his diary as one who had "come nearer to my heart than any other human being"[49] and again, "one who to me is too much to speak of; one who would give up all for me."[50] But she had come into his life too late. A more irresistible love than that of any woman had won him and he could never forsake it. His vision of the "angelic being" continually hovered before him and its beauty prevented him from accepting any human being, no matter how attractive. He knew he could never marry. There is no way of knowing if Hecker told this to Almira, or if he did, whether she thought she could prevail upon him to change his mind. After he left Brook Farm they corresponded regularly, but she was not pleased with his letters.[51] They were too cold, too impersonal. Realizing she was fighting a losing battle, she finally stopped writing and left him to go his own way.

After his fortnight in New York, Hecker took a greater interest not only in the company around him, but also in study. He attended classes in French and Latin and started reading the Bible in both languages. He listened to Mr. Ripley's lectures on Kantian philosophy and also went to the Botany and Agriculture courses. In addition to these studies, he was reading Schlegel, Leroux, Hume, and Goethe.[52] Isaac was also interested in Moehler's *Symbolik*, and when he could not get it in New York, Charles Dana borrowed it for him from Theodore Parker. *Symbolik* was written by a Catholic theologian, explaining the doctrinal differences between Catholicism and Protestantism, and Hecker found it enlightening and informative.[53]

Gradually he began to think of the Church in relation to his own spiritual problem. Perhaps the fact that his brother John had become an Episcopalian* affected him.[54] But it is much more likely that he was influenced by his great friend Brownson. Hecker had read Pusey's two volumes on German theology in the 16th and 17th centuries, and when he visited Brownson, he discussed the Oxford Movement. Together they contrasted the views of the Puseyites with those of the Catholic bishops of Prussia as well as the Bishop of Geneva. Hecker was struck by the similarity in ideas held by such widely separated thinkers who had not been in contact with one another. To him it seemed to augur the time when all sects would resolve their differences and unite in one Church.[55]

This too was the hope of Brownson who had changed radically in his attitude toward the Church and the priesthood. The road that Brownson had traveled since the days of his "Essay on the Laboring Classes" was labyrinthian to most everyone but Brownson. He had become convinced after his disillusioning experience of 1840 that man needed a power outside of himself to elevate himself. This fact now quite obvious to Brownson, demanded answers to two simple questions: Why did man need help? What was the nature of this help? After much thought and study Brownson finally found his answers in the doctrine of Original Sin. Since the fall, all men were turned off the path of virtue and the road to heaven. That is "why" they needed more than human aid to lead them back to God. This help was divine grace and answered Brownson's "what." Grace was the lever that could alone elevate man and society. All Brownson needed then was a channel to bring this supernatural aid into man's life. This must be the Christian Church, but here he moved cautiously, refraining from specifying which particular sect was truly Christian. He was fascinated by the goal of uniting all Christendom and hoped to draw attention to the Church as the medium through which divine grace pours into the soul. He spoke of this Church as Catholic, but denied it was Roman, Anglican, or Protestant.[56]

---

* John Hecker was baptized in All Saints Church March 31, 1843. In 1846 he was elected a vestryman and in 1857 he purchased *The Churchman* and made it the organ of the Episcopal Church. Under his direction it more than doubled its circulation. Later in the same year he opened a collegiate school for boys at 256 Madison Street, New York City. In connection with this, he founded the Madison Street Mission Chapel where he introduced the full choral service in the Episcopal Church in America.

As a result of his new position, Brownson was defending the very doctrines he had denounced in 1840. Hecker wrote to his family: "Brownson, like Paul (I make the comparison with reverence), who was the chief in opposing the Church and her priests is now in the midst of her enemies, battling alone against them, amidst the laughs of his former friends and the jeers of his enemies."[57] In these anguished days, Hecker was a great comfort to the lonely Brownson. On his way back to Brook Farm, Hecker stopped to visit the embattled warrior who told his young friend he had been studying intensely the history and doctrine of the pre-Reformation Church which he planned to defend while he carefully avoided "criticizing any sect or favoring any." After talking to Brownson for only a few moments, Hecker said to himself "he shows a greater affinity with the Catholic Church than before."[58]

It is quite likely that this conversation with Brownson directed Hecker's attention to the Church for that same night he wrote in his diary: "O Lord, lead me into Thy holy Church, which I now am seeking for, by the aid, I hope, of Thy Holy Spirit, wilt Thou lead me in the road by which I may come into Thy fold."[59] Though Hecker believed he was looking for the true Church, in reality he was trying to discover if he needed a Church. His supreme ambition was to live and grow in his new life with God and his only obligation was to accept or reject whatever aided or impeded that life. Ever since he was convinced that the Holy Spirit was guiding him, Hecker was extremely wary of moving without that guidance. He hesitated to take even a step for fear of losing the divine life God had given him. Repeatedly he had asserted that to lose that life would be death and he would accept any fate rather than jeopardize his union with his Creator. With this conviction, he approached the problem of Church affiliation.

On Easter Sunday, April 17, 1843, Hecker visited the Catholic Church in West Roxbury and found the services "impressively affecting."[60] But then the next day he comments: "The Church is not sufficient for my wants . . . I do not feel as if it had something to give; or what it has to give is not what my soul is aching for."[61] He does not, however, dismiss Catholicism completely, for four days later, during which he had been reading Moehler, he

makes the surprising admission: "The Catholic Church alone seems
to satisfy my wants, my faith, life, soul. . . . My soul is Catholic
and that faith answers, responds to my soul in its religious aspirations and its longings. I have not wished to make myself Catholic,
but it answers to the wants of my soul; it answers on all sides;
it is so rich so full."[62]

What produced such an amazing change of mind, Hecker does
not say. *Symbolik* may have impressed him with the beauty of
Catholicism but it was only an impression, not a conviction. If
he profoundly believed that the Catholic Church was the true
Church, Hecker would have felt compelled to become a Catholic.
He admitted this after hearing Brownson announce his intention
of preaching Catholic doctrine and administering the sacraments.
Hecker claimed that Brownson was at least conceding the Catholic
Church was nearest the truth and therefore he had the obligation
to join it.[63] But Hecker was not in this position. To him, "the
Church" was not "the great object of life" and he felt that it
was his duty "to live my own nature rather than to attempt to
mold it like some object." Neither the Protestant nor the Catholic
religion satisfied him.[64]

Isaac Hecker, at this stage of his development, was in no state
of mind to investigate methodically and critically the claims of
any Church. For him, there was a much more immediate and
pressing problem: what was he going to do with his life? During
the last two months of his stay at Brook Farm, he had crystallized
his thinking on the kind of life he must lead. He must live
constantly in the presence of God and whatever he did must
be motivated by the spirit and love of Christ. "What I do must
be Christ in me doing and *not me*. . . . To give Christ room for
action in my heart, soul and body, is my desire, my aim, purpose, being. I deny Christ in every act that I do which is not
done with and from His Spirit."[65] Total dedication to Christ
was Hecker's goal, but he knew not where he could achieve it.

The time fixed by his family for his stay at the Farm was
rapidly drawing to a close and Isaac still had no practical plan
for the future. Because of the expense, he could not hope to
stay much longer at West Roxbury as a full boarder. He thought
of becoming an associate member, but if he did, he would have
to spend so much time working to support himself, he would

neglect the spiritual. This was the crux of his difficulty, how to harmonize the material with the spiritual without detriment to the latter. He knew, as he wrote to his brothers, man could not live by spirit alone, but neither could he live by bread alone. "To be lost in either is not perhaps the true destiny of our being. Heroic spiritualism leads to martyrdom here, but eternal life hereafter. Selfishness or materialism leads to the death of all, the soul in time and eternity."[66] For Isaac there was no choice. Never would he sacrifice his spiritual progress.

An interesting sentence in Hecker's diary suggests that he suspected that the religious life alone would give him peace. "I would prefer adopting the life of the monastery to that of the world."[67] But he pursues the thought no further for he sees a possible hope in another Utopia, Fruitlands.

This was a new-type community established by Bronson Alcott and Charles Lane in June of 1843 near Harvard village about forty miles from Boston. Hecker had heard about it at Brook Farm and his close friend, Almira Barlow, had received an interesting letter months before the project was launched, from Bronson Alcott. She not only told Isaac about it but gave him the letter to read.[68] Though the new venture sounded very promising in writing, Hecker wanted to see it in operation. On June 19th he went to Fruitlands and met Mr. Alcott, his wife and children, Charles Lane and his son William, Samuel Larned, and Abraham Everett.[69] During the few days Hecker spent there, he was impressed by the spirit of self-denial and the desire for a more perfect life among its members. He was half inclined to give it a try. Alcott urged him to join the group, but Hecker did not commit himself. Since he was expecting his brother George to visit him, he decided to wait and discuss his plans with him.[70]

Suspecting that Fruitlands could not give him what he was seeking, Isaac saw three paths open to him: First, he could return home, go back to work in the bakery, and try to put into effect his concept of a Christlike life. But he recognized many difficulties in this plan. The spirit of the world was in opposition to the spirit of Christ and he did not feel he was yet strong enough to insure the triumph of the spiritual. The second possibility was to forsake all hope of trying to harmonize the two, "upturn all my former views of life and go into the blind world of chaos and live on." The third he found much more attractive. He could buy a small farm, gather a few like-minded friends, and live a simple, ascetic life. After reading Carlyle's *Past and Present,* he thought the great goal in his life should be: "To make some nook of God's creation, a little fruitfuller, better, more worthy of God; to make some human heart, a little wiser, manfuller, happier, more blessed, less accursed!" His own Utopia seemed to him the best way to fulfill this noble ambition.[71]

While he was turning these thoughts over in his mind, his brother George arrived on June 29th and stayed with him until after the fourth of July. Since this seems to have been George's first visit to New England, Isaac took him on a sight-seeing tour around Boston, Mount Auburn, the Bunker Hill monument, and other points of interest.[72] They also took time for serious discussion. Learning from George that he and John had realized their own need for a more spiritual life, Isaac wondered if he might not find what he was seeking at home. Since he was not sure, he and George decided he should try Fruitlands. If it proved to be the "Eden" Alcott said it was, he would become a member. But if it were just an empty dream — he preferred "not to speculate on the future, but look to Him who is above for a wise direction in all that concerns my life."[73]

The evening of July 11, 1843, Isaac Hecker arrived at Alcott's Eden. It was in marked contrast to the Utopia he had just left at Brook Farm where life was full, exuberant, and spontaneous. At Fruitlands, it was subdued, austere, and suppressed. Bronson Alcott had explained the underlying principle of the new venture as "the narrow way of self denial." The only road to happiness was a total renunciation of everything that prevented complete submission to Divinity — Alcott did not say God. These obstacles were primarily in the individual. The evils of life, he maintained, were not so much social or political, as personal, and only a personal reform which refused all self-gratification could remove them.[74]

This approach differed sharply from that of the founder of Brook Farm who believed that the inequality of workers, the impossibility of freeing the "Spirit of man" in a society of high-geared competition, and the almost total opposition of intellectual and physical labor prevented man from living according to the plan of God. When these conditions were changed, Ripley contended, man would achieve his highest development.

Briefly, the difference between the two projects was simply that at West Roxbury the Brook Farmers believed that improved circumstances would elevate mankind, while at Fruitlands the reformers maintained that improved men would change the world. Through strict diet and ascetic habits of life, they hoped to produce these men.[75]

Young Hecker was by no means repelled by the austerity practiced at Fruitlands, for while he was at West Roxbury he was abstemious at table, and occasionally spent the whole day in prayer and fasting.[76] In his first Fruitlands letter to his family, Isaac summed up his opinion of the philosophy of the movement: "Instead of 'acting out thyself' it is 'deny thyself.' Instead of liberty it is mutual dependence. Instead of the doctrine 'let alone,' it is 'help each other.' Instead of tolerance it is love." The theory, he conceded, was Christlike, but its practical fulfillment would depend on the sincerity of the members. Until he could gauge that, until he could discover if the Paradise Planters were what they seemed to be, he could not say how long he would remain in Alcott's Eden.[77]

As soon as Isaac arrived, he entered into the life of the new community but did not take over the baking. Since Alcott reserved that to himself,* Isaac helped in the fields, raking and piling the hay. Before the first crop was stored, Lane stood bareheaded in the middle of the barn and said: "I take off my hat, not that I reverence the barn more than any other place, but because this is the first fruit of our labor; I am conscious that what prompts my speech is felt by others as well as myself." For a few moments everyone kept silent "that holy thoughts might be awakened."[78]

Briefly and in stilted style Hecker records in his diary some of the after-breakfast conversations in which he took part. The

---

* Alcott used unbolted flour in the baking which did not make the bread too tasty. He tried to overcome this deficiency by forming the loaves in the shape of animals or other pleasing figures. How this stratagem affected the baker from New York who knew "how to make good bread" he doesn't say.

first one was on "Friendship and its laws and conditions. Mr. Alcott named Innocence; Larned, Thoughtfulness; I, Seriousness; Lane, Fidelity."

The following morning while Mrs. Alcott and her daughters cleared away the breakfast dishes, the discussion centered on "Man's highest Aim" which was much closer to Hecker's heart, though it is doubtful if he learned very much from the Orphic sayings of his companions. Alcott answered that he thought it was integrity; Lane, progressive being; Larned, annihilation of self; Bower, repression of the evil in the soul; and Hecker, "Harmonic Being."[79]

For more than a year Isaac had wrestled with the problem of harmonizing the spiritual and the material. He had gone to Boston, to Brook Farm, and to Fruitlands hungering for the answer but that "how" still remained a mystery. After a week with Alcott and Lane, he seemed to think that they might be able to help him reach a solution. But no sooner had he written this in his diary, than he was forced to admit they could not: "They are too near to me; they are not high enough to awaken in me a sense of their high superiority which will help me to be bettered, to be elevated." Readily he admitted their fine qualities which he admired, especially Alcott's iron will in the practice of self-denial and Lane's heroic generosity in money matters.[80] And when Brownson, who had tried to keep Hecker away from Alcott, wrote an unfavorable report of both the Paradise Planter* and his Eden to John Hecker, Isaac hastened to reassure his brother that the Boston Reformer was wrong: "They are the most self-denying, Christlike in spirit of any people, I ever met."[81] But despite all their excellent qualities, they could not give Ernest the Seeker what he wanted. He realized that although Fruitlands might be Alcott's paradise, it was not his. He must continue his search.

George Curtis once said of Hecker, "he was the dove floating in the air not yet finding rest."[82] After seven months circling the Utopias of New England, Isaac's homing instinct directed his hopes toward New York. "I have thought of my family this afternoon, of the happiness and love with which I might live with them again," he wrote in his diary on July 18th.[83] Repeat-

---

* After Alcott had an interview with Thomas Carlyle in July of 1842, he contrasted the essayist and himself in the words: "He the Cynic and I the Paradise Planter."

edly he asked himself if he could return, take his place in the business and still continue the spiritual life that was so vital to him. One obstacle seemed insuperable, the difference in ideals between himself and his brothers, the conflict between the spiritual and the material. But when he recalled George's words during his Brook Farm visit, telling him of the family's awakened interest in "a life which is higher, nobler, more self-denying" than they had led,[84] he began to wonder if there were such a wide divergence in their views. On July 19th he sat down and wrote a long letter home to find out how far apart they really were. Showing the influence of the after-breakfast conversation with the Paradise Planters, he begins abruptly:

Dear Brothers:

Do you ask yourselves the question: "What is our aim?" And after you have asked this question, do you ask yourselves: "What are we doing to attain this aim in view?" It appears to me your answers to these two questions would certainly tend to draw us together if we are one in the spirit, which I trust we are: and if we are not, it will be the means of clearly seeing where and what we are, and that will give us quiet and peace in our minds, which we do not now feel being separated from each other. . . . If you desire to continue the way of life you *have* led and do *now* lead, be plain, frank, and so express yourselves explicitly. If not, and you have any desire or intention in your minds to alter, or to make a radical change in your external circumstances for the sake of a higher or better mode of life, be equally open, and let me know all your thoughts and aspirations that are struggling for expression, for real life. . . . We have labored together in union for material wealth, can we now labor in the same way for spiritual wealth? . . . I feel that the time has arrived when we should see where we are, and what we are, that we may either come together or separate, as the case may be.[85]

Until he wrote this letter, Isaac was convinced that it was utterly impossible for him to live a spiritual life at home unless there was a radical change in the family attitudes and interests. Although he was not aware of it, Isaac was following the Brook Farm principle that improved circumstances would uplift the human soul. If he were to continue his spiritual development, the family must change their way of life to correspond with his. It was not until after he had written this letter that he began to realize his request was essentially selfish and self-centered. What right had he to demand such a price for his return? he asked himself. Could he not go home and live his life and they theirs? As he had done at Brook Farm and Fruitlands, so too in New York he could follow a life of self-sacrifice and prayer, while he guarded himself against the spirit of worldliness.[86]

Unknown to Hecker, the ideas of Ripley and Alcott were battling for his allegiance and those of the Paradise Planter were winning out. Of course, Alcott would never have recognized his part in Hecker's approach: "live in the world but not of it." If he did, he would never have established his Eden. But his dictum that the evils of life are not social, but personal, led logically to the conclusion that no particular place is necessary to correct those evils. Since they are inherent in the person, not in the place, the individual could root them out wherever he might be, through determined effort and the faithful practice of prayer and self-denial. Isaac could be just as rigid in abstaining from food and drink in Rutgers Street as he had been at Fruitlands. Hecker's logical mind had finally pierced the fuzzy thinking of the New England Transcendentalists and discovered the truth buried in sophisms. He recorded this discovery very simply in his diary: "My life is not theirs; theirs is not mine, though they have been the means of giving me much light upon myself."[87]

Before resuming his place in the bakery of Hecker Brothers, Isaac saw only one more hurdle and he hoped it was not insurmountable; the question of private accounts among the three brothers. He regarded this practice as stemming from selfish motives and he could have no part in it. Love and generosity should govern their relationship, not distrust and greed. It mattered little to him, if spending ten times more than he did, they were using part of his earnings. That would give him great happiness, he wrote in his diary, since it would be a practical demonstration of his love for them. Once this matter would be settled, he could go home, "be true to the spirit with the help of God and wait for further light and strength."[88]

The day before Isaac reached this decision, he had discussed with Alcott and Lane his position with the family. In the course of the conversation, the Paradise Planter asked Hecker if he had found any hindrances in the New Eden. Alcott, who bristled under criticism, must have been very uncomfortable when Hecker told him bluntly he had found five obstacles: "His want of frankness; his disposition to separateness rather than win co-operators . . . ; his family who prevent his immediate plans of reformation; the place has very little fruit on it which it was and is their desire should be the principal part of their diet; . . . they had too decided a tendency to literature, to writing."[89] After this conversation Alcott could not have been surprised when Hecker told him he was leaving. He went to Lane and said: "Well, Hecker has flunked out. He hasn't the courage to persevere. He's a coward." Lane, who had a much deeper appreciation of Hecker's spiritual nature and who realized the strong bond between him and his family, answered: "No, you're mistaken. Hecker's right. He wanted more than we had to give him."[90]

On July 26, 1843, Hecker bade farewell to Fruitlands. Once he had made up his mind, he acted quickly and did not wait for an answer to the letter he sent to his brothers on July 19th. Since he had left most of his things at Brook Farm, he went there to await word from home and to spend a little time settling his accounts before he left New England.

Before he ever stepped on the train leaving Boston, Isaac was aware of the problems he would have to face in New York. He could almost hear, he wrote in his diary, his brothers saying, "Business will go backwards unless we make greater exertions; it will not answer not to do so."[91] He could not suppress the fear that his "life" could not be lived at home. Again he considered the possibility of getting a little country place where a simplified life, free from the spirit of competition, would remove all obstacles from his path to God. Yes, it might be the wisest, but he recognized it was also the easiest, and he did not want to give in to himself so soon. The time had come to face the issue, "to meet boldly and with mighty valor" the forces of the enemy and to test his mettle.[92] Conscious of his own weakness, he begged Almighty God to give him:

> grace and strength to keep getting better, to overcome all temptations that beset my path. . . . May I become more obedient, meek, humble, like Jesus Christ my Master. . . . Lord help me to overcome all self will, to crucify self that there may be nothing of the old man left and that I may be a new man, born, begotten, in the Lord Jesus

Christ. . . . Give unto me more and more of Thy loving Spirit. Fill my whole being that there may not anything remain but Thy loving kindness.[93]

When John's letter reached Brook Farm, July 29th, it gave Isaac great hope. It was so sympathetic and co-operative that he could no longer speak of impediments at home. His family was willing to do everything possible to make his life with them agreeable and pleasant. However, John saw no need of suddenly changing their way of living and Isaac completely agreed with him. Time, he said in his reply, would be the answer. If they could live a finer life without drastic modifications, so much the better. But if, despite all their efforts, the obstacles were too great, then they could consider necessary changes.

Four days before Hecker left Brook Farm, he was sitting in his room when he heard John Dwight playing a few chords on the piano. Immediately the music released a feeling of pent-up emotion and feeling for Brook Farm. Though happy to return home, he would say farewell with deep regret to all his friends, many of whom were strongly entrenched in his affections. To all he was deeply grateful but "inexpressibly" so to George Ripley: "Oh may I be able to manifest my gratitude to him in a way that will satisfy my heart.* To thee, I dare say, Friend Ripley, my heart is grateful from the very source of its life. May heaven lead thee."[94]

Like many another Brook Farmer, Hecker was charmed with West Roxbury. It was not a sentiment that would wane with time, for some years later, he wrote of it:

How many dreamers! How many dreams realized! How many expired in its expiration. It was not lost — not all. It was the greatest, noblest, bravest dream of New England. Nothing greater has been produced. No greater sacrifice has been made for humanity than

---

* Hecker always retained this deep and affectionate regard for Ripley which was reciprocated. After Father Hecker returned from Europe in 1851, he went to see Ripley who was then working on the New York *Tribune*. Ripley asked him if he could do all that any Catholic priest could do. Father Hecker assured him he could. Ripley answered: "Then I will send for you when I am drawing towards my end." When Ripley was dying, he asked for Father Hecker, but the message was never delivered. Learning of Ripley's illness, Father Hecker hastened to his bedside but Ripley's mind was gone and he could do nothing for him. Elliott, *op. cit.*, p. 90.

the movement of Brook Farm embodied. It collected the dreamers of New England. Brook Farm was the realization of the best dreams these men had of Christianity, it embodied them.[95]

The morning of August 14th when Isaac Hecker stepped on the porch of the "Hive" to leave Brook Farm, he said "Farewell" not only to his friends and acquaintances, but also to all man-made Utopias. After eight months' experience with them, he knew they were powerless to give him what he was seeking. Although they failed in this regard, they still had been very profitable. Because of the difference in principles and aims of the two groups, they naturally affected Hecker in different ways.

Brook Farm sought to provide a better external arrangement for the individual. Emerson, in his journal, testifies that they had succeeded in this: "The founders of Brook Farm ought to have this praise, that they have made what all people try to make, an agreeable place to live in. All comers and the most fastidious find it the pleasantest of residences."[96] Life at Brook Farm was a valuable experience and no one realized it more than Hecker. "They have improved, refined my being. Beautiful scenery, fine music, cultivated and more than ordinary society, intimate friends, and some whom I love, all these had been more to me than what I had."[97] None of these things, certainly not the cultivated society he found there, was possible in the life he had led in New York. For Brook Farm had drawn most of its recruits from the cultured life of New England society. Mingling with people of such a nature and living in an atmosphere of refinement, the finer qualities of Hecker's character were nurtured and grew to full vigor. Excellent as were the advantages such company offered him, Hecker also had a marvelous opportunity for study. He had not only the leisure time to give to books, but also immediate contact with men of superior minds and outstanding abilities. Ripley, Dana, Dwight, and Bradford were always available, if not in the classroom, then around the grounds. From these men Hecker received his first taste of organized and advanced study. His mind was taught to arrange and correlate orderly and clearly. More than that, he learned how to express his thoughts lucidly and forcibly. When he went there in 1843, as he admitted a few years later, he knew nothing of the necessary rules of grammar. "I look back for a few years when I was ignorant whether to commence a sentence with a capital or no, and many other such little things."[98] One has only to look through his early diary, or read his letters to his family, to recognize the truth of that statement. In style and expression he made great strides between the first letter he wrote to Brownson, which is stilted and forced with a series of short, staccato, poorly constructed sentences, and those of two years later. These latter have a certain charm and fullness of expression which could come only from extended reading. Some of his letters and particularly his diary reveal a familiarity with ancient as well as modern classical writers, which he acquired at Brook Farm.

Fruitlands, too, contributed its share to the development of Hecker's character. Its emphasis was all on the internal, the personal, and individual. Since Hecker was there but two weeks, that life had scarcely enough time to make a solid impression on him.* Still it did strengthen his inclination to the ascetic habits which he had formed while at West Roxbury. After he returned to New York, he carried them to an extreme, by trying to live only on grains, fruits, nuts, and water.[99] He persisted in his abstinence from flesh meat for reasons he undoubtedly gathered at Fruitlands.[100]

Although the Utopias of New England had given much to the aesthetic self-seeker, they had failed to supply what he particularly wanted: an answer to the questions that perplexed him. His inner experiences harassed him and neither Brook Farm nor Fruitlands could enlighten him. He had come, as George Ripley said, "an amateur, self-perfectionizer, an aesthetic self-seeker, willing to suck the orange of Association dry and throw away the peel."[101] Though he had sucked that orange dry, he was still thirsting for light and peace.

---

* From Wittem in Holland, Hecker wrote to Thoreau, May 15, 1847. "When I remember the dreams of Fruitlands and see how far their boldest aspirations fall from what has existed for centuries in the Catholic Church, and now exists, I am led to smile, but I esteem truly these men as far as they went." *Hecker Papers.*

CHAPTER IV

The Conviction Unfolds

BEFORE leaving Boston for New York, Hecker had firmly resolved he would not allow any human interest to interfere with his complete dedication to Almighty God. Of all the distractions of city life, he saw none more likely to challenge this resolution than his work in the bakery. Business, he felt, was pagan and governed by competition, whereas he wished his life to be Christlike and motivated by divine love. Aware of the danger of mixing the two, Isaac resolutely made up his mind on August 15th, the day of his return home, to stand guard and fortify himself with two of the most powerful weapons at his command: prayer and self-denial. He would continue his communion with God, not in the shaded and peaceful pine groves of New England, but in the sanctuary of his soul, amid the confusion and hubbub of New York. To steel himself against the allurements of the world, he would continue to practice the strictest self-denial by living solely on unleavened bread, fruits, and nuts, with nothing to drink but water. Serene in mind, he went back to his duties at the bakery the day after his return "feeling in the midst of many, but not one of them."[1]

For the first few weeks Isaac was back in the city, he found that not business but politics was his greatest distraction. His brother John, an active member of the Democratic Party, was among those pushing John C. Calhoun as his party's candidate for the presidential nomination in the 1844 elections.[2] Since there was strong sentiment for the South Carolinian in certain sections of the country, especially New York, Boston, and the southern states, Calhoun's supporters believed that if they could whip up public opinion for their candidate, he could win not only the nomination but the election.

Although the movement for Calhoun was gaining momentum in New York City, it needed more publicity. A newspaper with Brownson, a great admirer of Calhoun, as the editor would be the ideal sounding board.[3] Young Hecker was asked to contact Brownson and find out under what conditions he would accept.[4] Although Isaac faithfully forwarded this request, he was not enthusiastic about the proposal. He knew Brownson was thinking of reviving his *Quarterly* which he had merged with the *Democratic Review* in 1843, and that he expected to be renamed director of the Marine Hospital in Chelsea.[5] If the appointment were made, Isaac hoped Brownson would resume the *Review* and forget about the paper. "Would it not be more commanding and better suited to your tasks," he wrote on September 14th, "if you should receive the hospital appointment to start the B[oston] Q[uarterly] R[eview]? Much as I should desire your coming on here, still I would regret much more the loss of your pen in that higher sphere which the Review would be the channel of and the newspaper not." Not presuming to influence Brownson, he added: "Still this [editorship of the Calhoun paper] may present advantages to you that I am not aware of."[6]

The offer seemed very attractive to Brownson who answered on September 18th that he would be not only pleased but delighted to accept the editorship. Asking the New York people to specify his duties and his salary, Brownson laid down one condition: he would have nothing to do with the financial affairs of the paper. His responsibility would be entirely editorial.[7]

Within two weeks, Brownson changed his mind. The delay in hearing from New York led him to suspect that he would not be the unanimous choice of the Calhoun supporters. But there was a stronger reason for declining the offer. He had decided to resume his *Quarterly*. Whether Hecker's remarks had any influence on this decision, Brownson does not say. He had been having difficulty with O'Sullivan, the editor of the *Democratic Review*, about the type of articles he was writing. The Boston Reformer, who chafed under any kind of editorial supervision, willingly severed his connection with the magazine at O'Sullivan's suggestion and set about reviving his own journal with the title *Brownson's Quarterly Review*.[8] This new development ruled out the editorship of the New York paper so Brownson wrote to Hecker on October 3rd, "stop all proceedings on my behalf."[9]

During the year Brownson was merely a contributing editor to the *Democratic Review*, he did not have the freedom to write as strongly and forcefully as he wished on the one subject absorbing so much of his attention, the need for a Church. But now that he would be his own master, he told Hecker that he would "come out boldly for the Church . . . independent of, but not in opposition to, existing organizations." He was still working for the reunion of all Christian denominations and until that could be accomplished he hoped "to rally all the forces I can around the great central ideal of fraternity and Christian communism."[10]

Brownson's decision delighted Hecker. Admitting that his own interior struggles and his contact with the transcendental movements of New England had left him somewhat lukewarm to religion, he was beginning to realize that the Church movement was "infinitely" more important than any personal, social, or political reform. The Church, he wrote Brownson in mid-October, "was the soul centre of all life."[11] Again, as earlier, this was not a conviction with Hecker, but a theoretic notion producing no practical results. Previously, at Brook Farm, he had looked at the Church, but only in relation to his spiritual life. Now he regarded it in the light of its effectiveness for reform, and he was not yet persuaded, as Brownson was, that the Church was the only organization capable of aiding man. In neither case did he make a careful investigation of the claims of the various churches, since he was not aware that he had an obligation to become a member of any of them.

More than Church affiliation, the "externality" of city life disturbed Isaac and he still cherished the hope that he could flee from it and dedicate himself more completely "to the Spirit."[12] Shortly after his return to New York, he wrote to George Curtis about his dissatisfaction. Curtis advised Isaac to remain where he was and cautioned him against running away: "No retreat from this warfare must be suffered — where you are is your battle-ground, what you are doing the scene of your conflict. If you must fail, fail in the breach. . . . Men demand men who stand strongly upon their feet, not pigmies upon stilts."[13] This advice was reinforced by Edward Palmer, a New Jersey reformer, who told Hecker "Act in society and win the best you can."[14]

Following this advice, Isaac decided to put out of his mind any ideas of forsaking the battleground, although he was not very content with its ramparts. His brother John noticed he had not entirely adjusted to his environment and told Brownson "your Boston Transcendentalists have had too much influence on his mind which I am in hopes will wear off."[15] What disturbed Isaac would never wear off, for it was not a transient state of mind. Captivated as he was by the desire to see the spirit of Christian love permeate all human relations, he was appalled by the social conditions in his own city. After the panic of 1837, the situation of the workingman was worse than it had been for the previous ten years. During the crisis, with the collapse of business, thousands were thrown out of work. Poverty and suffering were rampant with mothers and children begging in the streets. The city was slow in recovering from the crash, and for more than five years failed to return to normal conditions. The workingman suffered even in the periods when he found work. Since competition for jobs was so keen, employers could and did exact long hours for miserably low wages. The twelve- and fourteen-hour day was the rule, rather than the exception. It was not until 1845 with the return of some prosperity that agitation began for the restoration of the ten-hour day.[16]

Men who gave so much time and effort to keeping the body alive had little interest or energy left for cultivating the soul. One so personally conscious of the importance of spiritual reality as Hecker, deplored this situation which forced human beings to live half-lives. Who would assist them, correct this unjust system, and open their eyes to the spiritual life? He asked: "Must the slave perish and the Drunkard die and the social ills that shake the world to destruction continue and I stand quietly beholding. Not so, I am here to succor humanity or to die."[17]

The improvement of the workingman's condition had always been close to Hecker's heart. He had worked for that goal through the political party in 1837, but politicians had failed him. Then his interest was humanitarian; to better the laborer's lot as an

end in itself. Now it was religious; to remedy the situation of
the workingman so he would have both the time and opportunity
to care for the needs of his soul. It seems never to have occurred
to Isaac that though his aim was noble, it had one glaring defect.
External circumstances alone could of themselves neither prevent
nor encourage the development of the spiritual life if the desire
for the things of the spirit were lacking. Brownson had learned
this lesson three years before, when he realized that man needed
an inner impulse to seek the good, and then concluded that only
divine help through the Church could supply it. But he had not
succeeded in imparting this lesson to his young friend, for although
Hecker understood the arguments, they did not convince him.
Unaware that he was using a subjective criterion, Isaac was
judging all men by himself. Since he desired a more intense
spiritual life, he believed the same desire was latent in others
and needed only the external opportunity to develop. Transcendentalism, no doubt, strengthened him in this belief with its
fundamental principle that all men were inherently good and,
given the conditions, would strive for the better things of life.
But how to provide these conditions was still a mystery for young
Hecker. Society and the Church had failed and he was at a loss
to find a substitute.[18]

The cumulative effects of the ideas of Curtis and Palmer,
together with the force of the more blunt and straightforward
expressions of Brownson, were gradually beginning to weaken
Hecker's confidence in the transcendental dream. Brownson had
told him "these communities after all are humbugs. We must
rehabilitate the Church and work under its direction."[19] Curtis
in a more poetic vein had written him: "Why seems the hope
for men almost hopeless, because neither Church — nor Society
— hang out any beacons of success? . . . Are you quite sure
that your Church, or your Free Labor Society — or your Temper-
ance meeting or your Fourier re-organization is the straight path
to universal redemption? Seriously entertain that question for a
while and see."[20]

Isaac thought seriously and prayed earnestly over that question. Gradually his thought became "clearer and more distinct
and my whole mind more systematic." He took a comprehensive
view of the reform movements of his day which he reduced to

four: personal, social, political, and religious. He depicted their relation to one another as a triangle. On each side of the triangle he wrote one of the three kinds of reform. The first was personal, with its formula of self-denial, holiness, and union with God; the second, social with its objectives of universal brotherhood and a just distribution of the profits of labor; the third, political with its aim, equality of persons and interest before the state. In the center, as the source of all others, was religious reform trying to unite all sects and giving inspiration, direction, and purpose to everything else. Then he repeated practically the same words he had written to Brownson: "The Church is the centre, the soul of all progress."[21]

However, it was not until a month later that Isaac seriously considered the question of joining a Church. He noted in his diary on November 5th, "Of late, my mind has been disposed to look into Church matters with more interest than it has for six months back." He called on the Reverend Benjamin Haight, the rector of All Saints' Church where his brother John had been baptized, and discussed, for an hour and a half, the differences between the Anglican and the Roman Catholic Churches. The two agreed on almost all points, especially the failures of both groups. "If the Church of Rome had fallen into corruption in her over warmth, the Anglican had neglected some of her duties through coldness." But they disagreed on the acceptance of the decrees of the Councils. Haight told Hecker the Episcopalians accepted the first five Councils of the Church as legitimate, but rejected the Council of Trent because neither the Eastern Orthodox nor the Protestant groups had been represented. Furthermore, the minister maintained, Trent's decrees were contrary to the Bible and Christian tradition. Although Hecker conceded that representation in the Council was incomplete, "still as an individual, I think and feel she did not establish or enjoin anything in those decrees which was not in harmony with the Spirit of Christ, the Scriptures and Tradition."[22] Evidently Hecker was relying on the ideas he had gathered from Moehler's *Symbolik* for a defense of his position.

Several days after this visit, Brownson wrote to Hecker hammering home the point that no work of reform can be effective or successful "until we have recovered the unity and Catholicity of the Church as an outward visible institution." Disputing Channing's thesis that the principle of union is love, he also struck at Hecker's ideas with the argument: "The precise difficulty is that men do not love and it is *because* they do not love that they are alienated and divided. . . . So far from seeking Christian love as the basis of the union of the Church, we must seek the unity of the Church as the condition of creating love." Transcendentalists and Unitarians are both in error because they maintain "you must be good in order to come into the Church, instead of coming into the Church on the condition of being good."* Knowing of Hecker's contact with Haight, the Anglican minister, Brownson gave him a puzzling bit of advice: "I hope you will find that you can associate yourself with Mr. Haight's congregation. I cannot myself go with any of the fragments."[23] This struck Hecker as surprisingly inconsistent, counseling him to take a step which he, Brownson, found impossible. He referred to it years later as the only time he knew his great friend to be illogical.[24] Incongruous as it was, Hecker seems to have followed Brownson's suggestion, and again called on Reverend Haight. This time the discussion centered not on points of doctrine or history, but the minister's views of individual, social, and political life. Although Isaac kept no record of the conversation, he does say that he regretted raising the question of politics. The Episcopal Church was all right, he wrote to Brownson, but it was not for him. "I cannot join a Church which asks no more of me practically than what I am."[25] This interview dampened Isaac's interest in church membership for some months.

During these days of political and religious activity, Hecker was faithful to his resolution to cultivate his spiritual life. His diary is filled with ardent outbursts of love and devotion to Almighty God, with gratitude for all His gifts, and with fervent pleas for divine help to keep him faithful to the Spirit guiding him. Constantly, he is puzzled about the results of this guidance and wonders where it is leading him. Never does he lose the conviction that God is calling him for a special work and confidently he awaits the moment when that work shall be revealed to him.[26] Though he was spending time in prayer and meditation, he com-

---

* Brownson's meaning would have been clearer if he had written "in order to be good" instead of "on the condition of being good."

plains that his various activities were encroaching on the time he would like to give to communion with God.[27] Occasionally he would spend the day in fasting which, he admits, he would like to do more often were it not that he feared injuring his health.[28] It is difficult to imagine what he meant by fasting — perhaps abstention from all food for the day — since his regular diet was so stringent: apples, potatoes, nuts, and unleavened bread. He had even limited the amount of water he would drink: "scarcely a mouthful a week."[29] Surprisingly, this did not seem to affect his health which he noted in his diary was better than ever.[30]

Shortly after his return to New York, Isaac had worked out an arrangement with his brothers about the amount of time he would spend in the bakery. They had agreed that if he worked all morning, he could have the rest of the day to himself.[31] Part of his free time he devoted to the study of German, Latin, and English grammar, as well as to extensive reading.[32] Occasionally he would attend the opera or see a play, or visit with his friend George Curtis who had come to spend the winter in New York.* Meanwhile he was keeping up a continuous correspondence with his Brook Farm friends, Mrs. Barlow, Ida Russell, Ora Gannett, and Charles Dana, with an occasional letter to George Ripley. Nor did he forget his closest friend and adviser, Orestes Brownson.

Although the Boston Reformer had hoped to get back his old post at the Chelsea Marine Hospital with its annual income of sixteen hundred dollars, the appointment never materialized. When he had severed his connection with the *Democratic Review*, he had lost another source of income and his financial condition was precarious. To support himself and his family, he had to go back to the lecture platform and he enlisted the aid of the Heckers to secure him an audience in New York.[33] When Isaac received this news, he told Brownson that if none of the usual committees sponsored him, the Heckers would do as they had done in the past, hire the hall, arrange publicity, and secure a good audience,

---

* Curtis left Brook Farm the end of October and came to his home at 27 Washington Place about three miles from Rutgers Street. He describes one of his visits to the bakery in a letter to Dwight: "A gentleman in never so ragged clothes is a gentleman still. You may be sure nothing has charmed me more than my meeting with Isaac in his mealy clothes and brown paper cap. His manner has a grand dignity because he was universally related by his diligent labor." George Cooke, *Early Letters of George William Curtis to John S. Dwight* (New York, 1898), p. 114.

if he wished.[34] While waiting for Brownson's reply, Isaac sent on to Mt. Bellingham a few barrels of flour which the Boston Reformer acknowledged on November 8th as a "valuable gift which in my present condition is no trifling affair."[35] Although the Heckers were anxious to know Brownson's plans, they had no word from him after November 8, 1843, until the following March 11th. Ill health had caused him to cancel any ideas of lecturing, and the pressure of constant writing forced him to neglect his correspondence. Three of Isaac's letters remained unanswered on his desk.[36]

Meanwhile, Isaac was thinking over Brownson's insistence on the need of the Church both to arouse a desire for reform and to successfully effect it. Contradicting his views were the Transcendentalists, especially Alcott and Lane, who held that any individual with the proper spirit could do both by his own efforts. Although Isaac had been giving considerable time and effort to his own spiritual needs, he realized he had done nothing to help those around him. Had not the time arrived, he asked himself, when he should begin to do something for others? According to his success, or lack of it, he would be able to decide who was right, the Boston Reformer or the Paradise Planters. He did not start with an ambitious program for the poor of the city, but confined his activity to the smaller sphere of his home and bakery. With his brothers' consent, he made their bedrooms more cheerful and attractive, as his first step "in ameliorating their condition."[37] Then he turned his attention to the employees of the Hecker Flour Company and outfitted a reading room with comfortable chairs and periodicals where they could come in their leisure time to relax and think over the more serious things of life.[38]

When Hecker recalled this experiment years later, he undoubtedly smiled at the naïve and almost childish measures he hit upon to initiate his reforms. But at the time, he was deeply in earnest and thought he was doing his share to help others. He would have attempted more if a temporary lull in business had not restricted the amount of money available for further improvements.[39]

How the employees responded to the new reading room, Isaac does not say, but he does record his brother John's reaction to his altruistic attempts. On New Year's Eve of 1843, the Hecker boys were discussing the past and the future of the bakery, when

Isaac spoke up and asked if there was "anything in our relations with each other which hindered or otherwise prevented them from actualizing their characters which they must feel is their duty and destiny." It is doubtful how much John understood this question so reminiscent of the after-breakfast conversations at Fruitlands, but he lost no time in saying that he was not satisfied with the way business was being conducted; he would prefer to have it better organized. Since this would require a greater exercise of authority which, he supposed, both Isaac and George would regard as tyrannical, he did not expect them to agree. Immediately Isaac assured him that he had no objection to authority as long as it violated no principle. Both he and George would like to regard the employees almost as brothers and treat them with kindness and charity. John objected to this and insisted that these men were servants and should be treated as such. If need be, he would not hesitate to act vigorously with them. Isaac significantly added that there "the conversation ended."[40]

Though the family discussion was over, Isaac's thoughts of social improvement continued. After months of experimenting with reform in his own immediate surroundings, he saw how little he was accomplishing. Realizing how much more remained to be done in the world at large, he knew that as an individual working alone he had little chance of success. He must join an organization and work within its ranks. He had tried political parties and they had failed him; he had lived in community associations and they were inadequate. The only agency left was the Church. He had come around to Brownson's point of view and the impact of the older man's arguments, coupled with his own jejune efforts at social reform, had swept away the last remnant of transcendental dreams. On March 10th he wrote in his diary: "I have made up my decision of giving up my life, my time to study for the field of the Church."[41]

This expression of Hecker's decision is a key to an understanding of his attitude on church affiliation. Since he had no concept of a divinely instituted organization or even a suspicion that one existed in the world, he could hardly say, "I must join a church." Neither could he consider membership in any church as binding in conscience or demanded by divine law. At this stage

THE REDEMPTORIST STUDENTATE AT WITTEM

FATHER BERNARD HAFKENSCHEID, C.SS.R.

in his life, the Church was little more than an effective force for good which a person could join or not, as he wished. He regarded it as the means to help establish the kingdom of God on earth, giving him the opportunity to work for the cause of Christ. As early as the previous June, he had come to the conclusion that for the salvation of mankind "Christ must reign in all," and for his own happiness he must "feel that I am building up Christ's kingdom in all that I do."[42] Working in the bakery, studying with no purpose in view, visiting with friends, he began to realize that he was doing nothing toward fulfilling the goal he had set for himself. Within the framework of the Church he could exercise what talents he had for the cause of Christ.[43]

If Hecker had been questioned at this time about the relationship between Christ and the Church, he would have answered that the Church had failed to carry out perfectly the work of Christ. Toward the end of January he had written in his diary that the Church does not hold up to mankind the ideal of Christianity, but in March he felt that though it was not perfect, the Church was the only organization that had Christ's aim for its goal. It alone was the embodiment of His ideal.[44] He shows no evidence that he ever considered the question: did Christ institute a Church to continue His work and did He endow it with any special helps to keep it faithful to His message? Such questions never crossed his mind. That is why he was in no hurry to select any particular church. He knew he would join either the "Roman or Anglican" since he had eliminated various forms of Protestantism as lacking the full spirit of Christ.* The choice between these two he left "to a future decision."[45]

What was more immediately important to Isaac was the preparation he would have to make before he could begin his studies for the ministry. This he would settle after he told his family of his newly formed plans. When he announced his decision to his brothers, it came as no surprise to them. They knew, as he told them, his heart was not in the business and that he was called to an entirely different kind of life. His conversation, his ascetic

---

* Hecker did not consider the Anglican Church as Protestant, probably as a result of his study of the Oxford Movement. The Tractarians had maintained that they held all the essentials of Christian teaching and practice and kept referring back to early Christian writings in an attempt to prove their position.

habits, his frequent periods of prayer and contemplation, convinced them he was deeply sincere. Although he faithfully performed his duties in the bakery, he was not there in spirit. Without hesitation, John and George agreed he should prepare himself to work for the Church and they offered to help him in any way they could.[46] With this decision Isaac had taken a giant stride toward clarifying his conviction that God had a work for him to do. That work would be Christ's; his field, the Church; his labors, for the souls of men. Joyfully he wrote in his diary: "Such peace, calmness and deep settled strength and confidence I have never experienced."[47]

As the future began to unfold before him, Isaac realized the amount of preparation his new vocation required. His education, meager in his early years, and fragmentary at Brook Farm, particularly concerned him and he thought of ways to supplement it. He could take some preliminary studies for college entrance and after a full college course enter a seminary. Or he could confine all his efforts to studying with a tutor who would prepare him for the ministry. Isaac preferred the latter because he knew the curriculum of a college education required courses that would be not only uninteresting but unnecessary for his purpose. Suspecting that the books used in college, though good, were often not the best, he concluded that he had not the time to read merely good books, he must concentrate on the best. This he believed he could do under the direction of a competent tutor.[48]

Unwilling to trust his own judgment in so important a decision, he turned to the man best qualified to advise him, Orestes Brownson. In a long letter, he outlined the steps that had led him to dedicate his life to the work of the Church and the two methods he considered as a preparation for the ministry, indicating his preference for the tutor. Which, he asked, did Brownson judge to be the better. Explaining that he regarded him as "a parent," Isaac hoped he would always "bear a love to you as a son." Then he assured Brownson he need not hesitate to express an opinion for fear of offending his brothers. For he had explained everything, and John and the family not only encouraged him, but promised to help him in any way possible.[49]

Fully aware that no man can ever be a judge of his own ability because of the danger of overestimating or underrating himself,

Isaac asked Brownson to tell him candidly and "in plain English" if he thought his young friend had sufficient talents to be a successful minister of the gospel. No matter what the sacrifice or the effort, he had the courage to face all difficulties if Brownson thought he had made the proper choice.[50]

When Brownson received Isaac's letter, he was somewhat puzzled. His young friend had made no mention of his choice of a Church and, without that information, Brownson was hesitant to offer any advice. However, he made perfectly clear in his answer that unless Isaac decided upon either the Episcopal or Catholic, he could not encourage him. Personally, Brownson explained, he was leaning toward the Catholic and, despite his reluctance to join it, he expected that "sooner or later" he must become a member. For the present he would continue working for unity while he stood outside the doors of Rome.[51]

Assuming that Hecker had selected either the Episcopal or Catholic Church, then Brownson told him he would be delighted to see him enter the ministry. "I believe it your vocation, I have believed so ever since I have known you, and on this point my own judgment is made up and I have no hesitancy in saying, devote yourself heart and soul to the ministry. . . . I want you to become a Christian priest, but I want you should prepare yourself thoroughly for the work." Since Isaac already knew French and German, Brownson would not recommend a college course, but he did advise Hecker to master Greek and Latin. Then with the help of a tutor, he could be ready to enter the seminary within four years. Anticipating Isaac's impatience with such a long preparation, he conceded that, "all things considered," his shorter plan might be more desirable.[52]

Brownson's encouragement not only dispelled any doubts Isaac might have entertained about his decision but gave him hope and determination. He answered immediately saying he would not decide which Church he would join until he had made some progress with his studies, but he assured Brownson it would be either the Roman or Anglican communion. He was waiting to see the effect of the Oxford Movement in the Anglican Church. If its progress were halted, then there would be no alternative. He would become a Catholic. Meanwhile, he told Brownson that he was trying to engage an Episcopalian minister as a tutor, and

that he would also call on Bishop Hughes to learn what preparation
was necessary for ordination to the priesthood in the Catholic
Church.[53]

The Episcopalian clergyman Isaac had in mind was a William
A. Norris, of Carlisle, Pennsylvania. Some months before, a letter
addressed to "A Sincere Enquirer" (published in the New York
Churchman) appealed to Hecker because its views on reform
and the Church were so similar to those of Brownson. He learned
from Reverend Haight that Norris was its author. On March 14th
Isaac wrote to the Pennsylvania clergyman explaining that although he was not a member of any Church, he looked upon the
Roman and Anglican as branches of the Catholic Church and
expected to join one of them. He would do so "as a Catholic to
labor for the reunion and Catholicity of the Church as the pre-
requisite to all movements which have for their object the advance-
ment of Humanity." Then he asked Norris if he were willing to
tutor him for the ministry.[54]

Gracefully Norris declined, and not without reason. Since his
own course in theology had been very inadequate, he could not
even supplement his deficiencies with his library which could "be
carried in his arms," much less could he prepare another for the
ministry. Recommending the General Theological Seminary, Norris gave Hecker the opportunity to call on the Reverend Samuel
Seabury, the editor of the *Churchman*. After the *Catholic Herald**
had published what Norris considered "harsh strictures" on his
Sincere Enquirer, he wrote a rebuttal which Seabury decided not
to publish. Norris suggested that Hecker call upon the editor and
ask to see that reply.[55] After Haight had given him a letter of
introduction, Hecker went over to Seabury's Church of the
Annunciation in Thompson Street.

The visit proved to be most interesting and Isaac found Seabury
one of the most affable men he had ever met. His ideas were not
only liberal, but in Hecker's judgment free from narrow partisanship. Discussing the Oxford Movement, Seabury admitted quite
freely that both sides had made mistakes in the controversy between the Holy See and the Anglican Church. As well as rejecting
the Council of Trent which he personally did not find too objec-

---

* The *Catholic Herald* was the weekly diocesan paper for the Philadelphia diocese.
It was begun in 1833.

tionable, he strongly opposed the power the Pope had assumed, especially infallibility and the oath of allegiance he required from the bishops. Nevertheless, in spite of the papal power, he thought that Rome presented many more attractive features than Anglicanism. Her ceremonies and discipline were much more impressive than the Episcopal. Although Hecker granted that Rome had made mistakes, he maintained they resulted from practice and not from principle. For his part he thought it was easier "to prune a luxuriant tree than to revivify a tree almost exhausted of life." Seabury believed that the only way to restore unity was through an ecumenical council of all those groups which have preserved the Catholic faith. As a final bit of advice, the minister told Hecker to examine carefully any objections which prevented him from joining either Church, before he reached a decision.[56]

During the interview, Brownson's name was mentioned and Seabury spoke of his *Quarterly Review* with enthusiasm. However, he had some misgivings about the editor who seemed to be drifting Romewards. Haight had said the same thing six months before, and when Isaac relayed this opinion to Brownson, he replied: "Tell him . . . I stop before I get to Rome."[57] The rumor had become so widespread that in January of 1844, the Boston Reformer wrote in his quarterly: "There is no truth in the report that I have joined, or am intending to join the Roman Catholic Church."[58] But in April Brownson made no comment on Seabury's opinion.

Hecker's visit with the editor of the *Churchman* was in direct contrast to one he had with Bishop John Hughes of New York. On March 20, 1844, Isaac called on the Catholic prelate to find out the requirements for the priesthood in the Catholic Church. This request, coming from one who was not a Catholic, must have seemed strange to that militant defender of Catholicism. He told Hecker he would have to be in the Church for two years and then, before he could enter the seminary, he would need the testimonial of a priest stating not only that he was of good moral character, but that he had the ability to pursue his studies successfully. From the nature of the conversation, Hecker gathered that the Bishop thought he had some "inborn protestant notions of the Church" and Hughes proceeded to give him quite a talk on the authority and discipline of the Church.[59]

Although Hecker was far from the Catholic doctrine of the divine nature of the Church, he thought he was quite orthodox. Since he had had no explanation of Catholic teaching, he could not be expected to recognize his error. It is surprising that the Bishop did not catch this and then explain why the Church maintained she was the one true Church established by Christ and suggest that Hecker look into her claims more carefully. Instead, he presented Catholicism solely as an authoritative body, and exhibited, as Canon Barry has written, "in the strongest relief that aspect of authority which Cardinal Newman has called the 'regal' or sacerdotal."[60]

Though strict discipline by no means repelled Hecker, the Bishop's presentation of Catholicism deterred him from joining the Church "at the present time, though probably I may eventually be led to take this path." The impression that Hughes made upon Hecker is extremely interesting in view of his later work: "The R[oman] C[atholic] Church is not national with us, hence it does not meet our wants, nor does it fully understand and sympathize with the experiences and disposition of our people. It is principally made up of adopted and foreign individuals."[61] The only change Hecker would have made in that statement years later would have been to insert after "The Roman Catholic Church" these few qualifying words "as represented by some of her spokesmen." For he learned later that the objection was not the Church which is as much at home in America as in Europe and Asia, but the colors in which some of her members paint her.

After this visit, Hecker allowed the issue of church affiliation to lie dormant until he had settled the question of his education. Since Norris had admitted he was unable to tutor Isaac for the ministry, Hecker decided to study Greek and Latin as Brownson had suggested. This he could do at home, but he was worried that the distractions of city life would take his mind from his books. Instinctively his thoughts turned to New England as the ideal environment and settled upon George Bradford in Concord as the ideal teacher. He knew the Harvard graduate was very competent and had heard that, since he had a small school which engaged him only about three hours a day, he would be quite willing to teach languages in his free time. Before deciding definitely, Isaac sought Brownson's advice. Knowing that the older man feared the effect of the transcendental influence on Isaac's mind, he hastened to assure Brownson there was no danger. He was sure he was "impregnable" to any such harm, especially since he would not be *"so* very *far* from the invaluable influence" of Brownson.[62] The usual trinity of excuses, ill health, work, and negligence, delayed Brownson's answer until April 10th when he told Isaac he approved of his plan of studying with Bradford since he could "think of nothing better at least for the summer."[63]

This letter cleared the way for Hecker's return to New England and he was returning a changed man. Nine months before, when he left Boston, Isaac had no definite plan for the future. His life, he said, was like a ship drifting on the sea without a guiding star. But during his time in New York, not only had his ship found its course, but he now had a firm hand on the helm. He was steering for the harbor of Christ with two ports open to him — the Anglican or the Roman. During his time in Concord, he hoped the Spirit which had led him this far would guide him safely to the haven of his Master.

CHAPTER V

Concord and the Church

WHEN Hecker arrived in Boston in mid-April of 1844, he did not go out to Concord immediately, but started for Chelsea to see Brownson. Almost a year had elapsed since he had talked with him and he was eager to discuss his plans for the future with his friend. No sooner had Isaac greeted Brownson and his family than he found the Boston Reformer engrossed in every aspect of the Oxford Movement and every facet of the Anglican conflict with the Roman Catholic Church. He wanted to know in detail how Seabury justified the separation from Rome. This was Brownson's biggest problem and until that was solved to his satisfaction, he could do nothing about church affiliation.[1]

The lonely Brownson had few friends with whom he could discuss the church question. His former associates were much more interested in social movements and reform and since Brownson's article in the January number of his *Review* had stressed the point that no reform could be effective without a church, they were no longer in sympathy with him. Moreover, they felt that he was coming closer and closer to Rome, was too strongly in favor of authority and allowed too little scope for human reason, so they left him to himself. In young Hecker, Brownson found not only an interested listener, but one with the same problem. Far into the night they talked over the church question and Brownson told Hecker that if the Anglicans could justify the separation under Henry VIII he would become an Episcopalian. Even if you admit the abuses and corruption within the Roman

Church, Brownson argued, you are not justified in breaking the unity Christ established. The only "Catholic" move would have been to remain within the united group and work to remedy the evils. When the Anglicans failed to do this, they acted in an unauthorized and revolutionary fashion and succeeded in establishing merely a national church, ruled by the king, therefore subject to the state. Since he saw no hope of separating the two, Brownson then turned his attention to the American branch of the Episcopal Church which had complete religious freedom. Could this Church restore true Catholic unity? Brownson required their leaders to justify the separation from Rome before he would be interested in their unifying efforts.[2]

Despite all his denials that he was drifting Romewards and his mental gymnastics to find justification for the Reformation cleavage, Brownson's logic was slowly pushing him to the inevitable conclusion that the Roman Catholic Church was the true Church of Christ. Loath to accept this conclusion because of his prejudices, he was searching desperately to find, if possible, some compromise, some middle ground on which he could be faithful to his Catholic tendencies without becoming a Catholic.[3] He made his position clear to Hecker who wrote to his family "he is *anxious* to unite himself to the Anglican Church if he can do so consistently with Catholic principles." But since this attitude of Brownson's was not generally known, ostensibly he was still working for the reunion of all Christendom, Isaac added: "All I have said of O[restes].A.B[rownson]., do not let it go further than your own minds."[4]

The visit resulted in Brownson's determination to present his position in the next issue of his *Review* and to declare his intention of becoming an Anglican if his Episcopalian friends could provide solid arguments to defend the action of the reformers. But solid arguments he must have before he could take such a step. Apparently neither Hecker nor Brownson came to any other conclusion than to wait for the appearance of this article in the July issue of the *Quarterly* and then to evaluate the reaction.

Isaac, who was not as engrossed in the church question as was his friend, seemed much more concerned about getting started with Greek and Latin. After spending the night at Brownson's home, he went to Concord the next day to arrange with Bradford about his studies and also to find a place to live. He and Bradford spent most of the afternoon searching for a satisfactory room but found nothing. One seemed quite ideal until Hecker heard the price, seventy-five dollars a year.

After supper they tried again, and finally found what Isaac wanted. At the western end of town, not far from the Cliffs near the Sudbury River, was the home of Henry Thoreau. His mother showed Hecker a large room with two windows facing on a street beautifully arched with trees. One of the windows was shaded with honeysuckle. All he needed was there — a good straw bed, a large table, a washstand, bookcase, and chairs, and all for seventy-five cents a week. Isaac was delighted and immediately accepted.[5]

By April 25th, Hecker was settled and ready to begin the intensive study of Latin and Greek. He started the day's schedule by going over the lesson thoroughly until he could repeat it without difficulty. Then he translated sentences, breaking them down into their various grammatical parts, noting the declensions, conjugations, and different types of phrases and clauses. From twelve to one, Bradford would come to his room and listen to his translations, making necessary corrections and suggestions and giving some explanations on the structure of the language. With the exception of the time he gave to Bradford, and the few minutes that Mrs. Thoreau took to clean his room, Isaac had the rest of the day for study, reading, and especially meditation and prayer.[6] His diary shows that he was enjoying what spiritual writers would call a period of consolation. Deeply conscious of the presence of God within him, he would have been perfectly satisfied to spend his time solely in adoration and love of God. "My soul would do nothing but praise and magnify Thy name." Experiencing great joy and happiness, he wrote in his diary: "O Lord, hath not Thy Spirit taken up its abode in my heart? Can anything give this delight that Thou givest? . . . I have been groping in darkness, seeking Thee where Thou wast not and found Thee not. But, O Lord my God, Thou hast found me, leave me not. . . . O my God Thou art loving! And thou, my soul, art happy."[7]

At first, Hecker began his studies with energy and enthusiasm and a rugged determination to continue them faithfully. Day after day he followed the routine he had set for himself and kept doggedly at his work. The first day he mastered two lessons in Latin and Greek which pleased his tutor. When he was able to write a Greek sentence on the second day, Isaac was quite delighted with his own progress.[8] But within a week or two, he was finding it more difficult to concentrate. For a while he thought this loss of interest was due partly to Bradford's lack of enthusiasm. Hecker gathered the impression that tutoring was more of a chore for Bradford than a pleasure and he wondered if it would not be wiser to change to Henry David Thoreau who had not only a better grasp of the languages, but more interest and leisure for study.[9]

But no sooner had he written this complaint than he realized it was unfounded. That same day he had a very pleasant and profitable session with Bradford and never again adverted to changing to Thoreau. His difficulty was not the tutor but rather his desire to spend more and more time in prayer. His great joy and his deepest peace were not in his books but in his union with God. Day after day he noted in his diary that his heart was overwhelmed with divine love and "would do nothing but love God," so much so that he "would die and be with God which is only desiring to live in a diviner life which I feel within."[10] Such outbursts of love and devotion recur frequently during the last days of April and the first weeks of May.[11] Becoming more and more conscious of God's presence, he could find in the beauties of nature added reasons for adoration and praise.

Occasionally he would take his Greek books and Shakespeare's sonnets out to the Cliffs near the Sudbury River. After reading a few sentences in Greek and analyzing their grammatical content, he would open his Shakespeare. Freed from the pressure of business and city life, unhindered by distractions of any kind, he would read a few sonnets. They were just enough to release his pent-up emotion and he wrote in his diary:

> Lying on the bosom of my mother, the earth, looking up into the heavens of my Father, while the birds are singing in the trees, the gentle winds filling all space with the fragrance of spring flowers, the water flowing so slowly along, mirroring the whole firmament above, I feel like being in my native home. This is Eden.
>
> My heart is like the blue vault above. Floating emotions, like

silver clouds, pass over its bosom, leaving no trace upon its pure surface.

To the birds I listened and saw them hop from branch to branch, from tree to tree as if they were of the same element in which they moved. I watched the skillful spider weave his web, and the busy ant build its cell, and felt how full of instruction is all, and how divine is man.

> "Thou gentle stream flow on,
>   How calm, how noiselessly thou art;
> Thus flows the stream of life
>   When Christ is in the heart.
>
> He calms the ruffled waves,
>   And bids the winds 'be still';
> And like the crystal breast,
>   The pure reflect His will."[12]

Then he wrote no more but gave himself to adoration and love of God.

These periods of contemplation were becoming more and more frequent and gradually encroaching upon the time he gave to study. But from Hecker's point of view, it was not prayer that curtailed his study, but study that infringed upon his prayer. He began to notice that as his knowledge of Latin and Greek increased, "my heart ceases to feel the constant inflowing of love and my communion with the invisible not so familiar, nor so frequent." Since he never questioned the supremacy of the spiritual, he now began to wonder about the wisdom of spending so much time in study. He asked himself if God anywhere promised that His truth and grace would be given through the medium of books. Try as he would, he could not shake off the fear that if he kept on studying he would "quench the flow of life from within." The conviction was becoming more peremptory that he should give up his whole life to contemplation and that through the action of the Holy Spirit upon his understanding, he could acquire all the knowledge God wished him to have.[13]

Unwilling to decide so important a question by himself, he turned, as he did so often in a crisis, to his friend Brownson. Explaining how much more important contemplation was to him than study, he wrote to Brownson asking if he would encourage him to fight against this tendency and by dint of sheer effort apply himself to the Latin and Greek. In reality, Isaac was not asking Brownson so much for advice as telling him why he could not study. If he were to make the effort to apply himself to his books, the result "would be to throw me on the bed [in] less than three days" despite his desire to acquire a knowledge of Latin and Greek. From an observation of his past life, Isaac wrote that it seems no sooner is he at peace for a while than the divine hand is laid upon him and a voice tells him "Go, this is not for you, go and suffer. Your cup has not been half drunk." He is convinced that his only course is to remain quiet and wait to see if a change will come so that he can resume his studies.[14]

After he finished writing this letter, Isaac read it over and decided not to send it. It seemed too subjective and perhaps reflected only a temporary condition. However, each succeeding day convinced him that his inability to study was not temporary for, rather than receding, it was growing. Nevertheless he continued his sessions with Bradford and gave what time he could to his books but without any great success. Gradually he began to realize "my study will have to be laid aside, for how long a time I cannot say, I hope not forever."[15] The same experience he had more than a year ago was repeating itself. Then it drew him away from New York, his family, business, and friends, breaking all human ties and concentrating his attention on the life within him. Now it was hampering his mental faculties so that his mind would concentrate only on divine love.

The first time Isaac was aware of the action of the Spirit, he fought against it but it was a losing battle. That experience was valuable for now he realized he had only one course open to him. He must submit. Since he was co-operating with the Spirit much more readily than he had done in the past and with greater confidence and faith, he was not so restless nor upset. Having made up his mind to submit to the divine guidance, he asked no longer where "it will lead me" but waited patiently for "God's watchful care."[16]

After this act of resignation, Hecker had the opportunity to find out if a change from his hermit life might not help him. George

Bradford had a week free from school and decided to take a short vacation.[17] This gave Isaac the chance for a change of atmosphere, so on May 25th he went to Brook Farm wondering if mixing with his friends might freshen his mind and allow him to return to his books with renewed vigor and interest. On his way through Boston to West Roxbury, Isaac met Brownson who seemed to be in such a hurry that he had time for scarcely more than an exchange of greetings. Little did Isaac know or suspect that his friend was on his way to see Bishop Fenwick about joining the Catholic Church. Since Brownson was not sure of the reception the Bishop would give him, he maintained a discreet silence about his plans and merely told Isaac that the next number of his *Review* would be a "severe" one.[18]

At Brook Farm, Isaac visited with his friends, Charles Dana, John Dwight, and George Ripley. He also went into Boston to check on some things his family had sent him and to see Brownson. Hoping for an extended visit with the Boston Reformer, Isaac made several calls on his publisher, Mr. Greene, but Brownson was not there.[19]

Although Hecker had planned to remain away from Concord for at least a week, he soon found social activity not at all to his liking. If his dissatisfaction had not been so marked, there were several inducements that might have kept him in Boston. Ole Bull, the Norwegian violinist whom he had heard in New York, was scheduled for a concert on Thursday night and Isaac would have loved to hear him again. The Mormon apostle, Parley Pratt, whom he had met in New York, was to be in town on Friday and Isaac would have welcomed a visit with him.[20] But he just could not stay since he "could no more keep myself there than one could sink himself in the waters of the Dead Sea. I feel that I move in an element as different from those around me as the bird does from the fish and to meet them is altogether out of the question." So on Thursday afternoon, May 30th, he left Boston and returned to Concord and his hermitage in Thoreau's home.[21]

Having made the experiment to see if even a temporary change would increase his ability to study, Isaac had found the expedient to be futile. His desire for contemplation had not abated, but deepened. Once again he was face to face with that perplexing question which he had asked so many times over the past two years and had never been able to answer: What does God want me to do? For a time he thought his vocation was to work for the cause of Christ in the Church, but if he could not apply his mind to studies, how could he prepare for the ministry. With a deep sense of humility, he admitted that his efforts were useless and his "ability to benefit or accomplish anything in the view of the world, Christian or worldly, is daily becoming fainter and fainter to me." Only one course remained: obedience to the Spirit guiding him, no matter where it would lead him, with the absolute confidence "that a holy, pure trust in God will do more than any other, than all other efforts, have the power of doing."[22]

Despite this growing conviction, Hecker was reluctant to surrender himself to contemplation and forsake all study without consulting someone. Reading the letter he had written to Brownson two weeks before but had not mailed, he decided that since it was a fairly accurate presentation of his difficulty, he would send it. Accompanying it was another letter in which he did not ask Brownson if he should forsake contemplation for study, but explained what happened when he tried to apply himself to his books: "If I make the attempt to force myself to study, it is as if my whole mind vanished and all is blank and void before me, thought, memory and feeling is gone and I stand alone like one without soul or heart and empty body void of any sense." On the other hand, his spiritual life was increasing and his communion with God was greater and richer than ever. Not for a moment, he protests, is his love for mankind any the less, but in his contemplation he is conscious that he is aiding others. Although he admits that he may be laboring under a delusion, then "it never has so well counterfeited the truth and I trust some friendly hand will strip it of its garb."[23]

Looking for a direct, clear answer, Hecker could have gone to no more reliable source than Orestes Brownson. If Brownson detected sham and delusion, his sharp, penetrating mind would unmask it with merciless logic. He lost no time in sending a reply that was more important to Hecker than anything he had ever said or written to him before. It directed the course of his life into channels that finally brought him peace and happiness.[24]

Mt. Billingham,
June 6, 1844.

My dear Isaac,

I thank you for your letter and the frankness with which you speak of your present interior state. You ask for my advice, but I hardly know what advice to give. There is much in your present state to approve, also much which is dangerous. The dreamy luxury of indulging one's thoughts and ranging at ease through the whole spirit-world is so captivating, and when frequently indulged in acquires such power over us, then, we cease to be free men. The power to control your thoughts and feelings, and to fix them on what object you choose is of the last necessity, as it is the highest aim of spiritual culture. Be careful that you do not mistake a mental habit into which you have fallen for the guidance of the All-Wise. Is it not the very sacrifice you are appointed to make to our cause, this spiritual luxury, and to become able to do that which is disagreeable? Where is the sacrifice in following what the natural tendency and fixed habits of our mind dispose us to? What victory have you acquired, what power to conquer in the struggle for sanctity do you possess when you cannot so far control your thoughts and feelings so as to be able to apply yourself to studies which you feel are necessary? Here is your warfare. You have not won the victory till you have become as able to drudge at Latin or Greek as to give up worldly wealth, pleasures, honors or distinctions.

But my dear Isaac, you cannot gain this victory alone, nor by mere private meditation and prayer. You can obtain it only through the grace of God, and the grace of God only through its appointed channels. You are wrong. You do not begin right. Do you really believe the Gospel? Do you really believe the Holy Catholic Church? If so you must put yourself under the direction of the Church. I have commenced my preparation for uniting myself with the Catholic Church. I do not as yet belong to the family of Christ. I feel it. I can be an alien no longer, and without the Church I know by my own past experience that I cannot attain to purity and sanctity of life. I need the counsels, the aids, the chastisements and the consolations of the Church. It is the appointed medium of salvation, and how can we hope for any grace except through it? Our first business is to submit to it, that we may receive a maternal blessing. Then we may start fair.

You doubtless feel a repugnance to joining the Church. But we ought not to be ashamed of Christ, and the Church opens a sphere for you; and you especially, you are not to dream your life away.

Your devotion must be regulated and directed by the discipline of the Church. You know that there is a large Roman Catholic population in our Country, especially in Wisconsin. The Bishop of that territory is a German. Now, here is your work, to serve this German population, and you can do it without feeling yourself among foreigners. Here is the cross you are to take up. Your cross is to resist this tendency to mysticism, to sentimental luxury which is really enfeebling your soul, and preventing [it] from attaining to true spiritual blessedness.

I think you better give up Greek, but command yourself sufficiently to master the Latin, that you need and cannot do without. Get the Latin, and with that and the English, French and German which you already know, you can get along very well. But don't be discouraged.

I want you to come and see our good bishop. He is an excellent man, learned, polite, easy, affable, affectionate and exceedingly warm hearted. I spent two hours with him immediately after parting with you in Washington Street, and a couple of hours yesterday. I like him very much.

I have made up my mind, and I shall enter the Church if she will receive me. There is no use in resisting, you cannot be an Anglican, you must be a Catholic or a Mystic. If you enter the Church at all, it must be the Catholic. There is nothing else. So let me beg you, my dear Isaac, to begin by owning the Church and receiving her blessing.

My health is very good. The family are all well. I hope you are well. Let me hear from you often. Forgive me if I have said anything harsh or unkind in this letter for all is meant in kindness and be assured of my sincere and earnest affection.

Yours truly

O. A. Brownson

When Isaac read this letter, he was not surprised. He had partially anticipated Brownson's answer and admitted that "I certainly should recommend any person in my position and disposition as O.A.B. has recommended me."[25] Since his visit in April, this was the first time Isaac had heard from his friend, with the exception of the few minutes he spent with him in Boston. Although Hecker suspected Brownson would eventually become a Roman Catholic, he did not know what had taken place within those six weeks. Brownson had reached the conviction that the Catholic Church was the true Church of Christ and that he must accept her teachings as authoritative. But one fear held him back. If the Catholic Church were the one, true Church, and his Protestant friends remained outside of it, then they would all be damned. This difficulty he brought to Bishop Fenwick on the afternoon of May 25th after he parted from Hecker in Washington Street. Cautiously, the Bishop did not give him a direct answer and did not explain that if a sincere non-Catholic was in good faith, had no suspicion that the Catholic Church was the one true Church founded by Christ, and was faithful to the grace God gave him, he had a chance of salvation. Instead, he told Brownson that "God is just and you may leave your Protestant friends in His hands: for he will not punish them unless they deserve it." But their salvation, he warned Brownson, was no reason for his remaining outside the Church and neglecting "to make sure for yourself." The two-hour interview ended with the Prelate suggesting that Brownson think over the whole matter.[26]

By June 5th, Brownson decided that though it was not an easy matter to take so serious a step, the Church was his "last plank of safety, that it was communion with the Church or death." He would have to enter into almost a new world and once he crossed the bridge, there would be no turning back. All this would be very unpleasant, "but" he reasoned "to be eternally damned would be a great deal unpleasanter."[27] So he made up his mind he would become a Catholic and he asked Bishop Fenwick to appoint someone to instruct him. For this preparation, the Bishop assigned his coadjutor, Bishop Fitzpatrick.

As a result of Brownson's letter, Hecker found himself, for the first time in his life, faced with an obligation in conscience to consider seriously joining the Church. Like Brownson, he too hesitated but not for the same reasons. There is no evidence that Isaac worried about the salvation of his family and friends, nor did he think that unless he became a Catholic he would be damned. As a matter of fact, he seemed to be at a loss to explain his hesitation. Reviewing the situation, he could find no objections to Catholicism. From his study of the Catechism of the Council of Trent, he knew of no doctrine that in his judgment violated reason. Logically, as well as "to be true to my convictions" he should readily become a Catholic. Having sought in all the Protestant sects for that which would satisfy his wants, he had examined Catholicism, especially through his extensive reading while at Concord. Of that Church alone could he say "she meets all my wants on everyside." Facing all this evidence, he asked himself some challenging questions: Why was he reluctant to take the step. Was it self-will refusing to submit to authority? Is the Church the body of Christ? Is she the channel of the Holy Ghost? Is she the inspired body illumined by Christ's Spirit? "In a word, if it is the Catholic Church, if I would serve God and humanity, if I would secure the favor of God and Heaven hereafter, why should I not submit to it?" To these questions he gave no reply.[28]

However, Hecker in his diary made a very significant reference to a part of Brownson's long letter, the only part that he copied, which gives a clue to his indecision. Brownson had clearly labeled Isaac's habit of prayer and contemplation as "a mental habit" and practically called it daydreaming which he urged him to control. Isaac singled this out and wrote: "He speaks strongly against my present tendency and asks me if I believe in the Gospel. 'Do you really believe the Holy Catholic Church? If so, you must put yourself under her direction, etc., etc.,' and says I must either join the Church or be a mystic."[29] Without any qualification of any kind, without differentiating between true and false mysticism, Brownson seemed to place the Church in direct opposition to contemplation and to make the two irreconcilable. The choice he left Hecker was either the Church with an active apostolate or mystical contemplation without the Church. Such a choice, in view of all Hecker had suffered, would naturally cause him to hesitate. He had given up all hopes of a business career, of marriage, of the usual comforts of home and family to live a greater spiritual life. Only in prayer and communion with God had he found any peace and happiness. To renounce this and join the Church, as Brownson seemed to require, meant that Hecker would have to admit that for the last two years he had lived and sacrificed in vain.

At first glance, Brownson's advice seems very puzzling, but granting the path he had taken to the Church, his absolute dependence on logic, his ignorance of the real nature of mysticism, and his slight knowledge of Catholic life, it is not surprising. He had taken the philosophic road to Catholicism by drawing out logically the discordant principles of Protestantism. Painstakingly, he had examined private judgment in all its ramifications in doctrine, morals, and social relations and had rejected it. Through the force of sheer logic, he had eliminated Protestantism and by the same logic had critically surveyed Catholicism, reaching the solid conviction, with the aid of divine grace, that it was the true Church of Christ. Therefore, he must become a Catholic.

But Hecker's search had not been a painstaking scrutiny of creeds. By no cold rational process of elimination of one theology after another that left his mind dry and his heart untouched, did he come to the conclusion that the Catholic Church is the true Church. Rather, it was the result of mystical longings which he thought could find their complete satisfaction only in Catholicism. Divine grace had moved his will to seek God and when he found Him in the Catholic Church, his intellect readily acquiesced without the necessity of reasoned arguments that this Church was the true Church of Christ. Through the aid of divine grace, he saw the truth and needed no extended proof of its validity. However, he still saw no immediate obligation to become a Catholic. He was waiting for the impulse from the Spirit guiding him, and until he was sure of that impulse, he could not take the step. The Spirit spoke to him through Brownson. It was Brownson's admonition that brought him face to face with his obligation.

The realization came so quickly, so sharply, and with such a dark threat of the sacrifice of his spiritual life that he was bewildered. After two days of mental anguish and painful scrutiny of soul, he finally decided to see Bishop Fenwick. Brownson arranged the appointment for June 8th and after some preliminary questioning, Bishop Fenwick referred him, as he had done with Brownson, to his coadjutor, Bishop Fitzpatrick. Hecker found both Bishops "men of remarkable goodness, candor and frankness."[30]

On June 10th, Isaac had a much longer visit with the Coadjutor who though only seven years older than Hecker had completed his theological studies in the Seminary of St. Sulpice in Paris. Ordained in June of 1840, he was consecrated a bishop four years later. The Boston born and bred Fitzpatrick was immediately attracted to the native New Yorker for whom he quickly "conceived much interest." As Isaac related the odyssey of his soul, the Bishop listened attentively. Then he gave Hecker a letter of introduction to Bishop McCloskey of New York and from it we can gather some idea of the interview. The Boston Prelate recognized that Hecker's path to the Church was long and painful without "any human guide but the Spirit of God." His absolute fidelity to the Holy Spirit brought him to the "full conviction that the Catholic Church has infallible and divine authority to lead him and that in obeying her he obeys God." Not for an instant should Hecker think that all his sacrifices and prayers of the last two years were vain and illusory. They had brought him to the haven of truth with a conviction "so thorough and practical" that in the Bishop's judgment, Hecker would not hesitate to face "any of the consequences." Then Fitzpatrick wisely noted that "he needs guidance yet in many respects more for moderation than incitement."[31]

This visit swept away any doubt or misgiving Hecker might have had about becoming a Catholic. He would join the Church, but since he wanted to talk to his family in New York before making his profession of faith, Bishop Fitzpatrick gave him a letter of introduction to the Coadjutor Bishop of New York, John McCloskey.[32]

Although Hecker had a theoretical knowledge of the Church which Bishop Fitzpatrick considered broad and accurate, he was not too familiar with the practical religious life of a Catholic. To see the faith in operation, the Bishop suggested that he visit Holy Cross College at Worcester and offered to give him a letter of introduction to the President of the college. This would also give Hecker the opportunity to learn something of the Catholic educational system, so he readily accepted the Bishop's suggestion.[33]

Hecker realized that his decision to become a Catholic was the most important he had ever made. "A serious, sacred, sincere solemn step." It left him in such perfect peace that no external circumstances could disturb "this unreachable quietness." He was convinced that he had acted only from a desire to please Almighty God and not from any unworthy motive. Had he considered human opinion, he would have joined the Episcopal Church, since the Catholic was "the most despised, the poorest and according to the world the least respectable."[34] She numbered in her fold the poor and the ignorant, the foreigner and the worker. But none of this caused Hecker to hesitate a second. The Catholic Church was the Church of Christ and that was all that mattered to him.

Turning his thoughts to his friends, he anticipated their reaction. At first they would be astonished and after the first shock of the news had worn off, they would probably call him deluded or blind or even a fanatic. But this would not surprise him, for "the Protestant world admires, extols and flatters him who will speak and write high-sounding words; who will assert that he will follow truth wherever she leads, at all sacrifices and hazards, etc., and no sooner does he do so than it slanders and persecutes the man for being what he professed to be."[35] He had put his finger on the Protestant inconsistency: private judgment is excellent until that judgment leads to the Catholic Church. Then it is condemnable. Hecker had written while at Fruitlands: "I have a life to lead; I am called upon to lead it; the influence of others shall not swerve me from it."[36] With greater determination, he could repeat that same conviction now.

The day after his visit with Bishop Fitzpatrick, Isaac announced his decision to his family in a very calm but definite letter. However, he said he would wait until he had a chance to discuss the matter with them before he entered the Church. For fear they might think he was still vacillating between the Anglican and Roman Catholic Church, he summed up the difference between the two by asking: "Why should one go to a weak and almost dried up spring when there is one equally as near, fresh, always flowing and full of life." For his part, he would drink at the spring of Rome for it had the life his "heart is thirsting for and my spirit is in great need of."[37]

Hecker had not left New England before he met the first opposition to the step he was about to take. This did not come from his family whose only reaction was his Mother's preference for the Anglican Church.[38] It came from the foremost of the Transcendentalists, Ralph Waldo Emerson. Hecker had promised Lane he would visit him again at the Shakers and decided to go there Saturday, June 15th. Emerson was going to visit Alcott at Still River, so the two went together.[39] Emerson knew of Hecker's intentions to become a Catholic, probably from Thoreau, who had heard it from Hecker himself. All the way over to Harvard,

Emerson kept leading up to the subject, trying to learn what Hecker's reasons for the step were, "with the plain purpose of dissuading me." Adroitly Hecker kept leading away, and Emerson would not bring the matter into the open. They spent the night together at Still River, possibly in Alcott's home. Both Alcott and Emerson, working together, finally cornered Hecker in a sort of interview. Alcott, who was hampered by no sense of delicacy in such matters, developed the subject with a view of getting an explanation from Hecker. No longer able to evade the issue, Hecker finally said: "Mr. Alcott, I deny your inquisitorial right in this matter." Temporarily, this removed Hecker's conversion from the conversation.[40]

On the way back to Concord, Emerson once more returned to the subject. "Mr. Hecker, I suppose it was the art, the architecture, and so on in the Catholic Church which led you to her?" Hecker answered: "No, but it was what caused all that." Emerson's attitude was no surprise to Hecker. Isaac had noted in his diary the day before he left to go to Harvard: "Tomorrow I go with R. W. Emerson to Harvard to see Lane and Alcott and stay until Sunday. We shall not meet each other. . . . We may talk intellectually together, and remark and reply and remark again."[41]

Hecker's friends, Curtis, Thoreau, and Lane, had a very high opinion of Emerson which Isaac did not share. He appreciated the brilliance of the Sage of Concord, but recognized the weakness of his character. In a letter to his family, April 24th, he spoke of his meeting with the great American poet in Concord and added that although Emerson considered himself "many sided," he was really narrow-minded.[42] And on the very day he was to go with Emerson to Harvard, he wrote in his diary a penetrating judgment both of him and the Transcendentalists in general.

A transcendentalist is one who has a keen sight but little warmth of heart. Fine conceits but destitute of the rich glow of Love. He is *en rapport* with the spiritual world, unconscious of the celestial one. He is all nerve and no blood, colorless. He talks of self reliance but fears to trust himself to Love. He never abandons himself to Love but always is on the lookout for some new facts. His nerves are always tightly stretched like the string of a bow; his life is all effort. In a short period they lose their tone. Behold him sitting on a chair! He is not sitting but braced upon its angles as if his bones were of iron and his nerves of steel. Every nerve is drawn, his hands are clinched like a miser's, it is his lips and head that speak, not his tongue and heart. He prefers talking about Love to possessing it, as he prefers Socrates to Jesus. Nature is his church and he is his own God. He is a dissective critic, heartless, cold, and what would excite love and sympathy in another would but excite his curiosity and interest. He would have written a critical essay on the power of the soul at the foot of the Cross.[43]

Hecker realized how utterly impossible it would be for this type of person, especially an Emerson or an Alcott, to appreciate his reasons for joining the Church. He might just as well try "to paint the heavens or utter the eternal word."[44] As he told Brownson, his reasons defied all thought and expression. If he tried to explain them, he knew he would not succeed in presenting a convincing explanation. Rather than attempt it, he decided silence would answer more effectively.[45]

The day after this visit, Isaac left Concord and went to Worcester to Holy Cross College. Bishop Fenwick had secured the services of the Jesuit Fathers to start this boarding school which was opened in November of 1843, with Father Thomas Mulledy, S.J., as president.[46] By the time Hecker arrived, an attractive four-story brick building had been completed and housed the faculty and student body. Here Isaac presented Bishop Fitzpatrick's letter of introduction to Father Mulledy whom he found not only sociable, frank, and warmhearted, but a man of wide reading and profound learning. During his two-day visit, Isaac asked many questions so that he could inform Brownson whether or not it was a suitable place to send his sons for their education. He found out that there were twenty-five students ranging in age from eight to fourteen years, taught by two Jesuit Fathers, one scholastic, and two laymen. The pupils followed a rather exacting schedule from five in the morning until the time they retired at eight in the evening. The food was good and the quantity generous. In his report to Brownson, Isaac commended the school as well suited for his sons.[47]

After he left Worcester, Hecker went back to Boston on his way to New York and stopped at Brook Farm to see Mr. and Mrs. Ripley. When he discussed with them his intention of becoming a Catholic, he found that both listened with great interest. Mrs. Ripley, who ordinarily was calm and quiet, particularly surprised him with "her warmth and earnestness of feeling."[48] This reaction was so noticeably different from that of Alcott and Emerson that it surprised Hecker. But not only was it spontaneous and genuine, it was lasting. When Hecker was a Catholic missionary in 1863, Ripley wrote and suggested that Father Hecker give a mission in Concord, promising any help he could give him. This offer was entirely unsolicited.[49] Emerson, however, was not so generous. During the Civil War, Father Hecker came to Concord to lecture on the Church. He asked Emerson to help him obtain a hall for the occasion. The great American poet refused. Alcott, who had not hesitated to accept Hecker's hospitality in New York, promised he would aid, but did nothing. When the hall was finally obtained, Alcott attended the lecture but Emerson did not. Hecker met the latter the next day, and later recalling the interview, said: "We had a little talk together. . . . He avoided my square look, and actually kept turning to avoid my eyes until he had quite turned round!"[50] Emerson was decidedly uncomfortable in the presence of this priest whom he had wanted to keep out of the Church.

After his interesting discussion with the Ripleys, Hecker stayed but one night at Brook Farm and left the next day for his home. Although he explained why he wanted to become a Catholic to his family, Isaac left no record of their reaction. His biographer, Father Elliott, indicates there was nothing but "the mildest criticism" and he attributes this to the spirit of courtesy in the family. When a friend of Mrs. Hecker once asked her how she reacted to her Catholic son, she answered that she would never interfere with his faith.[51] Apart from his family, Isaac did not discuss his new religion with his friends. His conversion was too sacred to become a subject for conversation.

On June 25, 1844, Hecker had his first visit with Bishop McCloskey, who impressed him immediately as a man of rugged integrity and unusual talents. The Brooklyn born prelate had studied in Rome for three years before his ordination in 1834. While in the Holy City he came in close contact with Dr. William Ellery Channing's brother, Edward, and had learned a good deal about Unitarianism. With this background he understood some of the ideas that had influenced Hecker. As well, he knew Emerson's writings and Brownson's *Quarterly Review* which he discussed with Hecker. Isaac was enthusiastic about him and wrote to Brownson that he was more delighted with him that any other Catholic he had ever met. Describing him as an extremely well-read man with a mild and gracious disposition, he hoped to gain a great deal from his company.[52]

This first visit was mainly social and the Bishop did not question Hecker on his knowledge of the Church. Since he had to leave for Troy, he gave Isaac some books to read until his return in two weeks. One of these, an English translation of Abbé Gerbert's *Considerations on the Eucharist,* Hecker later recommended to Brownson as well worth reading.[53]

While waiting for the Bishop to return, Isaac also called on the Episcopalian Rev. Haight and told him of his decision to become a Catholic. This probably came as no surprise to the minister who could not help remembering Isaac's Roman leanings from his previous visits. But he did want to know what were Hecker's objections to Anglicanism. Isaac singled out the Episcopalians' lack of discipline and unity, as well as their lack of any clear-cut principle used in selecting doctrines retained from pre-Reformation days. Reverend Haight admitted these weaknesses, but apparently made no effort to justify them, nor did he criticize the Catholic Church. The interview was friendly with no long, involved partisan arguments and before Isaac left, the minister gave him two books to read.[54]

Little study, but considerable reading occupied Isaac's time after he finished his morning's chores in the bakery. Apart from contemplation, he found little else that interested him and he began to look to the future. What was to be his role in life? He still had the desire to work for the Church but seriously doubted he could do anything worthwhile for souls. As he wrote to Brownson: "I do not see what I can do and be useful." However, he was not discouraged, hoping that after he became a Catholic, his future would unfold. Until then, his only desire was to live in perfect obedience to the Holy Spirit guiding him.[55]

"Self-taught" is perhaps the best expression to describe Isaac Hecker in his knowledge of the Catholic Faith. For although he never had a formal course of instructions, he was well versed on the divinity of Christ, the divine foundation of the Church, the infallibility of the Pope, the nature and effects of the Sacraments, the Communion of Saints, and life after death. Bishop McCloskey discovered this in his second interview with Isaac and realized that the young neophyte not only accepted these cardinal doctrines of Catholicism, but could offer solid reasons for believing them. His study of Moehler and the *Catechism of the Council of Trent*, as well as the hours he spent in meditation, had been most rewarding. Since Isaac needed only a few explanations on the practices of the Catholic Church, which the Bishop could give without much delay, he told Isaac he could be baptized within a week or ten days.[56]

Delicately, the Bishop asked about Isaac's future plans and characteristically Hecker answered that he hoped to live the life the Holy Spirit had given him. A man with Bishop McCloskey's spiritual perception recognized immediately the contemplative character of his convert and explained that the Church in America was young and growing. She needed many hands to take care of the spiritual demands of her children. Did he think, the Bishop asked Isaac, that his vocation was to work for these souls in the priesthood? All he could give at the time was the uncertain reply, "I do not know." Then the Bishop went on to say that Europe had much greater opportunities for a full contemplative life than America; he hinted that perhaps Isaac could find his happiness in a community of brothers dedicated to prayer and sacrifice. The monastic life! Isaac remembered how he had thought about it more than a year ago at Brook Farm, and now his adviser in the Faith mentioned it. However, he could not decide now. He needed time and prayer. The Bishop was no more anxious to rush Hecker than Isaac was to be rushed. So the future was left to the future and Isaac prepared for the day of his baptism.[57]

On the morning of August 2, 1844, Isaac went quietly to the Old St. Patrick's Cathedral in Mott Street where Bishop McCloskey waited for him. Kneeling before this representative of Christ on earth, with his right hand on the Sacred Scriptures, Isaac read the profession of faith with deep and settled conviction. Because he had been baptized in infancy, the Bishop administered the Sacrament conditionally. The next day Isaac returned to the cathedral and made a complete confession of the sins of his whole life and received conditional absolution.[58]

Isaac Hecker was now a Catholic. He had found peace in the Church which he firmly believed was founded by Jesus Christ for the salvation of mankind. After years of wandering, his long journey was over. His search had been long and trying, his indecision and uncertainty painful, his devious path agonizing. But now it was all behind him. He had come much closer to understanding the conviction of his childhood: God has a work for me to do. The first step toward accomplishing that work he had taken. He had become a Catholic and he knew the Church was his "star, which will lead me to my life, my destiny, my purpose."[59] His heart was filled with love and gratitude to Almighty God and he broke forth in exulting praise:[60]

My soul is clothed in brightness. Its youth is restored. No clouds obscure its lustre. O blessed, ever blessed, unfathomable, divine faith! O blessed faith of Apostles, Martyrs, Confessors and Saints. O Holy Mother of Jesus, thou art my mother. Thy tender love I feel in my heart. O Holy Mother, thou hast beheld me! Bless me, Virgin Mother of Jesus.

CHAPTER VI

Watchful Waiting

WHEN Isaac Hecker became a Catholic in 1844, the Church in America was sorely in need of priests. Bishop McCloskey intimated this to his young convert a short time before he received him into the Church and he had ample grounds for his concern. In 1840, there were some 663,000 Catholics in the United States and only 482 priests to minister to their spiritual needs. The diocese of New York alone, which comprised the entire state of New York as well as eastern New Jersey, had about 80,000 Catholics but only 71 priests. Within the next ten years, the number of Catholics almost tripled, due to immigration. Viewing these incoming waves of migrants, critics described them as the "Irish Invasion" and the "Teutonic Tide." For the most part, the Germans journeyed to the Midwest while the Irish settled in the cities along the eastern seaboard. This tremendous influx created a demand for priests far greater than native vocations could fill. To help preserve the faith of the flock entrusted to them, the American bishops were forced to look to Europe for coworkers.[1]

For a recent convert like Isaac Hecker who cherished the desire to work for Christ, the priesthood provided a glorious opportunity. But Isaac did not respond. Even when Brownson bluntly told him to dedicate his life to the salvation of the Germans in the Midwest, Isaac showed no interest. Later when Bishop McCloskey more suavely suggested the priesthood in his native New York, Hecker seemed diffident. His reluctance stemmed, not from any loss of interest in the cause of Christ, but from a lack of confidence in his own ability to do anything for souls. About a year before, this same hesitancy first gripped him, but then Brownson's enthusiastic encouragement to enter the ministry swept it aside. However, Isaac's experience in Concord had revived it to such a degree that he was almost convinced he could never be of any value in the active work of the Church.[2] After his conversation with the Bishop, Hecker suspected that his vocation was to the contemplative life. Since there were no purely contemplative communities in the Church in America — the Trappists were the first to come, but they did not arrive until 1848* — he might be able to find what he wanted in Europe. He was not sure that this was his true vocation, but contemplation for a certain length of time under the watchful eye of experienced guides in the spiritual life appealed very strongly to him.[3]

In the days before his baptism, he directed his thoughts constantly to the monastic life abroad and asked himself why he should not go to Europe and investigate for himself. This soon gave rise to the possibility of making a genuine medieval pilgrimage to Rome. It would not be expensive he hoped, for he could work his way across on one of the ships, then beg for his food, living on bread and water, and traveling on foot to the Holy City. There he could see the monastic life in operation as well as visit all the hallowed spots of Catholic tradition. Not wishing to take such a trip alone, he thought of Henry Thoreau as the ideal companion, for he too "could live on bread and water and sleep on the earth."[4]

The day before he was received into the Church, Isaac wrote to his Concord friend and invited him to join his pilgrimage. While waiting for an answer, he also discussed the plan with Bishop McCloskey who did not disapprove, but "seemed inclined to favor it." However, he strongly advised his young convert to take some money with him and not to depend solely on the alms of Europeans. Having studied abroad, the Bishop was speaking from personal observation. Circumstances would arise, he said, when money would be absolutely necessary.[5]

---

* The Trappists had come from France in 1805 but returned to Europe a short time later. In 1848 they made a second attempt that was successful and established the monastery of Gethsemani in Kentucky.

Hecker's letter reached Concord while Thoreau was away on a walking trip through the Catskill Mountains where he lived on bread and berries, "slumbering on the mountain tops."[6] After Hecker had received no reply within two weeks, he wrote again hoping to stimulate Thoreau's interest, telling him that no sooner had he thought of the pilgrimage than Thoreau's name popped into his mind as the only companion for the journey. Mentioning the Bishop's admonition not to undertake the venture without money, he said: "If this makes it practicable for others, to us it will be sport." Then he sounded the motto for the journey: "Tis impossible, therefore we do it."[7]

Thoreau returned and found Hecker's invitation which he was strongly tempted to accept. Even Channing wondered how he could resist. But because of his recent activity, Thoreau decided it would be best to retire for a while into a "Brahminical, Artesian, Inner Temple life." With regret he declined, "sorry that the Genius will not let me go with you."[8]

Isaac's friend, Burrill Curtis, was a little alarmed when he heard of the project and asked the city-bred New Yorker: "Have you an accurate idea of the magnitude of the undertaking?" Still he was not too surprised, for Hecker's "preparedness for any fate" was one of the attractive features of his character. Nevertheless he thought the medieval tour of Europe was a manifestation of Isaac's restlessness which "is uppermost just now, not as a contradictory element — for it is not; but as a discovering power."[9] Curtis was very close to the truth. Hecker was restless and anxious to discover where he belonged.

When Thoreau refused the invitation, Isaac gave up further thought of the Roman pilgrimage and planned a more intensive spiritual life in New York. Continuing to live on his strict diet of nuts, apples, and bread, he decided to attend daily Mass, make an evening meditation, and devote more time to spiritual reading. Monthly confession was also included in his schedule, with the reception of Holy Communion as often as his confessor, Bishop McCloskey, would recommend.[10] How much the Bishop knew of Isaac's ascetic habits is difficult to ascertain. However, it would seem that he was not aware of his penitent's extreme mortifications or he would have cautioned him against too much severity.

As well as discussing spiritual matters with Hecker, the Bishop found time to talk about Brownson. Through some of the Boston clergy he was kept informed of Brownson's progress toward the Church. Sometimes rumors reached New York that were premature. In late August, McCloskey had heard that Brownson had already been to confession, but the editor of *Brownson's Quarterly* had to tell Hecker that he was making slow progress with his instructions but hoped the time would soon come for him to receive the Sacraments.[11]

Both Bishops Hughes and McCloskey were awaiting word of Brownson's reception into the Church. Both anticipated great results from his conversion. Bishop McCloskey told Hecker of a "day-dream" that he hoped would become a reality: an American Catholic review with the fiery and capable Brownson as editor. This appealed to young Hecker who wrote enthusiastically to his friend and suggested he come to New York and visit Bishop McCloskey. You would like him, Hecker wrote, better than either of the Boston prelates, or even Bishop Hughes.[12]

Two weeks later when Isaac called upon his spiritual director, the Bishop again brought up the question of the Catholic review. Not only he, but Bishop Hughes as well, was heartily in favor of it and was thinking of inviting Brownson to come to New York and become the editor of the proposed review. Reporting the visit to Brownson, Hecker had no doubt that Bishop Hughes would write and he was hoping that when the offer would be made Brownson would accept and move to the diocese. In no state of the union would he find a more able bishop than Hughes whose "patronage" would be all important. Furthermore Isaac was confident that the "heads of the Church" in New York would be more sympathetic to Brownson's ideas than the prelates of Boston. More progressive, more fearless, they would give him greater support and encouragement. No doubt hoping to offer additional encouragement, Isaac added "they look to your union with the C[atholic]. Church as an era in Catholic America."[13]

But Brownson was not to be swayed. By this time he had come to know both Boston Bishops very well and had no intention of leaving his beloved New England. He had no complaints about Bishop Fenwick, whom he loved as a father and revered as a saint. Nor had he any fault to find with Bishop Fitzpatrick, a man "of a powerful intellect" and completely devoted to the Church. Brownson could imagine nothing more painful than separating from his "confessor." Furthermore, the Boston Reformer was not in sympathy with a distinctly Catholic review for a limited circle of Catholic readers. He preferred to continue the *Quarterly* which circulated among non-Catholics as well. The Boston Prelates were of the same opinion. Ten years later, Brownson would sing a different tune and acknowledge that he would leave the confines of Boston not with pain but with a joyful feeling of deliverance.

Brownson's humility, which he was trying desperately to nurture, shrank from any idea that his conversion was a blessing to Catholicism. He was coming into the Church not because she needed him, but because he needed her. What was he bringing with him? he asked. Nothing but "my sins" and a desire to obey and "be saved." If he could aid the Church, he would be grateful. But he wanted to hear no more of compliments. "I am proud and vain enough and have hard work enough to acquire the humility that becomes me."

In this same letter, the persistent Brownson again spoke of Isaac's vocation. He encouraged him to resume his studies, and hoped he would prepare for the priesthood. The need was great and every young man who had any vocation owed it to his country to work for the good of America through the Church. But since "you have a spiritual advisor more competent to advise you than I am," Brownson prudently left this decision to Bishop McCloskey.[14]

Part of Brownson's well-meaning advice was unnecessary, for when nothing came of Hecker's proposed European pilgrimage, Isaac decided to continue his studies. But he still could not make up his mind to go on for the priesthood. Bishop McCloskey, far more skillful than Brownson in dealing with a budding vocation, knew it would bloom in its own good time and could not be forced or hurried. When Hecker laid before him his plan of study, the Bishop approved but asked no questions about the purpose of the study. The time was not yet ripe for such a discussion and the knowledge of Greek and Latin could prove very useful.[15]

With no specific goal before him but with supreme confidence that God in His providence would reveal His divine will, young Hecker enrolled in the Cornelius Institute on October 17, 1844.[16] Begun in 1840 by a few wealthy New Yorkers in memory of the Christian minister Elias Cornelius, this school was located in the basement of the Presbyterian Church in Sixth Street just east of Second Avenue, and offered a free academic education to men studying for the Christian ministry. An excellent Greek scholar, the Rev. John J. Owen, was the principal as well as professor of Greek and Latin. At the time Isaac went to the school, there were about thirty students, all of whom were Protestants but not all became ministers.[17]

One of Isaac's classmates, William D. Porter, wrote some years later that Isaac was always dressed in a black but not clerical suit, with his blond hair combed behind his ears and a small breast pin in his shirt. Always punctual, he was at his place at nine o'clock when the classes opened with the singing of a hymn from the old Carmina Sacra Collection. Then Dr. Owens read three verses from the Scriptures and each student in turn followed with two more verses. Isaac always used a small Bible he carried in his pocket. After the principal had said the prayer, studies began. Isaac took courses in Latin and Greek and also in music.[18]

Associated with the school was a literary group, the Adelphic Society, which Isaac was asked to join. Every Wednesday evening with Dr. Owens presiding, the members either discussed a paper which one of their number had read, or followed a debate on a current problem, or listened to a "declamation." The program attracted Hecker, but also presented both a problem and a challenge. How would the principal react to the presentation of the Catholic position in a professedly Protestant school for future ministers? The challenge was an excellent opportunity to explain the true Catholic attitude to future non-Catholic leaders who had either a distorted or inadequate notion of the Church. If Hecker accepted the challenge, he might not only draw down on himself the ill will of the principal, but also the indictment of using fifth column, proselytizing tactics. Isaac decided the only honest and fair course was to tell the principal that if he participated in any discussion or read a paper, he would do so only as a Catholic. How Dr. Owens reacted to this proposal, Hecker does not say. But Isaac did join the group. Some of the papers he read had a distinctly Brownsonian flavor: Subject and Object; Characteristics of the American People and the Tendency of their Civilization; the Criterion of Judgment; and the Objects of Modern Reformers.[19]

Before Isaac began his studies at Cornelius Institute he had to settle his obligations to the growing Hecker Flour Company. After he returned from Concord, he had been working all morning but had his afternoons and evenings free. Since he could no longer continue this schedule, Isaac decided this was the time to sever all connection with the firm. Although both John and George had every reason to believe that Isaac meant what he said, they did not change their trade name but continued as Hecker and Brothers. Neither did they dissolve the partnership the three had formed in 1842.[20]

Hecker began his study of Latin and Greek with some fear that he would not succeed but he was soon pleasantly surprised with his progress. After a week of classes he wrote to Brownson that he was getting along very well with no recurrence of the condition that had hampered him at Concord, but he cautiously added the hope that this time his spiritual life would not force him from his books.[21] From time to time, he questioned the wisdom of devoting so much of his day, which could be much more profitably spent in contemplation, to acquiring languages. Nevertheless he attended classes faithfully and prepared his recitation carefully. By the end of January he could report: "I find myself making gradual and respectable progress in my studies." But then he adds: "To what end?" To that question he could give no answer.[22]

Though Hecker could not conjecture what use he would make of his studies, he knew he wanted to consecrate himself to God. As the year 1844 was drawing to a close, he dedicated himself completely and without reserve to the service of Christ. He did it with greater self-surrender "than I have ever done, for the good of the kind of which I am a part, for the sake of the love of God." Firmly convinced that the only field of action is in, with, and for the Church, he wrote to Brownson, "My heart burns to realize the Catholic Church." Humbly he asked of Almighty God: "Oh may I be a brave and valiant soldier in Thy cause."[23]

But despite this complete consecration to the cause of Christ,

Isaac took no step toward the priesthood or even entertained the thought of going to the seminary. Two basic realities in his mind explain this apparent contradiction: his respect for the priesthood and his knowledge of himself.

From the very beginning of his Catholic life, he had held the sacred character of the priesthood in the highest regard. Contrasted with the Protestant ministry, which he had thought of entering, holy orders were immeasurably greater since they were supernatural in character. The priest acting in the place of Christ exercised the powers of his divine Master and had the responsibility of leading the faithful to sanctity of life and union with God. Therefore, Hecker reasoned, anyone aspiring to be Christ's minister must first have considerable natural ability and an abundance of supernatural virtue.[24] But Isaac sincerely believed he had neither. His gifts of mind he described as less than mediocre: "I look upon myself as belonging to that class of decidedly unfortunate beings who have no particular talent." His virtues, he regarded as non-existent and the longer he spent in contemplation, the louder grew his cry of unworthiness. He was becoming deeply conscious of the infinite perfection of God. This made him realize his own wretchedness and misery with ever increasing clarity. Complaining that his soul was filled with all kinds of sin, he wrote in his diary almost daily such sentiments as these: "Sin has disabled me. . . . My sins are unspeakable." "Nothing I can say is adequate to the weight of sin I feel." Accurately he described his state of mind in the words: "This is my theme and my only theme — my sins and ingratitude. Oh what defilement, ugliness and deformity of heart! Hard, obdurate, wicked, doubting, unbelieving, wayward heart that I have! Lord I cry from the depths of depths to Thee in heaven."[25]

This was not a morbid, crippling wail of despair, but a humble and penitent cry of a soul supremely conscious of the beauty and goodness of God. A comparison of the limitations of the soul with the infinite perfection of God must always bring forth protestations of utter unworthiness. And Isaac seeing himself against the splendor and magnificence of God could find nothing in himself to praise, but everything to condemn.[26]

And yet despite his sincere and constant protestations of sinfulness, the only faults he could discover were his lack of devotion in prayer, his lack of recollection at Mass, his neglect of spiritual exercises, and his carelessness in studies. When preparing for confession, he complained he could only accuse himself "in a general manner" and though he was sure there were many specific transgressions that he had committed, he was at a loss to name them. The consciousness of the heinous character of sin had become so real to him that even though he had not fallen into any sins, the slightest faults assumed great proportions in his eyes.[27]

Someone, he does not say who, had told him he had a very tender conscience "approaching to scrupulosity." But Isaac found that when he compared his conduct and habits to those of the saints, he did not think he was too scrupulous. They practiced much more self-denial than he did. They held the pleasures of the world, even the most innocent, in greater disdain than he. If he would imitate these heroes of Christ, he must regard all reality not in the light of time but of eternity.[28]

Since the priest reflected Christ to the world and, in a sense, shared in His divine power, he could never aspire to so sacred a vocation. The only help he could give to the cause of Christ was prayer for the salvation of souls. With this thought in mind, toward the end of February of 1845 he began to recite the Litany of the Blessed Virgin every night for the conversion of his friends. Gratefully mindful of all the blessings and graces God had given him through the Church, he longed to see others sharing those same blessings. First in his intentions was his own family, particularly his brother George, who, as yet, belonged to no Church. Although he too had an earnest desire to come closer to Christ, Isaac knew desire alone was not enough. The grace of God was necessary and he would do what he could, through his prayers and sacrifices, to obtain that grace for his brother.[29]

When Isaac made up his mind to join the Catholic Church, he wrote to George from Concord: "Shall we go arm in arm in our heavenly journey as we have on our earthly?"[30] Within less than a year Isaac's hopes were fulfilled. George took instructions from Bishop McCloskey and received baptism at his hands. On May, 18, 1845, the two brothers received the Sacrament of Confirmation. As they had been from their earliest days the closest of friends, they became even more so now through this new bond of faith.[31]

Wisely and carefully, Bishop McCloskey had been guiding Isaac's spiritual life. Since his penitent had opened his soul completely, and the Bishop knew Hecker's state of mind, he did not think it advisable to mention the priesthood to him until the end of March. Then he asked him if he thought of devoting his life to the service of the Church. Immediately the specter of his own unworthiness rose up before Isaac's eyes, and he could not say yes. But was he a competent judge in his own case? His confessor knew him thoroughly, he knew what the priesthood required and he seemed to be calling him to enter it. Rather than trust himself, Isaac decided to put his soul into the hands of the Bishop. He would do "whatever" his confessor "directed me to do" and told him "the more he gave me direction, the happier I should feel."[32] Very prudently the Bishop declined to make the decision. That must come from Isaac himself. So he directed him to think and pray about it with confidence that God would reveal His will. Two weeks later, he suggested that Hecker read the lives of two illustrious Jesuits: Saint Ignatius the founder and Saint Francis Xavier his devoted disciple.[33]

From the suggestions the Bishop was giving, it seems clear that he thought Isaac had a vocation to the religious life and that he might find his place with the Jesuits. He proposed that Hecker visit St. John's College (later Fordham) at Rose Hill where he could meet some of the convert professors. Although Hecker carefully read the lives of the Jesuit saints recommended by the Bishop, he knew he did not want to join the Society.[34]

Bishop McCloskey was not the only one interested in Isaac's vocation. A Catholic friend of Hecker's had mentioned the young convert to the Redemptorist Fathers at Holy Redeemer Church on Third Street, a little east of Avenue A, and one of the Fathers — Hecker does not give his name — said he would like to see him.* On April 21st Isaac went over to the rectory behind the frame church and had a very interesting visit with a German priest. Quite unlike the patient and unhurried method of the Bishop, the Re-

---

* In August of 1842, Bishop Hughes invited the Redemptorists to take charge of the German Catholic congregation in New York. The Community had come to America in 1832 to work in the Diocese of Cincinnati. Within the next ten years, they had houses in Baltimore, Pittsburgh, New York, Buffalo, and Rochester, where they worked zealously with the German-speaking Catholics. All the American Redemptorist houses were under the jurisdiction of the Belgian Province.

demptorist was all for a faster course of action. He wanted young Hecker to make a spiritual retreat "immediately and at their place" to discover what religious order in the Catholic Church suited him. During the course of the retreat he could make a general confession of his whole life which would aid the confessor to direct him. This procedure seemed much too fast for Isaac and he decided against it. The priest, Hecker conceded, was zealous "too much so it seems to me." However, he did agree with the Redemptorist's observation "that the discipline and standard of religion is not so high among the English and Irish Catholics."[35]

Whether Isaac told the Bishop of the German priest's observation on the English and Irish Catholics, he does not say. He did, however, speak of the retreat and the general confession. Quietly the Bishop explained that the Redemptorists were "zealous" for their order and would naturally like to secure candidates. But this zeal could create a "bias" in their judgment and might induce them to be less objective in their choice of an order for Hecker. As to the general confession, he had made one less than a year ago to the Bishop when he came into the Church. If he wanted to make another, though the Bishop seemed to think it unnecessary, he suggested the Jesuits. After this conversation, Isaac decided he would follow his confessor's direction and wait for the grace of God to enlighten him.[36]

Although Hecker was still persuaded of his lack of talent and virtue for so sacred a vocation, he had come to realize that whenever Almighty God calls a soul for a particular work, he always gives that soul the grace to accomplish that work. "God gives grace according to the destiny to be realized."[37] Could he be sure that God was calling him? The only test he had was the voice of his confessor who seemed to think he had a vocation. As long as he was faithful to his direction, he knew he had nothing to fear. From his reading of spiritual authors he had learned "it never has been known at any time that a soul has been lost that has obeyed its director." Neither would he make any mistake in following his. Through prayer, silence, interior recollection, and self-abnegation, he would make his soul more receptive to the grace of God.[38]

By the end of April Isaac had come to the conclusion that he

had a vocation. But he could not decide whether it was to the
secular priesthood or a religious community. Although he still
felt very much attracted to a life of contemplation, he realized
that he could not be satisfied in a contemplative order. For a
time he would be very happy, but he knew that he "could not
permanently remain in such a state without some disinclination."[39]
His vocation was a combination of the two, the active and the
contemplative. Could he find this combination only in the religious
life? As he weighed the question, he realized that the secular
clergy had ample opportunity for prayer and discipline. The life
of a diocesan priest could be just as severe as that of a religious.
Administering the Sacraments and dealing with penitents could
provide him with many occasions for patience, self-denial, humility,
and "self-forgetfulness." Above all, to be at the beck and call
of souls in spiritual distress would require one of the greatest
disciplines, the sacrifice of the will. Added to all these reasons
was the great need for priests in America, priests who would
be answering the call of Christ to work in His vineyard. But
this he could also do as a religious. He still could not decide.[40]

    During the month of May, Isaac visited the Redemptorist
Fathers frequently. One of them seemed to be particularly helpful
to him. In all likelihood this was the rector, Father Rumpler, a
learned and able man of mature spirituality. What advice he
gave him, Isaac does not say, but he did tell him to read St.
Alphonsus' treatise on the choice of a vocation in the religious
life. This was very fine, Isaac wrote Brownson, but "books and
men are books and men and it requires as much right judgment
to discriminate in their advice what strictly is applicable to one
as it does in them to give the right advice." As a result of his
questioning and reading, Isaac found he was "unable to choose"
but perfectly willing "to obey." The only thing he could do was
"knock, seek, pray, ask for. God has promised to give a response
to all these."[41]

    Another devout Catholic who was very anxious that Hecker
devote himself to the priesthood in America was his guide of
earlier days, Orestes Brownson. He had made his profession of
faith on October 20, 1844, and received Holy Communion on the
following day. Since that time, he told Isaac, he had grown more
and more Catholic and "less and less of a Protestant." He was

dismayed to find that the mass of Catholics were not completely Catholic, and he believed that America needed "American priests as fast as we can get them."[42]

Because of this positive attitude, Brownson urged young Hecker to work for the Church in America. Conceding that Isaac's disposition might lead him to the Carthusians, he asked him: "Could you not content yourself with the Dominicans?" The Redemptorists even though they do not have a strict monastic rule should offer some attractions. Bishop Fitzpatrick, Brownson added, recommended the Dominicans. Whatever the choice, the Boston Reformer had only one plan: Stay and work in America where the Church needs priests.[43]

Brownson wrote this letter on June 25th. Four days later he came to New York and stayed with the Heckers. Although Isaac merely intended to note in his diary that Brownson was there, he wrote an estimate of his great friend that is perhaps the most accurate and succinct characterization of Brownson that any of his contemporaries ever drew. It came from the pen of one who not only knew the great American philosopher intimately, but respected and admired him greatly. Still, he was not blind to his shortcomings as his observations show. Paying tribute to Brownson's extraordinary mental ability that enables him "to think for a dozen men," Hecker writes:[44]

No man thinks and reads more than he. But he is greater as a writer than as a person. . . . His presence does not change us.* Nor do we find ourself where we were not after having met him. He has not the temperament of genius, but more of a rhetorician and declaimer. He arrives at his truths by a regular and consecutive system of logic. His mind is of a historical rather than a poetical mould. He never startles us with profound truths rushing from his brain like Minerva from the head of Jupiter, already armed. We see both the genesis, exodus, and revelation of his thoughts. He never will be charged with holding two doctrines, one esoteric and the other exoteric. As a man, we have never known one so conscientious and self-sacrificing. This is natural to him. His love of right is supreme, and his great [horror], the thing he detests, is bad logic. This makes him peevish and often riles his temper. He defeats but will never

* The use of the plural pronoun in reference to himself becomes quite prominent after July 31, 1844, when Hecker noted in his diary, "Somehow or other, we have passed from I to we."

convince an opponent. This is bad. No one loves to break a lance with him, because he cuts such ungentlemanly gashes. He is strong and he knows it. He has more of the Indian chief than of the chivalrous knight in his composition. He has both — though nothing of the modern scholar, so-called. He is wholly wanting in genuine pathos. He whines when he would be pathetic. His art is logic but he never aims at art. He is a most genuine and true man to his nature. None so much so. . . . There is a pure and genuine vein of poetry running through his nature, but not sufficient to tincture the whole flow of his life. He is a man of the thirteenth or fourteenth centuries and not of the nineteenth. . . . He is genuine, we love him for this.

There is no doubt that Hecker "loved" Brownson whom he called "Father, Brother and Friend."[45] His friendship with the older man was frequently a surprise to many of Hecker's intimates who, with good reason, regarded the Boston Reformer as harsh and dictatorial.* But Hecker never found him that way.[46] Though he sought Brownson's counsel in his difficulties, he never followed his advice blindly. He always maintained the right to evaluate the older man's opinions. Even though Isaac knew that Brownson wanted to keep him away from Alcott and Lane, he still went to Fruitlands. And when Brownson wrote to the Heckers in New York what Isaac considered an unfair opinion of the Paradise Planters, he did not hesitate to disagree with him. Isaac also refused to join the Episcopal Church when Brownson suggested he should.[47] But these and other differences of opinion, which show Isaac was never under Brownson's domination, did not weaken the bond between them.

Perhaps the friendship of Hecker for Brownson is not nearly so remarkable as Brownson's interest in Hecker. When the two met, the Boston Reformer was a prominent public figure because of his writings and lectures. He could number among his friends political stalwarts such as Calhoun and Van Buren; he could find a welcome among religious leaders of the stamp of Channing, Ripley, and Parker; he could be at ease with the intellectual

---

* Georgiana Bruce, one of the Brook Farmers, said that "Brownson was not the prince of gentlemen in debate. He raised his voice and pounded the table and when worsted declared his opponents could not place him — nor herself — on his standpoint." G. B. Kirby, *Years of Experience* (New York, 1887), p. 147. And Swift says Brownson's appearance at Brook Farm was "no signal for mirth." *Brook Farm* (New York, 1900), p. 54.

Emerson or the garrulous Elizabeth Peabody. But what could he find to attract him in the young, uneducated, unimportant, confused baker from New York?

Brownson himself, in 1855, gives the answer to this question when he reviewed Father Hecker's book, *Questions of the Soul*. Referring to his early acquaintance with Hecker, Brownson said he found him: "Simple, unpretending, playful and docile as a child, warm and tender in his feelings, full of life, cheerfulness of manner . . . he infuses as it were his own sunshiny nature into your heart. From his youth he has been remarkable for his singular purity of heart, the guilelessness of his soul, the earnestness of his spirit, his devotion to truth and his longing after perfection."[48]

In this same review, Brownson also makes clear that this was not a friendship without benefit to himself. Freely, he admitted he owed a debt of gratitude to his young friend who never realized how much he helped both him and his wife to the Church. Although Hecker thought Brownson was giving him direction and guidance, the Boston Reformer, never lavish with praise, stated emphatically: "Each perhaps was of service to the other, but he aided us more than we him, for even then his was the master mind."[49] When he wrote this statement, Brownson had in mind the many hours the two spent together at Mt. Bellingham when Isaac came from Brook Farm, Fruitlands, or Concord. These were hours which were not only pleasant and interesting, but profitable, and gradually led both men to the Church.

In Brownson's judgment, Almighty God had given Hecker "a mission of vital importance" to America,[50] and he did not want him to bury himself or his God-given talents in a monastery. Although Hecker made no mention of his conversation with Brownson in June, 1845, there is little doubt that he stressed his conviction that Isaac should remain and work in America. Aware of the mystical bent in Isaac's nature, he urged him to sacrifice that tendency for the cause of Christ in his own country.[51]

Naturally Isaac did not share Brownson's conviction that he could play any significant role in the Church in America. On the contrary, he was obsessed with the thought that his "want of humility, talent and culture seem insuperable barriers to my usefulness in the priesthood." But at least he would do his very best. What he lacked in natural attainments, he confidently hoped God would supply through His divine grace.[52]

Before Bishop McCloskey left New York City early in June for a two months' visitation of the diocese, he suggested that Isaac wait until September and then enter the diocesan seminary at Fordham. If, after a time, he still felt drawn to the religious life, then he could decide which order he should join. When Isaac talked with Bishop Hughes during his confessor's absence, the Bishop expressed the same opinion.[53] But there was one difficulty in this plan. Isaac feared that if he stayed in the city, there would be too many distractions from his family and friends. Rather than gradually withdraw from the environment so familiar to him, he wanted to make a sharp, clean break with the past. This he could do so much better in Europe where there were stronger Catholic influences and where he would be under more severe discipline than in America.[54]

Two weeks later, Isaac again called on Bishop Hughes and mentioned his objections to Fordham. Anxious to keep the young man for the diocese if he could, the Bishop suggested the Seminary of St. Sulpice in Paris where he would be under strict discipline and the guidance of wise and prudent men who were also successful teachers. While he was preparing for the priesthood in the diocese, he would also see various religious orders and be in a much better position to decide if any one of them appealed to him. The Jesuits, Dominicans, Franciscans he knew only through the reports of others and through reading. Although he was quite familiar with the Redemptorists, the Bishop thought he should know more of other communities before he decided on any particular one. No doubt the New York Prelate was hoping that once the young convert was under the care of the Sulpicians, he would decide to remain among the diocesan clergy.[55]

But Isaac saw a practical objection to this plan. If he were to study in Paris, the expenses would be rather heavy and he was extremely reluctant to burden his family. Moreover, his brothers had started building a much larger flour mill which absorbed all their extra capital and were in no position to take care of his education in Europe. Even if they could, he saw no advantage to the plan. Why spend a year in Paris deciding on a religious order when he had practically decided he wanted a stricter life than that of the secular clergy? Just as he could leave St. Sulpice for the monastery, he could leave the religious order for the seminary, if he were not satisfied. Moreover, he preferred beginning with the more severe, rather than the less strict.[56]

Young Hecker's thoughts were settling more and more on the Redemptorists. In their convent on Third Street, he observed their way of life and was strongly attracted by their poverty and the atmosphere of prayer and recollection.

Another circumstance which influenced him was the fact that two young American converts, Clarence Walworth and James McMaster, had made application to the Redemptorists.[57] Both had been Anglicans but under the influence of the Oxford Movement had come into the Church the previous May and had received the Sacraments at Holy Redeemer Church. They had decided to become Redemptorists while the Belgian Provincial, Father de Held, was making his visitation of the New York house, which together with the other American Redemptorist houses, was attached to the Belgian Province. After he had given them a brief examination, the Provincial approved them for the novitiate. At first, they were directed to go to Baltimore, but after Father de Held's visitation of that house, he decided to send them to St. Trond in Belgium. They were to sail on August 1st.[58]

Father Rumpler arranged to have Hecker meet the two prospective Redemptorists before they would leave for Europe. How much this meeting influenced Hecker's decision to join them is difficult to know, but on July 29th he called on Bishop Hughes and told him he intended to apply for admission to the sons of St. Alphonsus. Since Hecker had already made up his mind, the Bishop could hardly do anything but approve and he gave Isaac his blessing.[59]

Only one more obstacle still remained in Hecker's path. Before he could go with Walworth and McMaster, he needed the Provincial's permission and he was in Baltimore. It was then Friday and the boat was due to leave the next afternoon. Not much time remained to see Father de Held and to prepare for the trip. Isaac made a quick decision. George could pack his trunk, arrange his passage, while he took the night train to Baltimore. At four o'clock in the morning he arrived at the Redemptorist house and asked to see the Provincial. After hearing the purpose of his call, Father de Held said he needed time to consider. But Isaac explained that if he were to sail with McMaster and Walworth, he would need an immediate decision. The earnestness and sincerity that had captivated Brownson won the Provincial. He told the young man to go to the chapel and hear Mass and then after breakfast he would see him. When Isaac saw him the second time, Father de Held handed him a Latin version of the *Imitation of Christ* and asked him to translate a few passages. After having plowed through Caesar and Cicero, Hecker had no difficulty with Thomas à Kempis. Father de Held was satisfied, gave his approval, and Isaac dashed for the eight-thirty train to take him back to New York.[60]

When the *Prince Albert* sailed out of the harbor, the three young aspirants for the Redemptorist Community were standing at the rail watching their native shore disappearing from view. Different emotions welled up in the hearts of Hecker and Walworth. The young convert from Episcopalianism found it "a bitter thing" to leave his country and his friends for a new strange land.[61] But Hecker had no such reaction. He had said good-by to his mother and the farewell filled her eyes with tears and her heart with sadness. John, too, had a difficult time controlling his emotions. But it was different with George who understood Isaac so well and could read the happiness in his eyes. He knew his brother was leaving without regrets, and if ever he were sent back to his native land as a priest of God, he would labor for "its true enlightenment and progress."[62] But Isaac alone knew the real cause for his joy and peace. He was coming ever closer to understanding his childhood conviction, "God has a work for me to do." He had not found that work in America; maybe he would discover it in Europe.

CHAPTER VII

Testing a Vocation

THE three young men traveling second class on the *Prince Albert* were an interesting group. They were about the same age, though Hecker was six months older than Walworth and Mc-Master. Hecker was born and bred in lower Manhattan, while the other two were natives of upstate New York where they met for the first time as students at Union College in Schenectady. After graduation, both took up the study of law, Walworth in Albany and McMaster in New York City at Columbia Law School. Neither practiced law for any considerable length of time and, quite independently of each other, both decided upon a career in the Episcopalian ministry. In 1840, McMaster entered the Protestant Episcopal General Seminary in New York City and two years later Walworth enrolled there, being assigned to a room just across the hall from his former college companion. Ardent Puseyites, they had traveled to the Church along a different road from that taken by Hecker. His was the philosophical and more mystical approach; theirs the historical and theological. They had watched with careful interest the Oxford Movement in England, while Hecker, though familiar with the Tractarian writings, was much more concerned with absolute obedience to the voice of the Holy Spirit within him. A year after Isaac, in the presence of Bishop McCloskey, had wholeheartedly pronounced his profession of faith, Walworth knelt before Father Rumpler in Holy Redeemer Church on May 16, 1845, and enunciated his credo.[1]

Some weeks before that, McMaster had called on Bishop Mc-

Closkey. Calmly he told the Bishop he wanted to become a Catholic, receive the Sacraments, but without making a profession of faith. When the Bishop told him such a condition was impossible, McMaster waited awhile and then called upon Father Rumpler. Finally consenting to waive all conditions, he made his profession to the Redemptorist Rector on June 7th and received conditional baptism.[2]

Their journey to the Church now successfully completed, the three converts began a new search, this time together, to discover if their true vocation would be found in the Redemptorist Community. If it were, then they would be the first native Americans to become Redemptorists. Although the Community had come to the States in 1832, it recruited priests and brothers from Redemptorist houses in Europe. When the three Yankees sought admission to the Community, the Redemptorist Fathers were devoting their efforts and attention almost entirely to German-speaking Catholics.[3] The demands made upon the Fathers were much greater than they could meet but despite their number they labored mightily to minister to the spiritual needs of the souls under their care. Overworked and understaffed, they gladly welcomed the three Americans who wanted to join their ranks and they confidently hoped that many others would soon follow their example.

During the twenty-five-day Atlantic voyage, the three converts had plenty of time to discuss their newly found faith and their plans for the future. Though they had come to know each other very well, they had little knowledge of the fascinating, but at times disturbing, history of the Redemptorist Community. Begun in 1732 by St. Alphonsus in Scala, Sicily, to preach the Gospel to the poor and most abandoned sinners, the Community grew slowly, first in Sicily and Naples, and then spread to the Papal States. In 1764, Alphonsus presided over a General Chapter that drew up a body of constitutions, in conformity with the rule approved by Benedict XIV, that was to govern the Community for some years to come. But no sooner had the Chapter made this first move to strengthen the foundation of the growing group than the hampering and detrimental influence of the state threatened to crush the future development of the Redemptorists. This was not the first time nor would it be the last when the government would attempt to control the destiny of the Community.

In the days of St. Alphonsus, it was the King of Naples who wanted to bring the Redemptorists under his domination. When Alphonsus tried in 1780 to obtain the approval of Ferdinand IV for his Congregation, government officials replied that certain changes had to be made in the Constitutions before any royal approval would be given. Never suspecting the sweeping character of the revision that would be demanded, and unfortunately trusting too much to one of his assistants, Alphonsus left the negotiations in the hands of his consultor, Father Majone. Msgr. Testa, the Grand Almoner of the King, undertook the revision which effectively mutilated the Constitutions Benedict XIV had approved. Alphonsus had been tricked and betrayed before he realized what had happened. If he refused to accept the royal revision of the Rule, the Community would be suppressed. Rather than face such an unwelcome fate, he and the majority of the Neapolitan Fathers provisionally accepted the radically emended Constitutions. This acceptance so dismayed that portion of the Community outside the king's jurisdiction that the Redemptorists in the Papal State petitioned the Holy See to allow them their own superior until the Neapolitans adopted the original Constitutions. Granting this request, Pius VI declared that a government had no authority to modify a canonically approved rule. Since the Neapolitan Fathers had submitted to this unwarranted assumption of royal power, they were no longer members of the Congregation sanctioned by the Holy See. Because of this decree, St. Alphonsus was excluded from, and died outside of, the Congregation he had founded.

Although the breach was finally healed in 1793 with the restoration of the old Constitutions throughout the kingdom of Naples, the situation was far from ideal. Owing to royal interference and domination, the Superior General could not personally direct the destinies of the Community beyond the Neapolitan domains. As the Redemptorists spread to Poland, Switzerland, Germany, and Belgium, through the zealous efforts of St. Clement Hofbauer and his disciple the Blessed Joseph Passerat, two branches of the Community began to appear: the Cisalpine, those within the king's domains, and the Transalpine, those outside. To guide the activities of the Transalpine group, a vicar-general was chosen.

The first to hold this office was St. Clement who was succeeded by Father Passerat.

As the Community expanded, this arrangement became less and less desirable. Since the King of Naples regarded the Redemptorists as a Neapolitan institution founded for his kingdom, he would not permit the Rector Major to leave the confines of his domains. The General Superior of the Order had therefore no personal knowledge of the houses existing in other parts of Europe and could hardly exercise the office entrusted to him for the general good of the Community. In 1841 with a view toward ultimately correcting this situation the Holy See divided the entire Community into six provinces subject to the Rector Major. However for closer supervision three of these were placed directly under him and three under the Vicar-General. Father Passerat was given jurisdiction over the provincials of Austria, Switzerland, and Belgium.

At the time of this division, the American houses became the care of the Austrian Provincial, but after the Congregation had established foundations in England which were attached to the Belgian Province, it seemed more natural to put the American establishments under the same jurisdiction as those of England. In August of 1844, Father Passerat wrote to the Rector Major asking that the change be made. The following November the Holy See transferred the American Redemptorists to the Belgian Provincial, Father de Held. As a result of this move, Hecker, Walworth, and McMaster were seeking admission to the Belgian Province of the Community.[4]

These grim facts of ecclesiastical history meant little to the three neophytes at this stage of their lives although they would note them carefully later on. At this time they knew nothing of the maneuverings or the crippling effects of State-Church politics, nor were they interested in them. To be Redemptorists was their one ambition and to reach the novitiate the fastest way possible was their fervent desire. When the *Prince Albert* stopped in the bay at Portsmouth on Wednesday, August 27, 1845, they boarded the pilot boat, went ashore, and took the train to Westminster.[5] There they arranged for passage to Antwerp, but despite their impatience to be on their way to St. Trond they had to wait until Sunday. Taking advantage of the delay, McMaster fulfilled a long-cherished hope before the doors of the cloister would close behind him. He wanted to see Newman and Dalgairns, the renowned Puseyites with whom he had corresponded while still at the General Theological Seminary. Hurrying to Oxford, he took the coach to Littlemore where he caught his first glimpse of Newman. Ushered into the library, McMaster saw the future Cardinal in a very unconventional pose. He was standing with one foot on the seat of a chair, a book in one hand and a sandwich in the other. With unruffled dignity, the Oxford scholar who had not yet come into the Church received his Yankee visitor and asked many questions about the Anglican movement in America. Graciously he invited McMaster to spend the night at Littlemore.[6]

Meanwhile Hecker and Walworth had found rooms in a small inn over a pastry shop near the Vauxhall Gate in Westminster. Not particularly interested in sight-seeing, they visited only Westminster Abbey, the tomb of Edward the Confessor, and the Church of St. Saviour close by London Bridge.[7] On Sunday, September 1st, both were delighted to take the boat from Folkestone to Antwerp, and the next day they completed their journey to St. Trond, about thirty-five miles southeast of Antwerp. Without much difficulty they soon located the novitiate in a narrow street of the little Belgian town. The house, a large rambling building, had a spacious garden of three or four acres in the back. As the newcomers entered the monastery in the dusk of evening, they could see a long corridor with novices' rooms on either side.[8]

This solid old structure, built in the first half of the 15th century, had served as the Redemptorist novitiate and house of studies from 1833 until 1836 when the studentate was moved to Wittem in Holland.

The newcomers scarcely had time to glance around before Father Leopold Ottmann, the novicemaster, met them and gave them a cordial welcome. Showing them their rooms which he called cells, he left them for the night. Each cell had a bed with a small wooden cross on the pillow, a table over which hung a large crucifix, a chair, and a washstand.[9] Isaac was delighted. The monastery was what he had dreamed about and hoped for and now at last he was within its sheltering walls. Immediately he felt as though he had been transported to a "lovelier, purer and better world." For three days his heart was filled with an indescribable joy and gladness greater than he had ever experienced in his life before. Finally he could say: "All my seeking is now ended. I can say with some degree of certainty I have found all that I have ever sought."[10]

The next day the Americans met their fellow novices, numbering between twenty and thirty, who had come from various villages and hamlets in Germany, Holland, and Belgium. Their ages ranged from eighteen to thirty. French was the language of the novitiate, though as Hecker noted "all are understood" even in their native tongues. However, before a novice could become a member of the Community, he had to know how to speak French. When Isaac learned this, he began to study the language "with all diligence."[11] Before long, some of the novices told the Americans they would like to learn English, so Isaac wrote to his brothers in New York asking them to send him "a half-dozen of Townsend's Analysis" as well as pocket dictionaries and grammars.[12]

Father Ottmann gave the newcomers a few weeks to get accustomed to their surroundings and companions before they began a retreat which would officially inaugurate their novitiate year. He told them that at the close of the retreat on October 15th they would receive the distinctive habit of the Redemptorist Community.[13] Clearly and definitely the novicemaster informed his charges about the purpose of their stay at St. Trond. They would have a year in which they would live the life of a Redemptorist, study the Rule and Constitutions of the Community, develop the virtues so necessary to a religious, and eradicate faults and failings detrimental to a true spiritual life. During this time they would decide if they were called to the Redemptorist life, while the novicemaster would observe them carefully to see if they measured up to Community requirements. If they did not, if in his mature judgment they had no vocation, he would tell them so. Any novice, satisfactorily proving himself, would at the end of the year's time take his vows as a Redemptorist.

As aids to the formation and development of the religious character, Father Ottmann detailed the helps which the novices would receive. They would follow a specific schedule beginning at 4:30 in the morning and ending at 9:30 at night. Every hour of the day would be occupied with particular duties and exercises carefully chosen to offer "agreeable variety." Apart from two hours devoted to physical exercise and recreation, the whole day was spent in prayer, spiritual reading, and various novitiate exercises performed in common. Each day the novicemaster gave a half-hour talk on some spiritual topic or some point of the Rule and Constitutions. To break the routine and provide relaxation, every Thursday was a day of recreation. Then the novices took what they called a promenade which Hecker described as a "good long walk which we enjoyed."[14]

Very quickly Isaac realized that the faithful carrying out of the schedule demanded a complete surrender of his will. It did not allow the luxury of following his own desires as he had done in New York and Concord. "To go to walk when you would remain at home retired; to converse with cheerfulness when you would remain silent, to eat when you would fast, and such like duties often cost more than what may be looked upon by some as the severest penances." Walworth too found the schedule exacting and life at St. Trond a "sober, every day sort of business." For him, the convent clock calling the novices to their various exercises was "a remorseless clock which makes no account of the particular inspirations you may have at the moment." The American novices soon became accustomed to the routine. Their cheery contentment more than compensated for any sacrifices they were called upon to make. Isaac, within two weeks of his arrival, found the situation so ideal that he summed it up in one word, "perfect." Severe and rigorous discipline, Hecker had told Bishop McCloskey, was what he wanted. At St. Trond he found it and was completely satisfied.[15]

Though Isaac was perfectly happy at the novitiate, his novicemaster was not so sure of him. This new novice understandably puzzled Father Ottmann. Ordinarily those who enter a novitiate have a strong desire to live a life in imitation of our divine Lord, but at the time they begin their training, they have not progressed much beyond the stage of simple desire. They need to be trained in the art of prayer and meditation; they must be schooled in the practice of self-denial and mortification; they must be taught to surrender their own will to the will of God reflected in their rules and the direction of their superior. And it is the

duty of the novicemaster to introduce his novices to this new
way of life and guide their progress along the way.

When Father Ottmann came to deal with Isaac Hecker, he
found a soul far in advance of the usual aspirant to the religious
life. For two years Hecker had been accustomed to what spiritual
writers call the higher forms of prayer. He quickly passed beyond the first stages of mental prayer and meditation in which
the memory and intellect, dwelling on some spiritual thought,
arouses the will to make acts of adoration, thanksgiving, and
penance. He had been in the habit of spending long periods of
time in contemplation of God and His divine perfections, pouring
forth his soul effortlessly in fervent and devoted love and adoration. It would seem that if he had not reached what mystical
authors call affective prayer, he was given to what they term the
prayer of simplicity.[16] When he came to St. Trond he had reached
a state of prayer that one would rarely find in a novice at the
end of his training, much less at the beginning.

Further, he needed no encouragement to practice mortification
and self-denial. Ever since 1843 he had followed a most rigid
diet to such an extent that he did not find it difficult to abstain
from food. All the normal and natural pursuits of life he had put
behind him, and he had separated from his family and friends
until he had no human ties holding him back. He had only one
path "one of love of God" and all his efforts were "cheerful
labor."[17]

Because every novice was required to open his soul to the
novicemaster, Father Ottmann soon learned of Hecker's advanced
spiritual development. Since this had taken place without the
help of a trained spiritual director and before Hecker had come
into the Church, Father Ottmann's duty and obligation were clear:
he must make sure that the young man had not been deluded and
that the state of his soul was the result of grace. To test him,
he demanded strict obedience in following the course of spiritual
activity prescribed for all the novices. Wisely he would not permit
him to exercise all the mortifications Isaac's zeal desired. He would
frequently demand a sacrifice of his will that was not only
humiliating but painful. When the weekly Thursday walks came
around, Isaac was delighted and enjoyed the hike through the
countryside with his brother novices. But just as he was about

to start, Father Ottmann occasionally would stop him and say: "Brother Hecker, please remain at home, and instead of the walk, wash and clean the stairway." As he turned way from the group and went to his task, Isaac's disappointment and humiliation were no small sacrifices. But he accepted them with resignation and humility.[18]

After nine months of trial, the novicemaster no longer had any doubts that God had singularly blessed this novice. He recognized the "hand of God" in his soul and granted him a privilege that Isaac earnestly longed for but would not request: the daily reception of Holy Communion.* He also allowed him to practice some of the mortifications he had previously refused him. Never for a moment of his novitiate did Isaac doubt his vocation to be a Redemptorist; never for an instant was he tempted to leave the cloister walls and return to the secular life. He was happy; he was at peace; he was walking the path of the love of God.[20]

Though he kept no diary while he was at St. Trond, we know from written statements he gave to his directors a few years later that God had granted him special gifts of prayer and also manifestations of his future work and suffering. How explicit they were, how clearly they were made known to him, and how much attention he devoted to them, he does not say. It would seem that his spiritual director prudently advised him not to regard them as prophetic utterances, nor to use them as guides for his conduct, but rather to consider them as intimations of what God had in store for him. At no time of his life did these manifestations lead him to plan his life according to their message. When these promised events came to pass, he was not surprised. His novitiate days had prepared him for them.[21]

All the spiritual joy and consolation Isaac received at St. Trond did not make him forget his family. Rather they increased

* Until the recommendations of St. Pius X urging Catholics to receive Communion frequently were put into practice, the faithful were accustomed to receive no more than three times a year. The majority did not go that often. This was not true of religious communities where members ordinarily went to Communion two or three times a week. According to the Redemptorist Rule, those who were not priests received the Blessed Sacrament on Sundays, Wednesdays, and Fridays of every week; as well as on holy days of obligation. The confessor, if he judged his penitent worthy, could permit him daily Communion. Father Ottmann without any request on Hecker's part granted him this unusual privilege showing his confidence in Isaac's sincerity and virtue.[19]

his love for them "more, greatly more." His letters home are filled with his great devotion for each one of them, but especially with his anxious concern for their eternal salvation which he maintained they could hope to secure only in the Catholic Church. Before he left the States, Isaac thought of conversions solely in terms of the great happiness and peace the Church could give to those outside her fold. But after he went to Europe, he focused much more attention on the grave danger of damnation facing those who were not Catholics. He manifested the same state of mind Brownson had shown shortly before he became a Catholic. Practically all his letters from St. Trond and later from Wittem expressed this fear and he constantly begged his family to become Catholics.[22]

Interestingly enough, Walworth and McMaster made the same urgent request in their letters, but not with a vehemence equal to Isaac's.[23] Since the Heckers could offer no solid arguments against the Church, he could not understand why they had not sought admission to her fold. Almost daily he was expecting to hear that at least his mother had become a Catholic. When no such word was forthcoming, he continued to stress the threat of damnation.

Apparently the three zealous convert novices had not learned that a person can investigate the claims of Catholicism, find them reasonable and understandable, yet fail to discern any obligation to become a member. Such an investigation does not necessarily result in the conviction: "I must be a Catholic. I have an obligation to join the Church." Human reason can demonstrate the credibility of the Church, but reason alone can never lead a person into the Church. To take the decisive step, divine grace is necessary and this grace does not always come at the time of the investigation. Such grace is a free gift of God; He gives it according to His divine providence. Seemingly, this all-important fact the three novices overlooked. They did not ignore its necessity, since they were praying constantly for their friends and family, but they seemed to think that those for whom they prayed were not co-operating with grace.[24]

Constantly Isaac asked Almighty God to give the gift of faith to those most dear to him and asked his brother George to do the same thing: "The next duty, after gratitude to God for having blessed us with the true faith, is to pray for the conversion of our friends, especially our parents and those that are nearly related to us. . . . We know not: God may connect the conversion of our friends, and hence their salvation, with our prayers."[25]

In this same letter, Isaac gives the first indication of his future hopes. When John had expressed the wish that his brother would soon return to America, Isaac replied: "With the grace of God I shall never return otherwise than as a missionary priest to labor and suffer for the salvation of the most abandoned souls . . . and for the conversion of our country."[26] Shortly after having taken his vows, he wrote in a similar vein to Bishop McCloskey: "Perhaps it is not simply for the salvation and sanctification of my soul that our blessed Lord has bestowed upon me so many favors . . . and should it be His will, it would be my greatest delight to be with His grace and in His time, an aid to you, Rt. Rev. Father, in converting our country to the Holy Church of our Lord and the honor of the Blessed Virgin Mary."[27] This desire and hope soon brought Isaac closer to answering the question that had plagued him for so many years: "What does God want of me?" As the answer became clearer he wondered if he would be able to acquire the necessary knowledge for the exercise of the priestly ministry. Expressing his fears to his novicemaster, he was told to cast them aside and, when the time would come, to take his vows with confidence and trust in God.[28] With this assurance, Isaac was convinced that his true vocation was the combination of the active and contemplative life which he found in the Redemptorist Community.

As the year of probation and training was drawing to a close, the novices eagerly awaited the day when they would take their vows and become members of the Redemptorist Community. Before that happened, one of the three Americans had a very serious and momentous visit with the novicemaster. This was McMaster. From the beginning of the novitiate, Father Ottmann doubted that this demonstrative and impulsive American had a vocation to the Congregation. As time wore on, he became more convinced of it, and the month before the group was to take the vows, he told McMaster that although he had been an exemplary novice, he had no vocation to be a Redemptorist. Realizing the truth of

Father Ottmann's words, McMaster asked his novicemaster if he could give him any advice for the future. The wise and discerning priest told his friend that he should seek a career in journalism. Though this advice was prophetic in view of McMaster's later life and success,* at that time the young man looked upon such a career "with abhorrence and contempt." On September 14, 1846, he left St. Trond with the prayers and good wishes of all the priests and novices, who deeply regretted his departure.[29]

For several years Isaac had been a puzzle to himself, his family, and his friends. During the agonizing days of Brook Farm, Fruitlands, and Concord, the mystifying influence that had driven him from home baffled him. Although he recognized this was God's divine action, he could not imagine where it was leading him nor could he understand why it was causing him so much pain and anguish. Not until the closing days of his novitiate when he read the writings of renowned mystics such as St. John of the Cross, St. Teresa, and St. Catherine of Genoa did he understand the divine operations of God in his soul. He found in their writings the answers to all his perplexing questions and the key to unlock the secrets of his soul.

Who had more right to know of his discovery, he reasoned, than his family and Brownson. They had no more understood him when he was home than he had understood himself. But now that the past was no longer obscure and mysterious, but crystal clear, he had the duty to share his discovery with them. He wrote to each a long and detailed letter describing the purpose and the effect of the divine action in his soul. In both letters, though the language differed, the message was identical. Without any merit on his part, Almighty God had infused into Isaac's soul His own divine love which soon absorbed all his attention. Once captivated by this love, he had to sever all ties so he could give himself completely to his Master. Human nature often rebels at so severe a deprivation of its interests and cries out in pain with every wrench from its normal objects. But the grace of God, Isaac continued, triumphs over nature and pours itself more unreservedly into the now undivided heart. While all this was taking

---

* After his return to New York, McMaster followed Father Ottmann's advice and did some editorial work for the *Freeman's Journal*. Then in 1848 with George Hecker's financial assistance, he bought the paper and began a most successful and brilliant career as a journalist.

place in Isaac's soul, he had submitted, though not without a struggle. The divine hand of God led him away from his former friends and companions, first into the Catholic Church and then into the religious life where he would grow more and more in divine love. Now there remained for him but one more step — to consecrate by vow his whole being forever to God and His service.[30]

On October 15, 1846, a half hour after he wrote to his mother, Isaac Hecker made his vows of poverty, chastity, and obedience. Kneeling before Father Ottmann, he assumed as well the added obligation to persevere in the Redemptorist Community until the end of his life. His consecration was complete and he could say in his heart, as he had written in his letter: "What peace, what happiness. To live alone for His love, and to love all for His love, in His love, and with His love! We leave nothing in leaving all for God, for in God we find Him and all, and the foretaste of our future joy and happiness."[31]

Back in his cell after the ceremony was over and while he was gathering together his clothes and the few books he would take with him to Wittem the following day, Isaac realized that though man does not live by bread alone, he does live by bread. All during his novitiate, he had been clothed and fed and housed by the Community of which he was now a member. But he had contributed not a penny to this expense. So he sat down and wrote a "begging letter" to his brother John. After telling him that he had taken his vows, he reminded him that: "We eat, and we sleep, and wear out clothing as other men do; we make use of books and other human things, and thus being subject to human wants, we must depend within the limits of our rules, upon human aid and means." All his wants the Community had supplied without asking for any family aid. Not even when the novitiate year had been completed were they told to ask for financial assistance. However, since John had "heretofore often expressed" his willingness "to do this and more," Isaac thought he might like to contribute something toward his brother's expenses. If so, Isaac suggested that he deposit the money with Father Rumpler at the Redemptorist house in New York.

One other matter Isaac called to John's attention. Before he left for the novitiate, John had said he would leave Isaac's name associated with his own and that of George in the firm and not dissolve the partnership agreement they had formed, in case he decided not to remain with the Redemptorists. Now that Isaac's decision was final, he asked both George and John "in respect to the business" to regard him as though he "had never been connected with it nor had any title or claim upon it whatever." Because of this he suggested that his brothers destroy the agreement and thus eliminate him from their business partnership.[32] Now he had only one contract that would bind him for life, his solemn promise to labor for the cause of Christ in the religious community he had chosen.

On October 16, 1846, Isaac Hecker with seven other newly professed Redemptorists left St. Trond and started by stagecoach for the house of studies in Wittem. This little village in the southern end of the Netherlands was about thirty miles southeast of St. Trond and almost midway between Maastricht and Aix-la-Chapelle. The pleasant journey led through a rolling and somewhat hilly country which reminded Hecker of New England. But never around Concord or Harvard Village had he found such tangible manifestations of a fervent religious spirit. As the carriage rolled along, he could see in the distance large crosses on the hillsides and, a little closer to the road, statues of the Madonna and her Son. Simple but devotional shrines appeared at almost every crossroad. The Catholic faith was strong in these small outlying districts of Holland, the land and the faith Hecker's ancestors had forsaken almost three hundred years before. But through the grace of God, he had recovered that faith and now in the land of his forefathers he would study for the priesthood in the Catholic Church.

After they left Maastricht and had traveled almost nine miles, the students caught their first glimpse of their new home off to the left side of the road. It had been an old Capuchin monastery built by the Count of Plettenberg in 1732, the year St. Alphonsus founded the Congregation in Scala. After it had been deserted for some time, the Redemptorists bought the house in December of 1835 and the following January started classes with twelve students. As the number increased more rooms were needed and a year before Hecker and his companions arrived a new wing had been added.[33]

The studentate differed from the novitiate in many respects, but especially in the size of the community and in the daily round of duties. At Wittem there were more than a hundred Redemptorists under the guidance of the rector, the spiritual and scholarly Father Heilig, who had just published a new edition of St. Alphonsus' moral theology. The house was quite international in character with fifty-seven students who had come from Holland, Belgium, France, and Germany. From these very same countries had come the twenty-six Redemptorist priests living in the monastery who served either on the faculty or on missions.[34]

The newly professed had to adapt themselves not only to their fellow students but also to a completely different schedule from that of the novitiate. At St. Trond spiritual exercises had occupied the greater part of the day, while at Wittem classes and study would absorb most of their time. However, they were clearly admonished not to neglect their spiritual exercises in their pursuit of knowledge. Morning and evening meditation, attendance at Mass, spiritual reading, and their various community and private prayers would be daily features of their program. Nor would they be left to their own devices for spiritual direction. Two prefects were selected to assist them in the development of the inner life they had begun at St. Trond. Father Lelouchier would guide the theologians and philosophers while Father Konings would direct those in the classical department.[35]

The new students were then assigned to their classes. According to their varied educational backgrounds, they entered theology or philosophy or the classical department. Of Hecker's group Walworth was the only one ready for theology. Three of the others began philosophy while the remaining four, including Hecker, were put in the classical course. All were told that although French was the language spoken in the house, Latin would be used in the classroom.[36]

Enthusiastically Hecker began his studies and was in no hurry to finish the course as quickly as possible. He was quite resigned to spend a long time in the studentate acquiring a "solid and general learning" for the priesthood. Convinced that he must acquire more than "ordinary knowledge to do good with the usual assistance of divine grace," he devoted more than the required amount of time to his books. But with all his good resolutions and firm determination, he realized that he would find study difficult. He would not have the time for contemplation that had been his at St. Trond and he wondered if his soul would be drawn away from his books to greater union with God. Would he be able to confine his spiritual activity to the usual periods of prayer, or would it keep breaking into his studies as had happened at Concord? He could only wait patiently while he placed all his confidence in God.[37]

Apart from his spiritual condition there were other formidable obstacles to Isaac's intellectual progress which apparently he had never considered. Since his early days in elementary school, he had spent only one year in regular class routine, that at Cornelius Institute. Both at Brook Farm and Concord he had studied under tutors whom he saw only an hour or two a day. But at Wittem he would have daily classes beginning at eight in the morning and continuing until noon. After dinner he would return for more lectures. Relentlessly the grind would go on week after week with continued concentration on subjects which might prove at times dull and uninteresting. He would also have to keep pace with the group, neither forging ahead nor lagging behind. A man twenty-seven years of age, such as Hecker, conforming for the first time to such a meticulous and exacting program would soon find both his mental powers and his physical energies taxed to the utmost.

In addition to this difficulty, Isaac would have to cope with the problem of language. His professors would conduct their classes in Latin which he regarded as a dead language, not as a flexible medium for living ideas. When he had struggled through Caesar and Cicero in New York he acquired some facility with Latin but not enough to express his thoughts in a recitation or write them out in an exam. The students who sat beside him in class were much more adroit with the Latin than was the earnest New Yorker. But he dug in with courage and dogged determination.

When the grades were posted at the end of the first semester, Hecker's success was in no sense phenomenal. He had not finished with flying colors. But neither had he done too badly. Although he was fifth in a class of six, he was still well above the passing grade. The second semester he was not so fortunate. He dropped down a grade, yet he received a rating listed in his professor's records as "good."[38]

Hecker knew why his marks had fallen. Although he had more than average intelligence, with a keen penetrating mind, he was finding it more and more difficult to apply himself to study. All the energies of his soul were drawn to contemplation and his spiritual faculties were turning constantly to God. He was beginning to feel himself "given, absorbed, taken entirely by the good God." Only with great difficulty could he keep his mind on his studies. To resist the desire to surrender his mind and will entirely to Almighty God seemed to him wrong and even sinful, for he was not so much seeking Him, as God was drawing him out of himself until He became the "centre of his soul." Any reluctance or refusal to co-operate appeared to him a rejection of the graces and gifts of God.[39]

During his first year at Wittem he alternated between these periods of contemplation and application to his studies. As the scholastic term drew to a close, he realized he was giving more time to "living a supernatural life" than he was to his books. Just before vacation his ambition was to give even more; he asked his superiors for permission to spend his vacation in solitude and retreat.[40] Wisely they refused to grant his request. He would need the relaxation and recreation to build up his energies for the year ahead. Isaac wondered how he would fare in that year. He could only surmise but he was not alarmed or disturbed. He was in the hands of God and he was perfectly content to submit to the divine will.

Though Isaac was drawn to prayer and recollection, he was by no means a somber monk with a long, forbidding face. He had a delightful sense of humor which he never repressed. At recreations he enjoyed the conversation and easy banter so characteristic of religious. Although he could and did hold his own in serious discussion, he would also take part in the usual bouts of repartee.

One afternoon the Community entertained a European bishop who soon heard that there were two Americans in the group. Addressing them in French, he told the Yankees that though he could read English he had never heard it spoken. Then he asked them: "Could you speak a little piece for me?" Immediately they consented. Putting their heads together, Walworth and Hecker held a hurried consultation. With mock seriousness they rattled off, without a slip, the tongue twister: "Peter Piper picked a peck of pickled peppers." English, the Prelate decided, sounded much stranger than he had imagined. Perhaps to hear a less explosive volume of sound, he suggested that the Americans sing a song. Not altogether in the tradition of classical harmony, they broke out with "The Carrion Crow." Leaving nothing to the imagination, they even filled in with gestures and imitations.[41]

After the summer vacation of 1847 the students resumed their classes, but not for long. Toward the middle of October several young men were taken down with fever but their illness gave no apparent cause for alarm. The superior did not suspect that it was the beginning of an epidemic that was to spread through the house with amazing rapidity. But when others began to show symptoms the doctor was hastily summoned. He pronounced it typhoid fever and advised segregating those who were still well. Before the plan could be put into effect, thirty-five of the young men were stricken. Father Heilig immediately sent twelve who had not been infected to St. Trond with Father Konings and two of the professors. Then he organized the house to care for the sick. Four of the brothers acted as infirmarians under two priests who were called prefects of the sick.[42]

Because of the large number of patients, the infirmarians needed help so three of the students volunteered. One of these was Isaac Hecker. The seven infirmarians faithfully attended their confreres neither deterred by the fear of contracting the disease nor repelled by the almost unbearable odors exuding from the most advanced cases. Getting very little rest day or night for almost six weeks, they cared for their patients conscientiously. The "student nurses" were dispensed from all spiritual exercises to devote their full time to the sick, though they were told to say their rosary. To sustain their health amid their fatiguing labors, they were allowed to eat at any time and were even ordered to drink a moderately large glass of wine a day. Following the advice of the doctors and their superiors, they managed to escape infection.

Among the thirty-five stricken students was Clarence Walworth who was kept in bed for six weeks. Hecker visited him regularly and did all he could to ease the patient's discomfort by his cheerful and patient ministrations. The vigilance and constant care of all the infirmarians prevented many tragic consequences of the epidemic. But despite all their efforts, five of the afflicted never recovered. Four died in November and one in December.

Not until mid-December did the doctors declare the worst was over. As a precautionary measure, however, the convalescents were not allowed to mix with the rest of the community until two weeks after they had left their beds. Eventually toward the end of December all danger had passed and the twelve theologians who had been sent to St. Trond returned on December 27, 1847. Classes were soon resumed and the studentate settled down to its normal routine.

Meanwhile, a change had taken place in the administration of the studentate. On December 10, 1847, Father Heilig, the rector, received word that he had been named the Belgian Provincial to succeed Father de Held.[43] This promotion, though richly deserved, deprived Isaac not only of a friend whom he cherished, but a spiritual director whom he trusted.* From one of Heilig's letters there seems little doubt that he had considerable regard for Isaac.[44] Convinced of the young man's sincerity and his desire to serve God, he wanted to see him complete his studies and enter upon his labors for souls as a Redemptorist. During Father Heilig's term as rector, Isaac was able to attend classes and make some progress in his studies. But when he returned to the study of philosophy after the typhoid epidemic, his absorption in the spiritual was becoming more constant. His mind was not on his work but was preoccupied with God. Though he attended classes faithfully, he was finding it increasingly difficult to focus his attention on studies. The stronger his concentration on spiritual reality, the weaker was his application to books. The situation was reaching a crisis when Father Heilig returned to preside at a faculty meeting in May of 1848. Apparently he had a talk with his former spiritual protégé who told him how impossible it was for him to follow the regular course of study. Hecker may have also suggested that if he were left to apply himself when his mind was

---

* Ordinarily the spiritual direction of the students was entrusted to a prefect. When Isaac was at Wittem, because of the large number of students, there were two prefects, Father Lelouchier and Father Konings. During his first year, Isaac's prefect was Father Konings. Hecker had scarcely begun his second year when Father Lelouchier, then his prefect, was made rector at Liége. Father Konings replaced him. Though he would then be Isaac's director, Hecker later maintained that he went to Father Heilig for direction and guidance.[45]

free, he was sure he could study. Whatever may have been the nature and extent of the conversation, Father Heilig announced to the faculty on May 25th that for reasons known to himself he was relieving Brother Hecker of all studies. He would no longer be required to attend classes.[46]

Five days after this meeting, Isaac sat down and wrote a remarkable statement for his spiritual director "to satisfy my sense of duty" and to aid his adviser in determining whether his ideas were "real or illusory." Briefly describing his spiritual condition, he devoted considerably more time to a discussion of his real vocation. Some, he said, had considered that he was called to a contemplative life; others to an active. For himself, Isaac believed that both were right. His true vocation was a combination of the active and the contemplative. To prepare for this he began his course of study firmly convinced that he needed to acquire as much knowledge as possible if he would be successful in God's work. But contrary to his wishes, divine action intervened and he was no longer able to concentrate on his studies. Nevertheless his conviction was just as strong that God had destined him for an active life. What was the precise character of that life? For the first time Hecker put in writing his answer to the tormenting question that had plagued him for so many years: What does God want me to do? Confidently but humbly, in direct and unmistakable language, he stated his conviction: "I believe that Providence calls me . . . to America to convert a certain class of persons amongst whom I found myself before my own conversion; I believe that I shall be the vile instrument which He will make use of for the conversion of a multitude of those unhappy souls who aspire after truth without having the means to arrive at and possess it."[47]

This declaration of so noble a vocation must have sounded very strange to Hecker's superiors. Here was a student stating very definitely that he believed God was calling him to work for the conversion of America, yet he was finding it all but impossible to follow the usual course of studies required for the priesthood. How could he harmonize his "vocation" with his intellectual ineptitude? Anticipating this difficulty, Isaac wrote: "To convince me that this work will not be mine and that I shall only be the mean instrument for the accomplishment of His design He wills me to be deprived of all human means, so that I shall not attribute His glory to myself." At first Isaac had thought that he would need "learning and eloquence" for the fulfillment of his goal. But he was mistaken. God would accomplish His design "solely by His grace and power. That is why I have been obliged to resign myself, in spite of my strong repugnance to seeing myself deprived of all learning and to abandon myself to the conduct of His divine providence." Did this mean that he was asking to be ordained immediately without any further preparation? Isaac was seeking no such extraordinary privilege. But he did have a practical plan: "Thus I think that could I be permitted to set myself to acquire what is absolutely necessary, chiefly the practical knowledge required to exercise the sacred ministry, God would abundantly supply all else of which I have need." Clearly Hecker did not expect that God was going to infuse knowledge directly into his soul without any effort on his part. He did not ask to be liberated from any further intellectual effort. All he sought was the permission to study when his mind would be free and could apply itself to books. If he were granted this privilege, he was convinced that he would acquire the knowledge necessary for the priesthood.[48]

Whether or not Hecker knew of Father Heilig's decision at the time he wrote this exposé of his state of mind, he does not say. But his wish was granted. On his own free time he continued his philosophy and, when he took the exams, the wisdom of Father Heilig's move was justified. In the orals he was classed as having made satisfactory progress and was rated again as "good." When his grades are compared with those of his fellow American, Clarence Walworth, Isaac is found to have had better marks. The former Phi Beta Kappa from Union College had varied from "fair" to "good." In all of Isaac's grades at Wittem, he had never gone below "good." Apparently Isaac would be far more successful studying on his own than following classes, so his superiors decided to let him continue his studies privately, but not at Wittem.[49]

Obviously it would not be the wisest move to let Hecker remain in the house of studies preparing for the priesthood but not attending any classes. His fellow students, though they considered him a mystic,* also regarded him as somewhat of a problem. Not familiar with his spiritual condition, they failed to understand why he could not follow the regular routine of class. Was he just stupid? Some thought so, and dismissed him as *minus habens* or, as we would say today, a boob. Others hearing him talk of his hopes for the conversion of America, but also knowing of his desperate struggle with his studies, regarded him as a fool. At times they even treated him as one.[50]

It did not take the provincial, Father Heilig, very long to make up his mind to send this unusual student to the newly established Redemptorist house in England. There he would be under the watchful eye of Father de Held who a few years before in Baltimore had accepted him for the novitiate. Also he would have the companionship of his fellow American, Clarence Walworth, who after two years of theology had been ordained on August 27, 1848. Father Walworth, with two other newly ordained Redemptorists, Fathers Theunis and Lefevre, had received their appointment to the recently acquired foundation in England and Brother Hecker went with them.[51]

On September 10, 1848, the four set out for London. They stopped first at the Redemptorist convent at Liége to be measured for suits. Since they were going to England where the cassock was not worn in the streets, they had to be outfitted. The tailor who was called in to take care of them could not quite understand the cut of the clothes they wanted. Doing his best, he produced a ridiculous compromise that was a cross between an Eton jacket and a fashionable frock coat. The waist was high and tight in front and the tails full and flowing in the back, flopping about their heels.[52] As the young Redemptorists went from Liége to Amsterdam and took the boat to London, people turned to stare, and some to laugh at the strangely garbed clerics. Chagrined and perhaps a little embarrassed, they finally reached London on September 23rd and made their way to St. Mary's in Clapham, three miles south of London Bridge.[53] Here they were greeted by Father de Held who had charge of all the Redemptorist foundations in England.

---

* During my researches in Wittem, one of the Fathers told me that there was a strong tradition that had come down from Hecker's day that he was a mystic.

Father Walworth stayed a month at St. Mary's before he was sent to the Redemptorist house at Hanley Castle in Blackmore Park, Worcestershire. To replace him, Father Louis de Buggenoms, who was soon to become Hecker's close friend and supporter, came from Falmouth.[54] He was very mild in disposition and character, sympathetic and understanding in manner, and lastingly loyal. Shortly after his arrival in November he became Hecker's confessor.[55]

When Isaac came under the jurisdiction of Father de Held, he found further trials awaiting him. How much his new Superior knew about him, contemporary evidence does not reveal. Necessarily he must have received some kind of report on his new subject since he would have the responsibility of deciding Hecker's future. No doubt Isaac had given him an explanation of his inability to attend classes and to follow the prescribed course of studies. This revelation of his soul to another superior was not an easy task for Hecker. If he spoke fully and in a straightforward manner his story would sound incredible, compounded as it was of two seemingly contradictory elements: a conviction that God was calling him to work for the conversion of America and an obvious lack of the qualifications for so gigantic a goal. On the other hand, unless Hecker did give a complete account of his spiritual state, his predicament would be ridiculous. If he had no valid explanation for his inability to study, how could he in conscience be seeking ordination in a Community dedicated to the active ministry?

From statements Hecker made toward the end of his life it seems evident that he opened his conscience to Father de Held.[56] As he unfolded his story, his new Superior's reaction was quite similar to that of his novicemaster, Father Ottmann: he must make sure that this young man's spiritual experiences were genuine and not exaggerations of a sensitive spiritual nature. And so he employed wisely and firmly the time-tried tests of obedience and humility. Borrowing an analogy from Blessed Henry Suso, Hecker described his method: "He treated me as a dog treats a rag — he took me in his teeth and shook me." But no matter how hard the Superior shook, he could not dislodge Hecker's confidence in the genuineness of his contemplation, nor weaken his conviction in the reality of his vocation. Isaac was certain that God had called him and would, in His own time, fulfill His divine designs. With resignation he submitted to the will of God as reflected in his superiors and he devoted as much attention as he could to his studies.

Amid all his trials, the stream of Hecker's spiritual life never abated and brought him many hours of divine consolation. During the time he spent before the Blessed Sacrament he experienced "a celestial joy and peace and a readiness to do all for Jesus Christ." The personal love of his divine Master poured in upon his soul in an intimate manner defying all human description. Even after he rose from his knees and went about his daily tasks the consciousness of that divine presence never left him. He was living constantly in communion with God.[57]

The study of theology which he began at Clapham was not as foreign to his spiritual life as were the classics and philosophy. The truths he laboriously extracted from his theology textbooks fused with his thoughts in contemplation and he became absorbed in the mysteries of Catholic Faith. Although he studied the nature of God in the writings of theologians, he received a much warmer appreciation of the divine Reality from his personal relation with Christ in the Blessed Sacrament. The eternal perfection of his Creator, "His immutability, sanctity, purity, beauty" became much more real in Isaac's hours before the tabernacle than in the didactic formula of a scholarly syllogism.[58] He had bridged the gap between what Newman once called notional and real knowledge.

Although Hecker was perfectly resigned to wait upon the divine will for the fulfillment of his vocation, he wanted to be sure he was following that will. For that assurance he turned to one who knew him well, his former spiritual guide and director at Wittem and now his provincial, Father Heilig. On March 18, 1849, he sent him a long and detailed letter explaining his state of soul. Frequently he quoted from the mystical writers and lives of the saints to describe his own spiritual experiences.[59] The discriminating use he made of these quotations reveals not only an unusual familiarity with the writings of St. John of the Cross, St. Teresa, St. Catherine of Genoa, Richard of St. Victor, and Blessed Henry Suso, but a remarkable appreciation of their meaning. Mystical authors are not easy to read and more difficult to comprehend. But this young religious, not yet five years a Catholic, had an insight into their thought that was more than merely academic.[60]

Less than a week after he received Isaac's letter, Father Heilig wrote a very careful reply "full of love, very charitable, but stern." He repeated his regard and esteem for his former student, who he was confident would "arrive at a great love of God" and who was "destined to do a great deal one day for the salvation of souls." But despite these sentiments, the Provincial felt that his former student had traveled too fast along the spiritual highway. "Your mistake is that you have passed too quickly from lower degrees to higher degrees of the spiritual life. You have sought the Lord with the greatest desire of finding Him. You have sought Him in the spirit of humility and in all the sincerity of your heart. That is why He has given you great graces." Then he went on to tell Hecker that he was too much concerned with the effects of grace in his soul and that he was attaching himself "rather to the gift than the Giver."[61]

Naturally Isaac was puzzled when he read this letter. His object in writing to Father Heilig was to explain what he was experiencing. How else could he do that except by describing as clearly as possible the effects of grace? Even more disconcerting were the Provincial's remarks about his quotations from the writings of the mystics. Father Heilig believed that Isaac, as a result of his extensive reading, had applied to himself the experiences of the saints. Even more dangerous than this was his tendency to imitate in his own life what had taken place in theirs. For this reason Father Heilig cautioned him against giving in to "the suspension of faculties" which Hecker had mentioned as curtailing his powers of study. The Provincial was not convinced that in reality God was actually absorbing Isaac's mental powers, but rather that Hecker imagined God was possessing them. All this delusion Father Heilig traced to what the modern psychiatrist would call transference.[62]

Admittedly there is always the danger that a person anxious to advance in the way of perfection may read into his own life what he has found in the lives of the saints. He may even induce in his own experience reactions similar to theirs; and he may produce these effects in the sincere and honest belief that he is specially favored by God. That is why the experienced spiritual director is very wary when he hears his penitent speak of unusual spiritual reactions. If he detects even the slightest indication that the soul under his care may be the victim of spiritual delusion, he immediately advises his penitent to ignore it and to put it out of his mind. This advice Father Heilig gave to Hecker and outlined three courses of action for him to follow. First, he must "believe blindly" that he was not in any extraordinary state of perfection but simply in the usual one granted to sincere and honest souls seeking greater union with God. Second, he must despise any manifestation of the extraordinary state, such as a suspension of his faculties. He should "pay no more heed" to such a reaction than a man gives to noisy children in the street. Third, if any idea that he is subject to unusual mystical experiences comes into his mind, he must reject it with scorn. Never should he speak or write of it "except with a supreme contempt."[63]

No wise director of souls could quarrel with these judicious words of advice. Nor would any soul, no matter how far advanced in the spiritual life, make any mistake in following them. They are cautious, prudent, and designed to avoid any possible danger of delusion. Apparently Hecker accepted these admonitions. He followed implicitly the injunction not to write of God's operations in his soul. Only once after that when he was in Rome in 1858 did he draw up a manifestation of conscience.[64] As a result, it is now all but impossible to trace the further intimate relationship of his soul with God, or to determine his progress in prayer and contemplation. The deeper recesses of his soul and the action of God's grace upon it, he sealed from further scrutiny for all time.

If the only evidence of mystical contemplation in Hecker's life was confined to his days of preparation for the priesthood, two questions would naturally arise. Did he imagine all these things in the fervor of his early religious life? Was he aware of them only after he had read mystical treatises and the lives of the saints?

Hecker's pre-Catholic years answer these questions. Before he ever knew there was such a volume as a treatise on mysticism, before he ever learned of the profound communion between the saints and God, he had received unusual gifts of prayer and contemplation. His early diary, especially the account of his days at

Brook Farm and Concord, clearly reveal this. At that time, he could not describe the condition of his soul with the clarity and precision found in his later statements. Then his spiritual life was so new to him that his explanations were awkward and stilted. But he could and did record clearly the overpowering effects of divine love. Five years before he ever heard the words "suspension of faculties" he had experienced the reality they express. At Concord and Brook Farm divine grace had so captivated his mind and will that, despite his strongest efforts, he could not study. He had not induced this state. On the contrary he fought against it and was baffled and mystified when he failed to succeed. He asked over and over again: Why has this happened to me? What is the reason for it?[65]

Not until he had read of similar experiences in the lives of the saints could he appreciate what had taken place in his soul. After years of perplexity and doubt, he was overjoyed to discover that God had dealt with him as He had done with others. Finding for the first time expressions and illustrations to mirror his experiences, he may have exaggerated their application to his state of soul. But this is a fact difficult to determine. There is no spiritual barometer to measure the precise degree of intensity of divine love in the human soul. But there are certain tests to evaluate its reality. All these solidly demonstrated that Hecker was not a victim of imagination or delusion.

The first Catholic he met who was adept enough in ascetical theology to determine this was Bishop Fitzpatrick. Meeting Hecker while he was still a non-Catholic, he realized what the young man had sacrificed for the love of God. He had given up his family, his friends, a life of luxury and ease, and the prospect of material wealth. Knowing that no normally balanced individual submits to such privations for the sake of a self-induced illusion, he also recognized the beneficial effects of grace in the life of Hecker. It had made him fervent in prayer, constant in mortification, and diligent in the practice of virtue. The Bishop had no hesitation in affirming that Isaac was led by the hand of God.[66]

In evaluating the reality of Hecker's life before he came into the Church, Father Heilig did not have this same advantage. He knew him only as a Catholic and only after he was familiar with the lives of the saints. And when Hecker described his pre-Catholic experience, as well as his subsequent spiritual development, he used the vivid phrases and illustrations of the experienced mystics, not the halting and vague language of the uninitiated. Naturally Father Heilig could not help wondering how much of the account was real and how much imagined. He did readily admit without question that God had given Isaac unusual supernatural gifts, that he was in an advanced state of spirituality, and that God would use him to lead many souls to Christ. But he also saw the dangers of too much soul searching and introspection. Apprehensive lest his young charge be led to spiritual exaggerations, he prudently warned him against excessive concentration on the divine operations in his soul. The one sure way to avoid that pitfall, he told him, was unquestioning obedience to his spiritual director.

Less than a year after he came to Clapham, the clouds hovering over Isaac's future began to disappear. After he convinced Father de Held that he had a vocation to the priesthood in the Redemptorist Community, the Superior's attitude changed. His severity gave way to kindness, his suspicion to confidence, his aloofness to friendship. No longer an adversary, he became Hecker's advocate.[67] Isaac's confessor, Father de Buggenoms, had no small part in effecting this change. Since Father de Held had known him from the beginning of his religious life and had a high regard for his judgment and spiritual discernment, he carefully considered Father de Buggenom's recommendations. Isaac, his confessor believed, was ready for ordination. Not only did he tell this to Father de Held but was willing to take full responsibility for his penitent if he were ordained.[68] Father Heilig, the provincial, had no opposition to the plan, knowing the high regard Isaac's superiors had for him. Moreover, he had a "firm confidence" that Hecker would "be very useful in the Congregation."[69] Although Hecker never had a formal course in theology, his superiors were satisfied that he had acquired sufficient knowledge to receive holy orders.

On the feast of the Most Holy Redeemer, October 23, 1849, Bishop Wiseman raised the young religious, prostrate before him, to the ranks of the priesthood of Christ. During the course of that ancient ceremony of ordination, Isaac received authoritatively and clearly the divine answer to the conviction of his childhood. This was what God wanted; this was why He had chosen Him; this was His divine design. He, Isaac Hecker, was now a priest forever.

CHAPTER VIII

Winning Souls for Christ

SIX years before Isaac Hecker was ordained a priest, this phrase in Carlyle's *Past and Present* captured his attention: "To make some human heart a little wiser, manfuller, happier, more blessed, less accursed." He found in those words his life's ambition. But he saw more than Carlyle had expressed, for he knew that the human heart could be genuinely happy only in living a Christlike life.[1] This he had discovered; how could he bring others to the same awareness? His experiences at Brook Farm, Fruitlands, and Concord had not given him the answer. Not until he became a Redemptorist and learned of the successful method of missions used by St. Alphonsus could he jubilantly proclaim his *eureka*. He had found what he had been seeking. Missions were his alchemy to purify the life of the soul and change it into the gold of divine life.

In the days following his ordination, Father Hecker thanked God for having led him to a Community whose specific objective was giving missions especially to the poorest and most neglected souls. The Founder of the Redemptorists had taken care to write this purpose into the Constitutions of the Congregation. No mere visionary, but an extremely practical person, St. Alphonsus clearly detailed the method his followers should use in conducting these "sacred expeditions," as Pius IX called them. They were to last at least ten or twelve days. Every morning there would be a Mass followed by a short instruction. Then in the evening, after an explanation of the mysteries of the Rosary, the entire con-

149

gregation would say the beads with the missionary. A brief instruction on the Commandments or on confession would precede the main sermon of the evening. This was to last an hour or an hour and a half and would treat of salvation, sin, death, judgment — one of the great eternal truths. Its purpose was to make the listener realize what God expected of him and to convince him that he should live according to God's expectations. The missionaries were to provide through their carefully prepared and simply delivered instructions and sermons the motives of sincere contrition for the sins of the past and a firm resolution to grow in the love and friendship of God. Then the penitent prepared for a worthy confession, would go to one of the missionaries, rid his conscience of the burden of sin, and receive absolution.[2]

Not only could Father Hecker read these detailed instructions in the Constitutions but he could see them effectively carried out in the missions his confreres were giving in England. The head of the English houses was a man completely devoted to achieving this external aim of the Congregation — Father Frederick de Held. Born of a noble Viennese family, he had established the Congregation in Belgium in 1833 and had initiated the system of fully organized missions according to the plan of St. Alphonsus. When he came to England, his great ambition was to inaugurate there the work he had started in Belgium.[3] He had under him an experienced and talented speaker in Father Vladimir Petcherine, a Russian-born convert, not the least of whose accomplishments was his facility with languages. He could speak fluently and effectively in Russian, German, Italian, French, and English. With him were Fathers de Buggenoms, Lans, and Ludwig who also knew English. When three more recruits arrived in September of 1848, one of whom was the American Father Walworth, Father de Held knew it was time to begin the work.[4]

Before the close of 1848 he had his first opportunity. Bishop Wiseman asked for a mission in his newly opened St. George's Cathedral in Southwark. Selecting Fathers Petcherine, Walworth, and Ludwig as his preachers, Father de Held took charge of the mission. He assigned Father Walworth to give the morning instructions as well as the explanation of the Rosary in the evening; Father Ludwig to explain the Commandments and the manner of making a worthy confession; Father Petcherine to deliver the main sermon. The mission was highly successful and the apostolic work of the Redemptorists in England was off to a good start. More requests from the clergy for these sacred expeditions began to come to Father de Held and he could see unfolding in England the same pattern he had witnessed in Belgium. It was not long before the name Redemptorist was synonymous with missions in the minds of English Catholics.[5]

The newly ordained Father Hecker watched with absorbing interest this apostolic work and looked to the future when he would take part in a mission. Never for a moment did he think that he could sway the hearts of a congregation as did the eloquent and magnetic Father Petcherine. It would be a long time, he thought, before he would be able to give an effective mission sermon. For the present, his work would not be in the pulpit but in the confessional. Though he doubted that he could speak to hundreds of people in the church, he knew he could deal with the soul of a single penitent seeking the mercy and forgiveness of God. He waited anxiously for the day when he would go out on his first mission.

Father de Held gave him his long-desired opportunity less than a year after his ordination, assigning him, with Father Petcherine, to a three weeks' mission at St. Nicholas' Church in Liverpool. On Sunday, May 12, 1850, the two Redemptorists began their work in the section of the city known as Copperas Hill. Their congregation was made up largely of the poorer classes of people and of inveterate sinners. With a little prodding, however, the people responded generously and the missionaries reported rewarding spiritual results. Moved by the stirring sermons of Father Petcherine, the people flocked to the confessionals. Here a large share of the work fell to Father Hecker. He spent many daylight hours and a good part of the evening after the sermon with penitents who had not been to the Sacraments for years. Patiently he assisted each one to receive the Sacrament worthily, helping them to unburden their consciences and encouraging them to remain loyal and firm in their good resolutions.[6]

After three weeks of this exacting and taxing work, he returned to Clapham weary but elated by the part he had played in bringing the grace of God to souls. Though his preparation for the priesthood had been irregular, since he had spent only one year in the study of theology, he found the hearing of confessions not at all difficult but, as he put it, "quite natural."[7]

The following July, October, and December, he was again out on missions where he spent most of his time in the confessional. In December he was at Clark's Well on the outskirts of London where the number of penitents was quite large. Long after the services were over, often as late as midnight he was still hearing confessions. His heart and soul were in the work and he was indefatigable in the discharge of his missionary duties for he was winning souls for Christ.[8]

During these days in England, Father Hecker's thoughts traveled across the ocean to his beloved America where he knew there were countless souls to be won for the cause of Christ. These were not only Catholics who had grown lax in the practice of their faith, but those who had never known the consolations of the one true Church. He was anxious to help them, to show them how Catholicism could make their lives "happier, more blessed." Never had he lost sight of that conviction he expressed at Wittem: God would use him as the instrument for the conversion of his non-Catholic fellow Americans. It was "ever before" his mind with a strength and reality that nothing could dislodge. Although God had left him "in ignorance how this was to be accomplished" he never doubted that divine Providence would reveal His design. Until that moment, he was content as he had been so often before in his life to wait patiently for the unfolding of that design.[9]

The Redemptorist Fathers had not forgotten or ignored Hecker's beloved America. In September, 1848, Father Heilig, the Belgian Provincial, selected as his vice-provincial for the United States one of the outstanding Redemptorist missionaries of his day, Father Bernard Hafkenscheid. A brilliant Hollander who had been a classmate of the future Leo XIII in the Roman College, he won his doctorate the year after his ordination. Forsaking a promising academic career, he applied to the Redemptorist Community and after he finished his novitiate, Father Passerat sent him to teach theology at the studentate. But within a year the superiors recognized his unusual abilities as a speaker and assigned him to the missions in Belgium and Holland. He could preach fluently not only in his native tongue, but also in French, German, and English. Tall, poised, and forceful in the pulpit with a vibrant clear voice, he was a born missionary. Immediately successful, he was known within a short time throughout Holland and Belgium as the eloquent Father Bernard.[10]

In 1845 he had come to America as Father de Held's companion. Alert and observant, Father Bernard had studied carefully the American character and the possibilities of the Church in the new land. When he returned as vice-provincial three years later, he had a clear idea of the work that awaited him. He knew that the situation of the Congregation in the New World was quite unlike its position in Europe. Since the bishops had asked the Fathers to take care of the German-speaking Catholics, they were engaged for all practical purposes in parish work. The numerous and exhausting duties demanded of them in the care of souls left little opportunity for missions. When Father Bernard arrived in January of 1849, he knew he could not inaugurate this work on the same scale as Father de Held had done in Holland, Belgium, and England. He made his beginning, however, in August when he gave a nine-day English mission in Detroit where he preached three and four times a day.[11] The results were immensely successful and consoling and the new Vice-Provincial awaited the day when he could initiate a full mission schedule. His first need was for more priests. What was more natural for him than to think of the two native American priests in England. He believed they should be working in their own country where they knew the people and the customs and where there was a great demand for priests.

It is difficult to say when Father Bernard first met the two Americans. He may have seen them before they left the States for Europe since he was the companion of Father de Held at the time. Perhaps he came to know them in Wittem since he lived at the studentate when he was not on missions. Certainly he became personally acquainted with them before he left Europe in December of 1848. On his way to America he had gone to Clapham to see his great and revered friend and former provincial, Father de Held. While he was there, he assisted at the first Redemptorist mission given in London at St. George's Church. Before he gave the evening sermon, he had heard Father Walworth give the instruction on the Rosary. And he had seen and talked with Father Hecker at St. Mary's in Clapham. A shrewd judge of future missionaries, he knew they would be invaluable in their own country.

Scarcely had he taken up residence in America as vice-provincial than Father Bernard began earnest efforts to reclaim the young Redemptorists for his territory. He asked not once "but again and again to have the American Fathers Walworth and Hecker whose help we now need so much returned to us and their native soil." But his plea fell on deaf ears. Father de Held wanted to retain them as long as he could for the English missions and he gave Father Bernard no hope that he would soon release them. Finally on March 4, 1850, the American Vice-Provincial together with his consultors sent a formal petition to the Rector Major in Pagani, Italy. Among other things he requested Father Trapenese to erect America into a province and to enjoin the Belgian Vice-Gerent* "to return to us at our pleasure those two American Fathers even though the English visitor [Father de Held] be unwilling."[12]

Success crowned this attempt. On June 29, 1850, America was made a province and Father de Held agreed to release Fathers Hecker and Walworth for their native land and the new province.[13] Joyfully Father Hecker wrote to his mother in September of 1850, "It is the intention of my Superior that Father Walworth and myself should return to the U. S. some time in the coming month of October."[14] Despite this news the two Americans did not leave England until the end of the year. Father Bernard had come to Europe to discuss the affairs of the American province with Father Smetana, the newly appointed Vicar-General, and he had decided to have his new subjects wait and return to the States with him.

It was not until January, 1851, that word reached Clapham that the Americans would sail at the end of the month. As soon as he heard the news, Father Hecker wrote immediately to tell his mother. He looked forward to the moment when he would see his family and tell them of his experiences in Europe. But he had another reason to rejoice. He thrilled at the thought of working for the non-Catholics in his own land. Prayerfully he

---

* At this time, the Belgian provincial, Father Heilig, was also a consultor to the Rector Major at Nocera. During his absence, Father Berset, his Vice-Gerent, handled the affairs of the Belgian province.

wrote: "May my arrival in America be for the good of many souls who are still wandering out of the one flock and the one Shepherd." He was advancing, he fervently hoped, one step closer to undertaking the great work God had called him to do.[15]

Two weeks before Hecker left London, he received a very friendly and cordial farewell letter from his former spiritual director and provincial, Father Heilig. "You return to your native country," he wrote, "and I shall depart for Coblenz." He was going there, he told his former spiritual protégé, to assume his new duties as consultor to the Vicar-General. "In a short time, we shall be very far from each other, but we shall remain united in spirit and heart. . . . I shall always carry a particular affection for your Reverence." Father Hecker was going back to old friends in the New World and he was leaving behind him new and devoted friends in the Old.[16]

On January 23rd, Fathers Hecker and Walworth, with Father Kittel also recruited for the American foundations, set out for Paris. They went by boat from Dover to Calais and then by rail to Paris. At the Hotel du Tours, they found not only Father Bernard, but seven other Redemptorists who would join them on the long voyage. Two were priests, Fathers Dold and Stiessberger, three were students, and two were novices. The group had a day for sight-seeing in the French capital before they set out for Havre. They visited the Luxembourg Gardens, the monument where the Bastille had stood, the Chamber of Deputies, the tomb of St. Vincent de Paul, and the Seminary of St. Sulpice.[17] As Father Hecker looked down the long corridors of the seminary with their brick floors, the thought flashed through his mind: this might have been my home. Had he followed the advice of Bishop Hughes, he would have come here instead of St. Trond. But he had no misgivings: he was very happy in the choice he had made.

The high point of the day was listening to the renowned Father Lacordaire preach in St. Roch's Church not far from the Champs Elysées. They heard his resonant voice ring clearly and distinctly through the vast edifice crowded to the doors. Every word was perfectly enunciated. Not a consonant or vowel was muted. He held his audience spellbound, "in the palm of his hand." The eloquent Dominican, they agreed, had measured up to his fame. But despite his pulpit mastery, they realized their model preacher was not in the pulpit before them, but in the sanctuary beside him. Father Bernard was their ideal missionary.* He would train them to give not rhetorical masterpieces with the finesse of a polished orator, but missions, real missions, that would move the hearts of the most wretched and abandoned sinners and bring them to the feet of Christ.[18]

Shortly after they set sail on the *Helvetia* from Havre early in the morning of January 27th, Father Bernard told the little group his plans for the future. His great objective was to establish solidly the Redemptorist missions in America. He wanted to form a trained group who would give these sacred expeditions regularly and constantly all over the country. He looked to the return of the two Americans "as a call from heaven" for they would form the nucleus of his mission band. One of the prime requisites, he told them, was to be truly American. If an apostle had no love for a country and its customs, he could hardly succeed with its people. The two Yankees needed no such encouragement but Father Bernard's words made them understand that their patriotism would meet not with opposition but with his heartiest approval.[19] He himself had realized that a missionary must have enthusiasm for the country in which he labored. Within a week after his arrival in Baltimore in January of 1849, he declared his intention of becoming an American citizen.[20]

During the long voyage, Father Bernard had ample opportunity to study his new missionaries.[21] While the seminarians spent some of their time absorbed in theology, Fathers Hecker and Walworth talked with Father Bernard about mission work in America. It is not unlikely that the Provincial started the two young missionaries on the preparation of their sermons. Because of his experience in England, Father Walworth thought he had little to learn, but a short time with the veteran missionary convinced him that he was still a tyro.[22] Listening to Father Hecker express his views on religion in America, Father Bernard saw the young priest's ability to present his points of view convincingly and cogently. These assets he was certain would be invaluable in the morning

---

* Writing years later, Father Walworth tells of having heard Lacordaire and Newman preach but despite their brillance his "model preacher" was Father Bernard. "From the first moment when I came under his care I felt myself standing, so to speak, at the base of a lofty tower. . . . He taught me how to be a missionary."

and evening instructions. These two men, Walworth with his oratorical ability and Hecker with his persuasive powers, would make a fine combination on a mission.

While the *Helvetia* was still on the high seas, Father Bernard had the opportunity to notice how clearly and persuasively Father Hecker could explain Catholic truth. The boatswain, a former college friend of Father Walworth, showed an interest in the Catholic religion. As soon as Father Hecker detected this, he had several discussions with him. Before the vessel docked in New York, the boatswain was in a "fair way of being converted to the Catholic faith."[23]

After fifty-two days of battling high winds and storms and dodging treacherous icebergs, the ship finally dropped anchor in the Narrows the evening of March 19, 1851. The next day a tugboat guided the *Helvetia* up the bay to quarantine where the passengers were given a medical examination. The doctor took care of the Redemptorist travelers first and told them two of their confreres were waiting for them. Father Mueller, the rector at New York, and his assistant, Father Bretschka, were the first to welcome the travelers to America. The priests at Holy Redeemer convent in New York had spent many anxious hours awaiting word that the *Helvetia* had arrived. Vessels that had left eight and ten days after it departed had all reached port and the Fathers began to fear that their brethren might have been shipwrecked or fallen victims in an outbreak of typhoid fever. Great was their relief when they found their fears were groundless.[24]

As the *Helvetia* was leaving quarantine for its berth in the harbor, the two Americans were standing on deck absorbed with the shore line. Father Hecker could almost see the street where as a boy he had worked in the type foundry; he could recall the various alleys and side lanes near the river where he had pushed his baker's cart. As he looked, reflecting on these scenes of his childhood, he saw a small tug moving slowly toward them. Three figures were waving furiously from the hurricane deck; one, taller than the other two, was swinging his battered hat wildly in circles over his head. There was no mistaking that human windmill. It was James McMaster, the onetime novice at St. Trond, who had willingly joined John and George Hecker on the tug they had hired to meet the *Helvetia* before it docked.[25]

The reunion of the Heckers was a happy one. After six years in Europe, their Isaac had returned, somewhat changed. He was much more poised and sure of himself with the unmistakable air of one who had found his place in life and was delighted with his discovery. No longer worried about his future, his anxiety had given way to tranquillity, his uncertainty to confidence. Peace and serenity were in his eyes. He greeted his family with his accustomed warmth and affection. As he spoke of his plans and hopes, optimism poured from his lips. Not only were his thoughts and ideas clear and comprehensible but he expressed them in simple and striking language. He had developed amazingly as a result of his religious training, his education, and his European travel. He was in many ways a better developed and more mature Isaac.

As the tired travelers made their way from the dock to the Redemptorist convent in Third Street, Father Hecker could see signs that spelled success for the firm of Hecker and Brother. The baking establishment on Rutgers Street had emerged into a profitable and extensive milling concern; the small Croton Flour Mill which they had built on the corner of Cherry and Pike Streets had expanded into a much larger and more imposing structure; the already widely known and fast selling Hecker Flour had added a successful partner in Hecker Farina.[26] But these were not the only changes he found in the family. He had met for the first time his Catholic sister-in-law, Josephine Mary Wentworth, whom George had married in 1849. He had seen his two and a half year old Episcopalian nephew, John Valentine Hecker, his brother John's second child.[27] Missing from the family circle was his sister Elizabeth who had died shortly after Isaac had gone to Europe. Though his parents looked well, Mrs. Hecker showed the effects of several prolonged illnesses she had suffered in his absence. But she was cheerful and uncomplaining, delighted that her youngest son was nearer to her than he had been for the past six years.[28]

Two days after his arrival, Father Hecker sent a note to Brownson telling him he was back in New York and expressing the hope that he could see him. "Perhaps you will be coming on here shortly?" he asked. If not, then his young friend would try to pay him a visit.[29]

The note was good news to Brownson and he answered immediately: "I want to see you much, very much. You have much to tell me that is needful that I should know and I beg you to come and see me. Tell your superiors from me that your visit to me will be more than an act of charity to me personally and that . . . I earnestly beg to have you come and spend a few days with me . . . I would willingly visit you at New York, or anywhere in the United States this side [of] the Rocky Mountains, but there is no place so appropriate as my own house." Then mindful of the many profitable hours he had spent with his young friend before his Chelsea fireplace, Brownson wrote: "I am more indebted to you for having become a Catholic than to any other man under heaven and while you supposed I was leading you to the Church, it was you who led me there. I owe you a debt of gratitude I can never repay. . . . My wife is a good Catholic and like me owes much of her conversion to you."[30]

The long-awaited visit was delayed for several months because of the unexpected opening of the mission field. Shortly after Father Bernard's return to the States with his little group, the rector of the Redemptorist houses in New York, Father Joseph Mueller, indicated to various pastors in the city the Community's readiness to give missions. The first to put in a request was Father McCarron of St. Joseph's on Sixth Street in lower Manhattan. He asked for a mission to open on April 6, 1851. Quickly Father Bernard made his plans. He would use Fathers Walworth and Hecker. In addition he could call on two other capable and available English-speaking Fathers.[31] One was the Irish-born John B. Duffy who had joined the Congregation in Baltimore and was ordained three months before Father Hecker. The other was Augustine F. Hewit, a Connecticut Yankee, who had been a Congregationalist minister and then an Episcopalian deacon before he presented himself to Bishop Reynolds of Charleston for reception into the Church. After the vicar-general, Patrick N. Lynch, the future Bishop of Charleston, had given him a course of instructions, Hewit made his profession of faith on Easter Sunday in 1846. Father Lynch continued as his tutor and guided his theological studies until Bishop Reynolds ordained Hewit a priest on March 25, 1847, in Charleston. Collaborating with Fathers Lynch and Corcoran in the publication of Bishop England's writings, Father Hewit visited Philadelphia and lived in the house of the Archbishop of Baltimore, Francis P. Kenrick. There he met the zealous Father Bernard and the saintly Father Neumann. Inspired by their example, he applied for admission to the Community although against the advice of Archbishop Kenrick who had hoped to win him for his archdiocese. In October of 1849, the month and year Hecker was ordained, Hewit began his novitiate. He made his vows on November 28, 1850, and was assigned to the Redemptorist house in Baltimore.[32]

The four Fathers, though eager and willing for missions, were a very inexperienced group. Only Hecker and Walworth had any previous background in the work, but neither of them had ever preached "the big evening sermon." As the mission *Chronicle* relates, all were "slenderly prepared with sermons and instructions." Under the experienced guidance of Father Bernard, however, this proved no serious handicap. He helped them with their sermons and encouraged them with his advice. In preparing his recruits for the mission, he was ably assisted by another veteran, Father Alexander Cvitkovicz, who for obvious reasons was always called Father Alexander.[33]

Father Bernard selected Fathers Walworth and Hewit to give the evening sermons and Father Hecker the instructions, though Walworth and Hewit helped with some of these latter. He assigned Father Duffy to instruct the children and also to preach one of the evening sermons.* Seeing the great crowds swarming into the church he called upon four English-speaking German Redemptorists to help with confessions. These Fathers, with the missionaries, spent many hours in the confessional and were the unsung heroes who contributed tremendously to the spiritual success of the mission. For the mission was undoubtedly a magnificent success. The church was jammed every night and more than five thousand adults received the Sacraments.[34]

This mission was particularly important since it marked the beginning of organized and systematic missions to English-speaking parishes in the United States. Previously the Jesuits had given parish retreats and the Redemptorists had conducted some German

---

* Shortly after the St. Joseph's mission, Father Duffy was assigned to the Redemptorist parish in New Orleans. In 1854 when the missionaries went to New Orleans, he assisted them on several missions. Most of his priestly life was devoted to parish work.

and occasional English missions, but no one had been able to set aside a trained group to devote themselves exclusively to English missions. This was Father Bernard's achievement. He had the unique distinction of being the first in the history of the American Church to inaugurate this work. To him must be given the credit for selecting as the nucleus of the first Redemptorist mission band in the United States the three American converts. He was quick to see their abilities and their talents: Walworth, the polished, powerful orator with a clear, musical voice and a flair for the dramatic which he could use to great advantage; Hewit, with an equally fine voice, a dignified manner, impressive bearing, and considerable oratorical ability; Hecker, with a natural grace and ease, a winning and persuasive appeal, an engaging personality that he could project and with which he could hold an audience. Above all, Father Bernard realized that these three had what every successful missionary must have, a love and enthusiasm for missions. He guided them wisely, trained them carefully, and patiently corrected their errors. From his own vast experience, he taught them how to prepare forceful sermons and how to use effective pulpit techniques. In a relatively short time his band of Redemptorist missionaries were in constant demand. Requests poured in from bishops and priests in various parts of the United States. In August of 1852, Father Hecker could say: "We have missions ahead for a couple of years or more."[35]

The exacting and time-consuming duties of provincial prevented Father Bernard from devoting all his efforts to this work. However, he did manage to participate in eight of these missions during the years 1851–1852 and on two of them he preached some of the evening sermons "to the great satisfaction of all." To take charge in his absence he appointed Father Alexander. This Hungarian-born veteran had come to America in 1841 and was superior of the American Redemptorists until 1845. He was admirably equipped to guide the young group, and they soon came to have personal affection as well as respect for him. Father Hewit has said of him: "It would have been impossible to find a superior more completely fitted for the position. . . . In the government of the fathers who were under him, he was gentleness, consideration and indulgence itself. In his own life and example, he presented a pattern of the most perfect religious virtue in its most attractive form — without constraint, austerity or moroseness and yet without relaxation from the most strict ascetic principles." Until he retired to parish work in 1854, Father Alexander was the constant missionary companion of the three converts. An indefatigable worker with tremendous energy, he would spend the greater part of the day in the confessional. Rarely did he preach, though he would occasionally assist with the instructions.[36]

The division of duties became quite fixed after the first mission at St. Joseph's. Fathers Walworth and Hewit would alternate with the evening sermon; Father Hecker would give the morning instructions and the explanation of the Rosary; Father Alexander would teach the youngsters their religion. All would hear confessions. Time after time, some of their confreres would assist in this arduous work, especially on the larger missions where they had a staggering number of penitents. At Old St. Patrick's Cathedral in New York City, for example, more than seven thousand people received the Sacraments. Without the help of their Redemptorist co-workers, the missionaries would never have been able to discharge this important feature of their work.[37]

Never one to do things halfheartedly, Father Hecker threw himself into the work of the missions. "We can do no good without enthusiasm" he had said to Brownson and he poured his heart unreservedly into his apostolic labors.[38] If the people were lackadaisical about attending the mission exercises, he would oftentimes go around from house to house and stir them up until the church was packed. When he led the congregation in the recitation of the Rosary, he expected a hearty response. If the people mumbled their replies, he would jump up from his place before the altar and tell them to put their heart and soul in their prayers. After his short but rousing plea they would shake themselves out of their mumbling and the walls would echo with a torrent of sound. His enthusiasm was infectious and he was described as "the most lively of the three."[39] When he was leaving Mount St. Mary's in Baltimore, after having given a retreat to the students, with Fathers Walworth and Hewit, the young men gathered outside the building to give the departing missionaries several cheers. Immediately, Father Hecker led them in "three cheers for our country, three more for its conversion and three for our Lady."[40]

Contrary to his own expectations, Father Hecker developed into a very capable speaker. His short and fervent explanations of the Rosary and the devotion with which he led the congregation in the recitation of the beads earned him the title "Father Mary" on his second mission given in Loretto, Pennsylvania. This title clung to him for years.[41] His morning and evening instructions were clear, lively, and convincing. At a mission given at the Baltimore Cathedral in April of 1853 he was reported in the newspapers as "a universal favorite with his hearers. His familiar instructions on the sacraments of Penance and the Holy Eucharist, the commandments, the Rosary of the Blessed Virgin Mary were given with an interest that charmed all. The most intelligent heard him with delight and profit, whilst his words went straight to the heart of the child and servant. We ought to be very grateful to the other Fathers for their excellent services, but Father Hecker taught us so many good things, we owe a double debt to him."[42]

A correspondent for the *Freeman's Journal* commented, after a mission in Schenectady, New York, on "the earnest attention" the congregation gave to Father Hecker's "admirable and systematic instructions."[43] Obviously the former "problem student" of Wittem could take his place on the mission platform and hold his own in the company of such eloquent and forceful speakers as Fathers Walworth and Hewit. Within a very short time he had proven himself a most effective and successful missionary.*

For the first year and a half the group worked solely in the archdiocese of New York and the diocese of Pittsburgh. But in the fall of 1852, they extended their labors as far west as the cathedral city of Cincinnati. There they met Archbishop Purcell who became a lasting friend of the three, but especially of Father Hecker. The mission *Chronicle* notes that Archbishop Purcell had as a visitor Bishop Fitzpatrick of Boston. This was probably the first time that Father Hecker had seen him since that memorable day in 1844 when he called upon him to discuss Catholicism. Both Prelates highly edified the missionaries for they not only attended the services, but also assisted with confessions "and re-

---

* At a mission given in St. Vincent's Church in Youngstown, Ohio, the Fathers tried the experiment of preaching from a platform at the back of which they had erected a large wooden cross some ten feet high. From the crosspiece they draped a white muslin cloth. This proved so effective, they used it regularly on all their missions.

mained one night until twelve." The Archbishop gave the concluding benediction of the Blessed Sacrament and then spoke to the people "with great feeling and emotion. . . . During his remarks, he said that that day had been the most glorious which the Catholic Church had ever witnessed in the valley of the Mississippi. His Grace even humbled himself to kiss our hands at parting."[44]

The next engagement on their missionary tour was the cathedral in Louisville where they met another outstanding member of the American hierarchy, Martin John Spalding (later Archbishop of Baltimore). Like Archbishop Purcell, Bishop Spalding was immediately attracted to the convert American missionaries and became their loyal and devoted friend. The people responded magnificently to the efforts of the Fathers and "the Bishop himself was greatly surprised and delighted" with the results of the mission.[45]

In January of 1854, the little band with Father Alexander still as its leader made its first invasion of the Southland. The four missionaries sailed from New York for New Orleans on the steamer *Crescent City*. The voyage was pleasant enough for all except Father Hecker, who had an attack of pneumonia. Since he was unable to open the mission at St. Patrick's in New Orleans, Fathers McGrane and Duffy took his place. Toward the end of the mission he had recovered enough to give some of the instructions and was his old self for the opening at St. Joseph's Church on February 12th. Father Walworth, however, came down with a very bad throat and preached only three times and was unable to hear confessions. One of the noteworthy facts of this mission was the presence of the nineteen-year-old James Gibbons, the future Cardinal of Baltimore. He was debating whether he should study for the priesthood or serve God in the world. Attentively he listened to the sermons and was particularly struck by the words of Father Hecker. Years later on the occasion of Father Hecker's death he wrote to Father Hewit: "When I was seriously reflecting on my vocation some thirty-five years ago, he [Father Hecker] gave me an impulse in the right direction in a course of sermons he preached in conjunction with yourself and Father Walworth."[46]

From January until May of 1854, the Fathers gave eleven weeks of missions in the South. With the exception of the first two weeks in March, which they spent at the cathedral in Mobile, all their labors were in the city of New Orleans where Archbishop Blanc presided at three of the closing services. This extended stay, together with the work Father Hecker had done in the East, was giving him an excellent opportunity to become familiar with Catholic life in America. His conviction deepened that "we as Catholics have a future; we alone have an ideal. By this I mean a beautiful and glorious future. . . . We are a young people, a vast immeasurable field is before us and [we] have no overpowering movements of the past to check our fresh enthusiasm or to dishearten us in any youthful attempts." Unlike Europe, America was not fettered with hidebound traditions. Hecker saw that the only obstacle to the progress of the Church was the spiritual life of many Catholic people. "Until we have a higher tone of Catholic life in our country we shall do nothing. We shall make some progress in material things, and perhaps in numbers, but in the end we shall do little for the greater glory of God, the good of souls, or for our country." One of the effects of the missions, he hoped, was to give the faithful a strong and vigorous impulse to lead a deeper and more intense Catholic life. Then these revitalized souls would be the leaven to act on the mass and influence the non-Catholic Americans to seek in the true Church the source of their happiness.[47]

In this way, Father Hecker regarded his missionary labors as a means toward the fulfillment of his conviction that God had called him to work for the conversion of his fellow Americans. And in this work he was intensely happy. He could conceive of no life more truly Christlike than that of an apostolic laborer winning souls for his Master. "It is a beautiful life," he wrote to his mother, "that of a Catholic Missionary who is freed from all the cares of this world and who in imitation of our Blessed Saviour and His holy Apostles, goes about preaching penance and doing good. Our work is nothing else than a continuation of the work of redemption begun by our Divine Redeemer. It is not inaptly we are called Redemptorists. . . . I can conceive of no life so like the life which our Saviour led when upon earth as that of the Catholic Missionary."[48]

While the missions gave Father Hecker the opportunity to study American Catholic life, they also gave the bishops of the country the occasion to observe him at close range. They heard him preach from the pulpit and then discourse on the future of Catholicism at the dinner table. The weeks he spent in various cathedral rectories allowed them to evaluate his abilities and his talents. It is rather significant that of the three American missionaries, no one stood out more prominently in their minds as a man of zeal, piety, and vision than did Father Hecker. In their judgment he had all the requisites for the bishopric. They would recommend him for the miter.

Less than six months after the close of the New Orleans missions, the Jesuit Bishop James Van de Velde of Natchez died. Since the See was in the Province of New Orleans, the bishops of the Province met with Archbishop Blanc to nominate a successor for the post. On January 27, 1856, they forwarded to the Holy See the names of three candidates in the following order: "1 — Rev. William Starrs, Vicar-General of the Archdiocese of New York; 2 — Rev. Isaac Hecker, the Redemptorist; 3 — Rev. William Elder, of Baltimore."⁴⁹

When Bishop Spalding heard of the choice, he recommended Father Hecker. Since some of the bishops thought that Hughes would not want to part with his Vicar-General, they expected the choice would be ultimately either Father Hecker or Father Elder.⁵⁰ But it was not the objection of the Archbishop of New York but the criticism of the Archbishop of Baltimore that removed Father Starrs from further consideration. In a letter to Cardinal Franzoni, Prefect of Propaganda, on February 28, 1856, he definitely disapproved of the New York Vicar-General. He recommended Father Hecker who "shortly after his conversion to the faith entered the Congregation of the Most Holy Redeemer" as a man "distinguished for his piety and zeal." However, he preferred the Baltimore-born Father Elder who was a doctor of theology, a graduate of Propaganda in Rome, and a professor at Mt. St. Mary's, Emmitsburg, Maryland.⁵¹ The Baltimore Prelate's choice prevailed and Father Elder was chosen as the third Bishop of Natchez.

It is unlikely that Father Hecker knew anything of these proceedings. Even if he had, he would not have been disappointed. He had no desire for honors for as he said: "Titles are easy to carry but to discharge the duties which they impose is not."⁵² He wanted to remain as he was, a missionary winning souls for Christ.

CHAPTER IX

Troublesome Days for the Missions

THE golden days of Father Bernard's Provincialate — this is how Father Walworth described them — were also glorious days for the missions. Under Bernard's guidance and spurred on by his zealous enthusiasm, the little band had carried the banners of St. Alphonsus into ten dioceses of the country. "Redemptorist missionary" had become almost a household word among the Catholics in the cities and towns where they had labored. Through the preaching of the American members of the Order, numerous bishops and priests had come to look upon the Community as an important factor in the work of the Church in America. They revered and admired Father Bernard as a talented and resourceful leader who had a keen perception of the needs of the Church in the new land.[1]

From the moment this fearless and energetic worker had taken over the leadership of the Redemptorists in 1849, he had striven to bring his Community to the attention of the American people. Before his coming, clergy and laity had regarded the Redemptorists as a foreign group, admirably suited to care for the German immigrant. Bishops appreciated their self-sacrificing labors for the Europeans in America. They recognized that without the assistance of these zealous priests, many of these Europeans would have lost the faith.[2] But it was not until Bernard sent forth his missionaries that they realized the Redemptorists could do more than merely minister to the Germans. They preached eloquently and forcefully to American Catholics. They filled churches to overflowing wherever they spoke and won the admiration and respect of their audiences. Their sermons prepared in clear, concise, and at times rhetorical language, were delivered with a brilliance seldom heard in the Catholic Church of that day. Charles A. Williamson, a trustee of the Baltimore Cathedral, who had listened to many speakers in his life, called the American convert Redemptorists "the most magnificent I have ever heard. . . . None that I have ever heard could equal them."[3]

In the spring of 1853, Father Bernard's term as provincial was drawing to a close. Custom required him to present personally to his superiors in Europe an account of his administration. On May 6th, Father Hecker arranged passage for him on the steamer *Asia*. When Father Bernard sailed from Philadelphia with Father Coudenhove on June 28th, his confreres, especially the missionaries, fully expected him to be reappointed provincial to continue the great work he had begun.[4]

Though the majority of Redemptorists working in America held their Provincial in high regard, he was not a universal favorite. A few resenting him, looked for opportunities to condemn and criticize his methods and policies. Not long after the *Asia* was on the high seas, rumors began to trickle back from Europe that Bernard would not be reappointed provincial. Complaints about his administration, the stories said, had reached the ears of his superiors in Europe. It is impossible to know now if such reports were sent to Europe and, if they were, how large a part they played in determining Bernard's career.[5] But the fact remains that the popular and successful Provincial did not return to America. The Vicar-General, Father Smetana, had other plans for him. He needed an experienced missionary to undertake the primary work of the Redemptorists in Ireland, so he appointed Father Bernard superior of the new foundation in Limerick where he remained until 1855 when he returned to his native Holland. Never again did he hold office in the Community but labored zealously as an effective and successful missionary almost to the day of his death on September 2, 1865.[6, *]

---

* When Canon M. J. Lans, who wrote a *Life* of Father Bernard, presented a copy to Leo XIII, Bernard's former classmate, the Holy Father said: "O! Bernard Hafkenscheid . . . he was a saint, really a holy man. He did an incredible amount of good and labored much for the conversion of souls. . . . I often think of him and have a portrait of him in my dining room." John F. Byrne, C.SS.R., *The Redemptorist Centenaries* (Philadelphia: 1932), p. 257.

Father Hecker and his companions were on missions in the South when a circular letter of January 30, 1854, announced the appointment of the new provincial, Father George Ruland. When the missionaries heard the news, they could not suspect the decisive role this man would play in their lives. Two years older than Father Hecker, Bavarian-born Father Ruland entered the Congregation as a priest a year after Fathers Hecker and Walworth. In May of 1848 he came to America where he labored in New York until 1852. Then he was made vice-rector at St. Alphonsus, succeeding the newly consecrated Bishop Neumann.[7]

The two Provincials, Bernard and Ruland, are an interesting study in contrasts. Though both were exemplary religious and devoted Redemptorists, they were widely different in temperament and character. Bernard had a dynamic personality, enthusiastic nature, remarkable vision, courageous spirit, great poise, and natural dignity. In his dealing with others, though strict and exact, he had a warm and expansive manner capable of evoking a generous response. By his word and example he could spur his subjects on to gigantic tasks for the glory of God. He was born to lead.

The extraordinary talents that distinguished Father Bernard did not adorn his successor. A rather negative person with a diffident manner, Father Ruland was not very impressive. Quiet and unassuming, he radiated no enthusiasm nor could he spark others to any unusual efforts. He chilled rather than warmed the hearts of his subjects. His shyness made him appear impersonal and aloof. At times he seemed to vacillate, not because he lacked a fixed purpose, but because he disliked a head-on clash of ideas or an open conflict. Rather than speak his mind out fearlessly, he preferred to convey his thoughts in writing. A man of details rather than ideas, he was inclined to lose himself in minutiae. Better fitted to execute plans than conceive them, he could more easily follow than lead. He was much more concerned about providing a Carthusian atmosphere in the houses than in stimulating the apostolic works of the Congregation. No one would have found it easy to follow in the giant footsteps of Father Bernard, but for a superior like Father Ruland, it was doubly difficult.[8]

A few months before the appointment of the new Provincial, word reached America that had far-reaching consequences for the

Redemptorist Community. On September 6, 1853, Pope Pius IX issued a decree dividing the Congregation into two separate communities, each with its distinct and independent government. After some years of trial, the Holy See had seen the futility of keeping the Transalpine followers of St. Alphonsus under the authority of the royally dominated Rector Major in Pagani. Though the creation of a vicar-general had worked fairly well, it was far from the ideal solution. Neither was Pagani the desirable seat of government for a congregation which had grown greatly outside the Neapolitan kingdom. Since the King of Naples had blocked all efforts to locate the Rector Major at Rome, the Holy Father authorized a complete division between the two groups. The Fathers in the kingdom of Naples would be subject to the Superior General at Pagani. Those outside the kingdom would be under the jurisdiction of Father Smetana whom Pope Pius named as vicar-general until a chapter could meet to elect a Transalpine Rector Major who would reside in Rome.[9]

The Transalpine Redemptorists looked upon the decree of Pius IX as the only practical solution to the impasse created by Ferdinand II. Immediately, Father Smetana set in motion the machinery for the General Chapter to be held in Rome in 1855. Every house of five or more Fathers in each of the seven provinces would hold a domestic chapter to elect a delegate who, with the superior of the house, would attend the Provincial Chapter. This group would then vote for two Fathers to represent the province with the Provincial in the General Chapter in Rome. There they would ballot in the election of the Rector Major and deliberate on the affairs of the Community.[10]

On October 4, 1854, the New York Domestic Chapter convened at Holy Redeemer rectory. The eight men assigned to the house were joined by five other Fathers from Buffalo and Rochester since neither of these houses had sufficient priests to elect its own delegates. On the first ballot, with thirteen votes cast, Father Hecker received seven and was declared the delegate to the Baltimore Provincial Chapter. The rector, Father Helmpraecht, as the superior was the other delegate.[11]

At nine o'clock on the morning of December 6, 1854, twelve delegates assembled at St. Alphonsus, the provincial house in Baltimore, with Father Ruland presiding. Father Hecker, the only

American to participate in the proceedings, came from St. Peter's in Baltimore where, on December 3rd, he had begun a mission with Fathers Walworth and Hewit.[12]

The Provincial Chapter did not dispatch its business as quickly as had the New York meeting. Father Alexander was elected first delegate but not until the fifth ballot when he received the required majority of seven votes. The second delegate, Father Joseph Mueller, was chosen in exactly the same manner. Since the instructions from Rome provided for two alternate delegates their selection was the next order of business. Again there were four fruitless ballots before Father Holzer received seven votes. The choice of the second substitute went a little more rapidly and with greater unanimity. Father Walworth was elected on the third ballot with nine votes, the largest plurality of the morning.[13]

The news of the election of the two delegates to the General Chapter was awaited with particular interest not only in America but also in Europe. Not only would the men chosen have a vote in the election of the Rector Major but they would also have a voice in the determination of policy. The Constitutions of 1764 needed some revision because of changing conditions and the growth of the Community. America especially presented a specific problem which became more noticeable in the years following Father Bernard's departure. When the superiors accepted foundations in the States, they necessarily bound the Congregation to engage in parochial work. The number of men required to maintain these stations prevented the establishment of mission bands which were the special objective of the Community. The European Redemptorists who came to labor in America soon found themselves in the role of parish priests.[14]

To readjust this situation was no simple matter. Because of their commitments to the bishops, the Congregation could not suddenly relinquish all parishes. Neither could it neglect to fulfill the duties associated with these churches which required men who might otherwise have devoted themselves to missions. The matter of finances was also a determining factor. Each house depended very largely on the income from the parish for its existence. If that source of revenue were suppressed, missions alone could not carry the burden of the foundations. No matter how much the superiors might want to establish mission houses, they could not dispense with parishes. At least, not according to the pattern that had already been established.

Father Hecker knew very well that it would not be easy to untie this Gordian knot. In a letter to Father de Held, January 23, 1855, after mentioning all the tangled circumstances that had entwined themselves over the years, he conceded that unraveling them was a Herculean task.[15] Replying on February 16th, Father de Held admitted the problem but maintained that time and good will could solve it. He believed that these three fundamental principles should be clearly established. First, the Redemptorists in America should no longer accept parochial foundations, nor should they permit the enlargement of the ones they already had. Second, determined and persistent efforts should be made to diminish parochial burdens until they would practically disappear. Granting that this could not be done immediately in every house, he believed that with patience and wisdom a way could be found to bring it about. Third, where it would be impossible to relinquish parishes, he thought some Fathers should be assigned "especially for this work and leave the others free to live as Redemptorists."[16]

Father de Held entertained no great hopes that his plan would receive universal support. But he did think there would be less opposition to his proposals in Europe than in America. Everything, he concluded, depended on the man who would be elected Rector Major. Great would be the hope for the future if he "truly unites in himself the qualities which form the essential spirit of our Congregation together with the talent and necessary virtues."[17]

Differences of opinion among Redemptorists existed not only in America. They were even more definite and clearly defined in Europe, especially on the interpretation of the Constitutions regarding the vow of poverty. The text of the Rule approved by Benedict XIV lent itself to two possible interpretations. One was quite strict and literal; the other more moderate and somewhat traditional. The Belgian group led by de Held favored the first; the "German" party with Smetana at its head, the second. The division was by no means on national lines since Fathers from various provinces were found in either camp. The labels followed the leaders rather than the followers. Not long before the Chapter opened, the Community looked to these two men as the leading candidates for the office of Rector Major.[18]

In view of this division, Father Ruland, who was decidedly anti-de Held, was not too happy with the choice of provincial delegates. Though not certain, he felt confident that Father Mueller would not join the Belgian group. Father Alexander was a question mark since it was impossible to sound him out. The Provincial had hoped to see certain delegates elected whom he knew were definite Smetana men. But they had not been too successful, receiving never more than five votes and sometimes none at all.[19]

When the General Chapter convened in Rome, April 26, 1855, the twenty-seven delegates were convinced the choice would be either Smetana or de Held. After disposing of preliminary matters, on May 2nd the Chapter turned to the election of the first Rector Major of the Transalpine Redemptorist Community. The first ballot made it obvious that the delegates had split on party lines. Smetana led with thirteen votes; de Held was second with eleven. Three votes were scattered. Since neither candidate had the required majority, the deadlock continued all morning with Smetana holding his thirteen votes for the first six ballots. Then there was a slight shift and the two candidates leveled off for the next four with eleven votes apiece. After the tenth attempt the Chapter adjourned for dinner and a recess was called until five in the afternoon. In the informal discussions that took place during the course of the afternoon, it became increasingly clear that neither Smetana nor de Held could obtain the required majority. The delegates began to look for a candidate who was not a partisan of either side. Finally, the French Provincial, Nicholas Mauron, emerged as the compromise nominee. When the Chapter convened at five in the afternoon, he was elected with twenty-two votes on the first ballot.[20]

Although the Belgian group thought Father Mauron was an independent, he was actually in the Smetana camp. Even before his election, some of the non-Belgians were aware of this. Joyfully Father Ruland wrote to his close friend, Father Rumpler, in America: "The Belgians will rub their eyes in surprise when they realize whom they have helped to elect."[21] Later Father de Held admitted the mistake in a letter to Father Hecker: "The General elected [Mauron] owed his office to the influence of Father Smetana as we very soon found out."[22]

Scarcely had Father Mauron assumed office when letters came

to him with news of an unfortunate situation in the American Province that reflected on the judgment of Father Ruland. When the new Provincial was appointed to office in 1853, Fathers Gabriel Rumpler and Francis Seelos were named his consultors. The capable Father Rumpler had served the Community in America very successfully as superior in New York and Baltimore and then as novicemaster. He had received Father Walworth into the Church and had encouraged both him and Father Hecker to join the Redemptorists. A strong-minded and energetic religious, he was very strict with the novices. Toward the middle of the year 1854, he was becoming so unusually severe and obviously tyrannical, that a number of the Fathers became alarmed. They questioned the wisdom of retaining him in his post and remonstrated with Father Ruland. Some were convinced that his mind was affected and that he was showing signs of a mental breakdown. But these observations had no effect on Father Ruland. He dismissed them as prejudices on the part of the Fathers and retained Father Rumpler in his post.[23]

Before the Provincial left for the General Chapter in Rome, he secured the appointment of Father Rumpler, his first consultor, as Vice-Gerent of the Province. This gave him full authority in the absence of Father Ruland. Fear and apprehension greeted the announcement of this appointment, fears which were soon realized. Growing progressively worse, Father Rumpler showed unmistakable signs of insanity. He became so deranged and so dangerous that finally several brothers had to seize him forcibly and tie him up until he was committed to Mt. Hope, a mental institution in Baltimore, on June 4, 1855. The doctor pronounced him a victim of acute mania.[24]

As second consultor of the Province, Father Seelos immediately assumed charge. But he did so not only by virtue of his office. Father Ruland, before his departure, had given Father Seelos a private document stating that he was actually the Vice-Gerent while Father Rumpler simply held the title. He empowered Father Seelos to produce and use this document whenever he saw fit. As soon as the Fathers heard of this, they realized that the Provincial had announced Rumpler's appointment, while entertaining grave doubts of his fitness for the office. Why, then, had he placed in charge one whom he suspected was mentally unsound?

Some concluded that the Provincial feared Father Rumpler and dared not cross him. All recognized the danger to which the Provincial had exposed the Province and they found his action inexcusable.[25]

Frightening as was this situation, it became tragic through the imprudent action of Father Seelos. When he visited Mt. Hope on June 20th, Father Rumpler seemed to him quite rational and sane. He begged Father Seelos to remove him from the institution. Heeding his pleas to let him come back to the Community, Father Seelos took him out without the permission of the doctor or the sisters who attended him. The Fathers at St. Alphonsus were aghast at seeing the unfortunate Rumpler at liberty even though he had been pronounced insane. He stayed overnight, said Mass the next morning, and then, to the consternation of all, Father Seelos accompanied him to the novitiate and remained with him. Knowing the shocking reaction this would have on the novices who had witnessed Father Rumpler's maniacal ravings, the Fathers in Baltimore took immediate action. Hastily they summoned Father Helmpraecht, the rector of New York. Early in the morning of June 23rd, he arrived with his admonitor, Father Hecker.* Knowing that Father Rumpler was still dangerously insane, and realizing that there was no time for delay, the Fathers met in council and delegated Father Walworth to go to the novitiate. They instructed him to put Father Rumpler back in Mt. Hope, by force if necessary. After a slight altercation, Father Walworth succeeded and by five o'clock that afternoon he had safely confined the deranged priest in the institution.[26]

Within less than three weeks after this tragic occurrence, at least six letters reached Father Mauron reporting all aspects of the affair and commenting on the condition of the American Province. Although all praised the religious spirit of Father Ruland and disclaimed any personal animosity toward him, they were critical of his leadership. Father Helmpraecht indicated he was too much concerned with unimportant details and not the man to govern the Province. He asked the Rector Major "to send us an

---

* An admonitor was one of the Fathers in the house appointed by the rector major who had the obligation to see that the rector faithfully discharged his duties. The Fathers in the house had full and confidential access to the admonitor to air their grievances. If these complaints were well founded, then the admonitor was to discuss them with the rector without revealing the source of his information.

energetic and prudent superior." Father Smulders related the common opinions without denying them: "They say he is shortsighted and attaches himself to some small details in losing sight of the principal thing." Father Van de Braak, not presuming to judge Ruland's abilities wrote: "They say he has not the tact to govern, he only sees things from one side, he sees only one thing at a time." Much more critical was the outspoken opinion of the Provincial Procurator, Father Anton Schmid: "Our government has been — it is true — rather despotic during these last few years. Our present Father Provincial . . . will not listen to any of his subjects, but deals ruthlessly without regard or consideration for the opinions and wishes of others. This has caused bitter feeling among them — and made him quite unpopular with many of them. Also he has shown himself to be petty and limited and gives too much importance to small details."[27]

Two others, Fathers Hecker and Walworth, were equally straightforward. Mincing no words, they spoke their minds with unmistakable clarity. Father Walworth told Father Mauron: "Since the departure of our former Provincial, this Province has been suffering the most deplorable mismanagement. . . . The Very Rev. Father Ruland although a good and well-meaning man, is manifestly incapable of government, being feeble in intellect, narrow-minded and timid." He called the Provincial's appointment of Father Rumpler as Vice-Gerent "the reign of terror." Father Hecker was no less forthright: "The truth is that the whole provincial government in America has fallen into wretched hands. There is perhaps not a dissenting voice that our present Provincial is not the man to be at the head of the Congregation."[28]

The discontent in the Province, as reflected in these letters, led Father Walworth to think that there would be "a general effort to displace" Father Ruland. If this were to happen, many hoped for the return of Father Bernard whose name was prominently mentioned in the letters to the Rector Major. Both Fathers Schmid and Smulders suggested him for the post. Father Walworth prayerfully wrote: "May it please God that this excellent Father return." And Father Hecker enthusiastically declared: "We would all hail his reappointment as one of the greatest blessings of God from your paternal hands."[29]

But these hopes were not to be realized. Father Mauron had

no intention of appointing Bernard to any superiority, much less a provincialate.[30] He decided to rename Father Ruland. Months before the appointment was official, Father Douglas, the newly elected consultor whom Father Hecker had known in England, wrote and told this to Father Hecker. Hoping, if possible, to head off the appointment, Father Hecker wrote a very strong, but not exactly diplomatic remonstrance to Douglas. Referring to America as "the fairest portion of our Congregation" he stressed the absolute importance of having the right man as provincial. Emphatically he maintained that Father Ruland was not the man. "You saw him. The Rector Major saw him. You must have heard and conversed with him too. Was that not sufficient? In my simplicity when he left for Rome, I imagined that this would be sufficient and more than sufficient. Let me ask you, my dear Father, does your judgment lead you to think that he is the man, or the best man, to meet the needs of our Congregation here at this moment? No man ever had less savoir-faire who held such a position. One's pity is excited to see him in the presence of a bishop. Is he the man to lay the foundations of the future prosperity of our Congregation in America? There is nothing in the man either in conversation or appearance which is attractive, and should not this too be considered in a country like this? He has not the confidence of his subjects, how can he excite that of others? I could furnish sufficient number of facts which I have witnessed as well as others to convince one of my statements." Then lest he be suspected of personal bias, he added: "I never had a cross word from Very Rev. F. Ruhland [sic]; he has always treated me kindly. I esteem him highly as a pious and strict religious. But as our Provincial I consider it a calamity that he should have been appointed. And it is solely in the interests of the Congregation and the hopes that it is not too late for a remedy that I have written this note, which I beg you to read to the Rector Major."[31]

All pleas coming from America were unavailing. Father Ruland was retained in office. However, the appeals may have led Father Mauron to name an American as an adviser to the Provincial. Father Hewit — the only one of the three Americans not involved in the Rumpler affair — was chosen second consultor and Father Joseph Mueller, first consultor. Although the Rector Major knew Father Mueller, who was a delegate to the Chapter in Rome, he had never met Father Hewit. Since he undoubtedly received the letters from America while the Chapter was in session, Father Mauron may have consulted with others apart from Father Ruland who were familiar with the American Province. Fathers Alexander, Bernard, and Coudenhove, all of whom were delegates, knew Father Hewit personally. Whatever the source of his information, Father Mauron made the appointments which were approved in Council on November 21, 1855. The next day they were forwarded to America.[32]

Devotion and loyalty to the Community and a sincere concern for its welfare prompted the Redemptorists in America in their efforts to secure the appointment of a new provincial. Particularly was this true of the missionaries. Having traveled extensively and visited many dioceses, they saw a glorious future for the missions. Until they started the work, the American Catholic had scarcely heard of a mission. They knew that without any difficulty a large band of missionaries could be actively employed all year around and do an immense amount of good for souls. This was the work of the Redemptorists, the Community they had joined, and they were convinced that Father Ruland was not nearly as much interested in it as he was in parishes.

In the fall of 1854, Father Walworth "had to implore and almost weep to get the consent of the Provincial to begin" the missions. Several of the German Fathers joined Walworth in his pleas and interceded with Father Ruland who finally consented.[33] But even though he gave his permission, he offered little co-operation. When a mission was given in a large city parish and the confessions were heavy, the missionaries knew that, according to their Constitutions, they should not call upon the local clergy to assist them.[34] But when they sought the aid of their confreres they were told "the Provincial had said there was no obligation to help out." Father Helmpraecht told Father Hecker in New York that Father Ruland had sent out a circular to all rectors containing this information.[35]

The American Fathers did not believe that the Provincial was deliberately hostile to missions or bore any personal animosity to the missionaries. They credited his attitude to his lack of mission experience. He had labored only in parishes since he entered the Community and his heart was in that work. Moreover, they were convinced that he was not aware of the magnificent opportunities the Church in America offered the Redemptorists. Neither was he familiar with the needs of the Church in this country.[36]

In justice to Father Ruland, it should be said that he found himself faced with practical difficulties. If he encouraged larger missions, he would have to take Fathers from parish work to assist the missionaries. This would double the burden of those already engaged in parochial duties which had increased since Father Bernard's time. He could assign only those familiar with the language and this requirement restricted him in the men he could choose. Understandably, he was hesitant to interfere with the efficient operation of the parishes since the Community depended on them financially. To do anything that might jeopardize that support would be unwise.

Despite these problems, there is no doubt that Father Ruland confided to Father Mauron serious misgivings about the missions and the missionaries. He believed that Father Bernard was "premature" in starting them. He should have waited until there were "sufficient forces to continue them." Also he was displeased with the way in which they were conducted. "Many evils and annoyances" had crept into them, although he did not specify what they were. He stated flatly "they have to be reorganized entirely in order to fulfill their purpose." How or in what way he proposed to reorganize them he does not say.[37] It seems odd that he would write that the missions were not fulfilling their purpose when the *Chronicle of Missions* lists an extraordinary number of souls who received the Sacraments. This, according to the Founder of the Congregation, St. Alphonsus, was the acid test of their success.[38]

Perhaps what disturbed the Provincial were certain circumstances of mission life which, in his judgment, were detrimental to the missionaries. He firmly believed the three Americans "suffered much" spiritually from their sacred expeditions. They traveled back and forth across the country "until they appeared like actors to the Community." Though they had publicized and brought the name Redemptorist before the American public, they themselves had also received undue notoriety. "There was always a fuss in the English religious newspapers after every mission." The American Fathers had gained too much prominence which he feared would inflate their pride and injure their religious spirit. Because of their missionary journeys, they spent a great amount of time away from the Community and when they returned they did not follow the Rule as closely as he thought they should. Yet they were not alone in this for in Father Ruland's report, there were not many Fathers who fulfilled the Rule to his satisfaction or who were as docile and pliant as he wanted them to be.[39]

Because of the Provincial's attitude and the limited number of available Fathers, the missionaries realized that the golden days of the missions were at an end. "The three regulars" were Fathers Walworth, Hecker, and Hewit, since Father Alexander had been assigned to parish work in New Orleans. Father Walworth had become head of the band in the fall of 1854. The year 1855 had scarcely begun when new difficulties arose to plague the little group. Toward the end of February while they were giving a mission in Utica, Father Hewit became sick. At first, they thought he had a heavy cold and would shortly recover. But they soon discovered that he was threatened with consumption. Ten years before, he had a similar attack and the doctors ordered him South for at least a year. This time the medical report was even more ominous. Though the physician said there were no immediate alarming symptoms, he prescribed complete rest for at least a year and advised a trip to Italy.[40]

This news discouraged Father Hewit, who apparently thought he would not recover. He looked to Rome as the place where he would like to breathe his last "at the center and source of faith and sanctity." He had soured somewhat on his native land, where his spirit was "thoroughly sickened with the infernal atmosphere of this infidel and heretical country." To secure permission for the journey, he wrote to Father Ruland, who was then at the Chapter, asking him to discuss the matter with the Superior General. At the same time, he wrote to Father Douglas "to request your good offices in the matter."[41]

Hard on the heels of this distressing news came another setback for the missionaries. They had scheduled a series of missions in western New York for the spring of 1855, when these were suddenly canceled. The Vicar-General of the Buffalo diocese had decided there was no need for missions and had "peremptorily" refused "to give any faculties whatever."[42]

Despite these reverses, Father Hecker was not discouraged. He placed all his trust in Almighty God and was confident that He would aid in this noble work for souls. In March of 1855 he wrote: "The future plan of missions depends . . . entirely upon Divine Providence. . . . The fact is we are afloat just at present and we shall steer according to circumstances."[43] Undaunted, they secured a mission for March 18th at Annunciation Parish in upper Manhattan, then called Manhattanville. After that, they went down to Kentucky and gave one mission in Lexington and another in Frankfort. Since these were not large missions, Fathers Walworth and Hecker handled them without having to call on their confreres for assistance.[44]

In July of 1856, the Rector Major answered Father Hewit's request for the European trip. Through the Provincial he gave his reasons for refusing which Father Hewit found "satisfactory even to myself."[45] But the European visit was not nearly so necessary as it had appeared. Despite the gloomy diagnosis of the physician, eight months of rest had worked wonders for Father Hewit's health and in October of 1856 he was ready to resume his missionary activities. Several large missions were scheduled for the fall of that year and a number of the Redemptorists generously pitched in to help the little band. Until January of 1856, they had the invaluable help of Father Smulders who joined them on five missions in Canandaigua, Pittsburgh, Sandusky, Cleveland, and New York.[46]

The year 1856 was the most promising for the future of English-speaking missions since the departure of Father Bernard. Two more American-born converts ordained to the priesthood in the Redemptorist Community swelled the ranks of the little band to five. The first was the former West Pointer and roommate of General Grant, Connecticut-born, Episcopalian George Deshon. He had an enviable record at the Point, graduating second in his class. While teaching mathematics and ethics at the Academy, he became a Catholic in 1850. Still in uniform, he called on the Redemptorists in Baltimore and asked to be admitted to the Community because he wanted "to preach the Gospel to the people." This fourth native American to be ordained a Redemptorist made his vows in June of 1852 and was ordained October 28, 1855, in the Baltimore Cathedral by Archbishop Kenrick.[47] Four months later he was on his first mission at Our Lady Star of the Sea in Brooklyn. Because of his teaching experience, he soon became quite adept in giving the morning instructions in a succinct and informative style.[48]

On his second mission in St. Patrick's in Newburgh, New York, March 2–13, 1856, Father Deshon became the subject of some good-natured ribbing. Shortly after it opened, he was taken sick and developed a sore throat. His companions jocosely observed that the strong and vigorous warrior, capable of enduring all the rigors of the apostolic life, crumpled on his second engagement. He reminded them, they teasingly told him, of the enthusiastic soldier hankering for combat who fell flat on his face in his first battle.[49]

The second acquisition to the mission band was the talented and saintly Francis Baker. Born in Baltimore, March 30, 1820, he graduated from Princeton in 1839 and two years later joined the Episcopalian Church. He met Father Hewit in 1843 when the two were studying for the Episcopalian ministry in the home of Bishop Whittingham. Ordained an Episcopalian minister in 1846, he served at St. Paul's Church in Baltimore until he was named rector of the fashionable St. Luke's Church in 1851. Within a short time he was recognized as one of the outstanding preachers in the city of Baltimore. Highly esteemed and loved, his conversion to the Catholic Church caused a sensation throughout the city.[50] The only consolation Protestants could find in his "capitulation to Rome" was that now at last the Catholic Church would have "one man who had read the Bible."[51]

On April 9, 1853, in the little chapel of the orphanage of the Sisters of Charity, Francis Baker made his profession of Faith to his close friend of Episcopalian days, Father Hewit. Father Hecker was also present on this occasion. Shortly afterward, to the great delight of the American missionaries, he joined the Redemptorists, pronouncing his vows on July 24, 1854.[52] While he was at the novitiate, Archbishop Kenrick visited Annapolis and later wrote to Dr. Kirby, rector of the Irish College in Rome: "The Redemptorists have their Novitiate there [Annapolis] in the old mansion house of the Carroll family. Francis Baker, a most distinguished convert is the humblest of the Novices."[53]

A little more than a month after Archbishop Kenrick raised him to the priesthood on September 21, 1856, Father Baker was on his first mission in St. Patrick's Church in Washington. Preaching the opening sermon, which, as the *Chronicle of Missions* said, "gave great satisfaction to all who heard it," he was hailed as a truly apostolic missionary by his companions. This mission had the unique distinction of catching the attention of the President of the United States, Franklin Pierce, and his wife. For the closing ceremony of the dedication to our Blessed Mother, Mrs. Pierce sent a beautiful bouquet of flowers "which the President assisted in arranging."[54]

From November 26, 1856, until February 8, 1857, the five convert missionaries gave missions throughout the South in the dioceses of Savannah and St. Augustine, preaching in the cities of Savannah, Atlanta, Macon, Augusta, and St. Augustine.[55] Success greeted them wherever they went and it looked as though the golden age of missions had dawned again. But no sooner had they finished their southern tour than it seemed as if the newly strengthened band would lose one of its original members, Father Hewit. This time the problem was not health but family.

In April of 1855, Father Hewit's younger brother Henry became a Catholic. Some time later his wife and children were also baptized. He had finished his medical studies but was having great difficulty setting up in practice. Knowing his financial distress, Father Hewit feared that unless he received assistance, his faith, as well as that of his wife and family, would be in danger. His debts were piling up, he had become discouraged, and his future seemed hopeless. Because of these reverses and their attendant dangers, Father Hewit believed he had an obligation in conscience to come to his brother's aid. In August of 1856, he decided the only way he could effectively remedy the situation was to ask for a leave of absence, take a parish temporarily, and then devote as much time as he could to lecturing and writing. With permission, he would be able to use whatever money he earned for the support of his brother and his family.[56]

When Father Hecker heard of Father Hewit's decision, he pleaded with him not to take that step and characteristically he offered to help him. First, he would see what he could do toward getting his brother some kind of employment. Second, he told his fellow missionary: "Consider $100.00 at your brother's demand with Father Rector. Write him to that effect." Undoubtedly this

sum came from the ever generous George Hecker. Then he begged
Father Hewit: "Keep up good courage. What! When we can do
greater things shall we not be able to do this with God's assistance?
I am ashamed of myself to think that this is a serious obstacle.
We shall succeed."[57]

For a while Hecker did succeed and the disaster was averted.
But six months later, the specter of ruin was again hovering over
Henry Hewit's head. Everything had failed. He was in debt for
over five hundred dollars and still he could not set up a medical
practice. After much prayerful thought and deliberation, Father
Hewit was convinced that the material, as well as the spiritual,
salvation of his brother and family fell upon his shoulders. Reluctantly on February 22, 1857, he wrote to Father Ruland who had
known of his difficulty to secure his release from the Rector Major.

This was the situation shortly after the missionaries had come
north from their second tour of the South. But again Father Hewit
was not forced to take the step which would have caused him
"intense pain." Father Ruland said he would allot some money
from the Province for Henry.[58]

At this time, Father Hecker was in Cuba for his health. After
his return, he came up with a practical plan. Contacting George
Ripley, who was then editing the *New American Encyclopedia*
with Charles Dana, he arranged for Father Hewit to write some
articles dealing with the Catholic Church. Whatever recompense
he received would be deposited with the Rector in New York and
made available to his brother.[59]

While they were trying to solve each problem that would put
their missions in jeopardy, the American missionaries were devoting more and more thought to establishing their work on a permanent basis. They realized its haphazard status and they saw many
difficulties looming up even more menacingly to threaten its future.
In their judgment, this all-important work of the Congregation
was slowly suffering extinction. To sit quietly and watch regret-
fully such a disaster taking place was, according to their conscience,
not only cowardly but sinful. Something had to be done to insure
the future of their apostolic labors. On a mission in Wilmington
in October of 1856, they decided their only hope was the establishment of an English-speaking house which had been the project of
the alert and perspicacious Father Bernard. Unanimously they

agreed that with courage and confidence, they "would use all lawful and proper means to hasten its foundation."[60] At the moment, they did not know what steps they could take. But while they labored zealously and enthusiastically in the fulfillment of their God-given missionary vocation, they had one dream, one hope, one ambition, an American Redemptorist mission house.

CHAPTER X

Appealing to the American Non-Catholic

DURING the first three years of Father Hecker's missionary career, he saw the immense amount of good the missions were accomplishing. More than one hundred thousand Catholics had received the Sacraments. Innumerable others had listened to solid and basic instructions on the truths of their Faith. Weak and timid Catholics, harboring feelings of inferiority so often character- istic of a minority group, took courage from the sight of the throngs of fellow Catholics in the nightly crowded churches. The careless and indifferent were spurred on to a new spirit of devotion and love for their faith. Confused Catholics adjusted their sense of values and attempted to maintain a proper balance between the spiritual and material needs of life. As a result of their newly made resolu- tions, the faithful raised the moral tone of their daily living.

Father Hecker noticed all these salutary effects on Catholics but he also saw that missions were making an impact on non-Catholics. Many of them watched with curious interest the phenomenon of churches crowded for eight or ten nights in succession. Some mus- tered enough courage to attend the exercises, listen to the speakers, and "see for themselves." Not a few, attracted by the forceful and convincing explanations of Catholic truth, sought further in- structions and eventually embraced the Faith. By the end of 1853, the Fathers could report that at least seventy Protestants had become Catholics in the preceding three years.[1]

In an enthusiastic letter to his English friend, the convert Richard Simpson, Hecker summed up the purpose of his missionary labors: "We must make Yankeedom the Rome of the modern world — at least we work hard to make it Catholic."[2] The positive conviction he formed at Wittem was ever in his thoughts and the conversion of the American non-Catholic was his "ardent and constant desire."[3] Although Catholic missions helped to satisfy that desire, he realized they were an indirect approach to his countrymen. Millions of Americans never set foot inside the doors of a Catholic church. No one seemed to be concerned about them. In their anxiety to preserve the faith of their flocks, Catholic leaders had overlooked those who had no faith. Either forgotten or ignored, they were still souls to be won for Christ, and Father Hecker was determined to help them.

Meditating on the gift of faith one day in his room, he was "suddenly struck" with the realization of his great happiness since he became a Catholic. He contrasted his present condition with the troubles and agony of soul he had experienced in the trying days before his conversion. The memory of Brook Farm, Fruitlands, and Concord arose to haunt him. "Alas! How many of my former friends and acquaintances, how many of the great body of American people are in the same most painful position. Can not something be done to lead them to the knowledge of the Truth? Perhaps if the way that Divine Providence had led me to the Church were shown to them, many of them might in this way be led also to see the truth." Knowing that he could not reach them through the spoken word, he decided he would try to speak to them through the written word.[4]

With this newest avenue open before him, he began to write in June, 1854. Within a month he had roughly sketched what ultimately became his first book, *Questions of the Soul*. From June until December of 1854, he worked feverishly at his writing, discussing it with Father Hewit, his brother George, Mrs. Ripley, and Brownson.[5] Because of his many duties, especially when the mission season opened in October, he could not give it his undivided attention. Nevertheless, in early December, he had practically finished the volume. Appleton had accepted it and his brother George offered to take care of the expenses of publication. Since Father Hecker was away from the city on missions, his friend, George Ripley, put it through the press, correcting and revising proof sheets.[6]

Questions of the Soul opens with a discussion of the very problems that had plagued Father Hecker from his early manhood: "What is my destiny? Have I a work to do? What is it and where?" Knowing that all men ask these perplexing questions, he quotes extensively from noted non-Catholic authors, Emerson, Channing, Milner, Lowell, Longfellow, Goethe, to show how they answered them. Though these writers admit the problem, they have no solution. Paraphrasing St. Augustine, Father Hecker wrote: "The soul finds no rest till it finds God." The destiny of every man is "to know, love and live for God."[7]

Mindful of his Brook Farm days, the author then addresses himself to those who can find no happiness in purely material pleasures or in the ordinary enterprises of life. This is not a small group but "a large class of persons in the United States who look for and seek a more spiritual and earnest life." Where can they find it? Not in humanitarian schemes such as Brook Farm and Fruitlands, nor in Protestant groups like the Brotherhood of the Holy Cross. All these noble and self-sacrificing ventures had failed. "They met with defeat instead of success, hopelessness instead of blessedness."[8]

Up to this point, *Questions of the Soul* is almost an autobiography with each chapter revealing different periods in the author's life. There is warmth and color in Hecker's prose and it becomes quietly inspirational as he speaks of Christ as the only Perfect Man who lived the Perfect Life. In quick strokes, with telling episodes from the history of the God-man, he establishes His divinity and the perpetuation of His work in the Catholic Church which he calls the only sure and certain way for man to reach his destiny. Citing Protestant authors, the writer shows the admitted inadequacy of man-made religion to satisfy completely the needs of the human heart. He rejects Protestantism "because it has no succor for man when he most needs it; and secondly because it fails to answer the mystic tendencies of the heart." Only a divinely established Church which watches over man from his birth to his death with the sacramental system "is adequate to all the wants" of his God-created soul. This is the Catholic Church, the answer to the questions of the soul. "All men so far as their nature is not perverted are Catholics and if they but knew their real wants, they would have to do violence to themselves not to enter the Catholic Church."[9]

In conclusion, Father Hecker admits that the Church is unknown to a vast majority of his fellow citizens. "This Church is here in the midst of us, but strange as it may seem, it is concealed from the minds of the American people by ignorance, misrepresentation and calumny as effectually as if it were once more buried in the Catacombs." But the Bride of Christ will not remain hidden. As soon as America comes to know her, "the Cross of Christ will accompany the stars and stripes." The Church will enhance the glorious future of America for "our people . . . if once Catholic, can give a new, noble and glorious realization to Christianity; a development which will go even beyond the past in achievements of zeal, in the abundance of saints as well as in art, science and material greatness."[10]

Father Hecker's approach marked a new departure in Catholic apologetical literature in America. He offered no logical or dogmatic defense of Catholicism drawn from Scripture or history. Neither did he set out to refute the errors of Protestantism or answer charges against Catholicism. He simply delineated in a positive, appealing, and non-controversial manner the instincts and desires of man's nature. Then he asked, can philosophy or the various forms of Protestantism adequately satisfy them? Investigating the different answers offered by representative philosophers and Protestants, he found them inadequate. When he applied the same criterion to the Catholic Church, he demonstrated that she alone could adequately satisfy the cravings of the human heart because she was divinely founded by Christ.

Anyone familiar with modern apologetic literature would see nothing unusual in the approach Father Hecker used. Today it is a recognized and accepted technique to tell those outside the Church: this is what Catholicism has to offer you; this is what the Catholic Church can do for you. Numerous apologetic books published today are based on this principle. But a hundred years ago it was a novel approach. As Father Gorman points out in his study of Catholic apologetic literature in this country, the Church in America until 1858 was "in a state of siege and quite generally misunderstood." As a result, Catholic writers concentrated on diminishing prejudice, correcting misrepresentations, and proving that the Church deserved equal rights with other religious denominations.[11] They concentrated on defense; Father Hecker on offense. He believed that the time had come to present to the American people a positive picture of what Catholicism could offer to satisfy psychological needs. Father Hecker believed his fellow countrymen were hungry for truth and desperately in need of divine aid, and that they were ready to listen to psychological arguments. Then, Father Hecker maintained, after hearing these arguments they would be more disposed to look into her historical claims and wholeheartedly accept the fullness of her teaching.

Eagerly Father Hecker awaited the public's reaction to his first appeal to the American non-Catholic. His interest was not simply that of a young author concerned with the fate of his first-born book. It was much deeper since he believed it would determine his whole future. He regarded the success or failure of *Questions of the Soul* as a test "whether God had really given me the grace and vocation to labor in a special manner for the conversion of the American people."[12]

Early in February, 1855, the volume was off the press and in the hands of the reviewers. The secular papers gave it considerable prominence with the New York *Tribune* carrying Ripley's two and a half column notice. Quoting freely from the volume, he judged that "in general the tone of the work savours more of sentiment than of reasoning, although it betrays more than a common degree of ability while its suavity of temper might spread its contagious sweetness without damage, among controversialists of every name." The *Boston Transcript* called it "A genial, though a Catholic book, evidently from the heart of the writer." The *Boston Atlas* described it as "well written, characterized by strong common sense views and from the pen of a sound, profound thinker."[13]

The non-Catholic religious papers, as Hecker said, "pitched into him with a vengeance." The New York *Observer* began its rather lengthy review with the caustic observation: "A queer title and a queerer book" and labeled it as "a cunning artifice of Popery to catch the unwary." The Philadelphia *Presbyterian* denounced Father Hecker's conclusion: "We have not much fear, notwithstanding the brazen designs of Rome that the free people of this land will ever be brought under the spiritual despotism which has enthralled the millions of Europe — most especially will they not come under the yoke at the call of such a two-penny trumpet as this book." The New York *Evangelist* protested that "Such works as this are an attempt to turn one of the chief arguments of Protestantism into the defense of the Papacy." The longest non-Catholic review was carried in the New York *Churchman* and lacked the invective found in other papers. This, Father Hecker credited to his brother John who "seems to have held his [the editor's] elbows while writing it."[14] Though disapproving of the volume, the reviewer concluded: "There is a vein of earnest though mistaken piety running through his volume, which occasionally almost wins one to his cause. But a moment's calm reflection dispels the delusion of it all."

The reaction of the non-Catholic historian, George Bancroft, was in sharp contrast with the caustic denunciations from his fellow co-religionists. Father Hecker had sent him one of the first copies of the *Questions of the Soul* to come off the press. In appreciation he wrote to the author: "Your volume is clear and simple in style (and clearness and simplicity are in writing the highest graces), rich in illustration; all the dwellers of Parnassus seem to bring their willing offerings to your writing table. I look upon your work as one of the signs of the times, that men are beginning to look inward and desire with loftier earnestness to solve the great problems of existence. I hope when I return to town I shall have the pleasure of seeing you often, and, old as I am, I shall be delighted to learn from one so sincere as you."[15]

The Catholic press was as laudatory as the Protestant press was condemnatory. The Detroit *Vindicator* praised it as a "beautiful and able work." The Pittsburgh *Catholic* called it "eminently practical and admirably adapted to the spiritual wants of our age and country. . . . The book itself is just what we would expect from the learned and zealous Father Hecker." The Cincinnati *Telegraph* commented that it would "guide many an ardent and inquiring mind to saving truth." The St. Louis *Leader* enthusiastically proclaimed it "THE book of the age. It is beautifully written, fervent, clear, candid and goes to the bottom of those very problems which now are agitating so many American hearts and minds."

The Catholic press in England unreservedly recommended *Questions of the Soul* to its readers. The London *Weekly Register* declared: "No book that we know of, which has been published during the last few years, appears so much calculated to clear away by Divine grace, those obstacles to conversion as the volume now before us. It . . . will be found as serviceable here as on the other side of the Atlantic." The *Rambler* for May, 1855, put it in the same category as Moehler, Lacordaire, Nicholas, and Balmes. A long three-page review in the October, 1855, issue of the Liverpool *Catholic Institute Magazine* praised the book and the author very highly.

The really "rave" review came from none other than the usually restrained and unusually critical Orestes Brownson. He devoted nineteen pages to it in the April, 1855, issue of his *Review* in which he wrote: "It is a genuine work of art in the highest sense of the term, as beautiful as true and as true as beautiful." Citing the chapters Father Hecker had devoted to Protestantism, Brownson called them the "most masterly refutation of it that we have ever read." The book, he said, was not only rewarding, enlightening, and satisfying, but a model for all future apologetical writers. "It shows how a Catholic can say all that is needful to say without giving offense to anyone." There were many things Brownson admired in the book "its sound theology, its rare philosophy and its deep thought." But he especially commended "its genial spirit, its youthfulness and freshness, its enthusiasm, its hopefulness and its charity."[16]

Shortly after *Questions of the Soul* had come off the press, Father Hecker cautiously gave his opinion of its sales potential. "I think it is likely that the book will be largely circulated."[17] In this he was not disappointed. Its first press run of one thousand copies was sold out almost within the first month of its appearance. A second was immediately prepared and by mid-June Appleton put out a third, each edition consisting of a thousand copies.[18] Gauged by modern book sales and best seller totals, three thousand copies can hardly be called a tremendous success. But in the 1850's it was considered quite a respectable press run, especially for a Catholic book. In 1840, *Brownson's Quarterly Review* had less than a thousand subscribers and in 1850, fourteen hundred, a figure which seemed quite satisfactory to the editor.[19]

The favorable reception given to the book by the press and the American public was most encouraging to Father Hecker. It deepened in him the conviction that God had called him to serve his fellow men. "Daily my confidence increases," he wrote to Brownson, "that Providence has destined me to do an important work for our country." The exact role he was to play in this work was still not clear in his mind. But he had no doubt that God would enlighten him as long as he remained "faithful to His grace and inspirations."[20]

The reaction to *Questions of the Soul* had not only made Father Hecker more certain of his vocation; it also convinced him that another book was needed. The comments of Ripley, Bancroft, and others did not deny that the Church meets the wants of the heart but they refused to admit that she satisfies the needs of the intellect. As Hecker put it: "the head was left to be con-verted." Early in April of 1855, he drew up a plan of a new book which would show that the dogmas and mysteries of the Catholic Faith "answer the requirements of reason."[21]

This book which he called *Aspirations of Nature* would be more ambitious in character and more fundamental in content. In the first section, he would describe the value and importance of reason which, although a God-given gift, had limitations. By its own natural powers, the human intellect could never know in all its fullness the divine plan of life. The sure way reason could be certain of the true and correct relationship between God and man would be to obtain God's manifestation of His design. Reason, Father Hecker concluded, must have divine revelation. But to direct man in the correct understanding of that revelation, reason further requires a teacher with divine authority not only to pre-serve God's message full and complete but to explain its true meaning with fidelity and accuracy. Before man can accept such a teacher, that teacher must prove his right to interpret God's revelation in full conformity with His divine mind.

After demonstrating the existence of these fundamental and undeniable needs, Father Hecker then proposed to examine them in the light of philosophy and Protestantism. He would show that the proponents of these systems through their own admissions must confess they are powerless to fulfill these needs. He would then call upon Catholicism to undergo the very same test. From its acknowledged and authoritative teachings, he would show that the Catholic Church alone meets all the requirements and answers all the demands of reason. "In her bosom, the whole man — reason, heart, senses, all is turned to the worship of its Creator."

Before he left for a mission in Covington, Kentucky, Father Hecker jotted down the whole plan of the book and sent it to Brownson. "How does it strike you?" he asked. Then conscious of his own limitations which always loomed larger in his own eyes than they actually were, he said to Brownson: "Should *I* undertake it? If so would you have it modified? You would do me a great favor to pen me a line or two in answer to these questions."[22]

Approving the plan without modifications, Brownson encouragingly replied: "I beg you to give yourself full freedom in your new book. What we want is free, fresh and spiritual writings. . . . I am more and more convinced of the necessity of presenting the positive side of Catholicity and of doing it in a way to meet the actual wants of our countrymen."[23] There was no doubt in Brownson's mind that Hecker was well qualified to undertake the task.

As soon as he received this heartening reply, Father Hecker began to put his thoughts on paper. In June of 1855, he wrote to Father John Duffy in New Orleans that he had made a beginning but its development would depend on "one who delights to help the helpless and to obtain grace for those who seek it from her merciful hands — our dear Lady. With her help it shall be well done; without, not done at all."[24] With his characteristic enthusiasm, Father Hecker continued his writing. He had to set his manuscript aside temporarily when he gave an eight-day retreat to the Sisters of Mercy in downtown Manhattan.[25] No sooner had he resumed his writing than a new turn of events on the American scene drew him away from his literary labors.

Father Hecker had published *Questions of the Soul* at the height of the political Nativist movement of the 1850's. This agitation was spawned and developed by the Know-Nothings who were an offshoot of previous organizations imbued with a hatred of the Church and all things Catholic. Bitter prejudice stirred up violent emotions which erupted in rioting and bloodshed in a number of cities. Because of the large numbers of Catholic immigrants, the

Nativists directed their attack against all foreigners, declaring "America for Americans." In their blind fury, they labeled all Catholics as aliens and un-American, tools of a foreign power anxious to control and destroy our national way of life.

Many ecclesiastics viewed the movement with great alarm and saw it as a crippling blow to all hopes for the future of the Church in America. But not Father Hecker. The attention of thinking men and influential citizens, he maintained, was drawn by the vehemence of the attack to consider the Church. Was she all her enemies said of her? Even a cursory examination of the absurd charges leveled against her would show how much she had been maligned. Fair-minded Americans, he was convinced, would become more kindly disposed to Catholicism and could be led to study her rather than ignore her. They would discover that a good Catholic because of his faith was a good American. Instead of any antagonism between Catholicism and patriotism, the Church provided the true foundation for genuine love and respect for one's country and demanded ready obedience to legitimately constituted and justly exercised authority.[26] This America needed to know, for as he wrote to Brownson: "the American people will never believe, or be convinced that we love our country, so long as we do not show genuine patriotic feeling for its interests and destiny."[27] As soon as the Catholic proves he is a true American then he can more easily prove to his fellow men that his Catholicism is the true religion.

Father Hecker's great friend Brownson was in the thick of the Nativist fight. In 1854, he wrote a vigorous article against the movement, deploring its existence not so much as antireligious as anti-American. It was against the very nature and principles of our Constitution and abhorrent to every right-thinking citizen. Recognizing that the main target of the movement was the Irish Catholic, Brownson pointed out that though they formed a large group in American life, they were not the whole of the immigrant population nor of the Catholic Church. While warmly defending the vast majority of the Irish, he strongly denounced an undesirable minority among them. In fairness to the majority, he begged his readers not to confuse them with this "miserable rabble." Above all, he pleaded with them not to judge the Church by this group.[28]

Brownson's caustic denunciation of this "miserable rabble" pierced the sensitive skin of those he was attempting to defend and wounded their feelings. Instead of concentrating on their common Nativist enemy, the Catholic press, especially the Irish papers in this country, turned against Brownson with a vengeance. In July and August of 1854, at least nine Catholic journals viciously denounced him. He was accused of vilifying the Irish, defaming their character, and attacking their religion. In no time, the veteran journalist found himself in the midst of enemies. He had to defend against Americans his right to be a Catholic, and against Catholics his right to be an American.[29]

After a conversation with Irish-born Bishop O'Connor of Pittsburgh, Father Hecker cautioned Brownson to be more prudent. "The Irish prelates and priests have become mighty tender on the point of Nationality. Your dose on Native-Americanism has operated on them and operated powerfully, especially in the West. They felt sore, and let me add, also weak from its effects."[30] Before Hecker had ever written this letter, Brownson was in the middle of the hornet's nest he had stirred up. But the stings were coming not only from the West. The waspish East was buzzing just as strongly. Archbishop Hughes, a native of Ireland, disliked the tone of the articles. Although he publicly opposed any comparison between native and foreign Catholics, he was privately convinced that the Irish immigrants would always be the backbone of the Church in America. He was quite displeased to see a distinguished Catholic declaring in print that some of his countrymen were no asset to either Church or country. Stirring appeals to patriotism roused little response in the heart of this churchman who could write to an American non-Catholic in public life: "I never voted but once in my life."[31]

The controversy became so bitter and so sustained that finally the Archbishop of Baltimore asked Brownson in February of 1855 to remove from the back cover of his Review the Bishops' letter of endorsement sent to him in 1849.[32]

The American-born Bishop Fitzpatrick, who had received Brownson into the Church, remained silent during the vituperative tirades against his distinguished convert. Although he was in Europe when Brownson published his controversial article, he had, before his departure, appointed Father John T. Roddan to act in his place as censor of the *Review*. When the Bishop returned, the storm was still raging. But he said nothing on behalf of Brownson either publicly or even privately to his brother bishops, although his designated censor had read and approved the article before publication.[33] Brownson was left to fight his battle alone. Disappointed and disillusioned, Brownson wrote: "there is hardly a Catholic voice raised publicly in my defense."[34]

The reaction of some of the hierarchy particularly pained Brownson. He was guilty of no error in faith and morals; he had uttered no heresy. Why the violent abuse? Why couldn't the bishops at least call upon the Catholic press to stop their torrent of invective and calmly point out his error? Brownson was convinced that they not only failed to rebuke his assailants but even encouraged them by remaining silent.[35] He regarded this attitude of the hierarchy as not only personally offensive but indicative of a prejudice against his fellow Americans. He wrote to Father Hecker: "Our great difficulty in getting our religion fairly presented to the American mind is the real dislike of the American people and character felt by a large portion of our bishops and clergy."[36]

Although Father Hecker might modify the word "dislike" to "distrust," he did not hesitate to admit that most of the foreign-born bishops in America favored their native flocks in this country and looked askance at American customs and traditions. Nationalism, he realized, was a highly inflammable issue and he feared that before long there would be an explosion "on this point in our Church." The American element was increasing numerically and exerting a much greater impact on the national consciousness than the immigrant. "This in itself must excite unpleasant feelings on the other side." The prudent and wise course to adopt was silence: silence on the emotionally charged question of nationalism; silence on the failure of the immigrant to adopt the American way of life. But speak out strongly and clearly, he maintained, on the tremendous benefits Catholicism offered to our country and its citizens.[37] This would steal the fire from the Nativists who prophesied ruin and destruction for the American nation if the Church were not suppressed and shackled.

Expressing his views to close friends, Father Hecker found in New York some who were imbued with the same ideas. He decided to bring them together so they could discuss more fully "the interests of the Church at the present moment in our country." In the second week of August he asked a chosen group of five to meet with him at the home of McMaster, the editor of the *Freeman's Journal*. Two were priests, the scholarly Dr. Cummings and the somewhat volatile Dr. Manahan; three were laymen, McMaster, Cavanagh, and Captain Monroe whom Hecker called a "capital man."[38] He was a relative of President Monroe. All were in agreement on presenting their views later expressed in the words: "We can be devout Catholics and at the same time enlightened and unflinching friends of both civil and religious liberty even in the American sense of the terms."[39]

After the meeting, Dr. Manahan had a long talk with Father Hecker about Brownson. Both men knew that the controversial editor was becoming increasingly lonely and discontented. Since his conversion, he had alienated his Boston Protestant friends; as a result of his Native American article, he had lost some of his New England Catholic followers. His place was in New York with the core of his loyal and devoted sympathizers who shared his ideals and hopes.[40]

In the summer of 1854, Brownson had discussed with Father Hecker the advisability of moving to New York. But his young friend was not in favor of it. Why he thought it unwise was apparently known only to Brownson and disclosed in conversation but not in writing.[41] There is a hint in one letter that Hecker had misgivings about Brownson's ability to get along with the Archbishop.[42] Both were strong men, outspoken and independent. Neither cared much to conciliate or concede. If the fiery Brownson were to clash with the implacable Hughes, there was sure to be an uproar. As long as the aggressive Editor was not in the diocese of the militant Prelate, such a tussle was less likely to occur.

A year later, Hecker no longer considered the move unwise. On August 23, 1855, he wrote to Brownson: "my views are changed. If you have still a notion to change your place of residence, I should like to know it. For if so, my intention is to do all in my power to prepare the way for it."[43]

Without delay, Brownson answered on August 29th that he was confident the move to New York would be beneficial for the *Review* as well as himself. Under Hughes's patronage, he thought he "could better breast the storm still raging and likely to rage for some time against me." His friends in New York were more loyal and devoted than those in Boston. He could exert greater personal influence if he were living in the fast growing metropolis. He would find there what New England no longer could give him — literary and cultured associates.[44]

Only one reason made him hesitate: the expense of moving and getting settled in a new home. Apart from this, he regretted leaving the Bishop who, though no active supporter, was "as warm a friend as ever."[45]

Brownson's difficulty was no problem for Father Hecker. After consulting with Brownson's supporters, among whom was George Hecker, he told Brownson the rent for his new home would be paid for the first year. Wasting no time, since his mission season was about to open, Father Hecker began to hunt for a suitable and reasonably priced house. He wanted to select two or three and then let Brownson make the final choice. Knowing the importance of having the Archbishop's approval, Father Hecker visited Hughes on October 1st. In the course of conversation, the Prelate mentioned that he heard Brownson was thinking of coming to New York. "Yes," said Hecker, "but with your approval." Immediately the Archbishop said he would be "quite pleased" to have the Boston editor in his diocese and asked his visitor to forward this information to Brownson.[46]

The way was now cleared and after the October number of the *Review* was off the press, the editor bade farewell to New England. He took his family, his *Review,* his library, and all his belongings to his new home. His son Henry said that after he left Chelsea, he produced "the profoundest and sublimest of his writings." Schlesinger describes the change as "stepping from darkness into daylight. Boston seemed tight and suspicious; New York open and tolerant."[47]

When Brownson moved to New York, he associated with such stanch believers in the future of the Church in America as McMaster, Cummings, Manahan, Cavanagh, and Monroe. The existence of this effective coterie of zealous workers increased Father Hecker's hopes for the conversion of his countrymen. Two of them were editors and converts who really understood the

American mentality. Like him, they wanted to show their fellow men that the Catholic Church was no enemy of their country but a powerful ally. Her teachings would not only strengthen the foundations of our nation, but would give peace and happiness to our citizens. Daily, in the Sacrifice of the Mass, Father Hecker prayed for the success of the group for "every day I am more and more under the conviction that God is preparing the way by special graces to converts of the faith for the conversion of our country."[48]

During the action-filled months of August, September, and October of 1855, Father Hecker had little time to devote to his second book, *Aspirations of Nature*. He had even less leisure for writing when the mission season opened in the fall. It was not until the spring of 1857 that he succeeded in putting his manuscript in final form. Meanwhile he kept the main ideas of the book firmly in his thoughts. In the spring of 1856 he received an unexpected opportunity to air them publicly before an audience made up of many non-Catholics. On March 30th, with Fathers Hewit and Bradley, he opened a mission at St. Patrick's Church in Norfolk, Virginia. The Fathers had been there almost three years before, but great tragedy had stalked the city since their last mission. Yellow fever had swept the area and claimed at least two hundred victims from the parish. In the neat new cemetery where the Fathers had seen only six graves in 1853, they counted one hundred and thirty-two in 1856. Immediately, the missionaries recognized that there was no need to arouse consciences or to thunder death and judgment. Their task was to console and encourage, "to instruct and build up."[49]

Noticing many non-Catholics in their audience, the missionaries did not adhere to their usual schedule but preached some dogmatic sermons instead of their customary moral exhortations. They spoke on the Divinity of Christ, the Mass, and the intercessory power of the Blessed Virgin. The effect on the non-Catholics was very noticeable. The *Mission Chronicle* relates that "as Virginians are a candid, frank and high-minded people, they did not hesitate to acknowledge it." Since there were many other Protestants who wished to attend the mission but who were pressured into staying away, the Fathers decided to try an experiment. They would remain after the close of the mission and give lectures specifically addressed to the non-Catholics for the following four nights.[50]

On Monday, April 7th, Father Hewit spoke on the need of faith; on Tuesday, the Bible and Tradition as the guides for man; on Wednesday, the divine foundation of the Church. The series closed on Thursday night when Father Hecker gave a popular lecture on the objections to Catholicism. As he later reported to Brownson, "I broke new ground, put Protestants on the defense and appealed to human nature for support."[51] As he had done in *Questions of the Soul,* he took a positive approach showing his audience that the Church did not shackle reason, but encouraged its fullest possible development. Catholicism, he pointed out, also provided divine safeguards to prevent reason from falling into harmful excesses. Rather than an enemy of man, the Catholic Church was his ally and defender. Father Hecker put his heart and soul into his talk and the *Mission Chronicle* described the lecture as "extremely eloquent and popular."[52]

Again, as with his book, Father Hecker looked upon the effect of this lecture as a further proof of God's divine call to labor for the conversion of his non-Catholic fellow men. The successful result far surpassed his wildest hopes. The large audience listened to him with rapt attention. Four or five expressed their desire to take instructions and become Catholics. His fellow missionaries were enthusiastic about his effectiveness. Father Walworth, who had finished a mission in nearby Portsmouth, listened carefully to the discourse and commended it highly. He told Father Hecker "it was the best lecture he had heard in the United States." He felt confident that Father Hecker's vocation was to work for the non-Catholic. Walworth realized that his companion had a knack of removing prejudices and exciting in others "an interest and desire to become better acquainted with the doctrines of the Catholic faith."[53]

The Fathers looked upon this attempt as a beginning of a great work in the Redemptorist Community. The Provincial, Father Ruland, had spoken of applying "the mission system" to the conversion of heretics. Brownson had also said that he considered such a work as "one of the chief branches of labor" for the Congregation.[54] But it was not until April of 1856 that it was first tried and proved successful.

Father Hecker had spoken many times before of a direct

appeal to the non-Catholic on the positive side of the Faith, but he found that his fellow missionaries were not entirely in sympathy with his views.[55] Father Walworth's main interest was in Catholic missions but after the Norfolk episode, he realized the potentialities in Hecker's approach. Before the year was out he had a chance to test his own abilities in this field. While on a mission in Macon, Georgia, in December of 1856, twenty non-Catholic men asked him if he would give a sermon on the Catholic religion after the close of the mission. Choosing for his topic the marks of the Church, he gave a positive explanation free of any attack or denunciation of Protestantism. Shortly after they left Macon, the missionaries heard that a Presbyterian minister began a series on Popery to counteract the effect left by the Fathers. His tirades against the Church offended his audience who contrasted his bombasts with "the calm convictions and good temper" of the missionaries.[56]

Father Hewit, in the early days of his conversion, was somewhat like Brownson in his intensity of faith and his disgust for the "infernal atmosphere of this infidel and heretical country."[57] But the optimistic attitude and cheerful spirit of Father Hecker drew his attention away from the somber side of the American scene and directed it to the spiritual possibilities of his countrymen. After the Norfolk mission he was "in great measure convinced of the correctness" of his companion's views.[58] He was aided in reaching this conviction through Brownson's unqualified endorsement of Father Hecker's ideas. In a letter to Father Hewit on March 17, 1856, the clear-thinking editor outlined the method he believed most effective in dealing with the American people: "My own conviction is that our true policy in dealing with the American mind is to study first to ascertain not its errors, but the truth it still retains, and to show that the truth can find its unity and integrity only in the Catholic Church. We must find our *point d'appui* in the sound principles it still holds, and lead it by arguments, drawn from those principles, of the justness of which they can judge without going out of themselves, to the conclusion to which we wish them to come."[59] These words were almost an echo of Father Hecker's thoughts. Certainly they describe the motives that activated him in writing *Questions of the Soul* and the ideas he kept before his mind as he selected and arranged his material.

Later on in this same letter Brownson characterizes the importance of showing that the Church does not suppress reason as "our work" at the present time. Hecker had some months before stressed the necessity of demonstrating that there was no antagonism between reason and grace. Impelled by this motive, he decided to write his second book, the plan of which he had sent to Brownson. It is interesting to find Brownson calling Father Hewit's attention to the very ideas Father Hecker planned to use in *Aspirations of Nature*. Brownson spoke of Father Hecker's approach as "the right view of this subject" while he calls his own "the worst of all."[60]

In October, Father Hewit acknowledged that he looked forward "to the conversion of a great number of the best part of our American fellow-citizens with confidence." He even hoped "for the conversion of the nation as such, though not so confidently." As long as God spared him, he wished to devote his life and all his energies to this "noble end." Like Father Hecker, he was now convinced that a glorious chapter was opening up for the sons of St. Alphonsus in the New World. "I trust Almighty God will soon give to the American Redemptorists the opportunity of acting more directly on the American people and laboring for their conversion."[61]

When Father Hecker found such encouraging support for his ideas, he thought it wise to send some information on this new development to his superiors in Rome. He expressed his views to Father Douglas in a letter of introduction he gave to a friend of his who was going to Rome. After outlining the condition of the Church in America, he wrote: "Our Congregation is growing rapidly in the United States and it is of course well that at headquarters our prospects here should be known and appreciated. There can be no doubt in the mind of any one whose eyes are open and [who] reflects that Divine Providence intends us for an important work in this country — blessing us as He has done with so many vocations, some of such an important character." Then he told Father Douglas he had formed a circle of Catholics numbering ten or fifteen, some of whom were converts, to pray for the conversion of their friends. Within a short time, they were thrilled "to see two of the number for whom our prayers were offered received into the Church, — a young man formerly a theological student in the Protestant Seminary (Anglican), the other a lady."[62]

As Father Hecker viewed the gradual unfolding of his conviction that God was calling him to work for the conversion of the American people, he realized that all the attempts he had made in this direction were individual and sporadic. They were neither unified nor concentrated. He had not hammered out a definite pattern for his project nor had his work been officially adopted as a specific goal of his Community. That, he trusted, would be the next step in the achievement of God's design. For in all his hopes, he associated this work with the Redemptorist Community.

The same idea was in the mind of Father Hewit. Both men realized that at the first opportunity they must take steps to follow out the resolution they had made in October of 1856 to secure an American Redemptorist house. This foundation would not only give stability and continuity to the mission work but would also enable them to act directly for the conversion of America.

CHAPTER XI

An American House

THE development of the Redemptorist Congregation in America
followed a pattern slightly different from that of the same Congregation in Europe. Wherever the Fathers began to establish
themselves on the Continent, they started immediately to preach
to the native population, and within a fairly short time they were
attracting native vocations. Young men sought admission to the
Community not only to live a religious life but also to work for
the spiritual welfare of their countrymen and preach in their
own language.[1]

In America, however, a different pattern evolved solely because
of the exigencies of the times. When the Fathers came to this
country, they found numerous groups of German Catholic immigrants who had come to a land where the customs and traditions
differed radically from those of their homeland. Since they had
been trained to identify their culture with their religion, they
clung tenaciously to their traditions.[2] To preserve the faith among
these immigrants, the American bishops saw the necessity of
forming national parishes and of providing priests who were
skilled in the use of the German language and familiar with the
type of life these people were accustomed to live. Because of their
backgrounds, the Redemptorists admirably filled this need. When
the American hierarchy called upon them for aid, they responded
generously and pledged themselves to minister to the German
immigrant. As their work increased, they requested priests from
their various houses in Europe. It was only natural, then, that

the Redemptorist foundations in America took on a distinctly foreign flavor. In their church, sermons and devotions were given in the German language. In their houses, their mother tongue was the medium of conversation as well as of official communications. Their way of life in manners and customs had a decided German touch. In many respects, to Americans these foundations seemed like sections of the fatherland transported to the New World. Yet despite the foreign tone, English-speaking Catholics were often attracted to these churches. The devotion of the Fathers and the dignity with which they carried out the liturgical services appealed to them.[3]

In the eastern cities where the Redemptorists had churches, they had to honor their agreement with the bishops to preach in German. The specialized character of their work allowed the Redemptorists neither the time nor the opportunity to address themselves to the American Catholic. However there were some deviations from this policy, notably in New Orleans, where there was an English sermon at one Mass every Sunday. The American congregation grew so rapidly that in 1850 a separate church was built for the English-speaking Catholics.[4]

When Father Bernard became the American vice-provincial in 1849, he quickly sized up the situation. From his personal observation of the Redemptorist development in Belgium and Holland, he knew the Congregation had not sunk its roots deep in American soil as it had done abroad. It was in this country but not of it. He recognized his Community's obligation to the American bishops but he also believed that without neglecting that commitment, the Redemptorists could appeal to the American Catholic. Until he had native vocations, however, he could not prove that both were possible. When Father Walworth was ordained in 1848, sixteen years after the Community had begun working in America, he became the first native-born Redemptorist priest. Father Hecker and then Father Hewit followed him. As soon as they were available, Father Bernard began the missions to American Catholics. But this was only the beginning of his program. His great ambition was to establish an American Redemptorist house where the Fathers would work for the American Catholic in the same way as the existing houses did for the German immigrant. This foundation would also serve as a headquarters for the American missionaries. Father Bernard did not remain long enough in America to see the fulfillment of his dream. He entrusted his hopes and plans to his American Redemptorist missionaries.[5]

Perhaps even more keenly than Father Bernard, did the little band realize how much an American house would help the spread of the Faith in this country and accelerate the growth of the Redemptorist Community. When the missionaries resolved to hasten the beginnings of their new foundation, American Catholics were desperately trying to prove against the Know-Nothings that they could be good Americans as well as good Catholics. In refutation of this claim, the Germanic character of the Redemptorist foundations could be cited as a telling argument. But if the Community could present a genuine American house, faithful in all the essentials to the spirit of St. Alphonsus, they could more easily make common cause with American Catholics to refute the Nativist. Thus they could show a patriotic love for American institutions which Father Hecker believed was a necessary prelude to a fair examination of the Catholic case by his countrymen.[6]

The missionaries were also firmly persuaded that the founding of an American house would provide a greater incentive to American youths to join the Community. One result of the missions was the increase of native vocations but the missionaries felt that the Congregation was not attracting as many candidates as it should. In the popular mind, Redemptorists were far too often regarded as a German group dedicated to the salvation of the immigrant. This characterization lessened their appeal for young men born and raised in this country. The American Bishop of Louisville, Martin John Spalding, also considered this an obstacle to the recruiting of vocations. He felt sure that a separate house for English-speaking religious with the special object of providing missions to American Catholics would appeal to "young men of talent who not rarely are converted to the Holy Catholic Faith in this country; but these American young men only with difficulty are persuaded to enter into a Congregation where for the most part the Superiors are German."[7]

Sometimes a young American consulting his spiritual director about joining the Redemptorists met with no encouragement. He might even find strong objections as had Father Deshon, whose confessor as well as his bishop objected to his entering the Congregation. They reasoned that the Redemptorist houses "were all German and that he would be cut off as a missionary from his proper relations with the people of his own country." It was only as the result of the "personal and sharp interference" of McMaster that the Bishop finally approved young Deshon's decision to join the Redemptorists.[8]

Then too the American Fathers believed that an American house was absolutely necessary for the stability and efficiency of their Catholic missions. There is no doubt that the missionaries were laboring under practical difficulties. They were stationed in three different and separated houses of their Community. Fathers Hecker and Deshon were in New York; Fathers Walworth and Hewit were in Baltimore and Father Baker in Annapolis. This was not an ideal situation since they had no opportunity to talk over their mission schedule and its development nor discuss their common mission problems. When the mission season began, each had to obtain the permission of his local superior before he could start out. Often the superior felt he needed an order from the provincial before he could grant such a request. The difficulty increased when the Fathers went from a small mission to a larger one requiring additional priests. Then they had to forward a request to the provincial after they found out where he might be, since his duties required him to visit the different houses. When he gave his consent, another letter had to go to the desired missionary or his immediate superior. Such a chain of command involving needless waste of time would be eliminated if all the missionaries were located in one house and living under the same superior. In effect this would create a central headquarters for the missionaries which would handle all their affairs including a prompt reply to a request for a mission.[9]

In the minds of the American missionaries these reasons more than sufficed for the establishment of their desired foundation. But there was one other of paramount importance to both Father Hecker and Father Hewit: it would give the Community a greater opportunity to work for the conversion of the American non-Catholic. Despite the wave of anti-Catholic bigotry stirred up by the Know-Nothing movement, Father Hecker was convinced that America was ready to listen to the claims of the Church. The success of the Norfolk mission and the reception given to *Ques-*

tions of the Soul demonstrated the importance of trying "to win and not simply beat our opponents." The way to capture the American mind was not by overpowering arguments that shattered all objections, nor devastating logic that demolished the citadels of error, but "the simple exposition of truth." A positive, appealing presentation, Father Hecker maintained, "attracts hearts." If the missionaries were together, they could collaborate in preparing this type of sermon and work out a program for presenting their views to the non-Catholic. The unified approach of a group of Redemptorists attached to an American house of the Community would give an official Redemptorist sanction to the movement for the conversion of America.[10]

When Father Ruland returned from the General Chapter in 1855, the American missionaries, especially Father Hecker, broached the subject of the foundation of a house for English-speaking Redemptorists. The Provincial said such a proposition was not feasible because of the limited number of Fathers. To start a new foundation with a shortage of personnel would be impractical and unwise. In the normal course of development, he explained, a house of this type would evolve naturally.[11] Apparently the missionaries saw the validity of these reasons and to Father Ruland's relief did not press the point further at that time.

Although Father Bernard had a high regard for both America and Americans, Father Ruland did not share his sentiments. At the height of the Know-Nothing movement, for instance, he thought the republic was close to dissolution. He was convinced, he wrote to Father Mauron, "that the *Union has had her longest day.*"[12] Nor was he more enthusiastic about the American character. His observations led him to conclude, he told the Rector Major, that Americans had too much freedom and independence. The basis of all home training in this country was not blind obedience but reasoned obedience.* Children were told not only what

---

* Obedience, which is essentially the submission of the will to that of lawful superiors as the representatives of God, can be divided into blind and reasoned. Blind obedience means the submission of one's judgment without question to that of the superior. It places the person in the hands of the superior "after the manner of a staff . . . after the manner of a corpse." Reasoned obedience acts in this way with regard to rules and constitutions which a religious attempts to fulfill as perfectly as possible. However, it recognizes that a superior can be mistaken and if his command seems unwise will permit the individual to ask the superior for an explanation. If after the explanation, the reasons given fail to convince the subject,

they should do but why they should do it. Anything the American interprets as arbitrariness, "he simply disregards or ignores." The spirit inculcated in early youth grew stronger as the child developed into a man. It was directly opposed to the European discipline wherein instant and willing compliance to every command was drilled into the consciousness of the youngster.[13]

An American who goes into religious life does not, according to Father Ruland, lose the habit of reasoned obedience nor does he acquire the practice of unquestioning compliance. He still looks for reasons for his actions. Firmly persuaded that his analysis was correct, Father Ruland shuddered to think what would happen to the Congregation if it came under American leadership too quickly. The transition from German guidance must be gradual in the hope that American Redemptorists would imbibe the spirit that he so highly regarded in his own countrymen. Authority within the American Province should pass from the European German to the American born of German parents and then ulti- mately to the Americans of native stock. For this reason, he told the Fathers entrusted with the training of future members of the Community to be more severe with the Americans than with others. He wanted to promote "the admittance of German- Americans" more than that of the native of American ancestry.[14] Filled with these ideas, Father Ruland could never welcome the proposal of an English-speaking Redemptorist house. In all sin- cerity he believed that it would create a division between the Germans and the Americans which would lead ultimately to hostility and schism within the Community.[15]

Many Europeans shared Father Ruland's pessimistic evalua- tion of the American character. The Rector of the English College in Rome, Dr. Wiseman (later Cardinal), found out that an Ameri- can resented capricious and arbitrary action no matter what its source. He tried to persuade an American student at the college to vacate his rooms in favor of a young Englishman of distin- guished family. When persuasion failed, he moved the American's

---

he complies. But if he sincerely and honestly believes that the superior is acting contrary to the rules of the institute or in a way harmful to its best interests, he feels obliged to call the fact to the attention of higher authority, even the highest authority or the Holy See. Then having fulfilled the dictates of reasoned obedience, he accepts that decision without qualification.

possessions out of the room while he was at class and locked the door. But the evicted student did not let the matter drop there. He finally secured an audience with the Holy Father and explained what happened. The next day he was moved back into his room. After this incident Wiseman said: "So long as I am head of this college, no Americans shall get into it again. They won't obey anything but law."[16]

The alert Brownson had recognized how erroneously his fellow men were judged: "There are many wrong notions entertained abroad and by a portion even of our own clergy with regard to the American people. They are supposed to be at heart, when not in conduct, a nation of rebels and filibusters whom hardly the grace of God can render loyal and obedient." Then he went on to show where our critics had failed to distinguish: "Blind obedience and unreasoning loyalty certainly is not [to] be expected of them. They cannot be governed as stones or machines, but they are at heart a loyal people, only they will be loyal to law, not to persons; to principles and not to show. . . . They retain and will retain, even in the most perfect obedience, a certain independence of feeling in presence of authority which belongs to men brought up in freedom and which men accustomed to more supple and servile forms mistake for the spirit of pride and disobedience. But it is not so. No people are really more submissive or easily governed than Americans."[17]

There was another point on which the Provincial was mistaken. When the missionaries spoke of a house for English-speaking members of the Community, he understood them to mean only American subjects. All German Fathers would be excluded and the superior would have to be an American. But the missionaries had no such notions. What they were seeking was a foundation for Fathers who had a grasp of English, regardless of racial background. The language spoken in the house would be English; sermons as well as devotions and confessions would be exclusively in that language. Never once did they stipulate that they wanted an exclusively American house and superior.[18]

Other Redemptorists of the Province saw nothing unusual in the desire of their American brethren to have an English-speaking house. A Hollander, Father Giesen said: "What is surprising in the fact that these Americans wanted an English* house when so many Fathers proclaimed loudly: 'We are here only for the Germans.' "[19] The German-born Father Luette told Father Deshon that "an English Redemptorist Church" would be of incalculable advantage "for the good of souls."[20] Another foreign born, Father Leimgruber, freely admitted that there were some non-American Redemptorists who were in favor of such an establishment "as soon as possible." These Fathers saw nothing alarming or frightening in the type of foundation their American confreres were seeking.[21]

Many of Father Ruland's fears and suspicions were unknown to his Redemptorist brethren, especially the missionaries. That he harbored them is clearly revealed in his correspondence with the Rector Major, but he did not discuss them with anyone in the Province, least of all the missionaries. Had he done so, many of his fears would have been dispelled and his suspicions cleared away before they became firmly fixed in his mind. Rather than enter into any discussion or explain his basic objections, however, he preferred to let the issue lie dormant in the hope that it would gradually be forgotten. Until it should become a vital and pressing question, he wished to avoid discussing it, lest he provoke an "undesired controversy that would do much harm and serve no purpose."[22]

The desire for an American house was no passing fancy with the missionaries. It was deeply rooted in their devotion and loyalty to both the Church and the Congregation. They saw the future effectiveness of the Redemptorists in America as well as the spread of Catholicism in their country closely linked with that foundation and they were determined to take "all lawful and proper means to hasten its foundation."[23] They had their first opportunity in the spring of 1857 when Father Walworth called on Bishop Bayley to discuss a mission for St. James Church in Newark. During the course of the conversation, the Bishop suggested the possibility of the Redemptorists taking charge of an English-speaking parish in his diocese. Father Walworth regarded the offer as an answer to prayer, especially when the Bishop assured him that the Fathers would be responsible only for the particular congregation

---

* The terms "English house" and "English Fathers" frequently appear in the correspondence as synonymous with "American house" and "American Fathers."

attached to the church and left free to carry on their missions which "would always be a paramount object with us."[24]

Immediately after leaving the Bishop, Father Walworth sat down and wrote a long letter to the Provincial acquainting him with all the details of the proposal and adding reasons why he thought the Community should accept the Bishop's offer. Since there were eight English-speaking Fathers with three students to be ordained within the next two years, he believed the time had come to start such a foundation. It would give the Congregation a firm and permanent foothold in this country and would attract many American boys into the Community long before the tide of immigration had ebbed.

Then Father Walworth brought up the touchy subject of nationalism: "I have heard it said, although I don't remember when or where, that the establishment of an English house would make a separation in the congregation. It seemed to me a very thoughtless and ungenerous remark." As long as all the houses in the Province lived under the same Rule, the same superiors, and the same obedience in everything, he saw no danger to unity and harmony. "It makes no difference what language is spoken in the houses, the pulpit or the confessional. Our rule has no recognized language and God forbid it ever should." The real danger of a separation, Father Walworth contended, was in the principle: "the houses of this Province are to be exclusively German." If such a principle were admitted, none but Germans would ever join the Congregation and "those of us already in the fold would be made to feel like exiles in our own birthplace and with no possible relief but to be transferred to England or Ireland." Quickly he added that he did not think that Father Ruland "would harbor or patronize such an odious spirit of exclusion or forget that our order is Catholic and embraces the wide world."[25]

In conclusion, Father Walworth asked the Provincial to take no immediate action until he had spoken with him. He would return to Baltimore within two weeks and then he would discuss the proposition more at length. Meanwhile he wished him to keep the matter a secret.[26]

Before mailing this letter, Father Walworth gave it to the New York Rector, Father Helmpraecht, as well as to Father Deshon to read. Neither saw anything objectionable in it, so he sent it on to Baltimore.[27] But the letter had quite a different effect on the Provincial. It filled him with fear and worry and awakened all his old prejudices. Faithful to part of Father Walworth's injunction to keep the matter secret, he said nothing to his consultors. But he did write to the Rector Major. Perhaps because of his anxiety, he either misread or misunderstood what Father Walworth had written. He told Father Mauron that Father Walworth had sent "a formal program for the founding of a house for the *English* Fathers."[28] Actually there was neither a formal program nor a formal request in the letter. All that Father Walworth had done was to acquaint his superior with the offer of the Bishop of Newark and to express a hope that he would support it. But at the same time he asked him not to take any action until he could discuss the proposal further with him.

In his letter to the Rector Major, the Provincial made some statements that put the American Fathers in a very bad light with their superiors in Rome. He expressed his fear "that our English Fathers are driven more by natural than by supernatural motives and that is why I fear their plans are not free from danger." The dangers that he envisioned were nationalism and the harm that would result to discipline within the Community. He assumed that if a foreigner were appointed superior of the new foundation, it would be "distasteful to the Americans." Apparently he had forgotten that the American Fathers had been foremost in the move for the return of Father Bernard only two years before. There was not the slightest indication in Father Walworth's letter that the Americans expected to have a superior of their own choice. Further, he overlooked the expression that unity consisted "in the same obedience in everything." The Provincial was convinced that if an American house existed with an American superior, discipline would not only be "greatly altered but also very relaxed."[29]

Father Ruland's main reason for writing to the Rector Major was to ask for an official statement of policy on the question of nationalism. He asked: "What principles am I to follow generally, in matters which play a part in the 'national' sphere?" He told the General that, until he had word from Rome, he would parry the question of the American house by saying he was waiting for the Rector Major's decision. Also he added that whatever the decision might be, he thought the creation of the new foundation should be postponed.[30]

When Father Walworth returned to Baltimore the last week of May, he discussed Bishop Bayley's offer with the Provincial. Father Ruland told him he had written to Rome and was awaiting the Rector Major's decision. Although surprised that the Provincial had not acceded to his request to wait before taking any official action, Father Walworth said nothing about the precipitous move. Immediately he asked if he had written in favor of the proposal. The Provincial said he had not and could not since he believed such a foundation would ultimately lead to the ruin of the Congregation. During the course of the conversation, Father Ruland asked "directly and emphatically" if Father Walworth had in mind a house only for American- or English-speaking Fathers to the exclusion of all others. Promptly Father Walworth declared he had no such idea. All he desired was a foundation where English would be the accepted language in both house and church.[31] This answer pleased the Provincial who was concerned about the fate of the German-American members of the Community in the years to come when the German element would become extinct. After Father Walworth told the Provincial that the American Fathers would willingly accept a German Father as superior, all opposition seemed to crumble. Father Ruland said he would write to Rome giving his approval and encouragement. He gave both Fathers Walworth and Hewit the impression that he was so wholeheartedly in favor of the American house that Father Hewit wrote: "he entered into it *corde et anima.*"[32]

During the early part of these negotiations, Father Hecker was in Cuba. In the hope of speeding his recovery from an attack of pneumonia suffered in January of 1857, he left New York on March 10th with George Hecker and his wife. He did not return until May 22nd when Father Deshon acquainted him with all the details of the American house.[33] He was delighted with the news but felt that New York would be a much more central location for the new foundation than Newark. When Father Hewit wrote to tell him of the Provincial's hearty approval of the American house, he added: "Now do all you can by prayer and other means to get us a good place."[34] Apparently Father Hecker took these words of the Provincial Consultor to mean that he was free to seek a location in New York. Sometime before the Provincial was expected for his visitation, Father Hecker called on Archbishop Hughes who received him very cordially and offered the Community a location in the vicinity of 58th Street and 9th Avenue.[35] Since the New York Redemptorists were awaiting the arrival of the Provincial, Father Hecker did not write about the offer but waited to discuss it with him personally.

Not one of the American Fathers doubted for a moment that the American house was shortly to become a reality. They had the Provincial's word that he had written to the Rector Major favoring the proposition and they saw no reason to suspect any opposition. Their optimism would not have been so great nor their hopes so sanguine however, had they known the content of the Provincial's letter. He gave no hearty endorsement of the project but a very qualified approval, so qualified that it served to kill all their hopes. He told the Rector Major of his conversation with Father Walworth and the willingness of the Americans to accept German subjects as well as a German superior; that, according to them, they did not want an exclusively American house but only one in which "English would be preached as elsewhere German is preached"; that when he learned this, he told the American Fathers "he would even advocate" the new establishment. Father Walworth, he wrote, gave as an added reason: if there were such a foundation then they could assist in the church after they returned from missions since services would be conducted in their native tongue. This they could not do in their present foundations where they were reduced for all practical purposes to the status of "guests" in their own homes.[36]

As he had done in his previous letter, Father Ruland then made some observations on the character of the American Fathers. These observations were merely his own opinions but in the eyes of the authorities at Rome they appeared to be a grave indictment. He wrote: "I think some of the English Fathers have a bit too much national feeling which later on, when they shall have a house of their own, will develop more strongly and therefore become detrimental to the Congregation." His additional comments not only lent credence to the accusation of nationalism but added that of laxity. Father Walworth had said that the American Fathers would willingly accept a German superior but the Provincial found this difficult to believe: "I do not see how they will put up with a local or Provincial Superior who is not English." If the superior were to be an American, who would it be? If it were Hecker, Hewit, or Walworth, he had grave forebodings: "I do not know what should become of the Rules and Constitutions and even of the Congregation. . . . They would let rules remain rules and plan to do everything according to what they think proper, rather than according to the rules." He showed a preference for Father Baker who had "decidedly the best spirit of them all" but he was still too young and untried. In fact, he looked over the entire Province and could think of no one suitable for the post: "I do not know how to find [a superior] among the other Fathers." Finally he asked for a postponement of the foundation "until such time that a German Father can be included. The English Fathers, I think, will be satisfied if, for the present, they are given hope that they will get a house."[37]

Father Ruland's suspicions, which he regarded as facts, pivoted on the two thorny issues of nationalism and laxity. Both had caused considerable harm to the Community in the past, especially in the kingdom of Naples, and had led to the creation of two distinct Redemptorist Congregations. That had taken place four years before the American Fathers had made their proposal. Now the Provincial reported to the Rector Major in Rome that these same twin evils were appearing within his jurisdiction and would ultimately cause another separation. This was the problem Father Ruland handed to Father Mauron for a decision. The Rector Major had no choice. He must act decisively even if severely to root out any thorns of dissension. Accordingly, on June 28th, he took up the matter with his consultors. Telling them of the proposal for a foundation in Newark which Father Walworth had submitted, he said that the Provincial rightly saw in this petition "the spirit of nationality and division." No prolonged discussion was necessary to reach the decision that the American Fathers should be told the Rector Major would never accept a foundation "exclusively for one nation, nor could he tolerate the spirit of nationality. It would be better if they would depart than to disturb the Congregation with their spirit unsuited to Community life." He had no opposition to a foundation where the exercise of the pastoral office would be carried on in English when the number of people would warrant it. That would come about in time. It could not be considered at the present moment since a new foundation had been accepted in Canada "where Fathers well versed in English are necessary."[38]

On a warm sultry Tuesday, July 21st, the Rector Major's decision reached Baltimore. He had written a four-page letter in German that came as a bombshell which surprised the Provincial and shocked the American Fathers. A purely English house, he declared, would mean the destruction of the Congregation in America. Although he was consoled by the Provincial's second letter telling him that Father Walworth did not intend such a foundation, he wanted it clearly understood that he would not tolerate any plans "which are in direct contradiction to the universality, the nature and the spirit of our Congregation. If however such a thing should happen despite my expectation, you may be assured that I shall step in with energy and unremitting severity, since I would not wish to burden my conscience with the responsibility for the deterioration of our Congregation. However great the need for workers in America, I would in such a case have no hesitation in releasing from the Congregation such obstinate adherents of these ideas, rather than to allow them to take root in our Congregation."[39]

Referring to Father Walworth's added reason that in an American foundation the Fathers after their missions would be gainfully occupied and not merely guests, he said it neither pleased nor edified him. Recalling St. Alphonsus' desire that the Fathers should spend a part of each year on missions and the remaining time in recollection, prayer, and studies, he thought the Americans were complaining about an arrangement that in reality was a blessing. "It is certainly not such an unbearable fate to dedicate part of each year to regular observance, pious exercises and studies without being swallowed up by works of the ministry and by labors in the pulpit and in the confessional." Then he asked: "Have they not found the best, the most beautiful, the most enviable lot, who labor part of each year on missions and the remaining time on their own sanctification, the most magnificent, fruitful and blessed part of our vocation?"

Continuing the same theme, he thought that the Americans

"despite all their other good and praiseworthy qualities have not sufficient reverence for the authority of our Holy Rule and our saintly founder, nor do they lay sufficient emphasis on the strict observance of our Rule. They appear to consider it permissible to occupy themselves with thoughts of how to arrange better and more efficiently many of the things prescribed by our Rule and enjoined by our holy founder. Such an attitude is not in keeping with the known sayings of our holy founder, that the welfare of the Congregation, its growth and the happy result of its apostolic works and every blessing from above, depend upon the scrupulous observance of the Rule." Admitting that owing to local conditions, certain unessential modifications might be required, he laid down three principles to follow: first, the nature and spirit of the Rule concerning the spiritual life and domestic discipline was to be firmly maintained "at all times, in all places and among all nationalities"; second, superiors were the ones to judge what unessential modifications should be permitted; third, every true Redemptorist must be permeated not only with the greatest reverence for the Rule and the sayings of the Founder, but also "with the most ardent wish to observe the Rule, as closely as possible, in letter and in spirit." Finally, Father Mauron asked the Provincial to translate the letter faithfully into English, or have it translated and then "communicate it to his consultors as well as to the American Fathers."[40]

Within a day or two after he received this letter, Father Ruland read it first to Father Walworth and then to Father Hewit. Both were thunderstruck as they listened to the Rector Major's reprimand. They protested vehemently that they had been maligned, that the allegations sent to Rome against them were entirely unfounded. Never for a moment had they been motivated by a spirit of nationalism which they despised and detested. Father Walworth said he knew of no such spirit in the Province. Strangely enough, although the Provincial had written in a different vein to Father Mauron, he agreed with Walworth, and said: "I do not know of any such thing among us. If in any religious order and in any part of the world national spirit is lost in a common attachment to the order and in fraternal charity, I believe it is here."[41]

Perhaps at this point the Provincial might have thought he had misjudged the Fathers. Certainly he gave them to understand that he did not think they were infected with any such nationalistic virus. As he read further in the letter, he saw that Father Walworth was highly incensed because he believed someone had misrepresented him at Rome. So he decided not to translate Father Mauron's observations that the Americans seemed to lack the proper attitude toward the authority of the Rule and the sayings of St. Alphonsus. Omitting that paragraph, he read Father Mauron's three principles governing unessential changes. He did the same with Father Hewit.[42]

This letter particularly affected Father Walworth since the Rector Major seemed to consider him a discontented and unworthy subject. He begged the Provincial to correct this false impression and "to speak favorably about him" the next time he wrote to Rome.[43] Hoping that through the good offices of the Provincial he could salvage his reputation, Father Walworth's next concern was to save the American house. But the prospects were not very bright. Father Ruland gave him and Father Hewit the "disastrous news" that the Community had accepted two new posts which would fall within the jurisdiction of the American Province. One was in the Island of St. Thomas in the British West Indies, the other in Quebec. He explained that the Holy Father had asked the Rector Major to establish a foundation in St. Thomas which would require two English-speaking Fathers.[44]

The proposed foundation at Quebec stunned Father Walworth. He knew that the Vicar-General of the diocese, Father Cazeau, had come to Baltimore at the request of Bishop Baillargeon in May of 1856 to ask the Redemptorists to take over a parish in his diocese. Since Father Ruland was away when he called, Father Walworth spoke to him and found the offer very unattractive. The parish was small and uninviting, the property in the hands of trustees, and there was very little, if any, opportunity for mission work.[45] Contrary to Walworth's expectation, the Provincial had written to Father Mauron who told him to "continue the preliminary negotiations so as to begin at Quebec in 1858."[46] The Provincial explained to Father Walworth that with the consent of Father Mauron he had made a promise to Bishop Baillargeon and he would have to redeem it. Father Walworth asked him if he knew what he was getting into and explained the situation in Quebec. Father Ruland seemed surprised and said he was going to visit the diocese and if conditions were so unsatisfactory, he would undoubtedly decline. Then he told the Fathers not to give up hope; he thought they would have their foundation "soon after all." He promised he would write to Rome and push their project.[47]

After their conference with Father Ruland, both Fathers decided to write to the Rector Major and declare that they were innocent of the charges made against them and also to explain what they meant by an American house. On July 25th, Father Walworth wrote a long letter in which he quoted the Provincial's words denying the existence of nationalism within his jurisdiction. Then Walworth said: "So far, I have never seen that any of our German Brethren looked on us who are natives with less affection on that account, nor could we love them more if they had been born in this country, and if their native tongue were English." He asked the Rector Major: "If your Reverence, by any inquiries, can find evidence of so detestable a spirit in me, I beg of you, for the love of God to visit it with that unrelenting severity promised in your letter. But it will not be found necessary. We can love each other without a whip." Turning from the personal to the general issue of the American foundation, he detailed the difficulties they had experienced as missionaries living in different houses, difficulties which an American foundation would remove. An increase of vocations was an added inducement for establishing such a house "which cannot fail to recommend itself to your Reverence's watchful solicitude for the welfare of this Province."[48]

Mentioning that the Provincial had said "an establishment is contemplated at Quebec where an English congregation has been offered to our care," he detailed the shortcomings and problems that made the offer not only unattractive but highly undesirable. He concluded his letter by saying: "I am asking for no personal favors for myself, making no complaints of others. I am pleading only for what I know is important to the cause of souls and the interests of a Congregation dearer to me than anything else on earth. I have not written this letter without both prayers and tears."[49]

Two days later Father Hewit wrote a more restrained but no less emphatic explanation in the hope that he could "remove or greatly diminish some of the causes of anxiety" in the mind of the Rector Major "about the attitude of the American members of the

Community." Then he used a personal but effective argument to remove any stigma attaching to his own character: "At the time of my entry into the Congregation, I gave no concern whether or not other Americans were to be with me. I wanted only to become a Religious and had I felt any antipathy towards the Germans, I could very easily have entered the Jesuits where everything is English. It would be a great ingratitude towards the Fathers who, at that time received me kindly if I now should repay them with rejection or unreasonable contempt. Therefore, I do not aim at a separation, nor at a foundation that is to be exclusively American." Pointing out that all the Fathers in the Philadelphia houses were German and that all the Irish-born Redemptorists were together in New Orleans, he significantly noted: "But no one regards it as coming from enmity or rejection against others to have Fathers of the same tongue or nationality together." The implication was obvious: why then should the Americans be criticized and condemned for wishing to be together in the same house? He told Father Mauron that their motive was not nationalism but a desire to stabilize their mission work, adding that it would also give them "the opportunity to work together for the conversion of Protestants."[50]

The Provincial's attitude both during and after the reading of Father Mauron's letter encouraged Fathers Walworth and Hewit. In a letter to Father Hecker, giving him all the "disastrous news" they said Father Ruland seemed to be as much dejected and distressed by "the unfortunate turn of affairs" as they were. Describing him as being "heartily" with them, they looked upon him as their only hope. They urged Father Hecker not to wait for the Provincial's arrival in New York, but to go to Philadelphia and see him there since "his will is good" but he needs "a great deal of posting up." Father Walworth also suggested that Father Hecker call on Archbishop Hughes and Bishop Bayley and ask them to make their offers directly to the Provincial or the Rector Major. Their influence would be much greater coming personally than through the mediation of one of the Fathers.[51]

When Father Hecker received this letter, he did not share the confidence of Fathers Hewit and Walworth in the Provincial. He concluded that the Provincial had sent the information to Rome that drew such a sharp rebuke from the Rector Major and this despite the fact that he had assured Father Walworth in their first discussion of the Newark proposal that he was heartily in favor of the American house and would write to Rome endorsing the project. Either he had sent the letter and his words had no weight at Rome or he had failed to keep his promise and had written against the plan. In either case, they could not depend upon the Provincial for effective action. Father Hecker had also heard from other Fathers in the Community who had better sources of information than he that the Provincial had "constantly" reported "unfavorably" on the American Fathers. He knew too that the Rector Major dealt only with the Provincial and depended on him for all his knowledge of the Province. Letters of explanation and justification, Father Hecker concluded, would accomplish very little. Meanwhile St. Thomas and Quebec would be accepted, their little band would be tapped to supply subjects, and any prospect of an American house would be relegated to the distant future. Father Hecker saw only one course of action: one of their group must go to Rome and present their case personally to the Rector Major. If the Rector Major knew the true state of affairs in the American Province, Father Hecker was confident that not only would he cease to regard the American Fathers as rebels and malcontents but he would also recognize the urgency of an American foundation.[52]

Convinced that this was the only satisfactory way to deal with the problem, he offered to make the trip. He spoke to Father Deshon who was heartily in accord with the plan. When he told Father Walworth and Father Hewit, both not only agreed but added that it was very necessary: "It is impossible to explain all these matters by letter. It requires a great deal of talking to show how fatal those new establishments would be to our missions and how necessary a missionary establishment [is] here."[53]

The hearty and unqualified concurrence of his co-workers confirmed Father Hecker in his resolve. He would go to Rome. Before the Rector Major he would plead for an English-speaking house in America to advance the cause of the Church and insure a brighter future for the Redemptorists.

CHAPTER XII

A Controversial Circular

THE last week of July, 1857, was hectic for the American
missionaries and harrowing for the Provincial. It was a week of
discussions, explanations, and disputes which resulted in misunderstandings, disagreements, suspicions, and distrust. There was no
meeting of minds, no coming to grips with basic fundamentals.
The Provincial and the American Fathers began with different
sets of principles and proceeded along parallel lines. As neither
could agree on mutual rights, they drew farther apart as tensions
increased.

The fundamental disagreement arose over Father Hecker's proposed trip to Rome. After their sessions with Father Ruland,
Fathers Hewit and Walworth were convinced that the Provincial
would readily give their companion permission for the journey. All
he had to do, they told Father Hecker, was to explain his reasons
and Father Ruland would grant the permission. Acting on this
information, Father Hecker applied for his passport and booked
passage on the *Asia* even before the Provincial came to New York.[1]

But the Baltimore Fathers were mistaken. They had overesti-
mated the Provincial's seeming good will. While they supposed he
was willing to co-operate, in reality he was trying to compromise.
On his part, Father Ruland had underestimated the intensity of
the Fathers' desire for an American house. He seemed to regard
that desire as a purely personal concern for their own convenience
and happiness which he could parry with promises. But the missionaries were convinced that the immediate interests, as well as the

future success of the Redemptorists in America, demanded prompt and effective action to hasten the establishment of this foundation. Their duty as devoted and loyal members of the Congregation was to take that action.

While Father Hecker and Father Deshon awaited the Provincial's arrival in New York, they recognized two formidable obstacles in their path: the Rector Major's mistaken notion of their character and motives and his imperfect knowledge of the American scene. Until he had firsthand and accurate information on both points, he would never consent to the new establishment. Only a detailed explanation given by one of the missionaries could supply this information. To secure the Provincial's permission to carry out this undertaking, they marshaled their arguments and when he arrived in New York on July 27th, they began to plead their case. They opened by saying that the severe and extreme threat of expulsion contained in Father Mauron's letter was undeniable evidence that he regarded them as "rebels and partisans." This the Provincial denied and explained that Father Mauron was merely using his first letter of May 29, 1857, as a springboard for a general warning. In saying this, Father Ruland was equivalently admitting that his report was the cause of Father Mauron's reprimand. Father Deshon then asked why the Provincial had written about the Newark proposal which Father Walworth had asked him to keep secret until he could discuss it fully with him. Father Ruland replied that he interpreted the request to mean he was not to talk with anyone in America but he certainly never understood it to extend even to letters to Father Mauron. Such an interpretation surprised Father Deshon who said he had read the letter and thought its meaning was obvious.[2]

This statement of Father Deshon aroused the Provincial's suspicions. He immediately concluded that all the American Fathers had known of the Newark affair before he did and yet had asked him to keep the matter a secret. He believed that they had hatched a plot and were acting as conspirators to force him to grant their request.[3] The suspicion of course, was unfounded. Father Hecker was in Cuba when Bishop Bayley made his offer and did not learn of it until his return at least two weeks after Father Walworth had submitted the proposal. Father Hewit was in Baltimore and heard of it only after Father Walworth had returned from

Albany and had discussed it with the Provincial. The mere fact that Father Deshon had read the letter before it was mailed did not imply a conspiracy. If it did, then Father Helmpraecht would have been equally guilty since he too had seen the letter before it was mailed to the Provincial.[4] Had Father Ruland mentioned his suspicions, they could have been dissipated by a recital of facts. But he said nothing about them.

After this preliminary discussion, Father Hecker told the Provincial that there was only one way to clear the good name of the American Fathers and convince the Rector Major of the necessity and importance of their foundation: a personal visit to Father Mauron. Then he asked Father Ruland to give him permission to go to Rome. This unusual request amazed the Provincial. He told Father Hecker he could not grant such permission since there was no reason for him to go to Rome, and since the Fathers could accomplish their purpose just as successfully by writing. Father Hecker objected that they could never achieve their purpose through correspondence. He asserted that they had been so thoroughly discredited at Rome that no amount of mail would erase the blot on their reputations. Moreover, while they awaited word to travel from New York to Rome and back again orders would come from Father Mauron to staff Quebec and St. Thomas, leaving no personnel available for the American house. Father Ruland tried to counter this objection by quoting the General's words that he was not opposed to an English-speaking house which "must infallibly come about by itself."[5] Father Hecker had heard almost these same words from the Provincial some time before. On that occasion, Father Ruland had explained that in the course of time, with the gradual decline of immigration, German would no longer be spoken in the houses, and there would be not one but many American foundations. By that time, Father Hecker had replied, they would all be dead and buried: so too would be the glorious opportunities now awaiting the Community.[6]

Once again Father Hecker returned to his main argument. His interest in the new foundation was not personal and selfish. His only ambition was to promote the interests of the Community and the good of religion. Unless he could explain all this in detail and in person to the Rector Major, there was no hope for the American house.

Aware of Father Hecker's zealous determination and anxious to show his own good will, Father Ruland offered to write to Rome for permission to purchase property in New York for the foundation and to do everything in his power to establish that house before the one in Quebec. He even said he would find a way to nullify his promise to Bishop Baillargeon. Both Father Hecker and Father Deshon countered that all this would require time. Like the sword of Damocles, Quebec was hanging over their head and any moment orders which could not be countermanded might come from Rome to send English-speaking Fathers to Bishop Baillargeon's diocese. Then all would be lost.[7]

Both Fathers continued to urge the Provincial to grant permission for the Roman trip, but he refused to yield. Maintaining that he did not have the authority, he cited a special circular issued by the Rector Major forbidding such a journey without his explicit permission. Although the Fathers were familiar with this circular which had been sent to all the houses of the Province on June 12, 1857, they had not judged it pertinent to their case. It had derived from an entirely different set of circumstances and they considered it applicable only to that specific type of situation.

The Rector Major had issued this official letter as a result of the imprudent and scandalous action of Father Felix Bretschka, a German Redemptorist in the American Province. In November of 1856, Father Bretschka left the Redemptorist house in Rochester and departed for Europe. Because of an overwhelming desire to see his ailing mother before her death, he had simply walked out without saying a word to his superior or to the Provincial. After visiting in Germany, he finally appeared in Rome in January of 1857 to explain his action to the Rector Major. To justify his conduct, he quoted from the 1764 Constitutions which recognized the right of a Redemptorist to journey to Rome on urgent business which admitted of no delay. But the Constitutions also required that he must at least ask for the permission before he could start out. But Bretschka had no case. He had not sought any permission; his reason for leaving America was not urgent; he had not gone directly to Rome. He was clearly guilty of a serious violation of his vow of obedience. Knowing that he was facing the penalty of dismissal from the Congregation, Father Bretschka pleaded for leniency. However, his previous record was spotty. For two years before he left America, he had committed serious breaches of discipline. This double indictment sealed his fate and Father Mauron expelled him from the Congregation on January 9, 1857.[8]

Shortly after his dismissal, Bretschka again besought the General for clemency, denying the disciplinary charges against him. When two of his confreres in Europe interceded for him, Father Mauron decided to suspend sentence until he could obtain additional information from America. After new evidence substantiating the charges reached Rome, the Rector Major on May 5, 1857, reinstated the previous dismissal.[9]

When this incident first occurred, Father Mauron intended to send word to the States forbidding any of the Fathers to come to Rome without first obtaining his written permission.[10] When the Bretschka case was finally adjudicated, the Rector Major drew up on May 9, 1857, what was to become a highly controversial circular. In the first paragraph, Father Mauron spoke of his delight in hearing two bishops from America, as well as Archbishop Bedini, praise the wonderful work the Redemptorists were doing in the New World. But while he was heartened by this commendation, he was afflicted by the Bretschka affair. Briefly relating the action of this disobedient Redemptorist, who had come to Rome without the permission of his superiors, "nay without saying a word to them," he announced to all:

> the expulsion of Father Bretschka from our Congregation for divers causes, but chiefly for his scandalous departure from America; and at the same time I make known that no one is permitted to leave America of his own will under penalty of expulsion from the Congregation automatically incurred. It was declared in the General Chapter [of 1855] that whoever came to Rome without previous permission of the Rector Major should incur expulsion, which prohibition especially applies to America. Wherefore, by these presents, I declare that anyone who leaves America without permission is automatically expelled.[11]

During the last days of July, 1857, this circular was subjected to many long and vehement discussions and explanations. It was analyzed, evaluated, and interpreted in an attempt to determine its precise meaning and extent, especially its application to the Constitutions. One of the articles of the Constitutions specified that a Redemptorist desiring to visit the Rector Major on urgent and important matters should first request the permission of his local superior who should not refuse it. If, however, he did, the subject had the constitutional right to make the visit. Since, then, the local superior was obliged to give the requisite permission, he certainly had the authority to do so. The all-important question was just how far did the Rector Major intend to alter the provision of the Constitutions. The Provincial maintained that this circular abrogated this and forbade *"each* and *everyone* under all circumstances to go to Rome without a written permission" from the Rector Major. Consequently, Father Mauron alone could give the permission.[12]

Father Hecker and Father Deshon disputed this interpretation. In the first place, they pointed out that nowhere in the document had the Rector Major used the words "written permission." Furthermore Father Mauron had not said that his permission was required, but merely that "anyone who leaves America without permission is automatically expelled." Father Deshon claimed that the Rector Major did not specify who could grant the permission. If he had meant that he alone could authorize such a journey, why did he not say so in clear and unmistakable language: "It is as easy for Father General to say without *my* permission, or without the permission *of the Father General,* as to say, as he has done, simply without *permission."* Therefore he concluded "the absence of the words [my, or the Rector Major's, permission] is conclusive evidence against the intention" of Father Mauron to deprive the Provincial of his constitutional right to authorize the journey. Therefore, Father Ruland still had the authority and could allow Father Hecker to go to Rome.[13]

This argument was based on a solid legal principle that you may not read into the law a wider application than the words will permit. If you do, then you tamper with the meaning and purpose of the law as well as the intentions of the lawmaker. But Father Ruland maintained he was not reading anything into the circular which cited the legislation of the 1855 Chapter forbidding a subject to come to Rome without the Rector Major's permission. Since Father Mauron joined that statement so closely to his prohibition, the Provincial concluded, the context clearly showed whose permission was required: "Not that of the Provincial, or the local superior but the permission of the Rector Major himself."[14]

Against this, Father Deshon held that the 1855 Chapter's decrees had not been approved by Rome, nor had they been promulgated pending action of the Holy See. Consequently they did not have the binding force of law. Until they were approved by Rome, they could not be made obligatory on the Community. The Rector Major had made this clear in his first official communication after his election. On July 26, 1855, he declared that until the 1855 Constitutions received official approbation, they would not be in force. Then Father Deshon asked: "Has not the Circular of the R.P. General the binding force of law?" Answering with an emphatic no, he quoted the Constitutions to show that the Rector Major has no authority to make new laws and constitutions nor to modify those already made. And he added that Father Mauron had given no evidence in his circular that he intended the declaration of the General Chapter to be binding. He cited it to show the sentiment of the General Chapter "by way of justification for the extraordinary exercise of a derogating power." But in no sense did he intend his reference to the 1855 Chapter to mean that he was constituting "this unapproved Rule into a special law for the American Province." Consequently any reference to this Chapter, he concluded, has no relation to the matter at issue. "Nothing exists [in the circular] which has taken away the authority of the superior or the right of the subject in this case."[15]

Pursuing the matter further, Father Deshon argued that all participants in the dispute agreed that the circular deprived them of "important privileges conceded by those Constitutions [of 1764]." Since it curtailed their rights, it should be interpreted according to the legal principle, restrictive measures are to be strictly interpreted. Hence the circular should be restricted to those cases fairly described in the document itself and not to others of a different nature." The only case mentioned in the circular was that of Bretschka, who had left the Province in an unauthorized and unlawful fashion. The fair interpretation of the General's letter, Father Deshon continued, was that anyone who acts as had Father Bretschka, "obtaining no permission," shall be expelled.[16]

The four American Fathers vigorously contended that Father Mauron hand in mind only situations comparable to Bretschka's and he was notifying the American Province that a repetition of similar conduct would merit instant and automatic expulsion.[17]

Father Hecker advanced the further argument that the Rector Major was forbidding anyone to come to Rome on purely private errands. But the circular "does not touch in any way whatever the right to send one to Rome on important and urgent affairs," concerning the general good of the Congregation. No one could imagine, he held, that the Rector Major ever intended to imperil the vital interest of the Community by requiring a delay until permission could be obtained from Rome: "Everything may go to ruin while one is waiting on this side of the water until permission to send an agent to Rome can be sent for and returned across the Atlantic."[18]

Despite all their arguments and interpretations, Father Ruland remained adamant for he knew the actual subjective intention of the Rector Major. On December 25, 1856, the General Secretary of the Congregation, Father Haringer, had written that the Rector Major would send a circular letter to the American Province in which "he will surely make it clear that no one is allowed without a written permission of the General to come to Rome and that he will judge the arbitrary leaving of the American Province as equivalent to the leaving of the Congregation and will punish it with dismissal."[19] There is no doubt in the light of this letter and subsequent developments in Rome that the Rector Major fully intended to restrict the right of any Redemptorist in the American Province to travel to Rome without his written permission. But the American Fathers knew nothing of this letter or of Father Mauron's intentions. All they had to guide them was the circular, and that document was couched in such terms that they could sincerely and honestly judge that it did not restrict the Provincial's constitutional authority. So they reasoned that, if in his judgment he thought that recourse to the Rector Major was necessary, he could authorize it.

In this sense, the American Fathers understood the circular and they could defend their position with legal principles and cogent arguments. Nor did they stand alone in their opinion. The Rector of the Baltimore house, Father Leimgruber, as well as the New York Rector, Father Helmpraecht, agreed with them. Father Joseph Mueller thought that if Father Hecker did make the journey, he would not risk expulsion. Father Helmpraecht went so far as to say that even he could grant the permission.[20]

When the intrinsic merits of their arguments failed to convince
Father Ruland, the Americans added the extrinsic weight of the
authority of the two Rectors and the Provincial Consultor. But
still Father Ruland would not budge as the Fathers hammered
home their arguments. Finally he exclaimed: "Do not press the
matter or you will drive me crazy."[21] He knew, as he later wrote
to Father Mauron, that "he stood alone" with his opinion. He
sorely felt the need of advice but he found "no one in New York
who could be helpful."[22]

In a final attempt to win over the Provincial, Father Hecker and
Father Deshon invited him to inspect the site which the Archbishop
had approved for the American house. Looking over the property,
he thought it was admirably suited for the foundation both as to
size and location. He was so well satisfied with it that he thought
it should be purchased as soon as possible and asked Father
Hecker if he could raise the money to buy it. Remembering Father
Mauron's refusal to sanction the Newark proposition, Father
Hecker wondered about the Provincial's suggestion and asked him
if he had the Rector Major's permission to begin the foundation
in New York. When Father Ruland said no, Father Hecker refused to take any step whatever without that approval.[23] However, because of the Provincial's interest, Father Hecker again
asked for permission to bring the whole matter before the Rector
Major. This time Father Ruland declared that if he thought he
had the authority to permit such a move, he would readily authorize it. Would he put that statement in writing? Father Hecker
asked. The Provincial agreed to do so. On July 31st, as Provincial
Superior he signed the following declaration which he had written
in German:

I, the undersigned, at the request of the Reverend Father I. Hecker,
C.SS.R., declare that I have looked at the site which has been selected
by the above-mentioned Father in the City of New York for the
erection of a house of our Congregation, and that the same not only
pleased me very well, but that it seems to me very well suited for
the end in view. I furthermore declare, that if I believed myself in
possession of the authority to send a Father of Our Congregation
to Rome to the Most Reverend Father General, I would in reference
to the above matter, without the slightest hesitation, have decided
that a Father of the English language should go to Rome, as has

been wished and as was requested of me to present then to the Most Reverend Father General whatever they would consider as necessary or good and proper.[24]

Besides giving Father Hecker this statement, Father Ruland told him and Father Deshon he was sorry that they had not started the project a year sooner and he regretted that he could not take more positive action at this time. Approving all that the missionaries had done, he did not complain that they had usurped his prerogatives or "exceeded in any respect the limits within which humble and obedient religious should confine themselves."[25]

Father Ruland's attitude and comments to the Fathers are very surprising when compared with a letter he wrote to Rome that very same day. On July 31st he began a nine-page account written in German, which he finished on August 3rd. In considerable detail, he informed the Rector Major of the stirring events that had taken place during these days, especially the Fathers' reaction to the circular and their insistence on the New York foundation. He told Father Mauron that he had found out that Father Hecker had seen Archbishop Hughes and selected the site, and that he viewed this as one more proof of the conspiracy formed by the American Fathers to force his hand. He believed that Father Hecker had negotiated with the Archbishop and offered him a foundation, but that he himself had learned of it only after it was a *fait accompli*. He complained that the Americans "had dealt with Bishops and made offers to them without my having even the faintest knowledge of it."[26]

If Father Ruland had known the sequence of events, he would never have reached this unfortunate conclusion. Had he even suggested that the missionaries explain why they had taken matters into their own hands, they could have cleared up the misunderstanding quickly. Father Hecker could have called his attention to facts which would have melted his disturbing suspicions. They had "dealt" with only two Bishops, Bayley and Hughes.

After Father Walworth had seen Bishop Bayley, he had sent immediately to the Provincial a written statement of the Bishop's offer even before some of his fellow missionaries knew a thing about it. With regard to the New York proceedings, the explanation was simple and understandable. After Father Walworth had corrected the Provincial's error on their concept of the American

house, Father Ruland gave him the impression that he was heartily
in favor of the project and would write to Rome endorsing it. His
co-operation seemed so sincere and so wholehearted that Father
Hewit was convinced the Provincial would soon move to make
their hopes a reality. They would have their American house. In
their minds there was only one problem to be settled: where
should this foundation be established? The Bishop of Newark had
offered them a parish in his diocese, but if Archbishop Hughes
would approve, New York would be a more ideal location. So
Father Hewit asked Father Hecker to sound out the Archbishop
on the proposition.[27] The reasoning behind this gesture was apparently to make sure that the Archbishop would welcome such a
foundation. If he would, then the Provincial would have this added
reason to offer the Rector Major. Motivated by these factors,
Father Hecker had called on Archbishop Hughes who was not only
willing but "desirous . . . that there should be another house of
your Order in New York for the spiritual benefit of the Catholics
who do not speak German."[28] To expedite matters for the Provincial, Father Hecker selected a site which the Archbishop approved. Since all of this had taken place so close to the time of
the Provincial's expected arrival in New York, Father Hecker
waited to explain it personally instead of by mail.[29]

With this explanation, Father Ruland would have understood
that Father Hecker had made no agreements whatsoever with the
Archbishop nor had he acted in a clandestine and scheming fashion.
The mere fact that he told his immediate superior, Father Helmpraecht, what he had done rules out any charge of chicanery.
Unfortunately, the Provincial never mentioned his objections to the
Fathers nor gave them the opportunity to correct his misunderstandings. They had no reason to suspect he was harboring such
notions in view of the fact that he had commended them for their
action in seeing the Archbishop and selecting the site.

Even more puzzling is the Provincial's inconsistency about the
New York location. In his letter to Father Mauron, he said that,
after inspecting the site selected by Father Hecker, he found it
desirable and gave him a letter to that effect. But then he told
Father Mauron that he had "a strong objection" to locating the
house in New York. The Fathers have all their friends there, they
would have "visits upon visits" and also would "do a great deal

of visiting" with incalculable harm to discipline and their own spiritual life. He told the Rector Major that on mentioning this objection to Father Hecker, the latter said there was no need to entertain such fears. They were groundless. However, Father Ruland was not convinced and admitted to Father Mauron that while objectively New York was ideal for the foundation, subjectively it was undesirable in view of its possible effects on the Americans. He had told the Fathers he would encourage the New York foundation, and yet in the letter to Father Mauron he advised the Rector Major that if the Americans should have a house of their own, let it not be in New York or Newark, "but somewhere where they [the Fathers] would be more secluded."[30]

Father Hecker and his companions knew nothing of what the Provincial had written in his letter. They could proceed only on what he had told them — that he favored the foundation in New York. Although he would not authorize Father Hecker's journey to Rome to present the matter to Father Mauron, they had received what they considered a "qualified permission." Showing it to Father Helmpraecht, they pointed out that Father Ruland thought there was sufficient justification for the journey. Then they said to Father Helmpraecht: "We ask for the permission which you still affirm you have the power to grant."[31] By this time, however, the whole situation had become so complicated and involved that Father Helmpraecht decided he would have no part in it. He had taken up the matter with Father Leimgruber who, in turn, had consulted Father Mueller. The latter said that if the Provincial did not feel free to grant the permission then neither should Father Helmpraecht. Finally Father Leimgruber decided that the most prudent course to follow was to avoid the issue entirely so he wired the New York Rector not to become involved in the affair.[32]

Despite the reluctance on the part of the Baltimore and New York Rectors, the American Fathers did not waver in their conviction that Father Hecker had the constitutional right to present his case to Father Mauron. Until July 30th, Father Walworth and Father Hewit had assumed that the Provincial would readily give the necessary permission. When they learned that he had refused on the basis of the circular, they paused to reflect. Both were just as strongly convinced as the two Fathers in New York that the circular applied only to cases similar to that of Bretschka. They were just as firmly persuaded that important and urgent interests of the Community were at stake and honestly believed that the 1764 Constitutions, under which they lived, gave Father Hecker an undisputed right to present their project to the Rector Major. The Rule on the vow of perseverance stated that a subject could go to the Rector Major in any matter of importance which would admit of no delay. However, he must first ask the permission of his superior and, if he refused, he could undertake the journey since the superior should not deny this permission. Father Hecker had asked for Father Ruland's permission but the Provincial had refused it. Then, they reasoned, according to the Constitutions, Father Hecker was entirely justified in going to Rome.[33]

Although they had no doubts about the correctness of their position, they questioned the expediency of Father Hecker's "going directly against the judgment and will of the Provincial." They feared that the step was "too extreme and unsafe." Still counting on the Provincial's good will, they thought if he "would pledge himself to use his influence to get us permission for a house, it might be done through him."[34] But when they heard that Father Ruland had given his permission "insofar as he could" they hesitated no longer. Both agreed wholeheartedly that Father Hecker should act as their "minister plenipotentiary." Father Walworth felt that with the declaration of the Provincial, there was no further problem: "Morally speaking, it settles the affair already. The only difficulty now is a technical one."[35]

On July 31st, Father Hewit, as Provincial Consultor, wrote a formal defense of Father Hecker's conduct which he could present to Father Mauron if necessary. Fully approving of the journey, he cited the 1764 Constitutions which permitted such a move. Then he said: "Although the new Constitutions are reported to be different, yet as we know nothing officially of these new Constitutions, we have to abide by the old." Referring to the circular, he thought it applied "to malcontent subjects, who abandon their province without acquainting their Superiors or asking their permission." Since it did not apply to them, he gave his reasons for authorizing Father Hecker's visit to Rome:

The fact that several fathers of weight and influence in the Congregation wish to lay their affairs before your Reverence by a representative, constitutes of itself a very grave and important reason for Father Hecker's journey to Rome; and makes it evidently the duty of the Provincial to give him permission. The reason for doing so is made more imperative by the fact that the most serious interests of the Congregation are involved. The Very Rev. Fr. Provincial thinks he has not the power to grant this permission. It is my judgment, however, that the gravity of the matters in question makes it proper and advisable that Father Hecker should use the right given him by the Constitutions and still go to Rome.[36]

Two days later, he not only gave Father Hecker a personal letter of approval but cosigned a statement that Father Walworth had written to their newly designated emissary:

I heartily approve of your going to Rome and it seems to me the only way of representing our affairs as they truly are, and saving the best interests of this Province from the ruin to which they are fast hastening. As to your right to go, I cannot have any doubt, since you do not go except on matters of great general importance which clearly fall within the provisions of the Constitution which declares your right to do so. Besides this, you do not go against the will of the Provincial, for he tells you that he thinks there is reason enough to give you permission, if he had the power to do so. He fears only the responsibility of assuming that power. I am unable to understand the nature of his scruples, but I am clearly of the opinion that you may go in such case without any permission. You have my most hearty concurrence.[37]

Even though he had personally approved of every move Father Hecker had made, Father Deshon also put his consent in writing:

I consider your going to Rome at this time, as my act as much as it is your own, since I coincide entirely with you as to the right, propriety and necessity of taking this step, and I have advised with you and co-operated in all that you have done. I confide entirely in the purity of your intention, in your zeal and discretion, and shall pray heartily that God may bring everything to a successful issue for the sanctification of ourselves and the salvation of so many destitute souls who are crying out on all sides, for the truth and for instruction.[38]

After Father Hecker had received the unqualified approval of his fellow missionaries to act as their representative in Rome, he told Father Ruland on August 1st that he was using his constitutional right to lay his case before the Rector Major. He also said he would not burden the Province with the expenses of the journey since his brother George had offered to provide the money. Father Ruland did not protest his decisions. Never once did he forbid Father Hecker to make the journey, nor to accept money from his brother. Repeatedly he asked him "not to take any steps that might turn out badly" and told him he feared that this trip "under such circumstances where there is no urgent need for it" was too drastic. But, as he wrote to Father Mauron, he made "no unnecessary objections" nor issued any positive prohibition, for he supposed that Father Hecker in his "state of agitation" would ignore his commands and "thus become guilty of a further misdemeanor." He assumed, as he said, "a passive conduct" which seemed to him "the wisest and safest" course.[39]

No doubt Father Ruland believed he was playing a passive role, but actually his attitude was more active than he imagined. He not only approved of the New York location for the new house, but told Father Hecker it "ought to be founded first" and suggested that he raise the money to buy the property. He thought the foundation was so important that "without the slightest hesitation" he would have sent an English-speaking Father to the Rector Major if he believed he had the authority to do so. Father Hecker had every reason to believe that while the Provincial refused to give permission for the journey, he had endorsed the reasons for it. In brief, his handling of the affair seemed to bear the external appearance of approval.

Before Father Hecker left for Rome, Father Hewit had sent him a wise bit of advice: "Be careful that Father Provincial does not write to the General a letter of excuse representing your departure as a thing which he wished to prevent and could not. Be accredited by him if possible and in as strong terms as you can persuade him to use."[40]

There was no way of knowing if the Provincial would write or, if he did, what he would say. But if he should send a damaging report to Father Mauron, then a strongly worded testimony in Father Hecker's favor might offset it. So the delegate of the American Fathers acting on this suggestion, asked the Provincial for a character reference including a declaration that he preferred the New York foundation to any other. On August 3rd, Father Ruland wrote in German:

I, the undersigned, hereby testify, that the Reverend I. Hecker, a priest of the Congregation of the Most Holy Redeemer in the American Province has always enjoyed the full approval of his superiors as a good Redemptorist, full of zeal for souls. Although I must, according to my conscience, disapprove his intended step of going to Rome, because I consider it to be contrary to the will of the Superior General, and besides, as unnecessary and justified by no sufficient reasons and therefore have advised against it, yet I cannot refrain from giving the Reverend Father Hecker the above testimonial.

I furthermore declare, that I not only wished the establishment of a house for the American Fathers to their entire satisfaction, in the manner prescribed by the Superior General, preferably to that of any other house in America, but also that I offered, without the offer having been accepted, to secure the necessary agreement and permission of the Father General.[41]

On the same identical day on which he gave Father Hecker this testimonial, Father Ruland wrote in his long report to Rome some observations that reveal strange inconsistencies in his thinking. He depicts Father Hecker as a headstrong religious motivated by a "human" spirit heavily saturated with nationalism. He and his companions want to be "under their own regime and not under a foreign one." The Provincial regards Father Hecker's journey to Rome as a course he would expect from "none but an American Father." For fear Father Hecker would not obey, he did not forbid him to make the journey.[42] Comparing these statements with the testimonial, it seems odd that if Father Ruland were convinced that his analysis of Father Hecker's religious character was really accurate, he would declare in his testimonial that "he has always enjoyed the full approval of his superiors as a good Redemptorist."

Even in his letter to Father Mauron, it is difficult to discover what the Provincial actually thought of Father Hecker. On one page, he says he is good and he "will not count his present step against him." On another, he says he condemns his action even though "he would not condemn his intention." And yet he writes that he foresees Father Hecker would not obey a direct command to abandon the Roman journey.[43] In other words, in one letter he attributes a rebellious spirit to a subject whom, in another letter, he has described as a good Redemptorist.

In this same testimonial, Father Ruland stated that he advised Father Hecker not to go to Rome because the trip was unnecessary and unjustified. But three days earlier, he had seen the New York property and put in writing a formal declaration that if he thought he had the authority he would send an English-speaking Father to the Rector Major "without the slightest hesitation." Apparently on July 31st, he thought there were valid and grave reasons for presenting the entire proposition to Father Mauron. At least, they were such as to cause him no concern about the necessity of the trip. What brought about this change of mind between July 31st and August 3rd, he does not reveal.

The second paragraph of this testimonial is also puzzling. Father Ruland declares he offered to secure the Superior General's agreement for the establishment of the American foundation "to their [the missionaries'] entire satisfaction." They had made it abundantly clear that they wished to have the house in New York and as soon as possible. Yet Father Ruland had officially advised the Rector Major that this city was the last place in the world for the foundation. If Father Mauron should decide to accede to their request, then the Provincial asked that it be delayed until October, 1858, a full year after the Fathers had requested.[44] It is rather difficult to understand, then, what Father Ruland meant when he said that he not only wished the new foundation "according to their entire satisfaction" but would also secure the necessary permissions to establish it.

When the Rector Major severely rebuked the Provincial on September 3rd for giving this testimonial, the Provincial could only say "it was caused by the peculiar situation in which I found myself at the time." He said he did not want to increase the Fathers' "suspicions" nor strengthen "their irritation" against him. He wrote the testimonial, he sadly admitted, "without reflecting at the time, why or for whom" he was granting it. One thought guided him. He wanted to show Father Hecker that he sincerely meant what he said and was not afraid to put it in writing.[45] However, Father Ruland does not explain why he made promises which he was convinced he could not fulfill in good conscience.

While Father Ruland was surprisingly inconsistent in his statements, yet he seems to have acted from the best of intentions. In the good sense, he was "playing both ends against the middle."

He was trying to prove to the missionaries his desire to co-operate, while, on the other hand, he was attempting to stave off from the Province what he sincerely believed was dangerous and destructive. There is no doubt that when Father Ruland reached New York he found a blazing conflagration which he himself had unwittingly ignited. He could neither control the blaze nor extinguish the flames. He thought that by prudent compromise and calculated delay he could eventually put out the fire. But ineffective proposals and empty promises could never quench the burning zeal of the missionaries. To speculate on what might have happened if Father Ruland had used other tactics, or if he had taken a firm and straightforward stand without minimizing words or compromising issues, would be idle and fruitless. He did neither and as the Redemptorist historian, Father Wuest, has said: "the fault lay with the poor Father Provincial of the time, owing to his peculiar character and education."[46]

Of the four Americans, Father Hecker was the first to suspect that the Provincial was straddling the fence. He noticed a discrepancy between Father Ruland's promises and his messages to Rome. Although he never saw these messages, he could roughly guess their content from Father Mauron's reprimand. By the end of July, 1857, he was convinced that the cause of the American missionaries could not be entrusted either safely or successfully to Father Ruland. That responsibility Father Hecker took upon himself, realizing the risk he was running. But he could not sacrifice the sacred cause in order to avoid misfortunes, humiliations, sufferings, or sorrow. As he said: "If it will cause me some trouble and pain, what of that? Thousands go and have their heads knocked off for the glory of their country and why not do as much for the glory of God."[47] To insure the future of the missions and above all to initiate a move within his own community for the conversion of America, he would "risk everything."[48]

But despite his courage, Father Hecker was not foolhardy. If there were going to be a contest he knew he should prepare for it. He would not enter the Roman arena without weapons. He would select them in America: the endorsement and good will of the American hierarchy. Since the Church in the United States was under the jurisdiction of the Sacred Congregation of Propaganda, he knew that the Prefect of that Congregation, Cardinal Barnabò, could be of immense help to the cause. It was then imperative to have letters from American bishops introducing and recommending him to this illustrious Prelate. So he took means to obtain them. Through Father Hewit, he secured a testimonial from Archbishop Kenrick of Baltimore who spoke of Father Hecker as "outstanding in his zeal for the Faith, in virtue and in labors in the vineyard of the Lord."[49]

One of the key figures in Father Hecker's plans was New York's Archbishop Hughes who knew him well and who had heartily agreed to have the American house in his diocese. Father Hecker needed this endorsement in writing. On August 2nd he went to Saratoga and explained the situation to the Archbishop, who, after listening carefully to his visitor, realized he might have a hard path to travel in the Eternal City. Yet he did not advise him to forego the trip but, convinced of his good faith and good conscience, recommended him to Cardinal Barnabò. He described him as a convert who, with his companions, had successfully given missions in the principal cities of the United States "resulting in numerous conversions of Protestants to our holy faith and in bringing back many lukewarm Catholics to the practice of their religion." Then he said "he visits Rome on business connected with the Community to which he belongs and I have great pleasure in recommending him to your Eminence as a laborious, edifying, zealous and truly Apostolic Priest."[50] The Archbishop also gave Father Hecker a personal letter which he apparently expected Father Mauron to read: "As you are about to visit Rome, I think you would do well to make known to your Superior how desirous I am that there should be another house of your Order in New York for the spiritual benefit of the Catholics who do not speak German. You are aware of what I have already said to encourage the undertaking and I trust the General will not find it inconsistent with the rules or the interests of the Congregation to encourage it [in] like manner."[51]

On the same day, Father Hecker's former confessor, Bishop McCloskey, gave him a very interesting letter to present to Monsignor Kirby, the rector of the Irish College. Telling the Monsignor that Father Hecker was going to Rome on matters concerning the interests of his Order in this country, the Bishop wrote: "Should it be necessary for him to have recourse to the Card. Prefect of the Propaganda, he may need the counsel and direction of someone experienced in the *ways* of Rome, and I know of no one to whom he can be more safely commended than yourself. In any case, he will feel honoured to make your acquaintance and on your own part I am sure you will be glad to meet such a pure-minded, intelligent and thoroughly devoted priest as is Father Hecker."[52]

There can be no doubt that Father Hecker hid nothing from the two Prelates. Both were aware of the troubles he might encounter and both did what they could to smooth the path before him. In like fashion, the convert Bishop of Newark, James Bayley, supplied Father Hecker with three letters. One was to Cardinal Barnabò in which he said that Father Hecker with the approbation of his Provincial (the Bishop knowing of the letter Father Ruland had written, apparently considered his "qualified permission" approbation) was going to Rome "to confer with the Superior General on matters of extreme importance, not only for the Congregation but for religion in this country. He will explain to Your Eminence the object he has in view and of which I approve with all my heart. As I know that Your Eminence has nothing more at heart than what concerns the spiritual interests of this new country, I doubt not that you will take great pleasure in giving him the support of your powerful protection."[53]

In a somewhat similar vein, the Bishop wrote to the Secretary of the Congregation of Propaganda, Archbishop Bedini: "Father Hecker as you already know is one of the most distinguished converts of which our Religion can have flattered itself in this country, and has already rendered the greatest services to Religion by his writing as well as his apostolic works. As I know that your Excellency has a sincere affection for all honest, virtuous men, I do not doubt that you will show the greatest kindness to Father Hecker, and that you will aid him with all your power to obtain the important points which determined him to visit Rome."[54]

The third letter of the Newark Prelate was to Father Mauron. He told the Rector Major that "some months ago I had decided to obtain permission from the Reverend Father Provincial of the Congregation of the Most Holy Redeemer through the mediation of the Reverend Father Walworth to erect a house of the same Congregation in this city which might be conducted by priests who are well versed in the English language." Later he was told that this request should be made directly to the Rector Major. Briefly describing his diocese and the benefits such a house would bring to souls under his care, he said that if the General would approve this proposal, he would make arrangements for starting it and would use every means at his disposal to complete it. He spoke of Father Hecker as "well-known to all the bishops and priests in this region not only for his eminent virtues but also for the zeal with which he labors strenuously for the salvation of souls." Then he concluded by saying that since he knew the Bishop's mind on the whole matter of the new foundation, Father Hecker could more easily explain the Bishop's views orally than by lengthy letters.[55]

In addition to these letters from the hierarchy, Father Hecker obtained others from such prominent laymen as Brownson, McMaster, Terence Donnelly, and the former Episcopalian Bishop of North Carolina, Levi Silliman Ives, who had become a Catholic in Rome some years before. Personally acquainted with Archbishop Bedini whom he had met during the winter of 1854, Ives requested for Father Hecker "Your Grace's kind consideration in reference to his important mission to Rome relating to the extension of Catholicity in the United States."[56]

The morning of August 5, 1857, Father Ruland left for Rochester. That afternoon, Father Hecker left for Rome. He said good-by to his Redemptorist brethren in New York, some of whom thought he was going at the Provincial's request to arrange for the establishment of the American house. Apart from Father Deshon, only Father Helmpraecht and Father Petsch knew the true story. The Rector was very kind and co-operative, giving Father Hecker an enthusiastic letter of approval. Describing him as a Redemptorist who had received the well-deserved praise of all for his great zeal for souls, Father Helmpraecht also testified that his regular observance of the Rule and his discipline of life merited "the love and praise of his own Superior." Before Father Hecker left the house, he knelt for his Superior's blessing which Father Deshon called "his heartiest benediction."[57]

Two o'clock that afternoon, the *Asia* slid out of her berth and headed for the narrows. Waving from the deck to his brother

George and Father Deshon on the pier, Father Hecker was in good spirits. Never for an instant had he wavered in his resolve to make the trip.[58] Having consulted with his brethren and bishops, as well as seeking divine guidance in prayer and meditation, he had no doubts, no hesitations, no misgivings. His peaceful conscience and his tranquil mind approved the step he was taking.

In the steamer's mail, the *Asia* carried two letters of far-reaching importance. One addressed to Cardinal Barnabò would open a rich vein of strength and influence; the other to Father Mauron would obstruct the channels of investigation. The Consul General for the Papal States, Louis B. Binsse, had written the letter to the Cardinal. The Provincial had composed the letter to the Rector Major.

Since his role was that of a liaison between the Papal States and the United States Government, Binsse transmitted all dispatches between the two countries, and he held an important post in the eyes of the Vatican. The Papal Secretary of State, Cardinal Antonelli, had appointed him on the recommendation of Archbishop Hughes.[59] Although the duties of his office were limited to temporal affairs, he kept a watchful eye on Catholic interests in America and corresponded regularly with Cardinal Barnabò who valued his opinions and judgments. Binsse was familiar with the Redemptorist missions and knew the salutary influence they were exerting on American Catholics as well as the impact they were making on non-Catholics. A native New Yorker who had been in the importing business, he was personally acquainted with the missionaries, especially Father Hecker. When he heard of his proposed visit to Rome, he not only presented him with a letter of introduction to give to the Cardinal, but also mailed a four-page personal recommendation of him and his cause. Speaking of the effective work the Redemptorists were doing in America, he singled out the convert priests of the Order and gave a few words on the history of each. He was more detailed in his description of Father Hecker whom he praised as a zealous and devoted religious. He spoke of his instructions, his manner of speaking, and his presentation of ideas which endeared Father Hecker to the people not only while he was in the pulpit, but especially in the confessional. Binsse carefully noted that on this point he was speaking from his own experience as well as that of others. Because

of his extensive missionary travel Father Hecker was well versed
on the needs of the Church in this country and Binsse told the
Cardinal he could obtain some very useful insights on the religious
condition of America from Father Hecker. Especially valuable
would be his observations on the possibilities and opportunities
for American convert work. Commending Father Hecker to
the Cardinal, Binsse expressed an ardent hope that his mission
would be successful. When Barnabò received this letter he was
anxious to welcome this American priest whom the respected
agent for the Papal States had recommended so highly.[60]

Father Ruland's letter was of an entirely different character.
He had written it during the hectic days of July to give the
Rector Major a clear picture of the situation and to prepare him
for the arrival of Father Hecker. In it, he repeated his suspicions
and his evaluation of the motives and conduct of the American
Fathers who had turned a deaf ear to his pleadings, attempted
to pressure him into sending Father Hecker to Rome, disputed
his interpretation of the circular, and insisted on the New York
establishment. Without consulting him, they had called on bishops
and discussed foundations. Obsessed with a nationalistic spirit,
they insisted that only Americans must convert America. They
were dissatisfied with the spirit of the Congregation in this
country which they wanted to change for greater effectiveness.
The four Americans had been conspiring together by mail and
telegraph. They had shown such a spirit of rebellion that Father
Hecker remarked that the General was not the Pope and if the
General was un-co-operative, he would go over his head and
appeal to the Holy See. Such was the content of the Provincial's
letter.[61]

To his previous charges of nationalism and laxity which he
confirmed in this letter, Father Ruland added two new counts of
conspiracy and rebellion. Naturally this report would put the
Rector Major on guard, create a bias against Father Hecker, and
predispose the General to expect a headstrong and defiant religious who had little or no concept of obedience or submission to
authority. When Father Ruland sealed his letter, he buried the
American advocate's hopes for a favorable hearing from the Rector
Major of the Redemptorist Congregation.

CHAPTER XIII

Expelled!

WITHIN ten and a half days after leaving New York, the *Asia* docked at Liverpool. Father Hecker had enjoyed the voyage since the weather was pleasant, the ocean rather calm, and he had not been seasick. After a short visit with William Channing and his family at Liverpool, he went to the Redemptorist house at Clapham where his close friend and former confessor, Father de Buggenoms, welcomed him warmly. Enthusiastically Father Hecker told his English confreres of the harvest of souls awaiting the Redemptorists in America. The non-Catholic was ready and willing to listen to the claims of the Church, he said, and if the Community would establish an American house, that house would act as a center not only for Catholic missions but also for convert work. No society of priests in the States was making a direct appeal to those outside the Church, since every community was engaged in spiritual ministrations to the Catholic population.[1]

Distinguished Catholic laymen, Father Hecker continued, such as McMaster, Ives, Binsse, and Donnelly agreed that the Redemporist Community was the one group qualified to dedicate itself to the conversion of America. Of all the religious orders in America, the noted laymen observed, the Redemptorists alone had attracted to its ranks, not only converts, but converts of unusual ability and talents. Was that not an indication, they asked, that Divine Providence had singled out the Congregation to work for the conversion of the American people?[2]

Father Hecker reported that the illustrious convert editor,

247

Orestes Brownson, also believed that the long-awaited day had dawned "to institute measures to bring this great and powerful nation into the Church of God." However the Yankee editor was not so confident that the sons of St. Alphonsus were ideally suited to undertake the work. He leaned more to the hope that "a Congregation should spring up of native origin and growth" with that specific goal as its aim. Nevertheless from his knowledge of the Community and the fact that it was "still in its first fervor, animated by a true Missionary spirit" it was "better prepared to engage in the work of converting this country to the Catholic Church than any other body of religious I am acquainted with." The time, he thought, was ripe for the Redemptorists to make the experiment because they had in their ranks five missionaries who were "men of the country, well acquainted with the American people and fair representatives of the American mind." If anyone could influence the American non-Catholic, it would be these Redemptorists because of the respectful attention given to their words and arguments.[3]

As he talked, Father Hecker noticed that his English brethren did not possess the same enthusiastic hopes for the conversion of their country that he had for his. Although they had at least seven native vocations in Fathers Bradshaw, Furniss, Stevens, Plunkett, and Vaughan, with the distinguished converts Fathers Coffin and Bridgett, nevertheless they seemed to entertain little hope for a brighter future for the Church in England. In conversations he had with Faber and Manning, Father Hecker noted a similar reaction which led him to observe in a letter to his brother George: "Men's heads in Europe are turned quite around. They see the past, but cannot fix their gaze on the future." They appeared to him quite pessimistic focusing their attention on problems and difficulties but ignoring opportunities. Disquieted by obstacles to the faith, they assumed, he thought, an attitude of helplessness which crippled any effective action. Such a frame of mind, to the enthusiastic and optimistic Father Hecker, was deplorable. Since he always looked at the bright and hopeful side of any situation, he found it difficult to understand those who, concentrating so much attention on the dark side of problems, could see no portent of success and as a result hesitated to act. This he took to be a mark of inward weakness so conspicuously absent in the Apostles and their successors. From what he saw and heard in and around London, he concluded: "England will never be reconverted unless a change takes place in English Catholics."[4]

On August 20th, Father Hecker left London and went to Paris. He stayed there only one evening and then journeyed on down to Marseilles. This ancient port reminded him of Havana because of its similar houses, streets, parks, and walks. He saw men of various nationalities either working on cargo or idling on the pier. There were Frenchmen, Italians, Spaniards, Greeks, and Turks "and every other outlandish people." It was all very curious and engaging but he thought he would find it more enjoyable if he had a companion "for half the enjoyment of seeing what interests one is expressing it to another who sympathizes with you." In fact, he said, he would have been quite lonesome had he not been preoccupied with his coming visit to Rome.[5]

The evening of August 24th, he took the steamer from Marseilles to Civita Vecchia on the west coast of Italy and from there went to Rome by stagecoach, a twelve-hour ride. The evening of August 26th he arrived at the Redemptorist headquarters on the Via Merulana, just a short distance from the Basilica of St. Mary Major.[6] It was here that the General Chapter of the Transalpine Redemptorists had elected in 1855 the thirty-seven-year-old Father Nicholas Mauron as their first Rector Major. He had been in office just two years when he was called upon to deal with the delicate problem that had arisen in the American Province. Two years older than Father Hecker, the Swiss-born Superior General was rather frail in health. He had sharp features, a high forehead, prominent nose, and square chin. In his twenty years as a Redemptorist, he had taught philosophy and theology in his community's house at Fribourg, had spent several months giving missions, and had served as a superior for three years at Landser before being made provincial of the French Province. A combination of kindness and firmness had characterized his administration as he zealously insisted upon the strict observance of the Rule and absolute obedience to authority.[7]

A notable characteristic of Father Mauron both as provincial and superior general was his attitude toward superiors whom he trusted. The Redemptorist historian, Father Stebbing, says of him:

"Once he had given his confidence to a Superior he was slow to withdraw it."[8] He had no lack of confidence in the man he had chosen to govern the American Province who, he said, was "so dispassionate, just and truthful that I can fully trust his statements."[9] He accepted without question Father Ruland's July 31st detailed and damaging report of the American missionaries which he had received just four days before Father Hecker's arrival. Apparently he did not question the accuracy of the facts given in the report nor the judiciousness of Father Ruland's interpretation of the missionaries' motives. He believed that the Provincial had "rightly" detected the spirit of nationality and division in the desire of the missionaries for an American house.[10] Although Father Hewit, the Provincial Consultor, categorically denied these charges in his letter of July 27th which reached the Rector Major about the same time as Father Ruland's report, Father Mauron's confidence in Father Ruland remained unshaken. He did not ask for any statement from impartial witnesses such as the other Provincial Consultor, Father Mueller, nor from the superiors of the various houses in which the Americans lived.[11] Since he accepted Father Ruland's word as gospel truth, he was prepared to meet in the person of Father Hecker a recalcitrant subject who had not only defied his authority but was threatening the unity of the American Province with his nationalistic and revolutionary ideas. If these charges were true, and Father Mauron honestly believed they were, he had no other course but to take vigorous action to safeguard his authority and to preserve the unity and religious spirit of the Congregation entrusted to his care.

On Thursday morning, August 27th, the Rector Major summoned Father Hecker to his room. As the American priest walked down the long corridor for the momentous meeting with his Superior General, two thoughts were uppermost in his mind: he had come to advance the cause of religion in his beloved America and to further the best interests of the Congregation to which he had dedicated his life and his energies. Never for a moment did he consider that, as the representative of his three Redemptorist brethren, he had come to fight against the Congregation, but rather to fight for it. He had come, not as a disgruntled religious to complain about his Provincial nor to criticize the administration of the Province, but as a dedicated son of St. Alphonsus to explain to his Major Superior the opportunities awaiting the Community. He believed Father Mauron had been totally misinformed. As he entered the room Father Hecker's hopes of success were high, his enthusiasm undiminished; but they were not to remain thus for long.

There is no verbatim record of the conversation that took place in this first meeting between Father Mauron and Father Hecker, nor of the interviews that followed on Friday and Saturday. However the general tenor of the discussions can be gathered from the letters and subsequent written statements of the two men involved.

The Rector Major began his investigation by asking his American subject to justify his extraordinary conduct in coming to Rome. Apparently Father Hecker started with the argument most cogent to him: the wonderful opportunities awaiting the Congregation in the New World if the Community would establish an American house. But the Rector Major refused to discuss this subject since he had already expressed his views on this foundation in his July 2, 1857, letter to the Provincial. Further, he did not consider this project the important issue at the moment. The crucial question was why had Father Hecker presumed to come to Rome without first obtaining the Rector Major's permission? Father Mauron contended logically that if Father Hecker had made an unauthorized visit to his Superior General, he violated obedience, had committed a serious breach of discipline, and merited expulsion. If his conduct deserved this penalty, then he would no longer be a member of the Congregation and any question of a new Redemptorist house would be no concern of his. On the other hand, if he could justify his right to come to Rome, then the discussion of the American foundation and the reasons for it would be pertinent.[12]

In defense of his conduct, Father Hecker appealed to the 1764 Constitutions which gave him the right to present urgent matters to the Rector Major, but Father Mauron maintained that these Constitutions had no application to this situation because of the special May, 1857, circular he had issued. "Were you aware of this circular?" he asked Father Hecker. When his visitor answered yes, the Rector Major wanted to know why he had not written for permission before leaving the Province? Explaining that he did not think this circular suspended the Constitutions, Father

Hecker advanced the same reasons he had given Father Ruland. But Father Mauron dismissed this explanation as inadmissible because, he contended, his circular was a special precept for the American Province which by its very nature excluded any application of the 1764 Constitutions. No subject, he continued, has the right to interpret a special precept according to his own mind or intention. If he could, then its purpose would be defeated. Moreover the circular did not absolutely prohibit a subject from visiting his Superior General, but only required him to obtain permission before doing so.[13]

Then Father Mauron touched on what he believed was the core of the problem: Why hadn't Father Hecker written for the permission before setting out for Rome? The urgency of the situation and the grave reasons involved, replied Father Hecker, demanded prompt attention. Father Mauron considered this argument practically worthless. What was so urgent about the New York foundation that required such immediate action? Within less than two weeks a letter requesting permission could reach Rome and in two weeks more the reply would be in America. Father Hecker countered with the observation that both the Provincial and his own Rector thought the matter was both urgent and grave. Did either, Father Mauron demanded, give him permission to make the journey? Father Hecker answered no, but neither had forbidden him to leave the Province.[14]

The question of the expenses for the journey was also discussed and Father Mauron wanted to know if his American visitor had requested permission of his Superior or Provincial to accept money from those outside the Community. Explaining that he had wanted to relieve the Congregation of the financial burden of the trip, Father Hecker answered that he had told both the Provincial and his immediate Superior several times that his brother would give him the necessary money and neither had objected or told him he could not accept it. Consequently, since his superiors knew all about it, he interpreted their silence as consent. But Father Mauron did not consider this procedure in accord with the vow of poverty, maintaining that Father Hecker should have requested explicit permission from his superiors to accept funds and not merely announce to them he would receive them.[15]

Although the Rector Major refused to discuss the advisability or the opportuneness of the American house, he condemned the action of the missionaries in trying to secure one. He particularly objected to Father Walworth's interview with Bishop Bayley about the Newark house and the letter he wrote detailing the reasons for such a foundation. All matters concerning new foundations, even the opening negotiations, were reserved to the authorities of the Community and were no concern of ordinary subjects, he reminded Father Hecker. In order to set in proper focus the missionaries' dealings with Bishop Bayley and Archbishop Hughes, Father Hecker attempted to explain the sequence of events leading up to the Newark and New York proposals. As he did, he used the word "we." Immediately Father Mauron inquired who were the "we"? Father Hecker replied they were Fathers Walworth, Hewit, and Deshon whom he represented. Father Mauron protested any such representation and when Father Hecker added that he had letters from each one appointing him their ambassador, the Rector Major saw in this action "another proof that a formal plot had been staged."[16]

During the three interviews that Father Hecker had with the Rector Major which he described as "most painful" he was keenly aware that Father Mauron had taken a very unsympathetic, if not hostile, attitude toward him.[17] This, he believed, was the result of Father Ruland's letters which the Rector Major had obviously accepted as accurate statements of fact and which had created a bias in Father Mauron's mind which no explanation of his could dissipate. Any reasons he gave for his actions, Father Mauron rejected as irrelevant or as excuses to conceal unworthy motives. He found that the Superior General took what he said "in such a wrong way" that he was repeatedly insinuating that the American missionaries had acted "from low and ambitious motives."[18] It is clear that Father Mauron did not attempt to evaluate Father Hecker's good faith, nor consider that he might have been sincere though mistaken in his interpretation of the May, 1857, circular. Neither did he investigate the possibility that the American missionary might have been honest but mistaken in thinking that he had the right to come to Rome.

Perhaps Father Mauron might have approached the problem somewhat differently had Father Ruland's letters of mid-1857 been the only complaints against the American Fathers. But they were not. At the time of his election as Rector Major, Father Mauron later testified, he "was informed of the dangerous inclinations in these three Fathers [Walworth, Hecker, and Hewit]."[19] Who gave him this information, he did not say. It could have been the Provincial who was then in Rome. Certainly after his return to the States, Father Ruland clearly labeled the American missionaries as trouble makers. In October of 1855, he wrote in his letter to Father Mauron about "the tendencies of the English fathers which come to the fore more and more and may yet cause us great embarrassment." A month later he described them as lax religious who had "lost the spirit of a Redemptorist."[20] Then for almost two years there is no further criticism of the Americans until May and June of 1857 when the old charges of nationalism and laxity are repeated and a new one of conspiracy is added.[21]

If Father Mauron's confidence in the Provincial had not been so resolute that he was willing to accept Father Ruland's word in preference to that of the American missionaries, he might not have proceeded so rapidly. He might have delayed long enough to obtain evidence from disinterested persons that would have substantiated the one or the other of the parties involved. He fell into the mistake (always unfortunate in a major superior) of completely trusting an accusing superior and equally distrusting an accused subject. His unquestioning faith in Father Ruland hindered him from bringing to a judicial examination the impartiality his position required. Since he gave absolute credence to Father Ruland's reports, Father Mauron could not help regarding the American missionaries as disgruntled subjects who had persisted for over two years in trying to force their ideas on their lawfully constituted Provincial Superior. They submitted humbly neither to his decisions nor to those of their Rector Major. In addition to this, Father Mauron saw in Father Hecker a rebellious religious who had journeyed to Rome in defiance of a special prohibition of the Superior General.[22] Under the circumstances he could hardly be expected to allow for the possibility of good faith or honest error in his accused subject. In Father Mauron's judgment, Father Hecker had publicly and flagrantly flouted his authority and had scandalously violated his own vow of obedience. As he put it: "In my various conversations with him I well analyzed the whole affair, and in fact the matter was so simple and clear that it required no further investigation and thought. He himself admitted to me that he knew of my Circular letter of May 9th and yet despite this, without having been summoned by the Holy See and without any consent whatever of his Superiors, in defiance of even the repeated pleas of his Provincial, he undertook the journey. Since the matter was thus so clear, it was not difficult for me to form a judgment." Father Mauron saw only one way to vindicate his authority and preserve discipline. He must expel Father Hecker from the Congregation.[23]

However, the Rector Major postponed his final decision until he had conferred with his Consultors. Since one of them, Father Douglas, was out of the city, Father Mauron awaited his return before calling the meeting.[24] The Rector Major told this to Father Hecker in their first interview and added that he would call Father Hecker before the group to explain his reasons for thinking he had the right to come to Rome. Further, the Rector Major advised him to write down these reasons in English and if he had difficulty expressing himself in French — apparently the language spoken in the meeting — Father Douglas would translate the document for him and then hand it to the Rector Major. At this time, Father Hecker also understood his Superior to mean that he should put down in writing all that he had to say and not merely why he thought he was justified in coming to Rome.[25]

When Father Hecker heard these words he was greatly encouraged. The apparent unfriendliness of the Rector Major had made it difficult for him to give a clear picture of what had taken place in America. But when Father Mauron said — or in Father Hecker's words "promised" — that he would call him before the Consulta consisting of the Rector Major and his advisers, Father Hecker was considerably relieved. He understood this promise to mean that he would have a full hearing in the strict sense of the term. In fact he seemed to think that the Consultors would be somewhat like associate judges before whom he could refute point by point the charges made against him and to whom he could offer documentary evidence in support of his position. Consequently he regarded his interviews with the Rector Major as preliminary and informal hearings, important but not decisive.

He did not then present to Father Mauron a full defense of his conduct, nor did he show him the testimonials from members of the American hierarchy, nor from the Provincial, the Rector, and his fellow missionaries. As he expressed it: "I put all my hopes in being able to defend the cause of the Congregation . . . only before the Consultors."[26]

In adopting this line of action, Father Hecker had either overlooked the Constitutions regarding the scope of the Rector Major's authority or he had misunderstood Father Mauron's words. The Constitution clearly declared that the Rector Major had the "supreme and absolute power of dismissing subjects" although they directed him to discuss the matter with his six Consultors before taking such punitive action. But he was not obliged to follow their decisions since their vote was consultive, not deliberative. Further, the Rector Major was not required to summon the accused before the Consulta, question him in their presence, and then allow him to defend his conduct before them. As the Major Superior, he was "bound in justice to hear the excuse of the accused, not once but often; and also the reasons whence the accused draws his defense." He was cautioned to "proceed slowly and quietly, not coming to a final decision until after careful and mature deliberation." Then he was directed to call the Consultors together and "carefully set before them the arguments for and against the accused."[27]

There is no doubt that Father Mauron sincerely and honestly believed that in his three interviews with Father Hecker, he had heard the defendant's side of the story not once but often; that he had carefully and judiciously evaluated the reasons Father Hecker had given for his conduct; that he had proceeded slowly and deliberately, free of passion and prejudice. Satisfied in his own conscience that he had faithfully fulfilled these precepts of the Constitution, Father Mauron then planned to present to his Consultors a complete and objective report of all the evidence he had obtained. But he had no intention of doing this in Father Hecker's presence, nor did the Constitutions require him to do so. He did intend to call Father Hecker to the meeting after he had thoroughly discussed all aspects of the case with his advisers. But then he would narrow the interrogation of the American missionary to only one issue: Why did Father Hecker think he had the right to come to Rome?[28]

This was all Father Mauron had in mind when he promised Father Hecker he would hear him in the Consulta. But it was not Father Hecker's interpretation of the Rector Major's promise. Undoubtedly he was thinking in terms of the American tradition that a man was innocent unless proven guilty and before he could be judged guilty the accused must not only hear the charges leveled against him but have the opportunity to answer them before a fair and impartial tribunal. Certainly Father Hecker believed that since the Consultors would be called upon to express their conviction of his innocence or guilt, they should be thoroughly acquainted with his defense which he himself and not a third party should present. Convinced that Father Mauron intended to give him this opportunity, Father Hecker worked industriously on the statement of his case. From the time of his first interview with the Rector Major on August 27th until the day before the Consultors' meeting on August 30th he devoted himself constantly to the preparation of his brief. Not once in those three days did he step outside the grounds of the Villa Caserta. When not engaged with the Rector Major, he spent his time before the Blessed Sacrament or marshaling his arguments in his room and carefully formulating them on paper. His defense, he believed, embraced not only his personal reputation and character, but the cause of religion in America and the future of the Redemptorists in the New World.[29]

Father Douglas returned to Rome on August 29th and Father Hecker had his document ready for translation. But since the meeting was to take place the next morning, the Consultor did not have the time to put the lengthy document into French. Father Hecker then begged Father Douglas to meet with him early the next morning so he could fully explain before the meeting his side of the story and show him the letters and testimonials he had brought with him. On Sunday morning Father Douglas was delayed in seeing Father Hecker and before the American missionary was halfway through his explanation, he had to leave for the meeting.[30]

At nine o'clock on the morning of Sunday, August 30th, the

Consulta began its deliberations. Father Mauron presided with Fathers Pajalich, Lelouchier, Macchiusi, Verheijen, Haringer, and Douglas present.[31] The Rector Major opened the meeting by saying that its purpose was to consider how to deal with Father Hecker without impairing discipline and authority. Then he traced the history of the problem citing the petition of the American Fathers for an American house which Father Ruland had submitted on May 16th and which the Consulta had discussed on June 28th. Since the Rector Major had agreed with the Provincial that this would lead to a nationalistic division in the American Province, he rejected the petition. But the missionaries, he said, were unwilling to accept this decision and having progressed "quite far in their own plans unknown to the Provincial, decided to send one of their number to Rome to the Most Rev. General with this end in view that he might obtain a foundation for the English Americans in New York City and impede foundations already accepted in the Isle of St. Thomas." For this purpose they selected Father Hecker, who came to Rome personally "with no respect for the decree of the Most Rev. Father General, which had already been published in America forbidding under penalty of dismissal from the Congregation anyone to come to him in Rome without obtaining in writing the permission of the Most Reverend General." A further indication of Father Hecker's disrespect for authority was his expressed intention of appealing to the Holy See, for as he said "the Father General is not the Pope."[32]

Obviously this presentation of the case came from Father Ruland's letters which Father Mauron had with him in the meeting and which he consulted from time to time. There was no written statement of Father Hecker's which could have disputed, if not disproved, the Provincial's assertions. The Rector Major "fully explained" to the Consultors what Father Hecker had said to him in his private discussions but because of the nature of these interviews, they could hardly be called a full and clear presentation of Father Hecker's cause. He was interrupted, cross-questioned, and halted in his explanation whenever the Rector Major considered his reasons unsatisfactory, whereas Father Ruland's report received no such critical examination. The Provincial was not called upon by his Superior to verify his charge that the Americans had plotted for months behind his back; nor was he asked why he had misled the missionaries by promising to do all he could to secure an American house while condemning such a foundation to the Rector Major; he was not accused of impeding a foundation accepted by the Rector Major when he "promised" the American Fathers that he would do all he could "to prevent the house in Quebec."[33] The Consultors, following the example of Father Mauron, apparently accepted the Provincial's report without question and on the charges made in that report they formed their judgment.

After Father Mauron had presented the case, from both sides as he sincerely believed, he admonished the Consultors:

> that each one with full liberty reveal what he thought and what before God seemed to him should be done. All with a unanimous voice answered to this: Father Hecker gravely and formally violated the vow of obedience by undertaking a journey contrary to the express decree of the Most Reverend Father General which he personally knew and also against the direct wishes of the Provincial. Consequently he also offended against poverty when he procured without permission necessary money to make the journey. Also he gravely sinned against the Rule, discipline and obedience by previously undertaking on his own and unknown to the Father General and Father Provincial a new foundation. All consulted with his Reverence and beseeched him to dismiss Father Hecker immediately from the Congregation to repair the most grave scandal. . . . No other remedy for safeguarding authority can be found except dismissal. All the Consultors were persuaded that the Rector Major in conscience was obliged to dismiss Father Hecker, nor by his own free will could he weigh either to dismiss or retain the aforesaid Father, for the common good of the Congregation must always be considered more than the private good of an individual.[34]

After this unanimous decision in which no one spoke up for Father Hecker or sought in any way to exculpate him, the decree of dismissal was discussed. In its final form the document stated that the Congregation had previously forbidden its subjects to go to the Superior General without his written permission, a prohibition which the General had renewed as particularly applicable to the American Province. Then addressing Father Hecker, the decree continued:

> You, unmindful of the holy obedience you vowed, did not hesitate to set at naught the same prohibition and its special penalty; and

since, unmindful of the holy poverty you vowed, you procured money
from outsiders without permission from the Superiors; and since,
finally your way of acting and thinking in general is by no means
in harmony with the laws and the spirit of our Institute; we have
judged it such as cannot be tolerated without the greatest spiritual
harm, without the destruction of the common good, and without
breaking all the chains of religious discipline in our Institute; for
we have before our eyes particularly the repeated protest of our
Father St. Alphonsus, that once obedience is done away with, the
Congregation is ruined.

Therefore not to fail in any way in our duty, nor to hold ourself
accountable in conscience to the Supreme Judge, having weighed the
matter carefully and religiously before God, having taken counsel
with our Consultors, and having implored the Divine aid; in virtue
of the faculties of our Rule approved by Benedict XIV and the
supreme authority of the Holy See given to the Superior General:
We dismiss you by these presents from the bosom of the Congregation of the Most Holy Redeemer, and free you from the simple vows
of poverty and obedience as well as from the vow and oath of
perseverance.[35]

These deliberations lasted an hour and a half. Meanwhile Father
Hecker waited outside the council chamber for the moment when
he would be called to give his statement of the case. He had
drawn up a summary to guide him in his presentation and had
arranged the testimonials that would prove his points. Finally
at ten-thirty he was admitted to the meeting. After he entered
and had taken a seat, Father Mauron asked him the direct
question: Did he know about the May 9th circular of the Rector
Major forbidding a subject to come to Rome without his permission? When Father Hecker answered that he did, Father
Mauron wanted to know why he did not get the Rector Major's
permission before leaving his Province. Having humbly begged
the attention of his listeners, Father Hecker opened a copy of
the Constitutions and began to read the passage concerning the
vow of obedience which granted to any subject the right to come
to Rome on urgent business even though his immediate superior
refused to grant the permission. No sooner had he started to
quote the section than the Rector Major interrupted him and
asked to see the passage.[36] Hurrying over the words which granted
this right, Father Mauron emphasized the warning:

But these attempts are always full of danger and risk; therefore let them [subjects] beware lest they be deceived by temptation; for these plans indeed are received not through the inspiration of God but of the devil. Truly, many who are now outside the Congregation would still be in it if they had not taken such steps: wherefore if they [subjects] deem it necessary, let them write to the Rector Major rather than set out; he, if he shall judge it expedient that they should come to him, will write to the local rector granting the permission to depart. This will be the way subjects act who are prudent and animated by the Spirit of God and submissive to their Superiors.[37]

Continuing, the Rector Major asserted that the Constitutions cautioned subjects against any such action without permission. Moreover he had made it clear in his circular of May 9th that he was suspending this section of the Constitutions and expressly forbidding any such recourse to him without his previous permission. Since Father Hecker had ignored this prohibition, he was guilty of defying the authority of his Superior General. But he had done more than that. He had violated his vow of poverty by accepting money from those outside the Community without having previously obtained permission to receive it. In conspiracy with his American companions, he had negotiated with bishops about new foundations; not only without any authorization from his Provincial or Superior General, but completely unknown to them. Finally he had tried to obstruct the establishment of new posts already accepted by the Rector Major and his Consultors.[38]

While Father Mauron enumerated these charges, Father Hecker remained respectfully silent. Since he regarded them as an indictment which he would be permitted to answer, he waited patiently for the Rector Major to finish, fully expecting he would be given a chance to speak in his defense. But he received no such opportunity. As Father Mauron approached the conclusion of his remarks, while still speaking, he handed a paper to the secretary, Father Haringer. Then he told him to read it. Father Hecker was stunned as he listened and realized that this was the decree of expulsion dismissing him from the Congregation. He fell to his knees and when the secretary finished reading, he begged to be heard and to be allowed to present his reasons for thinking he had the right to take the action he did. Quietly, but emphatically, the Rector Major refused. He had already listened to his reasons, had discussed them with his Consultors, and had reached his decision. There was no need for further discussion.[39]

Shocked and shaken to the depths of his soul, Father Hecker arose and left the council. He went directly to the chapel and poured forth his anguish and disappointment before the Blessed Sacrament. After fifteen minutes in prayer, he regained his composure and believing that the Consulta "had acted in passion" he returned to the council. Again falling on his knees before them, he begged formally and expressly to be heard, to be given the opportunity to show that the prohibitions cited against him did not apply to his case and that they were never intended to cover such situations as his. Again the Rector Major refused. A second time, Father Hecker pleaded for the privilege to speak in his defense.[40] This time the Consultors joined in the refusal saying that "his cause is sufficiently examined and weighed and there can be no doubt about the facts, especially the open and flagrant fact of the vow of obedience . . . nor can the scandal given by him be repaired other than by dismissal." Then they added that they were not judging his conscience, nor would they presume to say he was guilty of sin. That they would leave to God.[41]

In astonishment Father Hecker looked at them and then scarcely able to believe what he had heard, he asked: "You condemn me then without a hearing?" Silently they nodded their assent. The highest authorities in the Redemptorist Community had spoken. The case was finished. Father Hecker knew that there was nothing more he could say. However, before leaving the Consulta, he assured them he had acted in good faith, that he and his companions had been guided by sincere and honest motives. Then he withdrew.[42]

In great distress of soul, Father Hecker returned to his room. He was crushed and heartbroken when he realized that he had been expelled from the Congregation he had loved and cherished. Never once during his religious life did the thought of leaving the Redemptorists enter his mind nor did he ever regret the choice he had made. The Community was the place of his "choice and love" and he had no other wish than to live and die as a devoted Redemptorist. All during his priestly career he had worked tirelessly and sincerely to further its noble aims. The conviction that he could further advance its cause had prompted his coming to Rome which had resulted in such disastrous consequences.[43]

The agonizing "why" welled up in his soul as he struggled to find the answer to the question: Why have they "driven me out of the home of my heart and love?" Carefully and candidly he examined his conscience but despite the most searching scrutiny he could find no unworthy motive or dishonest intention. With God as his witness, he could declare that his only desire had been to act as the Congregation's "truest and best friend." Though he was suffering intensely, his conscience did not upbraid him. It did not accuse him "of having acted wrongfully" nor of having behaved as he was charged. Looking at the decree spread out on the table before him, he realized that he had been "handed his walking papers." He found some consolation in the realization that "God has not handed to me my walking papers and this with His grace and our Lady's help, I trust shall never happen." Although by the terms of the decree he was released from his vows, he "did not consider myself free from my vows in conscience at all."[44]

Turning his thought to his fellow missionaries, he began to wonder what would be their fate. In his conversation with the Rector Major, he had associated them with his plans and projects and even spoke as their ambassador. Since they too had been regarded as unworthy religious, he feared he might have cast further blame on them in his interviews with his Superior. To exculpate them insofar as lay within his power, he went to Father Mauron the very afternoon of his expulsion and told him that since he had first proposed the American house, he was responsible for pushing the new foundation. Therefore he alone should bear the punishment.[45] The Rector Major received him kindly, listened to him patiently, and assured him he understood. Then, graciously, Father Mauron offered him the hospitality of Villa Caserta while he was in Rome. Father Hecker thanked him for his kindness and accepted his offer until he could find lodgings in the city.[46]

After he had offered Mass in the Community chapel the next morning, Father Hecker carefully studied the decree of dismissal. Two lines caught his attention. One was the opening statement that the Congregation had previously forbidden its subjects "to go to the Superior General without his special permission obtained in writing"; the other was the accusation that "your way of acting and thinking in general is by no means in harmony with the laws and spirit of our Institute." Both of these statements surprised Father Hecker. He had never heard of such a prohibition and the accusation was in complete contradiction to the testimonials of his immediate superiors. Again, Father Hecker went to Father Mauron's room and asked if he could look at the prohibition mentioned in the beginning of the decree of expulsion since he had never seen it before, nor had any of the German or English Fathers in America ever mentioned it to him. Father Mauron replied that the former Vicar-General, Father Smetana, who was still residing at Villa Caserta, had told him he had issued such a prohibition. Although Father Mauron did not have a copy of the Vicar-General's circular, he told Father Hecker that since Father Smetana had a good memory, he could be quite certain that such a prohibition had been issued.[47]

Referring to the accusation that his conduct was far from what was expected in a Redemptorist, Father Hecker told Father Mauron that he had the "best of testimonials from his Provincial" who had put in writing that he was a good and zealous Redemptorist who had always enjoyed the full confidence of his superiors. He also cited Father Helmpraecht's recommendation testifying that as his superior for four years, he was pleased to state that Father Hecker had won his praise for his regular observance of the Rule and for his excellent moral character. This information seemed to surprise Father Mauron who said he would take time to reflect. This ray of hope lifted Father Hecker's spirits but only temporarily, for when he returned, Father Mauron gave him his decision in the words of Pilate: "What I have written, I have written."[48]

The procedure followed in his dismissal from the Congregation distressed Father Hecker more than any other event that had taken place in the Villa Caserta. It is prominently mentioned in all his letters and brought forth strongly in his later statements to the Roman Congregations. He could not understand why the Rector Major failed to fulfill his promise to hear his defense before his Consultors. Since he was given no such opportunity, Father Hecker declared he had been condemned without a hearing.[49] On the other hand, Father Mauron was equally emphatic in declaring that he had listened to the American missionary and had given him his day in court with the Consultors.[50] Though these two statements are directly contradictory, yet each man in his own conscience could honestly affirm the truth of what he had said.

In defense of his position Father Mauron could declare that he had interrogated and listened to Father Hecker on three different occasions; that he had faithfully related to his Consultors what Father Hecker had said; that when Father Hecker was called before the group, he was asked to justify his journey to Rome. When Father Hecker began his defense with an appeal to the Constitutions which the Consultors recognized as the argument he had advanced in his interviews with Father Mauron, they apparently expected that he would restate all that he had told Father Mauron. This they regarded as a waste of time since in their judgment those reasons in no way excused or condoned his conduct.[51] In truth they could say, as they did, that they listened to all of Father Hecker's arguments. But of course, they heard them not from Father Hecker's lips, nor from any formal statement of his, but from the Rector Major. In this sense, they were informed and Father Mauron could maintain that Father Hecker had a hearing and was not condemned without the opportunity to defend himself.

In support of his statement, Father Hecker could point out that he did not consider the three "informal talks" with the Rector Major an impartial nor an objective hearing. Because of Father Mauron's attitude he found it "impossible that I could explain myself." Then when the Superior General told him he would be called upon to give in the Consulta his reasons for the journey, he understood this to mean a quasi-judicial trial. Consequently he made no attempt to overcome Father Mauron's unfriendly attitude and fully explain his side of the story.[52]

Father Hecker never contested the Rector Major's claim that he had acquainted his advisers with Father Hecker's defense as he had gathered it from the three interviews. However, Father Hecker did contend that this presentation was neither complete nor objective. It was not complete, since Father Hecker had not told the Major General the full happenings, nor had he offered in evidence his testimonials. It was not objective, since without this exposition, Father Mauron had only one half of the case, that of Father Ruland. Further, in his appearance before the Consulta, Father Hecker was asked only one question and had no opportunity to explain himself.[53] It is clear from the Consultors' later testimony, that there was no discussion with Father Hecker; they did not ask him any questions; they did not hear any testimony from his lips other than the admission that he knew of the Rector Major's circular of May, 1857. The only defense they heard him give was the appeal to the 1764 Constitutions. Consequently they had formed their judgment of the case before Father Hecker ever entered the Consulta. This fact is substantiated by their testimony that they "beseeched him [the Rector Major] to dismiss Father Hecker immediately from the Congregation." Then after they had reached this decision "Father Hecker was called to the Council." There is no doubt that before Father Hecker ever entered the room he was judged guilty of the charges and the decree of dismissal was prepared and drawn up.[54] Quite honestly and without any distortion of words, Father Hecker could declare that he was dismissed without a hearing.

Although Father Hecker was dismayed by the action of his superiors he was not embittered. He had heard his good intentions misconstrued and his highest motives distorted. But he did not believe that personal animosity or ill will had dictated his Superior's course of action. He could say he had no "feelings of resentment against any one of the actors; on the contrary I would embrace them all with unfeigned sentiments of love and charity. God has been exceedingly good not to leave me to be tempted even in this way."[55] His superiors, he was confident, had acted in what they believed were the best interests of the Community. But they had completely misunderstood him and his companions and were woefully ignorant of the religious and spiritual needs of America. As he wrote to Brownson: "I am fully convinced that had a full hearing been granted, it would not have helped me or our affairs in the least. These good men from their education, politically and religiously are led with bona fide intentions to misconstrue our motives, misinterpret our language and misunderstand our actions."[56] He gave a similar explanation in his letter to the American Fathers: "Candidly if I had been listened to all day in the Chapter [Consultor's meeting] and had said all that could be said by each one of you, after all, I should not have been heard; for in their minds our thoughts, language and actions are looked upon by them in such a light, that our affairs are judged before a word is spoken."[57]

When the Rector Major had denied all his appeals for a reconsideration of his case, Father Hecker decided that "after prayer and consultation with some prudent and learned men" he would "take another step."[58] But before he moved in any direction, he must first find a place to live during his stay in Rome. He decided against the area around the Villa Caserta because it was a little too far from the heart of the city where most of his activity would be centered. After a little investigation he selected an apartment in a side street adjoining the Piazza di Spagna. The rooms were pleasant with three windows overlooking the plaza. He could see the tall column crowned with a statue of the Immaculate Conception standing in the center of the square and a little beyond that the long flight of steps leading to the Church of Trinità dei Monti.[59] But there was a more important reason why Father Hecker had chosen this location. He was just a few steps away from the headquarters of the Congregation in charge of the affairs of the Church in America, the Sacred Congregation of Propaganda. Not only was all the business of the Congregation transacted there, but the influential Cardinal Prefect, Alessandro Barnabò, had his office and his apartments in the same building. No matter what action Father Hecker decided to take, he wanted to be close to the ecclesiastical body directly concerned with the growth and development of the Church in the United States and to be within easy reach of the man who guided its destinies.

On Monday, August 31st, Father Hecker with a heavy heart took leave of his Redemptorist brethren in the Villa Caserta. As he walked along the Via Merulana toward the Basilica of St. Mary Major, he felt that his former brethren regarded him as a degraded religious whose conduct had merited the extreme penalty of expulsion from his Community. The weight of the bag he carried in his hand was as nothing compared to the weight of sorrow that pressed upon his heart. He was only thirteen years a Catholic and not quite eight years a priest when he was called upon to defend his honor and his reputation in a strange city where he knew no one and where his ignorance of the language was an added misfortune. But despite all his difficulties and the tortuous road ahead of him, he was not discouraged. He looked to "God alone" for his consolation and strength. "Thus far God has strengthened me and our Blessed Mother, I am assured, does not forget me." He wrote to his brother George: "I put my trust in God alone, in the right of my (no, our) cause, the purity of our intentions and the protection of our ever-blessed Mother Mary." With the aid of divine grace, he resolved "to act with deliberation, advice and with much prayer and determination." He was sure of one thing: he would "never yield" his place "in the Congregation while there remains a spark of hope." Resolutely, he made up his mind that he would "endeavor by all means lawful and charitable to be reinstated in the place of my choice and love."[60]

CHAPTER XIV

Appeal to the Holy See

A S HE sat in his apartment near the Piazza di Spagna on the first day of September, 1857, Father Hecker faced the future realistically. He realized that his immediate aim was the cancellation of his sentence of dismissal and reinstatement in his beloved Redemptorist Community. But even if he were to succeed in achieving that, he would not consider his work completed. Never for a moment forgetting his reason for coming to Rome, he ardently cherished "the cause of God and His holy Church in our own dear country." That was his constant preoccupation and he believed that "if God grants me to be the means of having our country understood here at Rome and aiding in preparing the way for its conversion, all that I have suffered these few days past will be as nothing." It was clear, however, that he would be unable to enlist the support of high-ranking Roman officials for this special mission until the extreme penalty of expulsion had been removed and he was once more regarded as a loyal son of St. Alphonsus. His first move, therefore, must be to have his sentence of dismissal revoked.[1]

Although Father Hecker's objective was clear in his mind, the means to achieve it were shrouded in mystery. The intricacies of ecclesiastical procedure and the involved process of presenting an appeal were about as familiar to him as the unexplored reaches of the Antarctic. He needed advice and guidance. Immediately his thoughts turned to his devoted friend, Father de Held, rector of the Redemptorist house in Liége. Because of his long years in administrative posts in the Community and his previous experience in Rome, he would know the best way to approach the problem. Father Hecker also knew that he could place complete confidence and absolute trust in this devoted religious who had recommended him for ordination some years before. On September 1st he wrote to Father de Held explaining the purpose of his visit to Rome and its unfortunate outcome. Telling him of the Rector Major's reference in the decree of dismissal to the ban imposed by Father Smetana, Father Hecker said he knew nothing of this document and had based his right to make the journey on the 1764 Constitutions. However, his defense was not accepted and he was dismissed on the grounds that he had violated the circular of the Rector Major forbidding such a journey. Because of Father Mauron's unfriendly attitude, Father Hecker explained, his case had not been heard fully and impartially. Consequently he would try to have his sentence reversed. Then mentioning the letters to Cardinal Barnabò and Archbishop Bedini which had been given him, he asked Father de Held what steps he should take. Should he first call on these prelates, or should he appeal directly to the Holy Father? He also hinted in this letter that Father de Held, if he thought well of it, might write to his superiors asking for clemency on Father Hecker's behalf.[2]

The same day, Father Hecker also wrote to his three American confreres, Fathers Walworth, Hewit, and Deshon. Knowing that they would be anxiously awaiting word of his visit to Rome, he reported the events culminating in his dismissal. This letter, however, he did not send directly to the Fathers but enclosed it in one to his brother George. He did this for two reasons. Knowing his changed status in the Community, he feared that his letters might never be allowed to reach those for whom they were intended. Also he did not want to run the risk of having anyone except the American missionaries read his letters. Any hope that might exist for the revocation of his sentence would be jeopardized if news of the events of the past few days had leaked out through him before it issued from official sources within the Community. For the remainder of his stay in Rome, he continued to send his letters to the American Fathers through his brother George who delivered them personally. On all his correspondents, including

Brownson and McMaster, he enjoined absolute secrecy about his affairs.[3]

After telling the missionaries and his brother about the tragic conclusion of his visit to Rome, he assured them he was neither discouraged nor conscience-stricken: "Even now my judgment approves wholly of the course that has been taken. . . . If my letter seems cheerful under present circumstances, it is not put on but simply because my intentions have been God's interest and I have a stronger desire to love and serve Him. I feel more impressed than ever of my obligation to be a good religious; Our Lord help me that I may." At the moment he did not know what action he would take, but "after prayer and consultation with some prudent and learned men, I will take another step."[4]

The Redemptorist Rector Major was well aware that Father Hecker might appeal his sentence of dismissal to the Holy See. Father Ruland had told him that the American missionary had letters of introduction to Cardinal Barnabò and Archbishop Bedini. To prepare for such a move, he decided to call on Barnabò and also Cardinal della Genga, the Prefect of the Congregation of Bishops and Regulars. This latter group, the predecessor of the present Congregation of Religious, handled all affairs pertaining to religious communities and Father Mauron knew that any action Father Hecker might take would fall within its jurisdiction. He discussed the matter with Cardinal della Genga and then saw Cardinal Barnabò.[5] He did not go into any discussion with the Prefect of Propaganda about Father Hecker's dismissal nor did he mention the action he had taken. He merely told him that Father Hecker was in town and would undoubtedly call on him. Then he asked the Cardinal to form no judgment of the purpose of Father Hecker's visit until after he had discussed the matter with him, the Rector Major.[6]

Father Hecker had no illusions about the magnitude of the task confronting him. A lone American, dismissed from his Congregation, he was protesting the decision of his Rector Major, the prestige of whose office gave him a privileged position in the eyes of ecclesiastical officials. Further, as an expelled religious, Father Hecker would have to plead his cause before experienced Roman authorities professionally on guard against even the appearance of resistance to authority. As Father de Held expressed it: "It is difficult to be considered in the right as against superiors at Rome, because Rome sustains legitimate authority as far as possible."[7]

As for Father Hecker's great hopes for the future of the Church in America — they were hardly to be shared by many in the Papal Curia. They had known of the native American outbursts denouncing Catholicism as a foreign importation dominated by despotic and absolute ecclesiastical rulers in Rome. The very democracy which Father Hecker viewed so favorably was confused in Rome with European republicanism whose avowed aim was the subjugation of the Church to the State. The events of the Revolution of 1848 which spread persecution of Catholicism throughout Europe were all too fresh in the minds of ecclesiastical Rome. Even the Holy Father had experienced the fury of the unrestrained mob when shots were fired at his own residence in the Quirinal and he was forced to flee from Rome in disguise. Hardly, then, could he be enthusiastic about democracy which had proved to be nothing more than anarchy in Europe and he seemed to be apprehensive about its success in America: "In the United States there exists a too unrestrained liberty; all the refugees and revolutionaries gather there and are in full liberty."[8]

The goal that Father Hecker had set before him was truly gigantic and no one saw it more clearly than his loyal and devoted Redemptorist confrere, Father de Buggenoms: "I must confess that unless Our Blessed Lady work a miracle, it will be hard for you to carry the point which brought you to Rome, as it will be hard enough to be reinstated in the Congregation."[9] Father Hecker's confidence, however, was equal to the obstacles. It was rooted not in his own efforts, nor in the help he might receive from important and highly placed officials in Rome, but rather in "God and the Truth, these are my defense — and the Blessed Virgin my hope and protector."[10]

Yet, despite his trust in divine help, Father Hecker did not disdain the aid of influential men. In fact, he sought it. He immediately began to put to use the letters he had brought with him from the American bishops and from prominent Catholic laymen. Bishop McCloskey had given him one to the Rector of the Irish College, Dr. Tobias Kirby, which seemed made to order at this stage of his affairs. Anticipating that Father Hecker might encounter difficulties in Rome, the Bishop had written: "Should it be necessary for him to have recourse to the Card. Prefect of the Propaganda, he may need the counsel and direction of some one experienced in the *ways* of Rome, and I know of no one to whom he can be more safely commended than yourself."[11] Shortly after he was settled in his new apartment, Father Hecker called on Dr. Kirby and related what had happened. Realizing the seriousness of the situation and the importance of taking immediate action, Dr. Kirby arranged for Father Hecker to meet his former vice-rector, Bernard Smith, who was then teaching at the Propaganda College and who would have easy access to Cardinal Barnabò. This meeting with the Propaganda professor was the beginning of a most important and influential friendship that was to last until the closing years of Father Hecker's life.[12]

The Irish-born Bernard Smith had finished his studies for the priesthood at the Jesuit Collegio Romano where he obtained his doctorate in theology. Shortly after that he joined the Benedictines at Monte Cassino, but because of difficulties with the Italian Government, he left the community to assume the vice-rectorship of the Irish College. He also held the chair of moral theology at the Propaganda College. Shortly before Father Hecker met him, he had re-entered the Benedictine Community leaving his post at the Irish College but still retaining his professorship.[13] An affable man with a penetrating mind and shrewd judgment, he took a great interest in Father Hecker and arranged to have him meet the Cardinal and present his letters of introduction. Although the Cardinal was a stranger to Father Hecker, Father Hecker was no stranger to the Cardinal. He had first heard of him almost two years before when his name was sent to Rome as one of the three candidates for the vacant see of Natchez, Mississippi. The Cardinal had read the recommendations of Father Hecker sent over by the First Provincial Council of New Orleans and by Archbishop Kenrick. He could not fail to notice how highly these American bishops had regarded this American missionary.[14] He had also received, before Father Hecker's visit, two commendatory letters from one whose judgment he trusted, the American Consul General for the Papal States, Louis B. Binsse. One of these letters had left America on the very ship in which Father Hecker had sailed;* the other had arrived a few weeks later. The latter was the result of a lengthy conversation between Binsse and Father Hecker a short time before he boarded the *Asia* and as a result of which Binsse had acquired a more complete understanding of Father Hecker's mission to Rome. Because of his "regard for that worthy religious" and his deep concern "for the great cause which he heartily wishes to serve," the Papal Consul decided it was necessary "to talk a second time, but briefly with your Eminence on that subject."

After these introductory remarks, Binsse reminded the Cardinal that although the principal work of the Redemptorists in the United States had been the parochial care of German-born Catholics, the Congregation had attracted remarkable native-born converts. They had "seen quite naturally opening up before them a field as vast as that in which the German Fathers who first founded the Congregation in the United States have worked. They have immediately devoted themselves to missions of a character which is at present entirely particular to their Order in this country. The good which through the grace of God followed and will follow from these missions adapted to the practical intelligence and to the circumstances in which the country finds itself and to its needs is beyond calculation. For some interesting details, I refer Your Eminence to Father Hecker himself who enjoys as much as any priest I know the full confidence of all, clergy and laity, in the Church in the United States." Then citing the "very important fact" of the abundance of vocations to the Redemptorist Community, he mentioned that sixty young men were studying for the priesthood. This growth, he observed was in marked contrast to "the sterility which is noticed elsewhere."

After he had painted the brighter side of the picture, Binsse drew the Cardinal's attention to some somber tones that threatened to overshadow the glorious future of the Community: "But that state of things so consoling and encouraging is hampered by the circumstance that the Society has in this country only a German superior and German houses exclusively, and everything pertaining to the Order is German. It is then for the purpose of putting his Order in the way of entering more freely into a very vast way of utility to which evidently divine Providence is calling

---

* The content of this letter is given on pages 245 and 246 of this volume.

it in this country that Father Hecker has undertaken his journey to Rome."[15]

This information would immediately catch the attention of the Cardinal Prefect of Propaganda who was charged with the spread of Catholicism and with the regulation of ecclesiastical affairs in non-Catholic countries. He had shown special interest in the establishment of the hierarchy in England and Holland as a means of increasing Catholicism in those countries.[16] He would be no less concerned with any move to accelerate the growth of the Church in the New World.

In his letter, Binsse did not close the matter with these observations. He added a few words about Father Hecker personally whom he characterized as possessing "in a remarkable quality and in equal quantity the gifts of prudence and courage. . . . He has been the object of the most remarkable expressions of esteem not only on the part of prelates and distinguished Catholic laity, but also on the part of highly placed people in political life, of savants and littérateurs." Then Binsse requested the Cardinal's interest on behalf of Father Hecker: "Your Eminence can by the influence you exercise aid him with powerful and valuable assistance, if you judge after reflection that it is opportune to do so."[17]

On either September 6 or 7, 1857, Father Hecker called on the Cardinal. Before reaching the Prefect's office, the American missionary met the Secretary of Propaganda, Archbishop Cajetan Bedini, who was no stranger to American affairs. In June of 1853 he had come to the States on his way to his post as Apostolic Nuncio to Brazil, to investigate for Pope Pius IX serious trustee troubles involving the Church in America. Arriving at the height of the Know-Nothing movement, he had been the victim of numerous hostile demonstrations which in several cities almost reached the proportion of riots.[18] But despite his unpleasant experiences the Archbishop, who remained in this country until February of 1854, retained a friendly feeling for America and was delighted to meet Father Hecker. He listened attentively to the American priest's brief but complete account of what had taken place. He entirely approved of Father Hecker's actions and only regretted that when he arrived in Rome he had not first called on Cardinal Barnabò.[19]

After this interview Father Hecker met one of the most influential men in Rome, Cardinal Barnabò, who was to become his "Father, Counsellor and Protector."²⁰ Born in 1801 to a noble family of the Romagna in Umbria, not far from the home of Pius IX, he had gone through a course of military training at St. Cyr before he entered the priesthood. After serving as secretary of the Propaganda, he was appointed prefect of the Congregation and made a cardinal in 1856. He was of medium height, but very stockily built, with a large head, a broad forehead, a long thin nose, light gray eyes, and a wide, firm mouth. His slightly ruddy complexion blended with his light brown hair that was turning gray. Energetic and straightforward, he was regarded as a fearless defender of justice and truth and an unrelenting foe of arbitrary and dictatorial methods. Held in high esteem by the Holy Father, he was known to press his opinions with frankness and honesty even when he disagreed with the Sovereign Pontiff. One who as a student at Propaganda had known the Cardinal personally described him as "approachable and free of formalities when a worthy object was proposed to him."²¹ It was this quality that first struck Father Hecker. The Cardinal greeted him warmly and with real affection, so much so that Dr. Smith told the American priest "he never saw a bishop treated with the cordiality and distinction with which the Cardinal and the Archbishop treated me."²²

After Father Hecker had presented his letters of introduction from Archbishops Kenrick and Hughes and from Bishop Bayley, all of which spoke of his mission to Rome on behalf of an American house of the Redemptorist Community, Cardinal Barnabò told him to call on the Rector Major and "see what could be done." This, Father Hecker answered, he had tried to do but without success. He then gave the Cardinal an account of his dismissal. As he listened, the Cardinal's expressive face showed first surprise, then astonishment, and finally displeasure. This reaction puzzled Father Hecker until the Cardinal told him that the Rector Major had called on him but said nothing of the action he had taken, other than to inform him that he could expect a visit from the American priest. What particularly irritated Barnabò was the General's request that he form no judgment and take no action until he had consulted with him, while he kept silent on the dismissal. This attitude offended the Cardinal's forthright spirit as he exclaimed: "What! he has done all he could without giving me a word of information!" Referring to the General's action he said: "In Rome it is not customary to act in that way." Then he advised Father Hecker to draw up a statement explaining his purpose in coming to Rome, the reasons he had for thinking he could make the journey, and the way in which he had been treated since his arrival.[23]

Undoubtedly the Cardinal found it difficult to understand why a priest who had enjoyed such high favor with the American bishops, who was so well recommended by clergy and laity alike, who even had testimonials from his immediate superiors commending him for his zeal and piety, could suddenly become so perverse and incorrigible as to deserve the severe punishment of expulsion. As he looked at the honest face across the desk from him and listened to Hecker's calm, deliberate recital of his condemnation given without any feelings of bitterness or resentment, he felt sure the General had acted precipitously and without complete information. Reassuring Father Hecker, he told him not to worry or fear, that he would personally investigate the whole case. Then the Cardinal outlined the procedure that he would follow. After Father Hecker had submitted his statement, he would send it to the Rector Major for an answer. When both documents were in hand, he would bring the disputants together in his presence and after hearing from each, he would give a decision.[24]

However, the Cardinal observed, there is one difficulty: "That is not an identity but only a coincidence, which will not be in your favor, and that is the appearance of its [the project for an American foundation] being an exclusive American movement." Father Hecker answered that he was well aware of this danger but he trusted "that their intelligence and the grace of God would enable them to see that there was no foundation whatever for such a suspicion." Then to disprove any such charge, he quoted the recommendation of the Irish-born Archbishop Hughes, who would never favor a nationalistic movement. As well, he cited the encouragement he had received from Irish-born Catholics in New York such as Terence Donnelly and others. Moreover, he added there is not "the slightest accusation that can be brought against any of us [the American Fathers] as having during all our labors showed any exclusive and party spirit." The Cardinal was perfectly satisfied with this explanation and again assured Father Hecker of his co-operation and support.[25]

After a week of suffering and disappointment, of sleepless nights and worried days, this visit immensely consoled and comforted Father Hecker. He could write to his confreres in America: "The picture is not all black." He was still amazed at the Cardinal's reaction, which was most unexpected: "he was so quick in his perceptions, so candid and confiding in speaking to me." His first experience with Roman officials and his first visit with a Prince of the Church was most gratifying. It made him feel "as never before the presence of God in those who are chosen as rulers of His Church."[26] More than upon any other friend he made in Rome, Father Hecker relied completely upon Cardinal Barnabò. He made no moves and decided upon no course of action without first discussing them with the Cardinal who gave him "free access." When the Cardinal offered his advice, Father Hecker followed it implicitly with the greatest fidelity to every detail. As time went on the American missionary's gratitude to God increased for having given him such a stanch defender who took an active and personal interest in his affairs, almost as though the Cardinal himself were personally involved. On one occasion after Father Hecker heard the Prefect speaking in his defense, he thanked God: "that he was not against me, for he was a most imperious character when aroused and there seemed no resisting him."[27]

Shortly after leaving Propaganda, Father Hecker began to prepare his brief. He employed no canonist to advise him nor did he cite any theological or canonical principles in his favor. His document was a straightforward, clear, simple statement without legal phraseology or the amenities usually employed in such formal statements. It was the sort of presentation that an American, unfamiliar with protocol, would make. It lacked, for example, the commonly accepted Roman conclusion ordinarily addressed to a cardinal: "Kissing the sacred purple and with profound respect and the greatest veneration, I sign myself, Your most humble and obedient servant." Unfamiliar with the formula, Father Hecker merely signed himself: "Your most humble servant in the service of Jesus and Mary." When he handed his manuscript to a translator to be put into Italian, that learned gentleman thought this expression too informal and changed it to conform to custom.[28]

Following the threefold division suggested by the Cardinal, Father Hecker began by saying: "the prospects of our holy Faith were never so encouraging in the United States of America as at the present moment." He did not detail the reasons upon which he based this judgment but stated that not only intelligent and devoted Catholic laymen recognized this fact but even the Holy Father had declared in a recent letter to the American hierarchy: "the time had arrived when the most strenuous exertions and efforts should be made for the conversion of the non-Catholic people of the United States."[29] Then he asked who was called upon to initiate this glorious movement. The "leading Catholic minds in the United States" looked to the Redemptorist Fathers as the one group singled out by God for this glorious enterprise, because they numbered in their ranks converts who were thoroughly familiar with the non-Catholic mind.[30] Their experiences as Protestants gave them an intimate knowledge of the inadequacy of man-made religion and through the grace of God their discovery of the divine truth of Catholicism gave them an advantage in presenting their newly found religion to their fellow men. Not only would they understand their non-believing brethren but they would know how to offer them the divine help they were unconsciously seeking.

Proudly admitting the excellent work the German Redemptorists had accomplished among the German Catholics "by their preaching, their zealous labors in the confessional, and by their attractive display of religious ceremonies in their churches and by their example," he, with intelligent and zealous Catholics, thought the time had come to extend the work of the Community to the native-born as well. To do this an American house was necessary. It would be "a most fitting instrument to exercise a powerful influence not only upon the English-speaking Catholics, but even on the Protestant community. For it is well known that the non-Catholic community in the United States are [sic] desirous to hear Catholic preaching and are attracted in crowds to witness the ceremonies of the Church."[31]

But it was not only Americans who thought such a foundation highly desirable. It had occurred to Europeans within the Congregation as well. Then Father Hecker cited the attitude of Father Bernard whom he carefully identified as the former Provincial of the Congregation in the United States and a Hollander, who considered "such a foundation demanded both by the best interests of the Congregation and the general good of our holy Religion and often spoke of it as a work which he had at heart and as likely to take place." That was five years ago and despite the fact that there were six American-born Fathers and about twenty-five vocations in the studentate and novitiate, the Community had "established no other than German communities." To live a community life in these houses "as the Rules require, the English-speaking subjects have to learn German, and conform to the German way of living." This was in striking contrast to the course the Redemptorists had pursued in other countries. Citing the pattern followed in Poland, Germany, Belgium, England, and Ireland, he pointed out that in each of these countries "the Congregation has established itself in the language of the country." Father Hecker did not ask why there should be a different policy for America.[32]

The absence of an American house, he continued, hindered the flow of vocations, since "in the whole of the United States there is no Redemptorist community that presents itself to priests and Catholic young men other than German." American youths attracted to the Congregation would recoil from the necessity of learning the German language and conforming to German customs and "thus place themselves out of proper relations with their own countrymen." Nor would they be encouraged to take such a step by their spiritual directors or their bishops. Sensing the danger of the charge of nationalism in these words and mindful of Cardinal Barnabò's warning to avoid any semblance of a native American movement, Father Hecker emphatically declared: "the idea of our being actuated by an exclusive or national spirit is a baseless suspicion and an unprovoked calumny." It would be unreasonable to suppose, he added, that the Archbishop of New York and the Bishop of Newark would encourage an exclusively American foundation. Yet they were heartily behind the project as they indicated in their letters. At this point Father Hecker quoted the letter of Archbishop Hughes telling how desirous he was to have the proposed house. To this testimonial he added the additional information that those who have offered to give generous contributions were not Americans but Irishmen. "Our labors have been principally among the Irish Catholics in the United States; they are our warmest friends and supporters."[33]

After disposing of the question of nationalism, Father Hecker returned to the American Fathers' attitude toward the projected foundation. They did not force their views on their superiors but labored indefatigably for upward of six years on missions with the most gratifying results. During that time they gave seventy-three missions, heard more than one hundred and fifty thousand confessions and received from four hundred to five hundred converts into the Church. The conversions were all the more remarkable, he said, since the mission sermons were directed to the faithful and not to the non-Catholic. "This shows plainly that if there were preachings and exercises for the conversion of non-Catholics, the harvest of souls that could be reaped would be abundant beyond belief. Knowing this and witnessing the blessing of God on our labors, it could not but be near our hearts to have the opportunity of laboring for the conversion of our countrymen, not only on missions but at home where we could adapt our preaching, instructions and other exercises so as to bring about their conversion more generally and effectually."[34]

Father Hecker readily admitted that they had explained their views to their immediate superiors and had asked for an American house. Satisfied with the answer that there were not enough members for the foundation, they waited patiently continuing with their labors, until they heard from "strangers" that a new foundation was contemplated for Quebec which would necessitate sending American subjects to staff it. When asked if this report were true, the Provincial had said yes, "that the foundation had been promised two years ago and if found suitable would have to be accepted in the coming month of October, and the General had also written to that effect."[35] This news deeply disturbed the American Fathers who found it difficult to understand why a new foundation requiring English-speaking subjects was under consideration outside the confines of the United States when their request for a similar house had been denied. They could come to only one conclusion: "The Rector Major whose office it is to accept foundations would never have made such a choice had he known how things stood." But how were they to give him a true picture of the situation in the United States? Letter writing would be inadequate since they could never sufficiently explain on paper the religious needs of America, the impossibility of their existing foundations fulfilling these needs, and the consequent necessity of an American house. Moreover, correspondence would not only be time consuming, it would be ineffective since "certain unfavorable impressions had been made previously on the mind of the Rector Major on this and other affairs which there was no hope of removing by writing." The American Fathers saw only one way to clarify the situation: one of them must go to Rome and personally explain all their aims and hopes.[36]

Had they the right to take this step? Father Hecker answered this question by quoting from the Constitutions permitting such action when grave reasons are present. In his mind, as well as those of his confreres, there was no doubt that the importance of the projected American foundation was more than sufficient to justify the journey: "If an undertaking in which the general interests of Religion in a country like the United States and the best interests of a religious congregation are concerned, constitutes a grave reason, then surely there was here a grave reason. Several Fathers of the Congregation including the Provincial thought there was such a reason." After quoting the Provincial's words that he thought one of the Fathers should go to Rome, Father Hecker asked the question: "If the Provincial believed this why did he not give the permission?" Because he thought the General's circular of 1857 suspended this particular article of the Constitutions. After a discussion of the background of the circular and the American Fathers' interpretation of its precise meaning "which was shared by several German Fathers" including his immediate superior, Father Hecker concluded: "In brief, this journey to Rome was undertaken with the conviction that it was in strict accordance with the spirit and letter of the Constitutions, with the will of the Provincial and not against the wishes of the Rector Major."[37] Father Hecker did not quote from the Provincial's statement that if he thought he had the power to grant such a permission he would readily do so. Had he included these words, he would have clarified what he meant by "the will of the Provincial."

In brief but dramatic fashion, Father Hecker then told what had happened when he reached Rome. He mentioned his three visits with the Rector Major, visits which he described as "most painful because of the base motives he imputed to me and others who were interested." He saw some hope, however, in the promise of the Rector Major to allow him to appear before the Consultors "to explain and say all that I deemed necessary." Describing his appearance in the Consulta, he related his abortive attempt to defend himself, the totally unexpected decree of dismissal, and the General's refusal to grant him any further hearing.[38]

In his final summation, Father Hecker concluded: "Many other important things were not mentioned for fear of being too long; but I trust that your Eminence will discover by the above that all who desired this step were actuated by the true interests of our holy Religion, by real devotion to the Congregation of which they are members, and by zeal for the salvation of neglected souls."[39]

After his brief was put in final form, Father Hecker had it translated into Italian and presented it to Cardinal Barnabò on September 15th. The Cardinal was quite satisfied with it. So too was Archbishop Bedini who said it was "clear, logical and strong."[40] Three days later, Barnabò sent it to the Rector Major and asked him to answer it.[41] Before Father Mauron gave his reply he called on the Cardinal and the conversation centered on the circular of 1857. Barnabò said that even if the General had the right to suspend certain sections of the Constitutions, did he have the power to attach the penalty of automatic dismissal? Father Mauron replied that he had acted within his rights. "My good Father," said the Cardinal, "you had better reflect a little on the matter. You may have acted with precipitation." Then Barnabò sounded out the Rector Major about withdrawing the dismissal, but Father Mauron felt that to do so would result in the downfall of all religious discipline. "But," observed the Cardinal, "if you have done an injustice, ought it not to be repaired?" The result of the visit was the Cardinal's offer to act as a friendly mediator between the two contesting parties. If Father Mauron refused this offer, then the case would be given either to the Congregation of Bishops and Regulars or brought to the attention of the Holy Father for a settlement.[42]

At this stage of negotiations, the Cardinal was hoping for informal arbitration without recourse to any formal legal action. This too was Father Hecker's desire: "God knows that I would gladly settle all this amicably. . . . I am willing to make all reasonable sacrifices and abide by his [Barnabò's] decision."[43] But by September 19th, all hopes of avoiding a lengthy and prolonged litigation began to fade. Father Douglas had called at Father Hecker's apartment on the 18th, but he was not at home. The following day Father Hecker returned the call at the Villa Caserta and met the General with whom he discussed the situation. Father Mauron told him he would not reverse his decision, that he had acted according to the Constitutions, and that in his reply to the Cardinal he would uphold his right to dismiss this disobedient subject. When Father Hecker denied he had been disobedient, the Rector Major "attributed all kinds of motives" to him. Father Hecker countered by saying that if the charges Father Mauron alleged against him and his companions were true "his decision is just and I have merited dismission* and should be content." But he insisted they were not true in any sense and therefore he would do all he could to have the sentence of dismissal annulled. In further discussion, Father Mauron asked some questions regarding Father Walworth taking the first step toward securing the American foundation. Realizing that the General was not as well informed as he should be, Father Hecker simply answered that it was too late to speak of those things now. He saw no reason to fill in the gaps in the General's knowledge of the American project since the case might still come before an ecclesiastical tribunal. If it did, then Father Hecker would have the decided advantage of being personally familiar with the negotiations for the New York foundation while the General would have to depend solely on written reports from the Provincial.[44]

Although this visit practically proved to Father Hecker that Father Mauron was not disposed to submit the sentence of dismissal to mediation but was determined to uphold it vigorously, he made one more effort to avoid any protracted trial or an involved legal process. He called on Father Douglas and asked him to use his influence with the General "to have this matter

---

* In his correspondence and statements, Father Hecker constantly uses the word "dismission" rather than "dismissal."

settled amicably by means of Cardinal Barnabò." But the Consultor General refused saying that the case could not be adjudicated in this manner. It was obvious then that Father Mauron preferred to oppose Father Hecker's appeal in the Congregation of Bishops and Regulars than contest it before Cardinal Barnabò.[45] He could correctly reason that the Prefect of Propaganda's obvious partisanship for Father Hecker had ruled him out as an impartial judge and cast him rather in the role of a defender.

When Cardinal Barnabò heard of the General's reaction, he decided to acquaint the Holy Father with the case. He did not do it himself, but told Father Hecker to have Archbishop Bedini, in his audience with the Pope, explain the whole situation including the dismissal and the aims Father Hecker had in mind in coming to Rome. On September 20th Bedini briefed the Holy Father and suggested that he might like to see the American missionary, although he did not directly request an audience for him. The Pope replied that he would have to see the General first.[46]

During the course of these negotiations, Father Hecker received an answer to the letter he had sent Father de Held. The Belgian Redemptorist was very sympathetic to his young friend whom he called "Reverend and dear Father." Then he said: "I address you in this way because I believe that in heart and mind you are in the Congregation." He told Father Hecker he must take it for granted that someone had made erroneous reports to the General about him personally and about his journey to Rome. As for de Held writing to the Rector Major on behalf of his exiled confrere, he thought it useless: "I have not much influence with our Superiors at Rome and I ought for your own sake to abstain from writing to them." However, he urged Father Hecker to call on Cardinal Barnabò with perfect confidence and present his letters of recommendation. The best way for him to gain access to the Pope was through the English-born convert, Monsignor George Talbot, whom he was sure Father Hecker had met in England. "Go to him from me," said Father de Held.[47] This was excellent advice since Talbot was a power with the Holy Father. Pius IX had selected him as one of his private chamberlains and had given him an apartment near his own in the Vatican. He was known throughout Rome as the confidant and most intimate favorite of the somewhat impressionable Pontiff. Although Talbot had a tendency to exaggerate his influence — he once said that he had the Pope's ear and that no one knew the mind of the Holy Father better than he did — it was by no means insignificant.[48] Father de Held knew this and he reasoned that if Father Hecker could win Talbot to his side, his influence, together with that of Barnabò and Bedini, would practically assure his success. But what Father de Held did not know was that Talbot's lot was cast with the General. It was he who had suggested to Father Mauron that the Redemptorists accept the station in the Island of St. Thomas in the West Indies[49] and he would not welcome any move that might interfere with this foundation. The Rector Major could correctly represent to Talbot that Father Hecker was not in favor of this establishment but was pushing a plan of his own which might adversely affect Talbot's project. When Father Hecker followed de Held's advice and called on the Monsignor he quickly discovered that the papal chamberlain would hinder rather than help him.[50]

The lines of battle were beginning to form. On the one side was the Rector Major with the prestige of his office and the support of his consultors, aided by his "undercover" agents Talbot and de Merode (another one of the Pope's chamberlains) and by Cardinal Reisach who watched carefully at Rome the interests of the German people.[51] On the other was Father Hecker recommended by the American bishops, backed by his missionary companions and his European Redemptorist confrere, Father de Held, assisted by his own "undercover" agents, Bernard Smith and Tobias Kirby, and championed by Cardinal Barnabò and Archbishop Bedini. Father Hecker with a cause to advance was on the offensive with the resourceful Prefect of Propaganda masterminding his campaign. The Rector Major, forced to uphold his authority, was on the defensive determining his strategy according to the action of Father Hecker.

In late September of 1857, Cardinal Barnabò was awaiting the General's answer to Father Hecker's statement before advising the next step. On September 30th, Father Mauron submitted his reply. It was a legal document, well organized and well reasoned, including quotations from a papal brief, the Council of Trent, the Redemptorist Constitutions, and the writings of St. Alphonsus. It contained a clear statement of the Rector Major's rights and duties and a logical justification for his action granting the validity of the facts supporting it. Father Mauron divided his treatment of the case into two questions: did he act legitimately in expelling Father Hecker; did he have just reasons for expelling him.[52]

In the first section, Father Mauron quoted from the Constitutions to vindicate his right to dismiss subjects who do not give edification. He added that according to a brief of Leo XII issued in March of 1828, the Rector Major "is not obliged to render an account of the reasons which had determined his action in expelling any subject . . . a declaration as wise as it is necessary to prevent infinite litigation, for otherwise every expelled member would institute a process against the Rector Major." Having clarified his position that he was under no obligation to reveal all the motives that prompted his action, Father Mauron answered Father Hecker's complaint that the Rector Major had not listened to his explanations. He clearly distinguished the issues involved and said that he repeatedly told Father Hecker he must above all else first justify his right to come to Rome. "With regard to this, I not only allowed him full liberty to explain himself, but I myself questioned him several times and compared his statements with the report received from his Provincial and other American Fathers."[53] Father Mauron continued: "The claimant complains further, or at least seems to complain, that my Consultors were not sufficiently informed, or that they had not consented to his expulsion."[54] This was a rather strange statement since Father Hecker had made no such complaint. He did complain that the General had promised to give him a hearing before the Consultors which he did not grant, but he did not say nor imply that the Consultors had not consented to his expulsion. In fact, he made very clear in his brief that they had acquiesced in the General's action.[55] However Father Mauron did not deny that he promised Father Hecker a full hearing before the Consulta.

In answering this "complaint" of Father Hecker, Father Mauron made the observation that the Constitutions did not require the consent of the Consultors and even if they "were not of my mind, the absence of their consent would never be a reason to impugn the lawfulness of his expulsion." However, he maintained his Consultors were fully acquainted with the case. He had held a discussion with them for almost two hours in which the facts were carefully examined, the explanations of Father Hecker seriously considered, and the reasons for and against expulsion fully evaluated. The consultors were all of one mind: Father Hecker should be expelled. Then Father Mauron added: "If the complainant should perhaps hold that I should have held the consultation in his presence, or have discussed the matter with him, such a pretension would not deserve consideration."[56]

The Rector Major then turned to a discussion of the question: Did he have sufficient reasons for expelling Father Hecker? Taking the decree of expulsion as the basis of his argument, he amplified the charges he had listed in that document. He naturally paid particular attention to the circular of 1857 maintaining that by its very nature it excluded any application of the 1764 Constitutions. The circular contained a particular command given to the American Province which would exclude every contrary interpretation permitting the journey to Rome. Moreover, he observed, this circular was merely an application of the general law of the Church as decreed in the Council of Trent which forbade religious to leave their convents even to visit their superiors, unless the superior sent for them. "Whoever shall be found without the said rescript in writing shall be punished by the ordinaries as a deserter of his institute." Father Mauron maintained that he had done nothing more than command under penalty of expulsion what had been decreed by the Council. By ignoring this circular, Father Hecker had merited the punishment promised in the document itself. Father Mauron maintained he had no other choice but to expel him. If he did not, "the vow of obedience that Religious profess is nothing but an illusory, absurd and ridiculous ceremony."[57]

Although Father Hecker had appealed to the Constitutions to justify his action, the Rector Major declared he had not paid sufficient attention to the section pointing out the grave dangers involved in departing without the permission of his immediate Superior. Father Hecker had no such permission. In fact, "the Provincial had begged him earnestly and for the love of God not to take this unlucky step but to write to me first instead of making the journey in vain."[58]

In this rebuttal Father Mauron did not touch the delicate question of the wording of the circular nor did he refute Father Hecker's argument that its lack of directness would allow of a contrary interpretation. He simply stated that the circular was clear and definite, that it admitted of no contrary interpretation and therefore Father Hecker was guilty of violating its prescriptions. Also he did not distinguish the time sequence in the reaction of the Provincial. When the Fathers first requested permission for one of their number to go to Rome, he begged them not to take such action without first securing the Rector Major's permission. But when Father Hecker told him he had decided he would invoke his constitutional privilege and make the journey, Father Ruland declared: "Against this, I had not wanted to protest from the beginning, so as perhaps not to bring on a greater evil." When he saw that Father Hecker was determined to go, he asked him repeatedly "not to take any steps that might turn out badly."[59] Such a request was sufficiently vague to include writing first to the Rector Major, but it was not clear enough to declare that Father Ruland "had begged him earnestly and for the love of God not to take this unlucky step but to write" to Father Mauron before beginning the journey.

To Father Hecker's alleged violation of the vow of poverty by taking money from his brother, Father Mauron devoted very little attention other than to say that the mere fact of Father Hecker telling the Provincial his brother was supplying the means for his expenses was not sufficient. He should have requested specific permission to receive such a gift.[60]

Despite Father Mauron's protestations that he would not discuss the projected foundation in New York until Father Hecker had first justified his action in coming to Rome, he listed the enterprise as a cause for dismissal. Obviously he had not heard Father Hecker's explanation of the actions of the Fathers or his own conduct in this matter. He accepted what Father Ruland had reported to him and repeated these charges in his reply to Cardinal Barnabò. They boiled down to the simple facts that Father Hecker had the caprice to project a new foundation on his own authority without the knowledge of the Rector Major or the Provincial, that he negotiated with the Archbishop of New York "in May of the current year" for the house in New York, and had even selected the site. Then he requested the Provincial "formally . . . to found at once an English Community."[61] In this recital of facts, Father Mauron had become confused. It was not Father Hecker but Father Walworth who mentioned to the Provincial the new foundation, but even then he presented no formal petition. He merely told the Provincial of the offer made by the Bishop of Newark, not the Archbishop of New York, for a house in the diocese of Newark and not in New York. The Bishop had made the selection of the site; not the American Fathers. Further, they had made no formal negotiations with the Prelate, but conveyed his request to the Provincial.[62] Perhaps if Father Mauron had discussed these transactions with Father Hecker before he expelled him, he would have received a correct understanding of what had happened. He made the unfortunate mistake of attributing to Father Hecker what Father Walworth had done and then accepting the Provincial's interpretation of these actions labeling them as formal negotiations unknown to the Provincial.

Before concluding the matter of the American foundation, the Rector Major referred to Father Hecker's statement that "he understood that some of the best American subjects were destined for Canada." Then he went on to say: "but in this point he does not tell the whole truth and intentionally passes over in silence an important fact. The Father Provincial, wishing to do his best to quiet the malcontents and keep them from any unwise step, through an excess of goodness and indulgence gave them an express promise that no American subject would be sent either to Quebec or St. Thomas."[63] When Father Hecker said he understood that some of the best American subjects were destined for the new foundations, he was practically quoting from Father Walworth's letter recounting his interview with the Vicar-General of Quebec. The latter had visited Archbishop Kenrick and asked him if he thought the Redemptorists would send two English Fathers for the new foundation. The Archbishop replied "he did not know of any they would be likely to spare, unless Father Duffy and Father Baker."[64] When the whole subject of the American house came to a head in late July of 1857, the Provincial declared that none of the missionaries would be sent to Quebec. However, he did not deny that English-speaking Fathers would be required. Then the Fathers reasoned that if one of their number would not staff the new foundation, at least some of the American missionaries would be needed to replace the men who would be sent to

Quebec.[65] This was the meaning of Father Hecker's statement, which unfortunately he failed to make clear in his brief, thus leaving himself open to the charge of refusing to go outside his country.[66]

With a strong peroration, Father Mauron concluded his discussion of the American house projected by four young Fathers who were not even local superiors: "What confusion, what disturbance of good order, what contempt of authority, what destruction of all obedience and all discipline does this not imply? What Superior General could govern a Religious community, and maintain in it discipline and the true spirit if such a democratic system were introduced? Our Holy Founder says in one of his Circulars, August 27, 1755: 'Once obedience is done away with, the Congregation dies; obedience [is] gone, and what would remain in our houses but trouble, opposition and sin?' "[67]

In the remaining four pages of his statement Father Mauron undertook to refute Father Hecker's "assertions" regarding the Redemptorist Congregation in America. He justified the Community's continued attention to the German Catholics on the grounds that they were the most neglected of the immigrants in the New World. For this reason "our houses and churches have had to do so much with the spiritual welfare of the Germans. All those who know the state of affairs in the United States agree that our Congregation is one of the principal props of the Germans in that country." Nevertheless as the number of native vocations increased, missions to Catholics were inaugurated with remarkable success. Then, Father Mauron quoted Father Hecker's statistics on the efficacy of the missions and their influence on non-Catholics. However, he sharply disagreed with the American missionary's contention that sermons addressed directly to non-Catholics were a more effective means to win converts than the traditional Catholic mission: "Experience sufficiently proves that the Apostolic missions are a much more efficacious means to attract and win the hearts of Protestants than all the conferences, controversies and demonstrations that may be carried on *ex professo* for their conversion, although sometimes and in certain circumstances these may be useful."[68] Here, of course, Father Mauron was not on solid ground. He was disputing an experienced missionary who had preached extensively in his own country, had given doctrinal explanations of Catholic Faith to non-Catholic audiences and had seen their effectiveness. Father Mauron, on the other hand, was theorizing about a country he had never seen and making emphatic pronouncements about the most effective way of convincing the American non-Catholic to whom he had never preached. Nor did he have any clear idea of the type of discourse Father Hecker had in mind as admirably suited to the needs and intelligence of those outside the Church. Raised as a Catholic in a Catholic European environment and dealing only with a Catholic audience all of his priestly life, he was hardly in as good a position as Father Hecker to determine the most successful way to win the Protestant mind in America.

Another point of wide divergence between the two priests was the German character of the Redemptorist houses in America. Father Mauron based his objection on a statement in Father Hecker's brief which he admitted must have been an error in translation: "I suppose that the complainant, not knowing Italian sufficiently well, has not expressed himself exactly, or that the translator of the pamphlet has not understood him. I know him too well to believe that he would deliberately tell a lie as manifest as it is monstrous."[69] Father Mauron had reasoned correctly. The translator had made a very serious mistake. Father Hecker had written in his manuscript: "In the whole of the United States there is no Redemptorist Community that presents itself to priests and Catholic young men other than German."[70] Father Hecker meant that because the Redemptorist churches in America were known as national parishes where services were conducted in German, sermons preached and confessions heard in that language, people would naturally regard the Fathers in charge of these churches as German. This, Father Hecker maintained, would be a barrier to vocations. This, of course, the translator did not gather from Father Hecker's statement. So he translated it: "Throughout all the U. S., there was not one Redemptorist who, though German-born, could carry on a conversation with priests and Catholic young men."[71] Naturally enough, Father Mauron seized on this as a vilification of the Community and vehemently denied the charge. What he refuted, then, was not Father Hecker's statement but what he admitted to be a garbled version of what Father Hecker had written.[72]

He also took strong exception to Father Hecker's declaration that because of the prevalent German tone of the American Redemptorist houses, the English-speaking subjects had to learn that language. Answering this, Father Mauron wrote: "We do not impose on our American novices the obligation of learning German."[73] Certainly there was no specific rule requiring the novices to learn German nor had Father Hecker said there was. However, practical circumstances demanded it. The Annapolis *Chronicle* noted on July 20, 1856, that the novicemaster gave his conference "for the first time in English."[74] And the *Annales* of the American Province for 1856 state that "German together with English" were carefully cultivated.[75] Official documents of the Provincial were written in German as late as 1858.[76] Even Father Ruland admitted that in the New York house in 1857, German was spoken during the recreation while in other houses "almost only English" was used when the American Fathers were present.[77] Father Helmpraecht had also stated that the American Fathers objected to the American students having to learn German, yet he did not deny that they were required to do so, thus implying that such was the case.[78] From all this evidence it would seem that Father Hecker had the better of the argument on the language problem, largely because he was speaking from firsthand experience of the situation in the American Province.

Toward the close of his statement, Father Mauron took notice of the testimonials from the American prelates "in which just praise is given to the Congregation in general and to himself [Father Hecker] in particular." He did not disagree with these commendations. "Indeed," he said, "it is a pleasure for me to add my own testimony that with regard to his habits and morals, his conduct has ever been blameless and edifying, and that outside of this matter, he is a zealous missionary, an excellent preacher and a man of talent. However all that I say against him has to do with him as a Religious, with his conduct in the matter discussed above and with his principles, which are destructive of religious discipline, and which once tolerated and propagated would ruin our Institute." For these reasons he dismissed Father Hecker from the Congregation and he notified the Cardinal that he could not rescind the dismissal and receive Father Hecker back into the Community because: "We never receive, on any condition whatever, in our Congregation a subject once dismissed; and in holding firmly to this rule we follow the ancient traditions, the example and admonition of our Holy Founder who although sometimes besieged by prayers, entreaties, intercessions, and appealed to by the love of the Madonna, did not yield, but protested that every exception to this rule would be an incurable wound to the discipline and spirit of the Institute."[79]

This position did not quite accord with Father Mauron's handling of the Bretschka case some months before. On January 9, 1857, the Rector Major had dismissed Father Bretschka from the Community for an unauthorized visit to Rome and for serious breaches of discipline. A month later Father Bretschka denied the charges alleged against him and two of his confreres interceded on his behalf. Father Mauron then suspended the sentence and allowed the expelled to be treated as a member of the Community until he received further information on the charges alleged against him. This information did not reach Rome until May and when the charges were substantiated, the Rector Major reinstated the dismissal.[80]

Before signing his document, Father Mauron assured the Cardinal that he "fulfilled" his duty "with great sorrow." "I regret having to send away a most useful worker and subject for the complainant possesses many good qualities; but in this matter one must prefer the common good to the particular good and Superiors must take care not to be carried away by a misplaced feeling of compassion."[81]

On September 30th, the Rector Major returned Father Hecker's statement together with his answer to Cardinal Barnabò. He also notified the Prefect of the Propaganda that he declined his kind offer to mediate the dispute between himself and Father Hecker.[82] As soon as he received this information, the Cardinal told Father Hecker to draw up a memorial* to the Holy Father petitioning for a commission of cardinals to examine the case and he would present it to the Pope in his audience of October 1st. After the Sovereign Pontiff had read Father Hecker's memorial, he asked Cardinal Barnabò to give him the American missionary's statement of the case together with the Rector Major's answer. After he

---

* Father Hecker used the word "memorial" to designate a formal petition to the Holy See.

had read both documents he would decide either to appoint a commission of cardinals or to send the case to the Congregation of Bishops and Regulars.[83]

This news meant one thing to Father Hecker: there would be no speedy settlement of his affairs. He would have to spend the winter in Rome and might even be detained longer. He was soon to learn what Talbot later told Manning: "Rome is properly called the Eternal City because they never decide a question before they have heard all the *pros* and *cons* which sometimes occupies much time."[84]

CHAPTER XV

Speaking Up for America

AFTER he had drawn up his statement for Cardinal Barnabò and while he was waiting for Father Mauron's answer, Father Hecker's thoughts turned to the cause so close to his heart. He was eager to initiate a movement for the conversion of America which would have the official approval of the Holy See. But everywhere he looked he saw obstacles and problems that threatened to stifle his hopes even before he could express them. The more he studied these hindrances, the more he could sum them up in the one frustrating word: misunderstanding. There was first the crushing blow of expulsion that had fallen because the authorities of his own Community had misinterpreted the purpose of his coming to Rome. Then there was the distressing information which he soon gathered that high-ranking ecclesiastical officials entertained exaggerated and uncomplimentary notions of his country which prevented them from seeing in it a fertile field for Catholicism.[1]

Father Hecker, however, was determined that he would not allow these difficulties to smother his resolve to work for the conversion of America. With a confidence vitalized by divine grace, he set himself to overcome them. While he waited for the decision of the Holy See concerning his own status, he approached with fresh enthusiasm the problem of putting his beloved America in its true light before the eyes of Europe. Strangely enough, both at home and at Rome, he found the chief stumbling block to the conversion of his fellow countrymen was misunderstanding:

in America, misunderstanding of Rome; in Rome, misunderstanding of America.

Father Hecker's missionary experiences in America had convinced him that the non-Catholics' distorted picture of the Church prevented them from examining the true Faith of Jesus Christ. They regarded Catholicism as inimical to human freedom, contrary to human reason, and uncongenial to American political and social institutions. If these prejudices could be swept aside and the fullness of divine revelation could be seen in all its splendor, he believed that American non-Catholics, enlightened by divine grace, would soon be led to enter the true Church. When he went to Rome, he entertained the hope that he might initiate a move which would result in bringing the truth of Catholicism to the attention of the American people. But he had not been in the Eternal City very long before he realized that Europeans had some strange and garbled views of Americans which, if true, would militate against any stirrings of faith in the New World. They regarded his countrymen as engrossed in the pursuit of wealth and consumed with a desire for pleasure and ease, with no concept of virtue and no interest in spiritual reality. Rather than look for the conversion of the American non-Catholic, the European was more concerned with preserving the faith of the American Catholic.[2]

As Father Hecker viewed the situation, he believed that "our country has been long enough calumniated in Europe" and that the shortcomings and weaknesses of the American people "in the darkest of colors has too long occupied the minds of men this side of the Atlantic." To correct this situation, he would speak up in favor of America and show another side of the Yankee character. Just as he had labored so strenuously in his own country to make America know the Church, now in Rome he would exert every effort to make the Church, or rather churchmen, know America. He was delighted to have this opportunity "of advocating at this moment her institutions and coming out boldly here in Rome in favor of her new civilization."[3]

Even before he had left the States, Father Hecker had something of this in mind. He had asked Father Hewit to write an account of the missions showing how faithfully Catholics had attended, how enthusiastically the press had hailed their efforts, and how frequently non-Catholics had received the gift of Faith during the course of these sacred exercises. He planned to have this article published in Rome, as well as Brownson's enthusiastic "Mission of America" which had appeared in the October, 1856, issue of his *Review*. Since he did not know what opportunity he himself might have for writing, Father Hecker came prepared bringing his sources with him: the *Catholic Almanac;* statistics and reports on the religious, social, and political condition of the United States; maps and several copies of *Questions of the Soul*. He had hoped that *Aspirations of Nature* would be off the press before he sailed, but since it had only reached the page-proof stage, he left instructions with the publisher to send him six copies as soon as they were ready.[4]

Father Hecker did not permit the anguish of his dismissal from the Redemptorist Community to diminish his resolve to make America better known in Europe. Although his totally unexpected release from the authority of the Rector Major had cut him to the heart, it also allowed him greater freedom to pursue his objective. Two days after his dismissal, he wrote to his brother George: "Now that there is an open field before me, with the help of God and the protection of our Blessed Lady, I will do my best to get some American ideas understood and appreciated here at Rome. . . . I will try to make the acquaintance of the editors of the newspapers and get some articles on the prospects of Catholicity in our country published." On the same day he wrote to Brownson: "Tomorrow I shall see the book publisher, with whom I am already acquainted about the translation and publication of 'Mission of America.' "[5] The gentleman he had in mind was Giuseppe Spithöver who not only had a bookstore in the Piazza di Spagna but also published books and maps.

After a little investigation, Father Hecker discovered that the most successful medium for bringing American conditions before the minds of prominent ecclesiastics was not a brochure but the pages of *La Civiltà Cattolica*. This influential publication was widely read in Rome and its opinions carefully studied by the Roman Congregations because of Pius IX's interest in it. The able and independent Jesuit, Father Carlo Curci, had projected the idea of this bimonthly magazine in 1849 to evaluate religious and political matters in the light of Christian principles. When he met with opposition from the General of his Order on the grounds that the Constitutions of St. Ignatius prohibited the Jesuits from dealing with political affairs, he enlisted the aid of Pius IX who told the General that the Sovereign Pontiff "had the right to dispense from a point of the rule." Exercising this right, the Holy Father not only encouraged Curci to begin the publication but gave him the necessary money to bring out the first issue in April of 1850. Although the *Civiltà* was not an official organ of the Holy See, it was regarded as the semi-official voice of the Vatican.[6] Knowing that this publication was all-important for his purposes, Father Hecker called on Father Curci whom he found much more receptive to new ideas than any man he had met in Rome. He was not a liberal and yet he was not ultraconservative. He had not followed the example of a number of Catholic journals of his day which loudly praised monarchies and roundly condemned democracy. He chose to maintain the position that the Church was not concerned with the form of government as long as she was free to exercise her divine prerogatives.[7] He was immediately interested in the religious condition of America as Father Hecker enthusiastically described it. However he did not care to carry a translation of an article that had already appeared in an American magazine. Rather than reprint Brownson's "Mission of America" he suggested that Father Hecker write an article which his assistant, Father Brunengo, would translate and prepare for publication.[8] With Father Hecker's consent and because of his questionable status as a dismissed religious, the editor decided to have the author remain anonymous.

With this opportunity before him, Father Hecker set to work. Between his visits to Cardinal Barnabò to find out how his case was progressing, and to the Rector Major to see if an amicable settlement could be arranged, he began his "Present and Future Prospects of the Catholic Faith in the United States of North America." Stating his purpose very clearly in the beginning of his article, he wrote: "The following pages are intended to show that God in His providence has prepared in our time, the American people for conversion to the Catholic Faith, and that the way is now fairly open to the Church to make a most glorious conquest." Then he asked his readers to give a fair and honest appraisal of the arguments he would offer, hoping that they would not only share his opinion but with a little deliberation develop, as he had done, a deep and settled conviction of the glorious opportunities awaiting the Church in America.[9]

The theme or general argument that he advanced was continued in the words: "It is now evident and it is daily becoming more so to all impartial men in the United States, that its [the American] political government and its institutions are based on principles decidedly in favor of the interests and success of the Catholic Religion." To prove this point, he proposed to discuss at some length the religious, social, and political conditions of the American people. But before he began, he paid a glowing tribute to the authors of the American Constitution: "Divine Providence so singularly watched over the framing of the American government, that it may well be doubted that if the Catholics of that country had it for a task to construct in our day its institutions, whether they would frame one so favorable to the cause of their own faith as the one under which they now live." These were very strong words to utter in 1857 about men who had written into the Constitution a clause prohibiting the federal establishment of Church and State. Realizing that to many a European who had been reared in the tradition of union of Church and State, this commendation would be suspect, he quoted the testimony of Gregory XVI in praise of the American nation: "Nowhere am I so much a Pope as in the United States of North America!"[10]

In his portrayal of the religious conditions of the United States, Father Hecker singled out New England as being more or less representative of the situation throughout the country. Calvinism was its predominant sect and remained practically unchallenged until the advent of William Ellery Channing. Rejecting the grim doctrine of the total depravity of human nature, he erected a new system with a more rational theology which in time became known as Unitarianism. Each system was radically different. Calvinism took a pessimistic view of human nature, while Unitarianism exalted it. Calvinism claimed its doctrines logically derived from the Trinity and the Redemption by Christ, whereas Unitarianism repudiated these doctrines and all forms of revealed religion. As a result it lapsed into Deism and naturalism. The conflict between these two ideologies, neither of which fulfilled the religious needs of man, left the average non-Catholic perplexed. He asked: "Where is the Religion to be found which is in harmony with the dictates of reason and commensurate with all the wants of man's religious nature? Is such a Religion yet to be revealed? Is it the task of the nineteenth century to construct from the materials in its possession this Religion which shall be adequate to the intellectual and moral wants of humanity?"[11]

Again Father Hecker realized that these questions would sound strange and almost incomprehensible to European Catholics reared in a Catholic atmosphere. He anticipated their reaction by asking rhetorically: "Why all this effervescence? Why this waste of time of noble impulses? Why these misspent energies?" The solution of the cradle Catholic would be a simple one: "Seek at once, where the truth may be found and found so easily in the bosom of the holy Catholic Church." Obvious as this answer might seem to them, it failed to touch the difficulty confronting the non-Catholic. "In the minds of the born and bred Protestant, it is a truth fixed almost as certain as one of Euclid, that the Catholic Religion is false and the last place of all to seek for true Christianity. It is only after having made the whole circuit of error that the suspicion has entered the mind that perhaps after all the charges made against the Catholic Religion may not be altogether true." Bearing in mind his own tortuous road to the Church but without specifying the difficulties he had to overcome, Father Hecker declared: "Many a convert to the Catholic Faith has given years of earnest labor and honest search to discover that amount of truth which suffices to create a rational doubt of the error of Protestantism. . . . Every other way under such circumstances will be tried before the right one."[12]

As evidence of the truth of this statement, Father Hecker cited the existence of Brook Farm and Fruitlands which attracted earnest seekers after truth. Quoting at some length from *Questions of the Soul,* which he did not identify as his own work, he showed the purpose, the nature, and finally the failure of these experiments. Despite their short-lived existence, they demonstrated an important fact: the desire for the spiritual in the

American people: "One might say that the longing after a more spiritual life is one of the principal characteristics of the American people." Then he took notice of the prevalent European notion that Americans were very materialistic minded: "Far from being a nation absorbed in commerce and in accumulating material wealth, there is no people who are so easily kindled to a religious enthusiasm. Hence the success of the Methodists among them. And few will be found who are more willing to make sacrifices for their religious convictions. Witness their countless churches, their bible and tract societies, spread over the country. We are told on good authority, that no less than one million pounds sterling was made in bequests and donations in the last thirty years by one state alone to religious, charitable, and literary institutions." Then he appealed to an argument that would be apt to win his readers: "What may not the true Religion anticipate from such a people if once they have been won to the faith and are under the immaculate influence of divine grace and guided by the Holy Church!"[13]

Then, lest this charitable tendency might be called Socialism and confused with its European counterpart, he high-lighted the difference between the two: "In Europe, socialism and communism are marked with a downward tendency and away from the Church; in America, their tendencies are upward and toward the Church. On this side of the Atlantic, such efforts are characterized with a spirit hostile to Christianity and involve a repudiation of its morals; on the other side they spring from a natural sympathy with the spirit of Christianity and an earnest desire to realize more perfectly its precepts."[14]

After a slight digression in favor of the American character, Father Hecker returned to his treatment of the disintegration of Protestantism in the United States. Unitarianism, Brook Farm, and Fruitlands were not the only protests against Calvinism. One of its own ministers and a prominent writer gave the development of his thought in a volume *The Conflict of the Ages*. Analyzing this book for his readers, Father Hecker showed the author's abortive attempt to find a satisfactory religion, after he had rejected Calvinism. Taking another volume, *Common Sense Applied to the Gospels*, Father Hecker described the same result. These explanations enabled him to hammer home his theme that if Catholicism and all its teachings were adequately known in the United States, many of these people would find their questions answered in the Catholic Church: "In the United States where the true revelation has not yet been published, one must not think that the repudiation of Protestantism is an evidence of infidelity, on the contrary it is a mark of an active intelligence, native integrity and an honest independent mind — dispositions most favorable to the reception of Catholic Truth. When we consider that of the twenty-four millions of inhabitants of the United States, that seventeen millions are of this class, who like a ripe and abundant harvest are ready for the sickle, where is there a Catholic heart which is not filled with zeal to undertake the noble enterprise of the conversion of this young and free people?"[15]

As his final example illustrating the religious conditions in the United States, Father Hecker chose the Anglican Church, pointing out a very essential difference between the American group and its parent stem in England: "In the United States, it has no support from the political government, no traditional sentiment in its favor and so far from being par excellence the established religion, it finds itself according to its own acknowledgments, unable to keep pace with the increase of population in the United States." Since it did not enjoy a favored position in America, Anglicanism had to struggle to hold its members, especially after the wave of Tractarianism had washed many of her adherents upon the shores of Rome. Her ministers had made strenuous efforts to adapt her teachings and ceremonial to American tastes, but even this proved unsatisfactory. In 1853, several of the most distinguished and outstanding Anglican clergymen presented a memorial to a congress of American Episcopal bishops meeting in New York. After enumerating their problems, the ministers asked (and here Father Hecker quoted from the document): "Whether the Protestant Episcopal Church, with only her present canonical worship and her tradition, customs and usages is competent to the work of preaching and dispensing the Gospel to all sorts and conditions of men and adequate to do the work of the Lord in this land and in this age?" This memorial was then submitted to a special committee of six bishops for further study. After an extensive investigation, they could not agree on any successful solution to the problem. This reaction led Father Hecker to conclude that the American people, not only among the Calvinists and Unitarians but even among the Episcopalians, were still searching for the religious peace and happiness that could be found only in the Catholic Church.[16]

At this stage in his writing, Father Hecker realized that he had filled twenty-six pages and he still had not treated the all-important subject of the relationship between Catholicism and the American political structure. He took what he had finished to the editor of the *Civiltà*, who, after reading the manuscript, told Father Hecker he would publish it as one article. Then he advised his American friend to finish the subject and he would carry it in a succeeding issue of the magazine.[17] This decision delighted Father Hecker since it gave him the opportunity to develop at considerable length his favorite thesis that the political philosophy underlying the Constitution was not opposed to, but in harmony with, the teachings of the Catholic Church.

Father Hecker opened his discussion by referring briefly to the persecutions of 1848 and the suppression of the rights of the Church in various countries of Europe. At that time, he wrote, the American nation opened its doors to those persecuted Catholics and offered them not only asylum but equal religious privileges with her own children. This was possible because: "The framers of the American Constitution were too wise to pretend to have it in their power to give liberty to Religion or the Church; they made no such absurd pretention, on the contrary, they made it unlawful for Congress to interfere with the divine prerogative of true religion — the freedom to exercise its divine mission over the whole face of the globe." This was not only his opinion but also that of the illustrious Archbishop of New York who did not hesitate to declare: "I regard the Constitution of the United States as a monument of wisdom, — an instrument of liberty and right, — unequalled, unrivalled in the annals of the human race. Every separate provision of that immortal document is stamped with the features of wisdom; and yet among its wise provisions, what I regard as the wisest of all, is the brief, simple, but comprehensive declaration that 'Congress shall make no law respecting the establishment of religion, or prohibiting the free exercise thereof.' "[18] Because of this provision, Father Hecker correctly concluded that the Church in America was free not only to exercise her God-given rights among her own children, but had a glorious opportunity to win the souls of those outside her fold.

But, he continued, it was not merely this external fact of non-interference that offered such a wonderful opportunity to the Church but the very nature of American political society which rested on principles essentially Catholic. Fundamentally the American nation was built on the maxim, man is capable of self-government. This dictum presupposed the Catholic doctrine of original sin and repudiated the Protestant principle of total depravity and predestination. For if man, by the fall of Adam, is totally corrupt, his reason and his will are debased. Not only is he then incapable of self-government but he cannot exercise the natural rights of justice and truth. If he is predestined for heaven or hell his obedience to law is forced and not free and he can neither be praised nor condemned for his action. No such effects followed from the Catholic teaching which repudiated the Lutheran theory and declared that although man's nature was affected by the Fall, it was still essentially good. Reason and free will were not destroyed. Consequently the basic substratum of American political life was in harmony with Catholic teaching and opposed to Protestantism. Thinking men, who analyzed the difference between the two groups, began to realize "that the Catholic religion is necessary to the support, perfection and perpetuation of American institutions."[19]

In this philosophical and theological analysis, Father Hecker did not cite any specific individuals who had come to this conclusion. He seemed to imply it was the work of the more speculative minds who in turn could, and in time would, influence popular thinking. But before that could happen, an organized movement had risen out of violent hatred of Catholics and the Catholic Church. This was the Know-Nothing outburst which vented its fury on the Catholic and the immigrant. Father Hecker emphasized that the party was as un-American as anti-Catholic. As such, Father Hecker maintained, it was doomed to failure because its aims and its methods were "as hostile to the spirit and genius of American institutions as they were to the Catholic religion." For a time the party was successful due to the machinations of "disappointed politicians and political parsons." But it soon overreached itself. Hecker cited the action of the Nunnery Committee appointed by the Know-Nothing Massachusetts Legislature with one of its own members as chairman. They investigated a convent school in West Roxbury where they ransacked the building intent on discovering "secret prisons, horrid instruments of torture and victims of shocking crimes." The conduct of this committee was so offensive that even the non-Catholic press condemned it and demanded that the Legislature investigate its activities. The result was that the committee was not only dissolved but its chairman was excluded from the halls of the Legislature.[20]

While Father Hecker did not ignore the harm the Know-Nothing movement had caused, he focused his attention chiefly on the good that it had unwittingly produced. The slanderous attacks on the Church led many Americans to investigate if the Church was what her enemies claimed her to be. Then when the party entered the political arena to elect its own condidates, "the Protestant parsons were so busy with political questions during the campaign that they forgot their ministerial duties and a great number of them made a stampede from their pulpits to the halls of legislation, while the Catholic priests were found quietly in their churches, attending to their religious duties and administering the consolations of religion to their flocks. The American people deprecated the bringing of religious questions into the area of political discussion, and beheld the parsons with the Know-Nothing party, calling out for political proscription of Catholics because of their religious creed. On the other hand, they saw the Catholics with the Democratic party advocating the American principle of freedom of religious worship, the keeping out of politics questions of religion, and their priests preaching peace!" Summing up the striking differences between the two groups, he continued: "What a contrast, the Protestant ministers with their Know-Nothing comrades acting contrary to the principles of the Republic and in a way offensive to the spirit of its people, while the Catholics were activated by the spirit of its institutions and in harmony with the genius of its civilization! The Protestant was anti-American because his religious opinions were anti-Catholic; the Catholic was all the better American because he was Catholic; for the principles of American civilization are consonant with the teachings of his holy Faith."[21]

Turning his attention to the thorny question of slavery, he found Protestantism hopelessly divided on the issue. The Methodists, Baptists, and Presbyterians had split into two groups: "the northern party holding slavery, in se, a deadly sin; the southern party defending it as a divine institution." This division was all the more deplorable because it threatened to split the Union and involve the country in a bloody war.[22]

Father Hecker summed up his arguments in the words: "The character of the political government of the United States, and the material advantages which this new country so abundantly offers, opens a wide door to the Catholic religion, and leaves its people free to adopt and follow the religion of their convictions. To gain the people of the United States, the Church has only to address their intelligence and convince them of the truth. And where is there a Catholic who doubts her future success on such a fair field?" In the ages past she had conquered the heathen and the barbarian, but in the New World it was "the contest of Catholic truth with an already civilized people, and a young and energetic nation; one to whom Providence has certainly entrusted important destinies. A more noble and glorious enterprise is difficult to imagine!" Then looking to the future, he exclaimed: "What will this young nation accomplish for religion when the energies which are now spent in her steamships, railroads and vast commercial enterprises are enkindled by the Catholic faith into a religious enthusiasm! The Church may yet look for the missionaries to convert the Japanese and Chinese among this enterprising and bold people.* We do not give voice to an enthusiastic sentiment when we say that America is the future hope of the Church."[23]

In the final pages of his article, Father Hecker noted that "until now" the Church in America was exclusively engaged in

---

* Fifty-four years after these lines were written, Fathers Thomas F. Price and James A. Walsh founded the Catholic Foreign Mission Society of America and seven years later this American Community sent its first missionaries into China. From that time on, they have labored in the Orient, together with other American-born priests of missionary communities. Within thirty years after the death of Father Hecker, his prophetic words were fulfilled.

caring for the spiritual needs of her children. But the time had arrived to broaden the scope of her activity, for she "cannot content herself with the mere possession of those born in the faith when there are millions of souls around her wandering into the paths of error. Her mission is as her name imports catholic, universal, including in her apostolic zeal and the embrace of her divine love, like her Divine Founder, all and every soul of the human race. She cannot therefore be content without making most strenuous efforts to win those who are without her fold, especially when the prospect is so promising as in this new and vast country. . . . The grace, the truth, the Gospel of Jesus Christ are confided to her alone. The American people are prepared and ready to receive these from her hand, let her but put forth the means with which she is so plentifully provided and they will be won to the cause of her Divine Master." Then briefly he enumerated the means to be used: "religious orders, missionaries, literature, journals and the press. And let the zeal of her children be stirred up to the glorious enterprise of winning this young nation of a virgin soil and the Divine Spouse of Christ will win one of the brightest jewels that ever encircled her heavenly crown!"[24]

In the last paragraph Father Hecker wrote a glowing tribute to the all-embracing zeal of the Vicar of Christ on earth and issued a fervent appeal to Pius IX to initiate and support a crusade for the conversion of America. After citing the Pope's words to the American bishops in 1855 counseling them to spare no efforts "to win for Christ every last unbeliever dwelling within the confines of your Dioceses" Father Hecker wrote:

Was this a wish on the part of the Holy Father or a prediction? Was it merely a hope springing from his apostolic zeal, or a sublime presentiment that one day would become a reality? It surely seems to us that on the lips of the Supreme Pontiff these words, with which he addresses his Church always ring with a kind of grand and divine note and ought to be interpreted in the light rather of heavenly communications than of human sentiments. . . . From the lofty watchtower of the Vatican, the Vicar of Christ observes and keeps focused within his sight all the nations of the earth entrusted and destined to his care; yet, guided by the light from above, he often anticipates their future destinies and in his well-informed zeal he prepares for and initiates the fulfillment of them. Who now knows but that among these might there not be the impending conversion of the United States of America to Catholicism? All things point up this hope in us; and the sublime words of Pius IX eminently confirm us in such a wondrous hope. Perhaps for his Pontificate, already renowned for so many accomplishments, God has reserved yet this one and if, in his day, we will not have the joy of seeing this great work brought to completion and seeing every last unbeliever over there who is sitting in darkness and in the shadow of death enter into the sheepfold of Christ, he, at least, will surely have the glory of having initiated and prompted it with a powerful impetus.[25]

In these two articles, Father Hecker publicly declared his abiding love for America and his steadfast conviction that the Catholic Faith was all she needed to achieve glorious conquests for Christ. He knew he had presented his country in its most favorable light and interpreted both its government and its people in the most laudatory terms. As he said in his letter to his fellow missionaries, he had painted his country in the *"couleur de rose"* to offset by contrast the somber grays in which so many Europeans had pictured his native land. He cited none of the obstacles to the conversion of America and touched but lightly on the evils of intolerance and bigotry. He saw no need to speak of the problems in America since they were only too well known in Europe. He raised his voice in defense of his country to tell Europeans of an America they had little known. As he laid down his pen in early October of 1857, he felt he had said as much as he could. Perhaps he had said more than he should at a time when democracy was not held in high esteem and in a city where political liberty and freedom were regarded as harmful to the cause of Christ.[26]

When he had put the final touches to his manuscript, he took it to Father Curci who was so pleased with the result that he decided to bring it before his readers as soon as possible. Important matter that the editor had intended publishing would have to wait. He would run the first section of Father Hecker's "Present and Future Prospects of the Catholic Faith" as the lead article in the November 21st issue of the *Civiltà* and give the second section the same prominence in the December 5th number. Since the author would remain anonymous, Curci decided

to identify him in a footnote only as "a learned and zealous
American writer" whose article was "worthy of the attention of
all our readers."[27] This was an encouraging reaction coming
from one so well informed as the editor of Rome's most influential
periodical, so Father Hecker decided to secure an even wider
audience for his views. He asked Curci to run off a hundred
reprints in pamphlet form and these he would send to the leading
Catholic journals in Germany, France, and England.[28]

When Father Hecker left the offices of the *Civiltà*, he knew
there was practically nothing more he could do for the present
toward furthering his hopes. He had appealed his sentence of
dismissal to the Holy See and he had written his manifesto for
the future of the Church in America. It would be at least a
month before his articles would appear and he could expect
no action on his appeal until early November. Since October
was the month for vacations in Rome, no business would be
transacted and both the Holy Father and Cardinal Barnabò had
left the city. Father Hecker welcomed this lull in activities and
the respite it brought from the terrific tension and the constant
pressure of his six weeks in the Eternal City. The disappointment, disillusion, suffering, and mental anguish he had experienced had sapped his energies and left his nerves on edge.
The added strain of keeping up a cheerful front to cover up his
heartache added to his burden. At night when he was alone in his
room he could relax by unburdening himself in prayer. When he
was unable to sleep, he would rise from his bed, go to his prie-
dieu and seek divine help and consolation. Often while he was
awaiting the first gray streaks of dawn, he would sit down at
his desk and write.[29]

After October 10th the strain had eased somewhat but all
he could do was watch and wait. Then he decided to follow the
Roman custom and take a short holiday away from his "sea of
troubles." But it would be more than a vacation. He would make
good use of this opportunity by combining pleasure with a
pilgrimage. There were many shrines he could visit, but he had
no hesitancy in making his choice. He chose to visit Pagani,
the final resting place of the revered Founder of the Redemptorist
Community, St. Alphonsus.[30]

On Wednesday, October 14th, Father Hecker left Rome for

Naples with Monsignor Bedini's secretary.[31] After a few days in this seaport town overlooking the Mediterranean, he continued on to Pagani, twenty-five miles to the south, where he had the privilege of offering the Holy Sacrifice of the Mass at the altar of St. Alphonsus and praying at his tomb. This closeness to the mortal remains of the Saint aroused "devout and noble thoughts" within him. He experienced a deep serenity and felt "consoled, supported and confident."[32]

But it was not only to visit the shrine of St. Alphonsus that Father Hecker had selected Pagani and Naples for his pilgrimage. He knew that the headquarters of the Cisalpine branch of the Redemptorists was located in the area and he would have the opportunity of talking with the Rector Major. This group had begun to occupy a larger share of his thoughts a few days before he left Rome. After he had witnessed Father Mauron's adamant refusal to receive him back into the Congregation and had seen the Rector Major's determined stand with Cardinal Barnabò, Father Hecker wondered if union with the Cisalpine Fathers might not be the solution to his difficulty. For even if Rome requested Father Mauron to rescind the decree of expulsion, he would not welcome his formerly expelled subject back into the Congregation. Since he also knew the attitude of Father Mauron toward his fellow missionaries, Father Hecker believed their lot would not be an enviable one.[33] On the other hand, if he and his companions were permitted to join the Neapolitan Fathers, all these problems might disappear. But before he could come to any conclusion, he wanted to know more about the group and to sound out the Cisalpine Rector Major on the possibility.[34]

With these thoughts in mind, Father Hecker called on Father Celestine Berruti who had been elected Rector Major of the Neapolitan Fathers the same year that Father Mauron took office.[35] Father Berruti received him very kindly and was most gracious and warm in his welcome. Since he spoke French, Father Hecker had quite a long conversation with him. After explaining his purpose in coming to Rome and its tragic outcome, the American missionary hinted at the possibility of casting his lot and that of his companions with the Neapolitan Fathers. Father Berruti told him he saw no great difficulties standing in the way of such a move. He had already made application to Cardinal Barnabò for a foundation in the United States since he had two Italian subjects who had made a vow "to labor for the conversion of unbelievers." Although he had received no reply to this request, he expected it would be granted. He also assured Father Hecker that if he and his companions were under his jurisdiction, they would be entirely free to carry on their missions and work for the conversion of America. After Father Hecker had explained that there was no final adjudication in his case as yet and that he would also have to obtain the consent of his companions, Father Berruti told him not to rush matters but to be patient, adding that if he would remain in Rome long enough, he would be successful.[36]

After this conversation, the Rector Major introduced Father Hecker to all the members of his house. The American missionary was impressed by the charitable spirit of the Fathers. It was so marked that he later wrote to his companions: "Indeed the spirit of St. Alphonsus reigns among these good Fathers. It seems at Naples and at Nocera as though you were in the presence of St. Alphonsus and breathed the same atmosphere. They are full of fraternal charity, without guile and most affectionate. I have never seen anything like it in the Congregation before." He summed it all up by saying that they seemed "more like a family than anything else," and he characterized the Fathers as "superior to any class of religious men whom I have seen in Italy."[37]

Despite the excellent impression the Cisalpine Redemptorists made upon Father Hecker, he came to no conclusion about petitioning for union with the group. He wanted more time to study the situation and to investigate at greater length the basic causes for the separation between the two groups. This he planned to do when he returned to Rome. But no sooner had he reached the Piazza di Spagna than he found some very important news awaiting him.[38]

CHAPTER XVI

Unexpected Difficulties

$\mathbf{T}$HE first official word of Father Hecker's expulsion reached the American Province on October 3, 1857. Four days after the dismissal, Father Mauron had written a long letter to Father Ruland enclosing the decree of expulsion and elaborating on the reasons given in that document. Although not as detailed, these were essentially the reasons he later advanced in his reply to Cardinal Barnabò. He explained that Father Hecker had appealed to the Constitutions of 1764, but that he had denied this appeal in view of the special circular of May 9, 1857. Refusing to admit any particular interpretation that would have permitted the journey, Father Mauron claimed that Father Hecker had scorned the Rector Major's authority and had deserved the penalty of expulsion contained in the circular itself. But in addition to this act of defiance, Father Hecker was guilty of three other transgressions. The first was his violation of the vow of poverty: he had accepted money from his brother without specific permission from the Provincial. The second was a violation of obedience: he had projected a new foundation without the knowledge of the Rector Major or his Provincial, even to the extent of dealing with bishops. The third was the formation of a "kind of conspiracy or plot" to force the establishment of an American house. In brief the Rector Major maintained that Father Hecker's conduct was so flagrant that he had no other choice but to expel him: "No other decision could have been reached without destroying first our American Province, then the entire Congregation, and loosening completely the bonds of authority and discipline."[1]

Then the Rector Major directed Father Ruland to tell the Fathers why he dismissed Father Hecker, but he told the Provincial not to show them the decree of dismissal. If the American Fathers should request their release from the Community, they were to write the Rector Major explaining their motives for taking such a step. Father Mauron said that after he had considered these reasons: "I shall thereupon not grant them simple release but likewise the expulsion since they are equally guilty.* Father Hecker told me that he had letters with him from Fathers Walworth and Deshon in which they accept full responsibility for their actions. This is another proof that a formal plot has been staged." He added that he did not think they would take such a step but would await the outcome of any action that Father Hecker might undertake.[2]

The contents of this letter disturbed Father Ruland. Though he had had vague misgivings that the General might dismiss Father Hecker, he had not anticipated such a move. It exceeded his "worst forebodings," and he feared it would have unfortunate repercussions in the American Province. As he told Father Mauron in his reply, Father Hecker had many influential friends among the laity and the hierarchy who, overlooking his rashness, would regard the action of the Rector Major as unduly severe. He became even more convinced of this after informing the Archbishop of Baltimore of Father Hecker's dismissal. Kenrick seemed quite surprised and dismayed by the news. This reaction prompted Father Ruland to discuss the matter with the Provincial Consultor, Father Mueller, and the Baltimore Rector, Father Leimgruber. All agreed that if Father Hecker could be readmitted, the move would have a salutary effect both within and without the Community. The Provincial sent this opinion to the Rector Major with apologies that perhaps he was arguing "along too worldly

---

* The simple release differed from expulsion in several important particulars. Expulsion was a punitive measure the Rector Major could employ to exclude an unworthy subject because of a serious infraction of the Rules of the Community. A simple release was an action of the Rector Major freeing a subject from his obligations upon the subject's own request and for personal reasons of an honorable character. The simple release could be compared to an honorable discharge, while expulsion could be likened to a dishonorable discharge.

and natural lines," but he thought it important enough to merit consideration. He was aware that the authority of the General would have to be upheld, but he thought that the sentence of dismissal in itself was sufficient punishment. Then if it were withdrawn, the Rector Major would be showing mercy and demonstrating that he had "dealt leniently with a Father who as a convert and enthusiast had transgressed more from ardour than malice." The fact of the expulsion would have beneficial results on the Fathers who would realize the seriousness of their actions and refrain from any such conduct in the future. The readmission of Father Hecker would heal all wounds and make the position of the Congregation in America more secure.[3]

Before he wrote to the Rector Major, Father Ruland also sent word to the various houses of the Province that Father Hecker "was excluded from our Congregation."[4] He enjoined on all the Fathers complete silence in the matter and ordered them not to discuss the case.[5] This was in line with Father Ruland's consistent policy of forbidding "discussion of matters concerning the government of our Congregation, or matters pertaining to it."[6] Possibly he also wished to head off any vocal criticism of either the Rector Major or Father Hecker in the event that later on the sentence of dismissal might be withdrawn.

The day after he received Father Mauron's letter, Father Ruland sent a report to the American Fathers as the Rector Major had ordered. Since they were conducting a mission in Newark he forwarded to Father Hewit a copy of sections of Father Mauron's letter which he asked him to translate "if necessary," since it was written in German, and communicate to his companions. In addition to giving his reasons for dismissing Father Hecker, Father Mauron had also told the American Fathers that he would never consent to the establishment of an exclusively American foundation. However, he did not oppose the idea of one in which the ministry would be exercised in English. This was simply a matter of time. But he reserved to his own "judgment and decision" the precise date when he would authorize such a foundation.[7]

Besides communicating this message from the Rector Major, Father Ruland added: "I will not conceal from your Reverence that I received a severe reprimand for having been so indulgent in my conduct in this matter, and for not having resisted the whole movement with all my energy." He admitted that he had failed to see the work of "the evil one" who under the guise of "doing good to the whole country and promoting the welfare of the Congregation instigated movements that are now likely to destroy the whole work of the missions and the hope of soon doing something towards the conversion of this nation to the Church." He should have realized this, he added, and "without human respect have resisted that anti-religious spirit to the utmost. . . . On account of my weakness and the want of judging this deplorable movement according to our Rule and the spirit of St. Alphonsus in its very beginning, I blame myself of being, at least in some way, the cause of so disastrous a result. May God pardon me for the past; in the future I will do my duty to its full extent."[8] In this last remark, Father Ruland believed that he had made clear to the Fathers that he would oppose vigorously any further attempt for an American house. This threat of strong action led him to believe that "he had won back the field against the English Fathers completely." Later, when the American Fathers had no comment to make upon his letter or the expulsion, Father Ruland reported to the General: "So far the American Fathers have kept rather peaceful and quiet. In their letters to me, Father Hewit and Father Walworth . . . have in no way insinuated even slightly about the entire incident." He believed that they had "come to have insight" and that "similar movements have, for all future purposes been thoroughly discouraged."[9]

The Provincial's letter came as no surprise to the American Fathers. They had learned of Father Hecker's expulsion a week before Father Ruland had received word from Father Mauron. They were in Newark to open a mission in St. James' Church on Sunday, September 27, 1857. Curiously enough, it was during the course of a conversation about the date of this mission that Bishop Bayley had made the first offer of a parish for an American Redemptorist house some months before. Fathers Walworth, Hewit, and Deshon had arrived on Saturday, September 26th. That afternoon while Father Hewit was on his way to the church, he noticed a carriage drive up to the rectory. As soon as it stopped, he saw George Hecker and Orestes Brownson hurriedly step out. He waved to them and they immediately came over to tell him the news. Then the three went into the rectory and George read the letters he had received from his brother and handed Father Hewit the one Father Hecker had written to the Fathers. At first, Father Hewit was stunned and could scarcely say a word. Then he became excited but not nearly as overwrought as Brownson who had known of the facts even before he left New York. Father Hewit left George to calm the fiery editor while he went to find his two companions. Their reactions were varied. Father Walworth became quite indignant while Father Deshon, although he deplored the action of the Rector Major, was the least surprised of all. He later told Father Hecker he had anticipated the expulsion. That evening Father Baker arrived and the Fathers took him into their confidence, giving him a full explanation of the dismissal. He too was quite dismayed at this unexpected turn of events and looked upon it as a move to tie the hands of the American missionaries.[10]

When the excitement of the first shock had worn off and they had a few leisure moments from their missionary duties, Fathers Hewit, Deshon, and Walworth wrote individual letters to Father Hecker. Each expressed his sympathy with his confrere in the blow that had fallen on him. But none of them could find any sufficient ground to justify the action the General had taken. Father Hewit gave Father Hecker "assurance that my approbation of your course remains unchanged." He said the Provincial had as yet given them no official word of the expulsion but when he did they would keep a very discreet silence. Meanwhile they could only hope for the best. He told Father Hecker he was not "at all cast down or discouraged. Let us pray to God and Our Blessed Lady and all will come out right." In closing he signed himself: "More than ever your devoted brother in the Sacred hearts of Jesus and Mary."[11]

Father Deshon wrote in a similar vein saying: "I cannot and do not believe that we are to be separated, but hope that this storm will eventuate in something good for us all. We must try to be good and better than ever before and pray for one another." He admitted that he wished Father Hecker had written more in detail telling them how many interviews he had with the General, whether he had presented all his papers, and if he still had all the documents he took with him. Then he advised Father Hecker that since he was "driven into a corner" he had the right to defend himself by all proper means even if it meant exposing the affairs of the American Province to their very roots.[12]

Father Walworth expressed a hope that Father Hecker would be able to reverse the sentence of dismissal "in a way which will be a complete remedy for that whole fatal course of administration which has already brought so much injury upon this Province and is likely to work its ruin." He told Father Hecker that he had written to the Provincial for a copy of his letter about the Newark house which Father Hecker had asked to see. But Walworth was rather surprised at the request since there was nothing offensive in the letter; he could not understand why the letter was so important. Then he concluded with a few sentences which differed in sentiment from that of his missionary companions and which indicated that he had more concern for his own immediate status than for that of his dismissed co-worker who had gone to Rome with his approval and to represent his interests: "You can easily understand our defenseless position at present and how little liberty we have to move, until you obtain a hearing upon the whole merits of the question before Higher Powers than those which have cut you off. I suppose that you consider the sentence otherwise irrevocable. When we are called upon by the competent authority to give our testimony, we can do it freely without danger of being crushed as rebels."[13]

Upon his return from Naples, Father Hecker found these letters awaiting him. This was the first news he had received from his American confreres since his dismissal from the Community and he was most anxious to know their reaction. Though the letters were not very long, they brought him a great deal of consolation and their messages of sympathy, confidence, and reliance on Divine Providence gave him additional courage and hope. He could see in their common trials only a greater bond of union. He told them: "How much these trials will endear us to each other! If we keep together as one man and regard only God, defeat is impossible. Do not forget to offer up continually your prayers for me."[14]

But it was not only from his American Redemptorist confreres that Father Hecker received sympathy and support. He had heard also from his former confessor and close friend, Father de Buggenoms who, although distressed, was not surprised at the outcome of his visit to Rome. He felt that the great work of initiating a move for the conversion of America was such that Father Hecker could not succeed unless the Holy See knew of that objective. And this could only happen when "the ordinary authority" had rejected his "case, or rather, the case of the Congregation in America." He hastened to assure Father Hecker: "I can certainly not imagine any reason for which you should have deserved to be dismissed." He counseled him to have patience and confidence in God: "Great trials make great saints and if God has chosen you to be the foundation or the instrument of some great work, He will know how to build upon your infirmities and to reach from end to end mightily though gently. For this reason, I think you must exercise an heroical [sic] patience and meekness together with prudence and confidence."[15]

Father Hecker's strongest Redemptorist supporter in Europe was Father de Held. From his post in Liége, he constantly counseled his former protégé, telling him that although the right to determine the opportuneness of any foundation fell within the province of the Rector Major, he "could not reasonably bear you ill will for desiring and proposing such a foundation." He advised him not to contest the General's right to issue the controverted circular of May 9th, but to maintain that in executing it, "he could not act contrary to the natural law and justice." Here Father de Held apparently had in mind the expulsion threatened in the circular. He held that according to both the natural law and the virtue of justice as well as the Constitutions of the Society, such a punishment could be inflicted only when a subject was guilty of a serious offense of major importance or when he constantly and contumaciously transgressed the Rule in lesser matters involving a serious injury to the Congregation. But Father Hecker was guilty of no such conduct. At most, Father de Held contended, he might have made a mistake in his interpretation of the circular "but certainly there was no sin." Since Father Mauron had refused to hear the case on these grounds, Father de Held said: "Take your affair to the other legitimate authorities. If my name can be of any use to you, avail yourself of it as you may see fit, — for after all, I fear no one but God." However, he doubted that his influence would be of much value since he believed that he was "not regarded very favorably by our Superiors and probably this sentiment had been communicated to the authorities at Rome. However that may be, I will reflect further and perhaps I will write to Cardinal Barnabò."[16]

After deliberating for a day, Father de Held decided he would speak up in defense of his former subject. On September 28, 1857, he wrote a letter to Cardinal Barnabò which he sent to Father Hecker to give to the Cardinal. "If it is of no very great use to you," he said, "it will not injure your cause."[17] Knowing the reputation that Father de Held had in official circles in Rome since his days as consultor and secretary to the Vicar-General, Father Hecker was sure it would greatly help him. Although he did not know its content, Father Hecker took it to the Cardinal who said that, after he had read it, he would decide how he would use it.[18]

The letters from the American Fathers, from Fathers de Buggenoms and de Held greatly encouraged Father Hecker. They lightened his burden of sorrow and made him realize that he had strong supporters within the Community who recognized that he was fighting for and not against the Congregation.[19] On their part they were willing to join their efforts to his to insure the success of the mission that had brought him to Rome. But no sooner had these assurances buoyed up his hopes than new and unexpected difficulties arose to cast them down. The first of these came from the critical pen of his friend of many years, Orestes Brownson, who had published an "unfortunate" review of *Aspirations of Nature* in the October, 1857, issue of his *Review*.[20]

Before Father Hecker had left the States, he had finished writing this book and had received the Provincial's permission to have it published.[21] When it appeared in proof sheets, he sent the proofs to Father Hewit who read them to Archbishop Kenrick, the foremost theologian of the Church in America. The Archbishop, having no particular criticisms to make, expressed "his high satisfaction with the work." Father Hewit, however, detected many errors in sentence structure, punctuation, and the use of capitals. He suggested to Father Hecker that he go over it carefully and make the necessary corrections before returning the proofs to the publisher.[22] Before Father Hecker could undertake the task of final revision, he was embroiled in the controversy over the American house which resulted in his departure for Europe. Before sailing he sent the proofs back to Father Hewit who promised to go over them carefully and make all the needed corrections.[23]

In the first letter Father Hecker sent to Brownson from Rome after his dismissal he told him: "Your notice of my new book if you will be so kind as to give one in your October number may be of the greatest service and the highest importance to me in getting a hearing in high and the highest quarters." Then Father Hecker suggested: "Make mention that now is the time to prepare the way for the conversion of the American people." Realizing that Brownson might have made up the magazine before his letter arrived, Father Hecker pleaded: "If this letter comes late and you find it necessary to delay some days the publication of your Review to accomplish this, I beg of you, do it. Now is the time to strike the blow. For God's sake and the love of our country and its free institutions do not let it pass. . . . George will see to any expense this undertaking may cost you."[24]

Almost the very day that Father Hecker wrote this letter to Brownson, Kirker, the publisher, had come out with the first edition of fifteen hundred copies. One of these went to Brownson who, after reading it, began writing a long review which he finished before Father Hecker's letter arrived.[25] He told Father Hewit's brother, Dr. Hewit, that it would be a candid and not too favorable criticism of the book. Sensing the danger that such a review could have at this stage of Father Hecker's affairs, Dr. Hewit got in touch with Father Deshon and suggested that Father Hewit should come up from Baltimore and get Brownson to modify his criticism. Immediately Deshon wrote to Hewit and told him the situation, but Hewit was not anxious to tangle with "the old bear" and on a pretext declined to make the trip. Meanwhile Dr. Hewit told Deshon he had read the review which was ready for the press and that it contained some statements that could be of great harm to Father Hecker. Father Deshon had no more desire to get into an argument with the formidable Brownson than did Hewit but he realized that if he stayed out of the fray and the review was printed as Dr. Hewit had reported, he could "never have forgiven" himself "for a gross negligence and dereliction of duty and friendship" for Father Hecker.[26]

When Father Deshon called on Brownson he found that he was in for a real fight. At the very outset of the visit, Brownson said that the review was the longest article in the magazine which would go to press in the morning. He had nothing to replace it and it was too late to make any extended changes. But Father Deshon refused to take this for an answer. He told Brownson that he "not only objected to particulars but to the whole article which was most unfortunate and injurious, that it was more than a criticism lugging in all sorts of odds and ends likely to prejudice" Father Hecker. Sticking to his guns, Father Deshon continued that he "regretted exceedingly that he [Brownson] should take such a course; that it would show only his own inconsistency."[27]

After battling back and forth for three hours, the former West Point lieutenant finally succeeded in getting the stubborn editor to change or eliminate "a number of very offensive expressions and ideas." Brownson did so reluctantly claiming that Deshon "had made him strike every thing in the article that had any point in it." The review as it finally appeared in the pages of *Brownson's Quarterly Review* was more of a triumph for Father Deshon's dogged determination than for his tact.[28]

In the first part of Father Hecker's book, Brownson found little to quarrel with although he took occasion to disagree with the approach that the author had adopted. Father Hecker's purpose was to show that the God-given gifts of reason and will could find their complete fulfillment only in the possession of divine truth and divine love. The function of religion was to help man achieve that goal. The only religion that could do it was Catholicism since it upheld the intrinsic worth of both faculties while Protestanism had taught that as a result of the fall of Adam these powers of man were essentially and permanently impaired. Catholicism on the contrary maintained that: "Original sin did not efface the image of God stamped upon the Soul. Reason and Free-Will remained in their essence unimpaired, uncorrupted, uninjured."[29] Brownson could find nothing heretical in what Father Hecker had written, for as he said: "It would be alike unjust to the author and to us to suppose that we are questioning any doctrine he asserts."[30] Nevertheless he believed that Father Hecker "in his strong desire to show the power of reason and the dignity and worth of human nature, has not made enough of the practical aberrations of reason and miseries of our fallen nature, or, rather, has not brought out as carefully as he might the other side of the picture."[31] This difference in approach revealed the difference in character and outlook of the two men. Brownson by temperament and habit was inclined to take a pessimistic view of reality; Hecker by nature and conviction had a bent for the optimistic. Brownson in his approach looked for what was wrong and insisted it must be removed before the good could prevail; Hecker ferreted out what was good and by intensifying it hoped to overcome the worst. Brownson in his observations and investigations had a nose for defects while Hecker saw the bright spots.

What disturbed Father Hecker when he read the review was not this difference of emphasis on the effects of original sin, but Brownson's observations on the future of Catholicism in America. Discussing the conversion of America, he wrote: "There is a great work to be done here before any direct efforts on a large scale can be attempted for the conversion of those who are without. If the souls of non-Catholics are dear to the Lord, the souls of bad Catholics are no less dear. . . . The conversion of bad Catholics, the proper training of Catholic children, the correction of the vice of intemperance and other immoralities, prevalent in a portion of our Catholic population of this city and the introduction of morality, good order, sobriety, and economy into what are now haunts of drunkenness, dens of vice and petty crimes, would do more for the conversion of non-Catholics than all the books and reviews we can write, all the journals we can edit, or efforts we can make expressly for their conversion."[32] In effect, Brownson was asking for the complete and absolute reign of virtue in the Catholic body before a step could be taken for the conversion of those outside the Church. He was taking the position of the traditional Catholics of England: we have enough to do to take care of Catholics without bothering with the souls of non-Catholics.

Then turning to an analysis of the American non-Catholic, he presented a very damaging picture of his countrymen: "There is scarcely a trait in the American character as practically developed that is not more or less hostile to Catholicity. Our people are imbued with a spirit of independence, an aversion to authority, a pride, an overweening conceit, as well as with a prejudice, that makes them revolt at the bare mention of the Church."[33] Because of this description of the American character, Brownson wrote in the closing pages of the review that Father Hecker "has a livelier sympathy with his own countrymen than we have and is less disturbed by the dangerous tendencies by which they are affected than we are. With him, hope is constant, ever-living and active; with us it is spasmodic, and is kept up only by an effort. We fear the tendencies now at work in our people will carry them so far, licentiousness and corruption of all sorts, in public and private life, will become so universal before the salutary influences of the Church can be brought to bear on them with the requisite power, that they will need to be visited by Almighty God in judgment rather than mercy. We fear also that they are more likely to carry away with them a large proportion of our Catholic population, than this population is to restrain them; we fear that even the salt that should save them will lose its savor and we tremble hardly less for our Catholic than for our non-Catholic population."[34]

Father Hecker saw in these lines ammunition that could be used against him. He had said that America was ripe for conversion, that this was the opportune time to initiate a direct move to bring the truth of Catholicism before the American mind. He had cited prominent men in private life who agreed with him, one of whom was Brownson. When the vacillating editor published this review, Father Hecker feared that the Rector Major could cite it as evidence that he had misrepresented the American scene and any move for the conversion of the American people was premature at this time.

The views that Brownson had enunciated in the *Review* were not only diametrically opposed to those of Father Hecker, especially as found in his *Civiltà* articles; they clearly contradicted what he had written in a letter he gave Father Hecker the very day he sailed for Rome. Brownson wrote this letter not merely as a personal communication but as a testimonial Father Hecker could use if necessary. Then Brownson had said the time was ripe "to institute measures to bring this great and powerful nation into the Church of God." His countrymen were ready to listen to the claims of Catholicism since "the dispositions of the American people are much less unfavorable to the Church than is generally supposed. . . . Their attention is turned to the study of Catholicity as it never has been before, and if approached now in a proper manner, with earnestness and charity, in their own language and tone by a clergy free from those foreign habits and manner which repel their confidence and who sympathize with their free and independent spirit, I cannot [but] believe that a rich harvest of souls will be reaped." He condemned the prevailing European concept of the American people which regarded us "at heart, when not in conduct, a nation of rebels and filibusters whom hardly the grace of God can render loyal and obedient." An idea which appeared in his review of *Aspirations of Nature* in October of 1857 he had disclaimed in his letter of August 5, 1857: "There need be no fear of the *rebellious* American. No people are more ready to submit to legitimate authority, and none will be more submissive than they when converted to the authority of the Holy See or more devoted to the successor of St. Peter."[35]

Within a short time after he had sent this review of *Aspirations of Nature* to the press, Brownson wrote Father Hecker a letter which again contradicted the ideas he had expressed in the article. Referring to Father Hecker's expulsion, he said: "Your good people at Rome seem to have a totally erroneous idea of us Americans. . . . There is not a more loyal people on earth than the American, or more ready to obey the law; but they, of course, cannot be made submissive to the arbitrary will of any man. They will obey cheerfully and scrupulously the law, or the man who governs in the name of the law, or as the vicar of our Lord, but will not obey arbitrary power and never can be made to submit to centralized despotism." He admitted that he was not as sanguine about the conversion of America as Father Hecker was and found as one of the chief stumbling blocks the attitude of Catholics: "The mass of our Catholics think only of enjoying their religion for themselves and lack everything like a missionary spirit. . . . Not a few are opposed to making efforts to convert the country because, in their view, conversion would increase the power of the American element and diminish that of the European. Hence there is not so hearty a response on the part of Catholics to our appeals as we would wish."[36]

Brownson was aware of his inconsistency and tried to explain it away in this letter. He said that his purpose was to head off any criticism of himself or Father Hecker, making clear that the move for the conversion of America was not a "hobby" but a very serious enterprise.[37] His justification was not successful. He had contradicted in his article everything he had written personally to Father Hecker both before and after he had left for Rome. The only plausible explanation for this strange mental flip-flop can be found in one line of the review and in the closing lines of his letter. In the article he admitted that: "It is always better to take counsel of our hopes than of our fears, and we will not dwell on our gloomy forebodings, which after all, may spring from the ill-health, under the depression of which, we are forced to write."[38] In his letter he added: "My own affairs are gloomy enough owing to the commercial collapse and money pressure. . . . I can but starve at worst and perhaps my friends will prevent that. I think it doubtful whether I shall be able to keep up the Review. I have been out of health and am more profoundly discouraged than ever before in my life."[39]

Later Father Hecker learned that Brownson greatly regretted the article he had written, especially when he heard the news of the American missionary's dismissal from the Redemptorist Community.[40] The treatment his friend had received "aroused all the noblest and generous part of his nature and brought back his former warm affection" for his companion of Transcendental days.[41] "If there is anything so feeble and uninfluential a man as I can do to serve your cause," he wrote Father Hecker, "I shall always be happy to do it."[42]

Though keenly disappointed in Brownson's article, Father Hecker entertained no harsh thoughts about the editor. His great worry was the use that might be made of the article, especially since its general tone was "condemnatory of any direct movement for the conversion of our people."[43] In reply he wrote to Brownson: "Surely it is a source of great regret that men who have the same noble and let me say divine work at heart, should find so many differences between them. This seems to be the usual accompaniment of all really good undertakings. It is however most unfortunate that these were put in print and made public at this juncture. The article will increase the unfounded suspicions of the General here and the Provincial in the U. S. A. What you say to exculpate me, however sufficient and true, will not be regarded by minds filled with suspicions. Parts of your letter which touch on these points, I will have translated to counteract this influence of the article if it is used in that way."[44] Personally Father Hecker thought that if Brownson had any advice to offer him or any admonition to give him, he should have done so privately and not through the medium of the public press. Charity and friendship, he felt, required this. Nevertheless he would say nothing. As he wrote to the American Fathers: "Having had to hear in patience and charity, my best motives and purest intentions grossly impeached and that from those who are bound to love me as Fathers and brethren, why it is not so difficult to bear lesser things and forget them from the hands of even old friends."[45] He would overlook this unfortunate incident occurring at a time when he was not in America to explain his position but when he was in Rome where he needed all the support he could get. He made up his mind that he would not allow the article to come between him and his friend of many years: "For my part I am determined to secure every honest man as my friend. Dr. B.[rownson] is all that; if there be any mortification to be taken, I willingly accept it, so that God's glory is advanced and souls gained to Christ."[46]

Had Father Hecker been in America, he would have known that the reaction of the Catholic press more than offset Brownson's critical review. Father Ruland reported to the Rector Major: "The religious press has taken notice of the book and poured many praiseworthy things upon it." Then he added that in his judgment the volume "surely did not merit" these commendations.[47] Archbishop John Purcell of Cincinnati, as well as the Catholic press, did not agree with the Provincial's judgment. The Archbishop took the occasion in one of his sermons at the Cathedral to publicly praise the book and to use it as the basis of his talk on nature and grace.[48] In a letter he wrote to Archbishop Kenrick, he said: "What a book for the times is the 'Aspirations of Nature' by Father Hecker. I had a chance of reading it while on my last visitation. Thanks be to God who raises up such men to illustrate His holy Truth and vindicate His Church by life and pen!"[49]

The review of *Aspirations of Nature* was not the only disappointing news that awaited Father Hecker after his return

from Naples. New currents had grown stronger in his absence
and they gave a severe jolt to his hopes. He had a suspicion of
them before he left Rome when he talked with Archbishop Bedini.
In his visit with the Holy Father in early October, the Archbishop
learned that the Pope had read Father Hecker's appeal to Cardinal Barnabò and the General's reply. When Bedini spoke in
Hecker's defense, the Holy Father said to him: "It seems that
you and the Cardinal have undertaken warmly the defense of
Father Hecker!" Then he returned both documents and told the
Archbishop that he had decided not to appoint a special com-
mission of cardinals to decide the case as Father Hecker had re-
quested. When Bedini reported this conversation to Father
Hecker, his visitor asked what was the next course of action.
The Archbishop replied that nothing more could be done until
Barnabò, who had gone to Foligno, returned to the city.[50]

Although Bedini did not indicate the next move, Father Hecker
thought it would be one of two things. Either the Pope himself
would decide the case or he would give it to the Congregation of
Bishops and Regulars for a hearing. Of the two, Father Hecker
preferred the former, as long as he would have the opportunity of
an audience with the Holy Father before he reached his decision.
This would have one advantage, there would be less delay. If
the case went before the Congregation, he knew that the hearings
and the examination would be a long-drawn-out affair and this
he wished to avoid. However, he could decide nothing, nor take
any action until after he had discussed the matter with Cardinal
Barnabò.[51]

On Saturday, October 24, 1857, Barnabò returned to Rome and
Father Hecker saw him that same evening. As he reached the
Cardinal's room, Monsignor Talbot was just leaving. Father
Hecker surmised that the Pope's chamberlain had relayed information to the Cardinal that would be important to him. No
sooner had he begun his conversation with Barnabò than he knew
he had guessed correctly. The Cardinal told him that the Pope
would not decide the case. Consequently, the only hope was an
official examination by the Congregation of Bishops and Regulars.
The Cardinal said he would give Father Hecker a personal letter
of introduction to the Secretary of the Congregation, Archbishop
Bizzarri, who would return to Rome on November 10th.[52]

This news meant one thing to Father Hecker: he would be detained in Rome all winter and would have to start his case all over again. In an effort to avoid this delay he tried one last stratagem. He had received an important letter from Father de Held written on October 14th and he thought if the Holy Father knew about it, he might change his mind and either give the case to a commission of cardinals or take it into his own hands. Father de Held had answered Father Hecker's letter of October 5th in which the American missionary reported Bedini's conversation with the Pope. This report Father Hecker had heard from the Archbishop himself who had told him that the Holy Father had remarked apropos of the Hecker case: "It is a crisis for the Congregation and a sign of dissolution."[53] This remark alarmed de Held who maintained that the trouble was not in the Community generally but in the governing body of the Community. Since this fact was not too well known at Rome and not likely to reach the official attention of the Holy See he took it upon himself to give an explanation of the situation as he knew it. In the first place, he contended that Father Smetana, "whose excessively violent and arbitrary government" as Vicar-General "had estranged a part of the Congregation," had tried to control the General Chapter of 1855. He attempted this by changing "the inferior superiors such as provincials, rectors, etc. immediately before the Chapter . . . to create docile and passive instruments." Although Smetana could not secure his own election as Rector Major, the candidate chosen, Father Mauron, "owed his office to the influence of Father Smetana." Also the Consultors who were elected were not only "agreeable to him . . . but nearly all of them at least had never known the general affairs of the Congregation." As a result, Father Smetana remained in Rome to assist Father Mauron in the government of the Congregation, although he had not been elected to any office. His influence, Father de Held described as "fatal." If Rome knew this, he believed that the Holy See would find a means to remedy the situation "without the body of the Congregation which is sound and has a future before it having too much to suffer." Father de Held gave Father Hecker permission to use this letter "as you think proper . . . but nevertheless be careful not to expose me uselessly."[54]

After Father Hecker showed this letter to the Cardinal, he

asked him if he thought it should be called to the attention of the Pope. Knowing that this information could have a bearing on Hecker's case, Barnabò did not hesitate a second: the Holy Father should see it. He told Father Hecker to take de Held's letter to Bedini and have him present it at his next audience. Then he added that if Bedini showed any hesitancy in taking it to the Holy Father, Father Hecker should send it by "post" to the Pope.[55]

This advice surprised Father Hecker who, knowing that Barnabò would have an audience with the Pope the following evening, wondered why he himself did not present the letter. Also he could not understand why Bedini would be reluctant to take care of the matter. Then the Cardinal explained. Since the Pope had remarked to Bedini that he and the Cardinal had undertaken warmly Father Hecker's defense, both had to proceed very carefully lest they be regarded as partisans who had already prejudged the merits of the issues involved. If the Pope were to come to this conclusion, then their efforts would be nullified. Moreover, since the contested dismissal was a dispute between a religious and his major superior, it came within the jurisdiction of the Congregation of Bishops and Regulars, not Propaganda. Were they to press matters, His Holiness would undoubtedly tell them the affair was no concern of theirs. After this explanation, Cardinal Barnabò assured Father Hecker that both he and Bedini were just as strongly interested in his success, but because of this new turn of events, they had to be cautious and prudent.[56]

When he left the Cardinal, Father Hecker went directly to Bedini's residence but the Archbishop was not at home. The next morning he returned and gave Bedini the de Held letter telling him that the Cardinal thought he should present it at his next audience with the Holy Father. After reading it, the Archbishop realized it would be of value in Father Hecker's case, but he was not anxious to take upon himself the task of showing it to the Pope. Since he had already been chided about his partisanship, he was unwilling to risk a further rebuke. However, since Cardinal Barnabò had suggested the "post," he thought Father Hecker should send it by mail with a personal note to the Holy Father. Then Bedini handed him another de Held letter. This one the Redemptorist Rector had written to Cardinal Barnabò on September 28th, and the Cardinal gave it to Bedini for the Pope. But

CLARENCE WALWORTH

AUGUSTINE HEWIT

The Five

American

Redemptorist

Missionaries

ISAAC HECKER

GEORGE DESHON

FRANCIS BAKER

CARDINAL BARNABÒ

he never found the opportune moment to present it. As long as
Father Hecker was forwarding the one de Held letter to the
Holy Father, Bedini saw no reason why he should not include
this letter as well.[57]

Although the American missionary had known of this letter —
Father de Held had sent it to him for Cardinal Barnabò — he did
not know its content other than that the Rector of Liége had said
a few words in his favor. But when he sat down in his apartment
near the Piazza di Spagna and read what his faithful friend had
written, he realized that he held in his hand "a complete and conclusive refutation of the calumnious charges of the General"
against him.[58]

Father de Held began by telling Barnabò the reason for his
interest and concern in Father Hecker: "It was I who as the then
Provincial received Father Hecker into the Congregation; it was
under my eyes that this Father passed his novitiate and the time
of studies; it was I who directed his first steps in the holy ministry
when I was Superior of our Congregation in England; and I can
affirm that I never had the least ground of complaint against the
conduct of Father Hecker. He has always been an excellent religious, *very pious,* very zealous and at the same time very obedient
and submissive to his superiors and since this Father has been
in America, I have never heard the slightest complaint against
him. On the contrary, he has seemed a model and pillar of the
Congregation. I ask then, very humbly in the name of justice
and in the name of the Congregation which appears to be threatened with a great misfortune, that Father Hecker may be heard
and his justification favorably received."

Why did the General take such strong punitive action against
such a worthy subject? "I cannot explain to myself," wrote Father
de Held, "the General's proceeding unless by supposing unhappy
and unjust prejudices and by influences which are brought to bear
upon him." Although he did not name the one responsible for
these influences, he mentioned a few circumstances that left no
doubt he was referring to Father Smetana. This part of de Held's
letter was not new to Father Hecker, since shortly after his arrival
in Rome, he had been told that the former Vicar-General still
"rules the Congregation."

Returning to Father Hecker's case, Father de Held told the

Cardinal that he was delighted that "Your Eminence desires to furnish Father Hecker with the means of justifying himself and I thank you with all my heart for this favor." He assured the Cardinal that he was not granting this favor to an unworthy religious, but to one who was convinced that the moment had arrived to extend the work of the Congregation to his fellow Americans. It was for this reason that he came to Rome to acquaint his superiors with the wonderful opportunity facing the Redemptorists in America. Then Father de Held continued: "Doubtless it pertains to the latter [superiors] to judge of the opportuneness of such a foundation, but certainly the step taken by Father Hecker with regard to the legitimate authorities does not appear to deserve the punishment with which this Father is threatened."

In conclusion, Father de Held wrote: "I am ready, no matter what consequences I may have to fear, to give any information that may be desirable." He added that Father Dechamps, the former provincial in Belgium, Father Lans who was then vice-provincial in England, and Father de Buggenoms who had been superior both in England and Ireland, all of whom knew Father Hecker, would give "information as favorable as mine."[59]

When Father Hecker finished reading this letter, he was pleased not only with Father de Held's opinion of him, but especially with his fearless loyalty to him. He still had powerful friends in the Congregation, he thought, who were willing to risk reprisals to come to his aid. The only jarring note to mar his happiness was that he had to use an indirect means to bring this testimonial to the attention of the Holy Father. For a while, at least, his stanch defenders in Propaganda must remain quietly in the background. They could not speak out on his behalf. He must speak for himself. But he could not do it in a personal visit to the Pope, but only indirectly through the mails. Sitting down at his desk in the last days of October, he wrote his first letter to the Vicar of Christ on earth:

Most Holy Father:

I have just received from the Reverend Father de Held, one of the oldest, most devout and greatly respected Fathers of the Congregation of the Most Holy Redeemer, formerly Provincial of Belgium and now Rector of the house at Liege, the letter herewith inclosed, containing matters of very great importance. I had thought it my duty to place it in the consecrated hands of Your Holiness through the mediation of the Sacred Congregation of the Propaganda, but Mgr. Bedini has told me that he has spoken of this affair to Your Holiness, and does not like to return to it unless You mention it to him; and having no other protectors in this city, I am compelled to send it by post. It makes it evident that the present difficulty is not confined to an individual, but extends to a great part of the Congregation. Alas! if Your Holiness would grant me the privilege of speaking to You, I could reveal many things concerning this. Although a very cruel blow has been dealt me, and I sincerely believe it would not have been so bad had I been given an opportunity to explain myself and make a categorical reply, still my affection for the welfare of the Congregation and my brethren remains unaltered, and this is my excuse for occupying [Your] attention and seeking to interest Your Holiness.

I have taken the liberty of transcribing the letter in order to facilitate the reading of it by Your Holiness, and also of accompanying it with another letter from the same father, which has been for some time in the hands of Mgr. Bedini.

Prostrated at the feet of Your Holiness, and asking Your blessing, I offer to Your Holiness the most humble and obedient submission.

I. T. Hecker[60]

After he had sent this appeal to the Holy Father, Father Hecker overcame his momentary depression and allowed his hopes to soar. He thought that the influence of Father de Held would be of such weight that the Holy See might decide to intervene in the affairs of the Congregation and order a new election. If so, this would materially alter his situation and he would be back once more in the Congregation under a new and different administration. Also he wondered if a change in the Rector Major and his Consultors might not restore unity in the Congregation bringing both Cisalpine and Transalpine groups under the one head.[61] If, however, Father Hecker had known of the other events that had taken place in the past weeks he would not have been so sanguine in his views for the future.

Shortly after the Holy Father had read Father Hecker's appeal to Propaganda and Father Mauron's reply, he granted an audience to the Rector Major on October 5th. During the course of this visit, Father Mauron had the opportunity to speak in greater detail of his reasons for the dismissal of Father Hecker and the difficulties that would result if he had to readmit him to the Community. The Holy Father listened carefully as Father Mauron explained that it was necessary to maintain simplicity, humility, and discipline. "And obedience," added the Pope. Then he told the Rector Major he had the right to do what he did; no one could contest it and neither would he. However, he said, "one thing only astounded" him and made him "reflect." This was the favorable testimony that both Fathers Ruland and Helmpraecht had given to Father Hecker. Father Mauron spoke up and explained that because "of the violence of the storm" both had "lost courage and had acted thus only to avoid," as they thought, even greater evils. This explanation seemed to satisfy the Holy Father and he terminated the interview.[62]

When Father Hecker first heard of this meeting between the Pope and the Rector Major is difficult to say. Certainly he knew it by November 9th, when he received a rather discouraging letter from Father de Held. The Rector Major had sent to the Provincial an account of this audience as well as a brief report on the Hecker case. He had said that the American Fathers wanted "to have houses composed exclusively of Americans"; that Father Hecker had taken his journey "against the formal prohibition of his superiors in America"; and that Father Hecker had fully three days in which to exculpate himself to the General and his Consultors.[63]

What was even more surprising to Father Hecker was the sentence: "I simply have to fear great difficulties if anyone comes to know of the letters I have written and which I do not regret, because convinced of your sincerity and truthfulness, I did what I thought right before God."[64] For a moment he wondered if Father de Held doubted him and had come to regret speaking in his defense. To clear up the situation, Father Hecker wrote to Liége immediately and took up point by point the statements that had appeared in the Rector Major's letter.

With regard to the Holy Father's reaction, Father Hecker said this could only result from the remarks the General made in the audience as well as in his report to Cardinal Barnabò. If, said Father Hecker, the facts as related by the General were true, then certainly the Pope would express himself as he did. In fact, if what Father Mauron had maintained were true, then Father Hecker would accept the dismissal and return to America. But he maintained the charges were false and emphatically and categorically denied each one. He declared that the American Fathers had never sought an exclusively American house: "There is not a word of truth in this; no one ever entertained the thought; no one ever expressed the thought; it exists only in the imagination of the Provincial in the U. S. who has excited it in the imagination of the General. . . . It is a sheer calumny."

Father Hecker was astounded when he read that he had undertaken the journey against the prohibition of his superiors. He told Father de Held that the Provincial issued no such prohibition but merely "expressed *his fears* that my journey would not prove successful." With regard to the circular, he said: "The Rector as well as the American Fathers thought it did not touch the affair in hand. If it does, we were mistaken, but we did not act in bad faith."[65]

The charge that he had three days in which to explain himself to both General and Consultors was an evasion of the real issue, Father Hecker maintained. He had never claimed that the General refused to hear him, but he did say that his prejudiced attitude prevented him from listening to an impartial and judicial defense. Because of this attitude and because of his promise to give his accused subject a full hearing before the Consulta, Father Hecker did not present his side of the story fully to the General. He put all his hope in the words of the General "who did not keep his promise."

Since Father Hecker wondered if Father de Held regretted taking part in the controversy, he decided to give his friend the opportunity to "back out" of the whole affair gracefully if he so desired. He wrote: "One thing I am sure of is your uprightness, fearlessness and zeal for God's interests. If God wishes me to stand alone, he will give me the grace to do so. From my whole heart I thank you for every little prayer you offer up for me. One thing my trials have taught me and this is the one thing important, to love God more. It almost seems that I did not know before what it is to love Him."[66]

But Father de Held did not forsake his friend. He rallied nobly after receiving this letter and urged Father Hecker to stay at his post: "It is not your personal or even your spiritual interest that is in question, but a much more general good, that is to say, that which our Congregation might do and seems destined to do in America. It is not merely a question of your vocation but that of all those who being Americans, have been called and may be called to the Congregation. . . . If I were free, certainly I would fly to your help, but in my actual position, all I can do is to tell you what I think and to pray that God may have pity on the Congregation and not withdraw His blessing from it."[67]

Before Father Hecker received Father de Held's letter telling him of the General's audience with the Holy Father, he had two visits with Father Mauron. The first was on October 22nd, the day after his return from Naples. The Rector Major said nothing about his papal interview, but Father Hecker noticed that he seemed subdued, ill at ease, and quite haggard. About the only information he gave the American missionary (and this he told him quite spontaneously) was: "Father Smetana had returned to Germany." Then he asked his former subject "to tell him when anything new turned up."[68]

The second visit, on November 6th, was not so tranquil. Father Hecker found that the General had been sick with Roman fever and was unable to leave his room. When Father Mauron asked him if he were going to the United States and labor as a secular priest, Father Hecker replied: "My future is undetermined, it is in the hands of Divine Providence and my actions would be [decided] according to my counselors." Then he added that if he were what the General thought him to be, he would be glad of the opportunity to return to America: "But I never violated my vows. The Congregation is as dear to me and [so too are] all its members without exception as on the days I made my vows. And thank God no one but my own unfaithfulness can rob me of my vocation; and I am ready with God's grace to suffer death rather than be unfaithful to Him."[69]

After this the conversation veered off on Father Mauron's report to Cardinal Barnabò which gave Father Hecker the opportunity to discuss some of its charges. He told the Rector Major he had "not a word of proof" accusing the American Fathers of conspiracy. Then he related the incident of Father Ruland asking

him to raise money for the property Archbishop Hughes had
designated for the proposed foundation in New York. Knowing
that it was the Rector Major's jurisdiction to decide on new
houses, Father Hecker refused to have anything to do with Father
Ruland's request when the Provincial admitted that he had no
permission for the foundation. The General was "stunned" when
he heard this and attempted to change the subject, but Father
Hecker refused to be sidetracked. Finally Father Mauron said
"the Prov.[incial] is weak and in the moment of excitement he
did not know what he did and he had reprimanded him for this."
All well and good, said Father Hecker, but "you trust the report
of such a man."[70]

Then Father Mauron accused Father Hecker of writing everywhere and saying that he had been condemned without a hearing.
The American missionary denied this and said that he had not
written "everywhere." Father Mauron replied that he knew of
letters Father Hecker had sent to England and America. Admitting
this was true, the American missionary declared that he had
simply stated the truth that the General "had frequently promised
to hear me in full Consulta and that instead he condemned me
without keeping his promise." The General countered by saying
that he had made his case known to the Consulta. "Yes," replied
Father Hecker, "you made it known in such a way that my condemnation would be certain." Then he told the General that if
the case were such as he had represented it in his report and if
"I had acted as he stated, I would be willing" to accept the dismissal and drop the whole affair. In this exchange the General
never said a word about his audience with the Holy Father nor
mentioned the Pope's words that he was right in doing what he
had done.[71]

News of Father Mauron's audience with the Holy Father
reached Cardinal Barnabò, possibly through Monsignor Talbot,
who exerted all his efforts on behalf of the Rector Major. When
both Barnabò and Bedini heard the report, they decided to avoid
all mention of Father Hecker in their dealings with the Pope.
They feared that the Holy Father had taken a decided stand
against the expelled religious and the only prudent course was to
await the outcome of Father Hecker's visit to Bizzarri before
making even the slightest move. They emphatically refused Father

Hecker's plea to secure a papal audience for him explaining that it was too risky a move at that time. The Pope, they explained, apparently entertained a very unfavorable impression of Father Hecker. Were he to see the American missionary while in this frame of mind, he would not be disposed to listen to any defense but would probably give him a "sharp reprimand" and send him "directly home."[72]

In view of this development the only hope lay with the Secretary of the Congregation of Bishops and Regulars, Archbishop Bizzarri. When Father Hecker finally managed to see him in the second week of November, he found that the Archbishop was not very anxious to review the case. Bizzarri had heard of the Pope's words that no one could contest the General's action and he took them to mean that nothing further was to be done on Father Hecker's behalf. In view of this reported declaration, Bizzarri did not want to start any action that would dispute the legality of the General's decree. Father Hecker answered that the Holy Father's decision was based on what Father Mauron had said, but that if he were given a chance, he could disprove the General's charges. Using all his powers of persuasion and "by dint of effort and courage" Father Hecker convinced the Archbishop that he should be given a hearing.[73] Finally Bizzarri told him to draw up a memorial to the Holy Father giving his reasons why the Congregation of Bishops and Regulars should review the decree of expulsion. If the Secretary judged that his reasons were sufficiently valid to bring the case to the attention of the Congregation, he would present this memorial to the Holy Father. But only when the Holy Father approved, could he take any action.[74]

During these days Father Hecker suffered intensely "from seeing the means resorted to against us [the American Fathers] and the helplessness of our position." It seemed to him that every way was blocked and "every side looked dark and nothing was left but to wait with the hope of a change." All he could do was "in silence cry to God and our Blessed Mother for help." Yet he let no one know the anguish he was enduring. People whom he met thought he was the happiest man in Rome.[75] At this time he kept out of his letters to the American Fathers the slightest trace of his trouble. Writing in a cheerful style, he kept insisting that all would turn out well. To keep up a front, every now and then he would throw in a little pleasantry into his letter. After he had seen Bizzarri, he told his confreres: "This morning I engaged a *canon* to draw up my document and brought to him the necessary papers. I think that having now cannon in the field we shall have some heavy reports."[76] Only occasionally did he hint to them the seriousness of the situation and the momentous issues involved: "If Mons. B.[izzarri] tells me to go on, go on it is; if not, then my separation from the Congr.[egation] is *un fait accomplis* [sic]."[77]

All this time, Cardinal Barnabò had not been idle. He had spoken with Bizzarri several times and had counseled Father Hecker's canonist in drawing up his statements. But this behind-the-scenes activity did not satisfy him. He did not relish the role of a silent partner. He wanted to come out boldly and fearlessly in defense of Father Hecker and the future of Catholicism in the New World. But as long as the case remained bottled up in the Congregation of Bishops and Regulars, he could do nothing.[78] Finally after much thought and many discussions with Father Hecker and his advisers, he came up with a plan that would give him a legitimate right to espouse openly the cause of the American missionary and the growth of religion in his native land.

CHAPTER XVII

A New Idea

SINCE the internal administration of discipline of a religious community was the concern of the Congregation of Bishops and Regulars, Cardinal Barnabò could not officially intervene in the dispute between Father Hecker and his religious superiors. However since he had been acquainted with the issues in the case nothing prevented him from reaching some very definite conclusions. He believed that Father Hecker was innocent of the charges alleged against him and that therefore the sentence of dismissal was unjust. Charity as well as justice demanded that Father Hecker's good name be restored and the decree of dismissal be withdrawn. After his first few interviews with the Rector Major, the Cardinal also realized that if Father Hecker were reinstated in the Community, his position would not be "of the pleasantest sort." So although he was determined to press for the cancellation of the decree, he was not convinced that Father Hecker should return to the Congregation while Father Mauron was Rector Major. Before telling this to Father Hecker, however, he remarked to him that if he were reinstated and "if it be for your sanctification and you are willing to suffer, you must return to the Congregation." Without a moment's hesitation, Father Hecker answered he "would most gladly" do this "even though the Gen.[eral] did not wish it."[1]

Satisfied with this evidence of compliance, the Cardinal then considered Father Hecker's future in relation to the general good of religion in the United States. After several lengthy conversations with the American missionary in which Father Hecker's intelligent enthusiasm for the conversion of his fellow men revealed not only apostolic zeal but deep spiritual resources, Barnabò asked him if he thought God was calling him for "a special work" in his own country. Father Hecker answered: "I could not think of this while a dismission was over my head." The Cardinal replied: "Of course not. If you are a mauvais sujet, as the General thinks, God will not surely use you for any special mission. That must be first determined."[2]

Apart from clearing his good name, Father Hecker had another reason for wanting to be reinstated in the Community in which he had made his vows and to which he had consecrated his life. From his student days in Wittem, he was firmly convinced that he would work for the conversion of America, a conviction that was always associated with the Redemptorist Community. He did not entertain the idea that God would call him to initiate any move for his non-Catholic fellow men apart from the vocation he had chosen. Even when he found himself expelled, he felt that it was his "first duty" to see whether this work could be accomplished within the Congregation.[3] Only when he would be convinced that he was completely cut off from the Community, with no hope of returning, could he seriously entertain any thought of working outside the framework of the Redemptorist Congregation. Nevertheless the Cardinal's words alerted him to the possibility of such a contingency arising and to the need of his being prepared for it.

In all his thinking, Father Hecker included his missionary companions. He had come to Rome as their representative solely to plead for an American foundation. At no time had they discussed any specific course of action if he were excluded from the Congregation. Now that this situation had arisen, it put a new aspect on their affairs. His expulsion affected them also since the Rector Major knew that they had been intimately associated with him in planning the new house. As a result, Father Mauron looked upon them as rebels and eyed them with suspicion.[4] Father Hecker realized that any decision in his case would inevitably influence their future. How would they react, he asked himself, if he were told to initiate a new movement for the conversion of America. Would they join him?

This was a momentous decision to make and Father Hecker was well aware of it. It should not be made hastily without evaluating the consequences. Before even suggesting the possibility of such a step to his missionary companions, Father Hecker took counsel with his spiritual director, "so that hereafter no scruples may trouble my conscience and God's blessing may be with me."[5] He had selected for his guide, Father Francis of St. Lawrence, a Passionist Father who had the reputation of being one of the most spiritually enlightened men in Rome.[6] When Father Francis approved of his speaking to the American Fathers on the subject, Father Hecker wrote on September 20, 1857, recounting the Cardinal's conversation and quoting his statement: "The Americans must separate from the Germans." However, he cautioned his companions not to draw too large an inference from the remark as it was intended only as an indication of what might happen. The case was still fluid and could take almost any direction. But, said he, "suppose . . . the dismission is removed and the Card.[inal] should say to me, it is not your duty to return, but to devote yourself to the English-speaking Catholics and to the conversion of non-Catholics. This is the will of God for you. And [if Barnabò] is willing to leave the door open to you to the same end, of course not to free us from our religious vows and obligations but as religious to enter upon this career with the approbation of competent authority — and if he approves of it we may be sure to have the Holy Father's blessing — are you willing to say Yes?"[7]

Realizing that this was a sudden and unexpected question, Father Hecker stressed that there was just "a *mere possibility*" of this happening, "but if it should turn out to be an actuality" he must know their reaction. His own decision, he said, would not be hurried but would be made only after prayer and prudent consultation: "But you must well understand that I should not accept such a proposition for myself before having the best counsel of men of God and their unhesitating approval of its being God's will." But once "assured of this on *competent authority*, with His Grace, whatever it may cost, I will not shrink from it. I call competent authority the approbation of good and holy men, one like the Cardinal who knows the country, knows *all* our affairs *now* and who has every quality of mind and heart to be a competent judge in this affair." If his advisers told him to go ahead, he would not hesitate: "If it should turn out that I am to act solitary and alone in this matter, my confidence is not shaken in God and I will comply."[8]

Loath to influence them, he told the American Fathers to act freely and according to their conscience keeping in mind "only the Will of God and the good of souls."[9] He reminded them that though they had appointed him to act in their name, this was a new and unexpected development and he did not feel free to assume the role of spokesman without their expressed authorization: "Though you made me your minister plenipotentiary, yet this is an individual affair, one we did not contemplate, one of the highest import to our salvation and sanctification and must depend on God and our individual conscience."[10]

In the midst of all this doubt and uncertainty about the future, one idea was clear, definite, and unassailable in Father Hecker's mind: the time was ripe to begin a sustained and intensive effort for the conversion of America. He cared little for his own reputation or for his future as long as he could initiate this work. As he later wrote to his English convert friend, Simpson: "God knows that I came to Rome for no personal objective and so that I succeed in getting something put on foot for the conversion of my fellow men, I don't care for having been kicked unceremoniously out of Villa Caserta, nor if I am kicked out of Rome — or to death. . . . My work is not a personal one. Either measures should be taken for the conversion of the American people or we should abandon our missionary vocation."[11]

That he would succeed in his objective, Father Hecker never for a moment doubted. The only question in his mind was how would it be done. He told Brownson: "Though I do not see the way in which it will be brought about, still my confidence increases that the special end of my journey will be granted."[12]

After a week of prayer, meditation, and consultation with his spiritual director, Father Hecker's thoughts of the future became a little clearer and more definite. When Barnabò told him that the Rector Major refused to readmit him unless the Holy See demanded it, Father Hecker saw his reinstatement as most unlikely. Since Father Mauron had taken such a positive stand,

it would be very difficult for him to back down. Although Father
Hecker was confident that the sentence of dismissal would be
nullified and his reputation as a worthy religious restored, he
saw no hope of being able to work as a member of the American
Province for the conversion of America. What, then, would he do?
Before he could answer this question, Father Hecker needed to
know the attitude of his missionary companions. Once again
he wrote to them. This time he was more specific as a plan was
gradually unfolding in his mind. He was rapidly approaching the
conclusion that "an independent band of Missionaries to be
devoted to the great wants of the country" was the best solution
of their problem. He had "considered and reconsidered, and
prayed and prayed, and in spite of my fears, this seems to me
the direction which D.[ivine] Providence calls us. . . . With
all the difficulties, dangers and struggles that another movement
presents before me, I feel more and more convinced that it is
this which D.[ivine] Providence asks of us." They could place
themselves under a bishop in the United States as their superior,
one who would sympathize with them and give them "full liberty
to work for the conversion of the country." Such a prelate, he
thought, would not be hard to find. Naming Bayley, Hughes,
and Kenrick, he favored Bayley as the best choice.[13]

After explaining this plan, Father Hecker asked his companions to let him know if they concurred. If so, then he advised them to draw up a memorial to the Cardinal Prefect of
Propaganda "stating your grievances, the interests and wants of
Religion and the Country . . . and asking to be permitted to
direct your labors in this direction." But he cautioned them that
such a memorial to be successful must have the endorsement of a
bishop who "by a strong and decided appeal" supported their
petition. He told them not to send the memorial directly to the
Cardinal but to him, "so that when the moment came I might
make use of it. Affairs might take such a turn as not to present
it at all. Still, if you approve, it ought to be here on hand in
case of need."[14]

Although Father Hecker thought that this new turn of events
might come as a surprise to the American Fathers, they had
been thinking along similar lines even before they received his
letters. When Father Ruland notified them of their confrere's

expulsion, and after they had read Father Mauron's letter of explanation, they believed that the future development of their American missions was hopeless. Writing in the name of the other two, Father Walworth told Father Hecker: "If things are to remain as the General and his party have determined, neither Father Hewit, Deshon or myself can find any vocation left to us in the Congregation." If, he said, Father Hecker could be reinstated in the Congregation "on terms which would restore yourself and us to our hopes and our true vocation" they would be eternally grateful to God. But if not, they instructed their companion "to procure a permission from the Holy Father for us to separate and form a distinct band or Society without relaxation of our vows."[15]

Hecker and his confreres, separated by the Atlantic, had arrived at the same conclusion, neither influencing the other. With this meeting of minds, all that remained was to work out details and to agree on a common course of action. In response to Father Hecker's request, they drew up a memorial signed by Fathers Walworth, Hewit, Deshon, and Baker. Although informal in character and lacking the details of an official petition it clearly expressed their desires:

We feel as well as yourself, that even supposing your dismission to be withdrawn, your position and ours would remain equally unhappy. We feel as well as you, that we have had, each and all of us, and still have, a special vocation in this country, indicated by the clearest marks of God's providence. We have not doubted hitherto that this vocation was to labor for God and for souls in the Congregation of the Most Holy Redeemer; and we still believe that in its original and true spirit this Congregation is admirably adapted to this country and calculated to develop and give employment to those means of doing good which God has bestowed upon us. We have always loved, and still love and cherish the Congregation and our religious vows. Nothing however is more evident to our minds than that the policy pursued by our Superiors in the Order for some time past in impeding our Missions, and opposing their natural development is contrary to the true interests of the Order, and especially fatal to [our] own plain vocation and all our hopes of usefulness in this land where God has placed our lot. If therefore those hopes which we entertained when you set out for Rome and which gave rise to the journey cannot be realized: — if as we fear the policy of the General is unchangeable, and it should prove impossible to arrange matters satisfactorily with the General and his Consultors, we most earnestly request that you will take what steps you can to relieve us from our present painful position. Any arrangement in accordance with the suggestions of your letter . . . by which we can be separated from the jurisdiction of the General, without detriment to our religious vocation as Missionaries and our vows of religion which we love and cherish, whether by making us more immediately subject to the Cardinal Prefect of the Propaganda, or by giving us new Superiors of our own, or in any other way which the Holy Father in his wisdom may approve, will meet our wishes. We not only consent to it, but most earnestly pray and petition for it.[16]

In sending this memorial Father Walworth explained to Father Hecker that they were authorizing him to secure relief for them "from the General's power" which he described as their "pressing necessity." Their position was one of uncertainty. Since the expulsion, they did not know what action the General might take against them. They might be separated as missionaries and then assigned to parochial duties in the various houses, a move which Father Walworth deplored. To give them security, the latter asked his confrere to take speedy action and not get embroiled in any long-drawn-out litigation: "In the meantime, be it remembered, our strength is not in technicalities and formalities and canons and precedents of every kind; in the midst of these, our very ignorance would drown us; but our true strength is in our plain good-will, our zeal for the glory of God, our favorable position in this country, and in the paternal heart of the Pope."[17]

In giving this advice, Father Walworth showed himself abysmally ignorant of canonical procedure. He seemed to think that a judicial tribunal would accept his statements and assertions as proven facts and demand no further proof; that all Father Hecker had to do was to present what Father Walworth had written and the case would be quickly decided! He saw no reason why Father Hecker did not go immediately to the Holy Father and hand him the memorial, as though — as Father Hecker said later — all he needed to do was to go to the Pope's apartment, "knock at his door and voila His Holiness!"[18]

What was even more surprising was Father Walworth's attitude toward the nullification of Father Hecker's expulsion. He told him: "The question of withdrawing your dismission is probably hopeless and in any case of minor importance." He viewed the removal of the stigma of a disobedient religious from Father Hecker's good name as of no consequence. So he advised him to drop all action on the decree and "urge the general cause which we have all at heart — our future vocation." If Father Hecker pressed "his private appeal" he would endanger this cause which was apparently more important to Father Walworth than clearing Father Hecker's good name and reputation. As long as he could secure "their vocation," Father Walworth was confident that Father Hecker would "not stickle upon a point of honor, or seek a personal triumph."[19]

Although he told Father Hecker that he was free to act, Father Walworth did not realize that the Holy See considered expulsion of more than minor importance. Until he could refute the charges alleged against him, Father Hecker was not free to act on behalf of his confreres and it was only as a result of continued correspondence that he finally made Father Walworth realize that he could not separate the two issues. Until the sentence of dismissal was removed, or at least a hearing given on its legality, Rome would not listen to any pleas for the formation of a group of independent missionaries.[20]

After sending this memorial as an emergency measure, Father Walworth told Father Hecker they were going to draw up a much longer and more formal document listing their reasons for desiring a separation and containing several proposals for their continued activity as missionaries. All their ideas were predicated on the assumption that "a better state of things for us in the Congregation has become hopeless." If, however, the government of the Community were changed and the Province returned to the golden days of Father Bernard, they much preferred to remain as they were.[21]

Father Hecker knew nothing of the American Fathers' attitude until the middle of November. Before their letters reached Rome, he had gone to Naples and met the Rector of the Cisalpine Redemptorists who not only received him most cordially but expressed his willingness to accept the American missionaries under his jurisdiction. Father Hecker had also received Father de Held's letter of October 14, 1857, stating his opinion that the core of the problem was the government of the Community and expressing his hope that Rome would find a way to remedy the situation.[22]

These new developments seemed to Father Hecker to open two new avenues for the future. If the Holy Father took cognizance of Father de Held's statements that the government of the Congregation was "in a bad way" and ordered a full investigation of the 1855 Chapter, the Holy See might very well demand the convocation of a new chapter and the election of new superiors. If this occurred, the American Fathers would no longer labor under the difficulties they had experienced and would be free to continue their missions for Catholics as well as to undertake special efforts for the conversion of non-Catholics.[23]

If, however, Rome hesitated to take so drastic a step as removing the first Rector Major of the Transalpine Community after he had been in office scarcely more than two years, the Americans could petition to join the Cisalpine group and place themselves directly under the jurisdiction of the Rector Major in Naples. Since the Neapolitan Rector Major seemed to agree heart and soul with the ideas of the American missionaries, he would readily grant their "just desire." This transfer would provide the least difficulty and consume the least amount of time, since it would simply mean changing from Rome to Naples, from one group of Redemptorists to another.[24]

Simple as this move might seem, Father Hecker knew he could not say a word about it until the Holy See had ruled on the legality of his expulsion. The slightest move toward union with the Cisalpine Redemptorists would expose him to the accusation of wishing to shake off the jurisdiction of his own Rector Major who had refused to bow to his wishes. If Father Mauron's action were upheld, then both Father Hecker and his companions would be regarded as "conspirators exclusively American, founders of houses on their own authority" who refused "to leave" their native land for distant posts in the Congregation. If, however, the Holy See declared the decree null and void, then the Rector Major would have failed to prove his charges. The burden of suspicion would then fall on him and not on them.[25]

But to obtain a judicial decision on the legality of the decree was no easy matter. After Father Mauron's audience with the

Pope, Father Hecker's chances of securing a hearing, to say nothing of proving his case, seemed doomed. His two defenders, Bedini and Barnabò, could take no official action. The only man who had the right to open the case, Bizzarri, was reluctant to touch it.[26] At this critical stage of Father Hecker's affairs, Cardinal Barnabò decided on a bit of strategy that would give him a free hand. Although basically the fundamental issue was the good of religion in America, it had manifested itself only as a contest between a few religious and their superiors. Before the Cardinal could intervene, this issue must be brought out beyond this narrow sphere and called to the attention of the American bishops. If they would take a stand and voice their opinions on the importance of an American Redemptorist house and the extension of the Community's labors to the American people, this would involve the hierarchy as well as a religious community and Propaganda could press for action on the dispute.

In the closing days of October, 1857, Barnabò came up with his plan. He told Father Hecker that he could interfere only if the general interests of religion in America were at stake. If, then, the American Fathers would prepare a memorial for the Holy Father telling him of their difficulties and how these were impeding the growth of the Catholic Faith in the New World, they would put the issue on a broader basis. They should list the extent of their labors, the opportunities available in America for the good of souls, the difficulties they had encountered, and their reasons for desiring an American house. In this approach they would be showing that they were "laboring for the interest of religion" in the United States and that "the opposition sprang from a want of knowledge of the interests of the country" on the part of their superiors.[27]

But valuable as such a document could be, it would be useless if not supported by at least one bishop. The Cardinal stressed the need of documents from the American hierarchy showing their reaction to the policy of a religious community unaware of its tremendous opportunities. The bishops' statements would then come under the jurisdiction of Propaganda and Barnabò could openly espouse their cause. Barnabò also suggested that the Fathers represent to the bishops that if the action taken against Father Hecker were sustained, it would adversely affect the good of religion in the United States. Since he was a convert, widely known and respected as a missionary and writer, such punitive action against him would be regarded as inimical to the interests of religion in America and to the hopes of the conversion of non-Catholics.[28]

Father Hecker saw clearly the nature and the purpose of the Cardinal's approach and the importance of the bishops' support. In his letter of October 31, 1857, to the American Fathers telling them of Barnabò's plan, Father Hecker emphasized the need to secure episcopal sanction. Asking them to prepare a good document, he insisted it must be "backed up with *episcopal authority*"; that they must have their "views sustained by one bishop, if you cannot get more," that "all the influence you can get in this direction is *powerful*."[29]

Although the future was gradually unfolding it was far from definite in Father Hecker's mind. Possibilities, contingencies, and new developments were constantly cropping up to change the situation from day to day. As he had told the Fathers: "Things shift here often and oftener than the wind. No one can foresee the result." However, it was becoming more obvious to him that the likelihood of their continuing their missionary career as Redemptorists was daily growing more and more remote. If there were an upheaval in the government of the Transalpine Redemptorists, they could remain as they were. But this seemed most unlikely. It would be a sharp blow to established authority and could threaten the permanence of the Community, a step which he believed Rome could hardly countenance. Union with the Cisalpine group at Naples or the foundation of a distinct group of Redemptorists in the United States under Propaganda would create so many practical problems that Villa Caserta would register the strongest opposition and Rome would bow to their demands.[30]

When he looked at the whole picture and added up the various possibilities with all their complex problems, Father Hecker saw as the most feasible solution the complete separation of the American Fathers from the Redemptorist Community and their authorization to organize as an independent group of missionaries to work for the general good of religion in their own country. As he told the Fathers in his letter of November 12, 1857: "What

appears to me *more and more probable* is that we shall have to
start entirely upon our own hook. That is perhaps the best of
all, all things considered. There are many things in our Con-
greg.[ation] which would hinder us to respond to the new demands and fresh wants of our country. Such a movement has from
the beginning seemed to me *the one D.[ivine] Providence calls
us to,* but I always felt timid as long as any door was left open
for us to act in the Congr[egation]."[31]

Before the American Fathers had received Father Hecker's
letter, they had finished their long memorial to the Holy Father —
an eighteen-page document in clear and strong language stating
their grievances and asking aid from the Holy See.[32] Signed by
Fathers Walworth, Hewit, Deshon, and Baker, the memorial
contained a statement of their past history as American Protestants who through the grace of God had received the gift of the
true Faith. Once they were in the Church, the Redemptorist
Community with its special missionary character had attracted
them to its ranks. As loyal sons of St. Alphonsus, they had given
missions in numerous dioceses of the United States benefiting
multitudes of souls and delighting "various Bishops and Pastors
of the country." As the work progressed and prospered, they saw
the need for an American house. Then listing their reasons for
desiring such a foundation, they told the Holy Father it would
serve as a nucleus for the effective arrangement of missions and
as a center for missionaries. It would be "the natural and only
practical avenue by which the Congregation" could work for
the American Catholic and direct its efforts toward "the conversion of the Protestants of this country"; it would more closely
fulfill the precepts of the Constitution which "suppose that the
missions are to be given ordinarily by subjects of the same house
and designated for that purpose by the Rector of the house, to
whom also it belongs in the ordinary cases to select and appoint
the time and place of each mission"; it would act as a training
center for prospective Redemptorist missionaries and serve to
attract vocations to the Community; finally, it would preserve
the missionary spirit of the order which "in this province is in
great danger of being lost."[33]

After enumerating these reasons, the American Fathers then
gave a brief history of Bishop Bayley's offer and its subsequent

reception by the Provincial and the Rector Major. Although they were keenly disappointed by Father Mauron's refusal to accept the Newark offer and his announcement of the new foundations for Quebec and the Island of St. Thomas, they were alarmed by his deep feeling of suspicion toward his American subjects and the spirit of exclusiveness and nationalism he imputed to them. Deploring this attitude, the Fathers assured the Pope in all sincerity of heart "that we have never been conscious of any such unworthy spirit of nationality, but utterly detest it; that we have always lived on terms of the utmost cordiality with all our brethren of every nation and language; and that we do not know of any of our brethren in this Province, with the exception perhaps of our Provincial, who impute to us any such exclusive or national spirit."[34]

At this critical stage of their affairs, they continued, Father Hecker offered to go to Rome to present their petition personally to the Rector Major. They heartily endorsed this measure as the only possible means to ameliorate the situation in America. Since the General depended on the Provincial alone for his knowledge of the American Province, he had received a very distorted picture from a man who was incapable "of representing the true interests of the Province." Letters would be inadequate to correct mistaken impressions.[35]

The Fathers did not deny in their statement that they had it in mind, in case of necessity and as a last resort, to appeal to the Holy See through Father Hecker: "We knew that in all ages of the Church Rome had been the refuge of the feeble and oppressed, and we trusted that in that sacred asylum our feeble and dependent condition would be no bar to our plea, nor the strong arm that afflicted us an argument against our cause."[36]

Then turning their attention to the controverted circular of May, 1857, they did not think that it could act as "a bar to Father Hecker's journey, even had we intended no appeal in any case beyond the General himself." After they had stated their reasons for thinking that the circular did not apply to their case, they added: "If your petitioners should have misjudged in this respect, they trust that the urgent necessity of their cause and their intention as a dernier ressort to appeal by means of Father

Hecker to the Holy See, will suffice to explain and justify their step."[37]

When they approached the Provincial for permission for Father Hecker to go to Rome, he at first refused because of the circular. However, he did not hesitate to say that if he thought himself authorized he would not hesitate to grant the requested permission. Relying then on the privileges of the Constitution and considering the Provincial's declaration as tantamount to a conditional permission, Father Hecker with their approval set out for the Holy City. His reception in Rome was to them as unexpected as it was disastrous. They had learned of his dismissal from the Provincial who told them the General's reasons for his action. Taking the various charges made against their confrere, the Fathers refuted them one by one. They put special emphasis on their opinion founded in natural law that Father Hecker should not have received an automatic expulsion "without regard to the nature of his cause or the rectitude of his motives."[38]

The General's manner of dealing with Father Hecker they considered unduly harsh and severe. Nor had he shown any indication of treating them with any less severity. The Provincial admitted he had received a sharp reprimand for his weakness and want of judgment in handling the situation but that in future he would fulfill his duty "to its full extent." Since they were convinced that "the ancient spirit of their Order which was one of missionary activity, of community life and of confidence and sympathy between Superiors and subjects" had radically changed, all hopes of their future usefulness in their own country were "cut off." Seeing no hope for a change of policy, they humbly presented their petition to the Holy Father "the last and only refuge left us in this world."[39]

We beseech Your Holiness to separate us from the jurisdiction of the Superior General, or Rector Major of the Congregation of the Most Holy Redeemer, and to authorize us to elect a superior of our own, or to receive one by the appointment of the Holy See, subject either immediately to Your Holiness, or to the Cardinal Prefect of the Propaganda . . . or to such other administration as Your Holiness in his wisdom may judge expedient. We desire however to retain our present vocation, our vows and the Rule of our Founder St.

Alphonsus, approved by Benedict XIV of blessed memory, predecessor to Your Holiness, to which vocation we are most ardently attached.

If however it should not seem fit and expedient to Your Holiness that this our first and most earnest petition should be granted, then, bowing submissively to the will of God, we ask at the hands of Your Holiness as our last resort the relaxation of our vows of religion and with the apostolic benediction such counsel and assistance for our future direction as Heaven to Your Holiness may inspire. And we further request that the Rev. Father Hecker beforementioned may be accepted as representative in person before Your Holiness of the interests of your petitioners in the matters herein set forth.[40]

This memorial was sent to Father Hecker on November 14, 1857. It was followed by a special letter addressed to Cardinal Barnabò by Father Hewit in his official character as Provincial Consultor.[41] This was a detailed account of the affairs of the Province that caused the unhappy situation then existing. Father Hewit first assured the Cardinal that he had been "devoted to my Superiors, full of confidence in them and inclined to support their measures with my whole heart." Only gradually and by degrees did he realize that they were pursuing a policy detrimental to the best interest of the Congregation in the United States. He did not charge them with any malicious intentions but simply with an ignorance of the true nature of the Congregation and a failure to realize the extraordinary opportunities unfolding before their eyes. Tracing the root of the trouble to the administration of Father Ruland which "was professedly one of reform" he pointed out that the missionary endeavors of Father Bernard were pushed into the background and those who attempted to keep them alive were immediately suspect. The distrust of Fathers Hecker and Walworth was further intensified because of the part they played in the closing days of Father Rumpler's career which he related in considerable detail. Not only did the Provincial entertain a prejudice against them but so too did the General because of the action they had taken in removing this mentally unbalanced priest to a mental institution.[42,] *

Although in Father Hewit's judgment his two confreres rendered the Community a "most meritorious act of service," neither the

---

* The details of this incident are on page 174 and following of this volume.

Provincial nor the General thought so. They maintained a "deep and unwavering prejudice" against both Fathers and the American missionaries associated with them. "The Provincial has been imbued with . . . a spirit of hostility and we have good reason to believe that he has fed the General 'hostility' by constant letters and representations against us of an unfavorable character. The General was therefore prepared beforehand to condemn the proposition for an English house, especially after the Provincial had written to him, misrepresenting in the most unwarrantable manner our intentions and accusing us of exclusiveness, nationalism, a wish for separation, etc."[43]

Again Father Hewit was careful to remind the Cardinal that he did not impute any unworthy motives to Father Ruland. He cherished, he said, great esteem and affection for him "as a man and as a religious," but he ascribed the measures he had taken to a lack "of practical knowledge of the missionary life and the wants of the country."[44]

The only possible way to correct the unfortunate impressions formed by the General was a personal and detailed explanation of the situation. For this reason and because he was convinced that Father Hecker had every right to go to Rome Father Hewit in his official character as Provincial Consultor had approved the journey.[45]

Before concluding his letter, Father Hewit took the occasion to say a few words about the scandal and injury that would result to religion from Father Hecker's expulsion. As a result of their labors "Redemptorist missionary had become a household word among the Catholics of the United States, from New York to Florida and Louisiana, to Michigan and Kentucky. And that name is indissolubly associated with the persons of Father Walworth and Father Hecker." Then because Father Hecker's character had been assailed and undeserved blame inflicted on him, Father Hewit gave a spirited defense of his missionary companion: "It would be difficult to convey to Your Eminence a just idea of the veneration and affection which the Catholics of all classes, from the lowest to the highest, cherish towards this truly Apostolic man, who has thrown lustre on the Congregation, both by his writing and his labors. There was no Father in this Province who was a more devoted son of St. Alphonsus, a more ardent lover of the Congregation, or more completely animated with the religious spirit. Not only did he renounce great wealth to enter the Congregation, but he also made free use of the resources which have been placed at his disposal by generous and wealthy relatives, for the benefit of the Order, and was disposed to confer on it still greater benefits of the same kind."[46]

Not only, Father Hewit continued, would the news of his expulsion shock the Catholic community, but it would affect adversely the non-Catholic as well. Since he was formerly a Protestant as were his companions, their movements were watched with interest by their non-Catholic friends and relatives. Father Hecker's unjust expulsion would create a "most unfortunate impression" on them as well as on "the holy Faith and . . . Religious Orders." All this, said Father Hewit, may be prevented if the Holy Father would place them on an independent and honorable footing. In this way any disagreement between them and their superiors would not be apparent and the formation of a new group would "assume the guise of an arrangement made by authority. But for this, we shall be indebted to the wisdom and clemency of the Holy Father and, as we confidently trust, to the good offices of Your Eminence."[47]

Before the American Fathers' memorial to Pius IX and Father Hewit's long report to Cardinal Barnabò were put in the mails, the missionaries had received Father Hecker's letter of October 3, 1857, telling them of the necessity of getting episcopal support for any action they might take. In reply, Father Walworth explained that they were not in a position to contact bishops about their affairs. If they did, word of their appeal to the Holy See might leak out and reach the Provincial, making their position very difficult. Besides, Father Walworth questioned the propriety of discussing community affairs with outsiders.[48]

Father Hecker could appreciate the missionary's hesitancy in mentioning their difficulties to a bishop but he knew there was no longer any need for secrecy. The Rector Major had announced his dismissal officially both in America and in Europe. He had also written to Archbishop Hughes. When the Holy Father had read in Father Hecker's report to Barnabò that Hughes had approved of the American house, the Pope suggested to Father Mauron that he had better write a letter of explanation to the

Archbishop. This Father Mauron did on October 8th telling the Archbishop that he had expelled Father Hecker because his journey to Rome was a flagrant violation of the General's special circular of May 9, 1857. By this act, Father Hecker had merited the penalty of expulsion threatened in the letter and the Rector Major was obliged to enforce it. With regard to Hughes's letter of recommendation for Father Hecker, the Rector Major said he had no wish to oppose this testimonial. "On the contrary, it has been for me a consolation that I could declare that Father Hecker was not only a man of ability and zealous as a missionary, but also that his conduct as a priest was free from blame. What I have to lay to his charge, has reference only to his character as a religious and to the obligations of that state. I am persuaded that as a secular priest, he will persevere in zeal, and will do much good."[49]

On October 31st, the Archbishop sent a reply to this letter which could have been very damaging to Father Hecker's cause. He told Father Mauron that he had not "the slightest part either in encouraging or approving the step which F.[ather] Hecker had taken." Although he had freely given Father Hecker a letter of recommendation he added "in truth, I hardly knew the specific nature and object of his going to Rome." Although the Archbishop pleaded ignorance of Father Hecker's purpose, he admitted that he knew a new foundation was in the offing for Quebec and that he had been asked if he would permit the establishment "of a new community of Redemptorists in my diocese consisting of those Fathers who speak the English language and who understand the German perfectly." He consented to this as long as the superiors of the Congregation approved such a foundation.[50]

Obviously the Archbishop did not want to become involved in the conflict between Father Hecker and the Rector Major. But in trying to remove himself from any part in the dispute, he left Father Hecker in a very false light. The Archbishop was well posted on the reasons for the American missionary's visit to his Rector Major. Father Hecker had gone to Saratoga, explained the situation to him and the reasons why he thought he could go to Rome.[51] As Hughes later told Father Smith, he knew "that Father Hecker in going to Rome, considered himself as acting in good faith, under the privileges secured to every member

of his order at that time and this I know further that it was
only under a well-founded conviction on my part that he was
asking in good faith that I gave him a letter of introduction and
to some extent of recommendation, to his Eminence, the Cardinal
Prefect of Propaganda."[52] But after Father Hecker's expulsion,
the Archbishop apparently considered it more prudent to say
nothing of this visit and to give Father Mauron the impression
that his letter to Father Hecker was just a routine recommendation.[53]

When the Rector Major received the Archbishop's reply, it
could only confirm him in the opinion that Father Hecker had
misrepresented Hughes's interest in the project. He had Father
Douglas send a copy of the New York Prelate's letter to Monsignor Talbot asking him to read it to the Holy Father. Then
Douglas said: "It is clearly shown that the extreme desire of
this prelate for the house and for the presence of F.[ather]
Hecker as a Redemptorist at New York existed only in the
imagination of those who favored the project."[54] The Rector
Major also sent a copy of the letter to Cardinal Barnabò. But
its influence was partially offset by one the Archbishop had
written to the Cardinal on October 30th. He told Barnabò that
he had understood the purpose of Father Hecker's visit was
to obtain permission to establish in his diocese a new house of
the Order distinct from the houses of the German Fathers. If
such a project had the consent of the Superior General, Hughes
said, he would "willingly cooperate" since it would open a "greater
field for their American Fathers' zeal in the works of the Holy
Ministry." He also said he had reasons to suspect the absence
of harmony between the German and American Fathers who were
converts and who "seem to believe that the German Fathers do
not understand as much as they do, the needs of this country
and that it would be better for the Community and the Church
if, while still being a part of the Community, they had a separate
house from that of the German Fathers." Assuring the Cardinal
that he had no cause for complaint with either group, Hughes
concluded that he had no desire to meddle with this matter
but preferred to leave it to the wisdom of the Holy See and
the superiors of the Congregation.[55]

As soon as Father Hecker saw this letter, he decided to write to the Archbishop himself. He had thought of doing it shortly after his expulsion but delayed. Now he saw it was necessary to correct any false impression Hughes might have received through Father Mauron's letter. Writing on December 4th he told the Archbishop he had hoped to confine his recent difficulties within the Community but since the Rector Major had already written to him, he thought a word of explanation was necessary. Stating once more the purpose of his visit to Rome, Father Hecker briefly recounted the General's action in dismissing him and his failure to fulfill his promise of a hearing before his council. He spoke of the favorable reception Cardinal Barnabò had given him and how generously he had espoused his cause. Since his first meeting with the Cardinal, Father Hecker said he had done nothing without his advice and counsel. At Barnabò's suggestion, he had offered orally and in writing to accept his sentence of dismissal and accept any punishment if the General "would prove to any impartial men or man any one of the serious charges he makes against me."[56]

After he had finished this letter, Father Hecker talked to Dr. Smith and suggested that he might drop a note to the Archbishop telling him of Barnabò's interest in the case. Smith readily consented and wrote to Hughes on December 5th.[57] Telling the Archbishop about Father Hecker's expulsion, he said: "I can safely state that Propaganda is all for F.[ather] Hecker and that they would even wish *in the present case to have aid from the American Prelates*. The Bishops, My Lord Archbishop, you know are constituted by the Holy Ghost; not so with the Religious Superiors. Without trespassing on the province of Religious Superiors, Bishops can and *sometimes should* speak out and say which is just for the good of religion. This, my Lord, is confidential but Dr. Baley [sic] might hear of it."[58]

Father Hecker sent both of these letters to his brother George, asking him to mail Smith's but if any of the missionaries were in New York, they could take his personally to the Archbishop.[59] What Father Hecker did not know at this time was that on December 1st, Fathers Deshon and Baker called to see Hughes who, after keeping them waiting a long time, played the part "of a crafty politician." Admitting that he had heard from Father Mauron, he thought Father Hecker's expulsion was "not a thing

accomplished but only under consideration." Then he made the
surprising statement that he had not answered either Father
Mauron's or Cardinal Barnabò's letters, but when he did he
would "be true to what appears to me right."[60]

The interview terminated without any tangible result other
than to leave in the minds of the two Fathers an unfortunate
impression. As Father Deshon expressed it: "If we succeed without him, he will be our friend; if we do not, he will be ready
to lend a parting kick." When Father Walworth heard of the
visit, he characterized him "a heartless friend, as well as an
ungenerous foe."[61]

After George Hecker had heard of the Archbishop's reaction,
he decided to call on Hughes "on my own hook to see what he
would say." Hughes received him kindly on December 18th
while George gave an account of Father Hecker's dismissal and
the General's conduct in the affair.[62] Then George said he "feared
that perhaps the Gen.[eral] had written to him and poisoned
his mind with false accusations." Hughes answered that he had
heard from the General but only to the effect that Father Hecker
had been dismissed for violating his order about coming to Rome.
Again the Archbishop said that he had not answered Father
Mauron's letter. Closing the interview Hughes asked George to
tell his brother that he did not esteem him any the less because
of his dismissal. When George had received Father Hecker's
letter for the Archbishop, he decided to deliver it personally on
December 27th, but since the Archbishop "was not well" he
could not see him. Leaving the letter, George said he would
call again.[63]

The effects of these visits and Dr. Smith's letter prompted the
Archbishop to send two letters to Rome on December 29th. One
was to Father Hecker; the other to Dr. Smith. In the former,
Hughes said he could not imagine what word in his reply to
Father Mauron "could be construed in a sense adverse to yourself." Since he had never heard a single word of complaint against
Father Hecker or his companions, he wanted it understood that
"I should not be brought in as having formed an opinion on
one side or the other and it would be very contrary to my intention if any word in my letter should be found susceptible of
an interpretation either pro or con in your case." If Father

Hecker should return to America without having had a trial, he would welcome him "the more heartily." If however he were given a hearing and the decision was against him, the Archbishop added: "Then I should not hail your return with the same full heart as I can do and shall do considering you expelled from your Society without a candid and patient hearing of your case."[64]

In his letter to Dr. Smith, Hughes regretted that he could not find Mauron's letter to him nor a copy of his reply "If indeed I kept a copy of my answer to the Superior." But he knew that he had written "in the true spirit of one who recognizes the legitimate exercise of ecclesiastical authority." Then he disclaimed having said anything detrimental to Father Hecker whom he regarded as a most excellent priest, learned, zealous, edifying, and energetic in his ministry. He and his companions, wrote the Archbishop, enjoyed the well-earned respect "of the Catholic Bishops, Clergy and laity of this country." Only because the Archbishop was assured of Father Hecker's good faith had he given him a letter of recommendation to the Cardinal Prefect of Propaganda. Hughes then made clear that he wished to have nothing further to do with this dispute between a religious and his superior. In the past he had not interfered in such matters, "nor is it my intention to do so hereafter." Although he had washed his hands of the case, Hughes had said enough to offset any use that the Rector Major might make of his letter to the detriment of Father Hecker.[65]

When this information reached Rome, it did not discourage Father Hecker. He had never expected "anything positively favorable" from the Archbishop. His only concern was that he might say something that could be used against the American missionaries.[66] If the Archbishop had written to Father Mauron a few weeks earlier, his letter might have made Bizzarri more cautious about opening Father Hecker's case. However by the time the Rector Major had sent copies to the Roman officials, Father Hecker had submitted for Bizzarri's consideration his memorial to the Holy Father. This was not a defense of the American missionary's conduct, nor was it a refutation of the charges made against him. Rather it was a petition asking for an official review of the decree of expulsion and a request for a hearing on the accusations made in the decree.[67]

This document was not a long and involved statement but a simple four-and-one-half page declaration of the issues of the case. After stating his length of time in the Redemptorist Community and his constant occupation as a missionary, Father Hecker cited the number of missions he and his companions had given and the number of non-Catholics who had become Catholics during these spiritual exercises. The success of this work prompted the bishops in whose dioceses they had worked to encourage the American missionaries to devote themselves "with greater zeal and energy" to the conversion of the non-Catholic. To enable them to carry on this work, the Fathers realized the need of an American house "under the rule of the same Institute and the same superiors, excluding any idea of separation." Then Father Hecker submitted the letters of Archbishop Hughes and Bishop Bayley who had expressed their desire to have such a foundation in their dioceses. Because of this approval and with the encouragement and approbation of his confreres, Father Hecker went to Rome to secure the permission of the Rector Major for the proposed house.[68]

Then Father Hecker briefly related his reception by the Rector Major and his subsequent expulsion. He spoke of the General's promise to allow him to justify his conduct before the Consulta, a promise which he failed to fulfill. When his pleas to be allowed to defend himself proved fruitless, he tried through the intervention of "two distinguished persons — among them, His Eminence, Cardinal Barnabò" to persuade the General to rescind the decree of expulsion. But in this he also failed. Finally there was only one avenue open to him: to entreat the Holy Father to grant him a defense "and to call for an examination of the decree by the Sacred Congregation of Bishops and Regulars, or by a special Congregation of Cardinals at the good pleasure of Your Holiness."[69]

There were several valid reasons why the decree should be annulled. Here Father Hecker had the aid of his canonist who offered three legal causes for the nullity of the expulsion: defect of form; a disproportion between the crime and the punishment; the false application of law. The approved order before proceeding to issue a sentence of dismissal required that the accused be given a hearing and the opportunity to defend his conduct. But

PIUS IX
(Alinari)

ARCHBISHOP CONNOLLY
From the Cathedral rectory
in Halifax, courtesy
Rev. John DeLouchry.

Decretum.

Nuper nonnulli ex Presbyteris Congregationis Smi Redemptoris in provincia Americae Septentrionalis foederatis existentibus Smo D.N. Pium IX supplici prece deprecabantur, ut eis ob specialia circumstantias emediret et auctoritate et jurisdictione Rectoris Majoris subtrahi, ac a propria Superiore Apostolica Sedi immediate subjecta juxta regulam a Benedicto XIV Smo approbatam gubernari. Quod si eis id datum non erit, dispensationem a votis in dicta Congregatione emissis humillime expostulabant. Re vocata per partes Sanctitati Sua aestimavit hujusmodi separationem unitati Congregationis officere, et S. Alphonsi instituta minime respondere, ideoque haud permittendam esse. Cum autem votatum sit Antoni stualti libere parcere in sacris appellitionibus peragendis, et ex jure minimum conveniri, christianaeque institutione curanda, et idcirco a pluribus Antistitibus commendentur, visum est Smo Dno magis expedire eos a praefata Congregatione eximi, ut in sacri Ministerii genere permaneant ad directione Antistitum locorum incumbere possint. Quapropter Sanctitas Sua Presbyteros Clementem Walworth, Augustinum Hewitt, Georgium Dahm et Franciscum Baker, una cum Presbytero Isaac Hecker, qui eorumdem postea laboribus quoad dispensationem a votis adhaesit, a votis simpliciter, etiam permanentia in Congregatione Smi Redemptoris emissis hujus Decreti tenore Apostolica Auctoritate dispensat,

et dispensatos, ac prorsus soluti esse declarat, ita ut ad eamdem Congregationem amplius non pertineant. Confidit vero Sanctitas Sua memoratos Presbyteros qua quae, qua exempla qua sermone in vinea Domini jus directione et jurisdictione Antistitum locorum, ad praecipitum Il Canonum adlaborant, ac aeternam animarum salutem alacriter curent, atque proximorum sanctificationem pro viribus promoveant.

Datum Romae ex Secretaria Sacrae Congregationis Episcoporum et Regularium. Die 6 Martii 1858.

A. Carlus de Ferge Praefus.

L✠S.

A. Archiepus Philippen. Secrius.

In fidem copiae -
Romae die 23 Martii 1858.

Nic. Mauron C. SS. Rr
Sup. gen. et Rect. maj.

"NUPER NONNULLI" The decree which dispensed the American missionaries
... Redemptorist Congregation

Father Hecker had no such opportunity. True, he said, the General had questioned him, but "such a brief interrogatory given privately" could hardly constitute a hearing in the true sense of the word. Had he been permitted to speak in his own defense, he could have proven "that neither the Provincial nor the local Rector had forbidden the journey but on the contrary had favored it so far as lay in their power. He could have given evidence of his good faith and innocence; he could have shown conclusively the uprightness of his intentions, his obedience, his union with and total dependence on his superiors." Even if he were at fault in making the journey, the punishment of expulsion "equivalent to civil death and infamy" was out of all proportion to the charges alleged against him. As Benedict XIV had said: "Even bishops in decreeing penalties . . . must not forget the penalty must be in proportion to the crime." Moreover the universal law of the Church ordains that no one can be dismissed from his congregation "arbitrarily and without reason."[70]

Turning to the charges alleged against him, Father Hecker maintained they were gratuitous assertions without a word of proof. The General had not cited a single document nor a proven fact to sustain his allegations. In a strong summation, Father Hecker put the issue squarely on its merits when he declared that he was

> ready to accept the decree and condemnation when the Rev. Father General shall succeed in proving before the Sacred Congregation or the judges deputed by it, either that he conspired with the other Fathers of the Order to separate from the Institute, or that he wished of his own will to found an independent house exclusively for American subjects, or that he ever refused to leave his home in the United States, or that he had not observed the rules of the Congregation, or that he had not given an edifying example of religious life.[71]

After this document was put in final form, Father Hecker took it to Cardinal Barnabò who read and approved it. On November 21, 1857, he submitted it to Archbishop Bizzarri who said he would present it to the Holy Father. In conversation with Bizzarri, both Barnabò and Bedini remarked of Father Hecker that if the manner in which he had been treated were known in the United States "It would operate very detrimentally to religion." This argument seemed to impress Bizzarri who began to take a greater interest in the case.[72]

When Father Hecker spoke to Bizzarri, early in December, he asked him if he had presented his memorial to the Holy Father. The Archbishop avoided answering the question but told the American missionary to submit another brief. This time he wanted him to prove in detail and with documents two points: first, his good faith in coming to Rome; the second, that the General had no right to expel him automatically without granting him a hearing. This request for further testimony convinced Father Hecker that the Archbishop must have given at least a report of his petition, even if he had not submitted the document, for Bizzarri would never have consented to open the case without the Pope's approval.[73]

A month later Father Hecker learned what had taken place in the audience. When Bizzarri brought up the subject of the American missionary, the Pope cut him off with the remark: "Authority must be sustained." Slowly and emphatically he repeated these words. "But Your Holiness," said Bizzarri, "if authority had committed an injustice?" The Pope hesitated a moment and said: "In that case, the matter must be examined." That was the authorization Bizzarri needed. It proved that, regardless of the common opinion, the Holy Father had *not* decided the case. Bizzarri could then conduct an impartial investigation without risking the Pope's displeasure[74] and Father Hecker had the long-awaited opportunity to prove that he had acted with a clear conscience and for the best interests of the Congregation as well as religion in America. Since this might be his last chance, Father Hecker was determined to spare no trouble or expense in drawing up his brief. He took all his papers to his canonist and left in his hands the preparation of the argument. Before beginning it, the canonist consulted with Cardinal Barnabò and Archbishop Bedini who advised him on the approach to be adopted and the issues to be stressed.[75]

This was the most encouraging development that had occurred since Father Hecker was expelled. He knew that the Pope had formed an unfavorable impression about him and his companions because of the General's report and the influence "of others who have whispered things into the Pope's ear." But he was also con-

fident that with a little patience and continuous prayer the Holy
See would grant him a hearing. As he told the Fathers: "Our time
will come." After Bizzarri had told him to submit the extended
brief, he announced to his confreres that "Our time is *coming*."[76]

It was the first break in the tight chain of circumstances that
had bound him on all sides. Other unexpected and fortunate
events hammered away at the remaining links until he was free
not only to clear his own name but to help in the reaping of
fields white to the harvest.

CHAPTER XVIII

The Turning of the Tide

SHORTLY after he left America, Father Hecker made a remark to his brother George which every American who has ever gone to Europe would heartily endorse: "Money does not go, but flies out of the purse of a traveller."[1] Even in 1857, Europeans seemed to think that Yankees were made of money and they sought every opportunity to profit by their presence. In Father Hecker's case, this became obvious after he settled down for his long stay in Rome. He had to pay not only the ordinary living expenses for his apartment, his clothes, and his food, but also to provide inevitable tips for domestics who would omit the most necessary duties if not periodically rewarded. He soon learned that he was expected to offer a gratuity in exchange for such favors as introductions to important and influential people.[2] He discovered that there were always some underlings, imperious and unapproachable, who would mellow at the sight of a sizable lira note. In addition to these "hidden taxes" he found that postage was quite expensive, especially with his voluminous correspondence; that the cost of translating and copying documents was mounting; that his lawyer's fee was substantial. Despite these financial obligations he always managed to help the needy. Sensitive to the needs of the poverty stricken, he could not neglect the poor and would occasionally give twenty-five dollars to help some destitute family.[3]

Fortunately for Father Hecker, in all his trials and difficulties, he had no worries over money. His brother George, who took care of all his expenses in Europe, was always ready to send him a bank draft whenever his finances were running low. But Father Hecker did not permit this generosity to become an excuse for luxurious living. Contrasting his Roman days with the time he had spent in Cuba with George and his wife, he could write to his brother: "My style of living is poor enough, not by any means *a la Havana!*"[4] Having rented a modest apartment, he took his meals at moderately priced restaurants. His favorite haunt for the continental breakfast of coffee and rolls was the Café Greco,[5] a sort of rendezvous for artists and men of letters, where in late October of 1857 Father Hecker met an American non-Catholic who was to play an important though indirect role in changing his fortunes at Rome, George Loring Brown.[6]

Brown was an artist who had studied under Washington Allston in Boston and Jean Baptiste Isabey in Paris and who later won renown for his paintings, notably the *Doges Palace and Grand Canal* and his *Crown of New England*.[7] At the time Father Hecker met him, he had acquired a solid reputation as an outstanding landscape artist. A Bostonian by birth with no definite church affiliation, Brown discovered he had many interesting topics to discuss with the easy, pleasant-speaking former Transcendentalist. It was not long before Father Hecker deftly but inoffensively introduced the subject of religion, which captured Brown's attention. As Hecker put it: "finding him ready to hear the truth, *I gave it to him!*"[8] After eight weeks of discussion, explanation, and instruction, which Father Hecker often gave over a cup of coffee in the café, or surrounded by easels in Brown's studio, the artist finally decided to become a Catholic. On December 5, 1857, he told Father Hecker he was ready to be received into the Church and, two days later, he made his profession of faith.[9]

News of the conversion of the popular artist spread quickly in Rome especially since a number of important ecclesiastics in the Roman Curia knew him.[10] Brown himself, essentially an extrovert, made no secret of his newly found faith and the part Father Hecker played in leading him to it. When Bedini and Barnabò heard about it, they were delighted. To them, it was one more proof that Father Hecker could not be the incorrigible religious he had been depicted since God Himself was using him as an instrument for bringing the gift of faith to one outside the Church. Moreover it seemed to bear out the assertions Father Hecker had made in his articles in the *Civiltà*. The willingness of the American artist to accept the truth when correctly presented to him tended to confirm Father Hecker's claim that America was ripe for the harvest.

Brown's conversion, together with the *Civiltà* articles, marked a change in Father Hecker's prestige in Rome. Although the articles were anonymous, in no time their author became known. After Father Curci had called the Pope's attention to them, he remarked to Father Hecker: "Your name cannot be altogether unknown to his Holiness?" In reply, Father Hecker merely shrugged his shoulders and exclaimed: "Ah!"[11] Many ecclesiastics soon discovered the name of the American priest then in Rome who had written the thought-provoking study of religious conditions in America. They looked upon him as a capable and zealous missionary who not only knew his country, but was vitally interested in its conversion. His role as an apostle for his native land began to overshadow his position as an expelled religious. As he told the Fathers, the articles had given him "a status."[12]

Within a few days after the November 21st issue of the *Civiltà* appeared, Father Hecker, at the suggestion of Cardinal Barnabò, called on Cardinal Reisach who had read the American priest's article and seemed quite interested in it. It diverted the Cardinal's attention from the personalities involved in Father Hecker's difficulties and roused his interest in the possibilities of religion in America. For almost two hours the two men discussed questions close to the missionary's heart. When the Cardinal said some positive steps should be taken to check the rationalistic tendency in America, Father Hecker agreed, adding that since the same ideas had occurred to him, he had published them. Then he offered to give the German Prelate a copy of *Aspirations of Nature*. Since Reisach knew English, he said he would be glad to accept and read the volume. Immediately after leaving the Cardinal, Father Hecker went back to his apartment, and having inscribed his appreciation of Reisach on the flyleaf, sent him the book.[13]

Through his writings in the *Civiltà*, Father Hecker had at-

tempted to present America in a more favorable light and to alter
the commonly held opinion that the United States was irreligious
and materialistic. After the first article appeared, he could feel
that he had met with some success. Men in Rome began to take
more of an interest in the progress of the Church in America and
its opportunities for future success. The obstacles formerly considered so formidable were soon regarded as challenging opportunities which could not be overlooked.[14] But how could the
Church avail herself of these opportunities? Father Hecker had
only hinted at the means to be used but had not gone into any
specific details. Recognizing this, Barnabò told his American
friend that he should publish his ideas on overcoming the obstacles
to the conversion of America.[15]

The next time Father Hecker met the editor of the *Civiltà*,
he outlined a plan for future articles. Although quite interested,
Father Curci could not promise to run them for two or three
months, because he was so backlogged with material. This answer
did not faze Barnabò who told the American missionary to write
out his ideas. Perhaps when Curci saw them, he would do as he
had done before: set aside the other material in their favor.[16]

Before Father Hecker had a chance to start writing, more
pressing matters demanded his immediate attention. Since his
appeal to the Holy Father had been successful, Bizzarri told
him to present a brief implemented with documentary evidence
proving his good faith in coming to Rome and the General's
error in automatically expelling him. From this request it was
obvious that the real point at issue was the General's circular
of May 9, 1857. What was the purpose and the meaning of the
prohibition contained in that document? If Father Hecker could
show that after an honest appraisal of this circular he sincerely
believed he had the right to make the journey, then the General
should not have dismissed him without evaluating the sincerity
of his interpretation. This was clear enough, but Father Hecker
lacked the all-important document for establishing his defense:
the controverted circular. On the advice of Cardinal Barnabò,
he called on Father Mauron December 5th and asked him for a
copy but the Rector Major refused to let him have it. Bedini
then told him to write to his confreres in America immediately,

have them procure an authentic copy, and send it without delay. Meanwhile the American missionary left a note for Bizzarri telling him of the General's refusal.[17]

Even without this circular, all important as it was to his defense, Father Hecker's canonist believed he could build a strong case by using the letters and statements in Father Hecker's possession. The brief, as it was finally presented to Bizzarri, seems to have been largely the work of the lawyer. Since the Archbishop had asked for a formal statement in legal style, Father Hecker apparently felt this was too much of a task for him. He entrusted this work to his canonist to whom he gave his letters and testimonials, his report to Barnabò as well as the General's answer to that statement.[18] The finished document written in legal phraseology and buttressed with numerous quotations from papal pronouncements, canonical authorities and moral theologians could never have come from Father Hecker, but only from a specialist in the field.

How much of a hand Father Hecker had in the preparation of the document and to what extent he approved its contents is difficult to say. Oddly enough, among his papers, this is the only statement he presented to the Roman authorities for which there is no English copy. Previously he had drawn first drafts, corrected them, and then had them translated into Italian.[19] But the only rough copy of this brief is in Italian. Since he was not familiar with that language, he would have had to have a translation before he could pass on the merits of the arguments it contained. There is one interesting difference between this brief and his other statements. In his previous documents, he always speaks in the first person offering his own evidence and explanation. But in this one, he is spoken of in the third person as though someone else were speaking for him.[20]

Taking as his starting point the high esteem in which Father Hecker was held, the lawyer stressed that even the Rector Major "was compelled by the very force of truth to write of him . . . to the Cardinal Prefect of Propaganda after he had inflicted the penalty of expulsion . . . that with regard to his habits and morals his conduct has ever been blameless and edifying and that outside of this matter [the journey to Rome] he is a zealous missionary, an excellent preacher and a man of talent." How then, asked the canonist, could a man who enjoyed such universal respect suddenly deserve "a penalty that brands him with infamy and is on a par with the Church's punishment of apostasy and civil death!"[21] In conscience, Father Hecker could not accept such a sentence but was honor bound to clear his priestly and religious reputation. For one month he had tried every means at his disposal to secure a reversal of the sentence but was blocked at every turn. Finally, he was forced to appeal to the Holy Father for a hearing before the Congregation of Bishops and Regulars. Then, listing the arguments that Father Hecker had advanced in his petition asking for this hearing, the canonist proposed to prove at much greater length that the decree was illegal in form as well as substance and therefore null and void. He begged the Sacred Congregation to study carefully the documents he would submit since they "set forth in unmistakable terms his [Father Hecker's] good faith which alone . . . would thereby exempt him from all penalty."[22]

After this introduction, the lawyer divided his subject into two well-defined sections to establish the points indicated by Bizzarri. First he set out to prove Father Hecker's good faith in going to Rome and, second, to show that the General did not have the right to inflict an automatic expulsion. In defense of Father Hecker's action, the canonist cited a universally accepted canonical and moral principle concerning the extent to which ignorance and error could exculpate a transgressor of a command. Under no circumstance could either or both excuse one who had committed an act recognized as intrinsically evil, such as murder, since right reason independent of any command would tell him that such a crime was wrong. However, when an action with no moral significance in itself, such as taking a journey, is forbidden because of the command of legitimate authority, the transgressor could be excused if he were ignorant of the prohibition or misunderstood its meaning. No one could deny that Father Hecker's action in going to Rome was in itself an indifferent action. By no stretch of the imagination could it be called intrinsically evil. The only fact that called it into question was the Rector Major's prohibition of the journey contained in his circular of May 9, 1857.[23]

Thus far no one could quarrel with the lawyer's argument.

He had come to the core of the question and needed only to show that the meaning of the circular was ambiguous or at least misleading. Consequently, in his interpretation of it, Father Hecker could honestly believe that it did not forbid his journey to Rome. But the lawyer failed to touch these points. Undoubtedly he was at a serious disadvantage. Without the actual wording of the circular before him, he could not prove that the General had failed to state in clear and unmistakable terms who could grant the necessary permission for the journey. In the absence of the document the canonist elected to show that Father Hecker was in good faith because he had the approval of Archbishop Hughes and Bishop Bayley for the new foundation, as well as the encouragement and support of his confreres. But this was begging the question. For his argument to be valid, the canonist would have had to prove two points: first, the Bishops' approval of the foundation conferred their permission to make the journey; second, the prelates and Father Hecker's companions had the right to grant such permission despite the prohibition in the circular. Apparently the lawyer did not see this and assumed what he should have first established.

In themselves the letters of both Bayley and Hughes could permit the canonist to say: "It was not Father Hecker who started the idea of opening other houses of the Institute in the United States, but the Reverend Bishops."[24] Bayley left no doubt that he had sought such a foundation on his own initiative. He had said in his letter to Mauron which was still in Father Hecker's possession: "Some months ago I decided to obtain permission from the Reverend Father Provincial" to erect a house of the Congregation in the Newark diocese. He had asked Father Walworth to present this request to the Provincial, but when the Bishop learned that it would be better to seek the foundation directly from the General, he decided to do it by means of his letter.[25]

The words that Hughes had used in his testimonial could also admit of the same interpretation. He asked Father Hecker "to make known to your Superiors how desirous I am that there should be another House of your Order in New York."[26] But this did not necessarily mean that the Archbishop had come to this decision of his own accord. It was true that Father Hecker had said nothing to Bayley about a new foundation, since he was in Cuba when the Bishop made his original offer through Father Walworth. However, Father Hecker had taken the initiative in suggesting the American house to Hughes, but only after Father Hewit had written to him that the Provincial was heart and soul behind the new foundation.*

The canonist stretched the meaning of the Prelates' letters further still when he wrote: "It was at the prayer of the bishops and his confreres that Father Hecker was chosen for this unlucky journey."[27] Neither Bayley nor Hughes had anything to do with Father Hecker's decision to go to Rome. They heard of it only after he had made up his mind to make the journey, though by their letters they had approved of his step. Both had known of the Provincial's attitude but considered that nevertheless Father Hecker was still acting within his rights guaranteed by the Redemptorist Constitutions. Hughes specifically stated that only after he was convinced that Father Hecker was justified in going to Rome did he give testimonial letters.

Had the canonist been able to focus his attention on the meaning of the circular, he would have presented a much stronger defense of Father Hecker's good faith. This is what the American Fathers did in their November, 1857, memorial to the Holy Father. Giving a true and complete presentation of what had occurred, they wrote:

> We did not suppose however that this circular could under the circumstances operate as a bar to Father Hecker's journey. . . . The said circular had been sent on occasion of a certain subject, the Father Bretska [sic], who had left his house for Europe clandestinely, on matters of personal interest only, and without any notice or consultation with his immediate Superiors. Your petitioners on the contrary proposed to send one of their number on matters of general interest and with the permission, which they believed could be obtained, of the Provincial, since the said Provincial professed himself favorable to their desires. Moreover, the Constitutions of the Order expressly provide that a subject shall have a right to go to the General Superior, in any matter of great importance which will not suffer delay, and that even although permission shall have been denied him by the local Superior. Your petitioners believed that, even

---

* A fuller explanation of this and the following paragraph is contained in Chapter XII of the present volume.

supposing a right on the part of the Superior General to limit the
privilege of the Constitutions under certain circumstances, and for
good reasons, he had not the right to abrogate it entirely and in all
cases, and could not have so intended. If your petitioners should
have misjudged in this respect, they trust that the urgent necessity
of their cause . . . will suffice to explain and justify their step.

In consequence of the circumstances above stated, sometime about
the close of the month of July past, the Rev. Father Hecker applied
to the Provincial for permission to set off for Rome. The Provincial
replied that in consequence of the aforesaid circular he did not think
he had the right to give such a permission. He therefore declined,
but at the same time said that if he believed himself authorized he
would not hesitate to accord the permission. It was nevertheless the
opinion not only of the Rev. Father Hewit, one of your petitioners
and Consultor of the Province, but of the Rectors of the houses of
Baltimore and New York, who were consulted upon the question,
that the Provincial had such power in this case, and that the said
circular could not be construed as a bar. Relying therefore on the
privileges of the Constitutions and the necessities of the case, and
considering also the above declaration of the Provincial as tantamount
to a conditional permission, the Rev. Father Hecker departed for
Rome on the 5th of August, 1857.[28]

Such a clear-cut and definite statement of fact would have
shown that Father Hecker had not ignored nor disregarded the
circular, but after mature deliberation and consultation with
prudent men in the Community, had arrived at a sincere conviction that he had the right to make the trip. Consequently,
he acted in good faith. Although Bizzarri might not come to this
conclusion from the canonist's argument, he could not escape it
when he read the American Fathers' memorial which he received
a short time later.

The second section of the canonist's brief was much stronger,
more to the point, and dealt with the issues involved. He proposed to show that the decree of expulsion was null and void
because it violated the prescriptions of the Redemptorist and
Apostolic Constitutions. Then he cited the 1764 Constitutions
of the Community concerning the procedure in the dismissal of
subjects: "Men who are turbulent, irreverent, and disobedient
and who when rebuked and corrected continue committing the
same faults, are alien from our Institute. In addition to grave

crimes, frequent violation of the rules without any hope of amendment is sufficient cause for expulsion. Let him [the Rector Major] treat the accused with the greatest charity and kindness, leaving nothing untried to recall him to his duty and make him repent; and let him not use the knife until he perceives that the wound is already rotten and incurable. He is bound in justice to hear the excuse of the accused, not once but often; and also the reasons whence the accused draws his defense. Moreover he is bound to use the greatest care that by frequent inquiries, he obtain a complete knowledge of the case from God-fearing men."[29]

This injunction, said the canonist, conformed to the common law of the Church formulated in the decrees of Urban VIII and Innocent XII. They prescribed that a subject to be expelled must have committed a grave crime; there must be legitimate proof through the testimony of witnesses that he had committed this crime; he must be given a fair trial with full proof of the cause of the expulsion. This legislation, the lawyer noted, is proof "that the Church is a foe of arbitrary methods. . . . The dignity of man requires that his rights be safeguarded and the wisdom of Mother Church has ever done so."[30]

The next step in the lawyer's case was to apply these norms to the case of Father Hecker. Had the American missionary been guilty of serious and frequent violations of the Rule? The testimonials of his immediate Rector as well as his Provincial belied such a charge. According to their declarations freely given, "his virtue stands untarnished." The Rector Major, even after expulsion, had willingly acknowledged the excellence of Father Hecker's virtue as a priest, although he condemned him for his conduct as a religious in the matter of the American house. But, said the canonist, "surely it is impossible for a man of such great virtue, morality, zeal and Christian spirit (as they pictured Father Hecker) to lay aside his lamb's clothing and be at the same time a wolf within the cloister. No. His actions are one and indivisible — in the house and outside it — just as the soul which moves and controls the body is one and indivisible."[31]

Could his journey to Rome be construed as a grave crime because of the circular? Such a judgment, argued the canonist, would violate the dictates of right reason and justice, especially since Father Hecker thought the circular did not prohibit such a journey. But even if one were to view "the voyage in the most damaging light possible, can we call it a crime? Can we say it is the atrocious, infamous, inexpiable, most grave sin required by law in strict proof? This would be a violation of all reason and sense."[32]

Furthermore Father Hecker was never granted the guarantees required by law, especially an impartial trial and an opportunity for defense. On the contrary, "without being allowed to exculpate himself, without receiving any papers relative to the case, without being admitted to a defense" he was summarily expelled. The canonist emphatically declared that "the very brief and obscure questioning by the Rev. Father General in two private meetings could by no means take the place of the regular proof or defense, for the law requires formal acts or processes in writing."[33]

As the final point in Father Hecker's defense, the lawyer called attention to the disproportion between the alleged crime and the penalty. Carefully noting that the Rector Major had not offered a single bit of evidence in support of his charges against Father Hecker, the canonist declared: "If all the charges were proved in detail and were accounted crimes, even then there would be by no means a proportion between the charges made and the penalty inflicted which is civil death and dishonor and against one's spiritual welfare. It is an axiom of eternal justice that penalties should stand in direct relation to the faults committed. In the case before us there is no proportionate penalty. Although the charges are not atrocious, or public, or grave, or inexpiable, the penalty on the other hand is the greatest and severest possible. The Apostolic Constitutions do not permit the penalty of expulsion . . . unless proof can be adduced of repeated nefarious crimes, of admonitions, of punishments administered, of insubordination and of incorrigibility." If the accusations were proven, "the only penalty possible would be the deprivation for two years of all active or passive voice in the Congregation."[34]

The canonist concluded by beseeching the Holy Father, in accord with his supreme authority in the Church, to nullify the decree and reinstate Father Hecker in the Community. Then he appended to his brief, as evidence, eight documents: Father Helmpraecht's testimonial of Father Hecker's good character;

Bishop Bayley's letter to Father Mauron requesting a foundation; the American Fathers' statement assuming their share of responsibility for Father Hecker's action; Father Walworth's letter countersigned by Father Hewit as Provincial Consultor declaring that in their judgment Father Hecker had the right to make the journey; Father Ruland's declaration about the importance of the New York foundation and his willingness to give permission to bring the matter before the Rector Major if he believed he had the authority to do so; Father Hewit's letter as Provincial Consultor to the Rector Major giving his reasons for approving Father Hecker's journey which was not forbidden by the circular; Father Deshon's letter to Father Ruland showing why he believed the circular did not abrogate the Provincial's right to give permission for the journey; and Hughes's letter to Father Hecker signifying his desire to have an American house in his archdiocese.[35]

On December 9, 1857, Father Hecker reported to the American Fathers that the statement of his case requested by Bizzarri December 5th was completed. It is quite likely that he gave it to the Secretary on December 12th, since Saturday was the day he usually saw Bizzarri in his office.[36]

During the closing days of November, 1857, Propaganda had not been idle. After the Holy Father had told Bizzarri to examine the merits of Father Hecker's case, both Barnabò and Bedini knew that the Pope had not decided in favor of Father Mauron. Barnabò then sent to Bizzarri another letter he had received from Father de Held. This was the third time the Liége Rector had written in defense of Father Hecker and the Secretary of the Congregation of Bishops and Regulars added it to his rapidly expanding file on the Hecker case.[37] Bedini also decided to make a move and to mention the American missionary's affairs in his November 29th audience with the Holy Father. He began by presenting copies of Father Hecker's *Questions of the Soul* and *Aspirations of Nature* together with a reprint of the *Civiltà* articles "bound in rich style." The Holy Father thanked him for the gifts and said that he regretted that he did not read English.[38] Bedini then called his attention to the articles and began to speak of Father Hecker's difficulties. The Pope listened and then said: "But I have not seen Père Hecker!" Bedini answered that Father Hecker was waiting to make his report to Bizzarri and, depending on the outcome of that appeal, he would seek an audience.[39]

When this word reached Barnabò, he decided there was no need to wait. "Strike while the iron is hot," he told Father Hecker and advised him to request an audience. Excitedly, Father Hecker wrote the great news to the American Fathers and said: "I should not be surprised if I kissed His Holiness' 'big toe' provided I don't bite it by mistake before my next letter."[40] On December 12th Father Hecker drew up a formal petition to Bedini asking him to obtain an audience since "it appears that it would not be displeasing to him [the Pope] to see me."[41] That evening Bedini told the Holy Father of the request and also spoke of Brown's conversion in which, as Father Hecker told his confreres, the Archbishop "amplified my part."[42] Bedini had done all he could to prepare the way for Father Hecker. Now it was up to Hecker.

One week before Christmas, at half past twelve on a Thursday afternoon, Father Hecker was ushered into the presence of Pius IX. Prostrating before the Pope, he reverently kissed his slipper. Gently the Holy Father touched him on the shoulder and told him to rise. Then saying that he knew all about his affairs, he asked Father Hecker what he desired. The American missionary replied that he hoped the Pope would examine the purpose of his coming to Rome. The conversion of America, he told the Holy Father, was a glorious goal dear to the heart of intelligent and pious Catholics, to men such at Dr. Ives whom he was sure the Pope knew. "Yes," replied the Holy Father, and then he inquired: "Has his wife become a Catholic?" When Father Hecker answered in the affirmative, the Pope returned once more to the question of his difficulties. "Your case," he remarked, "is being examined by Monsignor Bizzarri and nothing can be done until he gives in his report. Then I will give my opinion and my decision." With deep sincerity, Father Hecker answered: "Your decision, Most Holy Father, is God's decision and willingly and humbly I will submit, whatever it may be."[43]

This act of ready and filial obedience touched the Holy Father who looked at his visitor with great kindness. Father Hecker noticed that the Pope watched him very closely with a penetrating though paternal gaze. From this reaction, the American missionary knew that the Pope had taken an interest in him since he had been warned that when the Holy Father did not care to spend time with anyone he would shuffle the papers on his desk or look out the window.[44]

Although he kept his eyes fixed on Father Hecker, the Pope moved his head slightly to indicate a change in the conversation as he began to talk about the conversion of America. "The American people are so engrossed in worldly things and in the pursuit of wealth and these are not favorable to the spread of the Gospel. It is not I who say so but Our Lord." Quickly Father Hecker came to the defense of his countrymen: "The United States is in its youth and is like a young father of a family who is occupied in furnishing his house. While this is going on he must be busy. But the American people do not make money to hoard, nor are they miserly." Not wishing to be misunderstood, the Pope replied: "No, no, they are willing to give when they possess riches; the Bishops tell me that they are generous in aiding the building of Churches." Then he smiled as he added: "You see I know the bright as well as the dark side of the Americans!" But his next remark indicated that he was a little more impressed with the somber: "In the United States, there exists a too unrestricted freedom. All the refugees and revolutionaries gather there and are in full liberty." While admitting this, Father Hecker, with his characteristic optimism, pointed out that even this seemingly unfortunate situation had its merits. "True, Most Holy Father, but this has a good side. Many of these seeing in the United States that the Church is self-subsistent and not necessarily connected with what they call despotism begin to regard her as a divine institution and return to her fold." This impressed the Pope as he said: "Yes, the Church is as much at home in a republic as in a monarchy or an autocracy." But then he implied that other problems blocked the progress of religion in America: "You have the abolitionists and their opponents who get each other by the hair!" But said Father Hecker: "There is also the Catholic Truth, Holy Father, which if once known would act on these parties like oil on troubled waters. Our best informed statesmen are becoming more and more convinced that Catholicity is necessary to sustain our institutions and enable our young country to realize her great destiny." Sensing a glorious opportunity, Father Hecker then remarked humbly but confidently: "Allow me to add, Most Holy Father, that it would be an enterprise worthy of your glorious pontificate to set on foot the measures necessary for the beginning of its conversion." The Holy Father looked at his visitor, smiled, and motioned him to kneel for his blessing. Then he said in a low voice as Father Hecker knelt before him: "Bravo! Bravo!"[45]

As he left the Vatican after his audience, Father Hecker was delighted. He had not only talked with the Vicar of Christ on earth but had received his blessing. The Holy Father had not regarded him as an expelled religious but as a loyal and dutiful son of the Church. He had not upbraided him for his defense of America but seemed pleased that the American missionary had spoken in favor of his country. He had not labeled this zealous apostle as an enthusiastic visionary but had listened with interest as he talked of the future of the Church in his native land. Father Hecker felt confident that Pius IX would grant his desire, that he would examine the cause that had brought him to Rome. He believed more than ever that God was blessing his efforts. The conversion of Brown and his articles in the *Civiltà*, Father Hecker reflected, had helped to temper any false impressions that the Holy Father had received from previous reports.[46] Now the American missionary would have a chance to defend himself and to exert all his energies for the good of religion in America.

With an overflowing heart, Father Hecker thanked God for all the graces He had bestowed on him, especially for the many "warm friends" He had given him in Rome. He took no credit to himself for the success of the audience and never considered for a moment that his sincere, honest, and unaffected manner had won the heart of the Sovereign Pontiff. He believed that he owed a great deal to his two stanch defenders, Barnabò and Bedini.[47] After he had written an account of his conversation with the Holy Father, while it was still fresh and full in his mind, he gave a report of his success to the Cardinal. As Barnabò listened, he was delighted and exclaimed: "Did I not tell you that if you followed my counsel you would be successful?" Father Hecker replied that he had followed and always would follow Barnabò's advice and would take no step without consulting him. However he added: "I fear that in my calling on you so often I may be troublesome to Your Eminence." In surprise the

Cardinal asked: "Why do you say that? Am I not always glad to see you?"[48]

When Father Hecker wrote to his brother and the American Fathers about his interview with the Pope, he restrained his enthusiasm with the simple expression: "I can assure you it is a source of joy to me to have had the opportunity of speaking with him." Referring to his conversation with Barnabò, he spoke of the Cardinal's paternal affection for him, remarking that Barnabò was like "a father" to him; so too was Bedini. He assured the Fathers that both had not only his but their interests at heart and would do everything possible to bring them to a successful issue.[49]

By this time the American Fathers' memorial and Father Hewit's long letter to Barnabò had reached Rome. Father Hecker read them several times and summed up his opinion in the sentence: "They are in one word *the* thing."[50] After he had them translated into Italian, he gave them to Barnabò who sent the Italian, as well as the English, copies to Bizzarri on December 28, 1857.[51] The Cardinal was adding fuel to the gradually growing fire. There was only one inadequacy about the documents. There was not a single letter from a bishop to accompany them. When Father Hecker read Father Walworth's explanation that they were not free to deal with bishops because of their position and the need of secrecy, he wrote a very strong plea begging them to put aside all delicacy and interest the hierarchy in their behalf. He asked: "Shall I entreat, beg and pray . . . in order to induce you to take this step and overcome your scruples or yield up your opinions to the wishes of Card.[inal] Barnabò and Mons.[ignor] Bedini? The Propaganda *needs* help of this kind, so as to act more powerfully in our, in *your* favor, and are you unwilling to *try* and get it? . . . Surely you would not wish me to return to the United States to obtain this support by my own personal exertions. You have had the opportunity again and again to accomplish this and my entreaties till now have had no effect. God grant that you have done this before this letter reaches you and that the successful results of your zeal are on the way here."[52]

Pointing out the absolute importance of the Bishops' support, he asked his confreres to call on Bishop Bayley and tell him that "Propaganda would feel grateful" for his assistance. They must take this approach, Father Hecker insisted, since neither Barnabò nor Bedini could write in this fashion. No matter how strongly the Fathers believed that justice and truth were on their side in this dispute, they must remember that it was not a "pleasant thing for those in authority to take the side of simple subjects against their superiors." However, if the Bishops identified themselves with the American missionaries' cause, then the Holy Father would see that authority was balancing off against authority. Borrowing a phrase from Dr. Smith's letter to Hughes, he wrote: "But the episcopate is of Divine right and hence superior in authority to that of Generals of Religious Orders." Therefore the Holy Father would feel much freer in deciding the issues involved.[53]

Before this letter reached the States, the Fathers had responded to Father Hecker's previous appeals. On December 2nd, Walworth had called on Bayley and told him of the expulsion and all their difficulties "from beginning to end." The Bishop not only approved of everything that the Fathers had done but promised to write a strong letter to Barnabò emphasizing the value of the missions to the whole country "and the manifest ignorance of our Superiors in regard to American affairs and the interests of their own Order here." Since the cause of the missionaries was that of the cause of the Church in America, Bayley told Walworth that every bishop "was bound to see that we were not crushed." He then advised Walworth to write to Archbishop Kenrick in confidence and explain what had happened. However, Walworth was reluctant to make this move since the Redemptorists were in charge of all the German Congregations in his archdiocese and Kenrick might hesitate to compromise himself with the superiors of the Redemptorists. "We shall look carefully before we leap in that direction."[54]

The month of December had not yet run its course when the Fathers threw off all timidity and contacted ten bishops throughout the United States. Father Hewit had written to Archbishop Kenrick, Bishops Portier of Mobile and Lynch of Charleston. Father Walworth had written to Archbishops Spalding of Louisville and Purcell of Cincinnati and to Bishops Barry of

Savannah and O'Connor of Pittsburgh. In addition he had spoken with Bishop Wood of Philadelphia and Bishop McCloskey of Albany. All had promised to write to Propaganda on behalf of the American Fathers.[55] However, their letters did not reach the Cardinal until the end of January, excepting that of Bayley which arrived in Rome on December 31, 1857.[56]

While Father Hecker was awaiting word from the American hierarchy, the fortuitous arrival in Rome of the Irish-born and Roman-trained Bishop Thomas Louis Connolly greatly helped Father Hecker's cause. Formerly a Capuchin, he had gone to Nova Scotia as secretary to Bishop Walsh of Halifax and had become vicar-general of the diocese in 1845 and Bishop of St. John, New Brunswick, in 1852. A vigorous, forthright individual, he was not only a great Churchman with generous impulses but he was, as the non-Catholic Nicholas Flood Davin said: "also sagacious . . . with admiration for all that is good and a divine superiority to the littleness which thinks everybody else wrong."[57]

The Bishop was on his way to Rome in December of 1857, and only fifty miles from the Eternal City, when a band of thieves stopped the coach in which he was riding and took his money, his watch, and his pectoral cross. When the Holy Father heard of this indignity inflicted within the papal domains upon a highly regarded Bishop, he was distressed. He did all he could to make amends and showed Connolly every favor. He conferred honors on him and made him an assistant at the papal throne. No one doubted that Connolly, who had lost his money and his episcopal insignia on the way to Rome, gained power and prestige when he reached the Chair of Peter.[58]

Shortly after his arrival in Rome, the Bishop met Father Hecker through Cardinal Barnabò who told him about the American missionaries' difficulties. Connolly immediately liked this American priest whom he had known by reputation before he ever left his diocese. Hecker's honest and sincere manner, his pleasing smile, and his delightful personality endeared him to the Bishop and they became fast friends.* Connolly found that they were "marvellously of the [same] way of thinking." He was convinced that "the greater glory of God and the greater

---

* This friendship begun in Rome continued over the years until the Bishop's death in 1876.

good of religion in America" motivated Father Hecker in all that he had done and he offered to aid his cause "with promptitude and courage."[59] This forthright attitude "of the fullblooded Irishman" who was willing to work "like a trooper" for Father Hecker and the American missionaries was exactly what Cardinal Barnabò needed to keep the tide flowing in Father Hecker's favor. Connolly told the Cardinal and the American missionary that he would speak to the Pope telling him that in his judgment Father Hecker's cause was God's cause. Since part of his diocese was in the States, he believed that he had every right to intercede for the American priest. To make sure that the Bishop had a comprehensive grasp of the situation, Father Hecker briefed him on all phases of his case, before Connolly saw the Pope on January 10, 1858. The very morning that the Bishop was going to the Vatican, Father Hecker met and walked with him to Barnabò's residence "so that if anything is done, it may be done with a mutual understanding."[60]

The audience was a complete success so far as Bishop Connolly was concerned. He later told Father Hecker that "he had a regular tussle with His Holiness." When Pius IX heard the Bishop talk of Father Hecker in the most glowing terms, he mentioned some of the derogatory remarks that had come to his attention. Connolly countered with the observation: "Your Holiness, I should not be at all surprised if some fine day you yourself would have to canonize one of these Yankee fellows!" After considerable discussion about the difficulties between a superior general and some of his subjects, the Pope suggested that the best solution would be to release the Americans from all their obligations to the Redemptorist Community and let them form an independent group of missionaries. When the Bishop said they were ready to do this, but were waiting for his approval, the Pope replied: "They cannot expect me to take the initiating step; this would be putting the cart before the horse. Let them do this and present their plan to me and if I find it good, it shall have my consent."[61]

After his "tussle" with the Holy Father, Bishop Connolly caught up with Monsignor Talbot who, he suspected, had been pouring unfavorable reports into the ear of the Holy Father. Mincing no words, he told the Monsignor how he felt about

Father Hecker and the great good he was destined to do for religion in his native land. Finally, after hearing the Holy Father's solution, Talbot agreed that the only way of settling the difficulties was "to give the American Fathers the liberty to form a new company for the American missions." This was an important gain since Talbot was the General's chief defender and would undoubtedly carry this word to the Villa Caserta.[62]

When Barnabò heard the report he was quite pleased. Since early October of 1857, he was convinced that this was the only practical solution. However he was not yet ready to make his move. He wanted to have the letters from the American hierarchy to prove that the bishops, in whose dioceses these missionaries had labored, supported their cause and would like to see them continue their great work for souls. With this evidence in his hand, he could work openly and fearlessly to nullify the sentence of dismissal. He was determined that he would never send Father Hecker back to America with the slightest stigma on his name.

But it was Bishop Connolly who had paved the way for Barnabò and had heard from the lips of the Holy Father the directive which the Cardinal so anxiously awaited: let the American missionaries separate from the Redemptorists and form their own company. Father Hecker was everlastingly grateful to the Bishop for the interest he had taken in his case. He told the American Fathers: "Should the good Bishop come your way, whether by writing or otherwise, you cannot be too grateful for what he has done for us. After Card.[inal] B.[arnabò] and Mon.[signor] B.[edini], we owe more to him than anyone else. He alone has turned the tide completely in our favor and there is no way in which we should not show [him] our gratitude and appreciation."[63] Father Hecker knew only too well that the forceful efforts of Bishop Connolly had worked wonders in Rome. The American missionary was no longer on the defensive, hoping, praying, and working for the chance to clear himself. His champions could now speak out in his behalf, without fear of rebuff. For many months success had seemed to be vanishing in the distance but now it appeared to be nearer at hand. "Wind and tide," he said, "are now in our favor and my policy is to keep quiet and close at the rudder to see that the ship keeps right."[64]

CHAPTER XIX

Rome Speaks

THE usual delays attendant upon an appeal to the Holy See were multiplied in Father Hecker's case. After three months in Rome, months in which he had submitted statements to two different Congregations and a special petition to the Holy Father, he had finally succeeded in entering his appeal before the proper tribunal. When the news of his various moves reached America, his confreres were plainly puzzled at his changing from one Congregation to another while apparently overlooking the importance of the Pope. Since they were totally unfamiliar with the intricacies of legal procedure, the Fathers thought all his maneuvers were time consuming and dangerous. There was, in their opinion, one simple and effective method of handling the problem: go directly to the Pope since he was the head of the Catholic Church and the servant of the servants of God. Having addressed their memorial to His Holiness, they saw no reason why Father Hecker should not send this petition directly to Pius IX. His plan of bringing the case before the Congregation of Bishops and Regulars and submitting their memorial to the same group when it arrived alarmed them. Father Walworth was particularly distressed since he feared that the Congregation might declare the decree of expulsion null and void, restore Father Hecker to the Redemptorist Community, and do nothing further with their appeal to the Pope. If this happened, they would all be subject to the Rector Major who, knowing what they had done, might take reprisals against them.[1]

To offset any such contingency, Father Walworth wrote a very strong letter to Father Hecker deploring his haste "in departing from your application to the Pope and trying a new expedient with Card.[inal]* Bizzarri. The Pope having plenary power was able to overlook technicalities and consider the general merits of the case; but at present you are likely to be smothered with precedents and decrees and technicalities beyond number." In biting terms, he admonished him: "It is of the last importance to pursue a steady, unwavering course, without changing ground in the least, or trimming our sails to catch the varying winds that blow over us. . . . How can we do anything to further matters on this side when the suggestions and plans of one letter are all changed and forgotten in the next?" Then he warned his confrere: "Do not fall in with every expedient proposed to you even if it be a Cardinal that proposes it. . . . Cardinals who are willing enough to befriend us if they could do it without trouble will soon grow tired and gladly propose expedients to get us quickly out of the way. But if we urge our claim and do not allow ourselves to be switched off the track, Rome must do something for us." The real cause of Father Walworth's concern became more apparent in his final words of advice: "Unite your cause closely with ours because the General can crush you more easily as a single man and then your defeat would be a precedent against us."[2]

Although this unjustified criticism pained Father Hecker, he realized that the long delay and the inevitable uncertainty was beginning to tell on Father Walworth. On January 1, 1858, he answered him and explained more fully why he had to introduce his case before the Congregation of Bishops and Regulars, assuring his confrere that he was not changing course in the middle of the stream, but following meticulously Cardinal Barnabò's directions. He intimated that the Secretary of the Congregation of Propaganda was better informed on ecclesiastical procedure than the former barrister and American missionary. He told the Fathers that he had presented their memorial and Father Hewit's letter to Barnabò and Bedini after he had them translated into Italian. Then the Cardinal decided to send the documents to Bizzarri with a pointed reminder that he should report on them

---

* Walworth mistakenly referred to Archbishop Bizzarri as a cardinal.

to the Pope. Everything would depend, Father Hecker said, on that report. In the hope that he could induce Bizzarri to give a complete account of the memorial as quickly as possible, Father Hecker had called at the Secretary's office at least half a dozen times. But despite all his efforts and many hours of waiting in an outer office, he was unable to see the Archbishop. He had even called on Cardinal della Genga, the Prefect of the Congregation of Bishops and Regulars, but he too was unavailable. Then the Christmas holidays had intervened and no official business could be transacted until after January 6th. As soon as the letters arrived from the bishops of the United States, he hoped for quicker action. After he had detailed all the steps he had taken, Father Hecker wrote: "When you will hereafter have learned what have been my personal efforts, you will see how misplaced were the complaints made on this point."[3]

Apparently Father Hecker then thought that he would have smoother sailing in Roman waters during the year 1858 than he had experienced in 1857. But he was soon to find out that the winds of rumor and the tides of expediency would not only delay his progress but would make his course more stormy. The New Year dawned very auspiciously with the arrival of the first letter from the American hierarchy, Bishop Bayley of Newark. He told Barnabò that he had heard with "deep sorrow" the unfortunate result of Father Hecker's visit to the Rector Major. Although he was unwilling to meddle in matters that were no concern of his, he could not forego writing a few lines about the case. He thought that he expressed "the unanimous sentiment of all the Bishops and priests of the United States" when he told the Cardinal that "we all consider the formation of a group of missionaries who speak English and who are formed according to the spirit of St. Alphonsus as a special blessing of Providence for the Church in the United States. . . . I do not believe that there would be a difference of opinion among those who have an insight into the state of things in the United States as regards the good that would result from the foundation of a house where they [the American missionaries] could find themselves united in order to labor with greater energy and effect in the work to which they are dedicated." Mentioning Father Hecker by name, he spoke of him "as most dear to us . . . because of his zeal and example." The General's action against "the good Fathers" he thought could be only the result of a misunderstanding. He was confident that they were animated "in all they have done or planned by the greater glory of God and the good of the Church." He asked the Cardinal to use his influence to see that the larger issue of the good of souls in America be examined before Father Hecker's case would be decided.[4]

Although Barnabò was satisfied with the tone of this letter, he waited for others before taking any action. He knew that one communication from an American bishop did not give him the strong ground he needed to operate effectively. He told Bedini to send this letter to Bizzarri with a note calling the Secretary's attention to the great proportions the controversy was assuming, a controversy which "in the beginning could have been solved in one person."[5]

While Father Hecker waited for the additional letters, he tried to prod Bizzarri into reporting to the Holy Father on the nullity of the decree of expulsion. Thinking that Cardinal della Genga as Prefect of the Congregation of Bishops and Regulars could exert some influence on his subordinate, he had an interview with the Cardinal and explained his situation. Although the Cardinal listened carefully, he gave the American missionary no hope for a speedy settlement. He said the Congregation would pass on the merits of the case after Bizzarri presented it for a formal hearing. After this Father Hecker knew that there was no way of getting around Bizzarri. He would have to see him personally.[6]

On January 16th, after waiting for more than two and a half hours, he finally managed to see the Secretary. Bizzarri seemed unusually pleasant and cordial and told Father Hecker that his affairs were becoming more and more complicated so he had not yet drawn up his report. Volunteering the information that the case would not go to the full Congregation of Bishops and Regulars but would be decided by the Pope, he said with a smile "it shall not be a perpetual thing." Then he asked his visitor a question which gave an inkling of his delay. He wanted to know why Father Hecker and his companions could not enter some other Congregation. The American missionary immediately recognized the import of the Archbishop's request. If they were to join another community, there would be no need for the Pope to rule on the legality of expulsion. Bizzarri knew that the question was a delicate one and any decision would put the Holy Father in a very difficult position. If he decided in favor of Father Hecker, he would weaken the authority of the Rector Major; if he decided against him, he might offend against justice. But he could avoid these difficulties if the Americans would drop all litigation and simply petition to associate themselves with another religious order. Knowing that Cardinal Barnabò would never willingly accept such a solution, Father Hecker politely declined Bizzarri's suggestion.[7]

A week later the American missionary was again cooling his heels in Bizzarri's outer office. After waiting for some time, Father Hecker saw Bizzarri who this time treated him with indifference. No, he informed his visitor, he had not sent in his report to the Pope. He had not even given Father Hecker's brief against the legality of the decree of dismissal to the Rector Major for his rebuttal, a document he must have before he could draw up any evaluation of his case. Although he voiced no opinion, Father Hecker wondered about this delay, since the Secretary had had his brief for at least six weeks.[8]

The American missionary knew that he had come up against a stone wall in the Secretary of the Congregation of Bishops and Regulars. He could see him only with difficulty and then he could neither learn anything nor spur him on to do anything. Dubious as to how he could break through this barrier, Father Hecker happened to meet a man who seemed quite interested in his affairs. Then he discovered that this same individual was a close personal friend of the Archbishop. Not only did he see the Secretary frequently during the week but he visited him often at his home, a privilege granted to very few. He enjoyed the confidence of Bizzarri who spoke openly and freely with him. When Bizzarri discussed Father Hecker's case with him, the Secretary had said that he could see reasons for and against the legality of the decree but found it difficult to come to a decision. Father Hecker soon found that this mysterious person, whom he never identified in his letters, was not only communicative but co-operative. Offering to do all he could for the American missionary, he promised not only to keep after the Archbishop but to tell Father Hecker "every step he takes and all he does" in his treatment of the case. The American missionary was deeply grateful for the interest his newly found friend took in him and for the help he promised to give him. He did not think it would be amiss to express his gratitude in a tangible manner, an offer which his friend willingly accepted.[9]

Toward the end of January, 1858, the voice of the American hierarchy was heard in Rome. Kenrick, Spalding, and Lynch, with very forceful letters, had spoken out in welcome defense of the American missionaries. And in February, Purcell, Barry, and de Goesbriand likewise added their words of protest. All these communications were important but those of Kenrick and Spalding had particular significance: Kenrick because he was archbishop of the oldest see in the United States and knew the Holy Father personally; Spalding because of his reputation as a hardhitting American and his forthrightness in expressing his views.[10]

The tone of Kenrick's letter surprised Father Hecker, who never expected him to speak so strongly in his favor. The Archbishop expressed his deep regrets to Barnabò over Father Hecker's dismissal for having made a journey to Rome "to set before the General a plan for the good of religion and of profit to his Order." Although the Fathers were aware of the General's circular forbidding such a journey, they were convinced that their Provincial's approval "though reluctant" had removed any hint of disobedience. Then the Archbishop spoke in short but pointed sentences of their backgrounds, their zeal, and the excellence of their religious life and their success as missionaries. If they had erred in sending a spokesman to the General, he believed that it should be chalked up "to their burning desire to draw their fellow citizens to the Faith." He saw no reason why Father Hecker who had acted on their behalf should be the only one punished. If he were, the others might be tempted to leave the Redemptorists "to the great triumph of the enemies of the faith." Then the Archbishop asked that this "mistake be overlooked and the distinguished Father be restored to his order and sent back to his own country, since there is reason to hope that the affair can be settled so as to aid the cause of religion."[11]

Almost equal in importance was the letter of Bishop Spalding who was a graduate of Propaganda and spoke out, as Father

Hecker said, like a true American. He told Barnabò that he had learned with great bitterness of heart the Rector Major's intentions "to take measures which would result in great *harm* if not the ruin" of the missions given by the American Fathers. He had heard that the General was not only opposed to the establishment of a separate house "to train religious who speak English, but he also proposes to send to Canada and to the western islands of America a few Fathers of this Province who are of American and Irish extraction." Such a move would deprive the American Province of the great advantages accruing to English-speaking Catholics from the labors of these apostolic and zealous Fathers. Since the Fathers had entered an appeal against the action of the General, he wanted to support "with all my might" this appeal. Then he listed five reasons why he was taking this action. First, the need for the Redemptorist missions was more urgent in the United States than anywhere else. Second, the superiors and the Provincial of the American Province as well as the greater number of Fathers were for the most part German. They were excellent in ministering to their own compatriots, "but they do not easily enter into the plan of giving missions to English speaking Catholics who have even more of a need of them than the Germans." Then he added "the Germans, the Americans, and the Irish get along with difficulty in the same religious house, since they are of quite diverse temperaments and sometimes incompatible." Third, he was persuaded that an English-speaking house would attract a good number of applicants to the community, particularly "young men of talent who not rarely are converted to the Holy Catholic Faith in this country. But these American young men only with difficulty are persuaded to enter into a Congregation where for the most part the Superiors are German." Fourth, he believed that such a house would act as a center of Redemptorist missionary activity for all parts of the United States. Fifth, he had no doubt that such a foundation could support itself with the donations given by the faithful to the missionaries. Then the Bishop asked the Cardinal to present these reasons to the Holy Father and he would have the "merit of warding off a great evil and performing a great service to our missions as you have already done many times in the years gone by."[12]

The other letters, though not quite as strong and forceful, called upon the Cardinal to use his influence to protect the missions and to support the cause of the American missionaries for the greater good of religion in the United States. When Father Hecker read in Bedini's office what Kenrick, Spalding, and Lynch had written, he was elated. He reported to the American Fathers: "Yankee stock stands high in the Roman market."[13] Barnabò was also delighted when he saw the Bishops' statements. They gave him the opportunity he had wanted to take an active part in the dispute and to spur Bizzarri to action. He told Bedini to take the letters with him in his audience of January 31st and to show them to the Pope and ask the Holy Father what answer Barnabò should give to the American Bishops. Since Bizzarri had done nothing in the case and the matter had become most serious, Bedini was to tell the Pope that Barnabò did not want to keep the American hierarchy waiting for an answer.[14]

During the audience, the Pope introduced the subject of Father Hecker and the American missionaries and said that the American clergy were too independent and wanted to withdraw themselves from authority. Bedini replied that *"some* had that spirit," but this was not the case with the American missionaries. To prove his point he offered to read to the Holy Father the letters in his possession from the American Bishops. The Pope replied that this was not necessary. He should give them to Bizzarri with instructions to report on them the following Friday. With this remark, the Pope closed any further discussion of the Hecker affair.[15]

On February 1st, Bedini sent the Bishops' letters to the Secretary notifying him of the Pope's wishes.[16] Two days later, Barnabò met Bizzarri who complained about Father Hecker's impatience with the delays in the case. The Cardinal answered that the American priest had every reason to be impatient. He had been in Rome almost six months and it was "high time" that he received some consideration. Bizzarri replied that when he had suggested that Father Hecker join another religious order he had offered an acceptable solution. But the American refused. "He does right," said the Cardinal. "You would wish him to demand dispensation and thus acknowledge his guilt and prove by his own confession that he was a liar!" Barnabò knew that if Father Hecker took such a step before the decree of expulsion was declared null he would condemn himself. The Rector Major could then declare that after the American missionary had been thwarted in his attempt to change the very nature of the Redemptorist vocation he sought haven elsewhere. Hence selfish motives and not the interests of the Redemptorists had motivated him. Since these charges were anything but true, Barnabò emphatically counseled Father Hecker to take no action that might clothe them with even the semblance of probability. The Cardinal told Bizzarri: "The question before you is the legality of his expulsion. If he be guilty, then hang him. But if he be innocent, declare him so." Bizzarri objected that if he pushed for the nullity of the decree "authority will be compromised." Barnabò shot back: "If he be innocent and you do not declare him so, Justice will suffer!" Then referring to the American Fathers, Barnabò told Bizzarri that he had sent their memorial and Hewit's accompanying letter only to give him a better understanding of the case. He need not "embarrass" himself with that. "Give that to me," said the Cardinal. He would take care of their requests since they concerned the Church in America.[17]

If Bizzarri were to wash his hands of the American Fathers' petition, Barnabò was ready with a well-defined plan. He would give the Rector Major the opportunity of setting up an American house where the Fathers would be free to carry on their missions and engage in work for the non-Catholic. Leaving nothing to chance or whim, he would demand a written statement signed by Father Mauron detailing the purpose of the house and the date for its establishment.[18]

Although Father Hecker saw many disadvantages in this arrangement, he was not disturbed since he was practically certain that the General would never agree to such a proposition. If Father Mauron refused to accept Barnabò's proposal — Father Hecker preferred to say "when" — the Cardinal planned to form the Americans into a new company of missionaries directly under his authority as Prefect of the Propaganda. Apparently Bizzarri could surmise what the Cardinal had in mind and decided to deal with the memorial himself.[19]

Whether Barnabò's conversation with Bizzarri spurred the Secretary to take action in the case is difficult to say. However, the very day that Barnabò spoke to him, he sent two documents to Father Mauron for an answer: Father Hecker's plea to the Holy Father for a hearing and his brief on the nullity of the decree of expulsion.[20] He did not include the memorial of the American Fathers nor Father Hewit's accompanying letter since they had no direct bearing on Hecker's expulsion. Although Father Mauron did not see the statements of the American Fathers, word had reached him that "a number of American Fathers have requested dispensation directly from the Holy See." He did not know who they were nor what reasons they had given for seeking their release. However he sent this information to Father Ruland and advised him to deal very carefully with the Americans.[21]

The long delay in Father Hecker's case was beginning to irk Barnabò and he went to his audience with the Holy Father the night of February 4th determined to speak openly and forcefully. From the long report he gave Father Hecker of his conversation with the Pope, the Cardinal must have been in a fighting mood. He began by telling the Pope that the American Fathers were all converts, men who had attained positions of prestige and wealth before they entered the Church. They had not become Catholics "for bread!" They had labored zealously and effectively for the cause of religion in their own land, a fact which the American Bishops had attested. Then he cited the substance of each Prelate's letter after mentioning his name. Although he was tempted to take out the copies he had in his portfolio, he was careful not to let the Pope see them for fear he might say: "What are you doing with that revolver?" Continuing his argument, Barnabò pointed out the harmful effect the shabby treatment of the American missionaries would have on their friends in and outside the Church. He told Father Hecker that he "struck out left and right at certain persons here unfavorable to Americans, Talbot among others." In an attempt to scotch the stories that he was strongly prejudiced in favor of the missionaries, he told the Holy Father: "I have been twelve years bringing matters before Your Holiness and I can raise my head with boldness and challenge a reply whether I have ever been actuated by passion or prejudice." The Pope answered: "No, no!" He knew the Prefect had never been governed by such motives.[22]

Defending the missionaries, the Cardinal took up the rumor that the Americans had no idea of obedience. If that meant blind and prompt compliance with every command, perhaps they were lacking in some of these qualities. But they had the substance of the virtue and it was the General's duty "to manage and not to attack them." The Cardinal concluded his vigorous and forthright defense by declaring: "My conviction as regards Father Hecker is that he is innocent and has been most unjustly treated. I know it is a delicate question for you to decide, but if he be innocent, it is not for your Holiness to suppress Justice!" The Holy Father replied that he would never trifle with justice. He would wait for Bizzarri's report. If the case had reached unusual proportions and required a detailed and legal examination, he would send it to the full Congregation of Bishops and Regulars. No matter what action might be taken, Father Hecker would receive just and fair consideration.[23]

When Father Hecker reported to his confreres the Cardinal's account of his conversation with the Holy Father, he could only speak of it as a "glorious" defense. Now they could be certain that the Pope was familiar with all the details of their side of the case. He knew which Bishops had written and what they had said. Father Hecker told them he no longer feared that the Pope might decide the issue without full and complete information. Barnabò had told him all, so the American Fathers could not be in a better position. There was no need to worry. Now it was "heads up and eyes to heaven."[24]

The day after Bizzarri had reported to the Pope about the Bishops' letters, Father Hecker met him. The Secretary was very affable and friendly, telling the American missionary that he had also sent his documents to the Rector Major. When the General answered, both his reply and Father Hecker's statements would be given to the Pope. Bizzarri again suggested a solution to the problem so as to obviate the need of the Holy Father deciding on the nullity of the decree of expulsion. He offered to obtain a withdrawal of the expulsion from the General if Father Hecker would first petition for a dispensation from the Holy See. But the order in which he listed the procedure made it impossible for the American missionary to accept without incurring the displeasure of Cardinal Barnabò. He knew that his great defender would refuse to accept any proposal that did not give first place to the nullity of the decree. Bizzarri had placed it second. Only after Father Hecker entered his petition for a dispensation would the Secretary secure the cancellation of the dismissal. Again the American missionary had to refuse the Archbishop's offer.[25]

Within a week after he had received Father Hecker's statements from Bizzarri, Father Mauron sent his reply. He submitted six separate documents: his first answer to Cardinal Barnabò; his refutation of Father Hecker's brief on the nullity of the decree of expulsion; a copy of the bull of Leo XII confirming the Rector Major's right to dismiss quarrelsome subjects; a declaration from his Consultors regarding the dismissal; his secret motives for dismissing Father Hecker; a résumé of the Community's condition in the United States. The rebuttal of Father Hecker's appeal and the manifestation of the General's private motives for the action he had taken, were two of the most important papers in this collection.[26]

In refuting Father Hecker's claim that the decree of expulsion was null and void, the Rector Major discussed his right to dismiss insubordinate subjects. Father Hecker's canonist had contended that the Rector Major ignored the procedure required by ecclesiastical authorities and various papal constitutions when he expelled the American missionary. Admitting that these directives called for a judicial and formal trial, the testimony of witnesses, a statement of the charges alleged against the accused, and full opportunity for him to answer them, Father Mauron declared that these prescriptions of law did not bind the Rector Major of the Redemptorist Community. Since they were in force before Benedict XIV's approval of the Redemptorist Constitutions, his solemn approval "acquired for our Congregation the force of law which surely abrogates the preceding laws insofar as they are contrary to it." Consequently he was obliged to follow only the Community's Constitutions which gave him absolute authority to dismiss a subject. The Rector Major "alone is the judge" who shall decide whether or not a subject merits dismissal. He could expel not only those guilty of serious crimes, but even those who "do not give proper edification." Before issuing a sentence of dismissal he was not required to wait until a member became incorrigible or had refused to amend his ways. Neither did he have to conduct a canonical trial. Although he was duty bound to request the opinion of his Consultors, he was not compelled to follow their opinions. Furthermore he was not "obliged to give [delinquent subjects] an account of his reasons for dismissing them." Since he was absolute and supreme in this matter, if in conscience he believed there was sufficient cause to expel a member, he was acting within his rights in doing so.[27]

Having established his constitutional right in this matter, Father Mauron then undertook to prove that he had "not only a just and serious reason, but a mighty just and a mighty serious one and even urgent" for expelling Father Hecker. The core of his argument was that the American missionary in going to Rome had "formally violated the obedience due to his Superior General and that he had with public scandal scorned and trodden underfoot my authority."[28] The proof of this charge, Father Mauron noted, was in the document he had submitted to Cardinal Barnabò on September 30, 1857.[29] But in neither that document nor in this one to Bizzarri did Father Mauron prove formal disobedience. To substantiate such a charge, he would have had to demonstrate that Father Hecker knowingly and willingly refused to fulfill the commands of his superiors. To be guilty of formal disobedience, Father Hecker must have known that the Rector Major had forbidden the journey to Rome and then despite this prohibition set out for the Eternal City. But these conditions were not fulfilled. Father Hecker had good reasons for sincerely believing that the General's prohibition did not apply to his case and that it did not abrogate his constitutionally guaranteed right of personal appeal to the Rector Major. Consequently, according to his conscience, he did not act against his understanding of his Superior's wishes. Never for a moment could he even think that he had "scorned and trodden underfoot" Father Mauron's authority.

Neither could Father Hecker be accused of disobeying his Provincial since Father Ruland never forbade the journey. Father Mauron told Bizzarri that he had learned from the Provincial that Father Ruland had tried to restrain Hecker as much as he could both by warning him, by pleading with him, by reasoning with him, and by trying in vain to dissuade him through pointing out "the disastrous consequences" of his intended step.[30] Even if this were an accurate statement of fact, it would not constitute formal disobedience. Not with the widest possible interpretation could the Provincial's words be construed as a command which Father Hecker ignored.

When he took note of the canonist's statement that the American Bishops had sent Father Hecker to Rome, Father Mauron asked: "Would the Bishops send a Religious to Rome to negotiate their affairs without first consulting the Superiors of his Order?" There is no doubt that the canonist had overshot the mark when he proposed this argument. But Father Mauron was guilty of the same mistake when he answered it. He said that although Hughes and Bayley had given letters of recommendation to the American missionary, "when they found out that Father Hecker had come to Rome in defiance of the will of his Superiors, they declared that they would not have recommended him had the true circumstances of the matter been known to them from the start."[31] Father Mauron offered no evidence to prove that either Hughes or Bayley had made any such declaration. He cited Hughes's letter of October 31, 1857, but the most liberal interpretation of the Archbishop's words would fail to produce such an assertion.

The Rector Major charged the American missionary with a flagrant invasion of his rights when he failed to deliver a letter Bishop Bayley had addressed to the Rector Major: "I could bring him to the bar of justice for his unjust and deplorable manner of acting, but I would rather denounce him before this very Sacred Congregation which can judge for itself whether or not this act of injustice be a genuine act of wickedness." Then Father Mauron made a statement which under critical analysis would lose its force: "During the many days that Father Hecker sojourned in this house he never, either to me directly or to the Eminent Cardinals or Prelates of the Holy Roman Church, gave indication of such letters."[32] Father Hecker arrived at the Villa Caserta on August 26, 1857, and left it on August 31st. During that time he did not show his letters of recommendation to the Rector Major, expecting to present them at the hearing before the Consultors which Father Mauron had promised, but never granted. Until the day of his expulsion, Father Hecker had not ventured outside the confines of the Villa Caserta and could not have shown these testimonials to "Eminent Prelates of the Holy Roman Church."[33] However, when he saw Cardinal Barnabò, he produced his credentials and included the letters Bayley and Hughes had given him in his report to the Cardinal.[34]

The Rector Major then went into a long discussion of the constitutional right of a subject to appear before the General. Admitting that the 1764 Constitutions conferred that right on every subject, Father Mauron maintained that the 1855 Constitutions had restricted it to the Provincial.[35] However, he did not answer the American Fathers' objection against using the new Constitutions since he had said in his circular letter of July 26, 1855, that they were not binding until approved. Until that time, the 1764 Constitutions remained the legal code for the Community.[36]

Father Mauron then turned his attention to the "true status of the question," the prohibition contained in his circular of May 9, 1857. Quoting from the Constitution, he proved that he had every right to forbid a personal appeal to him without his previous written permission.[37] But he ignored the charge that the wording of the circular was ambiguous and could be fairly interpreted in a sense permitting the journey. Neither did he refer to the subject of Father Hecker's good faith. Resolving the issue to its basic components, Father Mauron contended that since Father Hecker admitted his knowledge of the circular and his failure to secure permission for the journey: "The matter was so simple and clear that it required no further investigation and thought." Father Hecker had shown "little regard for obedience and poverty . . . he did not give good example as a religious but rather he was a source of scandal to others." Therefore he merited expulsion.[38]

In the document listed as "Secret Motives" for dismissing Father Hecker, the Rector Major revealed for the first time the motives that played a decisive role in his decision. Previous to this time, he had not even hinted that they entered into his evaluation of the American missionary. The burden of this confidential communication appeared in the extravagant accusation: "he [Father Hecker] is a bad religious and a dangerous subject of the Institute." In an attempt to substantiate this grave charge, Father Mauron gave a rather rapid survey of Father Hecker's life.

Stating that the American missionary before his conversion had been "a Calvinist, then a Methodist, then he associated with a group which ate only bread, fruit and herbs," the Rector Major believed this was sufficient evidence of Father Hecker's "very unstable character."[39] Here Father Mauron's ignorance of Father Hecker's background led him to misstate facts. Although the American missionary had investigated various religious and ascetical groups, he had never joined any one of them. But even if he had, this would hardly prove instability. Any priest experienced in dealing with converts realizes that successive dissatisfaction with man-made religions is often the result of divine grace drawing a soul to the Church.

Continuing his brief and hurried narrative, Father Mauron spoke of the young man's spiritual experiences at St. Trond and Wittem. He noted that "if the then Master of Novices (who no longer is such) had been more faithful to the Congregation than so considerate of Father Hecker, he would have dismissed him. Nevertheless to our misfortune he allowed him to be professed." Although Father Hecker's spiritual directors, men of the stamp of Fathers Ottmann, Heilig, de Held, and de Buggenoms, had tested his vocation and were satisfied that he was solidly grounded spiritually, Father Mauron, writing more than ten years later and with only the most fragmentary knowledge, could find "the presence of a deep spiritual pride eminently dangerous."[40]

After Father Hecker's return to America, the Rector Major continued, it became more and more obvious that "he was far from being all that one seeks in a son of St. Alphonsus." Then Father Mauron began to cull from the reports and letters of the Provincial and his charges became more detailed, selective, and specific. His caustic statements are but a recapitulation, more succinctly stated, of the unsubstantiated accusations that Father Ruland had made not only against Father Hecker, but against Fathers Walworth, Hewit, and Deshon. Since Father Baker had fared so well at the hands of the Provincial and his signing of the memorial had not been discovered, Father Mauron failed to charge him with contumacy and conspiracy as he did the other four.[41]

After he put the finishing touches to this damaging description of his expelled subject, Father Mauron exclaimed: "Behold the

man, Excellency, whom you wish to induce me to receive anew
in the Congregation!"[42] This fervid line seems to offer the only
plausible explanation for the extraordinary and intemperate indictment that Father Mauron entered against Father Hecker.
Since Archbishop Bizzarri was obviously putting some pressure
on the Rector Major to receive Father Hecker back into the
Community, Father Mauron wanted to block any such move if
he possibly could. In a letter accompanying these documents, he
told Bizzarri that Father Hecker's readmission would irreparably
impair his authority. He "would be truly reduced to the state
of pure nothingness with the title of Superior and of General
but without any power to counteract any evil among my so-called
subjects whom I would no longer have the courage to command
under obligation because I could no longer expect from them the
required submission, if they see me shorn of that authority
which hitherto has been entrusted to the Superiors General by
the Rule. . . . Such an act of charity shown Father Hecker would
be on my part an act of cruelty towards all the other members."[43]

The available sources for this period do not reveal the reasons
why Bizzarri wanted Father Hecker reinstated in the Congregation. Hence there is no way of knowing if he did so because he
believed the decree of expulsion was null or because he was still
looking for a way to free the Holy Father from the embarrassment of deciding the legality of the decree. However, this document to Bizzarri, as well as a letter he wrote to the Holy Father
on February 11, 1858, reveal that Father Mauron was genuinely
concerned that the Holy See might order him to restore Father
Hecker to the Congregation. In an effort to head off what he
regarded as an unmitigated calamity, Father Mauron explained
to the Holy Father why he opposed this move and offered a
solution "which would turn out to the satisfaction of all concerned."[44]

In the first section of his letter, Father Mauron extolled the
wisdom of Pius IX in constituting the Transalpine group as a
separate Community and in decreeing the location of the central
seat of government at Rome. Order and discipline were flourishing
and the members of the Community were inspired with love and
zeal for the rule. Although Father Mauron trusted that his subjects would continue to grow in spiritual stature through love

alone, nevertheless "they are men and they are held to their duty by the fear of individual inconstancy as well as the fear that one day through some serious act of disobedience they might be dismissed from the Congregation." This fear was most salutary and necessary to anchor their vocation in the Community.

But said Father Mauron, "if I am forced, as some wish, to admit once again into the Community a subject who in such evident and public manner has trodden under foot his sworn obedience due to me as his legitimate superior . . . if the friends of Father Hecker prevail in their attempt to have him readmitted into the Congregation, how can I ever maintain this salutary fear in the hearts of thousands of our Members who after so many vicissitudes only now begin to enjoy the fruits of the paternal arrangements of Your Holiness."

After this explanation, Father Mauron then submitted his solution of this thorny problem which he felt would neither discredit the Redemptorist traditions nor weaken the discipline of the Congregation. Despite his desire to help so many needy souls in the United States, he found it practically impossible at that time to establish a house such as Father Hecker desired. However if the Pope would permit the exclusion of Father Hecker to remain, "rather than the Congregation undertaking such an enterprise, the benefit of such a house of missionaries could be gained for the American Protestant if Your Holiness would permit the said Father to be entitled Missionary Apostolic. Adorned with such an honorable title, he could, with the consent of the Archbishop and without delay, open in New York such a house of missionary priests. He could also add other companions who, without being bound to the Rules of our Congregation or any other existent Order could follow that way of life which they feel is more in conformity with their proposed objective and which is adapted to the needs of their fellow Americans." Father Mauron was confident that Father Hecker would not want for associates. Three of his confreres in America, he had heard, had already petitioned the Holy Father for a release from their vows. Then the Rector Major added: "If your Holiness be not of the mind to grant them directly the requested release from their vows, I beg that permission be immediately given me as Rector Major to avail myself of the faculty with which I am empowered by the Rule, should they insist, of granting them the usual dismissal. They then can join Father Hecker and begin without delay the much desired house." The American Prelates, Father Mauron concluded, would welcome four such experienced missionaries to inaugurate this wonderful apostolate to the non-Catholic, especially since they had "contributed nothing either in expense or anxiety" for the education and support of these priests.[45]

The report of the Rector Major stymied all Bizzarri's efforts to bypass a decision on the real question at issue: the legality of the decree of expulsion. Father Mauron had adamantly opposed willingly readmitting the American missionary into the Community. Father Hecker had resolutely refused to seek a dispensation. This left the decision up to the Holy Father and as Father Hecker put it "whichever way the Pope turns he is in a fix." He saw the situation as two opposing forces contending for the Holy Father's approval. One was the Rector Major with his supporters, including cardinals and influential cammerati in addition to the "German nationality which is a power per se." The other was the five Americans representing their nationality and sustained by Barnabò and Bedini, as well as being stanchly supported by archbishops and bishops of the United States. Between them stood the imposing figure of the Pope. If he crossed to the American side, he would imperil the position of the General and imply that all the suspicions and charges against the Americans were false. If he joined the General's forces, he would crush the American missionaries, adversely affect the cause of religion in the United States, rebuff Propaganda, and repudiate the judgment of the American episcopate.[46] In an attempt to conciliate both sides, Bizzarri hopefully studied the manifold documents spread out on the desk before him preparatory to giving his report to the Holy Father on February 19, 1858. But on the day of his audience he was taken sick with Roman fever and another week of tormenting delay had to run its course.[47]

The long, agonizing weeks of watching, waiting, and hoping were beginning to take their toll on Father Hecker. He was fatigued and distressed. The strain of weighing carefully every proposal, evaluating cautiously every expedient, refuting honestly every suspicion, and dispelling candidly every prejudice consumed almost all the moral and physical strength he could muster. He found days when he had no appetite and nights when he could not sleep. In all his Catholic life, he wrote on February 27th, he had never experienced "the oppression and anxiety of mind in such a degree as I have these ten days past." He asked his confreres to write often "for words of sympathy, hope and encouragement are much to me now."[48] Had it not been for Barnabò's insistent refusal to allow him to petition for a dispensation, he would have requested his release in the middle of February.[49] He cared nothing for reputation. He had been "cut and slashed at in every direction" until he had lost "all idea of ever having had any character."[50] When Bizzarri's confidant told him confidentially that the General's "secret motives" for the dismissal "insinuated the blackest calumny" against him, he was not disturbed. "This only awakens in my heart gratitude towards God whose grace has preserved me innocent" of any such charges.[51] Free from any feeling of vindictiveness, he sought no personal triumph over the Rector Major. Only one ambition consumed him: to win his freedom to fight the enemies of the Church, not his religious cohorts. "I desire nothing upon earth," he told his brother, "except to labor for the good of our religion and our country, whatever may be the decision in our affairs."[52]

Despite his temporary depression, Father Hecker was never forgetful of Divine Providence. This, he told the Fathers, was a time of severe trial for all of them. He was particularly concerned about Father Deshon and Father Baker who "in almost the beginning of their religious life are placed in such perplexing circumstances." Surely God had some divine purpose in permitting these trials. "If God intends to employ us in any important work in the future, such an experience was absolutely necessary for us. It is a novitiate on a large scale. . . . Let us keep courage, united, confiding in God and the protection of our Dear Mother."[53]

Father Hecker also recognized the personal value of his trials. They had "laid in me the foundations of something much greater than the world imagines: that of becoming a Saint. For I am sure my present opportunities on that score are abundant and thank God, His grace is more abundant." Finding that his long months in Rome had weaned him away from the world, he was more determined than ever to devote himself wholeheartedly "to the interests of God alone. How few there are who have no other interests in view but those of God. This however only stimulates me to become one of those few."[54]

By the end of February, the long night of uncertainty began to give way to the first streaks of the dawn of a new hope. The Holy Father had told Bizzarri not only to prepare his report for the audience of February 27th, but to bring with him "all, all, all" the documents he had. This Bizzarri did, though he gave a verbal account of the case. The Holy Father, after listening to the Secretary, took the papers and said he would give his answer shortly.[55] Five days later, on March 4th, Barnabò had his audience and discussed the Hecker affair with the Pope. Referring to the Bishops' letters and the memorial of the American Fathers, the Cardinal said: "I told your Holiness in the beginning, it was a religious broil, but now it is an affair of the American Episcopate." The Pope answered: "We shall have to give these Americans dispensation and set aside the expulsion."[56]

Although this was welcome news to Father Hecker, he wondered if he ought not petition for the dispensation. He was afraid that the Pope, in the absence of such a request, might release his companions but refer his expulsion to the Congregation of Bishops and Regulars for further adjudication. Knowing that this would mean long months of aggravating delay and tortuous anxiety, he wanted to avoid that at all costs. His only problem was Cardinal Barnabò, who insisted the declaration of the nullity of the decree must come first. How could he persuade him to relent on this demand? Fortunately the Pope had pointed the way by saying that he would grant the dispensation and set aside the expulsion. Barnabò then told Father Hecker to notify Bizzarri that he would accept a dispensation if the Pope would cancel the expulsion.[57] More than likely it was Barnabò who dictated the message Father Hecker sent immediately after leaving the Cardinal. He addressed his request to André Balzani — possibly the unnamed confidant of the Archbishop:

My dear friend:

I authorize you to acquaint Monsignor Bizzarri that if His Holiness deigns to cancel my illegal expulsion and if he gives dispensation to the other American Fathers, I will be satisfied, seeing the circumstances that have supervened in my affair, to accept my dispensation as well as they.[58]

The last hurdle was cleared and the way opened for the long-awaited decision. By two o'clock on the afternoon of March 6th, Father Hecker knew that the Pope had spoken but his decision was not immediately released. Bizzarri told him that if the Americans were "discreet persons" they would be "content with it."[59] Two days later, the Secretary sent copies of the decree to Cardinal Barnabò and Father Mauron. Shortly after it was in the Cardinal's hands, he read it to Father Hecker:

> Certain priests of the Congregation of the Most Holy Redeemer in the United States of North America recently presented their most humble petition to our Most Holy Lord Pope Pius IX, that in view of certain special reasons he would grant that they might be withdrawn from the authority and jurisdiction of the Rector Major and be governed by a superior of their own, immediately subject to the Apostolic See, and according to the [Redemptorist] Rule approved by Benedict XIV, of holy memory. If, however, this should not be granted to them, they most humbly asked for dispensation from their vows in the said Congregation. After having carefully considered the matter, it appeared to His Holiness that a separation of this kind would be prejudicial to the unity of the Congregation and by no means accord with the Institute of St. Alphonsus, and therefore should not be permitted. Since, however, it was represented to His Holiness that the petitioners spare no labor in the prosecution of the holy missions, in the conversion of souls, and in the dissemination of Christian doctrine, and are for this reason commended by many bishops, it seemed more expedient to His Holiness to withdraw them from the said Congregation, that they might apply themselves to the prosecution of the works of the sacred ministry under the direction of the local bishops. Wherefore His Holiness by the tenor of this decree, and by his Apostolic authority, does dispense from their simple vows and from that of permanence in the Congregation the said priests, viz.: Clarence Walworth, Augustine Hewit, George Deshon, and Francis Baker, together with the priest Isaac Hecker, who has joined himself to their petition in respect to dispensation from the vows, and declares them to be dispensed and entirely released, so that they no longer belong to the said Congregation. And His Holiness confidently trusts that under the direction and jurisdiction of the local bishops, according to the prescription of the sacred

Canons, the above-mentioned priests will labor by work, example and word in the vineyard of the Lord, and give themselves with alacrity to the eternal salvation of souls, and promote with all their power the sanctification of their neighbor.

> Given at Rome, in the office of the Sacred Congregation of Bishops and Regulars, the 6th day of March, 1858.
>
> G. Cardinal Della Genga, *Prefect*.
> A. Archbishop of Philippi, *Secretary*[60]

As he listened to the words of the official voice of Rome, Father Hecker could only utter a grateful "thank God!" It gave him and the American Fathers the opportunity they had sought, to work together with devotion and zeal for the good of souls in America. There was not a word in the decree that could be construed against them. On the contrary, it spoke favorably of their apostolic labors and mentioned the commendations of the Bishops. After a moment's reflection, Father Hecker thought, it would have been "so easy to have worded it differently" and leave them under a cloud. When he wrote to tell his confreres the good news, he said: "Let us be thankful to God, humble towards each other and the world and more in earnest to do the work God demands of our hands."[61]

After he had finished reading the document, Cardinal Barnabò told Father Hecker to request an audience with the Holy Father to thank him personally for his great kindness and thoughtful consideration. Although Barnabò knew the American missionary yearned to return to his native land and to his missionary companions, he told him to postpone all hopes of leaving Rome until after Easter. Such a delay, Father Hecker realized, would cause him no uneasiness. If enough time elapsed between the date of his audience and his departure, he would go "to our Lady of Loreto to invoke her aid in our behalf and for her protection over us as a body and each one of us."[62]

When Father Hecker called on Archbishop Bizzarri to express his gratitude and that of the American Fathers, the Archbishop was interested to know his reaction. Father Hecker told him he was immensely pleased with the decision of the Holy See, since it gave them "entire liberty to act in the future as God and our intelligence shall point out the way." The Archbishop then remarked that since the Holy See had praised the American Fathers in the decree, he trusted that they would show themselves worthy of this commendation in the future. "Since the beginning of our Catholic life," answered Father Hecker, "we had given ourselves soul and body entirely to the increase of God's glory and the interests of His Church and it was our firm resolve to do so until the end of our lives."[63]

On March 16th, Father Hecker knelt for the second time before the Sovereign Pontiff, Pius IX, who called him by name and said: "At length your affairs have been determined. We have many causes to decide and each must have its turn; yours came finally and now you have our decision." Speaking with the fullness of gratitude, Father Hecker replied: "True, your Holiness. And your decision gives me great satisfaction and it appears to me that it should be satisfactory to all concerned." Referring to the biblical account of Abraham and Lot, the Pope motioned with his hand: "I told one to take this and the other that direction." Father Hecker assured the Holy Father: "I sought no personal triumph over the General, but entertained every sentiment of charity towards him and every one of my former religious brethren. I thought of your Holiness' decision in the Holy Mass of this morning when in the Gospel Our Lord reminds us not to decide according to the appearances of things but render a just judgment. Such was the one you have given." Moved by this manifestation of charity and confidence, the Holy Father replied: "As you petitioned with the other Fathers as one of the Congregation, in giving you dispensation, I considered you a member of the Congregation." Then the Pope inquired: "But you intend to remain together in Community?" Quickly Father Hecker spoke up: "Most assuredly, your Holiness. Our intention is to live and work as we have hitherto; but there are many privileges attached to the exercises of the Missions very necessary to their success and in which we would gladly participate." Smiling, the Pope looked at him: "Well, organize, begin your work and then request them [the privileges] and I will grant them to you." He hesitated a moment and then continued: "But the Americans are very much engrossed in material pursuits." This to Father Hecker's ears was like a refrain from his first interview with the Pope. "True, Holy Father, but the holy Faith is there. We five Missionaries are Americans and were like others, but you see the grace of God had withdrawn us from these things, moved us to consecrate ourselves wholly to God and His Church. We hope it will do the same for many of our countrymen and once our countrymen are Catholic, for they have enthusiasm, we hope they will do great things for God's Church and His glory. It would be a great consolation to me if your Holiness would accord a plenary Indulgence to my brethren and several of my friends in the United States?" Again the Holy Father smiled: "But I must have a rescript." When Father Hecker drew one from his pocket, the Pope looked at it and said it was too general. Then taking his pen, he wrote out the conditions for gaining the blessing and signed it. Before leaving, Father Hecker knelt at the Pope's feet and begged him to give "a large blessing" that he might "become a great missionary in the United States."[64]

With the rush of Holy Week and Easter closing in on the Holy City, Father Hecker had no opportunity to make his pilgrimage to Loreto. He planned to leave Rome for Marseilles on April 6th and then sail from Havre on the *Vanderbilt,* April 28th.[65] One of the last places he visited before he left Rome was the first place he had sought when he arrived, the Villa Caserta. On March 30th, he called to say good-by to Father Mauron. He found the General still suffering from the effects of illness and his hands trembled "like those of an old man." Before they parted, Father Hecker offered to transact any business for him in the States. He took several engravings of St. Alphonsus for the houses in the American Province. The two men then took leave of each other with the most cordial feelings and promised to pray *"pro invicem."* With a fervent "God bless you," Father Hecker shook hands with his former superior and they parted.[66]

Father Hecker also had a message from another Redemptorist, Father de Held. After he had received the American missionary's letter telling him of the decree of separation, the Belgian Rector wrote: "I cannot tell you how I am pained by this result." He had hoped and prayed for Father Hecker's restoration to the Congregation, but now that the Holy Father had spoken, the case was closed. Father de Held said he understood that the Holy Father's dispensation "necessarily implies the cancellation of the decree of your expulsion." By this he meant that the Pope, in dispensing Father Hecker from his vows, considered they were still in force and the American missionary was a member of the

Community. If Father Mauron's expulsion were in effect, that expulsion would have released Father Hecker from his obligations and he would no longer be a member of the Community. But the Holy Father joined him with his four companions "in respect to dispensation from the vows" and then declared that they were "dispensed and entirely released so that they no longer belonged to the said Congregation." By the force of these words, the Holy Father ignored Father Mauron's expulsion and regarded it as non-existing. However, since the Pope had not explicitly said he was setting aside the decree or annulling it, Father de Held advised Father Hecker "to obtain from Cardinal Barnabò some document stating that your dispensation implies the annulment of the decree."[67] This was wise and cautious advice since Father Hecker would then have in writing from an official of the Roman Curia almost the equivalent of a direct decision on the nullity of the decree. Whether Father Hecker followed this recommendation or not, he does not say. Nor is there among his papers any such document from Barnabò. Father Hecker could have decided that he needed nothing in writing as long as the Pope had told both him and Barnabò that he acted as though the expulsion was non-existent.

The week before Father Hecker left Rome, one of the converts he had instructed in the Holy City, Anna Baker Ward, had an audience with the Holy Father. Falling at his feet, she fervently acknowledged him to be the visible head of the Church. Then, as Father Hecker said, womanlike she burst into tears. The Pope was deeply touched and exclaimed: "How many graces Rome has for souls and for their conversion!" After she had composed herself, Mrs. Ward replied: "True, Holy Father, but pardon me, it was an American priest in Rome that was the means of my conversion. I read a book called *Questions of the Soul* by Père Hecker and for the first time I saw the beauty and truth of the Cath.[olic] Ch.[urch]. This conviction passed into my heart and I could have no peace until I was fully instructed and submitted myself to the Church of God." Then she explained that it was Father Hecker who had instructed her.[68]

While this story was making the rounds of the Vatican, the American missionary was becoming "an object of interest." He decided then "it is time therefore that this American priest should

leave Rome, otherwise he would become proude [sic] like the
hard shell Baptist."[69] During the trying days when success seemed
like a mirage, he told the American Fathers: "Should we meet
with success, this may be more difficult to support than adver-
sity."[70] The mirage was proving to be a reality and he was finding
it strange and unusual. He must leave the scene of his conquests
and return to the land of his challenge.

As he looked over the past seven months he had spent in Rome,
it seemed to him that he had crowded a lifetime into these eventful
days. The two conspicuous elements in any human life, sorrow
and joy, stood out vividly in these memories of the Eternal City:
"When I think of the kicks and cuffs received, the fears, the
anxieties and labors undergone, I say to myself: 'boys that's fun
enough for this time.' On the other hand when I remember the
warm and disinterested friends God has given to us through these
difficulties and the happy issue to which Providence has conducted
them, my heart is full of gratitude and joy." Since he was not one
to indulge in self-pity, he dismissed the past from his mind and
looked to the future. "To me the future looks bright, hopeful,
full of promise and I feel confident in God's Providence and assured of His grace in our regard."[71] He rejoiced that his mission
in Rome was a complete success. He was leaving "without having
any desire or wish unfulfilled or unanswered. And for this success
I take no credit to myself but regard it as the work of the Providence of God."[72]

The long siege was over, divine grace had sustained him, and
now the future was beckoning. With enthusiasm, with courage,
with confidence in divine grace, he left Rome to face that future
in his beloved America.

*   *   *   *

As Father Hecker stood on the deck of the *Vanderbilt* making
its way across the Atlantic to American shores, he knew his search
was over and he was beginning almost a new life. An era had
closed; another was opening. His heart was filled with gratitude to
Almighty God for His divine favors and graces as he promised
Him he would work faithfully and zealously in the fulfillment of
his newly found vocation. He could look back with gratitude upon
his days spent in the Redemptorist Community where he had

learned the fundamentals of religious life and perfection, where he had been raised to the dignity of the priesthood and where he had received his first opportunity to win souls for Christ. Mindful of the blessings he had received as a Redemptorist, he was grateful to all his former brethren in religion for whom he had the kindliest feelings and whom he could embrace with unfeigned charity. But he knew, as the Holy Father had said to him, he and they had come to the parting of the ways. He left them, sad with the sorrow that comes from farewells, but not grief-stricken with anguish that flows from bitterness of heart. They would always be dear to him and he would continue to thank God for them, ever mindful that under their spiritual guidance, his conviction of a call to labor for the conversion of America ripened and developed into maturity. It was at their hands that the full realization of his divine call burst upon his consciousness. He was leaving them not in anger or disappointment, but filled with gratitude and charity for their kindness.

As he looked out over the waters of the Atlantic, he could almost see stretched across the horizon the inviting challenge: "Make America Catholic." With the grace of God, he, Isaac Hecker, would labor, suffer, and die meeting this challenge.

Bibliographical Comment

THE most important and fruitful source of information on the life of Father Hecker has been the vast amount of unpublished material in various archives throughout the United States and Europe. Printed volumes were for the most part secondary and in the main served to set the activity and labors of Father Hecker in relation to his time. Since bibliographical data for these publications have been given in the notes, it is hardly necessary now to list each author and title in alphabetical sequence. Hence I shall confine my attention to pointing out the importance of the archival depositories for this biography and to listing the published lives of Father Hecker with a brief evaluation of each. Photostatic copies of all pertinent material from the various manuscript collections cited in this work are now in the Paulist Fathers' Archives in New York City.

ARCHIVAL SOURCES

Archives of the Archdiocese of Baltimore. The *Kenrick, Bayley,* and *Spalding Papers* shed interesting light on the relationship between these Prelates and the American Redemptorist missionaries. They also reveal the Bishops' attitude toward Father Hecker during his days as a Redemptorist and their co-operation during his months in Rome.

Archives of the Archdiocese of New York. The *Hughes Papers* contain a few letters of Father Hecker to the Archbishop which point up the fact that he was more than casually acquainted with Hughes. The letters of Bernard Smith in this collection

415

leave little doubt of the interest that Propaganda had taken in Father Hecker's case in Rome. In the *McCloskey Papers,* there is a very important letter of Bishop Fitzpatrick to the New York Auxiliary which gives an entirely different impression of his reaction to Father Hecker than has appeared in the previous Hecker biographies.

Archives of the Diocese of Charleston. Although there is only one letter of Father Hecker to Bishop Lynch before 1859, there are some of Father Hewit which indicate the interest of the Charleston Prelate in the work of the American Redemptorist missionaries and his desire to aid in the apostolate to the non-Catholic.

Archives of the English College in Rome. Among the *Talbot Papers,* there is a letter of Father Douglas to Talbot which corroborates Father Hecker's observation that the English Monsignor was relaying information to Pius IX which, while it aided the cause of the Redemptorist Rector Major, adversely affected the interests of the American Missionary.

Archives of the Irish College in Rome. The only letter in the *Kirby Papers* bearing on Father Hecker is one of McCloskey to Kirby. Its few lines are extremely significant in revealing McCloskey's awareness of the difficulty between Father Hecker and his Redemptorist superiors and they explain how Father Hecker obtained his introduction to important ecclesiastical officials in Rome.

Archives of the Paulist Fathers. 415 West 59th Street, New York City. The *Hecker Papers* contain the early diaries, memoranda, and notes made by Father Hecker as well as more than one thousand letters he received in his lifetime from his family, bishops, clerics, and laymen. These letters alone provide interesting sidelights on the America of the early 19th century and Father Hecker's relation to prominent literary and ecclesiastical figures of his day. It need hardly be said that this collection is indispensable for any correct understanding of Father Hecker's character before and during his days as a Redemptorist. The letters he wrote to his American confreres during the course of his litigation in Rome made it possible to chart the progress of his case since they are almost a day-by-day account of his activities. His copies of documents and testimonials he had received in the Holy City are the only available records of important facts since the originals could not be located. The *Hewit, Baker,* and *Rosecrans Papers* are noteworthy for their information on the pre-Redemptorist days of the American Fathers.

Archives of the Diocese of Charleston. Although there is only one letter of Father Heckeer to Bishop Lynch before 1859, Congregation of Propaganda were the *Lettere e Decreti della S.C. e Biglietti di Mons. Segretario* (Volumes 348 and 349) and the *Scritture riferite nei congressi, America Centrale* (Volumes 17 and 18). The former contains a digest of the letters sent by Propaganda to various individuals in answer to their correspondence and makes it possible to learn the content of the original letters where these were no longer available. The *Scritture riferite* is a collection of letters sent to Propaganda by the American hierarchy and the various correspondents of the Congregation. Numerous letters about Father Hecker including his nomination to the See of Natchez and the efforts of the American bishops to aid him in the successful prosecution of his case were found in this collection. The interest, co-operation, and activity of Cardinal Barnabò and Archbishop Bedini can be seen in the notations that were made on these letters. Some of the documents sent to Propaganda on behalf of Father Hecker exist only as a copy, since the originals were forwarded to the Congregation of Bishops and Regulars. These originals could not be located in any of the Roman archives. However, a study of the material in Propaganda Archives as well as those in the Paulist and Redemptorist Archives filled in the gaps occasioned by the absence of the documents originally sent to the Congregation of Bishops and Regulars.

Archives of the Redemptorist Fathers. These various archives in Wittem (Holland), Clapham (England), Brooklyn, and Rome were richly rewarding in details hitherto unknown of Father Hecker's life as a Redemptorist. The Wittem chronicles expand previous knowledge of Father Hecker's student days and his progress in his studies; the Clapham records give some idea of his priestly activity as a missionary in England. The most important sources for material on the troubles that led to the separation of Father Hecker and his companions from the

Redemptorist Community are the *Ruland Papers* in the Baltimore Provincial Archives now located at 526 59th Street in Brooklyn, and the papers of the American Province in the Redemptorist General Archives in Rome. Through both collections, the remote as well as the proximate causes of the separation of the American missionaries from the Redemptorist Community can be found. The correspondence between the American Provincial and the Rector Major leaves no doubt about the various issues involved in the controversy. Since Father Mauron also kept copies of documents he forwarded to the Holy See, they were extremely valuable for filling out the story when the originals could not be located in the Roman archives.

Archives of St. John's Abbey in Collegeville, Minnesota. The microfilm of the Smith papers made by Father Colman Barry, O.S.B., from the originals in the Archives of the Abbey of St. Paul's Outside the Walls in Rome gives the vital role of Dr. Bernard Smith in aiding Father Hecker's cause. They also show that he acted as the agent for a number of American bishops and as a liaison between Propaganda and the American hierarchy.

Archives of the University of Notre Dame, Notre Dame, Indiana. The *Brownson Papers* contain Hecker's letters to Brownson and are especially important for Hecker's pre-Catholic days and his progress to the Church. They also delineate the development of his plans and hopes for the future of the Church in America while he was a Redemptorist missionary. In the absence of any full-scale life of Archbishop Purcell, the *Cincinnati Papers* supplied data on the relationship between that Prelate and the American Redemptorist missionaries, as well as the high regard in which he held Father Hecker.

Hall of Records, New York City. The *Books of Conveyances* are transcribed records of the actual conveyances by deed of real property located in New York County. In the same building, the Registry of Wills is also kept. After the will has been probated, all the details are entered in this Registry. Both of these sources yielded definite and authentic facts on the Hecker and Friend families and also accurate information on the property transactions of the Hecker boys when they first established their bakery.

BIOGRAPHIES OF FATHER HECKER

Walter Elliott, C.S.P., *The Life of Father Hecker,* New York, 1891, is the first biography of the Paulist Founder and has served as the source for practically all subsequent accounts of Hecker. It is valuable for the abundant quotations from Father Hecker's diary and letters as well as for the observations of the author who was Father Hecker's constant companion in his last years. Since it was published serially as articles in the *Catholic World* and appeared in book form within three years after Father Hecker's death, Father Elliott had little time for research or even a critical examination of available sources. He depended almost entirely upon the letters and diaries in the Hecker collection and upon memoranda he made during the closing years of the Paulist Founder's life. The author selected from this abundant source such material as would "tell the achievements and chronicle the virtues of Father Hecker." In his narrative, Father Elliott presented Father Hecker as a mystic of a high spiritual order without elaborating on his relation to the men and women of his own day and the precise part he played in contemporary affairs. Orestes Brownson has written a few observations on the technique used by some biographers of religious which aptly describe Elliott's approach. He said that these authors "appear to count external facts as of little importance and to hold as important only the interior life. They give us, it may be, the religious, but rarely the man." This criticism in all fairness could be leveled against Father Hecker's first biographer. In the pages of his book, many of the personal characteristics of Father Hecker, his engaging personality, his appealing sense of humor, his unconquerable optimism, his practical grasp of problems, his resourcefulness in overcoming difficulties — in short, many of the human qualities that made him such a remarkable person — are submerged. Hampered by the lack of important contemporary material and guided by the specific purpose he had in mind when writing, Father Elliott has given an incomplete and at times inaccurate picture of the Paulist Founder. Archbishop Keane, a devoted admirer of Father Hecker who knew him intimately for many years, once remarked about the *Life:* "That is Elliott's Hecker, not Hecker's Hecker."

William Barry, *Father Hecker, Founder of the Paulists*, New York, n.d. This pamphlet of seventy-five pages is a reprint of a review of Elliott's *Life* in the *Dublin Review* of July, 1892. Though not a biography, it is a running commentary on Elliott's work, written in excellent style.

Walter Elliott, C.S.P., *La Vie du Père Hecker*, Paris, 1897, is a translation and adaptation of the English life made by the Countess de Revilliax, the cousin of the Count de Chabrol. To make it more appealing to a French audience, the translator not only abbreviated Elliott's longer volume, but "remelted" it. In the process some of Father Hecker's ideas and teachings were thrown out of proper focus. Coppinger and Canon Barry after a critical analysis of the English and French volumes found that the translation was inaccurate and had departed too much from the original. It must therefore be used carefully.

Charles Maignen, *Le Père Hecker, est-il un Saint?* Paris, 1898. An English translation appeared as *Father Hecker, Is He a Saint?* London, 1898. To offset the popularity won by *La Vie du Père Hecker*, Father Maignen, who was a priest of the Brothers of St. Vincent de Paul, wrote his volume at the height of the Americanism controversy to discredit the Paulist Founder. He depended solely on the French translation of Elliott and had no familiarity with any of Hecker's printed writings. True to his purpose, he produced a slanderous diatribe against Father Hecker. In "A Myth in 'L'Américanisme' " published in the *Catholic Historical Review* for July, 1945, I wrote: "There is no point in discussing this volume. It is known and acknowledged to be inaccurate, biased, vitriolic, libelous and venomous." Nothing I have seen or read since those lines appeared have caused me to alter that judgment in the slightest degree.

Henry D. Sedgwick, Jr., *Father Hecker*, Boston, 1900. This compact, pocket-size volume of one hundred and fifty-seven pages is one of the series of *The Beacon Biographies of Eminent Americans* edited by M. A. de Wolfe Howe. The author depended almost entirely on the Elliott *Life* and presented in condensed form the main incidents of Father Hecker's life. He has given almost a *précis* of Elliott's volume. In a final chapter on the Americanism controversy, he adds a brief and uncritical survey of the issues involved in the contest and a rather apt summary of Leo XIII's *Testem Benevolentiae*.

Vincent F. Holden, C.S.P., *The Early Years of Isaac Thomas Hecker, 1819–1844,* Washington, D. C., 1939. This was written as a doctoral dissertation at the Catholic University of America. It represents the first critical examination and evaluation of Hecker's early life, written from the *Hecker Papers* which had not been used since the appearance of the Elliott biography. With that collection and other contemporary material, I tried to set in better focus Father Hecker in relation to his time. Done in strict dissertation style with numerous references and copious quotations, the book is heavy reading. The narrative is frequently broken with much background material of various movements such as the New York City political and labor situations, the Brook Farm and Fruitlands experiments. Also it is lacking in interpretation and in certain sections is scarcely more than a stringing together of documents and letters.

Katherine Burton, *Celestial Homespun,* New York, 1943. This is a popular life of Father Hecker done in historical-fiction style. The author took considerable freedom with her material as she invented scenes and conversations purportedly based on the sources. Such a technique inevitably creates an impression stronger than the document warrants. As a result it is difficult to know where history begins and fiction ends. The volume takes no notice of published accounts of Redemptorist history and exhibits no awareness of any Redemptorist material. Because of this omission, it is unbalanced. Because of its style, it has little value for the historian. Because of its inaccuracies, it will not give the reader an accurate picture of Father Hecker.

Joseph McSorley, C.S.P., *Father Hecker and his Friends,* New York, 1952. Although not specifically a biography of Father Hecker, this volume treats in some detail the main aspects of Father Hecker's life and work. The author has depended on more than the Elliott biography and dipped into the *Hecker Papers* as well as other source material at his disposal. If however, he had had the documents in the Redemptorist Archives as well as those in the Roman depositories, he would have revised some of his conclusions. With these reservations, the volume is an interesting and highly readable account of a good portion of Hecker's life. Father McSorley's evaluation of Father Walworth in "The Walworth Episode" is an excellent, critical estimate of a somewhat puzzling personality. In fact, it is the only penetrating analysis of Walworth that has yet appeared in print.

Andreas Goy, C.SS.R., *Semblanza del P. Hecker, fundador de los Padres Paulistas*, Mexico, 1955. This pen picture of Father Hecker is marred by a lack of scholarship and draws a number of its conclusions from Maignen's volume. For the facts on Father Hecker's life, the author depended upon the French translation of Elliott. Though undoubtedly Father Goy thought he was presenting a sympathetic study, his work is filled with historical errors, inaccuracies, misrepresentations, and a distorted interpretation of a number of Father Hecker's ideas and published writings.

ABBREVIATIONS USED IN THE NOTES

A.A.B.   Archives of the Archdiocese of Baltimore.
A.A.N.Y.   Archives of the Archdiocese of New York.
A.D.C.   Archives of the Diocese of Charleston.
A.E.C.   Archives of the English College in Rome.
A.I.C.   Archives of the Irish College in Rome.
A.P.F.   Archives of the Paulist Fathers, New York City.
A.P.   *Lett. et Decreta.* Lettere e Decreti della Sacra Congregatio de Propaganda Fide e Biglietti di Mons. Segretario, in the Archives of Propaganda, Rome.
A.P.   *S.R.C., Amer. Cent.* Scritture referite nei congressi America Centrale, in the Archives of Propaganda, Rome.
A.R.B.   Archives of the Redemptorist Fathers, Baltimore Province.
A.R.C.   Archives of the Redemptorist Fathers, Clapham, England.
A.R.R.   Archives of the Redemptorist Fathers, Rome.
A.R.W.   Archives of the Redemptorist Fathers, Wittem, Holland.
A.S.J.A.   Archives of St. John's Abbey, Collegeville, Minnesota.
A.U.N.D.   Archives of the University of Notre Dame, Indiana.

Notes

For pages 2–5

CHAPTER I

1. Carl W. Schlegel, *German-American Families in the United States* (New York: 1916), I, pp. 32–42. This is the source for these and other facts about the Hecker family mentioned in this chapter.
2. *Ibid.,* pp. 42–44.
3. Walter Elliott, *Life of Father Hecker* (New York: 1891), p. 3; Schlegel, *op. cit.,* p. 44.
4. *City Directory,* 1812–1813; *Citizen's Directory of New York,* 1814–1815.
5. Elliott, *op. cit.,* p. 3.
6. After George Hecker's death, February 14, 1888, his wife, Josephine, wrote to Father Hecker saying: "You are very near to me now, as one who was always a part of dear George." When Father Elliott read this letter to Father Hecker, the latter exclaimed: "George and I were united in a way no words can describe. Our union was something spiritual and divine." A.P.F., *Elliott Papers,* June 13, 1888.
7. Elliott, *op. cit.,* p. 11.
8. *Ibid.,* p. 8.

9. A.P.F., *Hecker Papers*, selected memoranda, February 15, 1886.
10. Elliott, *op. cit.*, p. 5. This was the answer Friend gave when someone asked him why he never learned English although he had been in the country forty years. He replied: "What can one learn in forty years?"
11. *Young Catholic*, III, p. 1, "The History of a Clock."
12. *Ibid.*, V, p. 97. Father Hecker writing as Uncle Ned recalls this verse he sang as a youngster.
13. School Number 7 was a new building which had been opened the previous May by the New York Public School Society. It was not a public school as we know the term today, granting education without any tuition. Parents were then asked to pay for their children's instruction according to the subjects they studied. The fee was in reality little more than a token payment to remove any stigma that it was a charity school for poor children. In 1805 the city provided schools for children whose parents were unable to pay for their education. Cf. A. Emerson Palmer, *The New York Public School* (New York: 1905), p. 18. When the Society realized that a number of families could not provide the fee required in private and denominational schools and preferred to deprive their children of any schooling rather than publicly admit their indigence, they petitioned the Legislature to enact a law empowering the trustees of the Society to require a moderate fee suited to the means of the parents. The law was passed January 28, 1826, with the provision that no child who could not pay was to be denied the benefits of education. This system was finally abolished February 3, 1832, and the schools again became absolutely free. *Ibid.*, pp. 63–70. Although the file papers, vouchers, receipt books, and trustee minutes of the New York Public School Society are in the New York Historical Society Research Library (170 Central Park West, New York City), they simply record tuition money received. They do not specify from whom it came or how much was paid. Hence it is impossible to know if Hecker's family paid any fee for his education.
14. Palmer, *op. cit.*, p. 45 ff., gives in some detail the course that was given in the schools.
15. Elliott, *op. cit.*, pp. 4–5; on page 6, he reprints an account from the *Young Catholic*, p. 1, probably written by Mrs. George Hecker, the editor. It is a very interesting account with the clock giving something of its history and that of its maker. When the Methodist Church was torn down, the clock was returned to Father Hecker and it hung in the Paulist sacristy in New York for about ten years. Then it was taken to the country house of George V. Hecker where it was accidentally destroyed by fire.
16. The school census of 1829 reported that of the six thousand and seven children attending the public schools, none acquired any more than the first elements and a smattering of geography, grammar, and arithmetic. Frequently when a youngster reached the age of fourteen, that marked the end of his educational training. Thomas Boese, *Public Education in the City of New York* (New York: 1869), p. 57.

17. A.P.F., *Hecker Papers*, Early Diary, April 15, 1843.
18. Schlegel, *op. cit.*, pp. 32–44.
19. Cf.: Georgiana B. Kirby, *Years of Experience* (New York: 1887), p. 187; Clara E. Sears, *Bronson Alcott's Fruitlands* (Boston: 1915), p. 87; Elliott, *op. cit.*, p. 87.
20. A.P.F., *Hecker Papers*, Isaac to Dear Father. This, though undated, was written from Wittem either in 1847 or 1848.
21. Schlegel, *op. cit.*, p. 45; *City Directory*, 1827–1828.
22. Vincent F. Holden, C.S.P., *Early Years of Isaac Thomas Hecker* (Washington: 1939), p. 23.
23. *History of the People of the United States* (New York: 1907), V, pp. 274–275.
24. *City Directory*, 1834–1835.
25. Elliott, *op. cit.*, pp. 7–8.
26. *Books of Conveyances*, Hall of Records, New York City, *Liber* 335, 477.
27. *City Directory*, 1838–1839.
28. H. H. Manchester, "Millers Who Became Famous," *Northwestern Miller*, CXXXIX, pp. 431–432.
29. *City Directory*, 1838–1839.
30. Elliott, *op. cit.*, p. 12.
31. *The Epic of America* (Boston: 1931), p. 175. The author gives a very good picture of the industrialization of the North and its effect on the laborer in Chapter VII, "The North Begins to Hustle." See also Carl Russell Fish, *The Rise of the Common Man* (New York: 1927), pp. 109–120.
32. James Truslow Adams, *The Epic of America* (Boston: 1931), pp. 181–182.
33. James B. McMaster, *History of the People of the United States* (New York: 1907), V, 121.
34. This group had been meeting secretly in the Military and Civic Hotel in Broome Street until March of 1835. When the time for the party nominations arrived, the Tammanyites, of which they were a part, gathered at Tammany Hall on October 29, 1835. While the members waited outside the front door, the committee gained entrance to the hall through a back door and laid plans to secure the nominations for their candidates. As the opposition filed in, Isaac L. Varian was nominated for the chair. When he went to seat himself, the workingmen nominated Joel Curtis. A fight ensued to see who would finally be seated. The majority won out and Curtis was placed in the chair. The defeated minority left the hall, went downstairs, and turned off the gas leaving the meeting in total darkness. The workingmen had come prepared; for as soon as the lights were extinguished, they took out candles and lighting them with locofoco matches, then just coming into use, illumined the hall and continued the meeting. Since these matches had stood the workingmen in such good stead, the Whig papers applied the term to the group. F. Byrdsall, *The History of the Loco-Foco or Equal Rights Party* (New York: 1842), pp. 23–28. This book contains the most sat-

isfactory account of the Loco-Focos. It was published five years after the dissolution of the party by the recording secretary of the group and is indispensable for a study of the movement.

35. *Ibid.*, pp. 39–40. This Declaration of Principles is quoted in full in Holden, *op. cit.*, pp. 35–36.

36. Elliott, *op. cit.*, p. 15, erroneously states that Isaac Hecker and his brother joined the Workingmen's Party of 1829–1831 in the year 1834. For a detailed refutation of this error, see Holden, *op. cit.*, pp. 30–33.

37. "Dr. Brownson and the Workingman's Party Fifty Years Ago," *Catholic World*, XLV (May, 1887), p. 200.

38. Dixon R. Fox, *The Decline of Aristocracy in the Politics of New York*, Columbia University Studies in Political Science, LXXXVI (New York: 1919), p. 382.

39. Elliott, *op. cit.*, p. 17.

40. Byrdsall, *op. cit.*, p. 162.

41. *Ibid.*, The entire account of the steps toward gradual unity with Tammany and the action of the minority is told in detail by Byrdsall, *op. cit.*, Chap. xiii.

42. Isaac Hecker, "Dr. Brownson and the Workingman's Party Fifty Years Ago," *Catholic World*, XLV (May, 1887), p. 203.

43. A.P.F., *Hecker Papers*, document submitted in Rome to his director by Father Hecker, January 6, 1858.

44. "Our Future Policy," IV, p. 77.

45. *Ibid.*, p. 82.

46. Elliott, *op. cit.*, p. 18, states that Father Hecker met Brownson in the autumn of 1834. Henry F. Brownson, *Brownson's Early Life* (Detroit: 1898), pp. 159–160, places the date of the meeting as 1837. Holden, *op. cit.*, pp. 49–60, gives in detail the evidence to show that both dates are incorrect.

47. Arthur M. Schlesinger, Jr., *Orestes A. Brownson A Pilgrim's Progress* (Boston: 1939), p. 124. This is an excellent study of Brownson by an author who has thoroughly mastered his subject.

CHAPTER II

1. *Boston Quarterly Review*, III (July, 1840), p. 358 ff.

2. Orestes A. Brownson, *The Convert* (New York: 1857), p. 288 ff.

3. *Evening Post*, March 5, 1841.

4. Isaac Hecker, "Dr. Brownson and the Workingman's Party Fifty Years Ago," *Catholic World*, XLV (May, 1887), pp. 204–205.

5. Schlesinger, *op. cit.*, pp. 8–138, *passim*.

6. Hecker, "Dr. Brownson in Boston," *Catholic World*, XLV (July, 1887), p. 466.

7. *Oration of Orestes A. Brownson Delivered at Washington Hall, July 5, 1841*, pp. 4–6. This address was later published as a brochure and is now available in the Harvard College Library.

8. *Ibid.*, p. 7.

9. A.U.N.D., *Brownson Papers*, Hecker and Brothers to Mr. Brownson, November 14, 1841.
10. *Ibid.*
11. For evidence that Isaac Hecker wrote the letter, cf. Vincent F. Holden, C.S.P., *Early Years of Isaac Thomas Hecker* (Washington: 1939), p. 50.
12. *Tribune*, January 18, 1842; *Evening Post*, February 3, 1842. See also *Tribune*, January 20, 27, 1842.
13. Isaac Hecker, "Dr. Brownson and the Workingman's Party Fifty Years Ago," *Catholic World*, XLV (May, 1887), p. 206.
14. Walter Elliott, C.S.P., *Life of Father Hecker* (New York: 1891), p. 31.
15. Hecker, *op. cit.*, p. 206.
16. Orestes A. Brownson, *The Convert* (New York: 1857), p. 271.
17. "Reform and Conservatism." Cf. Schlesinger, *op. cit.*, p. 140.
18. O. A. Brownson, "Charles Elwood" (reviewed by the editor), *Boston Quarterly Review*, V (April: 1842), p. 149 ff.
19. Elliott, *op. cit.*, p. 18.
20. Isaac Hecker, "Dr. Brownson's Road to the Church," *Catholic World*, XLVI (October: 1887), pp. 7–8.
21. *Ibid.*, p. 10.
22. Brownson, "Leroux on Humanity," *Boston Quarterly Review*, V (July: 1842), p. 321.
23. A.P.F., *Hecker Papers*, Early Diary, February 3, 1843, recalls the beginning of this change as "nine months ago." He makes a similar observation in a letter to his brother George on March 6, 1843. *Ibid.*
24. *Ibid.*, Isaac Hecker to his family, December 26, 28, 30, 1842; March 6, 1843. In these letters Hecker gives the chain of events that led to his changed attitude and how he fought against it but without success.
25. *Ibid.*
26. *Ibid.*, Early Diary, January 10, 1843.
27. *Ibid.*, Isaac Hecker to his family, December 26, 1842.
28. *Ibid.*, Early Diary, April 24, 1843. He states the beginning of the dreams as "six months ago."
29. *Ibid.*, May 18, 1843.
30. Cf. Evelyn Underhill, *Mysticism* (London: 1930), 12th edition, revised pp. 279–293, where the author, after a critical analysis of visions in the authenticated mystics, lists common characteristics of these supernatural visitations.
31. A.P.F., *Hecker Papers*, Early Diary, May 18, 1843.
32. *Ibid.*, January 10, 1843.
33. A.U.N.D., *Brownson Papers*, John Hecker to Orestes Brownson, January 7, 1843. While Isaac was visiting Brownson, John wrote a long letter of explanation of his brother's condition and the family reaction to it.
34. A.P.F., *Hecker Papers*, Isaac Hecker to his family, December 28, 1842.
35. A.U.N.D., *Brownson Papers*, John Hecker to Orestes Brownson, January 7, 1843.
36. *Ibid.;* A.P.F., *Hecker Papers*, Isaac Hecker to his family, December 26, 28, 1842.

37. A.P.F., *Hecker Papers,* Isaac Hecker to his family, December 26, 1842; March 6, 23, April 14, May 16, June 24, July 1, 1843.
38. A.U.N.D., *Brownson Papers,* John Hecker to Orestes Brownson, January 7, 1843.
39. A.P.F., *Hecker Papers,* O. A. Brownson to Hecker Brothers, November 28, 1842. The reports of these lectures are in the *Tribune* for December 7 and 9, 1842.
40. The awakening and development of Brownson's religious sense is traced in Arthur M. Schlesinger, Jr., *Orestes A. Brownson* (Boston: 1939), pp. 136–149.
41. A.U.N.D., *Brownson Papers,* Isaac to Friend Brownson, December 19, 1842. This letter makes it clear that Brownson extended the invitation to Hecker to make the visit.
42. A.P.F., *Hecker Papers,* Isaac Hecker to his mother, December 24, 1842.
43. Schlesinger, *op. cit.,* p. 155.
44. I. T. Hecker, "Dr. Brownson in Boston," *Catholic World,* XLV (July: 1887), p. 471.
45. *Ibid.,* p. 468.
46. A.P.F., *Hecker Papers,* Isaac to his family, December 26, 1842. This letter is published in Holden, *op. cit.,* pp. 77–78.
47. *Ibid.*
48. *Ibid.*
49. *Ibid.,* Early Diary, January 11, 1843.
50. This letter of Brownson to John Hecker has not been found. Part of its content can be known from John's letter of January 7, 1843, to Brownson.
51. A.U.N.D., *Brownson Papers,* John Hecker to Orestes Brownson, January 7, 1843.
52. A.P.F., *Hecker Papers,* Isaac Hecker to his brother and family, December 28, 1842.
53. *Ibid.*
54. *Ibid.,* Isaac to his family, January 3, 1843.
55. *Ibid.*
56. *Ibid.,* January 7, 1843.
57. *Records of the Brook Farm Association,* January 7, 1843. These records are in the Massachusetts Historical Society.
58. A.U.N.D., *Brownson Papers,* John Hecker to Orestes Brownson, January 7, 1843.
59. A.P.F., *Hecker Papers,* Early Diary, January 11, 1843.
60. *Ibid.,* Isaac Hecker to his family, January 7, 1843.
61. *Ibid.,* Early Diary, January 10, 1843.
62. *Ibid.,* January 11, 1843.
63. *Ibid.*   64. *Ibid.*
65. *Ibid.,* Isaac Hecker to Henry F. Brownson, April 17, 1876. This letter sent on the occasion of Orestes Brownson's death, was later returned to the Paulist Fathers by Henry Brownson's widow.
66. *Ibid., Hecker Papers,* Early Diary, June 29, 1845.

CHAPTER III

1. Octavius B. Frothingham, *George Ripley* (Boston: 1882), p. 109.
2. Eight of these associations were established in Ohio, six each in New York and Pennsylvania, three in Massachusetts, two in New Jersey, and others in Illinois, Michigan, Wisconsin, Indiana, and Iowa. After 1850, with the return of economic prosperity, they gradually disappeared. Cf. Carl Russell Fish, *The Rise of the Common Man* (New York: 1927), p. 189; Zoltan Haraszti, *The Idyll of Brook Farm* (Boston: 1937), pp. 10–11.
3. The development of Ripley's thought which finally culminated in the establishment of Brook Farm is given in some detail in Vincent F. Holden, C.S.P., *Early Years of Isaac Thomas Hecker* (Washington: 1939), pp. 91–96.
4. Lindsay Swift, *Brook Farm* (New York: 1900), pp. 18–20. This book is by far the best factual presentation of Brook Farm. J. T. Codman, *Brook Farm Memoirs* (Boston: 1894), is a comprehensive account written by a former member of the group. It is filled with personal reminiscence of his stay there. Unfortunately, it is not accurate. A succinct and interesting summary of the project has been given by Haraszti, *op. cit.*, which contains a good working bibliography of the experiment.
5. Swift, *op. cit.*, pp. 27–33, has a description of these various cottages. The Eyrie was spelled in various ways. Ripley used Eyry, others Eyrie and Aerie. Hecker spelled it Erie, leaving no doubt about the pronunciation.
6. George W. Cooke, *Early Letters of George William Curtis to John S. Dwight* (New York: 1898), p. 9.
7. Swift, *op. cit.*, pp. 110–198, gives a short sketch of each one of the members.
8. A.P.F., *Hecker Papers*, Early Diary. This entry is written on a four-page folded sheet. The beginning of the entry is missing, but is followed by February 3rd. It was probably written the end of January. John Van der Zee Sears, *My Friends at Brook Farm* (New York: 1912), p. 57, writes: "Always at Brook Farm, anyone not strictly in it . . . was absolutely out of it."
9. Ora Gannett Sedgwick, "A Girl of Sixteen at Brook Farm," *Atlantic Monthly*, LXXXV (March: 1900), p. 402.
10. A.P.F., *Hecker Papers*, Isaac Hecker to his family, January 26, 1843. In this letter Hecker reports he has taken over the bread baking, how he is proceeding, and the success he has had.
11. George William Curtis to Father Elliott, February 28, 1890; Walter Elliott, C.S.P., *Life of Father Hecker* (New York: 1891), p. 55.
12. Georgiana B. Kirby, *Years of Experience* (New York: 1887), p. 121.
13. A.P.F., *Hecker Papers*, Early Diary, April 15, 1843.
14. Anon., "Girl's Recollections of Brook Farm School," *Overland Monthly*, *N.S.*, *LXXII* (September: 1918), pp. 235, 236; Amelia Russell, "Home

Life of the Brook Farm Association," *Atlantic Monthly,* XLII (1878), p. 461.

15. Codman, *op. cit.,* pp. 10–11, gives the complete educational program.
16. A.P.F., *Hecker Papers,* Isaac Hecker to his brothers, January 26, 1843.
17. *Ibid.,* Early Diary, February 4, 1843.
18. *Ibid.,* January (cf. note 8 above), February 3, 1843.
19. *Ibid.,* Isaac Hecker to his brothers, January 26, 1843. Holden, *op. cit.,* p. 113, mistakenly has the length of the subscription to the *Weekly Herald* as three weeks instead of three months.
20. The letters of Hecker's family to Isaac are no longer extant. However their content in part can be reconstructed from the answers Isaac sends home.
21. A.P.F., *Hecker Papers,* Isaac Hecker to his family, February 8, 1843.
22. *Ibid.,* Isaac Hecker to his family, February 22, 1843.
23. *Ibid.*
24. *Ibid.* This family reaction is apparent from Isaac's letter to George, March 6, 1843.
25. *Ibid.*
26. *Ibid.,* Isaac Hecker to George, March 6, 1843.
27. *Ibid.,* Isaac Hecker to his family, March 14, 1843.
28. *Ibid.,* Isaac Hecker to his family, March 23, 1843.
29. *Ibid.,* Isaac Hecker to his family. April 13, 1843; Early Diary, April 15, 1843.
30. *Ibid.,* Isaac Hecker to his family, February 22, 1843.
31. *Ibid.,* Isaac Hecker to his family, April 13, 1843.
32. Elliott, *op. cit.,* p. 55.
33. George Wm. Curtis was born in Providence, Rhode Island, February 24, 1824. He received his early schooling in Jamaica Plain and in Providence. As a youth he had come under Emerson's spell while listening to him lecture on the "Over-Soul." He was taken out of this environment when the family moved to New York in 1839. His studies were continued at home under the guidance of tutors. Both he and his brother, Burrill, very much interested in Transcendentalism, asked permission of their father to go to the Brook Farm school. They arrived in May, 1841, and paid tuition and board, since they never became members of the Association. They returned to New York for the winter of 1843–1844, going back to Concord the following spring. In 1846 they went to Europe. After his return, George took up writing. He published *Nile Notes of a Howadyi, Howadyi in Syria, Potiphar Papers, Prue and I.* He became editor of *Harper's New Monthly Magazine.* Edward Cary, *George Wm. Curtis* (Boston: 1894).
34. In A.P.F., there are twenty-six unpublished letters of George Curtis to Isaac Hecker, between the period August 18, 1843, and July 9, 1845. Hecker's letters to Curtis have disappeared as Curtis admits in a letter to Walter Elliott, February 28, 1890, Elliott, *op. cit.,* p. 56.
35. A.P.F., *Hecker Papers,* Isaac Hecker to his brothers, May 2, 1843. There

are seven unpublished Dana letters in this collection and the usual salutation is "Mein liebster Isaac."

36. *Ibid.*, Ida Russell to Isaac Hecker, September 21, 1843. In this letter Miss Russell recalls such scenes.

37. *Ibid.* There are four unpublished letters of this correspondence in the Hecker Papers.

38. Randall Steuart, *The American Notebooks by Nathaniel Hawthorne* (New Haven, 1932), p. 78.

39. Ora Gannett Sedgwick, *op. cit.*, p. 402.

40. *Ibid.* There are six unpublished letters of Ora Gannett's to Hecker in the Hecker Papers.

41. A.P.F., *Hecker Papers*, Early Diary, May 11, 1844.

42. *Ibid.*, Ora Gannett to Isaac Hecker, July 28, 1844.

43. *Ibid.*, Early Diary, May 16, 1843. The vision of angelic being is given on page 27 of this book.

44. Cooke, *op. cit.*, p. 74.

45. Haraszti, *op. cit.*, p. 20.

46. A.P.F., *Hecker Papers*, Early Diary, April 18, 1843.

47. *Ibid.* Hecker not only tried to obliterate her name in this entry, but every time it occurred in the diary. Apparently about a year after he left Brook Farm, he reread the diary and tried to make the name illegible by writing over it. But despite the curves and circles he made, there is no doubt that he had written sometimes Almira Barlow; other times Almira. He also altered the originally written pronouns, her and she, to him and he. Holden, *op. cit.*, pp. 135–139, discusses in detail why the scratched-out name is Almira Barlow.

48. Haraszti, *op. cit.*, p. 21.

49. A.P.F., *Hecker Papers*, Early Diary, August 13, 1843.

50. *Ibid.*, July 7, 1843.

51. *Ibid.*, October 17, 1843. Hecker's diary shows clearly he received a number of letters from Mrs. Barlow, yet not one of them was preserved, although he saved others from his Brook Farm friends. For a more detailed discussion of this matter see Holden, *op. cit.*, pp. 135–141.

52. *Ibid.*, Isaac Hecker to George, May 12, 1843.

53. *Ibid.*, Isaac Hecker to his family, April 19, 1843.

54. Carl W. Schlegel, *German American Families in the United States* (New York: 1916), Vol. I, pp. 49–50.

55. A.P.F., *Hecker Papers*, Isaac Hecker to his family, February 22, 1843.

56. Arthur M. Schlesinger, Jr., *Orestes A. Brownson* (Boston: 1939), pp. 150–185. In the sixth chapter of this volume, Schlesinger gives a very clear and concise account of this development in Brownson's life. Henry F. Brownson, *Orestes A. Brownson's Early Life* (Detroit: 1898), pp. 453–470, recounts this phase of Brownson's religious development, but he is more diffuse and not nearly as readable as Schlesinger.

57. A.P.F., *Hecker Papers*, March 1, 1843.

58. *Ibid.*, Isaac Hecker, to his family, April 13, 1843.

59. *Ibid.*, Early Diary, April 15, 1843.

60. *Ibid.*, April 17, 1843.
61. *Ibid.*, April 18, 1843.
62. *Ibid.*, Early Diary, April 24, 1843.
63. *Ibid.*, Isaac Hecker to his family, May 9, 1843.
64. *Ibid.*, Early Diary, April 28, 1843.
65. *Ibid.*, June 26, 1843.
66. *Ibid.*, Isaac Hecker to his family, May 23, 1843. These ideas are found in his letters home, May 12, 16 and June 18, 1843. Also in his diary, April 24, June 1.
67. *Ibid.*, June 1.
68. A. Bronson Alcott to Mrs. Barlow, February 15, 1843. This letter was found among the *Hecker Papers*. Clara E. Sears, *Bronson Alcott's Fruitlands* (Boston: 1915), p. 12, mistakenly writes that Alcott sent this letter, part of which she prints, to Hecker. Hecker had heard both Alcott and Lane speak at Brook Farm. A.P.F., *Hecker Papers*, Isaac Hecker to his brothers, January 26, 1843. Holden, *op. cit.*, p. 157, says: "Hecker gives no indication that he ever heard Alcott speak at the Farm." When I wrote that statement this letter was not available but it is now in the A.P.F. From his letter to his family, June 18, 1843, it is obvious that he had received a good deal of information about Fruitlands.
69. Sears, *op. cit.*, p. 26.
70. A.P.F., *Hecker Papers*, Isaac Hecker to his family, June 24, 1843.
71. *Ibid.*, Early Diary, June 24, 28, 1843.
72. *Ibid.*, Isaac Hecker to his family, July 1, 1843.
73. *Ibid.*, Early Diary, July 5, 1843.
74. A.P.F., *Hecker Papers*, A. Bronson Alcott to Mrs. Barlow, February 15, 1843. Although Alcott's first name was Amos, he never used it after 1820 but shortened it to an initial.
75. Clara E. Sears, *Bronson Alcott's Fruitlands* (Boston: 1915), p. 44. This is a letter written by Charles Lane and Bronson Alcott to A. Brooke of Oakland, Ohio, August, 1843, on "The Consociate Family." Miss Sear's book is the best account of the Fruitlands' community yet in print. Odell Shepard, *Pedlar's Progress* (Boston: 1937), has a fine treatment of the background out of which Fruitlands grew. He has added little about external events because he felt that Miss Sears had told them "with such accuracy and sympathetic justice" that a repetition was unnecessary.
76. A.P.F., *Hecker Papers*, Early Diary, April 15, May 18, 1843; John Van Der Zee Sears, *My Friends at Brook Farm*, p. 72, was also aware of this, when he wrote of Hecker, "He was a faithful and competent baker for several months; usually happy and cheerfully interested in all that was going on, but occasionally taking a day off for fasting and prayer."
77. A.P.F., *Hecker Papers*, Isaac Hecker to his family, July 13, 1843.
78. *Ibid.*, Early Diary, July 7, 1843; Isaac Hecker to his family, July 13, 1843. Sears, *op. cit.*, p. 39, quotes from Carter's account of Fruitlands in *Century Magazine* about the baking by Alcott.
79. A.P.F., *Hecker Papers*, Early Diary, July 12, 13, 1843.

80. *Ibid.*, July 17, 1843.
81. *Ibid.*, Isaac Hecker to his brothers, July 19, 1843.
82. Elliott, *op. cit.*, p. 56, quoting a letter Elliott received from Curtis, February 28, 1890.
83. A.P.F., *Hecker Papers*, Early Diary, July 18, 1843.
84. *Ibid.*, July 5, 1843.
85. *Ibid.*, Isaac Hecker to his brothers.
86. *Ibid.*, Early Diary, July 23, 1843. Although Hecker has the date July 22nd in his diary, it should be 23rd. The clue to this is given in the preceding entry where he writes, "21, Sat." July 21st was a Friday, while Saturday was 22nd. From this entry until he left Fruitlands, the day of the week is accurate, but the date is not. This is borne out by checking with Anna Alcott's diary.
87. *Ibid.*
88. *Ibid.*
89. *Ibid.*, July 22, 1843.
90. Elliott, *op. cit.*, p. 81. That Lane did not share Alcott's view of Hecker is further borne out by a letter he wrote to Oldham, July 30, 1843: "Mr. Hecker, a very spiritual-minded young man, also has been with us. He is partners with his brothers at New York in a very extensive baking and corn mill business. He has resided several months at West Roxbury, but is by no means satisfied with their school boy dilettante spiritualism. He will, I believe, go to New York to clear up if possible with his family as to the relations in which they are in future to stand to each other. They appear to be so loving and united a family with such strong human attachments that, although he has done much toward breaking away, I fear that in the desire to bring his brothers further into the inner world, he will himself be detained." Clara Sears, *op. cit.*, p. 30.
91. A.P.F., *Hecker Papers*, Early Diary, July 29, 1843.
92. *Ibid.*
93. *Ibid.*, August 9, 1843.
94. A.P.F., *Hecker Papers*, Early Diary, August 13, 1843.
95. *Ibid.*, undated memorandum on Brook Farm.
96. Emerson and Forbes, ed., *Journals of Ralph Waldo Emerson* (Boston: 1909), Vol. VI, p. 43.
97. A.P.F., *Hecker Papers*, Early Diary, August 9, 1843.
98. *Ibid.*, Early Diary, June 28, 1845. His handwriting improved a bit, but not much. It is not easy to read as Richard B. Elliott, the brother of Walter Elliott, observes in the *Detroit Evening News*, January 25, 1899: "On Father Hecker's death, he [Walter Elliott] set about writing the story of his life, injuring his eyesight pouring over the manuscripts Father Hecker left behind him, written in a microscopic hand."
99. A.P.F., *Hecker Papers*, Early Diary, August 30, December 2, 6, 1843; *ibid.*, Isaac Hecker to his family, April 25, 1844; A.U.N.D., *Brownson Papers*, Hecker to Brownson, September 6, 1843.
100. A.P.F., *Hecker Papers*, Early Diary, September 16, 1843. The reasons given by Hecker are: "It does not feed the spirit. It stimulates the

animal propensities. It is taking animal life when the other kingdoms are sufficient, and better increment. Slaughter exercises the lower propensities and stimulates them. It is the chief cause of the slavery of the kitchen. It generates in the body the diseases the animals are subject to, and encourages in man their bestiality. Its odor is offensive and its appearance unaesthetic."

101. *Ibid.*, Ripley to Hecker, September 18, 1843.

CHAPTER IV

1. A.P.F., *Hecker Papers*, Early Diary, August 15, 1843.
2. From the time of his affiliation with the Equal Rights Party until 1865, John Hecker kept up an active interest in politics. He was the chairman of the Seventh Ward Citizen's Association for some time; in 1854 he was elected alderman and again in 1863. The political ring refused to seat him in 1863, but he secured an injunction against them and won out. In 1865 he was nominated for mayor by the Citizen's Association and ran on an independent ticket. He lost the election and after that retired from active participation in politics and devoted himself to educational movements in the city. Schlegel, *German American Families in the United States* (New York: 1916), Vol. I, pp. 46–48.
3. Since 1841, when Calhoun had written Brownson a very appreciative letter after reading his "Social Evils and their Remedy," the Boston Reformer had favored the Senator. The correspondence continued and when the move began for Calhoun's candidacy, Brownson endorsed him with enthusiastic articles in the *Boston Quarterly Review* and later in *Brownson's Quarterly Review*. The story of the attempt to secure the Democratic nomination for Calhoun is told by John B. McMaster, *History of the People of the United States* (New York: 1910), Vol. VII, p. 332 ff.
4. This was not the first time the Calhoun Democrats requested the services of Brownson's pen. On August 20, 1844, John Hecker had written to know if the Boston Reformer would write a fiery, persuasive speech for a New York rally on September 14th (A.U.N.D., *Brownson Papers*). But John had made a mistake in the date of the meeting which was September 4th. When the error was discovered, John was out of town, so Isaac was asked to notify Brownson and find out if he could have the speech ready by September 4th (*ibid.*, Isaac Hecker to Brownson, August 30, 1843). The time was much too short for the overworked Brownson and he had to decline (A.P.F., *Hecker Papers*, Brownson to Hecker, September 2, 1843). Henry Brownson, *Orestes A. Brownson's Early Life* (Detroit: 1898), p. 336, not knowing of this letter mistakenly writes: "Brownson having sent the address in time for the mass meeting an additional one was wanted after that meeting as Hecker writes under date of September 6, 1843."
5. A.P.F., *Hecker Papers*, Brownson to Isaac Hecker, September 2, 1843, in

which he writes: "I am expecting to get back to the hospital, though I have not yet received my appointment."

6. A.U.N.D., *Brownson Papers,* Isaac Hecker to Brownson, September 14, 1843.

7. A.P.F., *Hecker Papers,* Brownson to Isaac Hecker, September 18, 1843.

8. Henry Brownson, *op. cit.,* pp. 157–160, gives the full account of these difficulties.

9. A.P.F., *Hecker Papers,* Brownson to Isaac Hecker, October 3, 1843. Henry Brownson, *op. cit.,* p. 340, did not know of his father's reaction as expressed in this letter when he wrote: "He was hardly required to deliberate, however, on the matter, for the letter proposing was almost immediately followed by another recalling the suggestion, because it had been decided not to have a regular editor, but to leave his duties to one of the contributors, there being difficulty in collecting funds." The letter referred to as recalling the suggestion was written by Isaac Hecker to Orestes Brownson, October 16, 1843, which was more than a week after he received Brownson's decision not to accept the editorship. Henry Brownson had Hecker's letter of October 16, 1843, which he printed, *op. cit.,* p. 504, omitting the first paragraph in which Hecker wrote: "Your letter came just in time to prevent me from writing at that time the case as it then stood, which was not very helpful. Not having collected all the means that were expected, they now have finally agreed to start the paper without an exclusive editor, but under the supervision of one of the many contributors. That is now McCracken." A.U.N.D., *Brownson Papers,* Isaac Hecker to Brownson, October 16, 1843. Arthur Schlesinger, Jr., *Orestes A. Brownson* (Boston: 1939), pp. 161–162, also unaware of Brownson's letter to Hecker, writes: "In 1843, Brownson was offered the editorship of a pro-Calhoun paper to be established in New York; but the offer was recalled because of financial difficulties that made a regular editor impossible." In this, he accepts Henry F. Brownson's position.

10. A.P.F., *Hecker Papers,* Brownson to Isaac Hecker, October 3, 1843.

11. A.U.N.D., *Brownson Papers,* Isaac Hecker to Brownson, October 16, 1843.

12. A.P.F., *Hecker Papers,* Early Diary, August 29, 1843.

13. *Ibid.,* George Curtis to Isaac Hecker, September 3, 1843.

14. A.U.N.D., *Brownson Papers,* Isaac Hecker to Brownson, September 6, 1843. Edward Palmer, who lived in New Jersey, was one of the "Newness" group. He was a neighbor of Robert Carter, who mentioned him in his article "The 'Newness,' " *Century Magazine,* N.S., Vol. XVII, p. 129. Hecker first met Palmer August 17, 1843, and saw him several times after that. A.P.F., *Hecker Papers,* Early Diary, August 19, 1843; A.U.N.D., *Brownson Papers,* Isaac Hecker to Brownson, September 6, 1843.

15. *Ibid.,* John Hecker to Brownson, August 20, 1843.

16. Carl R. Fish, *The Rise of the Common Man* (New York: 1927), p. 273.

17. A.P.F., *Hecker Papers*, George Curtis to Isaac Hecker, October 8, 1843, quotes this as coming from Isaac's letter to him.
18. *Ibid.*
19. *Ibid.*, Brownson to Isaac Hecker, September 2, 1843.
20. *Ibid.*, George Curtis to Isaac Hecker, September 2, 1843.
21. *Ibid.*, Early Diary, October 17, 1843.
22. *Ibid.*, November 5, 1843.
23. *Ibid.*, Brownson to Isaac Hecker, November 8, 1843.
24. Isaac T. Hecker, "Dr. Brownson in Boston," *Catholic World*, XLV (July, 1887), p. 472.
25. A.U.N.D., *Brownson Papers*, Isaac Hecker to Brownson, December 14, 1843.
26. A.P.F., *Hecker Papers*, Early Diary, September 24, October 28, November 3, December 2, 6, 9, 14, 18, 1843.
27. *Ibid.*, September 24, 1843.
28. *Ibid.*, December 14, 1843.
29. *Ibid.*, December 6, 1843.
30. *Ibid.*, November 20, 1843. G. W. Cooke, *Early Letters of George W. Curtis to John S. Dwight* (New York: 1898), p. 123, prints Curtis' letter of November 20, 1843, in which he says that Hecker "looks fresh and well. Seems better in every way than I ever knew him."
31. A.P.F., *Hecker Papers*, Early Diary, October 17, 1843.
32. *Ibid.*, December 14, 1843.
33. *Ibid.*, Brownson to Isaac Hecker, October 3, 1843.
34. A.U.N.D., *Brownson Papers*, Isaac Hecker to Brownson, October 16, 1843.
35. A.P.F., *Hecker Papers*, Brownson to Isaac Hecker, November 8, 1843.
36. *Ibid.*, March 11, 1844. Hecker had written on December 14, 1843, January 21, and March 9, 1844.
37. *Ibid.*, Early Diary, October 17, 1843.
38. James Parton, "Our Roman Catholic Brethren," *Atlantic Monthly*, XXI (May, 1868), p. 561. These facts Parton could only have gotten from Father Hecker whom he interviewed before writing the article.
39. A.P.F., *Hecker Papers*, Early Diary, December 14, 1843.
40. *Ibid.*, December 31, 1843.
41. *Ibid.*, March 10, 1844. Hecker describes this development in a letter to Brownson, March 9, 1844, A.U.N.D., *Brownson Papers*. This letter printed in Vincent F. Holden, C.S.P., *Early Years of Isaac Thomas Hecker* (Washington: 1939), pp. 198–199.
42. A.P.F., *Hecker Papers*, Early Diary, June 26, 1843. From this time on Hecker refers constantly to the importance of Christ in human life and shows a strong personal devotion to Him. These reflections are in his diary for June 28, July 28, 29, August 2, 8, 9, 10, 26, November 3, 15, 23, December 6, 14, 18, 31, 1843; January 20, February 19, 29, 1844.
43. *Ibid.*, March 8, 10, 1844.
44. *Ibid.*, January 20, 1844; March 27, 1844.
45. *Ibid.*, March 10, 1844.

46. A.U.N.D., *Brownson Papers*, Isaac Hecker to Brownson, March 9, 1844. In this letter, Hecker tells of his brothers' reaction.
47. A.P.F., *Hecker Papers*, Early Diary, March 17, 1844.
48. A.U.N.D., *Brownson Papers*, Isaac Hecker to Brownson, March 9, 1844.
49. *Ibid.*
50. *Ibid.*
51. A.P.F., *Hecker Papers*, Brownson to Isaac Hecker, March 11, 1844.
52. *Ibid.*
53. A.U.N.D., *Brownson Papers*, Isaac Hecker to Brownson, March 15, 1844.
54. *Ibid.* Hecker includes in this letter a digest of what he had written to Norris.
55. A.P.F., *Hecker Papers*, William Norris to Isaac Hecker, March 25, 1844.
56. *Ibid.*, Early Diary, March 30, 1844; A.U.N.D., *Brownson Papers*, Isaac Hecker to Brownson, April 9, 1844, in which Hecker gave an account of his interview with Seabury.
57. A.P.F., *Hecker Papers*, Brownson to Isaac Hecker, September 2, 1843.
58. *Brownson's Quarterly Review*, January, 1844, p. 15.
59. A.P.F., *Hecker Papers*, Early Diary, March 22, 1844. Walter Elliott, C.S.P., *Life of Father Hecker* (New York, 1891), p. 137, quotes this entry: "I had some loose notions of the Church" but the original reads: "I had some inborn protestant notions of the Church."
60. Wm. Barry, *Father Hecker, Founder of the Paulists* (New York, 1892), p. 29. This is a reprint in pamphlet form of Barry's article in *The Dublin Review*, July, 1892.
61. A.P.F., *Hecker Papers*, Early Diary, March 22, 1844; A.U.N.D., *Brownson Papers*, Isaac Hecker to Brownson, March 28, 1844. Henry Brownson, *op. cit.*, p. 517, quotes this letter as of March 25th, but the date is clearly March 28th.
62. A.P.F., *Hecker Papers*, Early Diary, March 30, 1844; A.U.N.D., *Brownson Papers*, Isaac Hecker to Brownson, March 28, 1844.
63. A.P.F., *Hecker Papers*, Brownson to Isaac Hecker. Although undated, this letter was written after April 6, 1844. On that date, Hecker had written mentioning that he was reading Scotus Erigena. In reply, Brownson asks to see it. Allowing time for Hecker's letter to reach Boston, this undated letter of Brownson's was probably written April 10, 1844, at the earliest.

CHAPTER V

1. A.P.F., *Hecker Papers*, Isaac Hecker to his family, April 19, 1844. Though this letter was written on the 19th, it was postmarked the 22nd.
2. This train of thought and argument Brownson developed in his article "Bishop Hopkins on Novelties," *Brownson's Quarterly Review*, July, 1844.
3. Henry F. Brownson, *The Works of Orestes A. Brownson* (Detroit: 1844), p. 159.

4. A.P.F., *Hecker Papers*, Isaac Hecker to his family, April 19, 1844.

5. *Ibid.*, May 31, 1844.

6. *Ibid.*, May 2, 13, 1844.

7. *Ibid.*, Early Diary, April 25, 1844.

8. *Ibid.*, April 26, 27, 1844.

9. *Ibid.*, May 6, 1844.

10. *Ibid.*, May 1, 1844.

11. *Ibid.*, April 29, 30; May 1, 2, 3, 4, 5, 8, 1844.

12. *Ibid.*, May 5, 1844.

13. *Ibid.*

14. A.U.N.D., *Brownson Papers*, Isaac Hecker to Brownson. Although this letter is undated, it is possible to fix the proximate time when it was written. The reference to study, and his difficulty in concentrating on it, places this letter within the time he spent at Concord. When he did decide to send it, he continued: "Let me add a short note to this which was written three weeks ago." In his diary June 5, 1844, he speaks of sending a letter yesterday to Brownson that he had written some weeks ago, but did not send because it was too subjective. Consequently, this undated letter was probably written about May 16, 1844. This is one of the unpublished letters in the Brownson collection. Most of this letter is printed in Vincent F. Holden, C.S.P., *Early Years of Isaac Thomas Hecker* (Washington: 1939), pp. 216–217.

15. A.P.F., *Hecker Papers*, Early Diary, May 19, 1844.

16. *Ibid.*, May 23, 1844.

17. *Ibid.*, Isaac Hecker to his family, May 23, 1844.

18. *Ibid.*, May 28, 1844.

19. *Ibid.*; A.U.N.D., *Brownson Papers*, Isaac Hecker to Brownson, June 4, 1844. Though Hecker wrote the date as April 4th, it should have been June 4th as an entry in his diary for June 5th clearly shows.

20. A.P.F., *Hecker Papers*, Isaac Hecker to Mrs. John Hecker, May 31, 1844. Parley Parker Pratt was born April 12, 1807, in Burlington, New York. In 1829, he first came into contact with Mormonism when he met one of its advocates, Sidney Rigdon. He accepted the new sect, became an Elder and in 1835, one of the Mormon Apostles. He preached not only in New York, Missouri, Ohio, and Canada, but also in England and South America. He was murdered May 13, 1857, by the husband of one of his converts to Mormonism. Hecker probably met Pratt during the winter of 1843–1844. The reference to Pratt and Mormonism in this letter and in his diary for May 30th are the only information Hecker gives of his contact with Mormonism. Carl W. Schlegel, *German-American Families in the United States* (New York: 1916), Vol. I, p. 53, says that Hecker investigated Mormonism under its most prominent and able expounder, Parley P. Pratt. Walter Elliott, C.S.P., *Life of Father Hecker* (New York: 1891), p. 133, writes: "A singular episode in his search was his meeting with two enthusiastic Mormon apostles and a long and careful examination, under their guidance, of the then newly-delivered revelations and prophecies of Joseph Smith." Father

Elliott does not say who the two men were. There is not much doubt that Hecker was familiar with Mormonism. When he was in Rome in 1857, after he had written two articles on the Church in America for the *Civiltà Cattolica*, Cardinal Barnabò suggested that he continue writing on the same subject. Father Hecker decided to write on Mormonism: "I will show the origin, nature and bearing of Mormonism, Spiritualism, etc., which are little understood here." A.U.N.D., *Brownson Papers*, Isaac Hecker to Brownson, November 27, 1857. Presumably, he was writing from his own knowledge of it, since when he left for Europe he had no intention of writing any articles, and made no provision for material. Because of other events, Hecker never wrote the article. Just when he investigated Mormonism, and to what extent, it is impossible to say with certainty, due to an absence of contemporary material.

21. A.P.F., *Hecker Papers*, Early Diary, May 30, 1844.
22. *Ibid.*
23. A.U.N.D., *Brownson Papers,* Isaac Hecker to Brownson, June 4, 1844.
24. A.P.F., *Hecker Papers.*
25. *Ibid.*, Early Diary, June 7, 1844.
26. Henry F. Brownson, *Brownson's Early Life* (Detroit: 1898), pp. 472–473.
27. Henry F. Brownson, *The Works of Orestes Brownson* (Detroit: 1884), Vol. V, pp. 164 and 166.
28. A.P.F., *Hecker Papers,* Early Diary, June 7, 1844.
29. *Ibid.*
30. *Ibid.*, Isaac Hecker to his family, June 11, 1844.
31. A.A.N.Y., *McCloskey Papers*, A-22, Fitzpatrick to McCloskey, June 17, 1844. Part of this letter has been quoted by Edward T. Harrington in *History of the Archdiocese of Boston* (New York: 1944), Vol. II, p. 727. In a footnote Father Harrington writes. "I believe that this letter throws an entirely new light on the Bishop's relations with Father Hecker as they are described by Father Hecker in 'Dr. Brownson and Bishop Fitzpatrick.' *Catholic World*, XLV, 1st seq." A careful comparison of this *Catholic World* article with the contemporary accounts of the interview leaves the reader somewhat confused. Father Hecker in "Dr. Brownson and Bishop Fitzpatrick" recalling his own visit with the Bishop, gives the impression that it was not particularly pleasant. In fact, he wrote that the Bishop "attacked" him on various socialistic questions because of his association with Brook Farm and Fruitlands. He described the Bishop as "the embodiment of a purpose to refute error and to refute it by condemnation, direct and authoritative" (*Catholic World*, April, 1887, p. 3). A few years before he wrote this article, he spoke of his interview with the Bishop to Father Elliott who published Hecker's remarks in his *Life of Father Hecker* (New York, 1891), p. 161. "He [Bishop Fitzpatrick] tried to get me started on questions of modern theology such as he suspected I might be (as he would doubtless think, knowing my antecedents) unsound on; for example, rights of property

etc. I refused to speak my sentiments on them. I said I had no difficulties about anything to submit to him."

This aspect of the visit does not appear in the three documents written within a short time after the interview itself. Bishop Fitzpatrick's letter introducing Hecker to Bishop McCloskey shows no distrust of the prospective convert but rather a sympathetic appreciation of the difficulties Hecker encountered on his road to the Church:

Boston June 17, 1844

Rt. Revd Sir:

Allow me to introduce to you the bearer of this letter Mr. Isaac Hecker, a young gentleman for whom I have conceived much esteem and in whom I take a very considerable interest although our acquaintance is of but recent date. He will himself relate to you the details of his history. The summary is this: after a long and somewhat painful investigation, in which he had no human guide, but only the Spirit of God, he has arrived at the full conviction that the Catholic Church has infallible and divine authority to lead him and that in obeying her he obeys God. This conviction is in him thorough and practical and he stops not at any of the consequences. He presented himself to me with this mind and with it I refer him to you. His desire now is to join the Church after having gone through the preliminaries that may be deemed necessary, and he prefers to take this step in New York his native city where he has many friends. He needs guidance yet in many respects more for moderation than incitement. You will be better able than I to judge of the most judicious treatement [sic] in these matters. I recommend him therefore with confidence to your prudent and charitable attention.

Your obedient servant in Xt
✝ J. B. Fitzpatrick Coadjr Bost

Neither does anything Hecker wrote in 1844 about the visit indicate that the Bishop acted the part of the heresy hunter. In a letter to his family on June 11th, the day after his visit with the Coadjutor, Hecker wrote that he had met Bishops Fenwick and Fitzpatrick who were "men of remarkable goodness, candor and frankness" (A.P.F., *Hecker Papers*). And in his diary for the same date, he simply noted that he had spent some time with Bishop Fitzpatrick the day before and "I inquired particularly as to the preliminary steps in entering the R. C. Church" (A.P.F., *Hecker Papers*).

This comparison between the contemporary accounts of Hecker's visit with Bishop Fitzpatrick and the *Catholic World* article written some forty years later suggests several questions. Could Bishop Fitzpatrick have been somewhat critical at the beginning of the interview but after Hecker explained his situation become quite friendly and sympathetic? If this happened, then it is very strange that Hecker would have made no mention of the Bishop's changed attitude in his article. Also, Hecker gives no indication in his diary that the Bishop was in any way critical. This absence of any such comment becomes all the more significant when we read in the diary Hecker's report of his visit with Bishop

Hughes the year before: "He [Hughes] said the Church was one of discipline. I thanked him for the information that he gave, and said that it was for just such information that I sought him, because he seemed to think I had inborn Protestant notions of the Church" (*ibid.*, March 22, 1844).

Is it likely that Hecker erroneously, though sincerely, attributed to Bishop Fitzpatrick the attitude he found in Bishop Hughes? Certainly what Hecker had written about Fitzpatrick in the April, 1887, issue of the *Catholic World* could be said of his interview with Hughes. It seems quite clear from the tone of the entry in Hecker's diary that Hughes questioned him on points of Catholic doctrine in an aggressive manner. Unless Hughes was "searching for error instead of truth" (this, Hecker said Fitzpatrick had done, *Catholic World; loc. cit.*, p. 2), how would Hecker have received the impression that the New York Prelate suspected he had "inborn Protestant notions of the Church"? The emphasis Hughes put on the "discipline of the Church," which stood out in Isaac's mind, would lead one to suppose that Hughes was not presenting a positive picture to his visitor.

Bishop Hughes did not accelerate Hecker's progress toward the Church, for, after the visit, Hecker decided he would not become a Catholic "at present" (Early Diary, March 22, 1844). On the other hand, the few hours spent with Fitzpatrick made Hecker certain he wanted to enter the Church (*ibid.*, June 11, 1844). It is conceivable that after a lapse of forty years, Hecker confused the two visits.

In viewing this problem created by Hecker's article in 1887, it must be kept in mind that at the time he wrote "Dr. Brownson and Bishop Fitzpatrick" Father Hecker was a very sick man who died the following year. His memory had lost some of its accuracy as the article itself reveals. For example, Hecker says he visited Fitzpatrick "some months before Brownson did" (*Catholic World, loc. cit.*, p. 2). Actually Brownson had seen Fitzpatrick first and arranged the visit.

Hecker also says in the article he regretted the fact that Brownson at Fitzpatrick's direction began to write about the historical argument in defense of the Church while completely ignoring the philosophical. The latter was the one that had led Brownson to the Church and the one the readers of his *Quarterly* had associated with him. This change of approach seemed to Hecker very ill-advised and in the *Catholic World* article (*loc. cit.*, p. 7), he wrote: "When shortly after my conversion, I went to Europe, all the letters I wrote to him were filled with complaints that he had given up his first principles, or at any rate ignored them" (*Catholic World*, April, 1887, p. 7). In the Notre Dame University Archives there are three letters of Hecker to Brownson while Isaac was abroad (*Brownson Papers*, September 18, 1845; September 13, November 1, 1846). Not one of them has even a passing reference to Brownson's new apologetics. Hecker could hardly have known too much of what Brownson wrote; during the year he spent at the Redemptorist novitiate at St. Trond, he never saw Brownson's *Quarterly*. When Hecker was at the studentate in Wittem, only three numbers of the periodical were available to him.

However, there is no doubt that after his return to the States, Hecker was convinced that Brownson had lost a lot of his effectiveness by his change of apologetics. He knew too, as Brownson had explained in the *Convert*, that a considerable part of his following had deserted him because of this new — new for Brownson — approach to the Church (H. F. Brownson, *Works of Orestes Brownson*, Detroit, 1884, pp. 168–169). Since Brownson had adopted the new policy at the direction of Bishop Fitzpatrick, Hecker attempted to explain why the Bishop made such a move. Then as a further explanation of the Bishop's attitude, Hecker cited his recollections of his interview with Fitzpatrick (*Catholic World, loc. cit.*, p. 1 seq.)

In the light of documents written so close to the time of the visit, Hecker's *Catholic World* account, published forty-five years later, is difficult to explain. Although the 1845 material does not refute certain statements in the 1887 article, the contemporary accounts do leave some of the later observations open to question. Whatever may be the explanation for the discrepancy between the two, until *more* contemporary material is discovered, greater weight must be given to the reports made in 1845. For this reason, I have followed the account of the interview given in Bishop Fitzpatrick's letter to Bishop McCloskey and in Hecker's diary and letter to his family, while omitting any reference to the account of this visit found in the *Catholic World* article.

32. A.P.F., *Hecker Papers*, Early Diary, June 23, 1844.

33. *Ibid.*, June 11, 1844.

34. *Ibid.;* June 13, 1844.

35. *Ibid.*, June 11, 1844.

36. *Ibid.*, July 23, 1843.

37. *Ibid.*, Isaac Hecker to his family, June 11, 1844.

38. *Ibid.*, June 14, 1844, in which Isaac refers to George's letter telling him of his mother's reaction.

39. *Ibid.*, Early Diary, June 13, 1844. Emerson in his journal noted this visit: "A second visit to the Shakers with Mr. Hecker." Ed. W. Emerson and W. E. Forbes, *Journals of R. W. Emerson* (Boston, 1911), Vol. VI, p. 523.

40. The account of this visit is based upon a memorandum made by Father Elliott. Father Hecker recalled this visit on the occasion of Emerson's death. Elliott, *op. cit.*, p. 88 ff.

41. A.P.F., *Hecker Papers*, Early Diary, June 13, 1844.

42. *Ibid.*, Isaac to his family, April 24, 1844.

43. *Ibid.*, Early Diary, June 13, 1844.

44. *Ibid.*, Isaac Hecker to his family, June 19, 1844.

45. A.U.N.D., *Brownson Papers*, Isaac Hecker to Brownson, June 24, 1844.

46. R. H. Lord, J. E. Sexton, E. T. Harrington, *History of the Archdiocese of Boston* (New York: 1944), Vol. II, pp. 326, 327.

47. A.U.N.D., *Brownson Papers*, Isaac Hecker to Brownson, June 24, 1844.

48. A.P.F., *Hecker Papers,* Father Hecker's tribute to Mrs. George Ripley.
49. *Ibid.,* George Ripley to Father Hecker, January 12, 1863.
50. Elliott, *op. cit.,* p. 90.
51. *Ibid.,* pp. 4 and 150.
52. A.U.N.D., *Brownson Papers,* Isaac Hecker to Brownson, July 15, 1844; A.P.F., *Hecker Papers,* Early Diary, June 25, 1844.
53. A.U.N.D., *Brownson Papers,* Isaac Hecker to Brownson, July 15, 1844.
54. *Ibid.*
55. *Ibid.*
56. A.P.F., *Hecker Papers,* Early Diary, July 15, 1844. In Hecker's letters to his family, he shows his grasp of Catholic doctrine in explaining the reasons for his choice of Catholic doctrine, especially June 11, 14, 19, 1844. Also, Early Diary, July 18, 24, 1844.
57. *Ibid.,* Early Diary, July 15, 1844.
58. *Ibid.,* August 2, 1844. Hecker records his baptism in his diary under the heading, "Fri. August 1." This is another instance of the correct day, but the wrong date. Friday was August 2nd. According to Catholic theology, the Sacrament of Baptism may be received validly only once. Hecker in his infancy had been baptized by a Lutheran minister. The possibility in such a situation always exists that because of some defect in the conferring of the Sacrament, e.g., absence of the right intention on the part of the minister, the baptism was not valid. Because of the importance of this sacrament, the Church advises her ministers to baptize converts conditionally, unless the certainty of the first baptism is established. The condition is: "if you are not baptized." If the recipient were validly baptized the first time, the condition is not fulfilled and the sacrament is not conferred. If the first baptism were not valid, then the condition is present and the convert receives the sacrament. Since baptism with contrition remits all sin, whenever conditional baptism is administered, a double possibility exists. If the first baptism received were valid, and if sins were committed since that time, they must be submitted to the power of absolution. If the first baptism were invalid, then the second would be valid and all sins would be remitted. As in Hecker's case, the procedure is to have the convert make a full confession of all the sins he has committed. Then absolution is given conditionally.
59. A.P.F., *Hecker Papers,* Early Diary, July 28, 1844.
60. *Ibid.,* August 3, 1844.

Chapter VI

1. Richard J. Purcell, *The American Nation* (New York: 1931), p. 405; Peter Guilday, *History of the Councils of Baltimore* (New York: 1932), pp. 130, 131.
2. A.U.N.D., *Brownson Papers,* Isaac Hecker to Brownson, July 15, 1844.
3. *Ibid.;* A.P.F., *Hecker Papers,* Early Diary, July 15, 1844.
4. A.U.N.D., *Brownson Papers,* Isaac Hecker to Brownson, August 2, 1844.

5. A.P.F., *Hecker Papers*, Early Diary, August 14, 1844.
6. E. H. Russell, "A Bit of Unpublished Correspondence Between Henry Thoreau and Isaac Hecker," *Atlantic Monthly*, XC (September, 1902), p. 373, Thoreau to Hecker, August 14, 1844.
7. *Ibid.*, Hecker to Thoreau, August 15, 1844. Arthur M. Schlesinger, Jr., *Orestes A. Brownson* (Boston: 1939), p. 182, says that Hecker "actually made a strenuous but vain effort to persuade" Thoreau to take instructions in the Catholic Faith. There is no contemporary evidence to show that Hecker made any such effort at this time. His attitude as revealed in his diary and letters is all to the contrary. Lawrence Willson, "Thoreau and Roman Catholicism," *Catholic Historical Review*, Vol. XLII (July: 1956), pp. 158–159, says that Hecker "indeed cherished the illusion that he might convert Thoreau to Catholicism" and for this reason proposed the trip to Europe. But neither Hecker's letters nor diary give any indication of this motive. His reasons for inviting Thoreau were the latter's love for walking trips and his strict diet. Nowhere does Hecker give any impression that he hoped to convert Thoreau to Catholicism. In the same article, Willson says that Brownson's conversion inspired Hecker to follow him. Since Hecker was in the Church more than two months before Brownson, he could hardly have followed Brownson.
8. E. H. Russell, *op. cit.*, Thoreau to Hecker, August 14, 1844.
9. A.P.F., *Hecker Papers*, Burrill Curtis to Hecker, August 15, 1844.
10. *Ibid.*, Early Diary, September 21, November 27, 1844.
11. *Ibid.*, Brownson to Hecker, September 24, 1844.
12. A.U.N.D., *Brownson Papers*, Hecker to Brownson, August 17, 1844.
13. *Ibid.*, September 5, 1844.
14. A.P.F., *Hecker Papers*, Brownson to Hecker, September 24, 1844.
15. *Ibid.*, Early Diary, August 26, September 27, October 14, 1844.
16. *Ibid.*, October 17, 1844.
17. *Ibid.*, *Elliott Papers*, Wm. D. Porter to Father Elliott, May 15, 1891.
18. *Ibid.*
19. *Ibid.*, Early Diary, November 27, December 8, 1844; March 15, 1845.
20. *Ibid.*, October 14, 1844. *New York City Directory* for 1844–1845 lists the firm as Hecker and Brothers. It was not until the year 1847 that the plural is dropped and the trade name becomes Hecker and Brother. The *Co-Partnership Directory* 1843–1844 has the entry "Hecker and Brothers (John, Isaac and George)."
21. A.U.N.D., *Brownson Papers*, Hecker to Brownson, October 29, 1844.
22. A.P.F., *Hecker Papers*, Early Diary, January 20, 1845.
23. *Ibid.*, December 18, 1844; January 30, 1845. A.U.N.D., *Brownson Papers*, Hecker to Brownson, January 14, 1845.
24. *Ibid.*, Hecker to Brownson, October 29, 1844; A.P.F., *Hecker Papers*, Early Diary, April 2, 24, 1845.
25. *Ibid.*, October 29, December 18, 1844; January 3, 13, March 15, 1845.
26. *Ibid.*, January 20, February 16, March 12, March 15, 1845.
27. *Ibid.*, December 8, 18, 1844; January 3, June 3, 1845.
28. *Ibid.*, April 2, 1845.   29. *Ibid.*, March 15, 1845.

30. *Ibid.*, Isaac to his family, June 11, 1844.
31. *Ibid.*, Early Diary, June 1, 1845; A.U.N.D., *Brownson Papers*, Hecker to Brownson, May 4, 1845. Henry F. Brownson, *Brownson's Early Life* (Detroit: 1898), pp. 530–532, incorrectly dates this letter as 1844.
32. A.P.F., *Hecker Papers*, Early Diary, April 2, 1845.
33. *Ibid.*, April 19, 1845.
34. *Ibid.*, April 2, 1845.
35. *Ibid.*, April 24, 1845.
36. *Ibid.*, April 25, 1845.
37. *Ibid.*, April 27, 1845.
38. *Ibid.*, June 21, April 27, 1845.
39. *Ibid.*, April 26, 1845.
40. *Ibid.*, May 2, 1845.
41. A.U.N.D., *Brownson Papers*, Hecker to Brownson, May 4, 1845.
42. A.P.F., *Hecker Papers*, Brownson to Hecker, June 25, 1845.
43. *Ibid.*
44. *Ibid.*, Early Diary, June 29, 1845. Walter Elliott, C.S.P., *Life of Father Hecker* (New York: 1891), p. 180, incorrectly gives the date as June 22, 1845.
45. A.U.N.D., *Brownson Papers*, Hecker to Brownson, March 9, August 17, 1844.
46. A.P.F., *Hecker Papers*, Early Diary, June 29, 1845.
47. *Ibid.*, Isaac Hecker to his family, July 17, November 8, 1843.
48. *Brownson's Quarterly Review*, Vol. III (Third Series), April, 1855, p. 209.
49. *Ibid.*, p. 210.
50. *Ibid.*, p. 209.
51. This is the advice Brownson gave Hecker on June 25, 1844, and undoubtedly repeated on this visit. A.P.F., *Hecker Papers*, Brownson to Hecker, June 25, 1845.
52. *Ibid.*, Early Diary, June 15, 1845.
53. *Ibid.*
54. A.U.N.D., *Brownson Papers*, Hecker to Brownson, July 25, 1845.
55. *Ibid.*
56. *Ibid.*; A.P.F., *Hecker Papers*, Early Diary, July 27, 28, 1845.
57. A.U.N.D., *Brownson Papers*, Hecker to Brownson, July 29, 1845.
58. Clarence A. Walworth, *Reminiscences of Edgar P. Wadhams* (New York: 1893), pp. 80, 87, 88.
59. A.U.N.D., *Brownson Papers*, Hecker to Brownson, July 29, 1845.
60. Elliott, *op. cit.*, pp. 198, 199. Hecker reported his progress in Caesar and Cicero to Brownson, May 4, 1845. A.U.N.D., *Brownson Papers*.
61. Walworth, *op. cit.*, p. 89. He gives the name of the ship as *Prince Albert* in a letter to Wadhams dated July 25, 1845. Elliott, *op. cit.*, p. 199, calls it the *Argo*, which is incorrect. The New York *Herald*, August 9, 1845, lists the *Argo* as sailing that day while its issue of August 1, 1845, announces the *"Prince Albert,* for London, will sail tomorrow."
62. A.U.N.D., *Brownson Papers*, Hecker to Brownson, July 29, 1845.

CHAPTER VII

1. Clarence A. Walworth, *Reminiscences of Edgar P. Wadhams* (New York: 1893), p. 80.
2. Sister Mary Kwitchen, *James Alphonsus McMaster* (Washington: 1949), pp. 52, 53; John Cardinal Farley, *The Life of John Cardinal McCloskey* (New York: 1918), p. 153.
3. For a detailed account of the Redemptorists beginning in New York, cf. Michael J. Curley, C.SS.R., "The Redemptorist Pioneers in America," *Spicilegium Historicum*, Vol. IV (1956), pp. 121–155.
4. George Stebbing, C.SS.R., *The Redemptorists* (New York: 1924), pp. 20–26, has a very clear and concise account of the early Redemptorist history. John F. Byrne, C.SS.R., *The Redemptorist Centenaries* (Philadelphia: 1932), also treats of this history, pp. 1–41. Maurice deMeulemeester, C.SS.R., *Histoire Sommaire de la Congrégation du T. S. Redémpteur* (Louvain: 1950), presents a more detailed and factual picture. From these sources, I have gathered the material for the preceding five paragraphs. Curley, *op. cit.*, p. 108, follows Joseph Wuest, C.SS.R., *Annales Provinciae Americanae*, Vol. I (Ilchester: 1888), p. 147, in stating that the American Redemptorists, after the creation of provinces "remained immediately subject to the Vicar-General." But in A.R.R., there is a letter of Father Passerat to the Rector Major dated August 23, 1844, in which he states that in 1841 the American Mission was placed under the Austrian Provincial but he wanted to transfer it to the Belgian Provincial Father de Held who had the English houses under his jurisdiction. The Holy See by decree of November 16, 1844, authorized the change. A.R.R., X, D, 17. Wuest, *loc. cit.*, is also in error in saying that the provincial superiors were not elected before 1844. "Series Moderatorum Generalium Eorumque Vicariorum et Consultorum," *Spicilegium Historicum*, Vol. II (1954), p. 254, shows that the nomination of the Austrian Provincial, Father Francis Kosmacek, was confirmed by the Rector Major, December 15, 1841.
5. A.P.F., *Hecker Papers*, Hecker to his family, August 30, 1845. Hecker dates this letter the 29th and in it says: "Tomorrow, Sunday." The 29th was a Friday. This is just another instance where the date was incorrect, though the day of the week was accurate. Cf., also, Walworth, *op. cit.*, pp. 116–117, Walworth to Wadhams, February 7, 1846.
6. Kwitchen, *op. cit.*, pp. 58–61.
7. Ellen H. Walworth, *Life Sketches of Father Walworth* (New York: 1907), p. 93, Walworth to his father, September 18, 1845. Clarence Walworth, *op. cit.*, pp. 116–117, Walworth to Wadhams, February 7, 1846.
8. A.P.F., *Hecker Papers*, Hecker to his family, August 29, 1845; March 4, 1846.
9. Clarence Walworth, *op. cit.*, p. 117.
10. A.P.F., *Hecker Papers*, Hecker to his family, September 18, 1845.
11. A.U.N.D., *Brownson Papers*, Hecker to Brownson, September 18, 1845.
12. A.P.F., *Hecker Papers*, Hecker to his family, November 5, 1845.

13. Hecker and Walworth both received the habit on October 15, 1845, A.R.W., *Chronica Provinciae [Belgicae] et Collegiorum*, Vol. II, p. 197.

14. Walter Elliott, C.S.P., *Life of Father Hecker* (New York: 1891), p. 208. Hecker gave the novitiate schedule in great detail in a letter to his mother, March 4, 1846, A.P.F., *Hecker Papers*. Walworth writing to Wadhams, February 7, 1846, told of the schedule but not with as much detail. Clarence Walworth, *op. cit.*, pp. 114–115.

15. A.U.N.D., *Brownson Papers*, Hecker to Brownson, September 18, 1845; Clarence Walworth, *op. cit.*, pp. 110–111.

16. A. Poulain, S.J., *The Graces of Interior Prayer*, trans. from the sixth French edition by Leonora Yorke Smith (St. Louis: 1910), pp. 7–13, discusses these types of prayer.

17. A.P.F., *Hecker Papers*, Hecker to his family, September 18, 1845.

18. Elliott, *op. cit.*, p. 208, quoting from conversations he had with Father Hecker.

19. A.P.F., *Hecker Papers*, statement Father Hecker submitted to his spiritual director, January 6, 1858. The section of the Rule dealing with the subject of Holy Communion is found in *Codex Regularum et Constitutionum Congregationis SS. Redemptoris* (Rome: 1896), pp. 163–164, Sections 351–353.

20. *Ibid.*, Hecker to his family, January 1, October 15, 1846; Hecker to Bishop McCloskey, October 15, 1846.

21. *Ibid.*, statement Father Hecker submitted to his spiritual director, May 30, October 24, 1848; January 6, 1858; Elliott, *op. cit.*, p. 210.

22. A.P.F., *Hecker Papers*, Hecker to his family, November 5, 24, 1845; January 1, March 4, April 28, August 26, September 14, October 15, 1846.

23. Clarence Walworth, *op. cit.*, pp. 108–118, Walworth to Wadhams, February 7, 1846; Ellen Walworth, *op. cit.*, pp. 92–93, Walworth to his father, September 18, 1845; Kwitchen, *op. cit.*, pp. 62–63, McMaster to Wadhams, October 31, 1845.

24. *Ibid.;* A.P.F., *Hecker Papers*, Hecker to his family, November 5, 1845; January 1, March 4, April 28, August 26, 1846.

25. *Ibid.*, Hecker to his family, January 1, 1846.

26. *Ibid.*

27. *Ibid.*, Hecker to Bishop McCloskey, October 15, 1846. A photostat made from original in Dunwoodie Archives. This letter is printed in full in Farley, *op. cit.*, pp. 156–158.

28. *Ibid.*, Hecker to Mon. T. R. Père, May 30, 1848; statement Father Hecker submitted to his spiritual director, January 6, 1858.

29. Kwitchen, *op. cit.*, pp. 64–67, McMaster to Wadhams, November 5, 13, 1846; A.P.F., *Hecker Papers*, Hecker to his family, September 14, 1846; Clarence Walworth, *op. cit.*, p. 126, Walworth to Wadhams, December 1, 1846.

30. A.P.F., *Hecker Papers*, Hecker to his mother, October 15, 1846. This letter is printed in full in Vincent F. Holden, C.S.P., *Early Years of Isaac Thomas Hecker* (Washington: 1939), pp. 242–244. A.U.N.D., *Brownson*

Papers, Hecker to Brownson, November 1, 1846. (Though Hecker dates this letter October 1st, it could not have been written that early. He sent it from Wittem after he had taken his vows on October 15th. Undoubtedly the correct date is November 1st.) Poulain, *op. cit.*, pp. 64–120, describing the fundamental character of the mystic states, lists the various experiences the soul undergoes. These are somewhat similar to the descriptions Hecker gave in his letters to his mother and Brownson. During the height of the Americanism controversy, Father Poulain, who was writing an article on the word "mystic" sent a letter to Abbé Klein, the author of the preface to the French translation of Elliott's life of Hecker. Klein had said that "Aside from the writings of St. Theresa . . . there is hardly any book which can instruct us more clearly about events of this type [mystical experiences] than the journal and writings" of Father Hecker. Father Poulain was quick to see in this statement that Klein meant "Father Hecker felt or had some *interesting-curious* states of soul, about which he wrote exactly as St. Theresa has written." Poulain then asked the Abbé to clarify this for him since he had read nothing that would warrant such a statement. Further, he said that certain writers had described Father Hecker as a mystic. Poulain did not think this exact "at least on the basis of the documents given to us." Thomas à Kempis was not, Poulain continued, "a mystic but an ascetical writer. Father Hecker writes in the same way, although with a very different appearance" (A.U.N.D., *Klein Papers*, Poulain to Klein, May 16, 1898). Thomas McAvoy, C.S.C., *The Great Crisis in American Catholic History* (Chicago: 1957), p. 202, refers to this letter and says that Poulain suggests "that Hecker was not a mystic but an ascetic." This interpretation seems much wider than the letter warrants. Poulain said that "on the basis of the documents which have been given to us" it would not be "exact" to call Father Hecker a mystic. Comparing his writings to those of à Kempis, he said that Father Hecker's writings were more ascetical than mystical. Poulain was referring to his writings not his states of soul. Nor did he rule out the possibility of calling Hecker a mystic. He merely questioned applying this term to Hecker on the strength of the evidence he had read. If Poulain had studied Hecker's early diary, his letters, and his later statements, I believe he would have found parallels between Hecker's experiences and the characteristics he describes in his classic volume on prayer. Many of these documents in Hecker's papers did not appear in the Elliott life of Hecker.

31. A.P.F., *Hecker Papers*, Hecker to his mother, October 15, 1846.
32. *Ibid.*, Isaac Hecker to John Hecker, October 15, 1846.
33. M. Mulders, C.SS.R., "De Typhus-Epideme te Wittem in 1847," *Monumenta Historica* (Prov. Holland), Vol. III (1951), p. 14.
34. *Ibid.*, p. 18; Vol. II (1950), p. 166.
35. *Ibid.*, p. 162.
36. A.R.W., *Chronica Wittemiensis*, III, II, I, p. 129. One of the four who was put in the classical course with Hecker was Joseph Aertnys who

later became a well-known moralist, the author of a volume on moral theology that was widely used as a text in seminaries here and abroad; *Chronica Studendatus Wittemiensis*, Vol. I, p. gg.

37. A.P.F., *Hecker Papers*, Hecker to Mon. T. R. Père, May 30, 1848. In this letter to his director, Hecker describes his spiritual condition at Wittem. Though there is no indication of the name of the director, it would seem as though it were Father Heilig. Hecker maintained Father Heilig was his director while he was at Wittem and in the letter he says he "had told you and wrote you at the time" about his difficulties. This copy in the Paulist Fathers' Archives is a rough draft of the letter written in French. In it Hecker described what had occurred since he had arrived at Wittem.

38. A.R.W., *Chronica Studendatus Wittemiensis*, Vol. I, April 4, 1847. Walter Elliott, C.S.P., *The Life of Father Hecker* (New York: 1891), Chap. XXI, pp. 213–229, discusses Hecker's days at Wittem. Since Father Elliott did not have any contemporary documents for these days, he depended entirely on references to this period in three statements Hecker submitted to his director on May 30, October 24, 1848, and January 6, 1858 (A.P.F., *Hecker Papers*). These Father Elliott interpreted in the light of what he called "memoranda." These memoranda are accounts of conversations he had with Father Hecker when the latter was in broken health and nearing the end of his life. At that time, Hecker's memory was not reliable, as I have pointed out in detail in note 31, Chapter V of this volume, as well as in Chapters II and III of *Early Years of Isaac Thomas Hecker* (Washington: 1939). Father Elliott never questioned the accuracy of Father Hecker's recollections and after he left him, Elliott wrote down what he understood Hecker to have said. It is very difficult to distinguish how much of these recorded conversations is Hecker's and how much Elliott's. The latter published them as Father Hecker's exact words. Yet they can hardly be that. It is most unlikely that Father Elliott could have remembered these conversations so clearly after leaving Father Hecker that he could put them down verbatim. Nor is it beyond the realm of possibility that some of Elliott's own interpretation slipped into the record of the conversations which are quoted not only as Hecker's thoughts but his exact expressions. When I checked these memoranda against available contemporary evidence, I found them to be inaccurate and sometimes erroneous. Particularly is this true of Chapter XXI of the *Life*. That is why I have used the memoranda only when they are corroborated by contemporary evidence. To give a point-by-point refutation of the errors in Elliott's Chapter XXI would require almost a small volume. Rather than engage in such a tedious procedure, I will document my statements from contemporary material and where they differ from Father Elliott, he is differing from contemporary evidence without any substantiating proof except the inaccurate memoranda.

39. A.P.F., *Hecker Papers*, Hecker's statement to his director, October 24, 1848.

40. *Ibid.*
41. Elliott, *op. cit.*, p. 219.
42. For the account of this epidemic I have used Father M. Mulders, C.SS.R., *op. cit.*, pp. 12–18; A.R.W., *Chronica Wittemiensis*, III, II, I, pp. 144–146. Father Walworth writes of his illness in a letter to his father, January 1, 1848, Ellen Walworth, *Life Sketches of Father Walworth* (Albany: 1907), pp. 97–99.
43. A.R.W., *Chronica Provinciae Belgicae et Collegiorum*, Vol. II, p. 309.
44. A.P.F., *Hecker Papers*, Heilig to Hecker, March 24, 1849. Though this letter was written a year after Father Heilig left Wittem, it shows clearly the friendly feeling he had always entertained for Hecker. He said: "My heart has not changed in regard to you. . . . My reply is then a mark of particular confidence I have in you and in your virtue. . . . I wish especially that you may be and will remain assured of the affection, of the love and esteem which I have always borne for you and which I shall always bear for you." He refers to "your present director" which leaves the impression that he had been Hecker's former director.
45. M. Mulders, "De Inrichting van het Wittems Studendaat in de eerste tyd," *Monumenta Historica* (Prov. Holland), Vol. II (1950), p. 162. Hecker said later in life that Heilig was his director. Elliott, *op. cit.*, p. 222. This seems to be substantiated by Heilig's letter of March 24, 1849. Cf. note 44 above. The fact that he did not remain under the Prefect of Students is noted in Father Mauron's *Motivi Segreti* to Archbishop Bizzarri, February, 1858 (A.R.R., *Prov. Amer.*, I, 5). He said Hecker "was placed under the supervision of another Father" though Mauron did not name him.
46. A.R.W., *Chronica Studendatus*, Vol. II, May 25, 1848.
47. A.P.F., *Hecker Papers*, Hecker to Mon. T. R. Père, May 30, 1848. Cf. note 37 above.
48. *Ibid.*
49. Because of the typhus epidemic, there were no first-semester exams. Those for the second semester were held in the beginning of September before the vacation which began September 8th and lasted until October 8th. A.R.W., *Chronica Studendatus*, Vol. II, pp. ff, gg. Isaac's grade is listed for the scholastic year 1847–1848 which is evidence that although he was excused from class, he took the exams. *Ibid.*, Vol. I, "Année Scholaire, 1847/48." The system of grading used at Wittem followed a threefold division: *tres bien, bien,* and *assez bien*. Within each division there were first, second, and third. Hecker had received for this year "bien 2°"; Walworth, "assez bien 1° et bien." Elliott, *op. cit.*, p. 214, says: "All went smoothly with Brother Walworth." Ellen Walworth, *op. cit.*, p. 91, writes: "He [Walworth] bounded forward on his course with rapid strides." Both state further that while Walworth was so successful, Hecker was having great difficulty and Ellen Walworth, who was her uncle's amanuensis, adds that Father Walworth "soon outstripped" Isaac Hecker. Since neither writer had any contemporary

documents, but both knew Father Walworth personally, it is not inconceivable that they received this information from Walworth himself. Whatever may be the source of these statements, contemporary evidence from Wittem is quite to the contrary.

50. A.P.F. *Hecker Papers,* Hecker's statement submitted to his director, January 6, 1858. In this statement Hecker said: "One day my fellow-students were treating me as such [a fool] and throwing earth at me."

51. A.R.W., *Chronica Studendatus,* Wittemienses, Vol. I, September 10, 1848. Father Walworth's certification of ordination is in A.P.F., *Walworth Papers,* August 27, 1848.

52. Elliott, *op. cit.,* p. 220.

53. Following his term as Belgian provincial, Father de Held came to England in April of 1848. After he saw the marvelous opportunities for apostolic work in the suburbs of London, he bought the old-fashioned mansion with spacious gardens which had been the property of Lord Teignmouth in Clapham. Previous to Father de Held's purchase of it, the old house had been the headquarters for the English Bible Society. After the Redemptorists took possession on July 31, 1848, they quickly transformed the lower-floor parlors and corridors of the residence into a chapel. August 2, 1848, they had finished the work and celebrated the first solemn Mass for the Catholics of the district. Maurice de Meulemeester, C.SS.R., *Le Père Frédéric von Held* (Jette: 1911), pp. 199–204.

54. A.R.C., *Annales Provinciae Anglicae,* October 26, 1848.

55. Elliott, *op. cit.,* p. 222. In A.P.F., *Hecker Papers,* there are nine letters Father de Buggenoms wrote to Father Hecker after the latter's return to America.

56. Elliott, *op. cit.,* p. 222. This seems to be borne out by a letter of Father de Held to Father Hecker, September 27, 1857, and a copy of a letter of Father de Held to Cardinal Barnabò, September 28, 1857, A.P.F., *Hecker Papers.*

57. *Ibid.,* Hecker to Mon. T. R. Père, May 30, 1848.

58. *Ibid.*

59. Although this letter is no longer extant, it would seem from Father Heilig's reply of March 24, 1849, A.P.F., *Hecker Papers,* that Hecker had sent either the statement written October 24, 1848, or one very similar to it. There is no doubt from Father Heilig's reply that Hecker had written in detail about his spiritual condition and used quotations from spiritual writers to explain his state of soul.

60. A.P.F., *Hecker Papers,* Hecker to Mon. T. R. Père, October 24, 1848. This document is filled with quotations from recognized mystics that are relevant to Hecker's own spiritual condition.

61. A.P.F., *Hecker Papers,* Heilig to Hecker, March 24, 1849.

62. *Ibid.*

63. *Ibid.*

64. *Ibid.,* statement to his director, January 6, 1858. This Hecker wrote in English and then after it was translated into Italian submitted it to

Cardinal Barnabò, Mgr. Bedini, Father Francis of the Passionists, Father Gregorio of the Carmelites, and Father Druelle of the Holy Cross Fathers. This he did during the days following his dismissal from the Redemptorists so these men would be better guided in directing him.

65. These facts are all related in considerable detail in Chapters III, IV, V, of this volume.

66. The letter of Bishop Fitzpatrick to Bishop McCloskey which is the basis for these statements is given in note 31 of Chapter V. Fitzpatrick could hardly have written such a letter until he was assured of Hecker's sincerity and the objectivity of his account.

67. Elliott, *op. cit.,* p. 222. This is further borne out by Father de Held's letter to Cardinal Barnabò, September 28, 1857, A.P.F., *Hecker Papers.* There are nineteen de Held letters in the Paulist Fathers' Archives.

68. Elliott, *op. cit.,* pp. 222–223.

69. A.P.F., *Hecker Papers,* Heilig to Hecker, May 13, 1849.

Chapter VIII

1. A.P.F., *Hecker Papers,* Early Diary, June 28, 1843.

2. A.R.R., *Codex Regularium et Constitutionum Congregationis SS. Redemptoris* (Rome: 1896), pp. 29, 36–43, 49–57, 69–88. The Redemptorist Fathers in Rome graciously presented a copy of these Constitutions for the Paulist Fathers' General Archives in New York.

3. Maurice de Meulemeester, C.SS.R., *Le Père Frédéric von Held Rédemptoriste* (Jette: 1911), p. 211.

4. *Ibid.,* pp. 202, 204.

5. *Ibid.,* pp. 211–212; Clarence A. Walworth, "Reminiscences of a Catholic Crisis in England Fifty Years Ago," *Catholic World,* Vol. LXIX (June, 1899), pp. 400–401; Vol. LXX (October, 1899), pp. 59–60.

6. A.R.C., *Annales Provinciae Anglicae,* May 11, 1850. *The Catholic Standard* of London in its May 18th and June 1st issues carried an account of this mission and mentioned "the eloquent discourses of Father Petcherine."

7. A.R.C., *Annales Provinciae,* June 1, 1850; A.P.F., *Hecker Papers,* Father Hecker's statement to his director, January 6, 1858.

8. A.R.C., *Annales Provinciae Anglicae,* July 26, August 7, October 13, December, 1850. Walter Elliott, C.S.P., *Life of Father Hecker* (New York: 1891), pp. 230–231, says that Father Hecker was occupied "mainly in parochial duties at Clapham and some neighboring stations attended by the Redemptorists of that house" and "had only been at one or two small retreats." Since Father Elliott did not have the Clapham *Chronicle,* he did not know of the various missions in which Father Hecker assisted.

9. A.P.F., *Hecker Papers,* Father Hecker's statement to his director, January 6, 1858.

10. P. Claessens, *Life of Father Bernard,* translated from the French (New

York: 1875), *passim;* Augustine F. Hewit, C.S.P., *Memoir and Sermons of Father Baker* (New York: 1865), p. 120.

11. Claessens, *op. cit.*, p. 119.
12. Joseph Wuest, C.SS.R., *Annales Provinciae Americanae, Supplementum ad I, II, III, Pars II* (Maryland: 1903–1907), pp. 305–308; *Diary of Very Rev. Bernard Hafkenscheid,* March 4, 1850. An English translation of the French original is in the Baltimore Provincial Archives of the Redemptorists. Wuest, *op. cit.*, publishes the French, pp. 183–241. De Meulemeester, *op. cit.*, p. 208, implies that Father Hecker made an effort to be sent back to the States. The diary of Father Bernard shows that he initiated the move and there is no evidence to show that Hecker took any steps to secure his return to America.
13. A.R.B., *Diary of Very Rev. Bernard Hafkenscheid,* August 14, 28, 1850.
14. A.P.F., *Hecker Papers,* Father Hecker to his mother. Though this letter is undated, the reference to "the coming month of October" indicates it was written in September of 1850.
15. *Ibid.,* January 19, 1851.
16. *Ibid.,* Father Heilig to Father Hecker, January 11, 1851.
17. A.R.B., *Diary of Very Rev. Bernard Hafkenscheid,* January 23, 1851; Walworth, *op. cit.*, December, 1899, p. 414.
18. *Ibid.,* pp. 413–417.
19. *Ibid.,* p. 418.
20. A.R.B., *Diary of Very Rev. Bernard Hafkenscheid,* January 20, 1849.
21. Claessens, *op. cit.*, p. 288. He prints in full a very interesting letter written by Father Dold to the Rector at Wittem with many details of the journey.
22. Walworth, *op. cit.*, pp. 413–414, says he thought he knew his missionary vocation "well enough while living in England. . . . I was mistaken. I had much to learn yet."
23. Claessens, *op. cit.*, p. 312.
24. *Ibid.,* pp. 318–319.
25. *Ibid.,* p. 319; Walworth, *op. cit.*, January, 1900, pp. 512–513; A.R.B., *Diary of Very Rev. Bernard Hafkenscheid,* March 20, 1851.
26. H. H. Manchester, "Millers Who Became Famous," *Northwestern Miller,* CXXXIX (July 30, 1924), p. 432.
27. A.P.F., *Hecker Papers,* Hecker to his family, November 23, 1849, in which Isaac mentions George's marriage. Three girls and a boy were born of this marriage. In 1838, John married Catherine Gorham. They had three children, two girls and a boy. Carl W. Schlegel, *German-American Families in the United States* (New York: 1916), Vol. I, pp. 51–52.
28. *Ibid.,* November 5, 1845. In this letter, Hecker speaks of his sister's death. In those of December 8, 1848; February 8, November 7, 1850, he refers to his mother's illness.
29. A.U.N.D., *Brownson Papers,* Father Hecker to Brownson, March 22, 1851.
30. A.P.F., *Hecker Papers,* Brownson to Father Hecker, March 28, 1851.

31. *Ibid.*, *Chronicle of the English Missions given by the Redemptorist Fathers in the United States of N. America,* April 6, 1851, to March 28, 1858, pp. 1–2. This *Chronicle* made at the time of the separation from the Redemptorists is a copy of the "Record" the Missionaries kept of all their missions. The original record is in the A.R.B.

32. Henry E. O'Keeffe, C.S.P., *Thoughts and Memories* (New York: 1920), pp. 163–174. Joseph P. Flynn, C.S.P., *The Early Years of Augustine F. Hewit, C.S.P., 1820–1846,* has written this unpublished master's dissertation which is the finest and most complete account of Father Hewit's life up to his conversion.

33. A.P.F., *Chronicle of Missions,* p. 2.

34. *Ibid.*, p. 1; A.R.B., *Diary of Very Rev. Bernard Hafkenscheid,* April 6, 1851.

35. A.P.F., *Hecker Papers,* Father Hecker to R. H. Simpson, August 6, 1852. Cf. Walworth, *op. cit.,* January, 1900, pp. 508, 509, 513.

36. Hewit, *op. cit.,* pp. 121–122.

37. A.P.F., *Chronicle of Missions,* p. 18.

38. A.U.N.D., *Brownson Papers,* September 5, 1851.

39. A.P.F., *Baker Papers,* Chessie to her sister, April 16, 1853. This is a typed copy from the original with the notation "Letter of Ethel Morse's mother to her sister then at Manhattanville . . . Ethel and Evangeline Morse were friends of Father Fenelon." In this letter "Chessie" who was at the mission sends a full account of the services to her sister.

40. *Ibid.*, *Chronicle of Missions,* pp. 22, 69; *Hecker Papers,* Father Hecker to R. H. Simpson, August 6, 1852; A.U.N.D., *Brownson Papers,* Father Hecker to Brownson, January 6, 1852; December 2, 1854.

41. A.P.F., *Chronicle of Missions,* p. 6.

42. An undated and unidentified newspaper clipping pasted in the *Chronicle of Missions* after the account of the mission at Baltimore Cathedral, April 10–20, 1853. This is reprinted in Wuest, *op. cit.,* pp. 466–468.

43. October 20, 1854. This newspaper clipping is also pasted in the *Chronicle of Missions* (A.P.F.), p. 66.

44. *Ibid.*, p. 37.

45. *Ibid.*, p. 39.

46. A.P.F., *Hewit Papers,* Cardinal Gibbons to Father Hewit, December 24, 1888. This letter is in sharp conflict with a statement made by Ellen Walworth, *Life Sketches of Father Walworth* (Albany: 1907), p. 130. She states that the Cardinal, writing to Father Walworth to thank him for a volume of his poems, told him "in a few simple words" that his sermon at St. Joseph's Church, New Orleans, during the mission given February 12–21, 1854, decided his vocation. Apparently she did not have the Cardinal's note since she did not quote from it. If she did have it, it is very strange that she did not give it in full since she was very quick to publish any commendatory letter her uncle received from a prominent person. Apparently it was Walworth himself who told her about the letter, and she could have misunderstood him. Again it seems strange that he failed to preserve the Cardinal's letter if it were so

positive and laudatory as Miss Walworth leads one to believe. At no time in any of his published articles or in any recorded statements does Father Walworth mention this letter or the Cardinal's words about his sermon, except to his niece. On page 131, Miss Walworth further adds that, in 1902, she met the Cardinal in Baltimore and he substantiated this fact.

Against these statements of Miss Walworth we have the letter of Gibbons in his own handwriting saying that it was Hecker's words that turned his thoughts to the priesthood. As well, on two other public occasions, the Cardinal made the same acknowledgment. In January of 1910, the Paulist Fathers celebrated their fiftieth anniversary. Gibbons presided at the pontifical Mass celebrated by Bishop Farley and spoke at the end of the Mass. The press reported him as saying: "Cardinal Gibbons testified that it was the words of Father Hecker heard in a mission during a troubled time in his youth which under God decided his own vocation to the priesthood" (January 28, 1910). When the Cardinal celebrated his golden jubilee, the Paulist Fathers presented him with a shield emblazoned with his coat of arms. After he accepted it, he was heard to say: "It was a sermon by Father Hecker which I heard more than half a century ago that first turned my thoughts toward studying for the priesthood" (*Freeman's Journal*, November 20, 1913).

In addition to these testimonials of the Cardinal, several facts connected with the mission given at St. Joseph's make Miss Walworth's statements highly improbable. She contends that her uncle gave a sermon on the priesthood (p. 130), and then gives the outline of the sermon (pp. 137–140). An illustration used in the outline shows that it was written during the Civil War and not in 1854. Further it would be most unusual for Father Walworth, who gave the evening sermon, to depart from the regular schedule of subjects as demanded by the Constitutions of the Redemptorists. Especially would this be remarkable since he was ill at the time of the mission and only preached three times (A.P.F., *Chronicle of Missions*, p. 61). On the other hand, Father Hecker preached every morning at the instructions which the men attended so well that "even the sanctuary was crowded" (*ibid.*). In these instructions, he would touch on the duties of one's state in life and appealed frequently to the men telling them of the glorious future they had in the Church (A.U.N.D., *Brownson Papers*, Father Hecker to Brownson, July 29, 1851). It is not at all unlikely that it was words to this effect that stirred the future Cardinal.

Allen Sinclair Will, *Life of Cardinal Gibbons* (New York: 1922), Vol. I, pp. 19–20, says that Father Hecker was ill at the St. Joseph's mission and accepts Miss Walworth's position. John Tracy Ellis, *Life of James Cardinal Gibbons* (Milwaukee: 1952), Vol. I, p. 28, follows both Will and Walworth adding that Gibbons "did not have the good fortune to hear Father Hecker" because he was ill during the St. Joseph's mission. This is not correct. The *Chronicle of Missions*, p. 60, says that Hecker was sick during the mission given at St. Patrick's, New Orleans,

January 15–29, 1854, and was only able to give a few instructions at the end of the mission. However, he was completely recovered and gave all the instructions at St. Joseph's (*ibid.*, p. 61), which was the mission Gibbons heard Hecker preach. Joseph McSorley, C.S.P., *Father Hecker and His Friends* (St. Louis: 1952), also accepts the Will, Walworth, Ellis position.

47. A.U.N.D., *Brownson Papers*, Father Hecker to Brownson, July 29, September 5, 1851.
48. A.P.F., *Hecker Papers*, Father Hecker to his mother, January 22, 1852.
49. A.P., *S.R.C.*, *Amer. Cent.*, Vol. 17, 534, First Provincial Council of New Orleans to Propaganda.
50. A.U.N.D., *Cincinnati Papers*, Spalding to Purcell, March 29, 1856.
51. A.P., *S.R.C. Amer. Cent.*, Vol. 17, 573, Kenrick to Franzoni.
52. A.R.R., *Prov. Amer.*, I, 4, Father Hecker to Father Douglas, September 5, 1855. In this letter, Father Hecker refers to Father Douglas' election as a General Consultor and writes that "if ever the question should arise to take me from my simple duties in any way" and give him a position of honor and authority, then he begs Douglas to use his influence "to insist on remaining where I am." In 1857, Father Hecker knew of the nomination to the bishopric and refers to it in a statement he submitted to Cardinal Barnabò on September 15, 1857 (A.P.F., *Hecker Papers*). Stating his case for an English house for the missionaries, he cited this nomination as "the risk" he faced of losing his position in the Community.

CHAPTER IX

1. Joseph Wuest, C.SS.R., *Annales Provinciae Americanae* (Maryland: 1899), Vol. III, Pars I, p. 7. Brownson, who knew Father Bernard personally, wrote: "He had studied the American character and understood it better than any foreigner or native-born American it has been our happiness to meet and converse with. He had great respect for and confidence in the American people. He understood the wants of the country and had his plans which he was only waiting for time to mature." *Brownson's Quarterly Review*, Last Series, Vol. III (July 1875), p. 410.
2. Wuest, *op. cit.*, p. 7.
3. A.P.F., *Baker Papers*, Charles A. Williamson to My Dearest Daughter, April 17, 1853.
4. A.U.N.D., *Brownson Papers*, Hecker to Brownson, May 6, 1853; A.R.B., *Diary of Very Reverend Bernard Hafkenscheid*, June 29, 1853.
5. Wuest, *op. cit.*, p. 10; A.P.F., *Hecker Papers*, Hewit to Cardinal Barnabò, November 17, 1857 says: "The intrigues of Father Rumpler and several others combined with other causes which are unknown to us caused the substitution of Father Ruland as Provincial in the place of Bernard." I could find no letters in either the A.R.B. or A.R.R. on this matter.
6. P. Claessens, *Life of Father Bernard*, translated from the French (New York: 1875), pp. 131–136; 157–173.

7. A.R.B., *Provincia Baltimorensis,* pp. 182–184.

8. These characteristics will become evident as the story of Father Ruland unfolds. Some of them are given in brief in Wuest, *op. cit.,* pp. 11–13.

9. Maurice de Meulemeester, C.SS.R., *Histoire Sommaire de la Congrégation du T.S. Rédempteur* (Louvain: 1950), pp. 141–144.

10. Father Smetana presented this method of procedure to the Holy See who approved it, June 30, 1854. *Acta Integra Capitulorum Generalium* (Rome: 1899), pp. 307–309. Also in Wuest, *op. cit.,* pp. 324–327.

11. A.R.B., *Ruland Papers,* "Actus formalis Capituli Domestici," October 4, 1854.

12. *Ibid.,* "Actus formalis Capituli Provincialis," December 6, 1854; *Chronicle of Missions,* p. 70.

13. *Ibid.,* Ruland Papers, "Actus formalis Capituli Provincialis," December 6, 1854.

14. *Ibid.,* Ruland to Frischbier, August 16, 1855; A.R.R., *Prov. Amer.,* I, 3, Smulders to Mauron, July 3, 1855, wrote: "We wish to be Redemptorists rather than parish priests." *Ibid.,* 5, Giesen to Mauron, on May 26, 1858, remarked: "I am a quasi parish priest. . . . Never yet have I assisted on a mission since I have been a Redemptorist."

15. This letter is no longer extant but in his reply Father de Held refers to Father Hecker's observations which he admits are thorny problems.

16. A.P.F., *Hecker Papers,* de Held to Hecker, February 16, 1855.

17. *Ibid.*

18. De Meulemeester, *op. cit.,* pp. 151–154.

19. A.R.R., *Prov. Amer.,* I, 2, Ruland to Mauron, December 8, 1854. The delegates Father Ruland favored were Rumpler and Seelos.

20. De Meulemeester, *op. cit.,* pp. 152–153. He has a much more detailed account in his *Le Père Frédéric von Held Rédemptoriste* (Jette: 1911), pp. 268–275, in which he mistakenly says there were 26 delegates. A.R.B., *Ruland Papers,* Ruland to Rumpler, May 3, 1855, is a detailed report of the proceedings written the day after the session.

21. *Ibid.*

22. A.P.F., *Hecker Papers,* de Held to Hecker, October 14, 1857.

23. Wuest, *op. cit.,* pp. 164–165; A.R.R., *Amer. Prov.,* I, 3, Walworth to Mauron, June 21, 1855; Schmid to Mauron, June 28, 1855; Helmpraecht to Mauron, June 29, 1855; Walworth to Mauron, July 1, 1855; Smulders to Mauron, July 3, 1855.

24. A.P.F., *Hecker Papers,* Dr. Stoke's medical certification, October 21, 1856, mentions this diagnosis. The letters cited in note 23 verify the same facts.

25. Wuest, *op. cit.,* p. 171; A.R.R., *Amer. Prov.,* I, 3, Helmpraecht to Mauron, June 29, 1855; A.P.F., *Hecker Papers,* Hewit to Barnabò, November 17, 1857.

26. These facts are contained in the letters to Father Mauron cited in note 23 above. Father Rumpler remained in Mt. Hope for about a year when Father Hecker wrote and asked for the Provincial's permission to bring him to New York and put him under the care of Dr. Watson. Having

great faith in the doctor's skill with this type of patient, Father Hecker offered to provide for all his expenses and put the unfortunate priest "in a private house" with a Catholic nurse until he was well enough to return to the Community. Since, he said, he would do this for his own brother, "why should I not do it for Father Rumpler who ought to be to each one of us more than a brother" (A.P.F., *Hewit Papers,* Hecker to Hewit, June 30, 1856). Father Hewit, as Provincial Consultor, strongly opposed the move and said that he would not give assent until he had "evidence of a clear and satisfactory character from competent witnesses" that Dr. Watson had cured "worse cases than Father Rumpler" (*ibid., Hecker Papers,* Hewit to Hecker, July 4, 1856).

Whether Father Hecker produced the required proof is not known. However, on October 24, 1856, Father Ruland sent Father Rumpler to New York giving Father Hecker complete authority over him. He authorized him "to exercise all the powers" which he himself as Provincial possessed over the sick man. In Father Hecker's absence on missions, Father Helmpraecht was to take his place. Father Ruland was profoundly grateful for Father Hecker's kindness and said: "What many obligations we have to your Rev. for the troubles you have already had and will have with Father Rumpler" (*ibid.,* Ruland to Hecker, October 18, November 4, 1856). The Provincial notified the Rector Major of Father Rumpler's removal to New York but made no mention of Father Hecker's part in it (A.R.R., *Prov. Amer.,* I, 3, Ruland to Mauron, October 27, 1856). Although Father Rumpler never recovered his sanity, he had occasional lucid intervals. On one such occasion, Father Hecker heard his confession. Father Hewit later testified that Father Hecker "watched over him with the most tender charity and lavished on him every species of attention in the hope of doing him some good" (A.P.F., *Hecker Papers,* Hewit to Cardinal Barnabò, November 17, 1857). Two days before he died on December 13, 1856, Father Rumpler's mind was clear enough for him to make his last confession to Father Helmpraecht (Wuest, *op. cit.,* p. 233). At the time, Father Hecker was on missions in the South.

27. A.R.R., *Amer. Prov.,* I, 3, Helmpraecht to Mauron, June 29, 1855; Smulders to Mauron, July 3, 1855; Van de Braak to Mauron, July 12, 1855; Schmid to Mauron, June 28, 1855.

28. *Ibid.,* Walworth to Mauron, June 21, 1855; Hecker to Mauron, June 24, 1855.

29. *Ibid.,* Walworth to Bernard Hafkenscheid, July 3, 1855 (this letter is incorrectly dated June 3rd); Schmid to Mauron, June 28, 1855; Smulders to Mauron, July 3, 1855; Walworth to Mauron, July 1, 1855; Hecker to Mauron, June 24, 1855.

30. Mauron's attitude is clearly stated in council minutes. A.R.R., *Observantia,* Liber Consultationum, June 4, 1857. Father Swinkels, provincial of the Holland English Province, had reported that Father Bernard was distressed because he had not been appointed to any office in the Community. The General and his consultors decided that though he

was well regarded, he could not be appointed superior without detriment to discipline.

31. *Ibid., Prov. Amer.*, I, 4, Hecker to Douglas, September 5, 1855. Father Douglas' letter to Father Hecker is non-extant, though the latter refers to it in his reply.

32. A.R.B., *Ruland Papers,* Mauron's document of appointment, November 21, 1855.

33. A.R.R., *Prov. Amer.*, I, 3, Walworth to Mauron, July 1, 1855; A.P.F., *Hecker Papers,* "Memorial and Petition of the American Fathers to Pope Pius IX," November, 1857.

34. *Codex Regularium et Constitutionum* (Rome: 1896), p. 50, art. 55.

35. A.P.F., *Hecker Papers,* Hecker to Dear Fathers, October 26, 1857. While in Rome after his expulsion, Hecker wrote to call this to the attention of the Fathers who were preparing their memorial to the Holy See.

36. *Ibid.,* Hewit to Barnabò, November 17, 1857.

37. A.R.R., *Amer. Prov.*, I, 4, Ruland's report to Mauron on the Fathers in the Province, 1855. Though undated as to month, it was likely written November 21, the date for the sending of such a report. Ruland's observations on the missions are given in his estimation of Father Walworth.

38. *Codex Regularium et Constitutionum* (Rome: 1896), p. 50, art. 55.

39. A.R.R., *Amer. Prov.*, I, 4. Ruland's report to Mauron on the Fathers in the Province, 1855. See note 37 above.

40. *Ibid.,* Hewit to Douglas, April 17, 1855.

41. *Ibid.* In a letter of Ruland to Mauron, July 31, 1857 (*ibid.*), he refers to this request and imputes to Hewit a motive for wanting to go to Rome that clearly indicates Ruland's suspicious nature. He accuses Hewit of asking for the trip so he could be at Rome during the time of the General Chapter "to champion the American interests." This allegation was entirely unwarranted since Hewit's sole reason for the trip was health.

42. A.P.F., *Hewit Papers,* Hecker to Hewit, March 13, 1855.

43. *Ibid.*

44. *Ibid., Chronicle of Missions,* pp. 75–77.

45. *Ibid., Hewit Papers,* Hewit to Mrs. Henry Hewit, July 16, 1855. The letter of the Provincial to Hewit is non-extant.

46. *Ibid., Chronicle of Missions,* pp. 79–87.

47. There is no full-length biography of Father Deshon. The most recent account of his life is in Joseph McSorley, C.S.P., *Father Hecker and His Friends* (St. Louis: 1952), pp. 274–289. Father McSorley, p. 275, says: "Deshon was received into the Church in 1851." A letter of Deshon to his West Point friend, Rosecrans, dated November 28, 1850, speaks of his desire to be a Redemptorist but his director Father Slattery opposed it (A.P.F., *Rosecrans Papers*). At the time Deshon was a Catholic and more than likely had been received as a Catholic earlier in the year.

48. A.P.F., *Chronicle of Missions,* pp. 87–88.

49. *Ibid.;* Wuest, *op. cit.,* p. 194.

50. Augustine F. Hewit, C.S.P., *Memoir and Sermons of Father Baker* (New York: 1865), pp. 13–110, *passim.*
51. A.P.F., *Baker Papers*, Chessie to her sister, April 16, 1853.
52. Hewit, *op. cit.*, pp. 110–115.
53. A.I.C., *Kirby Papers*, Kenrick to Kirby, October 13, 1853.
54. A.P.F., *Chronicle of Missions*, pp. 106–110.
55. *Ibid.*, pp. 111–132.
56. A.R.B., *Ruland Papers*, Hewit to Ruland, February 22, 1857. In this letter Father Hewit discusses his brother's situation as he had explained it to the Provincial in August of 1856.
57. A.P.F., *Hewit Papers*, Hecker to Hewit, August 16, 1856.
58. A.R.B., *Ruland Papers*, Hewit to Ruland, February 22, 1857; A.R.R., *Amer. Prov.*, I, 2, Ruland to Mauron, March 13, 1857.
59. A.P.F., *Hewit Papers*, Hecker to Hewit, June 2, 1857; Hewit to his brother, July 27, 1857.
60. *Ibid.*, *Chronicle of Missions*, p. 106.

CHAPTER X

1. A.P.F., *Chronicle of Missions*, pp. 1–57.
2. Abbot Gasquet, O.S.B., "Some Letters of Father Hecker," *Catholic World*, Vol. LXXXIII (May: 1906), p. 235, Hecker to Simpson. Although Gasquet gives the date as January 27, 1853, it is incorrect. Hecker refers to a letter he received from Simpson which is dated April 4, 1853. More likely Hecker's letter was written June 27th.
3. A.P.F., *Hecker Papers*, document Father Hecker submitted in Rome to his director, January 6, 1858.
4. *Ibid.*, Hecker tells his director of the events leading up to the publication of his book.
5. *Ibid.*, *Hewit Papers*, Hecker to Hewit, June 29, September 9, 1854; A.U.N.D., *Brownson Papers*, Hecker to Brownson, September 14, 23, 1854.
6. *Ibid.*, December 2, 1853.
7. Isaac Hecker, *Questions of the Soul* (New York: 1855), pp. 10–33.
8. *Ibid.*, pp. 34–87.
9. *Ibid.*, pp. 88–289.
10. *Ibid.*, pp. 290–293.
11. Robert Gorman, *Catholic Apologetical Literature in the United States (1784–1858)* (Washington: 1939), p. 160.
12. A.P.F., *Hecker Papers*, document Father Hecker submitted in Rome to his director, January 6, 1858.
13. These and subsequent reviews are in A.P.F., *Hecker Papers*, Reviews on *Questions of the Soul*. Though the newspapers from which the clippings were taken are identified, the dates of the papers are not.
14. A.U.N.D., *Brownson Papers*, Hecker to Brownson, n.d.
15. A.P.F., *Hecker Papers*, Bancroft to Hecker, March 14, 1855.
16. *Brownson's Quarterly Review*, Vol. III (Third Series), pp. 215, 224, 227.

17. A.P.F., *Hewit Papers,* Hecker to Hewit, March 13, 1855.
18. A.U.N.D., *Brownson Papers,* Hecker to Brownson, April 7, 1855; A.P.F., *Hecker Papers,* Hecker to Duffy, June 18, 1855.
19. Arthur M. Schlesinger, *Orestes A. Brownson* (Boston: 1939), p. 195, n. 18.
20. A.U.N.D., *Brownson Papers,* Hecker to Brownson, April 7, 1855.
21. *Ibid.*
22. *Ibid.*
23. A.P.F., *Hecker Papers,* Brownson to Hecker, n.d. In this letter Brownson speaks of his lectures in the South. He had not returned to Boston until after May 12, 1855. So this letter was probably written in June.
24. A.P.F., *Hecker Papers,* Hecker to Duffy, June 18, 1855.
25. *Ibid.,* Mothers Augustine McKenna and Catherine Seton made notes of four retreats Father Hecker gave to the sisters in the summers of 1853, 1854, 1855, and 1856. They gave a copy of these notes which are now in the Paulist Fathers' Archives to Father Elliott.
26. Father Hecker gave his reaction to the Know-Nothing movement in an article he wrote for the *Civiltà Cattolica,* Vol. CLXXXV (December 5, 1857), pp. 513–529, while he was in Rome.
27. A.U.N.D., *Brownson Papers,* Hecker to Brownson, August 7, 1855.
28. Henry F. Brownson, ed., *The Works of Orestes A. Brownson* (Detroit: 1885), Vol. XVIII, p. 289 ff.
29. Henry F. Brownson, *Orestes A. Brownson's Middle Life* (Detroit: 1899), p. 567.
30. A.U.N.D., *Brownson Papers,* Hecker to Brownson, April 16, 1855.
31. John R. Hassard, *Life of the Most Reverend John Hughes* (New York: 1866), p. 351. On pages 378–379 Hassard publishes Hughes's letter to Cassius M. Clay, February 6, 1858, about his not voting.
32. Henry F. Brownson, *op. cit.,* p. 588, Kenrick to Brownson, February 12, 1855.
33. *Ibid.,* p. 535, Brownson to the editor of the *Catholic Mirror,* July 11, 1854.
34. *Ibid.,* p. 596, Brownson to O'Connor.
35. *Ibid.,* p. 583, Brownson to Corcoran.
36. A.P.F., *Hecker Papers,* Brownson to Hecker, June, 1855. Cf. note 23 above.
37. A.U.N.D., *Brownson Papers,* Hecker to Brownson, April 16, 1855.
38. *Ibid.,* August 23, 1855.
39. Joseph McSorley, C.S.P., *Father Hecker and His Friends* (New York: 1952), p. 229.
40. A.U.N.D., *Brownson Papers,* Hecker to Brownson, August 23, 1855.
41. *Ibid.*
42. A.P.F., *Hecker Papers,* Brownson to Hecker, August 29, 1855.
43. A.U.N.D., *Brownson Papers,* Hecker to Brownson, August 23, 1855.
44. A.P.F., *Hecker Papers,* Brownson to Hecker, August 29, 1855.
45. *Ibid.* Schlesinger, *op. cit.,* pp. 210 and 218, speaks of Brownson's "tense relationship" with Bishop Fitzpatrick and indicates that Brownson was

anxious to get away from the Bishop. If Schlesinger had seen this letter of Brownson's to Hecker, he would have revised those statements.

46. A.U.N.D., *Brownson Papers,* Hecker to Brownson, September 1, October 1, 1855.
47. Henry F. Brownson, *Orestes A. Brownson's Latter Life* (Detroit: 1900), p. 3; Schlesinger, *op. cit.,* p. 219.
48. A.U.N.D., *McMaster Papers,* Hecker to McMaster, November 23, 1855.
49. A.P.F., *Chronicle of Missions,* pp. 91–94; *Hecker Papers,* document Father Hecker submitted in Rome to his director, January 6, 1858.
50. *Ibid., Chronicle of Missions,* p. 92.
51. A.U.N.D., *Brownson Papers,* Hecker to Brownson, April 12, 1856.
52. A.P.F., *Chronicle of Missions,* p. 93.
53. *Ibid., Hecker Papers,* document Father Hecker submitted in Rome to his director, January 6, 1858; A.U.N.D., *Brownson Papers,* Hecker to Brownson, April 12, 1856.
54. A.P.F., *Chronicle of Missions,* p. 93.
55. *Ibid., Hecker Papers,* document Father Hecker submitted in Rome to his director, January 6, 1858.
56. *Ibid., Chronicle of Missions,* p. 125.
57. A.R.R., *Prov. Amer.,* I, 4, Hewit to Douglas, April 17, 1855. The letters Father Hewit wrote to his family after his conversion speak constantly of the absolute necessity of being a Catholic to merit salvation.
58. A.U.N.D., *Brownson Papers,* Hewit to Brownson, June 28, 1856.
59. *Ibid.,* Brownson to Hewit, March 17, 1856.
60. *Ibid.*
61. A.U.N.D., *Brownson Papers,* Hewit to Brownson, October 13, 1856.
62. A.R.R., *Prov. Amer.,* I, 4, Hecker to Douglas, July 29, 1856.

CHAPTER XI

1. A concise account of this development in Poland, Belgium, and England is given in George Stebbing, C.SS.R., *The Redemptorists* (New York: 1924), pp. 57–58, 74–75, 151–160.
2. Colman J. Barry, O.S.B., *The Catholic Church and German Americans* (Milwaukee: 1953), pp. 1–17, discusses the tenacity with which the German immigrants held to their cultural heritage and the problem they created for the American hierarchy.
3. A.R.R., *Prov. Amer.,* I, 4, Hewit to Douglas, August 20, 1856, in which Hewit says that St. Alphonsus Church in Baltimore was "a favorite resort for the high class of Catholic Americans. The rigid adherence to the German language is the only insuperable barrier that keeps them out."
4. John F. Byrne, C.SS.R., *The Redemptorist Centenaries* (Philadelphia: 1932), p. 203. English sermons were also preached at certain Masses in Monroe, Michigan, Annapolis, Maryland, and, a little later, St. Alphonsus in New York. *Ibid.,* pp. 119, 203, 241.
5. A.P.F., *Chronicle of Missions,* p. 106; *Hecker Papers,* Hecker's statement to Cardinal Barnabò, September 15, 1857; memorial of American

Fathers to Pius IX, November 15, 1857; Hecker to Bishop O'Connor, 1857.

6. A.U.N.D., *Brownson Papers,* Hecker to Brownson, August 7, 1855.

7. A.P., *S.R.C., Amer. Cent.,* Vol. 17, 791 — 2v, Spalding to Barnabò, January 2, 1858. Although the date on the letter is 1857, the content clearly shows it was written in 1858.

8. A.P.F., *Hecker Papers,* McMaster to Hecker, July 28, 1857. After he became a Catholic, Deshon decided to resign his lieutenant's commission in the army and enter the priesthood. His close friend, William S. Rosecrans (later General), advised him to enter the diocesan clergy. While he was hesitating, McMaster suggested he make a spiritual retreat with the Redemptorists at Baltimore where Father Rumpler "discouraged" him from becoming a secular "representing its great dangers." After the retreat he was drawn to the Redemptorists, but his director, Father Slattery, opposed it "bringing up objections on account of their being Germans" and recommended the Jesuits. *Ibid., Rosecrans Papers,* Deshon to Rosecrans, November 28, 1850. (These papers are photostats of the originals in the possession of General Rosecrans' grandson, William S. Rosecrans.) McMaster finally won Deshon over to the Redemptorists, a fact which Deshon freely admitted, calling him "the immediate instrument" through which he entered the Community. A.U.N.D., *McMaster Papers,* Deshon to McMaster, July 4, 1852. The Holland-born Father Giesen recognized other difficulties an American experienced in joining the Order. He wrote to Father Mauron: "No one doubts that Americans have been obliged to make great sacrifices in order to enter our Congregation. They had to live with Germans whose language and mode of living were different." He claims that the reason many failed to persevere was "because of the kind of life they are forced to live there." A.R.R., *Prov. Amer.,* I, 5, Giesen to Mauron, May 26, 1858.

9. A.P.F., *Hecker Papers,* Walworth to Mauron, July 25, 1857. Father Hecker took this letter to Rome but never found the opportune moment to present it to Father Mauron; *ibid.,* memorial of American Fathers to Pius IX, November 15, 1857; A.R.R., *Prov. Amer.,* I, 4, Hewit to Mauron, July 27, 1857.

10. A.P.F., *Hewit Papers,* Hecker to Hewit, April 24, 1857; A.U.N.D., *Brownson Papers,* Hewit to Brownson, October 13, 1857.

11. A.R.R., *Prov. Amer.,* I, 2, Ruland to Mauron, October 16, 1855; A.P.F., *Hecker Papers,* Hecker to O'Connor, 1857; Hecker's statement to Cardinal Barnabò, September 15, 1857.

12. A.R.R., *Prov. Amer.,* I, 2, Ruland to Mauron, October 27, 1856.

13. *Ibid.,* April 4, 1858.

14. *Ibid.,* October 16, 1855. Father Smulders was aware of the attempt to restrict the number of Americans as he wrote to Father Mauron: "I believe that they are afraid to diminish the German element and to increase the English element." *Ibid.,* I, 3, July 3, 1855.

15. Father Ruland first expressed this fear when he sent a report on the Fathers in the Province to the Rector Major. After Father Hecker's

name he spoke of his request for an American house and added: "But this would undoubtedly lead to a split between American and German Fathers in a few years." *Ibid.*, I, 4, Ruland to Mauron, 1855.

16. Clarence Walworth, *The Oxford Movement in America* (New York: 1895), pp. 151–153.

17. A.P.F., *Hecker Papers,* Brownson to Hecker, August 5, 1857.

18. A.P.F., *Hecker Papers,* Hecker's statement to Barnabò, September 15, 1857: "The idea of our being actuated by an exclusive or national spirit is a baseless suspicion and an unprovoked calumny"; *ibid.,* Hecker to de Held, November 9, 1857, says that "there is not a word of truth" to the charge "the American Fathers wished to compose a house exclusively American"; *ibid.,* memorial of American Fathers to Pius IX, November 14, 1857: "Your petitioners however assure Your Holiness in all sincerity of heart that we have never been conscious of any such unworthy spirit of nationality, but utterly repudiate and detest it."

19. A.R.R., *Amer. Prov.,* I, 5, Giesen to Mauron, May 26, 1858.

20. A.P.F., *Hecker Papers,* Deshon to Hecker, September 11, 1857.

21. A.R.R., *Amer. Prov.,* I, 5, protestation of loyalty of Baltimore house to Mauron, April 29, 1858. Besides Father Leimgruber, there were nine other foreign-born Redemptorists who signed this document containing this admission.

22. *Ibid.,* I, 2, Ruland to Mauron, May 15, 1857.

23. A.P.F., *Chronicle of Missions,* p. 106.

24. A.R.B., *Ruland Papers,* Walworth to Ruland, April, 1857.

25. *Ibid.*

26. *Ibid.*

27. A.P.F., *Hecker Papers,* Walworth to Hecker, September 28, 1857.

28. A.R.R., *Amer. Prov.,* I, 2, Ruland to Mauron, May 15, 1857.

29. *Ibid.*

30. *Ibid.*

31. *Ibid.,* Ruland to Mauron, May 29, 1857.

32. A.P.F., *Hecker Papers,* Hewit to Hecker, May 31, 1857.

33. The *Chronica* of the Baltimore Province (A.R.B., *Provinces*), p. 362, has the date for the departure and return of Father Hecker. He was taken down with pneumonia while on a mission in Savannah and did not give any more missions for the rest of 1857. In a letter to Bishop Lynch, he told why he had gone to Cuba. A.D.C., *Lynch Papers,* Hecker to Lynch, April 2, 1857.

34. A.P.F., *Hecker Papers,* Hewit to Hecker, May 31, 1857.

35. *Ibid., Hewit Papers,* Deshon to Hewit, August 5, 1857.

36. A.R.R., *Prov. Amer.,* I, 2, Ruland to Mauron, May 29, 1857.

37. *Ibid.* In this same letter, Father Ruland did not help the cause of the American missionaries when he wrote: "The advantage of an English house would be, primarily, in the fact of having the English Fathers contented."

38. A.R.R., *Observantia,* Liber Consultationum Curiae Generalis, June 28, 1857.

39. A.R.B., *Ruland Papers*, Mauron to Ruland, July 2, 1857. Father Ruland noted on this letter: "Received July 21st."
40. *Ibid.*
41. A.P.F., *Hecker Papers*, Walworth to Mauron, July 25, 1857. Father Hecker took this letter with him to Rome but never found the opportune moment to present it to Father Mauron.
42. A.R.R., *Amer. Prov.*, I, 2, Ruland to Mauron, July 31, 1857.
43. *Ibid.*
44. A.P.F., *Hecker Papers*, Walworth to Hecker, July 23, 1857.
45. *Ibid.* Father Caseau called at Baltimore on May 5, 1856, and presented a letter from Bishop Baillargeon to Father Ruland dated April 22. After seeing Walworth, he gave Father Seelos all the information "he could desire," and left a letter of his own, dated May 5th, for Father Ruland. Both letters are in the A.R.B.
46. A.R.B., *Provinces*, St. Thomas, 1856–1858, Douglas to Ruland, August 14, 1856.
47. A.P.F., *Hecker Papers*, Walworth to Hecker, July 23, 1857.
48. *Ibid.*, Walworth to Mauron, July 25, 1857. Cf. note 41.
49. *Ibid.*
50. A.R.R., *Amer. Prov.*, I, 4, Hewit to Mauron. Father Hewit also listed as further reasons: "to preach basically dogmatic and controversial sermons; if one should be sickly or unsuited for the missions, that he still have something to do in the English language; that the young priests, as regards sermons, etc., be trained and practiced by the older," and finally the increase of vocations.
51. A.P.F., *Hecker Papers*, Walworth to Hecker, July 23, 1857.
52. *Ibid.*, Hecker's statement to Barnabò, September 15, 1857; memorial of American Fathers to Pius IX, November 14, 1857; A.R.R., *Amer. Prov.*, I, 5, Helmpraecht to Mauron, August 17, 1857, states that the reasons motivating Father Hecker in his decision to go to Rome were: (1) The idea that only through an English house in New York can the Congregation become permanent and of value to America. (2) The great desire to remove from himself and his respective companions, and to prove, that they are not national and revolutionary. (3) The complete distrust of Rev. Father Provincial.
53. A.P.F., *Hecker Papers*, Walworth and Hewit to Hecker, July 27, 1857; "Memorial of American Fathers to Pius IX," November 14, 1857. Both these documents clearly reveal that Father Hecker independently of the others decided to make the trip to Rome. It was his idea. When he mentioned it to the other Fathers they heartily endorsed his decision and designated him as their representative. Walter Elliott, C.S.P., *Life of Father Hecker* (New York: 1891), p. 251, says that when the Fathers decided to send one of their number to Rome "the choice fell on Father Hecker." All those writing on Father Hecker follow Elliott in this. This statement is true only in the sense that they concurred in Hecker's decision and named him their plenipotentiary.

CHAPTER XII

1. A.P.F., *Hecker Papers*, Walworth to Hecker, July 27, 1857. The exact date Father Hecker applied for his passage and passport is not available. However his passport was issued July 31st. It is now among the *Hecker Papers* in A.P.F.
2. A.R.R., *Prov. Amer.*, I, 2, Ruland to Mauron, July 31, 1857.
3. *Ibid.*
4. A.P.F., *Hecker Papers*, Walworth to Hecker, September 28, 1857.
5. A.R.R., *Prov. Amer.*, I, 2, Ruland to Mauron, July 31, 1857.
6. A.P.F., *Hecker Papers*, memorial of American Fathers to Pius IX, November 14, 1857.
7. *Ibid.;* Hecker to Barnabò, September 15, 1857; A.R.R., *Prov. Amer.*, I, 2, Ruland to Mauron, July 31, 1857. There seems to be some question as to the nature of the promise Father Ruland made to the Bishop. John F. Byrne, C.SS.R., *The Redemptorist Centenaries* (Philadelphia: 1932), p. 352, says it was never "a *definite* and *positive* promise" since Father Ruland did not have the authorization to make such a promise. However, from a letter of Father Douglas to Father Ruland, it seems the Provincial had the authorization to proceed: "The Rector Major is pleased with the idea of a house in Canada. He wishes your Reverence to continue the preliminary arrangements with the Archbishop so as to be able to begin at Quebec in 1858." A.R.B., *Provinces*, St. Thomas, Douglas to Ruland, August 14, 1856. It seems to be even more clearly stated in the deliberations of the Consultors on June 28, 1857, when the Newark proposition of Father Walworth was discussed and rejected because, among other reasons: "A new foundation has been accepted for the year ahead in Canada." A.R.R., *Observantia*, Liber Consultationum. In his correspondence with Father Mauron, Father Ruland seemed to think he had made a promise which was binding. A.R.R., *Prov. Amer.*, I, 2, Ruland to Mauron, May 29, July 31, 1857. The foundation was refused September 2, 1857. Ruland to Baillargeon. A.R.B., *Provinces*.
8. A.R.B., *Provinces*, Chron. Prov. Amer., p. 336; A.R.R., *Observantia*, Liber Consultationum, January 9, 1857.
9. *Ibid.*, February 3, May 5, 1857.
10. A.R.B., *Ruland Papers*, Haringer to Ruland, December 25, 1856.
11. *Ibid.*, May 9, 1857. This is the original sent by Mauron. A copy was made and certified by Father Ruland on June 12, 1857, and sent to all the houses of the Province. One of these copies is in the A.P.F., *Hecker Papers*, May 9, 1857. Joseph Wuest, C.SS.R., *Annales Provinciae Americanae*, Vol. III, Pars I (Ilchester: 1899), pp. 266–267, prints the circular in full.
12. A.P.F., *Hecker Papers*, Deshon to Ruland, July 28, 1857, gives his reasons why he thought the Provincial could send a priest to Rome. Disagreeing with him, Father Ruland wrote his observations on this letter, July 31st, and returned it to Father Deshon; A.R.R., *Prov. Amer.*,

I, 2, Ruland to Mauron, October 12, 1857. The section of the Constitutions dealing with the subject's right to go to Rome is in *Codex Regularium et Constitutionum* (Rome: 1896), p. 159, Section 342.

13. A.P.F., *Hecker Papers*, Deshon to Ruland, July 28, 1857; Deshon to Hecker, December 14, 1857; Hecker to Barnabò, September 15, 1857. Memorial of American Fathers to Pius IX, November 14, 1857. Father Byrne, *op. cit.*, p. 266, says that the Rector Major in the circular forbade "any member of the Congregation in this country to go to Rome without his permission in writing." He follows Father Ruland's interpretation. Francis Du Mortier, C.SS.R., *Le Révérendissime Père Nicolas Mauron* (Paris: Firmin-Didot, 1901), p. 59, says the same, but as Father Deshon pointed out "in writing" was not in the circular.

14. A.P.F., *Hecker Papers*, Deshon to Ruland, July 28, 1857. Cf. note 12 above.

15. *Ibid.*, Deshon to Hecker, December 14, 1857. Mauron's circular letter of July 26, 1855, is in *Litterae Circulares Reverendissimi Nicolae Mauron* (Rome: 1896), pp. 1–3; also in Wuest, *op. cit.*, pp. 96–98.

16. A.P.F., *Hecker Papers*, Deshon to Hecker, December 14, 1857.

17. *Ibid.*, memorial of American Fathers to Pius IX, November 14, 1857; Hecker to Barnabò, September 15, 1857; Hewit to Mauron, July 31, 1857.

18. *Ibid.*, Deshon to Ruland, July 28, 1857. After Father Ruland had written his observation of Father Deshon's argument, Father Hecker added this interpretation. He repeated it again in his statement to Cardinal Barnabò, September 15, 1857. *Ibid.*

19. A.R.B., *Ruland Papers*, Haringer to Ruland, December 25, 1856.

20. A.P.F., *Hecker Papers*, memorial of American Fathers to Pius IX, November 14, 1857; Hecker to Barnabò, September 15, 1857; A.R.R., *Prov. Amer.*, I, 2, Ruland to Mauron, July 31, 1857.

21. A.P.F., *Hecker Papers*, Hecker to Hughes, September 30, 1857. This is a rough draft of a letter which Father Hecker rewrote and sent later.

22. A.R.R., *Prov. Amer.*, I, 2, Ruland to Mauron, October 12, 1857.

23. A.P.F., *Hecker Papers*, Hecker to the Fathers, November 7, 1857; Hecker to de Held, November 9, 1857. In this letter Father Hecker told de Held he could "prove" this point.

24. A.P.F., *Hecker Papers*, Ruland's opinion, July 31, 1857; Deshon to Walworth and Hewit, July 31, 1857, quotes this statement verbatim.

25. *Ibid.*, Deshon to Hecker, December 14, 1857, in which Deshon recalls the Provincial's words and actions.

26. A.R.R., *Prov. Amer.*, 1, 2, Ruland to Mauron, July 31, 1857.

27. A.P.F., *Hecker Papers*, Hewit to Hecker, May 31, 1857. Father Hewit said the Provincial had entered into the project of an American house *"corde et anima"* and told Father Hecker: "Do all you can by prayer and other means, to get us a good place."

28. *Ibid.*, Hughes to Hecker, August 2, 1857.

29. *Ibid.*, Walworth to Hecker, July 23, 1857. In this letter Walworth urges Father Hecker not to wait for the Provincial's arrival in New York

but to go and see him in Philadelphia, since he needs "posting up." From this letter it is obvious Father Hecker was waiting for his arrival to inform him as to what had taken place.

30. A.R.R., *Prov. Amer.*, I, 2, Ruland to Mauron, July 31, 1857.
31. A.P.F., *Hecker Papers*, Deshon to Walworth and Hewit, July 31, 1857.
32. A.R.R., *Prov. Amer.*, I, 2, Ruland to Mauron, July 31, October 12, 1857.
33. A.P.F., *Hecker Papers*, Hewit to Hecker, July 31, August 2, 1857.
34. *Ibid.*
35. *Ibid.;* Walworth and Hewit to Hecker, August 2, 1857.
36. *Ibid.*, Hewit to Mauron, July 31, 1857. Since Father Hecker never found the opportune moment to present this letter, Father Mauron did not see it. It was, however, presented to Cardinal Barnabò and later used in Father Hecker's defense.
37. *Ibid.*, Hewit to Hecker, August 2, 1857; Walworth and Hewit to Hecker, August 2, 1857.
38. *Ibid.*, Deshon to Hecker, August 4, 1857.
39. A.R.R., *Prov. Amer.*, I, 2, Ruland to Mauron, July 31, October 12, 1857.
40. A.P.F., *Hecker Papers*, Hewit to Hecker, July 30, 1857.
41. *Ibid.*, Ruland's testimonial, August 3, 1857.
42. A.R.R., *Prov. Amer.*, I, 2, Ruland to Mauron, July 31, October 12, 1857.
43. *Ibid.*
44. *Ibid.*, July 31, 1857.
45. *Ibid.*, October 12, 1857.
46. A.P.F., *Elliott Papers*, Joseph Hild, C.SS.R., to Walter Elliott, C.S.P., July 27, 1897. To this letter Father Elliott attached this very interesting memorandum: "In 1897, Father Hild, C.SS.R., a prominent member of the Order came to me in New York and said that their Father Wuest, he thought, was ill-advised in statements he was writing for the official Redemptorist Chronicle of their American Provinces. Father Hild requested to see any documents bearing on the separation of Father Hecker and our other Fathers from their order, so that he, Hild, could establish that they were not bad intentioned but acted in good faith, however mistaken. . . . I handed him a typewritten copy of all the correspondence of Father Hecker and his associates, and of the documents bearing on the question. After an interval, Father Hild returned the typewritten matter with the letter herein enclosed." In his letter, Father Hild said that Father Wuest copied the documents "word for word" and then both compared the copy with the notes Father Elliott had loaned them. Then he adds: "The material you have furnished us gives the altera pars, and you can hardly imagine how it has swept away prejudices and misunderstandings and has cleared the atmosphere. The Chronicler was simply amazed." On July 29, 1897, Father Elliott wrote this note on Father Hild's letter: "Father Wuest, C.SS.R., the Chronicler named herein called today and expressed the same sentiments as Father Hild." Although he had all the Paulist material on the separation, Father Wuest did not have all the Redemptorist sources. Also he treated the subject mainly from the point of view of the American Province and

did not follow the case through the Roman tribunals. Consequently he has not presented in his *Annales Provinciae Americanae* (Ilchester: 1899), Vol. III, Pars. II, a complete or balanced treatment of the subject.

47. *Ibid.*, *Hecker Papers*, Father Hecker to his brother George, August 18, 1857. Father Hecker wrote this letter from London and before he reached Rome.

48. A.R.R., *Prov. Amer.*, I, 2, Ruland to Mauron, July 31, 1857. Father Ruland gives these words as coming from Father Hecker to Father Helmpraecht with whom Father Hecker had lengthy discussions about his trip and his purpose.

49. A.P., *S.R.C.*, *Amer. Cent.*, Vol. 17, 1001, Kenrick to Barnabò, July 29, 1857. Father Hecker kept a copy of this letter which is in A.P.F., *Hecker Papers*, Kenrick to Barnabò, July 29, 1857. Father Hewit told Father Hecker, he had requested this testimonial, *ibid.*, Hewit to Hecker, July 26, 1857.

50. A.P., *S.R.C.*, *Amer. Cent.*, Vol. 17, 1023, Hughes to Barnabò, August 2, 1857. Father Hecker also kept a copy of this letter which is in the *Hecker Papers* under the same date. In a letter to Father Hecker (*ibid.*), written on December 3, 1857, Father Deshon tells of an interview with the Archbishop in which he reminds Hughes that Father Hecker had explained to him at Saratoga his grounds for going to Rome. In a letter which Hughes later wrote to Barnabò on September 30, 1857, he admits that he was aware of the difficulties. A.P., *S.R.C.*, *Amer. Cent.*, Vol. 17, 1125–1127. In a letter to Dr. Bernard Smith, December 29, 1857, Hughes said that he knew "that Father Hecker in going to Rome, considered himself as acting in good faith, under the privileges secured to every member of his order at that time, and this I know further, that it was only under a well founded conviction on my part, that he was asking in good faith that I gave him a letter of introduction, and to some extent of recommendation, to His Eminence, the Cardinal Prefect of Propaganda." A.S.J.A., *Smith Papers*.

51. A.P.F., *Hecker Papers*, Hughes to Hecker, August 2, 1857. Although Father Mauron never saw this letter, Cardinal Barnabò did and had Father Hecker submit it with his documents later on in the trial.

52. A.I.C., *Kirby Papers*, McCloskey to Kirby, August 2, 1857.

53. A.P., *S.R.C.*, *Amer. Cent.*, Vol. 17, 1027, Bayley to Barnabò, August 3, 1857. Hecker also made a copy of this letter which is in A.P.F.

54. A.P., *S.R.C.*, *Amer. Cent.*, Vol. 17, 1028–1030. Bayley to Bedini, August 3, 1857. Sister Hildegarde Yeager, C.S.C., *Life of James Roosevelt Bayley* (New York: 1947), pp. 175–176, n. 72, prints copies of this and the preceding letter which Bayley preserved and which she obtained from the New York Archdiocesan Archives.

55. A.P.F., *Hecker Papers*, Bayley to Mauron, August 3, 1857. This is Bayley's Latin original which Father Hecker did not have the opportunity to present to Father Mauron.

56. *Ibid.*, Brownson to Hecker, August 5, 1857; McMaster to Hecker,

July 28, 1857; Ives to Hecker, August 4, 1857; *S.R.C., Amer. Cent.,* Vol. 17, 1031, Ives to Bedini.

57. A.P.F., *Hewit Papers,* Deshon to Hewit, August 5, 1857; *Hecker Papers,* Helmpraecht's testimonial, August 4, 1857.

58. *Ibid.; Hewit Papers,* Deshon to Hewit, August 5, 1857.

59. Leo F. Stock, *Consular Relations Between the United States and the Papal States* (Washington: 1945). In his introduction, Dr. Stock gives a concise and accurate explanation of the origin and duties of the Consul General. On page 406 he prints Binsse's letter to Clayton, announcing his appointment to the post.

60. A.P., *S.R.C., Amer. Cent.,* Vol. 17, 1048–1050, Binsse to Barnabò, August 15, 1857.

61. A.R.R., *Prov. Amer.,* I, 2, Ruland to Mauron, July 31, 1857.

CHAPTER XIII

1. A.P.F., *Hecker Papers,* Isaac Hecker to George Hecker, August 18, 24, 1857. Joseph Wuest, C.SS.R., *Annales Provinciae Americanae,* Vol. III, Pars. II, p. 61, f.n. 1, says that Father Schauer told him of Father Hecker's visit to Clapham and his great plans for the new foundation.

2. A.P.F., *Hecker Papers,* McMaster to Hecker, July 28, 1857; Ives to Hecker, August 4, 1857; Binsse to Barnabò, August 15, 1857; Donnelly to Hecker, August 3, 1857.

3. *Ibid.,* Brownson to Hecker, August 5, 1857.

4. *Ibid.,* Isaac Hecker to George Hecker, August 24, 1857. It is interesting to note that Manning himself expressed a similar opinion. However, he placed the blame on the hereditary Catholics who opposed the progressive and missionary spirit of the converts. Edmund S. Purcell, *Life of Cardinal Manning* (New York: 1896), Vol. I, pp. 88–89.

5. *Ibid.,* Isaac Hecker to George Hecker, August 24, 1857.

6. *Ibid.,* September 1, 1857. This itinerary contradicts the position of Eugène Pladys, C.SS.R., *Le Cardinal Dechamps* (Brussels: 1903), T., I. p. 536. He says that on his way to Rome, Father Hecker stopped in Belgium and saw Fathers Dechamps and de Held; that the former was against the journey to Rome but the latter approved. Carl Dilgskron, C.SS.R., *P. Friedrich von Held* (Vienna: 1909), pp. 297–298, and Maurice de Meulemeester, C.SS.R., *Le Père Frédéric von Held* (Jette: 1911), pp. 281–282, following Pladys take the same position. So also Joseph McSorley, C.S.P., *Father Hecker and His Friends* (New York: 1952), pp. 48–50. However Father Hecker made no such visit. The chronology he gave to his brother George would not permit the trip to Belgium. Moreover, his passport (A.P.F., *Hecker Papers,* Hecker passport, July 31, 1857) bears out the route he gave to George. It is stamped for Paris, Marseilles, Civita Vecchia, and Rome, but not for Brussels. In discussing this matter personally with Father de Meulemeester in May of 1955, I asked him what was the historical evidence for his position. A strong tradition was his answer. He admitted, however, that the

tradition could not stand in the face of historical fact. It is quite possible that since Father Hecker visited Brussels on his return to America, this visit could have been confused with his journey to Rome.

7. F. Dumortier, C.SS.R., *Le Révérendissime Père Nicolas Mauron* (Paris: 1901), is the only *Life* of Father Mauron to appear. It is not critical and suffers from the absence of the perspective of time. Though not blessed with robust health, Father Mauron lived until July 13, 1893. The best account of Villa Caserta is the golden jubilee book, *Villa Caserta* (Rome: 1905).

8. George Stebbing, C.SS.R., *The Redemptorists* (New York: 1924), p. 124.

9. A.P., *S.R.C., Amer. Cent.*, Vol. 18, 139, Mauron to Barnabò, September 30, 1857. A copy of this statement of the Rector Major is in A.P.F., *Hecker Papers*, report of Rector Major, September 30, 1857; also in the A.R.R., *Prov. Amer.*, I, 5, Mauron to Barnabò, September 30, 1857.

10. A.R.R., *Observantia*, Liber Consultationum, June 28, 1857.

11. *Ibid.*, August 30, 1857, makes no mention of the source of the Rector Major's information. However in a statement submitted to Archbishop Bizzarri, probably during the week of February 19, 1858, the Consultors say that the Rector Major "consulted the letters which had come from the Superior Provincial and other Fathers" (A.R.R., *Amer. Prov.*, I, 5, Mauron to Bizzarri, February, 1858). The only letters dealing with this matter in the A.R.R. before August 30th are from Fathers Ruland and Hewit. There is one from Father Helmpraecht dated August 17, 1857, but it could not have reached Rome before August 30th, the date of the Consultors' meeting. Father Mauron could not have written to America to verify Father Ruland's charges since he received the Provincial's letter on August 22nd and expelled Father Hecker on August 30th.

12. A.P., *S.R.C., Amer. Cent.*, Vol. 18, 138, Mauron to Barnabò, September 30, 1857. In this report, Father Mauron mentions that Father Hecker told him these things orally. Consequently they were related in the interviews.

13. *Ibid.*, 138 v and ff.

14. *Ibid.*, 139.

15. *Ibid.*, A.R.B., *Ruland Papers*, Mauron to Ruland, September 3, 1857. In this letter Father Mauron gives in substance the interviews.

16. A.R.B., *Ruland Papers*, Mauron to Ruland, September 3, 1857.

17. A.P., *S.R.C., Amer. Cent.*, Vol. 18, 133, Hecker to Barnabò, September 15, 1857.

18. *Ibid.*, A.P.F., *Hecker Papers*, Hecker to the Fathers, September 1, 1857; Hecker to de Held, November 9, 1857. This is a copy of the letter that Father Hecker kept. None of his letters to de Held could be found.

19. A.R.R., *Amer. Prov.*, I, 5, Mauron to Bizzarri, Motivi Segreti, February, 1858.

20. *Ibid.*, 2, Ruland to Mauron, October 16, 1855; 4, November 21, 1855.

21. *Ibid.*, 2, Ruland to Mauron, May 15, 29, July 31, 1857.

22. A.P., *S.R.C., Amer. Cent.,* Vol. 18, 141 v., Mauron to Barnabò, September 30, 1857.

23. A.R.R., *Amer. Prov.,* I, 5, Mauron to Bizzarri. "Response to 2nd Defense of Father Hecker," February, 1858.

24. A.R.B., *Ruland Papers,* Mauron to Ruland, September 3, 1857.

25. A.P.F., *Hecker Papers,* Hecker to the Fathers, September 1, 1857; Hecker to de Held, November 9, 1857; A.P., *S.R.C., Amer. Cent.,* Vol. 18, 133, Hecker to Barnabò, September 15, 1857.

26. A.P.F., *Hecker Papers,* Hecker to the Fathers, September 1, 1857.

27. *Codex Regularium et Constitutionum* (Rome: 1896), pp. 159, 231–232.

28. That this was Father Mauron's intention is clear from his subsequent actions as related to Cardinal Barnabò. A.P., *S.R.C., Amer. Cent.,* Vol. 18, 138, Mauron to Barnabò, September 30, 1857. Also the minutes of the Consultors' meeting and the Consultors' later statement to Bizzarri reveal the same intention. A.R.R., *Observantia,* Liber Consultationum. August 30, 1857; *Amer. Prov.,* I, 5, Mauron to Bizzarri, February, 1858.

29. A.P.F., *Hecker Papers,* Isaac Hecker to George Hecker, September 1, 1857; Hecker to the Fathers, September 1, 1857.

30. *Ibid.;* A.P., *S.R.C., Amer. Cent.,* Vol. 18, 133, Hecker to Barnabò, September 15, 1857.

31. The names of Father Mauron's Consultors are given in *Spicilegium Historicum,* Vol. II (1954), p. 61.

32. A.R.R., *Observantia,* Liber Consultationum, August 30, 1857; *Amer. Prov.,* I, 5, Mauron to Bizzarri, Consultors' statement, February, 1858.

33. These statements appear in Father Ruland's letter of July 31, 1857, to Father Mauron, A.R.R., *Amer. Prov.,* I, 2.

34. *Ibid., Amer. Prov.,* I, 5, Mauron to Bizzarri, Consultors' statement, February, 1858.

35. A.P.F., *Hecker Papers,* decree of expulsion, August 30, 1857.

36. *Ibid.,* Hecker to the Fathers, September 1, 1857; Hecker to de Held, November 9, 1857; A.P., *S.R.C., Amer. Cent.,* Vol. 18, 133, Hecker to Barnabò, September 15, 1857.

37. *Codex Regularium et Constitutionum* (Rome: 1896), p. 159.

38. A.P.F., *Hecker Papers,* Hecker to the Fathers, September 1, 1857; A.R.B., *Ruland Papers,* Mauron to Ruland, September 3, 1857.

39. A.P.F., *Hecker Papers,* Hecker to the Fathers, September 1, 1857; Hecker to de Held, November 9, 1857; *S.R.C., Amer. Cent.,* Vol. 18, 133 v, Hecker to Barnabò, September 15, 1857.

40. *Ibid.*

41. A.R.R., *Amer. Prov.,* I, 5, Mauron to Bizzarri, Consultors' statement, February, 1858.

42. A.P.F., *Hecker Papers,* Hecker to the Fathers, September 1, 1857.

43. *Ibid.,* Isaac Hecker to George Hecker, September 1, 1857; A.P., *S.R.C., Amer. Cent.,* Vol. 18, 132 v.

44. A.P.F., *Hecker Papers,* Isaac Hecker to George Hecker, September 1, 1857; A.A.N.Y., *Hughes Papers,* Hecker to Hughes, December 4, 1857.

45. A.P.F., *Hecker Papers,* Hecker to the Fathers, September 1, 1857.

46. *Ibid.,* *Elliott Papers,* undated memorandum. Printed in Walter Elliott, *Life of Father Hecker* (New York: 1891), p. 254.
47. A.P.F., *Hecker Papers,* Hecker to the Fathers, September 1, 1857; A.P., *S.R.C., Amer. Cent.,* Vol. 18, 134 v., Hecker to Barnabò, September 15, 1857.
48. *Ibid.,* 135.
49. *Ibid.,* 133 v.; A.P.F., *Hecker Papers,* Hecker to the Fathers, September 1, 1857; Hecker to de Held, November 9, 1857; Hecker to Holy Father, November 21, 1857. The last document is a copy and though undated, a letter of Father Hecker to his brother George, November 20, 1857, fixes the date. There are also copies of these two documents in A.R.R., *Prov. Amer.,* I, 5. A.A.N.Y., *Hughes Papers,* Hecker to Hughes, December 4, 1857.
50. A.P., *S.R.C., Amer. Cent.,* Vol. 18, 138, Mauron to Barnabò, September 30, 1857; A.R.R., *Amer. Prov.,* I, 5, Mauron to Bizzarri, February, 1858; A.P.F., *Hecker Papers,* Ruland to Hewit, December 14, 1857.
51. A.R.R., *Amer. Prov.,* I, 5, Mauron to Bizzarri, Consultors' statement, February, 1858.
52. A.P.F., *Hecker Papers,* Hecker to de Held, November 9, 1857.
53. This is quite clear from the minutes of the Consultation held on August 30th, A.R.R., *Observantia,* Liber Consultationum, and in the Consultor's statement which Father Mauron submitted to Bizzarri in February of 1858, *ibid., Amer. Prov.,* I, 5.
54. *Ibid.*
55. A.P.F., *Hecker Papers,* Hecker to the Fathers, September 25, 1857.
56. A.U.N.D., *Brownson Papers,* Hecker to Brownson, September 1, 1857.
57. A.P.F., *Hecker Papers,* Hecker to the Fathers, September 1, 1857.
58. *Ibid.*
59. *Ibid.,* Isaac Hecker to George Hecker, September 1, 1857.
60. *Ibid.;* September 19, 1857; Hecker to the Fathers, September 1, 1857.

CHAPTER XIV

1. A.U.N.D., *Brownson Papers,* Hecker to Brownson, September 1, 1857; A.P.F., *Hecker Papers,* Hecker to the Fathers, September 1, 1857.
2. Father Hecker's letters to Father de Held are no longer extant. However, the content of this letter of September 1, 1857, can be deduced from Father de Held to Father Hecker, A.P.F., *Hecker Papers,* September 9, 1857. In this reply de Held says: "It seems to me doubtful that any Superior whatever could have the right to forbid what the rules permit. In any case you were ignorant of this prohibition." From this statement, Carl Dilgskron, C.SS.R., *P. Friedrich von Held* (Vienna: 1909), p. 300, and Maurice de Meulemeester, C.SS.R., *Le Père Frédéric von Held* (Jette: 1911), p. 282, assume that de Held was referring to the General's circular of 1857 and that Father Hecker led him to believe he was ignorant of the prohibition. For this reason, de Held supported his case. However, subsequent correspondence — A.P.F., *Hecker Papers,*

de Held to Hecker, September 27, November 1, 1857; Hecker to de Held (a copy of which Father Hecker kept) November 9, 1857 — all make very clear that Father de Held knew that Father Hecker was familiar with the circular but thought it did not apply to him. In the letter of November 9th, Father Hecker again mentions the circular and says, "Go back to my first letter and you will find that this one is but its repetition." In view of these letters and the fact that in his first letters back to New York as well as in his statement to Cardinal Barnabò (A.P.F., *Hecker Papers,* September 1st, September 15th) Father Hecker prominently mentions the Smetana prohibition, the only conclusion possible is that he also spoke of it to de Held thus accounting for the latter's statement: "In any case you were ignorant of this prohibition."

3. A.P.F., *Hecker Papers,* Father Hecker to George Hecker, September 1, 19, 21, 1857; Hecker to the Fathers, September 25, 1857. Father Hecker anticipated the action of the Provincial who gave orders to Father Helmpraecht to send him all letters to Father Hecker or from Father Hecker to Father Hewit, expecting that any letters from Rome would be sent to Father Hewit in his capacity as Provincial Consultor, A.R.R., *Amer. Prov.,* I, 2, Ruland to Mauron, December 11, 1857.

4. A.P.F., *Hecker Papers,* Father Hecker to George Hecker, September 1, 1857; Hecker to the Fathers, September 1, 1857. Frequently during his stay in Rome, Father Hecker would tell George to read his letters to the Fathers and also to show them the letters he received. This prevented a duplication of effort on his part.

5. A.R.B., *Ruland Papers,* Mauron to Ruland, September 3, 1857. Some months later in conversation with Barnabò, Mauron denied that he had concealed the fact of Hecker's expulsion in this visit to the Cardinal. According to Hecker's letter of January 18, 1858, Mauron told Barnabò that he would take his oath that he had explained it to him. The Cardinal replied: "You will take one oath that you told me of the expulsion at your first visit; and I before heaven will take three oaths that you did not; and my secretary, Mons. Bedini, will take three more. Now look at me, I am a Cardinal and my secretary is an Archbishop!" (A.P.F., *Hecker Papers,* Hecker to the Fathers, January 18, 1858).

6. A.P.F., *Hecker Papers,* Father Hecker to George Hecker, September 8, 1857; A.A.N.Y., Hecker to Hughes, December 4, 1857, A. 34.

7. A.P.F., *Hecker Papers,* de Held to Hecker, September 27, 1857.

8. *Ibid.,* Hecker to Fathers, December 17, 1857. E. E. Y. Hales, *Pio Nono* (New York: 1954), pp. 91–95, gives an interesting account of the Pope's flight. Dr. Joseph N. Moody in his "American Catholicism's Influence on Europe," *Historical Records and Studies,* Vol. XXXVIII (1950), pp. 9–10, has a concise explanation of the European attitude toward American democracy mistaking it for European republicanism.

9. A.P.F., *Hecker Papers,* de Buggenoms to Hecker, September 24, 1857.

10. *Ibid.,* Hecker to the Fathers, September 21, 1857.

11. A.I.C., *Kirby Papers*, McCloskey to Kirby, August 2, 1857.

12. There are 17 letters of Smith to Hecker in the A.P.F., as late as March 2, 1876. Hecker's letters to Smith are in the Benedictine Monastery of St. Paul's Outside the Walls. In 1951, Father Colman Barry, O.S.B., microfilmed the Smith correspondence and these copies are now in the archives of St. John's Abbey. Cf. *Scriptorium*, Vol. XI (March, 1951), pp. 21–35. There are 25 letters of Hecker to Smith in this collection.

13. A.S.J.A., *The Obituary Notice of Abbot Smith, O.S.B.*, Zelli to Most Reverend Father, December 12, 1892; *Scriptorium*, Vol. XI (March, 1951), pp. 24–25.

14. A.P., *S.R.C., Amer. Cent.*, Vol. 17, 534, 573.

15. *Ibid.*, 1047–1050. Binsse to Barnabò, August 15, 1857.

16. R. Aubert, *Le Pontificat de Pie IX* (Paris, 1952), p. 283; Hales, *op. cit.*, p. 146.

17. A.P., *S.R.C., Amer. Cent.*, Vol. 17, 1047–1050, Binsse to Barnabò.

18. Peter Guilday, "Gaetano Bedini," *Historical Records and Studies*, XXIII (1933), pp. 87–170.

19. A.P.F., *Hecker Papers*, Father Hecker to George Hecker, September 8, 1857.

20. *Ibid.*, Hecker to the Fathers, September 20, 1857. The historian of the pontificate of Pius IX, Aubert, *op. cit.*, p. 283, says: "The most marked influence [with the Pope] seems to have been Cardinal Barnabò." Both Talbot and Manning recognized how powerful he was with Pius IX. Cf. E. S. Purcell, *Life of Cardinal Manning* (New York: 1896), Vol. II, pp. 227, 232.

21. R. H[owley]., "Cardinal Barnabò," *Catholic World*, LXXVII (April, 1903), pp. 77–85.

22. A.P.F., *Hecker Papers*, Father Hecker to George Hecker, September 8, 1857.

23. *Ibid.*; A.A.N.Y., *Hughes Papers*, Hecker to Hughes, December 4, 1857.

24. A.P.F., *Hecker Papers*, Father Hecker to George Hecker, September 8, 1857. In a letter to his brother George on September 19, 1857 (*ibid.*) Father Hecker related Cardinal Barnabò's account of a conversation he had with Father Mauron: "He [Barnabò] told the General when he was laying charges at my [Hecker's] door, that I had abstained from all personalities and that I had not said one word to his disfavor."

25. *Ibid.*

26. *Ibid.*

27. *Ibid.*, Hecker to Fathers, January 18, 1857. In this letter Father Hecker says: "Card. Barnabò is my sole counsellor in everything however slight I say and do; there is no man in Rome with such a clear head, so broad and just in his views, so friendly to our cause and so powerful in his influence." Walter Elliott, *Life of Father Hecker* (New York: 1891), p. 255.

28. A.P.F., *Hecker Papers*, Hecker's statement to Barnabò, September 15, 1857. This is the copy Father Hecker wrote out in English. The Italian

translation he submitted to the Cardinal is in A.P., *S.R.C.*, *Amer. Cent.*, Vol. 18, 126–135.

29. A quotation from this letter of Pius IX was carried in a box square in the *Catholic Standard* of New Orleans, November 6, 1859: "Leave nothing untried by which our most Holy Religion and its salutary teaching may more increase in the United States, and unhappy wanderers may return to the safe path. Spare no cares, counsels, or labors that, — while in your dioceses any unbelievers may be found, sitting in darkness and the shadow of death, — you may enlighten them with the light of the Gospel and gain them for Christ."

30. A.P.F., *Hecker Papers*, Hecker's statement to Barnabò, September 15, 1857, p. 1; A.P., *S.R.C.*, *Amer. Cent.*, Vol. 18, 127 and v. In the following quotations from both documents, the first page number refers to the English document in A.P.F.; the second to the Italian in A.P., *S.R.C.*, *Amer. Cent.*, Vol. 18.

31. P. 3; 127 v.

32. Pp. 4 and 5; 128 and v.

33. Pp. 6–8; 128 v., 129 and v.

34. Pp. 8–9; 130.

35. P. 9; 130 and v. In this statement, Father Hecker compressed a time span of more than two years in a few lines. In May of 1856, Father Cazeau, the Vicar-General of Quebec, came to Baltimore at the request of Bishop Baillargeon to obtain a Redemptorist foundation for the diocese. Father Walworth met him and heard about the proposition. But he never thought the station would be accepted until Father Ruland spoke of it in July of 1857. This information, Father Hecker received from Father Walworth on July 23, 1857 (A.P.F., *Hecker Papers*). Father Hecker apparently had the letter with him in Rome and used it in preparing his document.

36. Pp. 10 and 11; 131.

37. Pp. 11–14; 131 v, 132 and v.

38. Pp. 14–17; 133 and v.

39. P. 18; 135 and v.

40. A.P.F., *Hecker Papers*, Father Hecker to George Hecker, September 19, 1857. The Italian translation of Hecker's statement is dated September 15, 1857, although the English original is undated.

41. A.R.R., *Prov. Amer.*, I, 5, Barnabò to Mauron, September 18, 1857.

42. A.P.F., *Hecker Papers*, Father Hecker to George Hecker, September 19, 1857.

43. *Ibid.*

44. *Ibid.;* Hecker to the Fathers, September 25, 1857.

45. *Ibid.*

46. *Ibid.* In this letter, Father Hecker said that Bedini was going to ask for an audience. Then in a postscript dated September 26th, he said: "he [Bedini] asked no audience." However in a later letter to the Fathers on November 20th, he said that "an audience was asked but the Holy Father said he would have to see the General first." Since the Pope

received Father Mauron on October 5th (A.R.B., *Ruland Papers*, Mauron to Ruland, October 8th), the request for an audience for Father Hecker would have had to be made before October 5th. More than likely Bedini mentioned to the Pope the possibility of seeing Father Hecker on September 20th but presented no formal petition for an audience.

47. A.P.F., *Hecker Papers*, de Held to Hecker, September 9, 1857.

48. Purcell, *op. cit.*, pp. 226 and 261. Hales, *op. cit.*, p. 240, says of Talbot: "Probably as persuasive an influence as any [on Pius IX] was the Englishman, Msgr. Talbot." Aubert, *op. cit.*, p. 284, describes him "as the confidant and most intimate favorite of Pius IX." Cuthbert Butler, O.S.B., *The Life and Times of Bishop Ullathorne* (London: 1926), Vol. I, p. 296, quotes Rymer: "he [Talbot] declared his conviction 'that there was nothing which, if he chose to act in an underhand way, he could not carry through.' " Sharing a somewhat different opinion, Lord Acton considered him one of "the most judicious of chamberlains." *Cambridge Historical Journal*, Vol. VIII (1946), p. 190. Talbot continued in favor with the Holy Father until his reason gave way and he was removed to an asylum at Passy, a suburb of Paris. Until his death in 1886, the Pope refused to allow his rooms to be disturbed, always hoping for his return to sanity. Purcell, *op. cit.*, p. 485.

49. Talbot had visited St. Thomas in 1855 and saw the great need for a religious community in the island. On his return, he suggested to the Holy Father that the Redemptorists should take the post. He then informed Father Mauron what he had done (A.R.B., *Ruland Papers*, Douglas to Ruland, August 14, 1856). The Rector Major decided to accept the foundation rather than run the risk of refusing and then being obliged to take it (A.R.R., *Observantia*, Liber Consultationum, July 16, 1856). The foundation was then assigned to the American Province since a knowledge of English was required in the priests who would labor there.

50. A.P.F., *Hecker Papers*, de Held to Hecker, September 27, 1857, an answer to Hecker's of September 17th in which Hecker evidently told de Held that Talbot was prejudiced against him. Father Mauron also told this to Ruland: "If Father Hecker flatters himself with the hope of gaining the support of Msgr. Talbot . . . he has made a serious miscalculation because Msgr. Talbot is much interested in St. Thomas" (A.R.B., *Ruland Papers*, Mauron to Ruland, September 3, 1857).

51. A.P.F., *Hecker Papers*, Hecker to Fathers, November 20, 1857, says that both Talbot and de Merode used their influence with the Holy Father in favor of the General. In his letter to the Fathers, November 26, 1857, Father Hecker says: "Card. Reisach is a friend of the Congregation." Aubert, *op. cit.*, p. 283, claims that Reisach had a role "not negligible" in regard to questions involving German people.

52. A.P., *S.R.C., Amer. Cent.*, Vol. 18, 137–142. A draft of this report is in the A.R.R., *Prov. Amer.*, I, 5. A copy made from the one submitted to Barnabò is in the A.P.F., *Hecker Papers*.

53. A.P., *S.R.C., Amer. Cent.*, Vol. 18, 138. At the time he wrote his reply

to Father Hecker's statement, Father Mauron had received a report which Father Helmpraecht on orders from Father Ruland had sent to Rome "on the curious Hecker affair." Perhaps this is what Father Mauron meant by "the report received . . . from other American Fathers." However, this Helmpraecht report has no information on the question of Father Hecker's journey to Rome. The New York Rector divided his observations into a statement of the facts in the case and his opinion on the American house. In the first section, he listed seven points which he labeled as "factual": the American Fathers would like to have the provincial chosen by the Province; they contended that America should be converted by Americans; they do not want the American students obliged to learn the German language; they are displeased that the government of the Congregation is German from top to bottom; they were offended that one of them was not a delegate to the General Chapter of 1855; they were discontented because there was no American represented in the Consulta at Rome; they do not like to give a mission with English-speaking foreign Fathers. Then he submitted his opinion on the advisability of a foundation consisting either of American- or Irish-born Fathers alone, or one such as Father Hecker wanted in New York made up of predominantly American Fathers. He was opposed to either because he saw in both the danger of a schism and also that the Americans would be concentrating on missions while the German Fathers would be confined to parish work. Then he made the astonishing statement that he believed an observant Redemptorist house would be impossible if there were a Father Hewit, Hecker, and Walworth in the house (A.R.R., *Prov. Amer.*, I, 5, Helmpraecht to Mauron, August 17, 1857). In view of the testimonial he gave to Father Hecker the day he left for Rome declaring him practically a model religious who gave delight and satisfaction to his Superior (A.P.F., *Hecker Papers*, Helmpraecht testimonial, August 5, 1857), his report to Mauron is difficult to understand. His testimonial to Father Hecker clearly contradicts his statement to Father Mauron. Father Hecker had no awareness of the feeling Father Helmpraecht expressed in his report to the Rector Major. Apart from the American Fathers, he was the only Redemptorist in America to whom Father Hecker wrote after his expulsion (*ibid.*, Hecker to the Fathers, September 25, 1857). Father Helmpraecht gave no indication to the American Fathers of his attitude as their letters show. Father Hewit said in his letter to Hecker, October 14, 1857 (*ibid.*): "His heart is yet good and well disposed"; and again on November 22, 1857: "Father Helmpraecht is very kind to us." Apart from Father Helmpraecht's letter to Father Mauron of August 17th and Father Hewit's of July 27, 1857 (A.R.R., *Amer. Prov.* I, 5), no other letters from Fathers of the American Province concerning the Newark or New York proposals were found in the A.R.R.

54. A.P., *A.R.C.*, *Amer. Cent.*, Vol. 18, 138, Mauron to Barnabò, September 30, 1857.

55. *Ibid.*, Vol. 18, 133, Hecker to Barnabò, September 15, 1857.

56. *Ibid.*, Vol. 18, 138 and 138 v, Mauron to Barnabò, September 30, 1857.

57. *Ibid.*, 138 v.

58. *Ibid.*, 139.

59. A.R.R., *Amer. Prov.*, I, 2, Ruland to Mauron, July 31, 1857.

60. A.P., *S.R.C.*, *Amer. Cent.*, Vol. 18, 139, Mauron to Barnabò, September 30, 1857.

61. *Ibid.*, 139 v.

62. A.R.B., *Ruland Papers*, Walworth to Ruland, April, 1857. These facts are also contained in Ruland's letter to Mauron, July 31, 1857, A.R.R., *Amer. Prov.*, I, 2.

63. A.P., *S.R.C.*, *Amer. Cent.*, Vol. 18, 139, v, Mauron to Barnabò, September 30, 1857.

64. A.P.F., *Hecker Papers*, Walworth to Hecker, July 23, 1857.

65. *Ibid.*

66. A.P., *S.R.C.*, *Amer. Cent.*, Vol. 18, 141, Mauron to Barnabò, September 30, 1857.

67. *Ibid.*, 140.

68. *Ibid.*, 140 and v.

69. *Ibid.*, 140 v.

70. *Ibid.*, 128 v, Hecker to Barnabò, September 15, 1857.

71. *Ibid.*, 140 v, Mauron to Barnabò, September 30, 1857.

72. *Ibid.*, 140 v, 141.

73. *Ibid.*

74. A.R.B., *Provinces*, Annapolis.

75. Joseph Wuest, *Annales Provinciae Americanae* (Ilchester: 1899), Vol. III, Pars. I, p. 257.

76. *Ibid.*, pp. 316, 341, 352; Vol. III, Pars. II, p. 293.

77. A.R.R., *Amer. Prov.*, I, 2, Ruland to Mauron, November 2, 1857.

78. *Ibid.*, I, 5, Helmpraecht to Mauron, August 17, 1857.

79. A.P., *S.R.C.*, *Amer. Cent.*, Vol. 18, 141 v, Mauron to Barnabò, September 30, 1857.

80. A.R.R., *Observantia*, Liber Consultationum, January 9, February 3, May 5, 1857.

81. A.P., *S.R.C.*, *Amer. Cent.*, Vol. 18, 141 v, 142, Mauron to Barnabò, September 30, 1857.

82. A.A.N.Y., *Hughes Papers*, Hecker to Hughes, December 4, 1857; A.P., *Lett. et Decreta*, Vol. 348, 635, 696.

83. A.P.F., *Hecker Papers*, Hecker to Fathers, October 3, 1857.

84. Purcell, *op. cit.*, p. 123, Talbot to Manning, January 29, 1860.

CHAPTER XV

1. A.P.F., *Hecker Papers*, Hecker to the Fathers, January 1, February 5, 1858. In another letter dated February 26, 1858, Father Hecker writes: "Rome entertains in a greater degree than it is willing to acknowledge, the prevalent notions of Europe in regard to the U. S. We are regarded

as rebels, without any true conception of Christian principles, who do not care for either God, man or the devil."

2. *Ibid.*, Simpson to Hecker, December 5, 1857. Simpson wrote: "A Church which says: 'Do not try after converts. They are more bother than enough. Look at home and stop the vices of our own people. That is our first duty' is ready to be supplanted." Happily, he continued, the Church in various countries had taken means to overcome this apathy toward conversions and he cited the activity of Father Victor de Buck of the Bollandist College for Belgium, Father Gargarin for France, the Baron von Hauthausen for Germany, and Wm. Palmer for Russia.

3. *Ibid.*, Hecker to the Fathers, February 5, 1858; A.U.N.D., *Brownson Papers*, Hecker to Brownson, November 27, 1857.

4. *Ibid.*, September 1, 1857, A.P.F., *Hecker Papers*, Deshon to Hewit and Walworth, August 5, 1857; Hecker to George Hecker, September 19, 1857.

5. *Ibid.*, Hecker to George Hecker, September 1, 1857; A.U.N.D., *Brownson Papers*, September 1, 1857.

6. E. E. Y. Hales, *Pio Nono* (New York: 1954), pp. 283, 284; R. Aubert, *Le Pontificat de Pie IX* (Paris: 1952), pp. 39–40.

7. Hales, *op. cit.*, p. 284. The author also says that "the Pope often expressed the keenest displeasure with what it [*Civiltà Cattolica*] said." However, Curci held his post as editor until 1863 when his writings, considered too progressive, clashed with the views of Pius IX and he was removed. *Ibid.*

8. A.U.N.D., *Brownson Papers*, Hecker to Brownson, October 24, 1857.

9. A photostat of the handwritten English copy of the article which Father Hecker gave to Curci is among the *Hecker Papers* in the A.P.F. This photostat was made in 1933 for Father John J. Burke, C.S.P., by Father M. Barbera, S.J., associate editor of the *Civiltà Cattolica*. When he sent the photostats, Father Barbera noted that the original manuscript "was translated into Italian by Father Brunengo, S.J., associate editor." The article appeared in two issues of the *Civiltà*. The first came out November 21, 1857, No. CLXXXIV, Third Series, Vol. 8, pp. 385–402; the second, December 5, 1857, No. CLXXXV, Third Series, Vol. 8, pp. 513–529. The Italian title was "Riflessioni sopra il presente e l'avvenire de Cattolicismo negli Stati Uniti d'America." In the following notes, the first page number referring to quotations from the article is the page of the English copy in A.P.F.; the second number refers to the pages of the *Civiltà* for the issues mentioned above.

10. P. 3; pp. 386–387.

11. Pp. 4–5; pp. 387–389.

12. Pp. 6–7; p. 389.

13. Pp. 7–13; pp. 390–394.

14. P. 13; p. 394.

15. Pp. 15–19; pp. 395–398.

16. Pp. 20–28; pp. 398–402.

17. A.P.F., *Hecker Papers*, Hecker to the Fathers, October 10, 1857.

18. Pp. 1–2; pp. 513–515. The editor appended a few lines to this section of the article pointing out that the relationship of Church and State in the United States though admirable should not be considered as applicable to all countries. A.U.N.D., *Brownson Papers,* Hecker to Brownson, November 27, 1857.

19. Pp. 4–6; pp. 516–517.

20. Pp. 7–10; pp. 518–520. This account of the Nunnery Committee is borne out by J. Allen Billington, *The Protestant Crusade* (New York: 1938), pp. 414–415. The un-American character of Know-Nothingism was advanced by Brownson in "The Native Americans" and "The Know-Nothings" in *Brownson's Quarterly Review* for July, 1854, and January, 1855.

21. Pp. 13–16; pp. 522–524.

22. Pp. 17–18; pp. 524–525.

23. Pp. 19–22; pp. 526–527.

24. Pp. 22–24; pp. 527–528.

25. This paragraph is not in the English copy but only in the *Civiltà*, pp. 528–529.

26. A.P.F., *Hecker Papers,* Hecker to the Fathers, November 20, 1857; A.U.N.D., *Brownson Papers,* Hecker to Brownson, November 27, 1857. When the American Fathers read the articles, they were quite surprised at Father Hecker's courage. Father Deshon wrote: "I tremble at your boldness in hazarding views and opinions which are likely to prove obnoxious to the prevailing current of the Italian mind" (A.P.F., *Hecker Papers,* Deshon to Hecker, December 14, 1857). Walworth wrote: "Bishop Bayley was struck by the articles . . . and thought they were likely to do us more harm than good in this present juncture of circumstances." Then he proceeded to lecture Father Hecker: "You are not in a position to open the eyes of people at Rome or in Europe to the true state of things here in America, for the truth will not bear to be told. The great difficulty in the way of converting America is in the weak, undisciplined and discordant elements which compose the Catholic body here and there is no one powerful enough to dare state the simple truth, for that truth is a scandal and he would be crushed if he did. Least of all should one attempt it who is in a position so delicate and dangerous as you and we are." (*Ibid.,* Walworth to Hecker, January 3, 1857.) That both Bayley and Walworth were wrong subsequent events proved. The articles were a great help to Hecker's cause. Even before hearing from America, Father Hecker knew the articles were extremely forthright. Cardinal Barnabò told him he was surprised that the *Civiltà* carried them (*ibid.,* Hecker to Fathers, October 10, 1857) and a member of the Holy Office told him "if an Italian had written them, they would have had him up at once" (*ibid.,* November 20, 1857).

27. *Civiltà Cattolica,* No. CLXXXIV, Third Series, Vol. 8 (November 21, 1857), p. 25.

28. A.P.F., *Hecker Papers,* Hecker to Fathers, November 12, 1857. In a

letter, February 1, 1858, Father Hecker reported that the articles "have been translated and published in France, Belgium and Germany."

29. *Ibid.*, Father Hecker to George Hecker, October 23, 1857; Hecker to Fathers, October 24, 1857.

30. *Ibid.* St. Alphonsus after reaching the age of ninety died at Pagani, August 1, 1787. His body was placed in a vault on the left of the high altar in the Redemptorist Monastery Church of St. Michael's in Nocera. Austin Berthe, C.SS.R., *Life of St. Alphonsus de'Liguori*, translated from the French by Harold Castle, C.SS.R. (Dublin: 1905), Vol. II, pp. 612–615.

31. A.S.J.A., *Smith Papers*, Hecker to Smith, October 13, 1857. Father Ruland had learned from Father Helmpraecht "which he had heard from a third mouth through a priest who was there" that Hecker had journeyed to Nocera with Cardinal Barnabò to see the Rector Major (A.R.R., *Amer. Prov.*, I, 2, Ruland to Mauron, January 5, 1858). After Ruland had related this information to Rome, Father Mauron replied: "The information that Hecker journeyed to Nocera with Cardinal Barnabò is a lie. Hecker was in Naples, while Barnabò was on vacation in Foligno" (A.R.B., *Ruland Papers*, Mauron to Ruland, January 29, 1858). Joseph McSorley, C.S.P., *Father Hecker and His Friends* (St. Louis: 1952), p. 61, makes the statement: "Hecker went with Barnabò to visit the Neapolitan Fathers at Nocera." Hecker had never said that he and Barnabò had made the trip together. In his letter to Father Smith he had written; "Tomorrow morning I leave Rome with the Secretary of Monsigneur Bedini for Naples and Nocera" (A.S.J.A., *Smith Papers*, Hecker to Smith, October 13, 1857); and in a letter to his brother George, he said: "The Pope was away and the Cardinal too, so I took a little recreation" (A.P.F., *Hecker Papers*, Father Hecker to George, October 23, 1857). There is a sentence in a letter Hecker wrote to the Fathers which if not carefully read might give the impression that Barnabò went to Naples with Hecker: "The Pope was out of the city and Card. B.[arnabò] and I took this opportunity of making a little recreation and pilgrimage" (*ibid.*, Hecker to the Fathers, October 24, 1857). In view of the letters mentioned above, Hecker meant that both the Pope and the Cardinal were out of the city, so he took a little vacation. If he were not writing so rapidly, he could have put a comma after Barnabò and then changed the "and" before the "I" to "so" and made his meaning much clearer. He did say further in this October 24th letter: "To-night I will try to see Card. B[arnabò] who returned this morning to Rome," leaving the rather definite impression that he had not been with Barnabò.

32. A.P.F., *Hecker Papers*, Hecker to Josephine Hecker (George's wife), October 24, 1857; Hecker to Fathers, October 24, 1857.

33. *Ibid.*, September 20, 1857.

34. *Ibid.*, October 24, 1857.

35. "Series Moderatorum Generalium eorumque Vicariorum et Consultorum," *Spicilegium Historicum*, 1954, p. 58.

36. A.P.F., *Hecker Papers,* Hecker to the Fathers, October 24, 31, 1857.
37. *Ibid.*
38. *Ibid.*

CHAPTER XVI

1. A.R.B., *Ruland Papers,* Mauron to Ruland, September 3, 1857. Father Ruland noted on the letter "Recd. Oct. 3."
2. *Ibid.*
3. A.R.R., *Prov. Amer.,* I, 2, Ruland to Mauron, October 12, 1857. In a letter to Mauron, November 2, 1857, Ruland again asks for the rein-statement of Father Hecker (A.R.R., *Amer. Prov.,* I, 2). Father Mauron refused these appeals of Ruland, and Father Douglas sent in early November of 1857 his reasons for not readmitting Hecker. Although this letter is not in the Ruland Papers in the A.R.B., Father Ruland quoted sections of it in his letter of December 14th to Father Hewit (A.P.F., *Hecker Papers*). He maintained that the same reasons for dis-missing Hecker militated against his readmission. In addition, he added that Father Hecker had shown no signs of contrition for what he had done, but declared he would do it all over again. Consequently Father Mauron "fears no consequences but is determined come what may to be faithful to his charge and to maintain obedience. He would prefer to abandon the whole American province and to be obliged to withdraw all his subjects from the United States rather than to admit amongst us principles subversive of the very essence of religious life and which St. Alphonsus himself has so strongly condemned" (*ibid.*).
4. A.R.B., *Provinces,* Chron. Balt., October 12, 1857, p. 48.
5. A.P.F., *Hecker Papers,* Deshon to Hecker, October 23, 1857; Walworth to Hecker, October 23, 1857; Hewit to Hecker, November 22, 1857.
6. A.R.R., *Amer. Prov.,* I, 2, Ruland to Mauron, March 2, 1858.
7. A.P.F., *Hecker Papers,* Ruland to Hewit, October 4, 1857.
8. *Ibid.* This rebuke is missing from Mauron's letter to Ruland, September 3, 1857 (A.R.B., *Ruland Papers*). Either Father Ruland or someone else removed this from the letter which is incomplete in A.R.B.
9. A.R.R., *Amer. Prov.,* I, 2, Ruland to Mauron, October 12, November 2, December 11, 1857.
10. A.P.F., *Hecker Papers,* Hewit to Hecker, September 28, October 14, 1857; Deshon to Hecker, September 28, 1857; Walworth to Hecker, September 28, 1857. The reaction of Father Baker is given in a con-versation he had with Father Ruland after the decree of dismissal and which Ruland reported to Mauron on April 4, 1858 (A.R.R., *Amer. Prov.,* I, 2).
11. A.P.F., *Hecker Papers,* Hewit to Hecker, September 28, 1857.
12. *Ibid.,* Deshon to Hecker, September 28, 1857.
13. *Ibid.,* Walworth to Hecker, September 28, 1857.
14. *Ibid.,* Hecker to the Fathers, October 24, 1857.
15. *Ibid.,* de Buggenoms to Hecker, September 24, 1857. After Father de Buggenoms had heard, through the Provincial, Father Mauron's reasons

for dismissing Father Hecker, he wrote on November 26, to Father Hecker: "I will always love you as I did before, if not more as regards praying for you for I cannot see, even after the explanation Fr. Douglas gave to Fr. Coffin of your dismissal, anything amounting to more than a material fault, or rather rash attempt, excused of course by the best motives. . . . I wish you would and I hope you will always preserve the same love for the Cong.[regation] and hope that sooner or later God and our Holy Mother Mary will reinstate you."

16. A.P.F., *Hecker Papers*, de Held to Hecker, September 27, 1857.

17. *Ibid.*, September 28, 1857.

18. *Ibid.*, Hecker to the Fathers, October 31, 1857.

19. The Redemptorist Fathers at Clapham were "grieved" at Father Hecker's dismissal. When people who learned of the dismissal asked about it, they were told "it was a very honorable one — the consequence of a mistake." (*Ibid.*, de Buggenoms to Hecker, November 26, 1857.) Although Father Hecker had written to Father Coffin after he was expelled, the latter did not reply since "he thought it better and more prudent not to answer his letter" (A.R.R., *Douglas Papers*, XLVII, II, Coffin to Douglas, November 10, 1857). Simpson, the editor of the *Rambler*, reported to Father Hecker, "Father Coffin and the rest . . . still love and admire you as before and treat your departure as an honorable one, necessitated by the service to which you felt yourself called" (A.P.F., *Hecker Papers*, Simpson to Hecker, December 5, 1857). When Father Prost, who was in Austria, heard of the dismissal, he wrote to Father Douglas: "Poor Father Hecker! May he come back again. As he did not leave the Congregation of his own will, it is in the power of the our Most Reverend Father Rector Major to be mercyfull[sic]." And on November 25, 1857, he again wrote to Father Douglas after his Provincial learned that Father de Held had written to Father Prost and said that he was surprised at "the rigour" with which the General treated Father Hecker: "I assure you that this surprise was greater in our Father Provincial and Father Coudenhove than in Father de Held" (A.R.R., *Douglas Papers*, I, a, Prost to Douglas, September 28, November 25, 1857). Although the Redemptorists in America could not write directly to Father Hecker, Father Hewit reported on November 22, 1857: "All the Belgian Fathers here are with us; also Father Klaholz" (A.P.F., *Hecker Papers*, Hewit to Hecker). After the decree of March 6, 1858, separating the American Fathers from the Redemptorists had reached America, Father Giesen wrote to Father Mauron: "It is true I love these Fathers" (A.R.R., *Prov. Amer.*, I, 5, Giesen to Mauron, May 26, 1858).

20. This review was published in the form of a long article which ran from page 459 to 503.

21. A.P.F., *Hecker Papers*, Ruland to Hecker, July 2, 1857. In this letter the Provincial said he found the "greatest pleasure" in reading the book which he hoped would "do a great deal of good. May God bless your

labors and by the instrumentality of your book draw many a soul to the Church."

22. *Ibid.*, Hewit to Hecker, July 22, 1857.
23. *Ibid.*, July 26, 1857.
24. A.U.N.D., *Brownson Papers*, Hecker to Brownson, September 1, 1857.
25. In his letter to Hecker on September 29, 1857, Brownson said his review "had been in print several weeks before your letter arrived." A.P.F., *Hecker Papers.*
26. *Ibid.*, Deshon to Hecker. Although undated, internal evidence of the letter fixes the date as December 3, 1857. He says: "Father Walworth went to Newark yesterday." From Walworth to Hecker, December 5, 1857 (*ibid.*), this visit took place on December 2nd; hence Deshon's letter, written a day later, should be dated December 3rd.
27. *Ibid.*
28. *Ibid.*
29. I. T. Hecker, *Aspirations of Nature* (New York: 1857), p. 197.
30. *Brownson's Quarterly Review*, N.S., Vol. II (October, 1857), p. 485.
31. *Ibid.*, p. 478.
32. *Ibid.*, p. 495.
33. *Ibid.*, p. 496.
34. *Ibid.*, p. 502.
35. A.P.F., *Hecker Papers*, Brownson to Hecker, August 5, 1857.
36. *Ibid.*, September 29, 1857. Henry F. Brownson, *Orestes A. Brownson's Latter Life* (Detroit: 1900), pp. 114–116, prints what apparently was a rough draft of this letter. It does not agree in many details with the one that Hecker received in Rome. For example, on p. 116, Brownson is quoted as saying: "I enclose a brief introduction to the *Mission of America.*" In the letter, Hecker received in Rome, he says: "If you publish the *Mission,* put such an introduction to it as you judge proper. The article was inspired by you and you stand its godfather." Of course Henry Brownson knew nothing of Deshon's visit and states, p. 116, that "Brownson's review of the book was already written when Hecker's letter was received and even if it had not been, he did not see how he could honestly have made it more acceptable to Hecker than it was." Then on p. 119, he writes, "On receipt of Hecker's letter copied above, Brownson added to his article some remarks that seemed to him reasonable and likely to assist Hecker in the accomplishment of the purpose for which he was at Rome." This conclusion on Henry's part is assumed and gratuitous. Contemporary correspondence reveals that any changes or additions were effected by Deshon. Cf. A.P.F., *Hecker Papers*, Deshon to Hecker, December 3, 1857.
37. *Ibid.*, Brownson to Hecker, September 29, 1857.
38. *Brownson's Quarterly Review*, N.S., Vol. II (October, 1857), p. 502.
39. A.P.F., *Hecker Papers*, Brownson to Hecker, September 29, 1857.
40. Abbot Gasquet, O.S.B., "Some Letters of Father Hecker," *Catholic World*, Vol. LXXXIII (May, 1906), Hecker to Simpson, December 28, 1857.

41. A.P.F., *Hecker Papers,* Hewit to Hecker, October 14, 1857.
42. *Ibid.,* Brownson to Hecker, September 29, 1857.
43. *Ibid.,* Father Hecker to George Hecker, October 23, 1857.
44. A.U.N.D., *Brownson Papers,* Hecker to Brownson, October 24, 1857.
45. A.P.F., *Hecker Papers,* Hecker to the Fathers, December 25, 1857.
46. Gasquet, *loc. cit.*
47. A.R.R., *Amer. Prov.,* I, 2, Ruland to Mauron, March 2, 1858.
48. A.U.N.D., *Brownson Papers,* G. H. Hilton to Brownson, October 20, 1857.
49. A.A.B., *Kenrick Papers,* Purcell to Kenrick, September 29, 1857.
50. A.S.J.A., *Smith Papers,* Hecker to Smith, October 13, 1857.
51. *Ibid.;* A.P.F., *Hecker Papers,* Hecker to the Fathers, October 3, 1857.
52. *Ibid.,* October 24, 1857; November 7, 1857.
53. Although the letter of Father Hecker to Father de Held is no longer
    extant (cf. note 37 Chap. XVIII), its content can be gathered from
    Father de Held's reply. He acknowledges he received Father Hecker's
    of October 5th and refers immediately to the words of the Holy
    Father. Writing to the Fathers five days later, Father Hecker repeated
    these words as he heard them from Archbishop Bedini. In view of Father
    de Held's reply to Father Hecker on October 14th where he mentions
    these words, and in view of Father Hecker's letter to the Fathers on
    October 10th, there can be no doubt that Father Hecker mentioned them
    to Father de Held on October 5th. A.P.F., *Hecker Papers,* Hecker to the
    Fathers, October 10, 1857; de Held to Hecker, October 14, 1857.
54. *Ibid.,* de Held to Hecker, October 14, 1857.
55. *Ibid.,* Hecker to the Fathers, October 24, 1857.
56. *Ibid.;* Hecker to the Fathers, October 31, 1857.
57. *Ibid.,* Hecker to the Fathers, October 24, 31, 1857.
58. *Ibid.,* Hecker to the Fathers, October 31, 1857.
59. *Ibid.,* de Held to Barnabò, September 28, 1857. This is a copy of the
    letter that Hecker made before he sent de Held's original to the Holy
    Father. De Held referred to Dechamps as "formerly Provincial in Eng-
    land." This was obviously a slip of the pen since the future Cardinal had
    never been provincial in England, but in Belgium. Cf. "Series Modera-
    torum Generalium Eorumque Vicariorum et Consultorum," *Spicilegium,*
    Vol. 2 (1954), p. 244.
60. A.P.F., *Hecker Papers,* Hecker to Pius IX. This is a copy in Father
    Hecker's handwriting. Though undated, it was probably sent on October
    27th, as two letters Father Hecker wrote to the Fathers on October 24,
    31, 1857, indicate.
61. *Ibid.,* Hecker to the Fathers, October 31, 1857.
62. A.R.B., *Ruland Papers,* Mauron to Ruland, October 8, 1857; A.P.F.,
    Hecker Papers, Ruland to Hewit, December 14, 1857.
63. *Ibid.,* de Held to Hecker, November 1, 1857.
64. *Ibid.*
65. *Ibid.,* Hecker to de Held, November 9, 1857. This is a copy of the letter
    that Father Hecker made and kept.
66. *Ibid.;* Hecker to Fathers, November 26, 1857.

67. *Ibid.*, de Held to Hecker, November 20, 1857.
68. *Ibid.*, Hecker to Fathers, October 24, 1857. This visit was the result of a note that the General had sent telling Father Hecker there was a package for him at the Villa Caserta. The package contained three copies of *Aspirations of Nature*. Father Hecker observed in his letter to the Fathers that the General could have sent the package along with the note "but he no doubt wished to hear some news from me, as I am near the Propaganda and am aware of all that takes place."
69. *Ibid.*, Hecker to Fathers, November 7, 1857; Hecker to de Held, November 9, 1857. Hecker made this visit "in accordance with the express wish" of Cardinal Barnabò. After giving an account of the interview, he told the Fathers in his letter of November 7th, "I felt that nothing could be gained by seeing the Gen.[eral] but I went in obedience to the Card.[inal]" (*ibid.*).
70. *Ibid.*, Hecker to Fathers, November 7, 1857.
71. *Ibid.*, Hecker to de Held, November 9, 1857.
72. *Ibid.*, November 20, 26, 1857; January 1, 1858. In this last letter, Father Hecker told the Fathers that if he had had an audience shortly after the General's, he would have risked "a coup de pied from his Holiness and a sharp reprimand." In his letter of November 20th, he told the Fathers that "Mons. Talbot and another, de Merode, have used their influence in favor of the Gen[eral] and of course adverse to us with the Holy Father. And you must know that the H.[oly] Father is a man who is quick in receiving impressions and at the same time they are not easily removed."
73. *Ibid.*, Hecker to Fathers, January 1, 1858. Father Hecker saw Bizzarri between November 9th and 12th. In his letter to de Held on November 9th, he said he was awaiting Bizzarri's return; in his letter to the Fathers on November 12th, he reported he had seen him.
74. *Ibid.*, Hecker to the Fathers, November 12, 1857.
75. *Ibid.*, January 18, 1858; December 5, 1857. In retrospect, Father Hecker refers to the difficulties he had encountered in getting his case before Archbishop Bizzarri.
76. *Ibid.*, November 12, 1857.
77. *Ibid.*
78. *Ibid.*, October 31, 1857.

CHAPTER XVII

1. A.P.F., *Hecker Papers*, Hecker to the Fathers, September 20, 1857.
2. *Ibid.*
3. *Ibid.*, Hecker to the Fathers, November 12, 1857.
4. *Ibid.*, September 21, October 3, 1857.
5. *Ibid.*, September 20, 1857.
6. Father Hecker noted on a document he had drawn up on January 6, 1858 (*ibid.*), that "Father Francis, Passionist" was his director in Rome. Joseph McSorley, C.S.P., *Father Hecker and His Friends* (St. Louis: 1952), p. 83, quotes a short biographical sketch of Father Francis from the "Necrology Register" of the Passionists.

7. A.P.F., *Hecker Papers,* Hecker to the Fathers, September 20, 1857.
8. *Ibid.*
9. *Ibid.,* September 25, 1857.
10. *Ibid.,* September 20, 1857.
11. Abbot Gasquet, O.S.B., "Some Letters of Father Hecker," *Catholic World,* Vol. LXXXIII (May, 1906), pp. 239–240.
12. A.U.N.D., *Brownson Papers,* Hecker to Brownson, November 27, 1857.
13. A.P.F., *Hecker Papers,* Hecker to the Fathers, October 3, 1857.
14. *Ibid.*
15. *Ibid.,* Walworth to Hecker, October 9, 1857. At the bottom of this letter Walworth added: "Consider this as written in the name of all."
16. *Ibid.,* Walworth, Hewit, Deshon, and Baker to Hecker, October 20, 1857.
17. *Ibid.,* Walworth to Hecker, October 23, 1857.
18. *Ibid.,* Hecker to the Fathers, January 1, 1858.
19. *Ibid.,* Walworth to Hecker, October 23, 1857.
20. *Ibid.,* Hecker to the Fathers, November 20, December 5, 18, 1857; January 1, 1858.
21. *Ibid.,* Walworth to Hecker, October 23, November 17, 1857.
22. *Ibid.,* de Held to Hecker, October 14, 1857.
23. *Ibid.,* Hecker to the Fathers, October 24, 31, November 7, 1857.
24. *Ibid.,* October 24, November 7, 1857.
25. *Ibid.,* November 20, 1857; January 1, 1858.
26. *Ibid.,* January 1, 1858, in which Father Hecker explains to the Fathers the delays that had taken place.
27. *Ibid.,* October 31, 1857.
28. *Ibid.;* November 12, 1857.
29. *Ibid.,* October 31, 1857.
30. *Ibid.,* November 12, 20, 1857.
31. *Ibid.,* November 12, 1857.
32. The original of this document went to Bizzarri, but could not be located in the Vatican Archives (cf. note 37, Chap. XVIII). A copy in the A.P.F. is in Walworth's handwriting. Apparently it was the first draft which the Fathers kept when they sent the finished manuscript to Rome. Although this draft is unsigned, the one sent to Father Hecker was signed by Walworth, Hewit, Deshon, and Baker. Cf. Walworth to Hecker, November 17, 1857. The document is not dated but was sent to Rome between November 11th and 14th. *Ibid.*
33. *Ibid., Hecker Papers,* memorial of American Fathers to Pius IX, November, 1857, pp. 2–6. In Father Walworth's manuscript, p. 5, no mention was made of "the conversion of the Protestants of this country." This was later written in by another hand. The writing seems to be that of Father Deshon.
34. *Ibid.,* pp. 7–9.
35. *Ibid.,* pp. 10–11.
36. *Ibid.,* p. 12.
37. *Ibid.,* p. 13. This is the first time in the correspondence that an appeal

to the Holy See was considered as sufficient reason for making the journey.

38. *Ibid.*, pp. 13–15.
39. *Ibid.*, pp. 15–18.
40. *Ibid.*, p. 18.
41. *Ibid.*, Walworth to Hecker, November 17, 1857. Father Hewit kept a copy of his letter to the Cardinal on which he wrote: "This with the erasures and alterations agrees with the copy sent to the Cardinal. Aug. F. Hewit." Though undated it was mailed November 17, 1857. It is in the *Hecker Papers*, A.P.F.
42. *Ibid.*, Hewit to Barnabò, November, 1857, pp. 1–18.
43. *Ibid.*, pp. 18–19.
44. *Ibid.*, p. 20.
45. *Ibid.*, p. 21.
46. *Ibid.*, pp. 24–25. Before the trouble about the American house broke, George Hecker had provided in his will for a bequest to be given to the Redemptorists for the proposed foundation. Father Hecker remembered this while in Rome and on November 7, 1857, wrote to his brother suggesting a change. He asked him: *"Do make some legal document to meet the present state of affairs —* and as at present I am bound by no vows you can leave what you please to me unconditionally. *Don't forget this* will you?" (*ibid.*, Father Hecker to George).
47. *Ibid.*, pp. 25–26.
48. *Ibid.*, Walworth to Hecker, November 17, 1857.
49. A.A.N.Y., *Hughes Papers*, Mauron to Hughes, October 8, 1857. Father Mauron sent a copy of this letter in German to Father Ruland on October 8, 1857, A.R.B., *Ruland Papers*. Joseph Wuest, C.SS.R., *Annales Provinciae Americanae*, Vol. III, Pars. II (Ilchester: 1899), pp. 265–266, reprints this version. In the A.R.R., *Prov. Amer.*, I, 5, October 8, 1857, there is a rough draft of the letter both in English and in French. Mauron also wrote to Kenrick on October 30, 1857, informing him of his action (A.R.B., *Ruland Papers*, Douglas to Ruland, October 30, 1857, enclosing a copy of the letter to Kenrick). There are only two differences between this letter and the one to Hughes. Writing to Kenrick, Mauron added that although he had asked the Provincial to inform Kenrick of the separation, he felt it was his duty to give the Archbishop a personal explanation. The other difference was the omission of the Rector Major's commendatory words about Father Hecker as a priest. There is no record in the A.A.B. or the A.R.R. that Kenrick acknowledged or answered the letter.
50. A.R.R., *Prov. Amer.*, I, 5, Hughes to Mauron, October 31, 1857.
51. A.P.F., *Hecker Papers*, Deshon to Hecker, December 3, 1857. (Although this letter is undated, the time it was written can be determined as December 3rd, from a comparison with Walworth to Hecker, December 5, 1857.) Relating his interview with Hughes, Deshon wrote that he said to the Archbishop: " 'Father H.[ecker] explained them [his reasons

for going to Rome] to you when at Saratoga.' He said not exactly but still he understood them in the main."

52. A.S.J.A., *Smith Papers*, Hughes to Smith, December 29, 1857.

53. A.R.R., *Prov. Amer.*, I, 5, Hughes to Mauron, October 31, 1857. This is clearly the idea expressed in this letter.

54. A.E.C., *Talbot Papers*, Douglas to Talbot [November, 1857]; A.R.B., *Ruland Papers*, Douglas to Ruland, December 2, 1857.

55. A.P., *S.R.C.*, *Amer. Cent.*, Vol. 17, 1125–1127, Hughes to Barnabò.

56. A.A.N.Y., *Hughes Papers*, Hecker to Hughes, December 4, 1857; A.P.F., *Hecker Papers*, Hecker to Hughes. This is a copy of the original letter made by George V. Hecker before he delivered the original to the Archbishop. Cf. *ibid.*, G. V. Hecker to Rev. and dear Father, December 28, 1857.

57. *Ibid.*, Father Hecker to George Hecker, December 5; Hecker to the Fathers, December 25, 1857. Father Hecker does not identify Smith by name but refers to him as "a friend."

58. A.A.N.Y., *Hughes Papers*, Smith to Hughes, December 5, 1857.

59. A.P.F., *Hecker Papers*, Father Hecker to George Hecker, December 5, 1857.

60. *Ibid.*, Deshon to Hecker, December 3, 1857 (cf. note 51 above for date).

61. *Ibid.;* Walworth to Hecker, December 5, 1857.

62. *Ibid.*, Walworth to Hecker, January 3, 1858.

63. *Ibid.*, G. V. Hecker to Rev. and dear Father, December 28, 1857.

64. *Ibid.*, Hughes to Hecker, December 29, 1857.

65. A.S.J.A., *Smith Papers*, Hughes to Smith, December 29, 1857. Smith gave the section of this letter dealing with Father Hecker to Barnabò in an Italian translation. This extract was later sent to Bizzarri on February 1, 1858. A.P., *Amer. Cent.*, Vol. 17, 1355. The statement of the Archbishop that he had not interfered in the internal affairs of a religious community in the past is not borne out by the prominent and forceful part he took in separating the Sisters of Charity in New York from their motherhouse in Emmitsburg. When trying to secure direct and independent control of the Sisters in New York, Hughes asked that the affairs of the Sisters be brought to the attention of the Baltimore Council in 1846. In a letter to Archbishop Eccleston: "He declared that there was a certain amount of dissatisfaction among the Sisters of Charity over what he described as the passing of 'the primitive spirit of their Institute' and among other things the failure to adhere strictly to the Constitution, with the result that 'they will find themselves in a religious Community entirely different from that which they intended to join and to which their first vows bound them.'" Hughes finally carried through the separation and set up an independent community under his own immediate jurisdiction, a move which Bishop Chanche of Natchez deplored: "I am very sorry that Bishop Hughes has taken the step which he has in relation to the Sisters of Charity." Joseph B. Code, *Bishop John Hughes and the Sisters of Charity*, n.d., pp. 9, 41, n. 74. In this brochure, which is a reprint from the *Miscellanea Historica*

in honorem L. Van der Essen, Father Code gives the history of the separation from documentary sources.

66. A.P.F., *Hecker Papers,* Hecker to Fathers, December 25, 1857.
67. The original which Father Hecker submitted to Bizzarri was given to Father Mauron for an answer in January, 1858. Before returning it, he made a copy which is now in A.R.R., *Prov. Amer.,* I, 5, February, 1858. Father Hecker's English original as well as an Italian translation are in A.P.F., *Hecker Papers.* Though the document is undated, it was submitted to Bizzarri, November 21, 1857. Cf. Hecker to Fathers, November 20, 1857 (*ibid.*) in which he says he will hand in his memorial on the next day. The following quotations from the memorial are taken from the copy in the A.R.R.
68. A.R.R., *Prov. Amer.,* I, 5, Hecker to Holy Father, p. 1, Appendixes 1 and 2.
69. *Ibid.,* pp. 2–3.
70. *Ibid.,* p. 3.
71. *Ibid.,* p. 4.
72. A.P.F., *Hecker Papers,* Hecker to Fathers, November 12, 1857.
73. *Ibid.,* Hecker to Fathers, December 5, 1857.
74. *Ibid.,* Hecker to Fathers, January 9, 1858.
75. *Ibid.,* December 5, 1857.
76. *Ibid.,* November 26, December 5, 1857.

Chapter XVIII

1. A.P.F., *Hecker Papers,* Father Hecker to George Hecker, August 24, 1857.
2. *Ibid.,* Hecker to the Fathers, February 19, 1858.
3. *Ibid.,* December 4, 16, 1857. (Although this last letter is dated December 26th, the date is obviously a mistake. Father Hecker says in his letter: "Indeed I hope to have a chance to have a private audience with the Holy Father." This took place on December 17th. Other internal evidence fixes the correct date as December 16th.) January 23, 1858.
4. *Ibid.,* Father Hecker to George Hecker, December 4, 16, 1857; January 23, 1858.
5. In the fall of 1857, Robert Seton, the grandson of Mother Seton, had come to Rome to study for the priesthood. Through Dr. Bernard Smith he met Father Hecker and shared the American missionary's apartment for several weeks. According to Seton, both he and Father Hecker went to the Café Greco for breakfast where the American missionary "took every opportunity to talk religion to anyone who understood English." In his discussions with Father Hecker about religion in America, Seton noticed that his friend avoided using the words "heretics, Protestants when speaking of those outside the Church" and called them "our separated brethren, our ill-informed friends." Writing more than sixty years later, he said that his host was "the pleasantest man to live with. . . . No one could meet him without feeling that he was one of God's

noblest works — an honest man." Robert Seton, *Memories of Many Years* (New York: 1923), pp. 122–123.

6. A.P.F., *Hecker Papers*, Brown to Hecker, May 8, 1859. In this letter Brown speaks of the café as their meeting place.

7. *Encyclopedia Americana* (New York: 1923), Vol. 4, p. 605, has a short biographical sketch of Brown.

8. A.P.F., *Hecker Papers*, Hecker to the Fathers, December 9, 1857.

9. *Ibid.;* notes made in Rome, December 8, 1857.

10. *Ibid.;* Hecker to the Fathers, December 9, 1857, which has a postscript dated December 12th.

11. *Ibid.*, Hecker to the Fathers, December 18, 1857.

12. *Ibid.*, November 20, 1857.

13. *Ibid.*, January 18, 1858. The same sentiment is in Hecker's letter to Brownson, November 27, 1857, A.U.N.D., *Brownson Papers*.

14. *Ibid.*, January 18, 1858.

15. *Ibid.*, November 7, 1857; A.U.N.D., *Brownson Papers*, November 27, 1857.

16. *Ibid.* Toward the end of December, Father Hecker had given up all idea of writing the proposed articles, A.P.F., *Hecker Papers*, Hecker to the Fathers, January 18, 1858. He had reached this decision before a letter of Father Hewit dated December 22, 1857, reached him. Hewit had said: "It is our unanimous opinion that the articles which you speak of as to be written are on ground too delicate and perilous to be ventured on while our common interests are in such danger and that we do not wish these latter to be identified with theories and projects likely to alarm prejudice and awaken opposition." In his reply of January 18, 1858, Father Hecker said the same reasons expressed by Father Hewit caused him to forsake writing the articles (A.P.F., *Hecker Papers*).

17. *Ibid.*, Hecker to the Fathers, December 5, 1857. In his letter of December 18, 1857, Father Hecker told the Fathers he had talked with the General who said Bizzarri "demanded the Circular and that he had sent it to him."

18. A.P.F., *Hecker Papers*, November 12, December 5, 1857.

19. These English documents are in A.P.F., *Hecker Papers*, Hecker to Barnabò, September 15, 1857; Hecker to the Pope, November 21, 1857. The Italian version of the statement to Barnabò is in A.P., *S.R.C., Amer. Cent.*, Vol. 18, 126–135 v. The Italian rough copy of the plea to the Pope is in A.P.F., *Hecker Papers*, and a copy of the final draft sent to Bizzarri is in A.R.R., *Prov. Amer.*, I, 5. When Bizzarri sent it to the Rector Major for an answer, Father Mauron had a copy of the document made before returning it.

20. In quoting from this document drawn up by the lawyer, I have used the copy in the A.R.R., *Prov. Amer.*, I, 5. The page numbers in the following citations refer to this copy.

21. *Ibid.*, pp. 1 and 2.

22. *Ibid.*, pp. 2 and 3.

23. *Ibid.*, p. 3.
24. *Ibid.*, p. 4.
25. *Ibid.*, pp. 15–16. The original of this letter is in A.P.F., *Hecker Papers*, and is dated August 3, 1857.
26. *Ibid.*, p. 21. The original of this letter to Hecker dated August 2, 1857, is also in A.P.F., *Hecker Papers*.
27. *Ibid.*, p. 21.
28. A.P.F., *Hecker Papers*, memorial of American Fathers to Pius IX, November [14], 1857, pp. 12–14.
29. A.R.R., *Prov. Amer.*, I, 5, Nullity of the decree of Expulsion, p. 8.
30. *Ibid.*, pp. 8–10.
31. *Ibid.*, p. 10.
32. *Ibid.*, pp. 10–11.
33. *Ibid.*, p. 11.
34. *Ibid.*, pp. 13–15.
35. *Ibid.*, pp. 15–21. All these documents are in A.P.F., *Hecker Papers*.
36. A.P.F., *Hecker Papers*, Hecker to Fathers, December 9, 1857.
37. On November 11, 1857, de Held wrote to Father Hecker and enclosed this letter to Barnabò who sent de Held an acknowledgment on November 30th. A.P.F., *Hecker Papers*, de Held to Hecker, November 11, 1857; A.P., *Lett et Decreta*, Vol. 348, p. 365, Barnabò noted that he sent the letter to Bizzarri. Apparently the letter was sealed and Father Hecker never saw its contents although Barnabò referred to it as a recommendation for Father Hecker. This plus the letters of September 28, 1857, of de Held to Barnabò and the letter of de Held to Hecker, October 14, 1857, were in Bizzarri's possession.

During the course of the trial, Barnabò sent numerous documents to Bizzarri, some of which were copied before they went to the Congregation of Bishops and Regulars. The documents of this Congregation are now in the Vatican archives. Father Hecker's case listed in the *Protocollo generale degli Affari della Segreteria della S. Congregatione de Vescovi e Regolari*,

dal numero $\dfrac{22511}{4}$ al numero $\dfrac{27260}{4}$, p. 23, was given the number $\dfrac{23524}{4}$.

The Redemptorist General Archivist, Father Sampers, and myself made an exhaustive search for the dossier containing the documents in this case. The attendants in the Vatican archives could not locate it. Neither was it in Bizzarri's or Bedini's personal papers in the Vatican. Through the kindness of Father James Risk, S.J., professor of Canon Law at the Gregorian University, we had Father Grisar, S.J., who teaches archive studies, make a search in other sections of the Vatican archives, but he could not find it. We also examined the dossiers in the present archives of the Congregation of Religious under both Redemptorist and Paulist, but it was not there. Neither could it be located in the Archives for Extraordinary Affairs. Knowing that Pius IX had called for all the documents in the case before he rendered a decision, we thought that the dossier might still be among his papers which are not available at the present time. However, Monsignor Serafini, the only one who has access to these papers, checked for us and said the dossier was not there.

In the absence of these papers, it is still possible to get a fairly complete picture of all that went before Bizzarri. Barnabò either sent copies, or copied originals, before he forwarded them to the Secretary and noted what was sent and on what date. Fuller statements were either in Propaganda Archives, the Redemptorist General Archives, or the Paulist Archives. About the only letters for which we could not locate any copies were two letters that Father de Held sent — one to Barnabò, November 11, 1857; one to Bizzarri, February 25, 1858. Since there were no written reports submitted to the Holy Father but only given orally, it is doubtful that the dossier would contain any decision on the legality of the decree of expulsion. Possibly there might be notes that Bizzarri made to guide him in the progress of the case or when he discussed it with the Pope. However, this question cannot be answered until the dossier is located, if it is still extant.

38. A.P.F., *Hecker Papers*, Father Hecker to George Hecker, December 16, 1857; cf. note 3 above for explanation of this date.
39. *Ibid.*, Hecker to the Fathers, December 5, 1857.
40. *Ibid.*
41. A.P., *S.R.C.*, *Amer. Cent.*, Vol. 17, 1332.
42. A.P.F., *Hecker Papers*, Hecker to the Fathers, December 18, 1857.
43. A.P.F., *Hecker Papers*, audience with Holy Father, December 17, 1857. Father Hecker recorded his interview after he left the Holy Father and then enclosed that in a letter to the Fathers dated December 18, 1857 (*ibid.*). Walter Elliott, C.S.P., *Life of Father Hecker* (New York: 1891), p. 267, incorrectly gives the date of the audience as December 22. After the volume was published, Father Elliott noticed the mistake and corrected it on typed copies of the correspondence that he used. Joseph McSorley, C.S.P., *Father Hecker and His Friends* (St. Louis: 1952), p. 66, speaks of the audience. Though he does not give the date, he places it in a sequence of events that might lead the reader to think it occurred in February of 1858.
44. A.P.F., *Hecker Papers*, Hecker to the Fathers, December 18, 1857.
45. *Ibid.*, audience with the Holy Father, December 17, 1857.
46. *Ibid.*, Father Hecker to George Hecker, December 18, 1857.
47. *Ibid.*
48. *Ibid.*, Hecker to the Fathers, December 18, 1857.
49. *Ibid.*, and Father Hecker to George Hecker, December 18, 1857.
50. *Ibid.*, Hecker to the Fathers, December 18, 1857.
51. A.P., *Lett. et Decreta*, Vol. 348, 778 and 779.
52. A.P.F., *Hecker Papers*, Hecker to the Fathers, December 18, 1857.
53. *Ibid.*
54. *Ibid.*, Walworth to Hecker, December 5, 1857.
55. *Ibid.*, Hewit to Hecker, January 11, 1858. Walworth's letter to Purcell is in A.U.N.D., *Cincinnati Papers*, December 25, 1857. Neither Hewit's

letter to Kenrick nor Walworth's to Spalding is in the A.A.B.

56. A.P.F., *Hecker Papers,* Hecker to the Fathers, January 1, 1858. A copy of Bayley's letter is in A.P., *S.R.C., Amer. Cent.,* Vol. 17, 330 and v. Barnabò sent the original of this letter to Bizzarri in January of 1858. Barnabò wrote to Bayley acknowledging the letter and told him he sent it to the Congregation of Bishops and Regulars which was handling the case.

57. *Catholic Encyclopedia* (New York: 1910), pp. 117–118. Joseph A. Chisholm's article on Halifax has a brief biographical sketch of the Bishop.

58. A.P.F., *Hecker Papers,* Hecker to the Fathers, January 9, 18, 1858. Connolly arrived in Rome the early part of December. Bernard Smith told Hughes of his accident on December 5, 1857 (A.A.N.Y., *Hughes Papers*). Hughes answered on December 29, saying: "I am exceedingly tickled at the adventures of good Dr. Connolly. I do not know any Bishop who could go through the ceremony of being robbed and plundered by bandits, more gracefully than his Lordship. . . . I enjoy this the more because he is exceedingly brave and speaks Italian almost like a Roman" (A.S.J.A., *Smith Papers*).

59. A.P.F., *Hecker Papers,* Connolly to Hecker, January 20, 1858. There are 22 Connolly letters among the Hecker Papers in A.P.F. All of Connolly's papers are missing from the archives of the Archdiocese of Halifax.

60. *Ibid.,* Hecker to the Fathers, January 9, 18, 1858.

61. *Ibid.*

62. *Ibid.,* January 18, 1858.

63. *Ibid.*

64. *Ibid.*

Chapter XIX

1. A.P.F., *Hecker Papers,* Walworth to Hecker, December 6, 11, 1857.

2. *Ibid.*

3. *Ibid.,* Hecker to Walworth, January 1, 1858.

4. A.P., *S.R.C., Amer. Cent.,* Vol. 17, 1330 and v, Bayley to Barnabò. This is a copy since Bedini sent the original to Bizzarri, January 4, 1858.

5. A.P., *Lett. et Decreta,* Vol. 349, 64.

6. A.P.F., *Hecker Papers,* Hecker to the Fathers, December 25, 1857.

7. *Ibid.,* January 18, 1858. This letter is misdated. It should be January 16, since Father Hecker refers to the day as Saturday. January 18 was a Monday.

8. *Ibid.,* January 23, 1858.

9. *Ibid.,* January 25, 1858. (This letter is also misdated and should be January 24 since Father Hecker refers to the day as Sunday. January 25 was a Monday.) February 19, 1858.

10. A.P., *S.R.C., Amer. Cent.,* Vol. 17, 1113 and v, Kenrick to Barnabò, December 30, 1857; 1133–1134, Lynch to Barnabò, December 30, 1857; 791–792, Spalding to Barnabò, January 2, 1858 (the year on the letter is 1857, but content shows it should be 1858); Vol. 18, 36 and v,

Purcell to Barnabò, January 23, 1858; 50 and v, Barry to Barnabò, February, 1858; 101 and v, de Goesbriand to Barnabò, February 27, 1858. One of the prelates whom the Fathers asked to write was Bishop Michael O'Connor of Pittsburgh. Although he did not write to Barnabò, he sent a letter to Dr. Smith in which he said, "I do not well know what I could say in any controversy that may exist as I scarcely know how I could interfere at all in the question . . . while my respect for Father Hecker is great, I have still greater respect for the Community which is now well established in the United States" (A.S.J.A., *Smith Papers*, O'Connor to Smith, January 6, 1858). In his letter to Smith of February 24, 1858, O'Connor was more explicit saying that with regard to the American Redemptorist house, he thought Rome should not "try much in that direction." Then he spoke of Hecker as "a worthy priest" and said that if he decided to remain a secular priest "He is just the kind of man I want at our Cathedral." Father Hecker saw these letters and years later said to Father Elliott that Bishop O'Connor "was the only one of the American Prelates who was against us" (A.P.F., *Elliott Papers*, Notes, November, 1885).

11. A.P., *S.R.C., Amer. Cent.*, Vol. 17, 1113 and v, Kenrick to Barnabò, December 30, 1857. Writing to Spalding on February 22, 1858, Kenrick said: "I wrote to Rome in behalf of Father Hecker to whom I had given a letter of recommendation to the Cardinal Prefect without being apprized of the object of his journey" (A.A.B., *Spalding Papers*). He is referring here to his letter of July 29, 1857. At the time Hewit asked for this letter, the Fathers were under the impression that the Provincial would give permission for the trip and did not expect trouble to arise. However, Father Hecker asked Hughes and Bayley for letters after the Provincial's refusal and both Prelates were informed of his action. Kenrick thought that it was "imprudent" of the Fathers "to press the matter of an English house" when they did.

12. A.P., *S.R.C., Amer. Cent.*, Vol. 17, 791–792, Spalding to Barnabò, January 2, 1858.

13. A.P.F., *Hecker Papers*, Hecker to the Fathers, February 1, 1858. Again Hecker had the right day, Sunday, which was January 31st, but the wrong date. The letter should be dated January 31st.

14. *Ibid.*, January 25, 1858. Beginning with this letter, Father Hecker kept a diary in his letters. He dated the letter the day he began, then before mailing it, he included events under the date he recorded them. The incident of Barnabò's reaction to the letters is dated January 28th.

15. *Ibid.*, February 1, 1858. Although dated February 1st, the day was a Sunday which was January 31st, the true date of the letter.

16. A.P., *Lett. et Decreta*, Vol. 349, 124.

17. A.P.F., *Hecker Papers*, Hecker to Fathers, February 3, in letter begun February 1, 1858.

18. *Ibid.*; February 11, 1858. Here Hecker put the wrong month on the letter, January 11th. Content obviously shows it was February.

19. *Ibid.*

20. A.R.R., *Prov. Amer.*, I, 5, February, 1858, Mauron to Bizzarri refers to Bizzarri's letter "dated the 3rd of the present month," sending Hecker's documents and requesting an answer. Bizzarri's letter of February 3rd is not in A.R.R.

21. A.R.B., *Ruland Papers*, January 29, 1858. In reply Father Ruland said he was quite disturbed by this news. He asked Father Mauron to do all he could to prevent the Holy See from granting the dispensation. Otherwise the consequences were to be very serious for the American Province. If the General dismissed the Fathers the results would not be as disastrous as if the Holy See dispensed them. A.R.R., *Amer. Prov.*, I, 2, Ruland to Mauron, March 2, 1858.

22. A.P.F., *Hecker Papers*, Hecker to the Fathers, February 5, 1858, in letter of January 31, 1858.

23. *Ibid.*

24. *Ibid.*

25. *Ibid.*, February 5, in letter of January 31, 1858.

26. A.R.R., *Prov. Amer.*, I, 5, Mauron to Bizzarri, February, 1858. Father Mauron kept copies of all these documents. Though his letter to Bizzarri containing them is undated, the date he submitted them was between February 3rd and February 10th. In his letter he acknowledged Bizzarri's of the 3rd. And in his letter to the Holy Father, February 11th (*ibid.*), he said he had submitted his reply to the Congregation of Bishops and Regulars.

27. *Ibid.*, Mauron to Bizzarri, February, 1858, pp. 1–4.

28. *Ibid.*, p. 4.

29. He enclosed a copy of this document with his reply. The original of the September 30th response is in A.P., *S.R.C., Amer. Cent.*, Vol. 18, 137–142.

30. A.R.R., *Prov. Amer.*, I, 5, Mauron to Bizzarri, February, 1858, p. 5.

31. *Ibid.*, p. 8.

32. *Ibid.*

33. A.P.F., *Hecker Papers*, Father Hecker to George Hecker, September 1, 1857.

34. A.P., *S.R.C., Amer. Cent.*, Vol. 18, 126–136, Hecker to Barnabò, September 15, 1857.

35. A.R.R., *Prov. Amer.*, I, 5, Mauron to Bizzarri, February, 1858, pp. 9–11.

36. *Litterae Circulares Reverendissimi Patris Nicolae Mauron* (Rome: 1896), p. 3.

37. A.R.R., *Prov. Amer.*, I, 5, Mauron to Bizzarri, February, 1858, pp. 11–12.

38. *Ibid.*, p. 13.

39. *Ibid.*, Motivi Segreti, pp. 1 and 2.

40. *Ibid.*, p. 2.

41. *Ibid.*, pp. 2–8.

42. *Ibid.*, p. 8.

43. *Ibid.*, Mauron to Bizzarri, February, 1858.

44. *Ibid.*, Mauron to Pius IX, February 11, 1858.

45. *Ibid.*
46. A.P.F., *Hecker Papers*, Hecker to the Fathers, February 26, 1858.
47. *Ibid.*, February 19, March 2, 1858.
48. *Ibid.*, February 27, 1858.
49. *Ibid.*, February 19, 1858.
50. *Ibid.*, January 18, 1858.
51. *Ibid.*, March 6, 1858, in letter begun March 5, 1858.
52. *Ibid.*, Father Hecker to George Hecker, February 19, 1858.
53. *Ibid.*, Hecker to the Fathers, February 19, 1858. The week before this, Father Hecker had received "an interesting and brotherly letter" from Father Baker (*ibid.*, Hecker to the Fathers, February 11, 1858) which left no doubt in Father Hecker's mind that the young missionary could see the lighter side of his troubles. He began by saying: "When I think of the feelings with which you will receive this letter, I am reminded of a story I once heard of a lady who had two children whom she loved very unequally. One day the less favored child came to her door and knocked. 'Is that you dear?' the lady answered from within. 'No, Ma,' the little fellow replied, 'it ain't *dear*, it's only me.' So I suspect that when you see this missive you will say, 'Ah, there's a letter from America! perhaps it's from Father Walworth, or perhaps it's from Father Hewit, or maybe Deshon has written it!' No, it's only *me*. It's only Father Baker. I thought I'd just write a line for old acquaintance sake, and to show that nowadays when everybody is writing to the Pope and Cardinals and Roman priests, I could do it as well as any body else." Then he told Father Hecker that the American Fathers were delighted he had presented their memorial because until he did they "were in a very unsatisfactory & nondescript position, but now it's all right and we are as proud as the paddy who had 'a reserved case' before the Archbishop of Dublin." Then he spoke about the success of the missions and added that he was "only too glad to take the lowest part in the glorious work to which we have given our lives." He concluded by asking Father Hecker to "accept these few lines as a token of the affectionate remembrance in which you are held by your confrere" (*ibid.*, Baker to Hecker, January 17, 1858).
54. *Ibid.*, Father Hecker to George Hecker, December 18, 1857; February 27, 1858.
55. *Ibid.*, February 27th in the letter begun February 26, 1858.
56. *Ibid.*, March 5, 1857.
57. *Ibid.*, March 11, 1858.
58. *Ibid.*, Hecker to Balzani, March 4, 1858.
59. *Ibid.*, Hecker to the Fathers, March 6th, in letter begun March 2, 1858.
60. A.P., *S.R.C.*, *Amer. Cent.*, Vol. 18, 122 and v, Nuper Nonnulli. Bizzarri sent a copy of the decree to Barnabò with a note saying it was the official decision "relative to the priest Isaac Hecker and other Liguorians of the United States." The copy to Father Mauron was enclosed in a letter of Bizzarri dated March 6, 1858, using the same expression and adding: "Further it is the wish of His Holiness that Your Paternity

must bring it about to provide that in the houses of the Liguorians of the United States, there be [stationed] some Subjects who understand the language of the place for the good of the residents" (A.R.R., *Prov. Amer.*, I, 5, Bizzarri to Mauron). On March 9th, Father Mauron acknowledged this letter and said: "I shall make it my duty to carry out his [Holy Father's] wishes." At the same time Father Mauron thanked the Archbishop "for the gracious part you played, to our great relief, in this affair" (*ibid.*, Mauron to Bizzarri, March 9, 1858).

In the A.P.F. (*Hecker Papers*, March 6, 1858), there are two copies of the decree. One is from the Congregation of Bishops and Regulars, labeled as a "Duplicat" and signed by Archbishop Bizzarri on March 13, 1858. The other is an authentic copy from the General of the Redemptorists and signed by Father Mauron on March 29, 1858. It was sent to Father Hecker at his own request. He had met the General in Archbishop Bizzarri's outer office on March 10th. When Father Mauron asked Father Hecker if he had received a copy of the decree, the American missionary said no. "You expect it from me, I suppose?" the General inquired. "Of whom else?" Father Hecker replied, "I never did and do not belong to Propaganda. You were my Superior until the Pope's decision." Then Father Mauron promised to send it in a day or two (*ibid.*, Hecker to the Fathers, March 11, 1858). By March 25th, Father Hecker still had not received the copy and he sent a note to Father Douglas asking him to remind the General to forward it since "it is from his hands I am instructed to expect it" (*ibid.*, Hecker to Douglas, March 25, 1858). The same day Father Douglas answered Father Hecker enclosing the copy: "The Father General had made me copy the Decree immediately after he had seen you a fortnight ago. As he had not seen you since and was ignorant whether you might not have received a copy from some other source, it has remained ever since in his room. He sends it therefore according to your wish" (*ibid.*, Douglas to Hecker, March 25, 1858). This copy was written by Father Douglas and was unsigned. When Father Hecker insisted on having the General sign it, Father Mauron did so four days later (*ibid.*, André Balzani to Hecker, April 13, 1858). In this letter, Balzani reports his conversation with Bizzarri who had asked how Father Hecker "had fared with the Father General." Apparently it was Bizzarri who had instructed Father Hecker to get an authentic copy from Father Mauron since the conversation concerned the American missionary's efforts to obtain a signed copy of the decree.

61. A.P.F., *Hecker Papers*, Hecker to the Fathers, March 11, 1858.
62. *Ibid.*
63. *Ibid.*
64. *Ibid.*, March 18, 1858, in which Father Hecker added as an enclosure his account of the audience.
65. *Ibid.*, Father Hecker to George Hecker, April 3, 1858.
66. *Ibid.*, Hecker to the Fathers, April 3, 1858.
67. *Ibid.*, de Held to Hecker, March 16, 1858.

68. *Ibid.*, Hecker to the Fathers, April 3, 1858.
69. *Ibid.*
70. *Ibid.*, January 18, 1858.
71. *Ibid.*, March 27, 1858.
72. *Ibid.*, March 19, 1858.

Index